THE PICKERING MASTERS

THE WORKS OF LADY CAROLINE LAMB
VOLUME 1

CONTENTS OF THE EDITION

Volume 1
General Introduction
Glenarvon

Volume 2
Graham Hamilton and Poems

Volume 3
Ada Reis, A Tale

THE WORKS OF LADY CAROLINE LAMB

Volume 1
Glenarvon (1816)

EDITED BY
Paul Douglass

LONDON AND NEW YORK

First published 2009 by Pickering & Chatto (Publishers) Limited

Published 2016 by Routledge
2 Park Square, Milton Park, Abingdon, Oxon OX14 4RN
711 Third Avenue, New York, NY 10017, USA

Routledge is an imprint of the Taylor & Francis Group, an informa business

© Taylor & Francis 2009
© Paul Douglass 2009

All rights reserved, including those of translation into foreign languages. No part of this book may be reprinted or reproduced or utilised in any form or by any electronic, mechanical, or other means, now known or hereafter invented, including photocopying and recording, or in any information storage or retrieval system, without permission in writing from the publishers.

Notice:
Product or corporate names may be trademarks or registered trademarks, and are used only for identification and explanation without intent to infringe.

BRITISH LIBRARY CATALOGUING IN PUBLICATION DATA

Lamb, Caroline, Lady, 1785–1828.
The works of Lady Caroline Lamb. – (The Pickering masters)
1. Aristocracy (Social class) – England – Fiction. 2. England – Moral conditions – Fiction.
I. Title II. Series III. Dickson, Leigh Wetherall. IV. Douglass, Malcolm Paul. V. Lamb, Caroline, Lady, 1785–1828. Glenarvon. VI. Lamb, Caroline, Lady, 1785–1828. Graham Hamilton. VII. Lamb, Caroline, Lady, 1785–1828. Ada Reis.
823.7-dc22

ISBN-13: 978-1-85196-902-9 (set)

Typeset by Pickering & Chatto (Publishers) Limited

CONTENTS

Acknowledgements   vii
General Introduction   ix
Introduction   xxvii
Bibliography   xlv
Chronology   xlix

Glenarvon
    Volume I   1
    Volume II   103
    Volume III   241
Appendix A: Preface to the Second Edition   353
Appendix B: Introduction to the Fourth Edition   357

Editorial Notes   363
Silent Corrections   377
Textual Variants   389

ACKNOWLEDGEMENTS

The editors would like to thank the many people at Pickering & Chatto who helped to see this large project through to fruition, especially Mark Pollard for his patience and guidance in so many editorial decisions. Several translators helped us to grapple with passages in Latin, French, Italian, Arabic and Greek, including Néhal Abuelata, Alan Harvey, Lisa Hopkins, Sam Hopkins, Guy Hopkinson and Danielle Trudeau. Ria Grimbergen receives our profound thanks for making us aware of the interesting copy of *Glenarvon* in the Koninklijke Bibliotheek, the National Library of the Netherlands, which contains Lady Caroline Lamb's editorial notes for the revision of *Glenarvon*.

Permission to reproduce Lady Caroline Lamb's poems contained in archive collections has been graciously granted by the following institutions and individuals:

The Brotherton Collection, Leeds University Library.
Castle Howard Archives, with kind permission of the Hon. Simon Howard.
Devonshire Mss., Chatsworth. By Permission of the Duke of Devonshire.
The Earl of Bessborough
Hertfordshire Archives and Local Studies Office, County Hall, Hertfordshire.
National Library of Scotland: The John Murray Archive.
Pollinger Limited and the Earl of Lytton.

Acknowledgement of permission to print specific poems has been made in the notes to the texts in Volume 2. We are grateful to Rosemary March for help in tracking down poems in the literary annuals. The editors would also particularly like to thank Dr Elizabeth Denlinger, Curator of The Carl H. Pforzheimer Collection of Shelley and His Circle of The New York Public Library, Dr Jill Barber of the Hertfordshire Archives and Local Studies Office, C. D. W. Sheppard of Leeds University Special Collections, David McClay of the National Library of Scotland, Andrew Peppitt of the Devonshire Collection at Chatsworth, Alison Brisby of the Castle Howard Archives, and Alison McCann of the West Sussex Record Office in Chichester. Thanks also to Virginia and John Murray for their enthusiastic and always helpful responses to inquiries. Their support for scholarship has been exemplary and unwavering. The editors have benefited from notes to *A New Canto* compiled separately by Peter Cochran and Duncan Wu, to whom they give profound thanks.[1]

Cochran and Wu are two among many scholars who have blazed the trail we have sought to follow toward a clearer and more objective view of Lamb's writing career. For their help (whether directly or through their work) in clarifying ideas and preparing notes for the present edition, the authors wish to thank the following: Frederick Burwick, Marilyn Butler, John Clubbe, Paula Feldman, Amanda Foreman, Caroline Franklin, Marilyn Gaull, Peter Graham, Jonathan Gross, Diane Hoeveler, Barbara Judson, Malcolm Kelsall, Christine Kenyon Jones, Ghislaine McDayter, Clark Olney, James Soderholm, Andrew Stauffer, Nicola Watson, Frances Wilson and Susan Wolfson.

Notes:

1. See D. Wu, *Romanticism: An Anthology* (London: Blackwell, 1994), pp. 695–703; and see Peter Cochran's online edition of *A New Canto* at *http://www.hobby-o.com/newcanto.php*.

GENERAL INTRODUCTION

Lady Caroline Lamb (1785–1828) was born Caroline Ponsonby.[1] Hers was a distinguished family. Her mother, Lady Bessborough, and her Aunt Georgiana, Duchess of Devonshire, were among the few politically influential women of the era. Marie Antoinette was a family friend, and so was the Prince of Wales (nicknamed 'Prinny' in the Devonshire–Bessborough circle). She married William Lamb, an important Whig politician who later became Queen Victoria's first prime minister. Lady Caroline Lamb's social, political and literary activities brought her the acquaintance of Charles Fox, Richard Brinsley Sheridan, social philosopher and novelist William Godwin, and other literary figures like Walter Scott, Thomas Moore, Samuel Rogers, Lady Morgan, Ugo Foscolo, Letitia Elizabeth Landon, Edward Bulwer-Lytton, Samuel Taylor Coleridge and, infamously, Lord Byron. Lamb lived a flamboyant life, and serious engagement with her literary work has generally been eclipsed by retellings of her supposed hysteria and obsession with Byron after the end of their four-month affair in summer 1812. Most fictional representations and biographical studies of Lamb portray her as unable to distinguish fact from fantasy due to emotional excesses she either could not or would not curb.

Criticism has also found fault with her literary work, starting with her first and most widely read novel, *Glenarvon*, which was believed to be the expression of Lamb's fixation on Byron, who left England amid a firestorm of negative publicity just a fortnight before *Glenarvon* rolled off the press on 9 May 1816. Lamb lamented from that moment forward that her work wasn't taken on its own merits: '[E]verybody wishes to run down and suppress the vital spark of genius I have, and in truth, it is but small (about what one sees a maid gets by excessive beating on a tinder-box). I am not vain, believe me, nor selfish, nor in love with my authorship; but I am independent, as far as a mite and bit of dust can be'.[2] Most critics and scholars have treated Lamb's novels and poetry as at best a devious attempt to hurt Byron, and at worst the production of a neurotic mind unable to grasp reality. The evidence of her writing suggests, however, that Lamb was all too acutely aware of her world, which she harshly critiques. In three novels – *Glenarvon* (1816), *Graham Hamilton* (1822) and *Ada Reis* (1823) – Lamb laments the loss of true nobility as a character trait in general, and as an aristocratic inheritance and guide for behaviour. She was a witness to the devolution of aristocrats into autocrats wielding arbitrary power, and she warned that their privileges would be wrested from them if they did not rein in their egocentrism. This theme compelled her as a novelist and as a writer of two narrative poems: *A New Canto* (1819) and *Gordon: A Tale* (1821) Her mature lyric poems – nearly a dozen of which were set and published as sheet music by her friend, composer Isaac Nathan – are preoccupied with themes of disappointed love, loneliness and the beauty of nature. Although diffident about her poetry, Lamb took care to preserve it in illustrated bound books, which she 'published' for her family and friends, who comprised an inner ring of remarkable power – and suffered from equally remarkable problems.

Social and Political Context

As a child, Lamb, lived in the highest circles without fully realizing her extreme privilege. She was precocious, and her talent for language, music, and art was encouraged by her indulgent grandmother, mother, and aunt. She begin writing in rhymes at the tender age of five, and by age twelve her letters were strewn with them: 'come sing row de low row de low ... I'm mad / that's bad / I'm sad / That's bad / I'm bad / That's mad...'[3] Her natural effervescence of verse on traditional subjects (spring, a favourite dog, sadness, joy and beauty) and others (the fierceness of pride, the pleasure of opium) would last her lifetime. Simultaneously, Lamb took a keen interest in the Whig politics in which her family was so deeply embroiled.[4]

As the opposition party to the King's government, the Whigs had been adopted by the Prince of Wales in a gesture of animosity towards his father, George III. However, when he became Prince Regent, the Prince abandoned the Whigs and embraced the Tories. During Lamb's lifetime the Whigs played second fiddle to Tory governments, and yet they viewed themselves as essential intermediaries between the parliamentary and public worlds. Nobody appeared to bridge this gap more effectively than Lamb's beloved aunt, Georgiana Cavendish, the Duchess of Devonshire, the leading Whig hostess of her generation, aided and abetted by her sister Harriet, Lady Bessborough, Lamb's mother. As Amanda Foreman reminds us, Devonshire House became the Whig party headquarters. Its vast spaces lent themselves to gatherings for social solidarity in times of celebration and commiseration, and Georgiana and Harriet were as much astute politicians as hostesses whose patronage of the arts increased the association of the Whigs with the fashionable culture of wit, taste and talent.[5] Georgiana's trend-setting celebrity made her the public face of the Whigs.

Georgiana's success was belied, however, by the calamity of her personal life. Her husband, fifth Duke of Devonshire, was indifferent towards her, and preferred her friend Lady Elizabeth Foster, who lived at Devonshire House with them in an uneasy triumvirate. Georgiana took Lord Charles Grey for a lover and eventually bore two children by him (one died at birth). The Duke temporarily banished Georgiana when he discovered her second illegitimate pregnancy. Similarly, Lamb's mother's marriage to Lord Bessborough was unsatisfying, and Harriet had affairs. Harriet's husband tried to control her behaviour by drugging her, which made even the Duke suspect he was trying to poison her.[6] Later, she fell in love with Granville Leveson Gower, by whom she had two children.

Georgiana and Harriet compensated for disappointments in marriage with love affairs, but also by becoming addicted to gambling and what Georgiana aptly described as 'a vortex of dissipation'.[7] Lamb uses these words in Glenarvon to describe Lady Calantha's immersion into London society, where 'every night was passed in the same vortex of fashionable dissipation'.[8] At the tables during the parties they attended, Georgiana and Harriet lost tens of thousands of pounds – sometimes in a single night. Their unhappy marriages may have provided the model for Lady Orville in Lamb's second novel, Graham Hamilton. Her husband's passivity drives Lady Orville to seek companionship in 'society'. Lord Orville is only roused to awareness of this fact by the impending financial disaster born out of Lady Orville's need to compensate for her empty marriage. In the end, Lady Orville is separated from her husband and children, and sent into the country to live quietly, where she finds fulfilment in charitable work, just as her mother Harriet found fulfilment in establishing a home for indigent single mothers, and Georgiana found it in politics and the role of a mediator.

As Whigs, the Devonshires and Bessboroughs embraced the establishment of a constitutional monarchy, a position in harmony with the initial principles of the French Revolution, which enshrined representative democracy. But as aristocrats and friends of Marie Antoinette, they abhorred the mob violence they had witnessed firsthand in 1789, and the mob rule that resulted in the violent deaths of several close friends, including the French Queen.[9] Their views on the Revolution epitomize a division within the Whig party between the 'new' Whigs led by Charles Fox and the 'old' Whigs led by Fox's one-time friend, Edmund Burke. Fox supported the Revolution as necessary and democratic, whereas Burke, who did not oppose the principle of reform, objected to drastic, uncontrolled change that placed power in the hands of amateurs with little or no political expertise.

Lamb was well aware of the politics of her era, and she wrote about them in her letters and fiction. Her novels were published in the period crossing from the Regency into the reign of George IV, who ascended to the throne 19 July 1821. Before 1780, aristocratic pre-eminence had rarely been questioned, and aristocrats never doubted their right to speak on behalf of their inferiors. After 1780, however, unquestioning acceptance of the natural aristocracy began to give way to criticisms of corruption and parasitism, as Frank O'Gorman and Linda Colley have shown.[10] The aristocrats represented in Lamb's novels fail in their obligations to those dependent upon them, nor do they generally exhibit classical traits of high character. In *Glenarvon*, for example, the Duke of Altamonte has retired from social and political life. Disappointed in his ambitions, he has retreated 'sullen and reserved' to his Irish estates, where he is ineffective when the Irish rebellion gathers momentum around him. His own tenants are 'mutinous and discontented' because he 'refused to attend to the grievances and burthens of which the nation generally complained'.[11]

Lamb's portrayal of a dissolute society is neatly illustrated by a scene in *Graham Hamilton* in which the hero is given ironic advice on his education from his Scottish moneylending uncle, Sir Malcolm. Hamilton is told to pay attention only to extrinsic things, 'to acquire an easy, and something of an insolent manner' and to practise blindness to moral challenge and eschew all 'genuine feeling of human nature'. He is sarcastically invited to form 'no intimate friendships ... [to] associate with the worthless', and to treat genuine feeling as if it were 'hypocrisy'.[12] The credo for this education is not noblesse oblige but superficiality. Lamb has Sir Malcolm point out to Hamilton, that 'exterior deportment' has achieved primary importance; codes of dress, speech and etiquette that previously denoted nobility are no longer reliable signifiers. Lamb's novels consistently portray the aristocracy as having self-destructively withdrawn itself from the rest of the nation. In *Glenarvon* the 1798 Irish rebellion gathers momentum around the Delaval family because of their neglect of duty. In *Graham Hamilton* Lady Orville dreads the 'tediousness of [country] neighbours',[13] preferring to remain within her own elevated circle despite imminent ruin. In Ada Reis we meet a character who seems to represent the aristocracy in extremis, for he is guaranteed impunity from a murder motivated by greedy acquisition, which in turn is part of a prophecy representing the fulfilment of an inheritance.

Lamb consistently shows how the Whigs, too long the opposition party, had become stuffed shirts and celebrities, losing their political credibility. She saw them giving up their integrity for an empty display of ostentation. This is clearly signalled in the introduction of *Ada Reis*, in which Lamb describes the famous adventurer Belzoni[14] as he breaks open a temple, 'the wonder and pride of man, perchance the sepulchre of kings', only to find 'a loathsome toad, its sole proprietor'.[15] This is a clear allusion to Christ's characterization of his opponents, the Pharisees, whom he denounces as 'whited sepulchres, which indeed appear beautiful outwardly, but are within full of dead men's bones, and of all uncleanness'.[16] The dazzling exterior of wealth and property is belied by the lack of inner substance, as Lamb illustrates with the revolutionary glamour of the political shape-shifter, Glenarvon; with Lady Orville feigning the appearance of wealth when actually crippled with debt; and with the brutality and greed of Ada Reis, masked behind the external accoutrements of the ruling elite.

The same themes are found in her narrative poems, *A New Canto* and *Gordon: A Tale, A Poetical Review of Don Juan*. Both satirize Byron's Don Juan, itself a mock-epic satire of British aristocracy. *A New Canto* presents an apocalyptic upheaval for Lamb's time: 'When doomsday comes, St Paul's will be on fire / (I should not wonder if we live to see it)...'.[17] The speaker describes the ball on the dome of St Paul's 'tumbling with a lively crash', as the Bank of England collapses.[18] London has become a volcano, and frantic crowds seek salvation in the church, where 'the font is hot, and fizzing'.[19] *A New Canto* charges Byron with writing literature that is 'worse than an emetic', its sole purpose to perpetuate Byron's fame and 'keep [his] name in capitals, like Kean', an allusion to the career of actor Edmund Kean and Byron's connection to Drury Lane Theater.[20] It thus attacks him as the scion of a British aristocracy for which everything is a show put on as a mere 'joke'. Similarly, *Gordon: A Tale* ends on an apocalyptic note. In a rising fury, the speaker spits venom on Byron's work, saying that Byron has squandered his genius merely to show off. His reward 'for such enormous pains / Is, "Byron did it!" – is this all he gains?'[21]

Whether in fiction or narrative verse, Lamb emphasizes that the aristocracy offers little but outward show – staged theatricality for public consumption – in the mode of her Aunt Georgiana's opening her opulent quarters for 'public days' or making appearances amongst the voters. These exercises in self-legitimization amounted to acts of propaganda, showcasing the desirable and acceptable face of the Whig aristocracy, who yet pursued a licentious and even gluttonous private life. Throughout her novels Lamb exposes that public face as a sham. The celebrity aspect of the split was functioning merely as a distraction from the Whig party's ineffectiveness as the opposition party. Leo Braudy writes of this transition occurring across Europe in the early part of the nineteenth century, that the 'Aristocracy, so used to considering its style a byproduct of status, now had to convince of status by its style'.[22]

The coronation of the Prince Regent as George IV is an example proving Braudy's point. It was an extravagant affair with a medieval motif intended to inspire loyalty and almost feudal enthusiasm for the tradition and authority of the monarch.[23] The overtly stage-managed royal ritual was criticized as a hollow and misguided sham that relied upon theatrical props and, as such, was ridiculous in an enlightened age; this is certainly how the new monarch was perceived, for the obese George IV was described as 'more like an elephant than a man'.[24] For Lamb the performance of the role is not enough, for it can be insincere, easily imitated. She peels back the veneer in her recurring portraits of aristocrats as fakes, offering versions of Byron as the epitome of contemporary aristocracy on a personal and political level. Though Lamb's fictional portraits of Byron, particularly in *Glena-*

rvon, have been read as an expression of her spleen, they were the vehicles, rather than the targets, for her critique of contemporary Whig politics.

Byronic Background

Lamb was pointing out a truth about Byron, for he was not exempt from the hypocrisies of his time. Despite the circuitous route that brought him to a Baronetage, Byron also practised rituals of self-legitimation, carefully controlling his aristocratic image. Christine Kenyon-Jones has shown how, despite the apparent informality of his portraits, Byron employed them to assert himself as nobleman rather than poet, resisting artists' attempts to add poetic paraphernalia to the picture.[25] Byron recognized the importance of showmanship in fulfilling the role of the governing class. On 27 February 1812, he chose the subject of the proposed capital punishment of the Nottinghamshire 'frame-breakers' for his maiden speech in Parliament. He performed his speech as an oration and wrote later that it was 'perhaps a little theatrical', following which he rarely fulfilled what he termed his 'senatorial duties' and wrote to his half-sister Augusta that he had 'no intention to "strut another hour" on that stage'.[26] He had taken an unpopular stand in favour of the workers, for even among Whigs the Frame Work Bill was thought a reasonable measure to prevent an uprising.

At this time, Byron was also correcting the final proofs of *Childe Harold's Pilgrimage*, a poem based loosely on his travels. Suddenly nervous about the parliamentary leadership, he became worried that *Childe Harold* contained an attack on Lord Elgin for taking marble statues from the Parthenon. His publisher, John Murray, commissioned the shrewd Samuel Rogers, poet and banker, to test out reactions to the poem, and Rogers loaned an advance copy to Lady Caroline to get her reaction. She wrote to Byron, and thus began their affair, which lasted from March through September of 1812, when Lamb's family removed her to Ireland and Byron tried to break off correspondence entirely. Whatever the effect upon her personal life, Byron's persona fired Lamb's literary endeavours, which had to this point been focused primarily on poems and lyrics, sparking her decision to start a novel about the heir to an Irish estate who betrays his country and his people: *Glenarvon*.

The art of speechmaking as a performance is at the centre of Byron's short parliamentary career and this is how he, as a representative of the Whig patriarchy, is portrayed as Glenarvon: a persuasive and charismatic man who seduces with rhetoric and legitimizes himself to the increasingly restless Irish in the identical ways their current rulers have done.[27] Lamb describes him as appearing 'amidst the grotesque and ferocious rabble, like some God from a higher world'.[28] Despite his apparent egalitarianism Glenarvon is not a democrat and insists that he must be called by his title, to which he has a very dubious claim, though others have renounced theirs.[29] His title and the ancestral lands that he recuperates in the name of Glenarvon – St Alvin Priory and Belfont Abbey – fulfil the same legitimizing functions as the trappings of achievement of the existing rulers; they mark Glenarvon out as a figure of distinction and authority, with a tradition of leadership in his genealogy.

Lamb also paints a fairly damning picture of Byron in *Ada Reis*, but that portrait is clearly intended as a condemnation of the society that lionised him rather than of Byron himself. In a letter to Lady Morgan, Lamb thanks her for her 'kind reception of Adamo el Reis' and responds to a query about the novel's apocalyptic conclusion by remarking that 'Condulmar not Ada is Ld Byron that is if there be a Byron in the Tale and as to the Radicals in Hell they must be some where you know & where the Deuce in these Aristocratic days can they be'.[30] It is not only the Radicals being punished in Hell, but also the aristocrats, those sinners of the fashionable world who have 'dreamed away life's little hour without committing any actual crime; but misspending every moment in idleness and folly, [who] have proved the cause of ruin to others, and have brought themselves, by mere wantonness and neglect of duty, into our abode'.[31]

Byron dismissed *Glenarvon*'s worth as a portrait of himself, saying the author had not written the 'truth' and that he did not 'sit long enough' for a good likeness to be made.[32] Yet his distancing himself from Lamb's creation was partly an exercise in damage control, since the book was published immediately after his departure from England. Some contemporary readers understood that *Glenarvon* was intended as a rendering of contemporary political and social life. Lady Byron herself reacted positively to the book at first,[33] and the British Critic, in reviewing *Glenarvon*, commented that if Lamb's work was a faithful delineation of the fashionable world, and if it was her intention to stem the tide of 'Continental profligacy', then she did not 'write in vain'.[34] It appears that Lamb's husband, William, was supportive of her novel-writing, even of *Glenarvon*, the subsequent editions of which he could have blocked, but didn't. This, however, is not to argue that Lamb's novel wasn't severely attacked by her contemporaries. It was. Indeed, some then, and later, denied that the book was a novel at all, but rather some sort of incomprehensible attempt at self-therapy in print.

Genre and the Politics of Form

Lamb's work has been largely discussed as an attempt by her to maintain a connection with Byron via literary imitation, transgression and forgery of him. James Soderholm attributes to Lamb a desire to 'recreate the Byronic hero in her own fashion'.[35] Nicola Watson suggests that Lamb 'pilfered Byron's authority'.[36] Admittedly, one of the present editors, Paul Douglass, has echoed this theme of identity theft, stating that the end of Lamb's life witnessed an abandonment of 'her abortive struggle to become a feminine novel-writing version of Byron'.[37] However, Lamb's choice of the novel as a vehicle for social and political critique is not necessarily a response to Byron. It follows the example of British writers of the 1790s, such as her correspondent and erstwhile mentor William Godwin, author of *Things as They Are; or, the Adventures of Caleb Williams* (1794), and Robert Bage, author of *Hermsprong; or, Man As He Is Not* (1796). As Gary Kelly observes, the Jacobin writers sought to shape the ideology of an emerging professional class.[38] In contrast, Lamb wrote to reform the aristocracy itself, knowing at the same time that her novels would be marketed to a wider consumer culture. The *roman à clef* in *Glenarvon*, the silver-fork resonance of *Graham Hamilton*, and the oriental and South American fantasy of *Ada Reis* were chosen with an understanding of the economic market place and readers' expectations. True, Lamb wrote verse in imitation of Byron's *Don Juan*, twice bringing that poem back to earth in London, but her satire constitutes not a forgery of, but rather a public response to Byron's work.

In Lamb's early life, her choice of genre was conventional for a woman: poems of love, loss, domesticity and nature. Yet this choice was made in a period when feminine lyric poetry was considered transgressive because of its emotionality and sometimes overt sexual content. One female writer of such verse was Charlotte Dacre (1782–1841). The author of Gothic novels like *The Confessions of the Nun of St. Omer* (1805) and *Zofloya* (1806), Dacre wrote under the Della-Cruscan[39] style *nom de plume* of 'Rosa Matilda'. Her *Hours of Solitude* (1805) contains sentimental poetry that some considered rife with sexuality:

> Reclining here, beneath the shade
> Sleeps a languid, half-dress'd maid;
> There, a youth, whose varying cheek,
> Seems disorder to bespeak...[40]

Dacre also describes the 'falt'ring sigh, / Voluptuous eye, / And palpitating heart' of 'rapture as it flow'd' between lovers.[41] Lamb's juvenilia and published lyrics exhibit traits similar to those of Dacre's verse and, over time, elegiac and mourning elements also found in *Hours of Solitude* occupied more and more of Lamb's poetical landscape. For example, such verses as 'Farewell' and 'Weep For What Thou Hast Lost, Love' were set and sold as sheet music by composer Isaac Nathan. In this, Lamb continued a pattern set by her Aunt Georgiana, Duchess of Devonshire, who had also published songs, one of which Jane Austen chose for her personal songbook: "I have a Silent Sorrow Here."[42]

Lamb was also preceded in prose-writing by her Aunt Georgiana, who published two novels, *Emma: or, the Unfortunate Attachment* (1773) and *The Sylph* (1779) and collaborated with her sister Harriet on an adaptation of a play titled *Siegendorf*.[43] Writing novels, songs, and plays was an acceptable mode of expression, so long as the pretence of anonymity was preserved. Lamb's choice of *roman à clef* was therefore deemed spectacularly inappropriate, a flouting of a conventional woman's role, and the content of *Glenarvon* was dismissed as mere 'kiss and tell' confessional, or as Byron damningly put it, '---- and publish'.[44] The novel has also been interpreted by modern critics as an act of compulsive self-revelation and confession. Clark Olney observed fifty years ago that *Glenarvon* was primarily 'an act of contrition and humility; a public confession of her sin'.[45] But what exactly was Lamb revealing or confessing, especially when her relationship with Byron was common knowledge?

Contemporary readers of the novel knew some of the external details of the affair, but not internal ones, such as Lamb's portrayal of her protagonist's dilemmas of being torn between duty and self-fulfilment, her intense feelings for Byron, his duplicity, and the way their affair ended. But if these were the elements of 'intrigue' for readers, they must have seemed tame. Any first novel will undoubtedly have autobiographical elements that can be labelled 'confessional', and *Glenarvon* is no different. Lamb claimed in a preface inserted into the second edition of the novel, published a few weeks after the first, that she had published it to correct 'excited misrepresentation[s]' of her own character (see Appendix A). She felt she had been treated unfairly because Byron was the favourite of her mother-in-law and other female acquaintances, while she was pilloried for her transgression with him. She had rebelled, refusing to be silent about what she saw as an unfair bias. It was an act of defiance that has, as Frances Wilson says, a modern day counterpart in a descendant of Lamb from the Spencer line, Diana, Princess of Wales.[46] Both women became an embarrassment to the establishment and their husbands and extended families because they publicly denounced an embedded hypocrisy that punished female transgression severely while tolerating egregious male vice. In choosing the *roman à clef* for her act of defiance, Lamb was aware from personal experience of the keen interest in the aristocracy within popular print culture.[47] Unfortunately, the book was treated as a monumentally tasteless act, even one of social suicide, and therefore the product of an unhealthy mind.

Despite the furore that surrounded the appearance of *Glenarvon*, Lamb was granted permission by her husband to allow a second edition to be printed, perhaps partly on the promise that she would extensively revise it, which she did. In the preface added to the second edition Lamb wrote that despite universal condemnation of the novel as being of an 'immoral tendency', it was the 'general tendency of the work [to be] favourable to the interests of virtue'.[48] In issuing the second, and then third and fourth editions, to which this preface was also attached, Lamb recognized that she must bow to the opinion of the public but questioned whether the morality of the tale had 'been injured by the description of desperate characters, depraved conduct, and daring crimes?'[49] The preface requests that readers distinguish between 'painting human nature as it is, and the base desire of deforming and degrading it'.[50] It is a preface that is simultaneously apologetic and unrepentant, arguing that similar or worse had already appeared in 'novels, romances and romantic poems', and that the offence taken by some was strictly due to the 'personal application' of the perceived imputations.[51] Critics of Lamb have read *Glenarvon* as a melodrama which she inhabited as the tragic heroine, and have suggested that this fantasy crossed over into the real world, so that she could no longer tell the difference. In this reading of *Glenarvon*, the text has produced the life, and the connotations of the *roman à clef*, through which Lamb sought to expose hypocrisy, have been lost. Such a reading cannot, for example, account for the obvious identification of the author with both Calantha and Glenarvon.

Lamb apparently sought advice about her second novel from Ugo Foscolo, the exiled Italian novelist who had found refuge with the Whig literati of Holland House. Foscolo advised her to 'write a book which will offend nobody, women cannot afford to shock'.[52] Whether Lamb heeded this recommendation or not, *Graham Hamilton* (1822) appeared superficially to avoid the faults of *Glenarvon*, and *Blackwood's Magazine* applauded it as belonging 'to the class of proper and of good novels' which presented a 'spirited picture of the manners and follies of the times'.[53] *Glenarvon* and *Graham Hamilton* were published by Henry Colburn, who brought out the majority of currently fashionable fiction, including the later 'silver-fork' novels, an immensely popular genre that flourished from the mid-1820s to the early 1830s.[54] The appeal of such novels was that one could gain an insider's view of high society, as seen by its members, or at least by someone in close proximity. Colburn recruited aristocratic writers like Lord Normanby, Lady Charlotte Bury, Lady Morgan and Lady Blessington, hoping for novels that would reveal the details of fashionable life – what to wear, how to behave, where to be seen and who to know – all imparted in witty dialogue. Ironically, however, the bestselling novelists of the genre, as Jump and Cronin both observe, came from slightly lower down the social scale and gleaned their authenticity by association rather than birthright.[55]

Although *Glenarvon* and *Graham Hamilton* predate the timeframe of the silver-fork genre, there are points where they seem to prefigure it, particularly in the case of *Graham Hamilton*. Lamb certainly fits the preferred profile of an author of the fashionable genre and both *Glenarvon* and *Graham Hamilton* contain some of its identifiable and desirable elements: *Glenarvon* is driven by the political situation in Ireland and features a duel between Glenarvon and Lord Avondale; *Graham Hamilton* also contains a duel, scenes at the opera and Lady Orville's ball, and the practising of the female arts of flirtatious wit upon Hamilton. The 'I-spy' nature of the *roman à clef* asserted the fashionable or aristocratic credentials of the novel's world and author, which Colburn effectively employed in his marketing campaigns.⁵⁶

As a genre, the silver-fork novel came to be associated with the thick description of an opulent consumer society. Lamb, by contrast, employs a didactic minimalism to great effect, introducing elements of luxury when it is offered as a stark contrast to necessity. Seemingly, Lamb delivers an authentic representation of the lives of the aristocracy, one that is based upon her own family experience. This authenticity not only subverts but pre-empts the expectations of the silver-fork genre in its early stages. Lamb had understood the basic reader's curiosity, but turned it toward criticizing the abuse of class distinction and privilege. *Glenarvon* and *Graham Hamilton* anticipate the politicized form of the genre as later practised by Edward Bulwer Lytton and Mary Shelley. By the time Bulwer Lytton published *Pelham: or The Adventures of a Gentleman*, in 1828, as Fiona Stafford and Harriet Devine Jump point out, the silver-fork novel was no longer regarded as mere frivolous escapism.⁵⁷ In *England and the English* (1833), Bulwer Lytton wrote that the authors of the genre had contributed to the necessity for parliamentary reform because they 'unconsciously exposed the falsehood, the hypocrisy, the arrogant and vulgar insolence of patrician life' and subjected the reader to a 'parade of frivolity, the ridiculous disdain of truth', which characterized aristocratic society.⁵⁸ Lamb similarly projected a picture of aristocratic life, deliberately exposing it as a parade of giddy gamblers and hypocrites with a contempt for 'truth'.

If *Graham Hamilton* was grudgingly acknowledged as a credit to Lamb, *Ada Reis* reconfirmed the conception of her as a dissipated and dysfunctional aristocrat. Reviewers found fault with its fantastical style and settings: 'Is this probable? Is that in nature?' asked the *New Monthly Magazine*.⁵⁹ The *Examiner* asserted that 'if these volumes were not the production of that gifted child the Opium-eater, they certainly ought to be'.⁶⁰ Nonetheless, reviewers involuntarily acknowledged the long list of precursors to Lamb's improbable tale, including *Anastasius, Don Juan, Faust, Vathek*, the works of Quevedo, and (by implication) the *Odyssey*, Dante's *Inferno*, and Milton's *Paradise Regained*, which provide chapter epigraphs in *Ada Reis*'s third volume.⁶¹ Her work stands in a literary tradition that invokes the supernatural, classical and exotic to critique excesses nearer to home.⁶² Lamb's introduction outlines the moral of the tale, which is guided by philosophical principles of Manichaeism, a severely ascetic teaching of radical dualism that represents the spiritual element of the world as Light, and the material element emanating from Darkness, a force driven by desire. The religious philosophy of Manichaeism provides the framework through which the novel should be read, and helps to explain its final allegory of spirituality and its apocalyptic climax.

As a fiction writer Lamb made use of Byron's persona to construct anti-heroes. In poetry she appropriated Byron's authorial voice, writing two anonymous imitations of *Don Juan: A New Canto* (1819) and *Gordon: A Tale, A Poetical Review of Don Juan* (1821). The former purports to be a continuation of Byron's mock-epic poem, the first two cantos of which had been published previously the same year. It is now generally accepted that Lamb is the author, and the poem has been reprinted under her name by Margot Strickland and Duncan Wu.[63] Like Lamb's other genre and subgenre choices, this one involved a setting yoked to its type, for it is satire of a deeply English character, and is therefore set in London. Despite their differences, Lamb never lost her wonder at Byron's poetic gifts. *Don Juan*, however, she described to Byron's publisher John Murray as 'neither witty nor in very good taste' and overall 'weak'.[64] As *A New Canto* demonstrates, she thought it a sacrifice of genius for mere publicity, a criticism that is continued in the anonymous *Gordon: A Tale*, published after the appearance of canto 5 of Don Juan, although the preface indicates that it was inspired by cantos 1 and 2 and was completed 'long before' cantos 3, 4 and 5.[65] Although there appears to be some confusion as to the author (the British Library erroneously attributes this manuscript to Byron himself), *Gordon: A Tale* is commonly attributed to Lamb and the criticism of Byron as the author of *Don Juan* is in keeping with that of *A New Canto*. The work again pays tribute to Byron's poetic power, and the narrator purchases a copy of *Don Juan* in eager anticipation, only to be grossly disappointed, crying 'Would that he used his talents for our good! . . . But oh! instead it serves but to infect: / Its powers perverted, all its time mis[s]pent'.

Lamb's appropriation of Byron's mock-epic satire and his voice depends upon a context and a readership that were well-known to Lamb, and she carefully set these, and all three of her novels, in geographical and imaginative spaces suited to her readers' experiences in and out of books.

The Political and Moral Landscape of Lamb's Novels

The settings of Lamb's novels are connected to their genres. A *roman à clef* cannot easily be set in a time and place far removed from the experience of the reader or the characters without the risk of making the fictional portraits unrecognizable. A silver-fork novel set in a wilderness would make nonsense of the generic conventions, though it might thereby reinvent the genre. Lamb's settings are all charged with significance on the map of Whig ideology.

The Ireland of 1798 in *Glenarvon* conveys a specific personal and political resonance. The Irish rebellion of 1798 was inspired by the American and French Revolutions. With the promised aid of the French, the Society of United Irishmen set aside their religious differences to, as Robert Kee succinctly puts it, 'eradicate the baneful English influence and destroy the aristocratic tyrants of the land'.⁶⁶ Critic James Garver has charged that the landscape of Lamb's Ireland is unknown and unknowable, a literary fantasy, 'sublimely wild and desolate; ominously castellated; infested by banditti variously known as rapparees [...] who reflected a historical muddle of Jacobite or Jacobin conspiracies of rebellion'.⁶⁷ Similarly, Malcolm Kelsall argues that there is no account of the oppression that provoked the rebellion, and there exists a naivety in a landscape of the 'picturesque imagination'.⁶⁸ True, Lamb's knowledge of Ireland was limited to a few months in 1812, but the rebellion conspiracy in *Glenarvon* is no fantasy. The landscape is wild, dangerous and untameable, seething with insurrection as the rebels have literally been driven under and into the ground – and in short appropriate to the genre and themes of the novel.

Likewise, the emphasis upon fashionable society in *Graham Hamilton* meant that it must take place in an urban setting – London, where Lamb and her family roamed and were recognized. Unlike the topographically indistinct Ireland of *Glenarvon*, this novel's landscape is signposted with recognizable features, which, though few, all point towards a criticism of the priorities and values of the aristocracy. Hamilton must learn to negotiate an alien environment where social hierarchy is based upon visual signs of status. His callowness allows Lamb to illuminate a complex and socially coded environment that undermines personal integrity. Hamilton's parvenu status is continually reinforced by his discovery of the invisible social boundaries that are embedded within a reduced cityscape of London, the type identified by Moretti in his discussion of the silver-fork novelists' attempts to address the complex urban locations of their fictions.⁶⁹ Lamb's London is an extremely simplified version of the binary representations of London by silver-fork novelists – of west and east, aristocracy and other. *Graham Hamilton*'s London story is retrospective, for Hamilton has banished himself from London and all Europe for the 'great prospects opening in the New [World]'.⁷⁰ With Thomas Paine's vision in mind,⁷¹ Whigs saw America as the embodiment of political and social liberty, and their political colours of buff and blue were adopted from the uniform of the 'American' army. The absence of an endemic caste system was the deciding factor in rejecting the 'Old' world of Great Britain and Europe in favour of the blank canvas of the 'New'. Can Hamilton, with his fortune, put himself and his money into what Lamb calls a 'field enterprise',⁷² or will he again be seduced by a simulacrum of superiority in the form of lovely Aristocratic women?

In contrast to her second novel, Lamb's *Ada Reis* employs an imaginative landscape fraught with the supernatural, one that Lamb shared with other readers of the Byronic Oriental or Eastern tale: Genoa, Tripoli, Lima, and ultimately a Catholic manifestation of Hell. As a landscape symbolic with the possibilities of rebirth and redemption, America has a significant role in *Ada Reis*, though this time it is not the newly liberated democratic north inhabited by settlers, but the dark and impenetrable interior of the southern hemisphere, the indigenous population of which divides into pre-civilization savages and pre-lapsarian innocents. Lamb represents all the native inhabitants of South America as Indians and, crudely drawn as they are, they provide an effective contrast to the notion of European superiority. Keen to ingratiate himself with the Spanish nobility, Ada Reis has been dazzled by their success in building an empire. During a feast for the Viceroy, over which Ada Reis presides, the ghost of one he has murdered approaches and, in the manner of Hamlet's father or Keats's cold philosopher, reveals to Ada Reis that his true nature is known and the day of retribution is at hand, due to occur on 28 October, the date of the earthquake. Ada Reis, personification of the desire for a crown, discovers the true weight of the mantle of authority which drags him straight to hell. Like Lamb's other novels, *Ada Reis* is set in landscapes that support her themes, revealing the Dantean inferno lurking behind the Mediterranean exoticism popularized by Byron's Eastern tales.

Conclusion

Lamb occupies a troubled – but highly interesting – spot in the timeline of feminism. If one considers the expectations of the era for a woman of her class, as well as the health problems that essentially ended her writing career in 1823, her productivity is surprising. In seven short years she published three novels, two substantial poetical satires, twelve songs printed as sheet music, and a number of lyric poems that appeared in newspapers and the annuals. Isaac Nathan's *Fugitive Pieces* (1829) gave posthumous publication to another dozen verses, and she recorded and had bound numerous other poems. By reputation immature, vengeful, melodramatic, nymphomaniacal, insufferable and unstable, Lamb managed to write some memorable fiction and touching verses while holding her marriage together, sustaining deep friendships, and bringing up an epileptic and retarded son. As Frances Wilson has pointed out, Glenarvon's warning is also her cry: 'I am not what I seem. I am not [her] whom you take me for'.[73]

Notes:

1. Caroline Ponsonby received the honorific 'Lady Caroline' when her father succeeded his own father as Count Bessborough in March 1793. She kept this title throughout her life, even after marrying, in 1805. Her husband became the second (and last) Viscount Melbourne in July 1828, but Lady Caroline had passed away the previous January, so that she never took the title 'Lady Melbourne'.
2. C. Lamb, *The Whole Disgraceful Truth: Selected Letters of Lady Caroline Lamb*, ed. P. Douglass (New York: Palgrave-Macmillan, 2006), p. 190.
3. Lamb, *The Whole Disgraceful Truth*, p. 8.
4. In numerous letters of her early teens Lamb writes of issues like treason against the government, the reform movement, and the comings and goings of the politicians with

whom her mother and aunt were so intimate. See Lamb, *The Whole Disgraceful Truth*, pp. 8–14.
5. A. Foreman, *Georgiana: Duchess of Devonshire* (London: Harper Collins, 1998), pp. 92, 139.
6. P. Douglass, *Lady Caroline Lamb: A Biography* (New York: Palgrave Macmillan, 2004), p. 6.
7. Foreman, *Georgiana: Duchess of Devonshire*, pp. 44–61.
8. C. Lamb, *Glenarvon*, 3 vols (London: Henry Colburn, 1816), vol. 1, p. 267.
9. Foreman, *Georgiana: Duchess of Devonshire*, pp. 234, 249.
10. See F. O'Gorman, *The Long Eighteenth Century; British Political and Social History 1688–1832* (London & New York: Arnold, 1997), p. 331; and see Linda Colley, *Britons: Forging the Nation 1707–1837*, (New Haven, CT: Yale University Press, 1992; London: Vintage, 1996), p. 162.
11. See below, pp. 8 and 32.
12. See Volume 2, pp. 20.
13. See Volume 2, p. 67.
14. Giovanni Battista Belzoni (1778–1823), an explorer who discovered the temple of Seti I in the Valley of the Kings, and was the first person to penetrate the second pyramid of Giza and locate the inner chambers.
15. See Volume 3, p. 5.
16. Matthew 23:27.
17. See Volume 2, p. 144.
18. Ibid.
19. Ibid.
20. See Volume 2, p. 50.
21. Ibid., p. 175.
22. L. Braudy, *The Frenzy of Renown: Fame and Its History* (New York: Vintage Books, 1997), p. 348.
23. M. Girouard, *The Return to Camelot; Chivalry and the English Gentleman* (New Haven, CT and London, Yale University Press, 1981), pp. 25-27.
24. D. Cannadine, 'The Context, Performance and Meaning of Ritual: The British Monarchy and the "Invention of Tradition", 1820–1977', in E. Hobsbawm and T. Ranger (eds), *The Invention of Tradition* (Cambridge: Cambridge University Press, 1994), pp. 101, 117.
25. C. K. Jones, 'Fantasy and Transfiguration: Byron and His Portraits', *Byromania; Portraits of the Artist in Nineteenth- and Twentieth-Century Culture*, ed. Frances Wilson (London: Macmillan, 1999), p. 114.
26. Leslie Marchand, *Byron; A Portrait* (London, Pimlico, 1993), pp. 114, 125.
27. Rodney Barker has described this process in *Legitimating Identities: The Self-Presentation of Rulers and Subjects* (Cambridge: Cambridge University Press, 2001): Revolutionaries can pose 'an acute challenge to the legitimating self-identification of rulers [by presenting] to the government its own mask carried by other players'. See p. 101.
28. See below, p. 250.
29. See below, p. 133.
30. Douglass, *Lady Caroline Lamb: A Biography*, p. 252.
31. See Volume 3, p. 170.
32. Marchand, *Byron; A Portrait*, p. 248.
33. Douglass, *Lady Caroline Lamb: A Biography*, p. 188.

34. *British Critic*, 5 (June 1816), pp. 627–33.
35. J. Soderholm, 'Lady Caroline Lamb: Byron's Miniature Writ Large', *Keats-Shelley Journal*, 40 (1991) p. 30.
36. N. J. Watson, 'Trans-Figuring Byronic Identity', *At the Limits of Romanticism: Essays in Cultural, Feminist and Materialist Criticism*, ed. M. A. Favret, and Nicola J. Watson (Indianapolis, IN: Indiana University Press, 1994), p. 190.
37. P. Douglass, 'Playing Byron: Lady Caroline Lamb's *Glenarvon* and the Music of Isaac Nathan', *European Romantic Review*, 8:1 (Winter 1997), p. 18.
38. G. Kelly, *English Fiction of the Romantic Period 1789–1830* (London and New York: Longman, 1989), p. 36.
39. The Della Cruscans were a group of English and Italian sentimental poets founded by Robert Merry (1755–98) who wrote in English, Italian, and French. The name comes from the Accademia della Crusca in Florence, which was founded in 1583 to purify the Italian language.
40. C. Dacre, *Hours of Solitude*, 2 vols (London: D.N. Shury, 1805), vol. 1, p. 7.
41. Dacre, *Hours of Solitude*, vol. 1, pp. 23, 110.
42. The song is in one of eight bound volumes of Jane Austen's personal music held at the Austen Memorial Trust in Chawton, England.
43. See P. Cochran, 'Harriet Lee's *The German's Tale*, *The Hungarian* by Georgiana, Duchess of Devonshire, and Byron's *Werner*', *Keats-Shelley Review*, 18:179 (2004); and Foreman, *Georgiana, Duchess of Devonshire*, p. 331. *Siegendorf* was probably never produced.
44. Lord Byron, *Byron's Letters and Journals*, ed. L. Marchand. 12 vols (Cambridge, MA: Belknap Press of Harvard University Press, 1973-1995), vol. 5, p. 85.
45. C. Olney, 'Glenarvon Revisited', *University of Kansas Review*, 22 (1955), p. 275.
46. F. Wilson, '"An Exaggerated Woman": The Melodramas of Lady Caroline Lamb', *Byromania: Portraits of the Artist in Nineteenth- and Twentieth-Century*, ed. F. Wilson (London: Macmillan, 1999), p. 217.
47. For example, newspapers and periodicals such as *Bon Ton Magazine*, *Morning Post and Gazetteer* (formerly known as the *Morning Post and Fashionable World*) and *Morning Herald*, all of which took a keen interest in the social life of the pre-eminent political families of the day and had reported extensively upon her own family.
48. See below, p. 353.
49. Ibid.
50. Ibid.
51. Ibid.
52. Douglass, *Lady Caroline Lamb: A Biography*, p. 225
53. *Blackwood's Magazine* (Tuesday 30 July), 1822, (1.4.1).
54. H. D. Jump (ed.), *Silver Fork Novels 1826–1841*, 6 vols (London: Pickering & Chatto, 2005), vol. 1, p. ix; G. Kelly, *English Fiction of the Romantic Period 1789–1830* (London and New York: Longman, 1989), p. 220; R. Cronin, R., *Romantic Victorians; English Literature 1824–1840* (Basingstoke and New York: Palgrave, 2002), p. 118.
55. Jump, *Silver Fork Novels 1826–1841*, vol. I, p. xii; Cronin, *Romantic Victorians*, p. 117.
56. Kelly, *English Fiction of the Romantic Period 1789-1830*, p. 221.
57. F. Stafford, '*Lodore*: a Tale of Present Time?', *Mary Shelley's Fictions from 'Frankenstein' to 'Falkner'*, ed. Eberle-Sinatra, M. (London: Macmillan, 2000), p. 185; Jump, *Silver Fork Novels 1826–1841*, vol. 1, p. xiii.
58. Quoted in Stafford, '*Lodore*: a Tale of Present Time?', p. 185.
59. *New Monthly Magazine,* No. 8 (1823), pp. 317–21.

60. *Literary Gazette*, No. 323 (1823), pp. 198–200; *The Examiner*, No. 796 (27 April 1823), p 284.
61. *Examiner*, p. 284. *Anastasius: or, Memoirs of a Greek; Written at the Close of the Eighteenth Century* (1819) by Thomas Hope. *Arabian Nights Entertainments* or *The Thousand and One Nights* was made available in Europe by the translation of Antoine Galland that appeared between 1704 and 1717. *Le Diable Boiteu x*(1707), written by Alain-René Le Sage, better know as the author of *Gil Blas* (1715–35); Le Sage's *Le Diable Boiteux* is not to be confused with Jacques Cazotte's *Le Diable Amoureux* (1772) whence Lamb acquired the name 'Biondetta'. The 'Visions of Quevedo' refer to the work of Spanish satirist and novelist, Francisco de Quevedo y Villegas (1580–1645) and his satiric account of the inhabitants of hell in his work *Los Sueños* ('visions'), first published in 1627 and which were later translated by Roger L'Estrange in 1667 and published in London under the title *The Visions of Dom Francisco de Quevedo Villegas, Knight of the Order of St. James*. *Vathek* (1786) by William Beckford; it was in Byron's copy of *Vathek* that Lamb famously inscribed 'Remember me', which in turn inspired Byron's composition 'Remember Thee! / till Lethe quench Life's burning stream'. James Soderholm notes that Lamb's inscription is reminiscent of the last words of the Ghost to Hamlet: 'Adieu, adieu, adieu! Remember me' as is Byron's reminiscent of Hamlet's repetition of 'Remember Thee!' Soderholm also recognizes that 'Remember me' is perhaps a conscious echo of 'Ricorditi di me che son La Pia' ('do thou remember me, who are La Pia'),Dante, *Purgatorio*, Canto 5, line 133. La Pia is among three sinners who were impenitent up to the last hour. See James Soderholm, 'Lady Caroline Lamb – Byron's Miniature Writ Large', *Keats-Shelley Journal*, 40 (1991), p. 42.
62. This is a point made by Marilyn Butler in 'Orientalism', in ed. D.B. Pirie (ed.), *The Penguin History of Literature, Vol. 5: The Romantic Period*, (London, Penguin, 1994), p. 396.
63. M. Strickland, *The Byron Women* (London: Peter Owen, 1974), pp. 212–16; D. Wu, *Romanticism, An Anthology*, 2nd edn (Oxford: Blackwell, 1994), pp. 650–7.
64. F. McCarthy, *Byron: Life and Legend* (London: John Murray, 2002), p. 349.
65. (I, 37, 39).
66. R. Kee, *The Green Flag, Volume 1: The Most Distressful Country* (1972; London: Penguin, 1989), p. 50.
67. J. Garver, (1980), 'Gothic Ireland: Lady Caroline Lamb's *Glenarvon*', *A Journal of Irish Studies*, 4:10 (1980), p. 216.
68. M. Kelsall, 'The Byronic Hero and Revolution in Ireland: the Politics of *Glenarvon*', *The Byron Journal*, 9 (1981), p. 6.
69. Moretti, (1999), p. 83.
70. See Volume 2, p. 4.
71. Thomas Paine, *Rights of Man, Common Sense and Other Political Writings*, ed. M. Philip, (Oxford: Oxford University Press, 1995), pp. 217–18.
72. See Volume 2, p. 4.
73. See below, p. 135.

GLENARVON

Introduction

Lady Caroline Lamb claimed she dashed *Glenarvon* (1816) off in a month, but in fact she worked on it over several years.[1] In fall 1812, after her family took her to Ireland in an attempt to end her affair with Byron, Lamb wrote songs and stories that would evolve into the novel, and the manuscript had been mostly completed before news of her brother Frederick's near-fatal injuries at Waterloo (in June 1815) diverted her attention and took her to Brussels. She arranged to have her manuscript delivered to Byron's publisher, John Murray, shortly after her departure for the continent.[2] After a long period of deliberation, Murray declined *Glenarvon*, perhaps because it did not meet his standards or because he felt Byron would object to his publishing an ex-lover's novel obviously based partly on their affair. He may also have feared that the powerful Melbournes, Devonshires, Spencers and Bessboroughs might become angry if the novel created a scandal. Murray's rejection arrived in February of 1816, when Lamb was undergoing severe stress.

Lamb's in-laws were pressing her husband William to separate from her. They had been upset by Lamb's public love affairs, first with Sir Godfrey Vassal Webster in 1810–11, and then Lord Byron in 1812. Lamb's behaviour was unpredictable, and she had fought violently, at times, with William. Even though the Lambs were no great respecters of propriety, she made them nervous. Her mother-in-law, Lady Melbourne, and sister-in-law, Lady Cowper, went so far as to call in a physician who was willing to declare Lamb insane and commit her to an asylum. Lady Cowper told Lamb's brothers that she had suffered a breakdown, produced the written diagnosis, and confronted Lamb, extorting her promise not to fight the separation. Lamb later protested to her mother-in-law over these strong-arm tactics: 'As to any promises I may have been forced to make when a straight waistcoat & a Mad Doctor are held forth to view – they cannot expect I should think them binding... it is too sad to hear all this is for my own good'.[3] The plan fizzled when William Lamb refused to cooperate.

Her second choice for a publisher was Henry Colburn, a highly successful purveyor of popular fiction who would soon pioneer the 'silver-fork' novel, a genre of which *Glenarvon* is sometimes thought a precursor.[4] While Colburn deliberated, Lamb felt a sudden foreboding that she would die before the novel could be published – before, that is, anyone could discover the 'anonymous' writer's identity: '[I]n such case', she told Colburn, 'I beg you to do justice to my little narrative – to have it published with my name [–] its errors will then be examined at once. A short preface and my name would make the sale such as to enable you to perform my wishes'.[5] Her first letters to Colburn had been diffident: 'You will easily see by the style of this book that it is written more from the feelings than the mind. However careless it may appear to a Critic's eye it has caused me much labour'. Cautious Colburn showed the manuscript to readers whose opinions (now seemingly lost) upset Lamb, but eventually he took the book, advancing her £200 with an agreement to pay £300 upon publication. He must have anticipated good revenue, for he had recently paid a successful writer £550 for a novel.[6]

As the first volume of *Glenarvon* was being set in type, Lamb went over the proofs, quickly detecting unwanted changes: 'I shall be seriously angry if any alteration is made whatever either in punctuation or orthography & I entreat you to send me the proof sheets. Remember and send the remainder of the 1st vol. – for I have been obliged to alter it all back again…'[7] Colburn apparently wanted to move ahead as rapidly as possible, but Lamb was struggling to finish proofreading. Thus distracted, she was caught off guard when Byron chose to flee the country rather than continue fighting with his estranged wife, Annabella, over custody of their daughter. He left England abruptly on 23 April, having been forced to sell most of his books to raise funds for his trip. He departed just minutes ahead of the authorities, who seized everything they could find in his apartments for debts still owed. Lamb wrote Byron offering to sell some 'trinkets & things' worth about £300 if it would redeem some of his property. At the same time she stated definitively to Byron's close friend, John Cam Hobhouse, that in the quarrel between Byron and his wife, Annabella: 'I … take her part not his'.[8]

On 27 April, as publication neared, Lamb's foreboding grew. Hobhouse thought she seemed 'ready to sink' with anxiety.[9] Colburn had agreed to print the music for two songs (set by Isaac Nathan) in the novel, but they were inadvertently left out: 'I am quite vex'd at seeing the songs without the music', Lamb wrote.[10] Perhaps Lamb felt Nathan's music would help to sell the novel because the second and final volume of Byron and Nathan's successful song collection, *Hebrew Melodies*, had just appeared in April 1816. The music was put back in, and when *Glenarvon* was published on 9 May 1816 and Lamb held it in her hands, she wrote with premonitory anxiety: '[I]t looks beautiful but made my heart beat!'[11] It had been a rush job, with multiple versions over a very short time, and a good deal of correspondence exchanged between Lamb and Colburn. There were typos. The numbering of chapters was confused.[12] But the author was proud of it, and sent copies to friends and acquaintances.

Reception

Though the novel was published anonymously, the public soon knew the author's identity. *Glenarvon* was viewed immediately as a 'kiss and tell' confessional, or as Byron damningly put it, a ' – and publish' betrayal.[13] The reaction was apparently not at all what Lamb expected. Family and friends felt she had acted treacherously, and the day after the novel was published, messages of outrage began to arrive. Henry Webster called to berate her for what he believed were unflattering portraits of his brother and mother.[14] Byron's close associate Hobhouse wrote to say he might retaliate for the supposed assault on Lord Byron's character by publishing some of Lamb's letters. This message caused Lamb nothing but 'great astonishment', according to her mother-in-law.[15] It is unclear whether Hobhouse had at that point actually read *Glenarvon* or was reacting to the gossip then circulating. Lamb's surprise at the hubbub seems genuine. She had not intended, either, to reignite a family civil war over her behaviour. Her brother-in-law Frederick and sister-in-law Lady Cowper redoubled efforts to effect William Lamb's separation from his wife. Lamb wrote with savage irony to friends whom she suspected of encouraging the separation that 'it is my wish that the utmost severity may be shown me by every body'.[16]

Glenarvon has been read as a compulsive act of confession. John Clubbe suggests that the novel 'forced itself out of her: she had to write it as much as Byron had to write his confessional poems'.[17] This is an impulse that Peter Graham likens to a volcanic explosion, over which Lamb had no control: by 'foolishly publishing a transcript of her own folly[;] Lady Caroline makes a good confession but a bad novel'.[18] Lamb defended herself in a preface to the second edition (see Appendix A below), charging that her relations and friends – especially her sister-in-law, Lady Cowper, mother-in-law, Lady Melbourne, and friend, Lady Holland – had 'supported Byron for four years even though it annoyed William [Lamb]', and that they had unfairly dredged up all Lamb's misdemeanours and crimes at once, 'stretching back to the days of infancy', and sought 'without mercy' to have her certified insane.[19] An echo of Lamb's rebellion against this double standard may be perceived, as Frances Wilson points out, in the story of Lamb's descendant from the Spencer line, Diana, Princess of Wales.[20] Like the author herself, *Glenarvon* was not 'tactful'.

Logically following from her tactlessness came charges that Lamb had committed a flagrant act of self-aggrandizement and made a shameless play for sympathy. She became untouchable, and her reputation for insanity is largely based upon her apparent act of social suicide. But if we recall Lamb's stated motives for writing and publishing the novel, then her work seems not much of a confession. Some characters and scenes were certainly recognizable as people and places she knew, but that is often true of novels. Unfortunately, her circle of acquaintance was comprised of very public figures. Moreover, contrary to Hobhouse's initial reaction, Byron was not the primary target for embarrassment. As she said herself, 'Had I chosen to be ill-natured [about Byron], God knows without deviating from the truth I had plenty of means'.[21] Admittedly, Lamb had mixed motives. She wrote to strike back at Byron and those who had snubbed her. She would accomplish this by exposing his shortcomings as a 'hero': Glenarvon – 'the idol they once adored ... a coward and a hypocrite ... smooth dissembler , and while he smiles he stabs'.[22] But her deeper intention was to reveal the warped values of a society that knowingly continued to abide behaviour that was more criminal then her own. Of Calantha, the novel's heroine, Lady Caroline wrote, '[S]he heard folly censured till she took it to be criminal; but crime she saw tolerated if well concealed'.[23] From this perspective, the novel dramatizes Calantha's refusal to learn 'the language of hypocrisy and deceit'.[24] A highly unflattering mirror was held up to English aristocracy.

In addition to the impropriety of exposing her affair with Byron and putting the aristocracy in a bad light, Lamb set her novel in Ireland during the uprising for Catholic emancipation of 1798, which was brutally repressed. The novel's scandal thus lay in at least two quarters: first, it made a public liaison even more public, dragging into the open a cast of characters from the highest aristocratic circles of England; second, it endorsed the political aspirations and military struggles of Irish Catholics, painting Glenarvon, its eponymous Byronic hero, as a traitor of their cause. For this and for his offences against women he is condemned to hell. If Lamb thought that Glenarvon's death, and the deathbed repentance of Calantha would put an acceptable moral context around the transgressions the novel describes, she was wrong.

Lamb's husband was reputed to be ignorant of his wife's authorial ambitions, but William Lamb knew *Glenarvon* existed long before it was published, and he apparently encouraged his wife's writing career. He claimed ignorance only to calm family indignation. Shortly after the novel was published, he wrote Henry Colburn to say his wife had proceeded 'without any consultation with her friends' and that 'there shall be published no second edition'. Colburn's 'knowledge of the world' would undoubtedly help him to understand William's decision.[25] William never said that he was himself ignorant of his wife's plans – only that her *friends* were. Gradually, his position altered, and scarcely ten days later he had admitted he knew about the novel but claimed that he had never seen the unpleasant parts.[26]

The reaction of family and acquaintances to *Glenarvon* was generally outrage at the apparent violation of their privacy, but this was not universal. Lady Byron's first response to *Glenarvon* was largely positive. She sat down a week after the novel had appeared and wrote out comments on the character of Calantha, whose creed she described as, 'I am thought of – therefore I am'. More tellingly, she conceded that the reader might involuntarily give in to Calantha's self-justifications, and that this could lead to adopting her view that Glenarvon embodied the ideals of love and poetry. Without the cosmetic treatment provided by Calantha's homage, Glenarvon seemed pitiless, a man whose 'rage was impotent in proportion to its impiety'.[27] Lady Byron recommended the novel to others, including Lady Melbourne and Mrs. George Lamb, who was flabbergasted: 'Your opinion of *Glenarvon* is very indulgent', she remarked with that exaggerated tact of her class. 'I agree with you in the tendency of the moral and the cleverness of many parts ... but I cannot forgive [Lamb], for the ridicule that she throws at William, by the publishing all their private secrets'.[28] The opinion that Lamb had done something 'unforgivable' was echoed in the reviews.

The *British Critic* described *Glenarvon* as composed of 'scenes of seduction and adultery' that would initiate innocent minds into 'the mysteries of profligacy'. The reviewer found Glenarvon himself an appalling figure, especially since he was presented as 'the idol of the female heart', and treated the book as representing the 'morals of Paris and Vienna' – shorthand for 'Sodom and Gomorrah' – written by an author who seemed bent on 'publishing to the world her own shame', and who seemed 'to glory in her guilt'. The reviewer dismissed the novel 'with a mixed feeling of abhorrence and pity'.[29] The *Theatrical Inquisitor* acknowledged Lady Caroline's 'animated style, brilliance of imagery, and [her] skillful delineation of gloomy and mysterious character', but decided that *Glenarvon* posed a 'tiresome and revolting task' for the reader. The author was charged with seeking to revenge herself upon 'the society from which she has been excluded', especially in assassinating Lady Holland's character in the personification of the Princess of Madagascar. Like the *British Critic*, the *Theatrical Inquisitor* argued that *Glenarvon* was a pornographic work dangerous to 'the young and the virtuous', and even compared it to John Cleland's *Fanny Hill*.[30]

Comparing *Glenarvon* to *Fanny Hill* was true hyperbole, and the suspicion of a campaign to brand the novel as grossly indecent is substantiated by similar exaggeration of its sexual explicitness in the *British Lady's Magazine*. The reviewer admitted ordering the book because he had 'been taught to expect allusion to existing character; and in truth, sent for these volumes with the idea of being entertained with all manner of fashionable scandal'. The reviewer went on to claim that he had never encountered 'a more senseless farrago of extravagance ... than this wretched production', which was 'disgusting, immoral, and tawdry' and on top of that, 'farcical'. Hoping to damn the author with her own words, the reviewer printed a lengthy extract from Glenarvon's death scene on shipboard, ending lamely with the statement that the novel was 'the silliest production in the world'. Acknowledging that the song lyrics in *Glenarvon* possessed 'both nature and feeling', the review described them as a failed attempt to dress up a tawdry item: like 'embroidery upon a blanket'.[31]

The *Monthly Review*'s short notice avoided discussion of *Glenarvon*'s assault upon public decency, if it detected any, and focused on the novel's 'strangeness'. Was it a romance or a biography?: '[I]t is of the *doubtful gender*, though a feminine production', but overall, simply 'wearisome'.[32] *The Augustan Review* first nodded to the widely-reported scandal of the author's having 'intended to delineate her acquaintance under the names of the interesting persons who figure in the work', but acknowledged not being 'sure whether this is the case'. The reviewer then followed the *Monthly Review* in criticizing the novel's artistry: 'There is a constant straining at *effect*, which often fails in a most lamentable manner', though the novel showed 'indications of genius' and 'gleams of tenderness and fancy' in its handling of the guilty passion of Calantha and Glenarvon.[33] Though the notice in the *Augustan Review* was not enthusiastic, Lamb liked it, 'because it takes the thing fairly, and not as real characters' – in other words, not as if she had simply transcribed her impressions of people she knew.[34]

A lone exception to the mostly negative reviews appeared in the *New Monthly Magazine*, which printed a short notice calling *Glenarvon* a history 'ably and vigorously drawn' of Byron's crimes, and therefore 'a fearful beacon to warn the young and inexperienced against the danger of talents unsanctified by a sense of duty', as well as 'an effectual antidote to the arts of deception and the blandishments of vice!'[35] Perhaps the reviewer was an acquaintance of the author, for he seemed to know her stated intentions.

Revision

William Lamb's complicity in his wife's writing career is proved by his giving permission for further editions, despite the wounded outrage of his friends and family. Within days of his statement that Colburn would print no more copies, Lamb wrote to her publisher, 'I am happy to say that I have obtained leave to publish a second Edition which will be greatly improved without delaying the Printer. I have also written a most beautiful preface'. Lamb wanted her name printed on the title page this time, and she promised to make improvements on the first edition expeditiously: 'I will learn all the marks to which the Printers are used ... I see so many errors I corrected last time'. She sent him the preface and asked him to 'get rid of the 1st Edition as quick as possible that I may correct some very ridiculous mistakes in the second'.[36] She strongly desired to appease critics within the Lamb–Bessborough circle. 'I am doing every thing I can to stop the further mischief', she told Lady Melbourne.[37]

Lamb did indeed revise *Glenarvon* carefully in an attempt to damp the fires of controversy, and she expended a lot of energy so that the printer would encounter minimal problems in re-setting the novel. For every word she added, she sought to subtract at least one. Revisions decreased the page count of volume I from 295 to 288. Remarkably, she kept the page counts for volumes II and III exactly the same: 390 and 322 respectively. The revisions were numerous; over 1,000 individual changes were made in the first volume alone, and a similar number in volume II. Volume III was relatively lightly edited, and edits from chapter 21 to the conclusion are especially light. Hundreds of the changes were minor punctuational ones: substituting a colon for a semi-colon and vice versa; putting in commas and taking them out; adding exclamation marks; subtracting dashes. These small edits show how carefully the author went over her text, though they changed little of substance. Hundreds of other changes were, however, substantive. She cancelled passages and added others in the attempt to assuage her critics and mollify her family. She changed the characterizations of Glenarvon and Calantha, dropped or modified some passages that supporters of Lady Holland and Samuel Rogers had complained about, and reduced the gothic elements. Glenarvon grew somewhat less Satanic, while Calantha and her family became Catholics.[38] Lord Avondale was made somewhat more noble and courageous; he also more specifically repented that he had not seized control of his errant wife. The duel between Avondale and Glenarvon was also altered so that Glenarvon commits a dastardly act, stabbing Avondale in the chest.

Most of Lamb's substantive revisions were aimed at deflecting charges of immorality. For example, direct references to God are often eliminated. 'God' becomes 'Heaven' or 'Being'; 'Oh God!' becomes 'Oh Heavens!'; 'for God's sake' becomes 'in mercy'. This attempt to deflect charges of blasphemy is accompanied by the effort to play down the carnal nature of the relationship between Glenarvon and Calantha. In a brief passage in chapter 12 of volume II,[39] Lamb alters the phrase 'fires of lust' to 'fires of passion', changes 'whirlwinds of passion' to 'whirlwinds', and substitutes 'pure' for chaste'. Another example may be found in chapter 23 of the second volume. There Lamb wrote originally, 'As he spoke, he again pressed her to his bosom, and his tears fell over her'. The second edition alters this to, 'As he spoke his tears fell upon her hand'.[40] In the fourth chapter of volume II, Lamb cuts several descriptions of physical attraction: '...but the kiss I have snatched from your lips is sweeter far for me. Oh, for another, given thus warm from the heart! It has entranced – it has made me mad'.[41] The sexual aspect of the relationship is not eliminated, but it is submerged. Similarly, in the first pages of volume III, Lamb reverses her statements about human frailty to avoid charges that she makes excuses for the heroine's misbehaviour: 'There are trials which human frailty cannot resist' becomes 'There is no trial which human frailty cannot resist ... if we call upon our God to assist us... '[42]

A good example of Lamb's revision technique may be found in chapter 16 of volume II of the novel. Changes include: deletion of two dashes; insertion of eight commas; deletion of six commas; conversion of one comma to a semicolon; capitalization of three words ('Greek Church' and 'Princess'); spelling out the word 'damn'd (rather than 'd – d'); correction of three typographical errors ('concietious', 'disconfiture', and 'change: his' (the latter a superfluous colon – all changes handled as silent corrections in the present edition); introduction of one error, probably by the printer ('exuberant' became 'exuberent'); change of a name spelt differently in the first edition ('Mowbray' becomes 'Mowbrey'); failure to correct a typographical error ('wispered' remains uncorrected; handled in this edition as a silent correction); and the substitution of one word for another ('pretty' becomes 'handsome'). In all, Lamb cuts twenty-eight words and adds fifteen. The deletions and additions have three apparent purposes: first, to add specificity (the word 'it' is modified to 'the partiality'); second, to change the sense of the activities at Castle Delaval (from 'an agreeable variety' to 'rational pleasure of the society'); and third, to tone down the passion of the relationship between Calantha and Glenarvon as exhibited in the scene in which he gives her a ring. The sentences in the first edition read:

> As he spoke, he pretended to pick up a ring. 'Is this yours?' he said. 'No'. 'It is', he whispered; and placed it himself upon her finger.

In the second edition, the same passage reads simply: 'He gave her a ring'. The changes here typify patterns of revision throughout the second edition of *Glenarvon*.

Not satisfied simply to minimize what offended – or at least recontextualizing it as less morally ambiguous – Lamb hit back at her critics in her preface. Lamb argues that the novel is not immoral at all, despite the inclusion of characters and actions that are reprehensible.[43] She asked that readers recognize her intention to describe, rather than to degrade human nature, and reminded them that most novels and narrative poems have such material in them. If some readers thought they were personally slandered, that was not her intention, she said.[44] Though some of the 'applications' detected by readers were undoubtedly intentional, Lamb apparently never meant to offend so many so personally. She extensively revised the second edition, then published a third 'edition' which did not differ from the second, except for a handful of minor edits in vol. II, the inclusion in some copies of her name as author, and frontispiece engravings taken from designs by Lamb herself. In a fourth edition (1817), Lamb further underscored her fidelity to her theme of the ineluctable passions, as her protagonist, Calantha, claims that a 'power stronger than reason... impelled me forward to my ruin'. The novel was later translated into Italian in 1817, and into French in 1819 and 1824. A severely edited, cheaply printed, and now very rare version was printed as *The Fatal Passion* in 1865 and 1866.

Glenarvon as Roman à Clef

Lamb apparently never intended her novel to be a simple *roman à clef* (a novel with a key), despite obvious allusions to real people whom she mocked or praised. Most readers, however, wrote 'keys' on *Glenarvon's* endpapers. In the end, most were so fascinated by this hunt for allusions to the denizens of London society that they really couldn't appreciate the novel as fiction. Lady Holland identified Caroline's cousin Harriet Cavendish as the character of Sophia (Mrs Seymour's daughter) because she was preoccupied with embroidery. The traitorous Lady Oxford, who had encouraged Byron to write cruelly to Caroline when he broke off their affair in 1812, was identified by Lady Holland and others as the character Lady Mandeville. Lady Holland also suspected that the character of William Buchanan was based upon her own son, Sir Godfrey Vassal Webster, with whom Lamb had carried on an affair in 1810–11: 'His hands were decorated with rings, and a gold chain and half-concealed picture hung round his neck: his height, his mustachios, the hussar trappings of his horse, the high colour in his cheek, and his dark flowing locks, gave an air of savage wildness to his countenance and figure, which much delighted Calantha'.⁴⁵ Naturally, Lady Holland disliked the character of the Princess of Madagascar, because 'every ridicule, folly and infirmity (my not being able from malady to move about much) is portrayed'. No doubt upset, she commented rather temperately, 'The work is a strange *farrago*', and confined herself to sympathizing with the *real* victims: 'I am sorry to see the Melbourne family so miserable about it. Lady Cowper is really frightened and depressed far beyond what is necessary'.⁴⁶ *Glenarvon* caused a mild hysteria among those who believed they had glimpsed their own caricatures. Many who took offence did so because of scenes in volumes I and II satirizing London society in the houses of Lamb's friends, especially Lady Holland. The Princess of Madagascar is accompanied by a cadaverous sycophant Fremore (the name is misprinted as 'Tremore' three times in the first edition), who was based upon Samuel Rogers, and a cast of characters from Holland House makes its appearance in those scenes. Rogers, a man with a famously sardonic tongue, was only one of several figures ripe for satire then and after. Miss Emily Eden later wrote of him:

> We have had the most alarming visit from Rogers the Poet this morning, the very recollection of which would make my hair, black pins, combs and all, stand on end, if they ever subsided since his first appearance. I never saw such a satirical, odious wretch, and I was calculating the whole time, from what he was saying of other people, what he could find ill-natured enough to say of us. I had never seen him before, and trust I never shall again.⁴⁷

As John Clubbe says, *Glenarvon* captured the 'wit and artificial bonhomie' of Whig culture so perfectly that twenty years after *Glenarvon* appeared, friends still called Lady Holland the 'Princess Madagascar' behind her back.⁴⁸

Some readers of *Glenarvon* could be dispassionate in assigning 'originals' to its characters. Robert Wilmot was an acquaintance of Lady Byron's, and he wrote to her with his own key to the novel, most of whose characters he perceptively described as 'compounds' rather than 'portraits':

> Of course Lady C[aroline] & W[illiam] L[amb] you will easily recognise. Miss Monmouth perhaps *you do not know*, but I do, & can assure you that she is a most delightful person [i. e., Lady Byron herself]. Lady Mandeville is Lady Oxford – P[rincess] of Madagascar, Lady H[olland] ... as to the other characters, I much question their being portraits, but rather compounds ... there are traits in Lady Margaret meant for your dear Aunt [Lady Melbourne]. Some say that Buchanan is Sir G[odfrey Vassal] Webster, others that Lady Augusta is Lady Jersey, others that Lady Margaret is the present D[uchess] of D[evonshire]. Mrs Seymour is I should think compounded of parts of the character of the late Duchess & Lady Bessborough [Lamb's mother].[49]

Wilmot was right that *Glenarvon*'s characters cannot be quickly and simply keyed to a list of real persons. The attempt to do so has led to highly contradictory lists of 'originals'. For example, Mrs Seymour was often understood by readers as a version of the sisters, Georgiana and Harriet (Lamb's aunt and mother). Yet Mabell, Countess of Airlie, thought that Lady Melbourne, Lamb's mother-in-law, was 'probably represented under the name of Mrs. Seymour'.[50] Another later commentator, Marjorie Villiers, tells us that the character of Lady Margaret is the Duchess of Devonshire.[51] And Paston and Quennell are confident that Lady Melbourne is represented in the novel by the character of Avondale's aunt, Lady Mowbrey (also called on one occasion Lady Monteith, after the estate on which she dwells).[52] This brings more confusion than clarity, and points to the limit of the *roman à clef* as applied to *Glenarvon*.

Often, readers apparently thought they knew the identity of a particular character when they recognized some element in the plot connected with that person. The story of the birth of Sidney Albert, the disappearing heir who reappears as Zerbellini, was read by some as based on a malicious rumour that the Marquis of Hartington – later the sixth Duke of Devonshire – had really been the illegitimate child of his mother's friend and father's lover, Lady Elizabeth Foster. To accept this reading meant equating the devious Lady Margaret with Georgiana, Duchess of Devonshire – a 'key' that makes little sense.[53] Similarly, assuming Lord Avondale is meant to stand for William Lamb, then Lady Elizabeth Mowbrey, sister of Lord Avondale, would seem to allude to Emily Lamb (later Lady Cowper), William's sister. And yet the name 'Elizabeth' recalls the hated Elizabeth Foster, who outraged Lamb when she married her uncle, the fifth Duke of Devonshire, after the death of her beloved aunt Georgiana. Alternatively, the name 'Elizabeth' also recalls Lady Melbourne – whose maiden name was Elizabeth Milbanke, and whose grandmother had been named 'Delavel'. Indeed, there is something uncanny about the names in *Glenarvon*. Lord Avondale shares certain characteristics with Lamb's husband William and with Lord Byron, and his name constitutes a mirror image of Glenarvon's: Glen and dale – these words evoke *Glenarvon*'s mystical Irish countryside.

If many originals may constitute one character, several characters may derive from one original—or if not traceable to originals, they may appear in alternate versions, a doubling effect of which Lamb seems to have been particularly fond. Byron's identity is manifested in Glenarvon, de Ruthven and Viviani (admittedly merely his alias), but also in William Buchanan, who flatters Alice Mac Allain, delights in being supposed her seducer, and even returns to flatter Calantha herself before Glenarvon makes inroads into her heart. Calantha, too, is only one of several characters with whom Lamb identified. Other reflections of Lamb are found in Alice Mac Allain, who becomes pregnant by Glenarvon and begs in vain for his help, and even in the little page-boy, Zerbellini (also known as, Sidney Albert, the Duke's heir).[54] Lady Caroline's breeches-roles often featured a page's outfit of hussar jacket, feathered cap and silver buttons, and she was sometimes called pejoratively, by her in-laws, 'Cherubina' – an Italian nuance retained in 'Zerbellini'. Elinor St Clare, with her penchant for playing the harp, writing songs and dressing like a man, also embodies aspects of Lamb, and after Calantha dies, Elinor steps forward to re-invoke the 'broken heart' motif before expiring herself in a suicidal leap on horseback, 'bleeding to death from her wounds' sustained in the ill-fated rebellion and in her affair with Glenarvon, whose estate is burning to the ground.[55] Even the scheming Lady Margaret herself exhibits characteristics derived from Lamb, for she has a 'fierce spirit which never yet had been controuled – which deemed itself born to command, and would have perished sooner than have endured restraint'.[56] Most readers, however, identified Calantha as Lamb's character, pure and simple, though they failed to appreciate the literary allusion which makes Calantha a symbol of her class.

Named after the protagonist of John Ford's *The Broken Heart* (1633), *Glenarvon's* Calantha Delaval is no simple authorial self-portrait. Parallels between the two Calanthas make it obvious that Lamb structured her novel around the allusion to aristocratic stoicism conveyed by the choice of the name.

Ford's Calantha is a princess of Sparta who is betrothed to her cousin, Nearchus, the Prince of Argos. She is in love, however, with Ithocles, and together they persuade Calantha's father – and even Nearchus himself – to accept their marriage. Ithocles's twin sister, Penthea, is in love with Orgilus, but her brother, despite his insistence on a love-match for himself, demands that she marry Bassanes, who is wealthier, but much older. Penthea eventually starves herself to death rather than continue in a loveless marriage to a jealous older husband. The spurned lover Orgilus murders Ithocles in revenge. In the ensuing scene at a festival dance Calantha hears that her father, her friend Penthea and her husband-to-be Ithocles are dead. Nonetheless she forbids the dance to stop. Once it has reached its conclusion, she takes up the mantle of queen, sentences Orgilus to death for the murder of Ithocles, then gives her kingdom to Nearchus. Her last acts are to put her wedding ring on the finger of Ithocles and to die of a broken heart. The scene is an exhibition of an aristocratic ideal of self-control under duress – an exemplification of how one must never forget one's place as a member of the nobility.

Ford had undergone a minor revival during the Romantic period. Charles Lamb had included an extended discussion of Calantha and *The Broken Heart* in *Specimens of English Dramatic Poets, Who Lived About the Time of Shakspeare*, which appeared in 1808, and in a new edition in 1811. As T. J. B. Spencer notes, contemporary critics William Hazlitt, William Gifford, and Francis Jeffrey all discussed Ford's accomplishments as a playwright.[57] As Leigh Wetherall Dickson has documented, Ford also drew Byron's attention for his candid approach to the theme of incest. Ford became a significant source for Lamb's writing because one of his major themes is the importance and integrity of the aristocracy as occupying an 'intermediary position between the people and the monarchy'. Ford's depiction of ideal behavior for the aristocracy provides Lamb with a framework for delineating the moral bankruptcy of the aristocrats of her era. Additionally, as Byron appreciated, Ford dealt non-judgementally with taboo sexual relationships, writing sympathetically about those who are trapped by their own strong passions.

Parallels between *The Broken Heart*, *Glenarvon* and Lamb's life are founded upon the heroine's rejection of what Wetherall Dickson labels the 'dynastic marriage' in favour of a love-match. Ford's Princess Calantha rejects Nearchus for Ithocles; and Lamb's Lady Calantha rejects her cousin William Buchanan for Lord Avondale, just as Lady Caroline Lamb rejected her own cousin, the Marquis of Hartington, for William Lamb. In several scenes of *Glenarvon*, Lamb borrows from Ford and revises his telling of the tragedy that ensues when true love (the love of Orgilus for Penthea in *The Broken Heart*, and the love of Calantha for Glenarvon) is thwarted. In many places in the novel Lady Calantha Avondale's stoicism is evoked. The literary allusion of 'Calantha' is driven home in chapter thirteen of volume two of *Glenarvon*, when Calantha's friend, Lady Augusta, asks her if she has ever read *The Broken Heart* (she has not). 'At this moment', continues Lady Augusta, 'you put me vastly in mind of it. You look most woefully. Come, tell me truly, is not your heart in torture? and, like your namesake Calantha, while lightly dancing the gayest in the ring, has not the shaft already been struck, and shall you not die ere you attain the goal?'[58]

John Ford's drama provides a touchstone for *Glenarvon*'s moral and dramatic structure, focusing as it does upon the failure of the aristocracy and the disaster of denying true love, even if it is taboo. Nowhere is the message more clearly stated than in Calantha's speech, delivered to her aunt, Lady Seymour, shortly before she dies in chapter 16 of volume III. It is a confession of the failure of the British aristocracy to adhere to the high principles of behaviour demanded of the privileged few:

'From the deep recesses of a guilty, yet not humble heart, in the agony and the hopelessness of despair', said Calantha, 'I acknowledge before God and before man, that for me there is no excuse. I have felt, I have enjoyed every happiness, every delight, the earth can offer. Its vanities, its pleasures, its transports have been mine; and in all instances I have misused the power with which I have been too much and too long entrusted. Oh, may the God of worlds innumerable, who scatters his blessings upon all and maketh his rain to fall upon the sinner, as upon the righteous, extend his mercy even unto me ... Tell them I do not hope that my example can amend them: they will not turn from one wrong pursuit for me; they will not compare themselves with Calantha ... Yet when they read my history – if amidst the severity of justice which such a narrative must excite, some feelings of forgiveness and pity should arise, perhaps the prayer of one, who has suffered much, may ascend for them, and the thanks of a broken heart be accepted in return'.[59]

The exact phrase, ' broken heart', occurs eight times in volume III of *Glenarvon*; and the word 'heart' occurs over 500 times in the novel. In Elinor's final appearance, her last words before plunging to her death from the cliffs of Heremon include, 'Peace to the broken hearts'.[60]

Glenarvon's Achievement

In her condemnation of the English aristocracy and her dissection of the disastrous relationship of Calantha and Glenarvon, Lamb explores the themes of Ford richly, sharpening them with political observations of the Irish rebellion. Perhaps contemporary reviewers treated *Glenarvon* with excessive harshness because they felt irritated with the author's eccentric personality and tactless exposure of private lives of the wealthy and famous. And certainly the novel has passages that are tiresome in their repetition: angst-filled trysts and overwrought exclamations of love, pain and self-recrimination. A disproportionate irritation with these failings has persisted, with twentieth-century condemnations of the novel as 'a deplorable production'[61] that is 'outrageous' and 'badly written'.[62] But if Lamb writes badly, and if her story is the 'silliest production in the world', how did she manage to satirize so many people so hilariously? With its flaws, *Glenarvon* is still the work of a literate and politically sensitive mind. The novel exhibits the fruits of its author's experience of Shakespeare, Byron, Cazotte, Moore, Marlowe, Voltaire, Dante, Tacitus and de Laclos.

Lamb also paid homage to literary foremothers, like novelists Germaine de Staël and Ann Radcliffe, and also to Lady Morgan, who had published *St. Clair, or the Heiress of Desmond* (1803) and *The Wild Irish Girl* (1806), her most famous novel, which focused on music and national identity. Many echoes of Morgan's work are found in *Glenarvon*. Glorvina O'Melville, the heroine of *The Wild Irish Girl*, first appears in the castle chapel playing the harp for her father and the chaplain, while the male protagonist spies upon her. Lamb introduces Elinor St Clair in *Glenarvon* in the same manner. Like Lady Morgan's heroines, the women of *Glenarvon* are mysterious, intelligent and passionate about politics. Caroline also emulated Lady Morgan by incorporating Irish myth and legend into the setting of her novel. Maria Edgeworth, too, influenced *Glenarvon*. For example, the first song that appears in the novel is the 'Pillalu', a 'song of sorrow' chanted by the 'tenants and peasantry' over the body of what they believe is the son of the local laird, the Duke of Delaval: 'Oh loudly sing the Pillalu, / And many a tear of sorrow shed. . .'.[63] Lamb could have observed an Irish funeral procession herself, but Maria Edgeworth's *Castle Rackrent* (1800) is a more likely source, with its Irish lamentation over the dead – sometimes called 'Whillaluh' or 'Ullaloo'.[64]

Consistent with Lady Morgan's focus on a nexus of song and national identity, Lamb included fourteen songs in *Glenarvon*, and in two cases printed music to allow performance. These songs, which she published in a separate volume titled *Verses from Glenarvon* (1819), allude to other songs. For example, when Glenarvon sings 'Farewell' in volume II he does so in strains reminiscent of Byron's well-known lyric, 'Maid of Athens': 'Maid of Athens, ere we part, / Give oh give me back my heart' is reflected in Lady Caroline's 'Come give thy hand, what though we part, / Thy name is fixed, within my heart', The final stanza of Byron's poem strikes a related chord: 'Maid of Athens, I am gone; / Think of me, sweet! when alone'. Caroline echoes: 'Thou'lt think of me when I am gone, / None shall undo, what I have done'.[65] Lamb obtained the help of Byron's partner in the *Hebrew Melodies* (1815–16), Isaac Nathan, who had also set 'Maid of Athens' to music during this period, to write the music for 'Farewell' printed in *Glenarvon*.

'Farewell' is symbolic of the political and personal betrayal that lies at *Glenarvon*'s core. Lord Glenarvon, like Lord Byron, perfected a method of riveting attention upon himself that often involved elaborate, dramatic departures – departures which promised but rarely delivered triumphant returns. Lord Glenarvon abandons his countrymen when they need him most, during Ireland's abortive 1798 rebellion. Hoping for the aid of the French, the Society of United Irishmen have set aside their religious differences to, as Robert Kee puts it, 'eradicate the baneful English influence and destroy the aristocratic tyrants of the land'.[66] Malcolm Kelsall has pointed out that *Glenarvon* gives little account of the oppression that provoked the rebellion, and that its landscape is a naïve representation.[67] Admittedly, Lamb had limited experience of Ireland, but the conspiracy to rebellion in *Glenarvon* alludes to historical fact well-known at the time, and its roots are certainly discussed in the novel.

While writing from the position of an English aristocrat, Lamb nonetheless faithfully records the disintegration of Anglo–Irish relations, about which she knew a great deal as the niece of the Lord High Treasurer of Ireland, the Duke of Devonshire, who was also the Governor of County Cork and owned Lismore Castle in County Waterford. Additionally, Lamb's father's owned Irish estates at Kildaton in County Kilkenny, given to his forebears by Cromwell; and Lamb's husband was heir to the Irish Viscountcy of Melbourne, seated at Kilmore in County Cavan.[68] Lamb portrays this complicated and fraught relationship of English aristocrats to their Irish lands and subjects in *Glenarvon*, depicting the Duke of Altamonte as a nobleman who has retired as a failure in social and political life, retreating 'sullen and reserved' to Ireland, where he proves ineffective as the Irish rebellion gathers strength. His own tenants are 'mutinous and discontented' because he 'refused to attend to the grievances and burthens of which the nation generally complained'.[69] Lamb sums up the state of Irish dissatisfaction with the occupation by the Anglo-Irish: 'Numerous absentees had drawn great part of the money out of the country; oppressive taxes were continued; land was let and sub-let to bankers and stewards of estates, to the utter ruin of the tenants; and all this caused the greatest discontent'.[70] She portrays the duplicity of the noble class in Glenarvon himself, the apotheosis of a Whig aristocracy whose stand against tyranny was just so much self-serving theatre, though admittedly she also implicitly endorses Avondale's and Glenarvon's contempt for the lawless rabble's vain desire to govern themselves.[71] In her revisions for the second edition, Lamb also attempted blunt somewhat her condemnation of Glenarvon's political hypocrisy.[72]

Nonetheless, Lamb depicts Glenarvon as a seducer and betrayer of women and of political rebels: 'Glenarvon it seems has left his followers, as he has his mistress', remarks Cormac O'Leary, one of the United Irishmen, in volume III.[73] Lamb's portrait of Glenarvon thus forms a political as well as personal observation – an anticipation of the twentieth-century feminist principle that the personal *is* political. Taking her cue from Mary Wollstonecraft, she decried those women who (like Lady Dartford and Sophia) succumbed to the magnetic pull of gowns, jewelry, balls, discreet affairs and paintings made on velvet – those 'spiritless immaculate prejudiced sticklers for propriety'.[74] In striving to claim a bigger world for herself, of politics, poetry, and passion, she became one of those writers who enlarged the possibilities for women.

Notes:

1. J. Clubbe, '*Glenarvon* Revised – and Revisited', *The Wordsworth Circle*, 10:2 (1979), pp. 205–6.
2. 'Miss Webster will send you my MSS'. Lady Caroline Lamb to John Murray, n.d. (June 1815). John Murray Archive. It is possible that Lamb was also spurred on to complete her book by the appearance of a novel based on Byron, *The Baron of Falconberg; or, Childe Harolde in Prose* (1815), by Mrs. Elizabeth Thomas, the wife of the Vicar of Tidenham, who wrote under the pen name of 'Bridget Bluemantle'.
3. Lady Caroline Lamb to Lady Melbourne, n.d. (April or May 1816). British Library Add MS 45546, f. 89–90.
4. The Silver Fork novel, popular in the 1820s and 1830s, was given its name by William Hazlitt in a review that mocked its focus on the social customs and etiquette of the upper

class. See William Hazlitt, 'The Dandy School', *The Examiner*, November 18, 1827. The text of this review is posted online at http://www.dandyism.net/?page_id=835.
5. Forster Collection, Victoria and Albert Museum, correspondence of Lady Caroline Lamb and Henry Colburn.
6. Colburn paid the sum of £550 to Lady Morgan for her novel, *O'Donnel*. See Lee Erickson, *The Economy of Literary Form: English Literature and the Industrialization of Publishing, 1800–1850* (Johns Hopkins University Press, 1996), p. 156.
7. Forster Collection, Victoria and Albert Museum, correspondence of Lady Caroline Lamb and Henry Colburn.
8. Lady Caroline Lamb to John Cam Hobhouse. n.d. (April 1816). John Murray Archive.
9. John Cam Hobhouse (Lord Broughton), *Recollections of a Long Life: With Additional Extracts from his Private Diaries*, Lady Dorchester (ed.), 4 vols. (London: John Murray, 1910; AMS 1968), vol. 1, p. 337.
10. Forster Collection, Victoria and Albert Museum, correspondence of Lady Caroline Lamb and Henry Colburn.
11. Ibid.
12. *Glenarvon* numbered its chapters with Roman numerals. Volume I omitted to use the ninth numeral (IX), throwing off the remaining count by one. Volume II mis-numbered chapter twenty-six (XXVI) as twenty-four (XXIV); chapter twenty-seven (XXVII) as twenty-six (XXVI); and chapter thirty-six (XXXVI) as thirty-four (XXXIV). The third volume of the novel numbered chapters from seventy-two (LXXII) to one-hundred six (CVI). All these errors have been silently corrected in the present edition.
13. Lord Byron, *Byron's Letters and Journals*, ed. Leslie Marchand. 12 vols. (Cambridge, Belknap Press of Harvard University Press, 1973–1995), vol. 5. p. 85.
14. Hobhouse, *Recollections of a Long Life*, vol. 1, p. 338.
15. George Paston [E. M. Symonds] and Peter Quennell, '*To Lord Byron*': *Feminine Profiles Based Upon Unpublished Letters 1807–1824* (London: John Murray, 1939), p. 73.
16. Lady Caroline Lamb to Lord Holland, n.d. (May 1816). British Library Add. MS 51558 f. 21.
17. Clubbe, '*Glenarvon* –Revised and Revisited', p. 205.
18. P. Graham, *Don Juan and Regency England* (Charlottesville: University Press of Virginia, 1990), pp. 99–100.
19. Lady Caroline Lamb, *The Whole Disgraceful Truth: Selected Letters of Lady Caroline Lamb* (New York: Palgrave Macmillan, 2006), p. 159.
20. F. Wilson, '"An Exaggerated Woman": The Melodramas of Lady Caroline Lamb' in Frances Wilson (ed.), *Byromania: Portraits of the Artist in Nineteenth- and Twentieth-Century* (London: Macmillan), p. 217.
21. Ibid., p.193.
22. See below, p. 342.
23. See below, p. 54.
24. See below, p. 71.
25. William Lamb to Henry Colburn, 17 May 1816. Forster Collection.
26. William Lamb to Lady Caroline Lamb, June 1816. John Murray Archive of the National Library of Scotland.
27. Lady Byron, Comments on Calantha in *Glenarvon*, 17 May 1816. Bodleian Library, University of Oxford, Dep. Lovelace Byron 118, ff. 7–8.
28. Mrs George Lamb to Lady Byron, 17 May 1816. Bodleian Library, University of Oxford, Dep. Lovelace Byron 78, f. 24.

29. *British Critic*, 5 (June 1816), pp. 627–31.
30. *Theatrical Inquisitor*, 9 (August 1816), pp. 122–5.
31. *British Lady's Magazine*, 4 (August 1816), pp. 101–3.
32. *Monthly Review*, 80 (June 1816), pp. 217–8.
33. *Augustan Review*, 3 (October 1816), pp. 350–4.
34. Lady Caroline Lamb to John Murray, n.d. (endorsed but not dated September 1816). John Murray Archive of the National Library of Scotland.
35. *New Monthly Magazine* 5 (June 1816), pp. 443–4.
36. Lady Caroline Lamb to Henry Colburn, n.d. [1816]. Forster Collection.
37. Lady Caroline Lamb to Lady Melbourne, n.d. (after 9 May 1816). British Library Add. MS 45546 f.91–2.
38. In revisions to the second edition of *Glenarvon*, the Duke of Altamonte is said to have 'married into a Roman Catholic family' in chapter 2 of volume I. Mrs. Seymour and her daughters, Frances and Sophia, are made specifically Catholic in an interpolated sentence in the second edition, chapter 8 of volume I: 'She was a Roman Catholic, and all who differed from that persuasion were, in her opinion, utterly lost'. Calantha's allegiance to Catholicism is similarly specified in an interpolated passage in chapter XVI of vol. 1. See below, pp. 383, 388, 393.
39. See below, p. 148.
40. See below, p. 423.
41. See below, p. 255.
42. See below, pp. 245 and 432 (textual variants).
43. See Appendix A: Preface to the second edition of Glenarvon, below, p. 353.
44. See below, pp. 353–4.
45. See below, p. 80.
46. Thomas Creevey, *The Creevey Papers: A Selection from the Correspondence & Diaries of the Late Thomas Creevey*, 3d edn, Sir Herbert Maxwell (ed.) (London: John Murray, 1905), pp. 254–5.
47. Letter to Lady Buckingham dated 4 June, 1819, in E. Eden, *Miss Eden's Letters*, V. Dickinson (ed.) (London: Macmillan, 1919), p. 35.
48. Clubbe, '*Glenarvon* Revised – and Revisited', pp. 209, 213.
49. M. Elwin, *Lord Byron's Family: Annabella, Ada, and Augusta 1816–1824*, Peter Thomson (ed.) (London: J. Murray, 1975), pp. 32–3.
50. Mabell, Countess of Airlie, *In Whig Society: 1775–1818* (London: Hodder and Stoughton, 1921), p. 184.
51. Villiers, *The Grand Whiggery* (London: John Murray, 1939), p. 321.
52. Paston and Quennell, '*To Lord Byron*', p. 72.
53. Villiers, *The Grand Whiggery*, p. 321.
54. In most "keys" to *Glenarvon*, characters who seem to personify other aspects of the author, like Zerbellini, Alice Mac Allain, and Elinor St Clare, are not listed at all. Calantha is actually taken for Zerbellini by Glenarvon, who greets her on the heath above the cliff with these words: 'Ah! my / little trembling page, my Zerbellini, welcome to my heart'. See below, p. 213.
55. See below, p. 343. Note that in speeches similar to Calantha's, St Clare has struggled with guilt over having incurred 'a father's curse', and confesses 'my heart is breaking'. See below, p. 220.
56. See below, p. 10.

57. See T. J. B. Spencer, 'Introduction' to John Ford's *The Broken Heart*, T. J. B. Spencer (ed.), (Manchester: Manchester University Press, 1980), pp. 27–9.
58. See below, p. 152.
59. See below, p. 292.
60. See below, p. 344.
61. D. Cecil, *Melbourne* (New York: Bobbs-Merrill, 1954), p. 70.
62. H. Blyth, *Caro: The Fatal Passion: The Life of Lady Caroline Lamb* (London: Rupert Hart-Davis, 1972), p. 196.
63. See below, p. 20.
64. M. Edgeworth, *Castle Rackrent* (Boston: T. B. Wait, 1814), pp. 11, 99–103.
65. See *Collected Poetical Works* of Byron and see below, p. 173.
66. R. Kee, *The Green Flag, Volume 1: The Most Distressful Country* (London: Penguin, 1989), 50.
67. M. Kelsall, 'The Byronic Hero and Revolution in Ireland: the Politics of *Glenarvon*', *The Byron Journal*, 9 (1981), p. 6.
68. T. Barnard, *A New Anatomy of Ireland: The Irish Protestants 1649–1770* (New Haven: Yale University Press, 2003), pp. 21–41.
69. See below, pp. 8, 132.
70. See below, p, 132.
71. See B. Judson, 'Roman à Clef and the Dynamics of Betrayal: The Case of *Glenarvon*', *Genre: Forms of Discourse and Culture*, 33:2 (2000), p. 160. Avondale expresses his contempt for the rabble when he is confronted by them on the mountain overlooking Glenarvon Bay: '"Fickle, senseless beings!" he said, with bitter contempt, as he heard their loyal cry. "These are the creatures we would take to govern us: this is the voice of the people; these are the rights of man."' See below, p. 307.
72. Lamb added the following passage to the third volume, chapter 32, in which St. Clare partly exonerates Glenarvon: 'Let not rage against Glenarvon actuate your resolves: whatever he may have done, "we shall not live to see his like again." Shew not such pleasure in trampling upon the high: my vengeance is just resentment – but how has he offended you?' See textual variants to Glenarvon below, p. 441.
73. See below, p. 309.
74. See below, p. 58.

BIBLIOGRAPHY

Works by Caroline Lamb

Novels

Glenarvon, 3 vols (London: Henry Colburn, 1816). 2nd and 3rd editions in the same year; 4th edn in 1817; also published in Philadelphia, PA and in Paris. Facs. 1st edn (Oxford and New York: Woodstock Books, 1993). Facs. 1st edn (Delmar, NY: Scholars' Facsimiles and Reprints, 1972). Facs. 3rd edn (New York: AMS Press, 1975).

Graham Hamilton, 2 vols (London: Henry Colburn, 1822).

Ada Reis, 3 vols (London: J. Murray, 1823). Also published in Paris by Galignani, 1824.

Poetry

Verses from Glenarvon, to Which is Prefixed the Original Introduction Not Published With the Early Editions of that Work, (London: Henry Colburn, 1819).

A New Canto, (London: William Wright, 1819).

Gordon: A Tale: A Poetical Review of Don Juan, (London: T. and J. Allman, 1821).

'To the Hon. William Lamb', *Friendship's Offering: A Literary Album*, ed. T. K. Hervey, (London: Lupton Relfe, 1826), p. 89.

'To a Friend, on Sending a Fancy Drawing, After Promising Her Own Picture in the Character of a Gypsey', *The Bijou; or Annual of Literature and the Arts* (London: William Pickering, 1828), pp. 89–90.

'Invocation to Sleep', *The Keepsake for 1830* (London, 1830), p. 202.

'Woman's Love', *The Keepsake for 1830* (London, 1830), p. 316.

Songs Set to Music by Isaac Nathan

'Would I Had Seen Thee Dead and Cold' (London, [1800s]).

'My Heart's Fit To Break' (London, [1810s]).

'Waters of Elle' (Arrangement of a Traditional Tune) (London, 1816).

Farewell (London, 1816).

'After Many a Well Fought Day' (London, [1820s]).

'Amidst the Flowers Rich and Gay' (London, [1820s])

'The Kiss that's on thy lip impress'd' (London, [1820s]).

'Thou Would'st Not Do What I have Done' (London, [1820s–30s]).

'Sir Henry De Vaux' (London, 1823).

'Sing Not For others, but for me' (London, 1823).

'Weep for what thou'st lost, Love' (London, 1823).

'Let the Harp Be Mute Forever' (London, [*c.* 1829]).

Letters

The Whole Disgraceful Truth: Selected Letters of Lady Caroline Lamb, ed. P. Douglass (New York: Palgrave, 2006).

Secondary Sources

Airlie, M., Countess, *In Whig Society: 1775-1818* (London: Hodder and Stoughton, 1921).

Blyth, H., *Caro: The Fatal Passion: The Life of Lady Caroline Lamb* (London: Rupert Hart-Davis, 1972).

Byron, G. G., *Byron's Letters and Journals*, ed. L. Marchand, 12 vols (Cambridge: Belknap Press of Harvard University Press, 1973–95).

—, *The Complete Poetical Works*, ed. J. McGann, 7 vols, vol. 6 co-ed. B. Weller (Oxford: Clarendon Press, 1980–93).

Clubbe, J., '*Glenarvon* Revised – and Revisited', *Wordsworth Circle*, 10 (1979), pp. 205–17.

Douglass, P., 'Isaac Nathan and Lady Caroline Lamb: A Response to Graham Pont', *Newstead Abbey Byron Society Review*, (January 2004), pp. 88–9.

—, *Lady Caroline Lamb: A Biography* (New York and London: Palgrave, 2004).

—, 'Lady Caroline Lamb Before Byron: The Godfrey Vassal Webster Affair', *The Wordsworth Circle*, 36:3 (Summer 2005), pp.117–24.

—, 'Lord Byron's Feminist Canon: Notes Toward Its Construction', *Romanticism on the Net*, 43 (August 2006). ISSN : 1467–1255 (electronic version) http://www.erudit.org/revue/ron/2006/v/n43/013588ar.html

—, 'The Madness of Writing: Lady Caroline Lamb's Byronic Identity', *Pacific Coast Philology*, 34:1 (1999), pp. 53–71.

—, 'Playing Byron: Lady Caroline Lamb's *Glenarvon* and the Music of Isaac Nathan', *European Romantic Review*, 8:1 (1997), pp. 1–24.

— and Rosemary March, 'That "Vital Spark of Genius": Lady Caroline Lamb's Writing Before Byron', *Pacific Coast Philology*, 41 (2006), pp. 43–62.

—, 'What Lord Byron Learned from Lady Caroline Lamb', *European Romantic Review*, 16:3 (July 2005), pp. 273–81.

—, 'Young Caroline: A Medea in the Making?' *A View in the Rear-Mirror: Romantic Aesthetics, Culture, and Science Seen from Today – Festschrift for Frederick Burwick on the*

Occasion of His 70th Birthday, ed. W. Pape (Trier: Wissenschftlicher Verlag Trier (Studien zur Englischen Romantik #3), 2006), pp. 73-88.

Eisler, B., *Byron: Child of Passion, Fool of Fame* (New York: Knopf, 1999).

Foreman, A., *Georgiana: Duchess of Devonshire* (New York: Random House, 1998).

Garver, J., 'Gothic Ireland: Lady Caroline Lamb's *Glenarvon*', *A Journal of Irish Studies*, 4: 10 (1980), pp. 213–28.

Graham, P., *Don Juan and Regency England* (Charlottesville, VA: University Press of Virginia, 1990).

—, 'Fictive Biography in 1816: the Case of *Glenarvon*', *The Byron Journal* 19 (1991), pp. 53–68.

Grosskurth, P., *Byron: The Flawed Angel* (New York: Houghton Mifflin, 1997).

Hofkosh, S., 'The Writer's Ravishment: Women and the Romantic Author – The Example of Byron', in A. K. Mellor (ed.) *Romanticism and Feminism*. (Bloomington, IN: Indiana University Press, 1988), pp. 93–114.

—, *Sexual Politics and the Romantic Author* (Cambridge: Cambridge University Press, 1998).

Jenkins, E., *Lady Caroline Lamb* (London: Victor Gollancz, 1932).

Judson, B., 'Roman Á Clef and the Dynamics of Betrayal: The Case of *Glenarvon*', *Genre: forms of Discourse and Culture*, 33:2 (Summer 2000), pp. 151–69.

Kelsall, M., 'The Byronic Hero and Revolution in Ireland: The Politics of *Glenarvon*', *The Byron Journal*, 9 (1981), pp. 4–19.

MacCarthy, F., *Byron: Life and Legend* (London: John Murray, 2002).

Marchand, L., *Byron: A Biography* (New York: Knopf, 1957).

McDayter, G., 'Hysterically Speaking: Lady Caroline Lamb's *Glenarvon* and the Revolutionary Voice', G. McDayter, G. Batten and B. Milligan (eds) *Romantic Generations: Essays in Honour of Robert F. Gleckner* (Lewisburg, PA: Bucknell University Press, 2001), pp. 155–77.

Melbourne, E. M. L., Viscountess. *Byron's 'Corbeau Blanc': The Life and Letters of Lady Melbourne*, ed. Jonathan David Gross (Houston, TX: Rice University Press, 1997).

Mitchell, L. G., *Lord Melbourne: 1779–1848* (Oxford: Oxford University Press, 1997).

Morgan, S. O., *Lady Morgan's Memoirs: Autobiography, Diaries, and Correspondence*, 2nd edn, 2 vols (London: William H. Allen & Co., 1863).

Nathan, I., *Fugitive Pieces and Reminiscences of Lord Byron: Containing and Entire New Edition of the Hebrew Melodies, With the Addition of Several Never Before Published; the Whole Illustrated with Critical, Historical, Theatrical, Political, and Theological Remarks, Notes, Anecdotes, Interesting Conversations and Observations, Made by that Illustrious Poet: Together with His Lordship's Autograph; also Some Original Poetry, Letters and Recollections of Lady Caroline Lamb* (London: Whittaker, Treacher and Co., 1829).

—, and Lord Byron, *A Selection of Hebrew Melodies, Ancient and Modern (1815–16)*, ed. F. Burwick and P. Douglass (Tuscaloosa, AL and London: University of Alabama Press, 1988).

Normington, S., *Lady Caroline Lamb: This Infernal Woman* (London: House of Stratus, 2001).

Olney, C., '*Glenarvon* Revisited', *University of Kansas City Review*, 22 (1955), pp. 271–6.

Paston, G. [E. M. Symonds], and P. Quennell, '*To Lord Byron*': *Feminine Profiles Based Upon Unpublished Letters 1807–1824* (London: John Murray, 1939).

Soderholm, J., *Fantasy, Forgery, and the Byron Legend* (Lexington, KY: University Press of Kentucky, 1996).

Stauffer, A., 'Byron, Medwin, and the False Fiend: Remembering "Remember Thee"', *Studies in Bibliography*, 53 (2000), pp. 265-76.

Strickland, M., *The Byron Women* (London: P. Owen, 1974).

Wetherall-Dickson, L., 'Authority and Legitimacy; Representations of the Aristocracy in the Novels of Lady Caroline Lamb', *Women's Writing*, 13: 3 (2006), pp. 369–91.

—, 'The Construction of a Reputation for Madness: The Case Study of Lady Caroline Lamb', *Working With English: Medieval and Modern Language, Literature and Drama*, 2 (2005–6), pp. 27–46

Wilson, F., '"An Exaggerated Woman": the Melodramas of Lady Caroline Lamb', in F. Wilson (ed.), *Byromania* (Basingstoke: MacMillan Press, 1999), pp. 195–220.

Wu, D., 'Appropriating Byron: Lady Caroline Lamb's *A New Canto*', *Wordsworth Circle* 26:3 (1995), pp.140–6.

Ziegler, P., *Melbourne: A Biography of William Lamb, 2nd Viscount Melbourne*, (New York: Knopf, 1976).

CHRONOLOGY

1778	Frances Burney's *Evelina, or a Young Woman's Entry into the World* published.
1779	Lamb's husband William Lamb born (15 March).
1781	Lamb's brother John William Ponsonby (later Lord Duncannon) born.
1783	Lamb's brother Frederick Cavendish Ponsonby born (6 July).
1785	Caroline Rosalie St Jules (illegitimate daughter of Lady Elizabeth Foster by the fifth Duke of Devonshire) born (16 August).
	Harriet Elizabeth Cavendish, Lamb's cousin born (29 August).
	Lamb (née Caroline Ponsonby) born (13 November).
1786	William Beckford's *Vathek* published.
1788	George Gordon, sixth Lord Byron born (22 January).
1787	Lamb's brother William ('Willy') Francis Spencer Ponsonby (her favourite) born.
1790	William Spencer Cavendish, Marquis of Hartington ('Hart'), Lamb's cousin (later sixth Duke of Devonshire) born (21 May).
1791	Lamb leaves for Europe with her mother and Aunt Georgiana, Duchess of Devonshire, who has been banished by the Duke for becoming pregnant by her lover, Earl Grey (November).
1792	Mary Wollstonecraft's *A Vindication of the Rights of Woman* published.
1793	Louis XVI of France guillotined (January).
	Lord Bessborough dies (11 March), making her father the third Earl Bessborough and Lamb becomes officially 'Lady Caroline.'
	Lamb's Aunt Georgiana and Lady Elizabeth Foster are permitted by the Duke of Devonshire to return to England. Lamb remains in Italy with her mother, Harriet, who is too ill to travel. (May).
	Marie Antoinette guillotined (16 October).
1793–4	Lamb suffers a life-threatening illness in Italy, and her mother, Harriet, falls in love with Granville Leveson Gower. They travel home to England.
1799	William Lamb takes degree at Cambridge and goes to Glasgow to study law.

1802	The ill-fated Treaty of Amiens signed, negotiated by Pitt the Younger (March).
	William Lamb meets his future bride; they are infatuated (August).
1803	Britain declares war on France (18 May).
1805	Caroline and William Lamb are betrothed and married. 'Hart' is devastated (3 June).
1806	Lamb delivers a baby girl who dies shortly after. On the same date, William is elected Member of Parliament for Leominster (1 February).
	Lamb's Aunt Georgiana, Duchess of Devonshire, dies (30 March).
	William gives opening address of Parliament; Lamb sneaks in dressed as a man to watch (November).
1807	Lamb's and William's son Augustus born. The Prince of Wales is his sponsor (29 August).
1809	Lady Elizabeth Foster marries the widowed fifth Duke of Devonshire, usurping the place of Lamb's Aunt Georgiana (19 October).
	George Lamb marries the new Duchess's daughter, Caroline Rosalie Adelaide St Jules (17 May).
	Granville Leveson Gower marries 'Hary-O' (Lady Harriet Elizabeth Cavendish), the niece of his long-time lover, Lady Bessborough (24 December).
1811	Regency bill becomes law, and the Prince of Wales assumes the royal duties because George III is incapacitated by what is now believed to have been porphyria (5 February). Lamb's affair with Sir Godfrey Vassal Webster draws negative attention, especially from his mother, Lady Holland (March/April). William Cavendish, fifth Duke of Devonshire, dies, making Lamb's cousin 'Hart' the sixth Duke (29 July).
1812	Lord Byron's *Childe Harold's Pilgrimage*, a poem in two long cantos, officially published. Lamb has read an advance copy and writes to Byron in verse (10 March). Byron attends Lamb's waltzing party. Their affair begins (25 March). Lamb runs away and Byron manages to bring her home to Whitehall (12 August).
1813	Lamb forges Byron's handwriting to obtain a painting from John Murray (January). Lamb cuts herself in a chaotic scene at Lady Heathcote's ball, and it is widely reported that she tried to kill herself (5 July). Austria declares war on France (10 August).
1814	Lamb's grandmother Lady Spencer dies (18 March). Lord Byron moves into the Albany, where Lamb sometimes visits him in men's attire (28 March). Lamb meets Isaac Nathan, who arranges music in honour of her brother Willy's engagement (Spring). Napoleon exiled; arrives on Elba (4 May). Lamb attends a masked ball at Burlington House held by Watier's Club to honour the Duke of Wellington's victory over Napoleon (1 July).

1815	Lord Byron is married at Seaham to Anne Isabella Milbanke, William Lamb's cousin (2 January). Napoleon returns to power in France (20 March). The Byrons settle at 13 Piccadilly Terrace (house of Elizabeth Foster, Duchess of Devonshire) (28 March). Nathan and Byron's *A Selection of Hebrew Melodies* volume 1 published (April). Napoleon defeated at Waterloo (1 July). William's father, the Viscount Melbourne, is created Lord Melbourne in the peerage (11 August). Granville Leveson-Gower created Viscount Granville (12 August). Lamb and her husband visit Brussels and Paris. Napoleon exiled to Saint Helena (16 October).
1816	Nathan and Byron's *A Selection of Hebrew Melodies* volume 2 published (18 April). Lord Byron signs deed of separation from his wife (21 April). Lord Byron leaves London for the European Continent, never to return (24 April). Lamb's first novel, *Glenarvon*, published by Henry Colburn (9 May). William is elected Member of Parliament for Northampton (7 July). Canto III of Byron's *Childe Harold* published in London (18 November).
1818	Lamb's mother-in-law, Lady Melbourne, dies (6 April).
1819	Lamb canvasses for William's brother George Lamb's election, in which he defeats Byron's friend, John Cam Hobhouse (February/March). Lord Byron's *Don Juan* Cantos I and II published (15 July). Lamb's *A New Canto* (a satire of *Don Juan*) published (October).
1820	George III dies (29 January). The Prince Regent, now George IV, opens Parliament (27 April). Lamb appears at Almack's dressed as Don Juan with attendant devils (Summer). Queen Caroline (George IV's estranged wife) is put on trial for adultery with her courtier, Bartolommeo Bergami (August). The trial lasts through November, when she is acquitted.
1821	George IV is crowned in an elaborate, medieval style ceremony at Westminster Abbey. Queen Caroline is prevented from attending (19 July). Queen Caroline dies (7 August). Lord Byron's *Don Juan* Cantos III–IV published (8 August). Lamb's *Gordon: A Tale* (another satire of *Don Juan*) published (Autumn). While they are travelling in Italy, the infant son of Lamb's brother William and Lady Barbara dies in Parma, and then Lamb's mother, Lady Bessborough, dies in Florence (5 November). Lamb is so distraught that she is unable to attend the services in late December.
1822	Lady Byron's mother dies (Lady Noel) and Lord and Lady Byron assume the additional name of Noel (28 January). Lord Byron's daughter Allegra dies in a convent (19 April). Lamb's novel *Graham Hamilton* published by Henry Colburn (Autumn).
1823	Lamb's novel *Ada Reis* published by John Murray (March).

1824	Elizabeth Foster, Duchess of Devonshire, dies (20 March). Lord Byron dies in Greece, partly the victim of his own doctors, who dehydrate him through bleeding (19 April). Byron's memoirs are burned at John Murray's offices in Albermarle Street, and it is disclosed that Murray has let Lamb read them (17 May). The *Florida* arrives in England with Byron's remains (29 June). Byron's funeral cortege leaves London and passes through Welwyn, Hertfordshire, where Lamb encounters it (12 July). Byron's funeral (16 July). Medwin's *Conversations of Lord Byron* published and Lamb reads his vitriolic poem 'Remember Thee' for the first time (23 October).
1825	William Lamb finally succumbs to family pressure to separate from Lamb, who signs separation agreement, meets obscure poet Wilmington Fleming, and departs for Paris (Summer). Lamb back in London; Doctor Goddard makes diagnosis of insanity (October).
1826	Lamb returns to Brocket (January).
1827	William appointed Chief Secretary to the Lord Lieutenant for Ireland; takes their son Augustus with him (April). Lamb becomes severely ill with 'dropsy' (September).
1828	William notified Lamb likely to die (15 January). Lamb dies, William having arrived just in time to speak with her (25 January). William's father dies at age eighty-three. William becomes Lord Melbourne (22 July).
1829	Isaac Nathan publishes *Fugitive Pieces and Reminiscences of Lord Byron: ... also Some Original Poetry, Letter and Recollections of Lady Caroline Lamb*.
1836	Lamb's son Augustus dies.
1830	George IV dies. His brother, Duke of Clarence, age 64, is crowned William IV (26 June).
1837	William IV dies (20 June). Victoria, a grandchild of George III, is crowned Queen at age eighteen. Lord Melbourne (William Lamb) becomes an important advisor to the young Queen.
1848	Lord Melbourne dies (24 November).

GLENARVON.

IN THREE VOLUMES.

VOL. I.

LONDON:
PRINTED FOR HENRY COLBURN.
1816.

GLENARVON.

VOL. I.

L'on t'a trop cheri?

GLENARVON.

Disperato dolor, che il cor mi preme
Gia pur pensando, pria che ne favelle.[1]

VOL. I. /

GLENARVON.

CHAPTER I.

In the town of Belfont, in Ireland, lived a learned physician of the name of Everard St. Clare.² He had a brother, who, misled by a fine but wild imagination, which raised him too far above the interests of common life, had squandered away his small inheritance; and had long roved through the world, rapt in poetic visions, foretelling, as he pretended, to those who would hear him, that which futurity would more fully develop. – Camioli was the name he had assumed.³

It was many years since Sir Everard last beheld his brother, when one night Camioli, bearing in his arms Elinor his child, about five years of age, returned, after his long absence[a] to his native town, and knocked at Sir Everard's door. The doctor was at the castle hard by, and his lady refused admittance to the mean-looking stranger. Without informing her of his name, Camioli departed, and resolved to seek his sister the Abbess of Glenaa.⁴ The way to the convent was long and dreary: he climbed, therefore, with his lovely burthen to the topmost heights of Inis Tara, and sought temporary shelter in a cleft of the mountain known by the name of the 'Wizzard's[b] Glen.' Bright shone the stars that night, and to the exalted imagination[c] of the aged seer, it seemed in sleep, that the spirits of departed heroes and countrymen, freed from the bonds of mortality, were ascending in solemn grandeur before his eyes; – the song of the Banshees,⁵ mourning for the sorrows of their country, broke upon the silence of night; – a lambent flame distinguished the souls of heroes, and, pointing upwards, formed a path of light before them; – the air resounded with the quivering of wings, as with one accord innumerable spirits arose, fanning the breeze with their extended plumes, and ascending like a flight of birds toward the heavens.⁶

Then, for the first time, Camioli beheld, in one comprehensive view,⁷ the universal plan of nature – unnumbered systems performing their various but distinct courses, unclouded by mists, and unbounded by horizon – endless variety in infinite space! Then first he seemed to hear the full harmonious cadences of the angelic choirs – celestial music, uttered by happy spirits in praise of the great Author of Existence, as directing their flight onwards from sphere to sphere, from world to world, they felt joyful in themselves, and rejoiced in the wonders and variety of creation.[d]

From visions so wild, yet delightful,ª the soft sweet⁸ voice of his child awoke him.ᵇ – 'How cold and dreary it is, dear father; how lone these hills. I am weary unto death, yet I fear to sleep.' – 'My comforter, my delight, my little black-eyed darling,' said Camioliᶜ (enveloping his childᵈ in his long dark mantle),ᵉ 'why do I thus sully the purity of your nature by leading you to the abode of misery, and shewing you the haunts of men! They are but as the flowers that blossom and wither, or as the clouds that pass along to shade for a moment the brightness of the heavens: – all here on earth is desolation and woe. But Iᶠ will soon take you, my lovely one,ᵍ to a place of safety. My sister, the Abbess of Glenaa, lives in the valley beneath the mountain: she will protect my Elinor; and, in her mansion, my child shall find an asylum. I shall leave you but for⁹ a short time; we shall meet again, Elinor; – yes, we shall meet again. – Continue to live with St. Claraʰ your aunt: obey her in all things, for she is good: and may the God of Mercy avert from you the heaviest of all my calamities, the power of looking into futurity.' – He spoke, and descending the rugged mountain path, placed his Elinor according to promise,ⁱ under the protection of his sister the Abbess of Glenaa, and bidding her farewell, walked hastily away.

The morning sun, when it arose, shone bright and brilliant upon the valley of Altamonte – its gay castle, and its lake. But a threatening cloud obscured the sky, as Camioli raised his eyesʲ and turned them mournfully upon the ruined priory of St. Alvin, and the deserted halls of Belfont.¹⁰ – 'Woe to the house of Glenarvon!' he said. 'Woe to the house of my patron and benefactor! Desolation and sorrow have fallen upon the mighty. Mournᵏ for the hero who is slain in battle. Mourn for the orphan who is left destitute and in trouble. Brightˡ shone the sun upon thy battlements, O Belfont, on the morn when the hero bade thee a last adieu. Cold are thy waters, Killarney;¹¹ and many a tree has been hewn from thy rocky bosom, thou fair mountain Glenaa, since the hour in which he parted. But not so cold, nor so barren is thy bosom, as is that of the widow who is bereft of every joy... Mourn for the house of Glenarvon, and the orphan who is destitute! No mother – no companion of boyish sports and pleasures yet lives to greet him with one cheering smile. – There is not left one tongue to welcome him to his native land; or, should he fall, one friend to shed a tear upon his grave!'

Thus sung the Bard, while the red deer were browsing upon the hills, and the wind whistled through the arches and colonadesᵐ of the Castle of Belfont,¹² as if in hollow murmurs for times which were long past. – 'Woe to the house of our patron,' said the frenzied old man, as with bitter tears he departed: – 'even in this moment of time, the fairest star of Belfont sets for ever: the widowed Countess of Glenarvon is dead – dead in a foreign country; and strangersⁿ hands alone perform her obsequies.' He spoke, and looked, for the last time, upon the land that he loved, then turned from it forᵒ ever... Previous, however,¹³ to his departure from Ireland, Camioli again sought his brother, (who was then an inmate in the family of the Duke of Altamonte,) for the purpose of commending Elinor to his care.

Castle Delaval,[14] the property of that nobleman, was situated in a valley sheltered from every keen blast by a dark wood of fir and elm.[a] The river Elle,[15] taking its rise amidst the Dartland Hills, flowed through the park, losing by degrees the character of a mountain torrent, as it spread itself between its rich and varied banks in front of the castle, till it joined the sea beyond the Wizzard's[b] Glen. The town of Belfont stands close upon the harbour, and from one of the highest cliffs, the ruins of the convent of St. Mary, and a modern chapel may yet be seen, whilst Heremon and Inis Tara,[16] raising their lofty summits, capped with snow, soar above the clouds.

The abbey of Belfont, and the priory of St. Alvin, both the property of the Glenarvon family, were now, in consequence of the forfeiture of the late Earl of that name, transferred to Lord de Ruthven,[17] a distant relation. The deserted priory had fallen into ruin, and Belfont abbey, as yet unclaimed by its youthful master, and pillaged by the griping hand of its present owner, exhibited a melancholy picture of neglect and oppression. – No cheerful fires blaze in its ancient halls; no peasants and vassals feast under its vaulted roofs. – Glenarvon, the hero, the lord of the demesne is dead: – he[c] fell on the bloody field of Culloden:[18] – his[d] son perished in exile: – and[e] Clarence de Ruthven, his grandson, an orphan, in a foreign land, has[f] never yet appeared to petition for his attainted titles and forfeited estates. – Of relations and of friends he has[g] never heard./

Where are they who claim kindred with the unfortunate? Where are they who boast of friendship for the orphan that is destitute and in trouble? The[h] Duke of Altamonte,[19] whose domains were contiguous, and whose attachment extended to the son of his ancient friend, had ofttimes written to his sister enquiring into the fate of the child; but Lady Margaret had answered her brother's letters with coldness and indifference. /

CHAPTER II.

It is the common failing of an ambitious mind to over-rate itself – to imagine that it has been, by the caprices of fortune,[a] defrauded of the high honours due to its supposed superiority. It conceives itself to have been injured – to have fallen from its destination; and these unfounded claims become the source of endless discontent. The mind, thus disappointed, preys upon itself, and compares its present lowliness with the imaginary heights for which it fancies itself to have been intended.[b] Under the influence of these reflections, the character grows sullen and reserved, detaches itself from all social enjoyments, and professes to despise the honours for which it secretly pines. Mediocrity,[c] and a common lot, a man of this disposition cannot bring himself to endure; and he wilfully rejects the little granted, because all cannot be obtained, to which he once[d] aspired.[20]

In this temper, the Duke of Altamonte had retired from public affairs, and had quitted the splendour and gaiety of the court, to seek in retirement that repose which, of all men, he was the least calculated to appreciate or enjoy.[e] In the society of the duchess, he[f] found all that could sooth his wounded spirit. In[g] Mrs. Seymour,[21] the duchess's sister, he[h] welcomed a mild and unobtrusive guest; and[i] the project of uniting the Lady Calantha Delaval, his only daughter, to her cousin William Buchanan,[22] heir presumptive to the Dukedom of Altamonte, and son of his sister Lady Margaret Buchanan,[23] for some time occupied his hours[j] and engrossed his attention.

To forward this favourite object, he communicated to them both, that they were destined for each other; and by employing them in the same occupations, instructing them in the same studies, by the same masters,[k] and in every way contriving that they should be continually together[l] he hoped that early habits, and the first affections of childhood, might unite their hearts in indissoluble bonds. But how short-sighted, how little founded in a right knowledge of human nature, was this project! Habituated to the intimacy which subsists between near relations, was it probable that love, when the age of that passion arrived, would be content with objects thus familiar; and that the feelings of the heart would quietly acquiesce in an arrangement which had been previously formed upon the calculations of interest and family pride? – On the contrary, the system pursued in their education, accustomed them to give way to their violent tempers, without restraint, in their intercourse with each other;[a] and the frequent recurrence of petty quarrels, soon produced sentiments, which bordered on dislike; so that at the moment, when the Duke exulted most in the success of his project, he was painfully undeceived.[b]

Happily, a new event which occurred at this time in the family of the Duke of Altamonte, soon turned his thoughts from the failure of his present system of education, the superintendence of which he relinquished with as much readiness, as he had once shewn anxiety to undertake it.[c] – The Duchess, after a long period of ill health, was pronounced by her physicians to be once more in a situation to realize her husband's most sanguine hopes. – 'If I have a boy,' he cried, 'from the hour of his birth all I possess shall be his. Give me but a son, ye powers who rule over destiny, and I am content to yield up every other claim, privilege and possession.' – The wish was heard, and at the appointed time, the Duchess of Altamonte, after a few hours[d] illness, was delivered of a son and heir. It was in vain for the Duke, that until this event he said to himself daily as he arose from his stately bed, that none other was his rival in wealth or power; – it was in vain that friends surrounded him, and flatterers attended upon his least commands: – until this unexpected, and almost unhoped for[e] event, he could not be said to have enjoyed one hour of felicity, so unwisely did he blind himself to every other blessing which he possessed; and so ardently solicitous did he suffer his mind to become, for that one boon which alone had been refused to his prayers. But since the birth of his son, he looked around him, and he had nothing left to wish for upon earth; his heart became agitated with its own satisfaction; and the terror of losing the idol upon which every feeling and affection was fixed, rendered him more miserable than he was even before the fulfilment of his wishes.

The education of the lady Calantha[f] and William Buchanan was now entirely laid aside; the feuds and tumults in the adjacent countries were disregarded; and he might be said to live alone in those apartments where, robed in state, and cradled in luxury, the little infant lay helpless[g] and unconscious of its honours and importance. Not a breath of air was suffered to blow too rudely upon the most noble and illustrious Sidney Albert, Marquis of Delaval. The tenants and peasantry flocked, from far and near, to kneel and do[h] him homage, gazing in stupid wonder on their future Lord. The Duchess feebly resisted the general voice, which encouraged an excess of care, hurtful to the health of him, whom all were but too solicitous to preserve. Yet the boy flourished, unaffected by this adulation, the endless theme of discussion, the constant object of still encreasing[i] idolatry.

Without delay, the Duke resolved to intimate to his sister, Lady Margaret Buchanan, who was at Naples, the change which had taken place in her son's expectations. He felt the necessity of softening the disappointment[j] by every soothing expression; and, as he loved her most sincerely[a] he wrote to urge her immediate return, with all the warmth of fraternal affection; – informing her at the same time of the circumstance which at once occasioned his delight, and her disappointment. With what fond overweening[b] vanity did he then flatter himself, that she, who was the next dearest object of his affections, would share his present joy; and forgetful of the entire ruin of her fondest hope, doat like him upon the child who had deprived her son of all his expectations! He knew not Lady Margaret: – less than any other, he knew that fierce spirit which never yet had been controuled[c] – which deemed itself born to command, and would have perished sooner than have endured restraint.

At this very period of time, in the prosecution of her sudden and accursed designs,[d] having bade adieu to brighter climes and more polished manners, with all the gaiety of apparent innocence,[e] and all the brilliancy of wit which belong to spirits light as air[f] and a refined and highly cultivated genius, she was sailing, accompanied[g] by a train of admirers, selected from the flower of Italy, once again to visit her native country. With their voices and soft guitars, they chased away the lingering hours; and after a fair and prosperous voyage, proceeded, with their equipages, horses and attendants,[h] to Castle Delaval.

Lady Margaret was received with delight at the house of her father, in her own native[i] land. A burst of applause hailed her first appearance before the wondering crowd assembled to behold her. Fond of admiration, even from the lowest, she lingered on the terrace, which commanded the magnificent scenery of which Castle Delaval was the central object,[j] – leaning upon the arm of the Duke[k] and bowing gracefully to the people, as if in thanks for their flattering reception. Buchanan alone met his mother without one mark of joy. Cold and reserved, from earliest childhood, he had never yet felt attachment for any other being than himself; and fully engrossed by the splendour with which he was at all times surrounded, he looked with indifference on every event which did not promote or prevent his own personal amusements. He saw many new guests arrive without experiencing the slightest accession of pleasure;[l] and when those departed whom he had been in the habit of seeing around him, it seldom cost him even a momentary regret. He had so long and so frequently been informed that he was heir of the immense possessions now belonging[m] to his uncle, that he was overpowered by the sense of his greatness; nor did the commiseration of his attendants, on his disappointed hopes, awaken him to the conviction of the great change which had occurred since the birth of the Marquis of Delaval. Indeed he seemed as indifferent on this occasion as on all others. Yet whatever his errors, he was at least in person and manner all that Lady Margaret could wish. She was also much pleased with Calantha, and thought she traced, in her radiant countenance, some resemblance to her own.

The Duchess of Altamonte had, in mind and person, won^a the affections of all who approached her. She had a countenance in which languor and delicacy added sensibility and grace,^b to beauty, – an air of melancholy half veiled in smiles of sweetness, – and a form soft and fragile as the bright fictions of a poet's dream; yet a visible sadness had fallen upon her spirits, and whilst she appeared alone to sooth and bless every other heart, she seemed herself in need of consolation. Lady Margaret's beauty irresistibly attracted; her wit enlivened; and her manners fascinated – but the dreadful secrets of her heart appalled!

Lady Margaret was not much liked by Mrs. Seymour, nor by many other of the guests who frequented the castle. Her foreign domestics, her splendid attire, her crafty smiles^c and highly polished manners, – all were in turn criticised and condemned. But neither prejudice nor vulgarity received from her lips the slightest censure. She did not even appear to see the ill will shewn to her. Yet many thought the discords and disasters which occurred after her arrival in Ireland, were the fruits of her intriguing spirit, and all soon or late regretted her presence at the castle, till then, the seat of uninterrupted harmony and almost slumberous repose. /

CHAPTER III.

LADY Margaret Delaval, only surviving sister of the Duke of Altamonte, was born in Ireland, where she remained until her marriage with Captain Buchanan. She then established herself at Naples; the fleet in which her husband served being stationed in the Mediterraneau sea. After the birth of her son William, she immediately sent him to Ireland, there to receive, under her brother's tuition, an education more fitting the heir of Altamonte, and the future husband of Lady Calantha Delaval.

Freed from the last tie which had bound her to one feeling of honour or of virtue, she, without remorse, gave way during the absence of her child and husband (who accompanied the boy to Ireland) to a life of extravagance and vice, ensnaring the inexperienced by her art, and fascinating the most wary by her beauty and her talents. The charms of her person and the endowments of her mind were worthy of a better fate than that which she was preparing for herself. But, under the semblance of youthful gaiety, she concealed a dark intriguing spirit, which could neither remain at rest, nor satisfy itself in the pursuit of great and noble objects. She had been hurried on by the evil activity of her own mind, until the habit of crime had overcome every scruple, and rendered her insensible to repentance, and almost to remorse. In this career, she had improved to such a degree her natural talent of dissimulation, that, under its impenetrable veil, she was able to carry on securely her darkest machinations; and her understanding had so adapted itself to her passions, that it was in her power to give, in her own eyes, a character of grandeur, to the vice and malignity, which afforded an inexplicable delight to her depraved imagination.

While she was thus indulging her disgraceful inclinations, her heart became attached with all her characteristic violence to Lord Dartford,[24] a young English nobleman, who had accompanied the Countess of Glenarvon to Naples, and who, after passing some months in her society, had already made her the offer of his hand. He no sooner, however, beheld Lady Margaret than he left that object of his first attachment; and the short-lived happiness of guilty passion was thus enhanced by a momentary triumph over a beautiful and unfortunate rival. – Lady Glenarvon lived not to lament it: the blow which was given by the hand she loved, went straight as it was aimed; it pierced her heart; she did not long survive.

Her son, already advancing towards manhood, she committed to the care of the Count Gondimar, the only being who, amongst the numerous attendants in the hours of her prosperity, had remained with her in this last trying scene, and received her dying wishes. – 'He has no father,' said she,[a] weeping in remembrance of the gallant husband she had lost; 'but to you I consign this jewel of my heart, the dear and only pledge of my true and loyal love. Whatever[b] crime I have committed since the loss of Glenarvon, my only protector, let not a shade of it be cast upon my son, to sully[c] the bright splendor of his father's fame! Promise a dying mother to protect her child, should he be restored to his grandfather's titles and fortunes. To you, to you I entrust him. Ah! see that he be safely conducted to his own country.'

The Italian Count promised all that Lady Glenarvon desired; and wept as he kissed the faded cheek of the English boy. But no sooner was the momentary interest which he had conceived for the unhappy sufferer at an end – no sooner had Lady Glenarvon expired, than, disregarding her last request, he sought only to render himself useful and necessary to her son. For this purpose he eagerly assisted him in all his pursuits, however criminal, and whilst he lived upon the sums which were regularly sent from Ireland to supply the necessary expences[d] of his charge, he lost no opportunity of flattering Lord de Ruthven, the present possessor of the estate, and conniving[e] with him in the means of detaining[f] Glenarvon in Italy, and thus depriving him of a great share of his property. Gondimar's lessons were, however, unnecessary;[g] Glenarvon soon emancipated himself from his tuition; and the utmost the base Italian could boast, was[h] that he had assisted in perverting a heart already by nature,[i] but too well inclined to misuse the rare gifts with which it had been endowed. /

Glenarvon passed the first years after his mother's death, in visiting Rome and Florence.[25] He, after this,[j] expressed a wish of entering the navy; and having obtained his desire, he served under the command of Sir George Buchanan. He even distinguished himself in his new profession; but having done so, abruptly left it.

Love, it was said, was the cause of this sudden change in Glenarvon's intentions. – Love[k] for the most beautiful woman in Florence. Young as he then was, his talents and personal attractions soon gained the object of his pursuit; but a dreadful tragedy followed this success. The husband of Fiorabella revenged the stigma cast upon his wife's fame, by instantly sacrificing her to his vengeance; and, since that fatal deed, neither the chevalier[126] nor Glenarvon had ever again appeared in Florence.

Some said that the unhappy victim had found an avenger; but the proud and noble family of the chevalier,[m] preserved a faithful silence concerning that transaction. Glenarvon's youth prevented any suspicion from falling upon him; and the death of Giardini was ascribed to another, and a more dangerous hand. Strange rumours were also circulated in Ireland, after this event; it was every where affirmed that Glenarvon had been secretly murdered; and Lady Margaret, then at Naples, had even written to apprize her brother of the report. /

CHAPTER IV.

ABOUT the time of the disappearance of Glenarvon, Captain Buchanan died; and Lady Margaret expected[a] that Lord Dartford would immediately fulfil his engagement, and reward her long and devoted attachment to himself by the offer of his hand. Count Gondimar was with her at the time. In all companies, in all societies, the marriage was considered certain. One alone seemed eager to hear this report contradicted – one who, dazzled by the charms and beauty of Lady Margaret, had devoted himself, from the first hour in which he had beheld her, entirely to her service. The name of the young enthusiast was Viviani. A deep melancholy preyed upon his spirits; a dark mystery enveloped his fate. Gondimar had, with some coldness, introduced him to Lady Margaret. He was the friend of the lost Glenarvon, he said, and on that account alone he had strong claims upon his affection. Lady Margaret received the stranger with more than common civility: his ill state of health, his youth, his beauty, were powerful attractions. He confided his sorrows to her bosom; and soon he dared to inform her that he loved.

Lady Margaret was now more than usually attentive to Lord Dartford: the day even for her intended nuptials was fixed.[b] 'Oh give not that hand to one who values not the prize,' said the young Count Viviani, throwing himself before her;[c] 'let not Dartford call himself your lord; his love and mine must never be compared.' 'Go,[d] foolish boy,' said Lady Margaret, smiling on her new victim: 'I can be your friend[e] as readily when I am Lord Dartford's wife as now.' Her young admirer shuddered, and rose from the earth: 'You must be mine alone: – none other shall approach you.' 'The disparity of our ages.' 'What of that?' 'Enough, enough. I will give my hand to Dartford; my heart, you know, will still be at your disposal.' A deep blush covered the pale cheeks[f] of Viviani, he uttered one convulsive sigh, and left her to ruminate on his hopeless fate; for every thing, he was informed, was prepared for the approaching nuptials.

But they knew little of the nature of man, who could conceive that Lord Dartford had even a thought[g] of uniting himself to Lady Margaret by any lasting ties. On the contrary, he suddenly and secretly, without even taking leave of her, departed for England; and the first letter which she received from him, to inform her of his absence, announced to her, likewise, his marriage with a lady of fortune and rank in his native country.

Lady Margaret was at dinner with a numerous company, and amongst them the young count, when the letters from England were placed before her. The quivering of her lip and the rolling of her dark eye might have betrayed, to a keen observer, the anguish of a disordered spirit; but, recovering herself with that self-command which years of crime and deep dissimulation had taught her, she conversed as usual, till it was time for her to depart; and only when in her own apartment, closing the door, gave vent to the fury that opprest her.[a] For some moments she paced the room in silent anguish; then kneeling down and calling upon those powers, whose very existence she had so often doubted;[b] 'Curse him! curse him!' she exclaimed. 'O may the curse of a bitter,[c] and deeply injured heart, blast every promise of his happiness; pursue him through life; and follow him to the grave! – May he live to be the scorn of his enemies, the derision of the world, without one friend to soften his afflictions! – May those, whom he has cherished, forsake him in the hour of need; and the companion he has chosen, prove a serpent to betray him! – May the tear of agony, which his falsehood has drawn from these eyes, fall with tenfold bitterness from his own! – And may this blooming innocent, this rival, who has supplanted me in his affections, live to feel the pangs she has inflicted on my soul; or perish in the pride of her youth, with a heart as injured, as lacerated as mine! – Oh if there are curses yet unnamed, prepared by an angry God, against offending man, may they fall upon the head of this false, this cold-hearted Dartford!'

She arose, and gasped for breath. She threw up the sash of the window; but the cool air, the distant lashing of the waves, the rising moon and the fine scene before her, had no power to calm, even for one moment, a heart torn by guilt and tortured by self-reproach. A knock at the door roused her from her meditations. It was the fair Italian boy; he had followed her; for, at a glance, he had penetrated her secret. With a smile of scorn he upbraided her for her weakness. – 'What! in tears lady!' he said: 'is it possible? can a marriage, a disappointment in love, overpower you thus!' Lady Margaret[d] affecting a calmness,[e] she could not feel, and opposing art to art, endeavoured to repel his taunting expressions. But he knew her thoughts: he saw at once[f] through the smiles and assumed manners which blinded others; and at this moment he watched her countenance with malignant delight. It was the face of an Angel,[g] distorted by the passions of a Dæmon;[h] and he liked it not the less for the frailty it betrayed.

It happened, however, that he had just attained the means of turning the tide of her resentment out of its[i] present channel, and,[j] by awakening her ambition – her ruling passion, of at once quenching the dying embers of every[k] softer feeling. 'You have read I perceive,' said he,[l] 'but one of the epistles with which you have been favoured; and I am already before hand with you[m] in hearing news of far greater importance than the loss of a lover. – The Duchess of Altamonte.' 'What of her?' 'After a few hours illness,' continued Viviani, drawing one of the English papers from his pocket, 'the Duchess of Altamonte is safely delivered of a son and heir.' The blood forsook Lady Margaret's lips: 'I am lost then!' she said: 'the vengeance of Heaven has overtaken me! where shall I turn for succour? Is there none upon earth to whom I can apply for assistance? Will no one of all those who profess so much,[a] assist me? Shall Dartford triumph, and my son be supplanted? Revenge – revenge me, and I will be your slave.'

If the name of love must be given alike to the noblest and most depraved of feelings, the young Viviani loved Lady Margaret with all the fervor of which his perverted heart[b] was capable. She had made him the weak instrument of her arts; and knowing him too well,[c] to place herself in his power, she had detained him near her, by all the varying stratagems of which she was mistress.[d] – He now knelt before her, and, reading in her fierce countenance her dreadful wishes, 'I will revenge thee,' he said,[e] 'yes it shall be done!' 'Blood – blood is the price!' said Lady Margaret. 'Seal the compact thus: – be mine but for one hour: – let me fancy myself blest – and: . . . .' 'My son[f] must be Duke of Altamonte,' returned Lady Margaret, deeply agitated. – 'He shall.' – 'Swear it, my loveliest, my youngest friend!' – 'By the living God of Heaven, I swear it.' – 'Ah! but your courage will fail at the moment: your heart, intrepid as I think it, will shudder,[g] and misgive you. – Say where, and how, it can be done with safety.' 'Leave that to me: keep your own counsel:[h] I will do the rest.' He spoke,[i] and left her. /

When they met again, the following day, not one word was uttered upon the dreadful subject of their former discourse: the compact between them was considered as made: and when once again the Count Viviani spoke of his passion, and his hopes, Lady Margaret reminded him of his vow; and a fearful silence ensued. Revenge and ambition had urged her to a determination, which a sentiment of prudence inclined her to retract. Viviani unconscious of her wavering resolution, enjoyed a momentary triumph. 'Is not this extacy?' he exclaimed, as he viewed the woman he now considered as entirely bound to him. 'Is it not rapture thus to love?' 'Revenge is sweet,' she answered. 'Will you give yourself to me[j] Margaret? Shall I indeed press you to my burning heart! say – can you love?' 'Aye, and hate too,' she replied, as, convulsed with agony, she shrunk from the caresses of her importunate admirer.

From that hour he courted her with unremitting assiduity: he was the slave of every new caprice, which long indulgence of every selfish feeling could awaken. But the promised hour of his happiness was delayed; and his passion thus continually fed by hope, and yet disappointed, overcame in his bosom every feeling of humanity, till he no longer cherished a thought that did not tend to facilitate the immediate gratification of his wishes. /

CHAPTER V.

It was not long after Lady Margaret's arrival at the castle that Count Gondimar, who had accompanied her to Ireland, prepared to return to Italy. A few evenings before he quitted her, he sought the secret habitation of his friend Viviani who had likewise followed Lady Margaret to Ireland, but in order to facilitate his designs,[a] had never openly appeared at the castle. 'How strong must be the love,' said Gondimar, addressing him, 'which can thus lead you to endure concealment, straits and difficulty! return[b] with me: there are others as fair: your youthful heart pictures to yourself[c] strange fancies; but in reality this woman is little worth you. I love her not,[d] and it is but imagination,[e] which thus deceives you.' 'I will not leave her – I cannot go,' said Viviani impatiently: 'one burning passion annihilates in my heart[f] every other consideration. Ah! can it merit the name of passion,[g] the phrenzy which rages within me! Gondimar, if I worshipped the splendid star, that flashed along my course, and dazzled me with its meteor blaze, even in Italian climes, imagine what she now appears to me, in these cold northern regions. I too can sometimes pause to think whether the sacrifice I have made is not too great. But I have drained the poisoned cup to the dregs. I have prest the burning firebrand to my heart, till it has consumed me – and come what may, now, I am resolved she shall be mine, though the price exacted were blood.' Gondimar shuddered.

It was soon after this,[h] that he returned to Italy. Before[i] he departed, he once more in secret affectionately embraced his friend. 'She has deceived me,' cried Viviani; 'months have glided by in vain attempts to realize her depraved wish. She evades[j] my suit. But the hour of success approaches: – to-morrow: – nay, perhaps, to-night...If thou, Gondimar – oh! if thou couldst believe: yet wherefore should I betray myself, or shew, to living man, one thought belonging to the darkest of human hearts. This alone know – I dare do every thing;[k] and I will possess her. See, she appears – that form of majesty – that brow of refulgent brightness. The very air I breathe speaks to me of her charms. What matters it to me, whilst I gaze entranced upon her, if the earth shake to its foundation,[l] and rivers of blood were streaming around me! – Pity me, Gondimar. – Pardon me. – Farewell!'

Hurried on by mad passion, Viviani, who constantly visited Lady Margaret, was now upon the eve of fulfilling her wishes. Yet once, in the hope of dissuading his savage mistress from her bloody purpose, he placed the infant in her arms, and bade her take pity on its helpless innocence. 'See thy own – thy brother's image in those eyes – that smile,' he whispered; 'ah! can you have the heart?' But Lady Margaret turned from the child in haughty displeasure, thrusting it from her as if afraid to look on it; and, for many days, would not vouchsafe to speak to the weak instrument of her criminal ambition. Yet he, even he, whose life had been one continued course of profligacy, who had misused his superior talents to the perversion of the innocence of others, and the gratification of his own ungoverned passions, shuddered at the thought of the fearful crime which he had engaged himself to commit!

His knowledge of human nature, and particularly of the worst part of it, was too profound to depend upon any personal or immediate aid from Lady Margaret: he, therefore, conceived a project which, by any one but himself, would, in every view of it, have been considered as altogether desperate and impracticable. It was, however, a maxim with Viviani, which his practice and experience had justified, that nothing is impossible to a firmly united league of time, money[a] and resolution. Alone, he could have accomplished nothing; but he had a satellite long trained in his service, who possessed every quality which fitted him to assist the designs of such a master. The name of this man was La Crusca. In spite of a seeming wish to conceal himself, in conformity, perhaps, with his master's designs, this man was known at the castle to be a servant to the count, and[b] by his flattery and the versatility of his genius, had become familiar with a few of its inhabitants; but shortly after his arrival, he had been dismissed, and it was now three months and more since his departure.

One evening, acccording to custom, Viviani having secretly entered the castle, sought Lady Margaret in her own apartment; his face was fearfully pale; his hand trembled. He found her in company with her son, Buchanan, and Calantha. Alarmed at his manner and appearance, the latter concealed her face on the white bosom of her aunt, nor guessed by what storms of fierce passion that bosom was disturbed. Viviani mistook the brilliant hue which heightened Lady Margaret's complexion for a softer feeling; he approached her, and, gently removing the child, whispered vows[c] of ardour and tenderness in the ears of his mistress, and urged his suit with every argument he could devise to overcome any remaining scruple.[d] But when he looked,[e] in expectation of a favorable[f] answer, he sprung back with terror from her; for it seemed as if the fiends of hell were struggling in her eyes and lips for looks and words with which to express their horrid desire, already[g] without the aid of words, but too sufficiently manifest! At length, breaking silence, and rising in scorn from her seat: 'Have I not promised myself to you?' she whispered indignantly, 'that you thus persecute me for the performance of a voluntary vow? Do you think your protestations can move, and your arguments persuade? Am I a timid girl, who turns from your suit bashful or[a] alarmed? Or am I one grown old in crime, and utterly insensible to its consequence? – Nothing, you well know, can make me yours but my own free will; and never shall that will consign me to such fate, till the sickly weed is destroyed, and the fair and flourishing plant restored to its wonted vigour and due honors. See there, there is the image of my brother, of all that is glorious and lovely.' As she spoke, she pointed to Buchanan... 'Lady,[b] the deed is already done! This night,' said the Italian, trembling in every limb, 'yes, on this fearful night, I claim the performance of thy vow!' He spoke with an emotion she could not mistake. – 'Is it possible?' said she,[c] 'my beautiful, my beloved friend:' and his hand trembled as he gave it her, in token of his assent. – Fearing to utter another word, dreading even the sound of their own voices, after such a disclosure, she soon retired.

Was it to rest that Lady Margaret retired? – No – to the tortures of suspense, of dread, of agony unutterable. A thousand times she started from her bed: – she fancied that voices approached the door – that shrieks rent the air; and, if she closed her eyes, visions of murder floated before her distracted mind, and pictured dreams too horrible for words half suffocated[d] by the fever and delirium of her troubled imagination. She[e] threw up the sash of her window, and listened attentively to every distant sound. The moon had risen in silvery brightness above the dark elm trees;[f] it lighted, with its beams, the deep clear waters of Elle. The wind blew loud at times, and sounded mournfully, as it swept through the whispering leaves of the trees,[g] over the dark forest and distant moors. A light appeared,[h] for one moment, near the wood, and then was lost. Lady Margaret, as if palsied by terror, remained fixed and breathless on the spot; – a step approached the door; – it was the step of one stealing along, as if anxious no one should hear it pass. Again, all was silent: – so silent that the grave itself had not been more tranquil, and the dead could not have looked more pale, more calm, more still, than Lady Margaret!

But how was that silence broken? and how that calm disturbed? – By the shrieks of an agonized parent – by the burning tears of a heart-broken father – by the loud unrestrained clamours of the menial train; and that proud mansion, so lately the seat of gaiety, whose lighted porticos[i] and festive halls had echoed to the song of joy and revelry, presented now a scene of lamentation, terror and despair. –[j] The heir of Altamonte was dead – the hope so fondly cherished was cut off – the idol, upon whose existence so many hearts were fixed, lay in his gilded cradle and costly attire, affording a lesson impressive[k] although every day repeated, yet unheeded although impressive,[l] – that it is the nature of man to rest his most sanguine expectations upon the most frail and uncertain of all his possessions.

The women who had been employed to attend upon him were weeping around him. His nurse alone appeared utterly insensible to his fate, – her eyes were fixed,[a] – her lips motionless,[b] – she obeyed every command that was given; but, when left to herself, she continued in the same sullen mood. Some called her hard and unfeeling, as in loud accents they bewailed the dire calamity that had fallen on their master's house; but there were others who knew that this apparent insensibility was the effect of a deeper feeling – of a heart that could not recover its loss – of a mind totally overthrown.

She had arisen that morning at her accustomed hour, to take to her breast the little infant who slept in the cradle beside her; – but[c] lifeless was that form which, a few hours before, she had laid on its pillow, in the full enjoyment of health. Spasms, it was supposed, had seized the child in his sleep; for his face was black and dreadfully disfigured. All efforts to recover him were fruitless. Physician nor medicine could avail,[d] – the hand of death had struck the flower,[e] – the vital spark was extinguished.

It was in vain that the[f] distracted mother, pressing his cold lips to hers, declared, in the agony of hope, that they still retained a living warmth. – It was in vain that she watched him till her eyes[g] deceived, fancied that they[h] saw a change imperceptible to others – a breath of life restored to that lifeless breathless form. It was in vain: – and floods of grief, with the sad rites of a pompous funeral, were all which the afflicted Duke and his sorrowing family had to bestow.

The tenants and peasantry were, according to an ancient[i] custom, admitted to sing the song of sorrow over the body of the child: but no hired mourners were required on this occasion; for the hearts of all deeply shared in the affliction of their master's house, and wept, in bitter woe, the untimely loss of their infant Lord. – It was thus they sung, ever repeating the same monotonous and melancholy strain.

> Oh loudly sing the Pillalu,
> And many a tear of sorrow shed;
> *Och orro, orro, Olalu*;
> Mourn, for the master's child is dead.
>
> At morn, along the eastern sky,
> We marked an owl, with heavy wing;
> At eve, we heard the benshees cry;
> And now the song of death we sing;
> *Och orro, orro, Olalu.* /
>
> Ah! wherefore, wherefore would ye die;
> Why would ye leave your parents dear;
> Why leave your sorrowing kinsmen here,
> Nor listen to your people's cry!
>
> How wilt[j] thy mother bear to part
> With one so tender, fair[k] and sweet!

Thou wast the jewel of her heart,
The pulse, the life,[a] that made it beat.

How sad it is to leave her boy,
That tender flowret[b] all alone;
To see no more his face of joy,
And soothe no more his infant moan!

But see along the mountains[c] side,
And by the pleasant banks of Larney,
Straight o'er the plains, and woodlands wide,
By Castle Brae, and Lock Macharney:

See how the sorrowing neighbours throng,
With haggard looks and faultering breath;
And as they slowly wind along,
They sing the mournful song of death!

O loudly sing the Pillalu,
And many a tear of sorrow shed;
Och orro, orro, Olalu;
Mourn, for the master's child is dead. /

Thus singing[d] they approached the castle, and thus[e] amidst cries and lamentations, was Sidney Albert, Marquis of Delaval, borne for ever from its gates, and entombed with his ancestors in the vault of the ancient church, which, for many hundred years, had received beneath its pavement the successive generations of the family of Altamonte. Heart-felt tears, more honourable to the dead than all the grandeur which his rank demanded, were shed over his untimely grave; while a long mourning and entire seclusion from the world, proved that the sorrow thus felt was not momentary, but lasting as the cause which had occasioned it was great. /

CHAPTER VI.

As sickness falls heaviest on those who are in the full enjoyment of health, so grief is most severe, when it comes unexpectedly, in the midst of happiness. – It was from this cause, that the Duke, more than any one in his family, gave vent to the sorrows of his heart; and murmured at the irrecoverable loss, by which he had been afflicted. The Duchess in vain attempted to share,[a] and lessen the regret of her husband: – he had that haughtiness of mind which disdains all confidence, and flies from all consolation. But of her far keener suffering, for the loss she had sustained, little shew was made; for real misery delights not in reproaches and complaints. It is like charity and love – silent, long suffering[b] and mild. /

There are virtues which admit of no description – which inspire on the first mention of them but little interest. Great faults[c] and heroic qualities, may be pourtrayed; but those milder merits[d] which contribute so much to the comfort and happiness of life – that sweetness of disposition, to which every hour that passes by,[e] bears an approving testimony, can be only felt, enjoyed[f] and regretted. Benevolence that never fails, patience under the heaviest calamities, firmness in friendship[g] under every trying change – these are among its characteristic features; and these were all possessed by the Duchess of Altamonte, who seemed to live for no other purpose than to endear herself to those who surrounded her.

With this consideration for others, and forgetfulness of self, she had apparently endured the loss of her son with greater fortitude, than had been expected: indeed she sustained it with a degree of firmness which religion alone could have inspired: she murmured not; but submitted to the trial with the meek spirit of pious resignation. – 'My dear, dear boy, my pretty Albert' would sometimes escape her, and a few tears would wait upon the exclamation; but her whole study was to share the disappointment, and lighten[h] the sorrows of her husband; as well as to check the intemperate complaints, and soothe the more violent agitations of Lady Margaret.

But while the soul of the Duchess[i] rose superior to the ills of life, her constitution, weakened by a long period of ill health, and by the agitations of extreme sensibility, was not in a state to resist so great a shock; and though she lingered upwards of a year, the real cause of her death could not be mistaken: – an inward melancholy preyed upon her spirits, which she combated in vain. – 'Many have smiled in adversity,' she would say; 'but it is left for me to weep in prosperity: – such[a] is the will of Heaven, and I resign myself as becomes me, to that power, which knows when to give, and when to take away.'

On her death-bed, she said to the Duke: 'This is a hard trial for you to bear; but God, who, when he sends trials, can send strength also, will, I trust, support you. – You[b] will pursue your career with that honour and dignity, which has hitherto distinguished it – nor would my feeble aid assist you in it; but[c] I, on the contrary, like a weak unsupported plant, must have drooped and pined away, had I lived to survive the tender and faithful friend, who has guided and sustained me. It is far better,[d] as it is. You will be a guardian and protector to my Calantha, whose quickness and vivacity,[e] make me tremble for her. I could not have watched over her, and directed her as I ought. But to you, while she smiles,[f] and plays around you, and fills the space which I so soon must leave,[g] – to you, she will prove a dear and constant interest. Never, my dearest Altamonte, ah! never suffer her to be absent, if possible, from your guiding care: – her[h] spirits, her passions, are of a nature to prove a blessing, or the reverse, according to the direction they are permitted to take. Watch over and preserve her – are[i] my last words to you. – Protect[j] and save her from all evil – is the[k] last prayer I offer to my God, before I enter into his presence.'.....[l]

Calantha! unhappy child, whom not even the pangs of death could tear from the love, and remembrance of thy mother, – what hours of agony were thine, when a father's hand first tore thee from that lifeless bosom,[m] – when piercing shrieks declared the terror of thy mind, oppressed, astonished at the first calamity, by which it had been tried,[n] – when thy lips tremblingly pronounced for the last time, the name of mother – a name so dear, so sacred and beloved, that its very sound awakens in the heart, all that it can feel of tenderness and affection! What is left that shall replace her? What friend, what tie, shall make up for her eternal absence? What even are the present sufferings of the orphan child, to the dreary void, the irreparable loss she will feel through all her future years. It was on that bosom, she had sought for comfort, when passion and inadvertence had led her into error. It was that gentle, that dear voice, which had recalled her from error,[o] even when severity had failed. – There is, in every breast, some one affection that predominates over the rest – there is still to all some one object, to which the human heart[p] is rivetted beyond all others:[q] – in Calantha's bosom, the love of her mother prevailed over every other feeling.

A long and violent illness succeeded, in Calantha, the[r] torpor which astonishment and terror at her loss had produced; and from this state, she recovered only to give way to a dejection of mind not less alarming: but[s] even her grief was to be envied, when compared with the disorder of Lady Margaret's mind.

– Remorse preyed upon her heart, the pride and hardness of which, disdained the humility of acknowledging her offence[a] in the presence of her Creator.

The great effort of Lady Margaret was to crush the struggles of passion; and when, at times, the agony of her mind was beyond endurance, she found it some relief to upbraid the wretch who had fulfilled her own guilty wishes. – 'Monster!' she would exclaim, 'without one tender or honourable feeling, take those[b] detested and bloody hands from my sight: – they have destroyed the loveliest innocent that was ever born to bless a mother's wishes: – that mother now appears in awful judgment against thee: – out, out, perfidious wretch! – come not near – gaze not upon me.' – Viviani marked the wild expression of her eye – the look of horror which she cast upon him; and a deep and lasting resentment succeeded in his breast,[c] to every feeling of attachment. Seizing her hand, which he wrung in scorn: 'What mean you by this mockery of tardy penitence?' he fiercely cried. – 'Woman,[d] beware how you trifle with the deep pangs of an injured heart: – not[e] upon me – not upon me, be the blood of the innocent: – it was this hand, white and spotless as it appears, which sealed his doom: – I[f] should have shewn mercy; but an unrelenting tigress[g] urged me on. – On thee – on thine, be the guilt, till it harrow up thy soul[27] to acts of phrenzy and despair: – hope not for pardon from man – seek not for mercy from God. – Away with those proud looks which once subdued me: – I can hate – I have learned of thee to hate; and my heart, released from thy bonds, is free at last: – spurn me,[h] – what art thou now? A[i] creature so wretched and so fallen, that I can almost pity thee. – Farewell. – For the last time, I look on thee with one sentiment of love. – When[j] we meet again, tremble: – yes – proud as thou art, tremble; for, however protracted, thou shalt find the vengeance of Viviani, as certain,[k] as it is terrible.

'Is it possible,' said Lady Margaret, gazing upon that beautiful and youthful countenance – upon that form which scarcely had attained to manhood, – 'is it in the compass of probability[l] that one so young should be so utterly hardened? Viviani smiled on her and left her. – Very[m] shortly after this interview, he quitted Ireland, vainly endeavouring in the hour of his departure to conceal the deep emotion by which he was agitated at thus tearing himself from one who appeared utterly indifferent to his hatred, his menaces, or his love. /

CHAPTER VII.

THE habit of years, though broken and interrupted by violent affliction or sudden prosperity, fails not in the end to resume its influence over the mind; and the course that was once pursued with satisfaction, though the tempest of our passions may have hurried us out of it, will be again resumed, when the dark clouds that gathered over us, have spent their fury. Even he who is too proud to bow his mind to the inevitable decrees of an all wise Creator,[a] – who seeks not to be consoled, and turns away from the voice of piety, even[b] he loses sight at length of the affliction, upon which his memory has so continually dwelt: – it lessens to his view, as he journies onward adown the vale of life, and the bright beam of hope rises at last upon his clouded spirits[c] and exhausted frame.

From a state of despondency and vain regret, in which more than a year had been passed, the inhabitants of Castle Delaval, by slow degrees, revived; and the Duke, wearied of a life so gloomy and solitary, summoned, as before, his friends around him. Lady Margaret, however, was no longer the gay companion of his morning walks, the life and amusement of his evening assemblies. The absence of Viviani filled her with anxiety; and the remembrance of her crimes embittered every hour of her existence. If she turned her eyes upon Calantha, the dejected expression of that countenance reproached her for the mother whose life she had shortened, and whose place she vainly exerted herself to fill; if upon the Duke, in that care worn[d] cheek and brow of discontent, she was more painfully reminded of her crime and ingratitude; and even the son for whom so much had been sacrificed, afforded her no consolation.

Buchanan estranged himself from her confidence, and appeared jealous of her authority. – He refused to aid her in the sole remaining wish of her heart; and absolutely declined accepting the hand of Calantha. 'Shall only one will,' he said, 'be studied and followed; shall Calantha's caprices and desires be daily attended to; and shall I see the best years of my life pass without pleasure or profit for me? I know – I see your intention; and, pardon me, dearest mother, if I already bitterly lament it. Is Calantha a companion fitted for one of my character; and, even if hereafter it is your resolve to unite me to her, must I now be condemned to years of inactivity on her account. Give me my liberty; send me to college, there to finish my education; and permit me to remain in England for some years.

Lady Margaret saw, in the cool determined language of her son, that he had long meditated this escape from her thraldom: – she^a immediately appeared to approve his intention^b – she said that a noble ambition, and all the highest qualities of the heart and mind were shewn in his present desire; but one promise she must exact in return for the readiness with which she intended instantly to accede to his request: – provided he was^c left at liberty till a maturer age, would he promise to take no decisive step of himself, until he had once more seen Calantha after this separation? To this Buchanan willingly acceded; his^d plans were soon arranged; and his departure was fixed for no very distant period.

The morning before he left the castle, Lady Margaret called him to her room; and taking him and Calantha by the hand, she led them to the windows of the great gallery. From thence^e pointing to the vast prospect of woods and hills, which extended to a distance,^f the eye could scarcely reach, 'all are yours my children,' she said, 'if, obedient to parents who have only your welfare at heart, you persevere in your intention of being one day united to each other. Ah! let no disputes, no absence, no fancies have power to direct^g you from the fulfilment of this, my heart's most fervent wish: – let this moment of parting,^h obliterate every unkind feeling, and bind you more than ever to each other. Here, Buchanan,' continued she,ⁱ 'is a bracelet with your hair: place^j it yourself around Calantha's arm: – she shall wear it till you meet.' The bracelet was of gold, adorned with diamonds, and upon the clasp, under the initial letters of both^k their names, were engraved these words: '*Stesso sangue, Stessa sorte.*'²⁸ 'Take it,' said Buchanan, fastening it upon the arm of Calantha, and remember that you are to wear it ever, for my sake.'^l

At this moment, even he was touched, as he pressed her to his heart, and remembered her as associated with all the scenes of his happiest days. Her violence, her caprices, her mad frolics, were forgotten; and as her tears streamed upon his bosom, he turned away, least his mother should witness his emotion. Yet Calantha's tears were occasioned solely by the thought of parting from one, who had hitherto dwelt always beneath the same roof with herself; and to whom long habit had accustomed, rather than attached^m her. – In youth the mind is so tender, and so alive to sudden and vivid impressions, that in the moment of separation it feels regret,ⁿ and melancholy at estranging itself even from those for whom before it had never felt any warmth of affection. – Still at the earliest age the difference is distinctly marked between the transient tear, that^o falls for imaginary woe, and the real misery which attends upon the loss of those who have been closely united to the affections by ties, stronger and dearer than those of habit. /

CHAPTER VIII.

THE accomplishment of her favourite views being thus disappointed, or at least deferred, Lady Margaret resolved to return to Italy, and there to seek for Viviani.ª Her brother, however, entreated her to remain with him. He invited his friends, his relations, his neighbours. Balls and festivities once more enlivened the castle: it seemed his desire to raze every trace of sorrow from the memory of his child; and to conceal the ravages of death under the appearance at least of wild and unceasing gaiety. – The^b brilliant *fêtes*, and the magnificence of the Duke of Altamonte and his sister, became the constant theme of admiration; from^c far, from near, fashion and folly poured forth their victims to grace and to enjoy them; and^d Lord and Lady Dartford naturally found their place amidst the various and general assemblage. To see Lord Dartford again, to triumph over his falsehood, to win him from an innocent confiding wife, and then betray him at the moment in which he fancied himself secure,^e this vengeance was yet wanting to satisfy the restless fever of Lady Margaret's mind; and the contemplation of its accomplishment gave a new object, a new hope to her existence; for Lady Margaret had preferred enduring^f even the tortures of remorse,^g to the listless insipidity of stagnant life, where the passions of her heart,^h were without excitement, and those talents of which she felt the power, useless and obscured. What indeed would she not have preferred to the society of Mrs. Seymour and her daughters?[29]

The Duchess of Altamonte had possessed a mind, as cultivated as her own, and a certain refinement of manner which is sometimes acquired by long intercourse with the most polished societies, but is more frequently the gift of nature, and, if it be not the constant attendant upon nobility of blood, is very rarely found in those who are not distinguished by that adventitious and accidental circumstance.

Mrs. Seymour had many of the excellent qualities, but none of the rare endowments possessed by the Duchess;ⁱ she was a strict follower of the paths of custom and authority;^j in the steps which had been marked by others, she studiously walked, nor thought it allowable to turn aside for any object however praiseworthy and desirable.^k She might be said to delight in prejudice – to enjoy herself in the obscure and narrow prison to which she had voluntarily confined her intellects – to look upon the impenetrable walls around her as bulwarks against the hostile attacks by which so many had been overcome.[a] The daughters were strictly trained in the opinions of their mother. 'The season of youth,' she would say, 'is the season of instruction;' – and consequently every hour had its allotted task; and every action was directed according to some established regulation.

By these means, Sophia and Frances were already highly accomplished; their manners were formed; their opinions fixed, and any contradictions[b] of those opinions, instead of raising doubt, or urging to enquiry, only excited in their minds astonishment at the hardihood and contempt for the folly which thus opposed itself to the final determination of the majority, and ventured to disturb the settled empire and hereditary right of their sentiments and manners. – 'These are *your* pupils,' Lady Margaret would often exultingly cry, addressing the mild Mrs. Seymour –[c] 'these paragons of propriety – these sober minded steady automatons. Well, I mean no harm to them or you. I only wish I could shake off a little of that cold formality which petrifies me. Now see how differently *my* Calantha shall appear, when I have opened her mind, and formed her according to *my* system of education – the system which nature dictates and every feeling of the heart willingly accedes to. Observe well the difference between a child of an acute understanding, before her mind has been disturbed by the absurd opinions of others, and after she has learned their hackneyed jargon: note her answer[d] – her reflections; and you will find in them, all that philosophy can teach, and all to which science and wisdom must again return. But, in your girls and in most of those whom we meet, how narrow are the views, how little the motives, by which they are impelled.[e] Even granting that they act rightly, –[f] that by blindly following, where others lead, they pursue the safest course, is there any thing noble, any thing superior in the character from which such actions spring? *I* am ambitious for Calantha. I wish her not only to be virtuous; I will acknowledge it,[g] – I wish her to be distinguished and great.'

Mrs. Seymour, when thus attacked, always permitted Lady Margaret to gain the victory of words[h] and to triumph over her as much as the former thought it within the bounds of good breeding to allow herself; but she never varied, in consequence, one step in her daily course, or deviated in the slightest degree from the line of conduct which she had before laid down.

Sometimes, however, she would remonstrate with her niece, when she saw her giving way to the violence of her temper, or acting, as she thought, absurdly or erroneously, and Calantha, when thus admonished, would acknowledge her errors, and, for a time at least, endeavour to amend them; for her heart was accessible to kindness, and kindness she at all times met with from Mrs. Seymour and her daughters. /

It was indeed Calantha's misfortune to meet with too much kindness, or rather too much indulgence from almost all who surrounded her. The Duke, attentive solely to her health, watched her with the fondest solicitude, and the wildest wishes her fancy could invent,[a] were heard with the most scrupulous attention[b] and gratified with the most unbounded compliance. Yet, if affection, amounting to idolatry, could in any degree atone for the pain the errors of his child too often occasioned him, that affection was felt by Calantha for her Father.[c]

Her feelings indeed swelled with a tide too powerful for the unequal resistance of her understanding: – her motives appeared the very best, but the actions which resulted from them were absurd and exaggerated. Thoughts, swift as lightening, hurried through her brain: – projects, seducing, but visionary crowded upon her view: without a curb she followed the impulse of her feelings; and those feelings varied with every varying interest and impression.

Such character is not uncommon, though rarely seen amongst the higher ranks of society. Early and constant intercourse with the world, and that polished sameness which results from it, smooths away all peculiarities; and whilst it assimilates individuals to each other, corrects many faults, and represses many virtues.

Some indeed there are who affect to differ from others: but the very affectation proves that, in fact, they resemble the ordinary mass; and in general this assumption of singularity is found in low and common minds, who think that the reputation of talent and superiority belongs to the very defects[d] and absurdities which alone have too often cast a shade upon the splendid light of genius, and degraded the hero and the poet, to the level of their imitators.

Lovely indeed is that grace of manner, that perfect ease and refinement which so many attempt to acquire, and for which it is to be feared so much too often is renounced[e] – the native vigour of mind, the blush of indignant and offended integrity, the open candour of truth,[f] and all the long list of modest unassuming virtues, known only to a new and unsullied heart.

Calantha turned with disgust from the slavish followers of prejudice. She disdained the beaten tract, and she thought that virtue would be for her a safe, a sufficient guide; that noble views, and pure intentions would conduct her in a higher sphere; and that it was left to her to set a bright example of unshaken rectitude, undoubted truth[f] and honourable fame. All that was base or mean, she, from her soul, despised;[g] a fearless spirit raised her, as she fondly imagined, above the vulgar herd;[h] self confident, she scarcely deigned to bow the knee before her God;[i] and man, as she had read of him in history, appeared too weak, too trivial[j] to inspire either alarm or admiration. /

It was thus, with bright prospects, strong love of virtue, high ideas of honour, that she entered upon life. No expence,[k] no trouble had been spared in her education; masters, tutors[l] and governesses surrounded her. She seemed to have a decided turn for every thing it was necessary for her to learn;[m] instruction was scarcely necessary, so readily did her nature bend itself to every art, science and accomplishment; yet[n] never did she attain excellence, or make proficiency in any; and when the vanity of a parent fondly expected to see her a proficient in all acquirements,[a] suited to her sex and age, he had the mortification of finding her more than usually ignorant, backward and uninstructed. With an ear the most sensible and accurate, she could neither dance,[b] nor play; with an eye acute and exact, she could not draw; with[c] a spirit that bounded within her from excess of joyous happiness, she was bashful and unsocial in society; and with the germs of every virtue that commands esteem and praise, she was already the theme of discussion, observation and censure.

Yet was Calantha loved – dearly and fondly loved; nor could Mrs. Seymour, though constantly discovering new errors in her favourite, prevent her from being the very idol of her heart. Calantha saw it through all her assumed coldness; and she triumphed in the influence she possessed. But Sophia and Frances were not as cordially her friends: – they had not reached that age, at which lenity and indulgence take place of harsher[d] feelings, and the world appears in all its reality before us. To them, the follies and frailties of others carried with them no excuse, and every course that[e] they themselves did not adopt, was assuredly erroneous.

Calantha passed her time as much as possible by herself;[f] the general society at the castle was uninteresting to her. The only being for whom she felt regard, was Sir Everard St. Clare, brother to Camioli the bard, and late physician to her mother, was[g] the usual object of ridicule to almost all of his acquaintance. Lady St. Clare in pearls and silver; Lauriana and Jessica, more fine if possible[h] and more absurd than their mother; Mrs. Emmet[i] a Lady from Cork, plaintive and reclining in white sattin and drapery; and all the young gentlemen of large property and fortune, whom all the young ladies were daily and hourly endeavouring to please, had no attraction for a mind like Calantha's. Coldly she therefore withdrew from the amusements natural to her age; yet it was from embarrassment, and not from coldness, that she avoided their society. Some favorites she already had: –[j] the Abbess of Glenaa, St. Clara her niece, and above all Alice Mac Allain, a beautiful little girl of whom her mother had been fond,[k] had already deeply interested her affections. [30]

In the company of one or other of these,[31] Calantha would pass her mornings; and sometimes would she[l] stand alone upon the summit of the cliff, hour after hour, to behold the immense ocean, watching its waves, as they swelled to the size of mountains, then[m] dashed with impetuous force against the rocks below; or climbing[n] the mountain's side, and gazing[o] on the lofty summits of Heremon and Inis Tara, lost in idle and visionary thought; but at[p] other times joyous, and without fear, like a fairy riding on a sun beam[q] through the air, chasing the gay images of fancy, she would join in every active amusement[r] and suffer her spirits to lead her into the most extravagant excess. /

CHAPTER IX.³²

LOVE, it might be conjectured, would early shew itself in a character such as Calantha's; and love, with all its ardour and all its wildness,ᵃ had already subdued her heart. What, though Mrs. Seymour had laid it down as a maxim, that no one, before she had attained herᵇ fourteenth year, could possibly be in love! What, though Lady Margaret indignantly asserted, that Calantha could not, and should not, look even at any other than him for whom her hand was destined! She had looked; she had seen; and what is more, she believed the impression at this time made upon her heart was as durable as it was violent.

Sophia Seymour, Mrs. Seymour's eldest daughter, in a month, nay in a week, had alreadyᶜ discovered Calantha's secret: – the same feeling for the same object,ᵈ had given her an acuteness in this instance, with which she was not at all times gifted: – Sheᵉ herself loved, and, therefore, perceived her cousin's passion. Calantha's manner immediately confirmed her in her supposition. She entered one morning into her room; – she saw the unfinished drawing; – she could not mistake it – that commanding air – that beaming eye – there was but one whom it could resemble, and that one was Henry Mowbray,ᶠ Earl of Avondale.³³ She taxed Calantha bitterly with her partiality;ᵍ 'But he thinks not of you,' she said, and haughtily left the room.

Admiral Sir Richard Mowbrayʰ was an old and valued friend of the Duke of Altamonte. He had served with Sir George Buchanan, brother-in-law to Lady Margaret. He had no children; but his nephew, the young Earl of Avondale, was, next to his country, the strongest and dearest interest of his heart. What happiness must the Admiral then have felt when he beheld his nephew;ⁱ and found that, in mind and person, he was distinguished by every fair endowment. He had entered the army young;ʲ he now commanded a regiment: with a spirit natural to his age and character, he had embraced his father's profession; likeᵏ him, he had early merited the honours conferred upon him. He had sought distinction at the hazard of his life; but happily for all who knew him well, he had not, like his gallant father, perished in the hour of danger; but, having seen hard service, had returned to enjoy, in his own country, the ease, the happinessˡ and the reputation he so well deserved.

Lord Avondale's military occupations had not, however, prevented his cultivating his mind and talents in no ordinary degree; and the real distinctions he had obtained, seemed by no means to have lessened the natural modesty of his character. He was admired, flattered, sought after; and the strong temptation[a] to which his youth had thus early been exposed, had, in some measure, shaken his principles and perverted his inclinations.[b]

Happily a noble mind and warm uncorrupted heart soon led him from scenes of profligacy to a course of life more manly and useful: – deep anxiety for a bleeding country, and affection for his uncle, restored him to himself. He quitted London, where upon his first return from abroad[c] he had for the most part resided, and his regiment being ordered to Ireland, on account of the growing disaffection in that country, he returned thither to fulfil the new duty[d] which his profession required.[e] Allanwater and Monteith, his father's estates, had been settled upon him;[f] but he was more than liberal in the arrangements he made for his uncle and the other branches of his family.

Many an humbler mind had escaped the danger to which Lord Avondale had, early in life, been exposed;[g] – many a less open character had disguised the too daring opinions he had once ventured to cherish! But, with an utter contempt for all hypocrisy and art, with[h] a frankness and simplicity of character, sometimes observed in men of extraordinary abilities, but never attendant on the ordinary or the corrupted mind, he appeared to the world as he really felt, and neither thought nor studied whether such opinions and character were agreeable to his own vanity, or the taste of his companions; for whom, however, he was, at all times, ready to sacrifice his time, his money, and all on earth but his honour and integrity.

Such was the character of Lord Avondale, imperfectly sketched – but true to nature[i] – He, in his twenty-first year, now appeared at Castle Delaval – the admiration of the large and various company then assembled there. Flattered, perhaps, by the interest shewn him, but reserved and distant to every too apparent mark of it, he viewed the motley groupe before him, as from a superior height, and smiled[j] with something of disdain, at times, as he marked the affectation, the meanness, the conceit[k] and, most of all, the heartlessness[l] and cowardice of many of those around him. Of a morning, he would not unfrequently join Calantha and Sophia in their walks; of[m] an evening, he would read to the former, or make her his partner at billiards, or at cards. At such times, Sophia would work at a little distance; and as her needle monotonously passed the silken thread through the frame to which her embroidery was fixed, her eyes would involuntarily turn to where[n] her thoughts, in spite of her endeavours, too often strayed. Calantha listened to the oft-repeated stories of the admiral; she[o] heard of his battles, his escapes and his dangers, when others were weary of the well-known topics; but he was Lord Avondale's uncle, and that thought made every thing he uttered interesting to her.

'You love,' said Alice Mac Allain,ᵃ one day to her mistress, as they wandered in silence along the banks of the river Elle,ᵇ 'and he who made you alone can tell to what these madning^c fires may drive a heart like yours. Remember your bracelet – remember your promises to Buchanan; and learn, before it is too late, in some measure to controulᵈ yourself, and disguise your feelings.' Calantha started from Alice; for love, when it first exists, is so timid, so sacred, that it fears the least breath of observation, and disguises itself under every borrowed name. 'You are wrong,' said Calantha,ᵉ 'I would not bend my free spirit to the weakness of which you would accuse me, for all the world can offer;ᶠ your Calantha will never acknowledge a master; willᵍ never yield her soul's free and immortal hopes,ʰ to any earthly affection. Fear not, my counsellor, that I will forsake my virgin vows, or bow my unbroken spirit to that stern despot, whose only object is power and command.'ⁱ

As Calantha spoke, Lord Avondale approached, and joined them. The deep blush that crimsoned over her cheek was a truer answer to her friend's accusation than the one she had just uttered. – 'Heremon and Inis Tara have charms for both of you,' he said, smiling: – 'youʲ are always wandering either to or from thence.'ᵏ 'They are our own native mountains,' said Calantha, timidly: – 'the landmarks we have been taught to reverence from our earliest youth.' 'And could you not admire the black mountains of Morne as well,' he said, fixing his eyes on Calantha, – 'my native mountains? – they are higher far than these, and soar above the clouds that would obscure them.' 'Theyˡ are too lofty and too rugged for such as we are,' said Calantha. 'We may gaze at their height and wonder; but more would be dangerous.' 'The roses and myrtles blossom under their shade,' said Lord Avondale,ᵐ with a smile; 'and Allanwater, to my mind, is as pleasant to dwell in as Castle Delaval.' 'Shall you soon return there, my lord,'ⁿ enquired Calantha. 'Perhaps never,' he said, mournfully; and a tear filled his eye as he turned away, and sought to change the subject of conversation.

Lady Margaret had spoken to Lord Avondale: – perhaps another had engaged his affections: – at all events, it seemed certain to Calantha that she was not the object of his hope or his grief. To have seen him – to have admired him, was enough for her: she wished not for more than that privilege; she feltº that every affection of her heart was engaged, even though those affections were unreturned. /

CHAPTER X.

To suffer the pangs of unrequited love was not,[a] in the present instance, the destiny of Calantha. That dark eye, the lustre of whose gaze she durst not meet, was, nevertheless,[b] at all times fixed upon her; and the quick mantling blush and beaming smile, which lighted the countenance of Lord Avondale, whenever her name was pronounced before him, soon betrayed, to all but himself and Calantha, how much and how entirely his affections were engaged. He was of a nature not easily to be flattered into admiration of others – not readily attracted, or lightly won; but, once having fixed his affections, he was firm, confiding and incapable of change, through any change of fortune. He was, besides, of that affectionate and independant[c] character, that as neither bribe nor power could have moved him to one act contrary to his principles of integrity, so neither danger, fatigue, nor any personal consideration could have deterred him from that which he considered as the business and duty of his life. He possessed a happy and cheerful disposition, – a frank and winning manner, –[d] and that hilarity of heart and countenance which rendered him the charm and sunshine of every society.

When Lord Avondale, however,[e] addressed Calantha, she answered him in a cold or sullen manner, and, if he endeavoured to approach her, she fled unconscious of the feeling which occasioned her embarrassment. Her cousins, Sophia and Frances, secure of applause, and conscious of their own power of pleasing, had entered the world neither absurdly timid, nor vainly presuming: – they knew the place they were called upon to fill in society; and they sought not to outstep the bounds which good sense had prescribed. Calantha, on the other hand, scarce could overcome her terror and confusion when addressed by those with whom she was little acquainted. But how far less dangerous was this reserve than the easy confidence which a few short years afterwards produced,[f] and how little did the haughty Lady Margaret imagine, as she chid her niece for this excess of timidity, that the day would, perhaps, soon arrive[g] when careless of the presence of hundreds, Calantha might strive to attract their attention, by the very arts which she now despised, or pass thoughtlessly along, hardened and entirely[h] insensible to their censure or their praise!

To a lover's eyes such timidity was not unpleasing; and Lord Avondale liked not the girl he admired the less, for that crimson blush – that timid look, which scarcely dared encounter his ardent gaze. To him it seemed to disclose a heart new to the world – unspoiled and guileless. Calantha's mind, he thought, might now receive the impression which should be given it; and while yet free, yet untainted, would it not be happiness to secure her as his own – to mould her according to his fancy – to be her guide and protector through life!

Such were his feelings, as he watched her shunning even the eyes of him, whom alone she wished to please: – such were his thoughts, when, flying from the amusements and gaiety natural to her age, she listened with attention, while he read to her, or conquered her fears to enter[a] into conversation with him. He seemed to imagine her to be possessed of every quality which he most admired; and the delusive charm of believing that he was not indifferent to her heart, threw a beauty and grace over all her actions, which blinded him to every error. Thus then they both acknowledged, and surrendered themselves to the power of love. Calantha for the first time yielded up her heart entirely to its enchantment; and Lord Avondale[b] for the last.

It is said there is no happiness, and no love to be compared to that which is felt for the first time. Most persons erroneously think so; but love like other arts[c] requires experience, and terror and ignorance, on its first approach, prevent our feeling it as strongly as at a later period. Passion mingles not with a sensation[d] so pure, so refined as that which Calantha then conceived, and the excess of a lovers[e] attachment terrified and overpowered the feelings of a child.

Storms of fury kindled in the eye of Lady Margaret when first she[f] observed this mutual regard. Words could not express her indignation:[g] – to deeds she had recourse. Absence was the only remedy to apply; and an hour, a moment's delay, by opening Calantha's mind to a consciousness of her lover's sentiments and wishes, might render even this ineffectual. She saw that the flame had been kindled in a heart too susceptible, and where[h] opposition would encrease[i] its force;[j] – she upbraided her brother for his blindness, and reproached herself for her folly. There was but one way left, which was to communicate the Duke's surmises and intentions to the Admiral in terms so positive, that he could not mistake them, and instantly to send for Buchanan. In pursuance of this purpose, she wrote to inform him of every thing which had taken place, and to request him without loss of time to meet her at Castle Delaval. Mrs. Seymour alone folded Calantha to her bosom without one reproach, and, consigning her with trembling anxiety to a father's care, reminded him continually, that she was his only remaining child, and that force, in a circumstance of such moment, would be cruelty.[k] /

CHAPTER XI.

Lady Margaret insisted upon removing Calantha immediately,[a] to London; but Lord Avondale having heard from the Admiral the cause of her intended departure, immediately declared his intention of quitting Ireland. Every thing was now in readiness for his departure; the day fixed; the hour at hand. It was not perhaps till Lord Avondale felt that he was going to leave Calantha for ever, that he was fully sensible how much, and how entirely his affections were engaged.

On the morning previous to his departure, Calantha threw the bracelet, which Lady Margaret and her cousin had given her, from her arm; and, weeping upon the bosom of Alice, bitterly lamented her fate, and informed her friend that she never, never would belong to Buchanan. – Lord Avondale had in vain sought an opportunity of seeing her one moment alone. He now perceived the bracelet on the floor of the room she had just quitted;[b] and looking upon it, read, without being able to comprehend the application of the inscription, '*Stesso sangue, Stessa sorte.*' – He saw her at that moment: – she was alone: – he followed her: – she fled from him, embarrassed and agitated; but he soon approached her: – they fly so slowly[c] who fly from what they love.

Lord Avondale thought he had much to say – many things to ask: – he wished to explain the feelings of his heart – to tell Calantha, once at least before he quitted her, how deeply – how dearly he had loved,[d] – how, though unworthy in his own estimation of aspiring to her hand, the remembrance of her should stimulate him to every noble exertion, and raise him to a reputation which, without her influence, he never could attain: – he thought that he could have clasped her to his bosom, and pressed upon her lips the first kiss of love – the dearest, the truest pledge of fondness and devotion. But, scarcely able to speak, confused and faultering, he dared not approach her: – he saw one before him robed in purity, and more than vestal innocence – one timidly fearful of even a look, or thought, that breathed aught against that virtue which alone it worshipped.

'I am come,' he said, at length, 'forgive my rashness, to restore this bracelet, and myself to place it around your arms.[e] Permit me to say – farewell, before I leave you, perhaps for ever.' As he spoke, he endeavoured to clasp the diamond lock; – his hand trembled; – Calantha[f] started from him. 'Oh!' said she,[g] 'you know not what you do: – I am enough his already: – be not you the person to devote me to him more completely: – do not render me utterly miserable.' Though not entirely understanding her,[a] he scarcely could command himself. Her look, her manner – all told him too certainly that which overcame his heart with delight. – 'She loves me,' he thought, 'and I will die sooner than yield her to any human being: – she loves me; and, regardless of fears – of prudence – of every other feeling, he pressed her one moment to his bosom. 'Oh[b] love me, Calantha,' was all he had time to say; for she broke from him, and fled, too much agitated to reply. That he had presumed too far, he feared; but that she was not indifferent to him, he had heard and seen. The thought filled him with hope, and rendered him callous to[c] all that might befall him.

The Duke entered the room as Calantha quitted it. – 'Avondale,' he said, offering him his hand, 'speak to me, for I wish much to converse with you before we part: – all I ask is, that you will not deceive me. Something more than common has taken place: – I observed[d] you with my child.[e] 'I must indeed speak with you,' said Lord Avondale firmly, but with considerable agitation. 'Every thing I hold dear – my life – my happiness – depend on what I have to say.' He then informed the Duke with sincerity of his attachment for Calantha,[f] – proud and eager to acknowledge it, even though he feared that his hopes might never be realized.

'I am surprised and grieved,' said the Duke, 'that a young man of your high rank, fortune [g] and rising fame, should thus madly throw away your affections upon the only being perhaps who never must, never ought, to return them. My daughter's hand is promised to another. When I confess this, do not mistake me: – No force will ever be made use of towards her; her inclinations will at all times be consulted, even though she should forget those of her parent; but she is now a mere child, and more infantine and volatile withal, than it is possible for you to conceive. There can be no necessity for her being now called upon to make a decided choice. Buchanan is my nephew, and since the loss of my son, I have centered all my hopes in him. He is heir to my name, as she is to my fortune; and surely then an union between them, would be an event the most desirable for me and for my family. But such considerations alone would not influence me. I will tell you those then which operate in a stronger manner: – I have given my solemn promise to my sister, that I will do all in my power to assist in bringing about an event upon which her heart is fixed. Judge then, if[h] during her son's absence, I can dispose of Calantha's hand, or permit her to see more of one, who has already, I fear, made some impression upon her heart.'

Lord Avondale appeared much agitated. – The Duke paused – then continued – 'Granting that your attachment for my child is as strong as you would have me believe – granting, my dear young friend, that, captivated by your very superior abilities, manners[i] and amiable disposition, she has in part returned the sentiments you acknowledge in her favour,[j] – cannot you make her the sacrifice I require of you? – Yes. – Though you now think otherwise, you can do it. So short an acquaintance with each other,ª authorizes the term I use: – this is but a mere fancy, which absence and strength of mind will soon overcome.

    Lord Avondale was proud even to a fault. He had listened to the Duke without interrupting him; and the Duke continued to speak, because he was afraid of hearing the answer, which he concluded would be made. For protestations, menaces, entreaties[b] he was prepared; but the respectful silence which continued when he ceased, disconcerted him.[c] 'You are not angry?' said he:[d][34] 'let us part in friendship: – do not go from me thus: – you must forgive a father: – remember she is my child, and bound to me by still dearer ties – she is my only one.' His voice faultered, as he said this: – he thought of the son who had once divided his affections, and of whom he seldom made mention since his loss.

    Lord Avondale, touched by his manner and by his kindness, accepted his hand, and struggling with pride – with love, – 'I will obey your commands,' he at length said, 'and fly from her presence, if it be for her happiness: – her happiness is the dearest object of my life. Yet let me see her before I leave her.' – 'No,' said the Duke, 'it is too dangerous.' 'If this must not be,' said Lord Avondale, 'at least tell her, that for her sake, I have conquered even my own nature in relinquishing her hand, and,[e] with it every hope, but too[f] strongly cherished by me. Tell her, that if I do this, it is not because I do not feel for her the most passionate and most unalterable attachment. I renounce her only, as I trust, to consign her to a happier fate. You are her father: – you best know the affection she deserves: – if she casts away a thought sometimes on me, let her not suffer for the generosity and goodness of her heart: – let her not.'[g] – He would have said more, but he was too deeply affected to continue: – he could not act, or dissemble: – he felt strongly, and he shewed it. /

CHAPTER XII.

AFTER this conversation, Calantha saw no more of her lover: yet he was very anxious to see her once again, and much and violently agitated before he went. A few words which he had written to her he gave into Mrs. Seymour's own hands; and this letter, though it was such as to justify the high opinion some had formed of his character, was but little calculated to satisfy the expectations of Calantha's absurdly romantic mind; or to realize the hopes she had cherished. It was not more expressive of his deep regret at their necessary separation, than of his anxiety that she should not suffer her spirits to be depressed, or irritate her father by an opposition which would prove fruitless. – 'He does not love you[a] Calantha,' said Lady Margaret, with a malicious smile, as soon as she had read the letter – (and every one would read it): – 'when men begin to speak of duty, they have ceased to love.' This remark gave Calantha but little consolation. Lord Avondale had quitted her too, without even bidding her farewell; and her thoughts continually dwelt on this disappointment.

Calantha knew not then that her misery was more than shared,[b] – that Lord Avondale, though too proud to acknowledge it, was a prey to the deepest grief upon her account,[c] – that he lived but in the hope of possessing the only being upon earth to whom he had attached himself,[d] – and that the sentence pronounced against both, was a death stroke to his happiness, as well as to her own. When strong love awakes for the first time in an inexperienced heart it is so diffident, so tremblingly fearful, that it dares scarcely hope even for a return; and our own demerits appear before us, in such exaggerated colours, and the superior excellence of the object we worship arises so often to our view, that it seems but the natural consequence of our own presumption, that we should be neglected and forgotten.

Of Admiral Sir R. Mowbray,[e] Calantha now took leave without being able to utter one word: – she[f] wept as children weep in early days, the hearts'[g] convulsive sob free and unrestrained. He was as much affected as herself, and seeking Lady Margaret, before he left the castle[h] and followed his nephew[i] who had gone straight to England, began an eager attack upon her, with all the blunt asperity of his nature. Indeed he bitterly reproached himself, and all those who had influenced him, in what he termed his harsh unfeeling conduct to his nephew[j] in this affair. – 'And as to you, madam,' he cried, addressing Lady Margaret, 'you make two young people wretched, to gratify the vanity of your son, and acquire a fortune, which I would willingly yield to you, provided the dear children might marry, and go home with me to Allanwater, a place as pretty, and far more peaceful than any in these parts: there, I warrant, they would live happy, and die innocent – which is more than most folks can say in these great palaces and splendid castles.'

A smile of contempt was the only answer Lady Margaret deigned to give. – Sir Richard continued, 'you are all a mighty fine set of people, no doubt, and your assemblies, and your balls are thronged and admired: but none of these things will make the dear child happy, if her mind is set upon my nephew. I am the last in the world to disparage any one; but my nephew is just as proper a man in every point of view[a] as your son; aye, or any body's son in the whole world; and so there is my mind given free and hearty; for there is not a nobler fellow, and there never can be, than Henry Avondale: – he is as brave a soldier as ever fought for his country; and in what is he deficient?' Lady Margaret's lips and cheeks were now become livid and pale – a fatal symptom, as anger of that description in all ages[b] has led to evil deeds; whereas the scarlet effusion has, from the most ancient times been accounted harmless. 'Take Lady Calantha then,' exclaimed Lady Margaret, with assumed calmness, while every furious passion shook her frame; 'and may she prove a serpent to your bosom, and blast the peace of your whole family.' 'She is an angel!' exclaimed the Admiral, 'and she will be our pride, and our comfort.' 'She is a woman,' returned Lady Margaret,[c] with a malicious sneer; 'and, by one means or other, she will work her calling.' Calantha's tears checked Sir Richard's anger; and, his carriage being in readiness, he left the castle immediately after this conversation. /

CHAPTER XIII.

It may easily be supposed that Lady Margaret Buchanan and Mrs. Seymour had a most cordial dislike for each other. Happily, at present, they agreed in one point: they were both desirous of rousing Calantha from the state of despondency into which Lord Avondale's departure had thrown her. By both, she was admonished to look happy, and to restrain her excessive grief. Mrs. Seymour spoke to her of duty and self controul.[a] Lady Margaret sought to excite her ambition and desire of distinction. One only subject was entirely excluded from conversation: Lord Avondale's name was forbidden to be mentioned in Calantha's[b] presence, and every allusion to the past to be[c] studiously avoided.

Lady Margaret, however, well aware that whosoever transgressed this regulation would obtain full power over her niece's heart, lost no opportunity of thus gaining her confidence and affection.

Having won, by this artifice, an easy and favorable audience, after two or three conversations upon the subject the most interesting to Calantha, she began, by degrees, to introduce the name, and with the name such a representation of the feelings of her son, as she well knew to be best calculated to work upon the weakness of a female heart. Far different were his real feelings, and far different his real conduct from that which was described to her niece by Lady Margaret. She had written to him a full account of all that had taken place; but his answer, which arrived tardily, and, after much delay, had served only to increase that lady's ill humour[d] and add to her disappointment. In the letter which he sent to his mother[e] he openly derided her advice; professed entire indifference towards Calantha; and said that, indubitably, he could not waste his thoughts or time in humouring the absurd fancies of a capricious girl,[f] – that Lord Avondale, or any other, were alike welcome to her hand,[g] – that, as for himself, the world was wide[h] and contained women enough for him; he could range amongst those frail and fickle charmers without subjecting his honour and his liberty to their pleasure; and, since the lady had already dispensed with the vows given and received at an age when the heart was pure, he augured ill of her future conduct, and envied not the happiness of the man it was her present fancy to select: – he professed his intention of joining the army on the continent;[i] talked of leaden hail, glory and death! and seemed resolved not to lessen the merit of any exploits he might achieve[a] by any want of brilliancy in the colouring and description of them.

Enraged at this answer, and sickening at his conceit, Lady Margaret sent immediately to entreat, or rather to command, his return. In the mean time, she talked much to Calantha of his sufferings and despair; and soon perceiving how greatly the circumstance of Lord Avondale's consenting to part from her had wounded her feelings, and how perpetually she recurred to it, she endeavoured, by the most artful interpretations of his conduct, to lower him in her estimation. Sarcastically contrasting his coldness with Buchanan's enthusiasm: 'Your lover,' said she,[b] 'is, without doubt, most disinterested! – His eager desire for your happiness is shown in every part of his conduct! – Such warmth – such delicacy! How happy would a girl like my Calantha be with such a husband! – What filial piety distinguishes the whole of his behaviour! – "Obey your father," is the burthen of his creed! He seems even to dread the warmth of your affection! – He trembles when he thinks into what imprudence it may carry you! – Why,[c] he is a perfect model, is he not? But let me ask you, my dear niece, is love, according to your notions and feelings, thus cool and considerate? – does it pause to weigh right and duty? – is it so very rational and contemplative?....' 'Yes,' replied Calantha, somewhat piqued. 'Virtuous love can make sacrifices; but, when love is united with guilt, it becomes selfish and thinks only of the present moment.' 'And how, my little philosopher, did you acquire so prematurely this wonderful insight into the nature of love?' 'By feeling it,' said Calantha, triumphantly; 'and by comparing my own feelings with what I have heard called by that name in others.'

As she said this, her colour rose, and she fixed her animated[d] blue eyes full upon Lady Margaret's face; but vainly did she endeavour to raise emotion there; that countenance, steady and unruffled, betrayed not even a momentary flash of anger: her large orbs rolled securely, as she returned the glance, with a look of proud and scornful superiority. 'My little niece,' said she, tapping her gently on the head, and taking from her clustering locks the comb that confined them, 'my little friend is grown quite a satirist, and all who have not had, like her, every advantage of education, are to be severely lashed, I find, for the errors they may inadvertently[e] have committed.' As she spoke, tears started from her eyes. Calantha threw herself upon her bosom. 'O, my dear aunt,' she said, 'my dearest aunt, forgive me, I entreat you. God knows I have faults enough myself, and it is not for me to judge of others, whose situation may have been very different from mine. Is it possible that I should have caused your tears? My words must, indeed,[f] have been very bitter; pray forgive me.' 'Calantha,' said Lady Margaret, 'you are already more than forgiven; but the tears I shed were not occasioned by your last speech; though it is true, censure from one's children, or those one has ever treated as such, is more galling than from others. But, indeed, my spirits are much shaken. I have had letters from my son, and he seems more hurt at your conduct than I expected: – he talks of renouncing his country and his expectations; he says that,ᵃ if indeed his Calantha, who has been the constant object of his thoughts in absence, can have already renounced her vows and him, he will never intrude his griefs upon her, nor ever seek to bias her inclinations: yet it is with deep and lasting regret that he consents to tear you from his remembrance and consign you to another.'

Calantha sighed deeply at this unexpected information. Toᵇ condemn any one to the pangs of unrequited love was hard: she had already felt that it was no light suffering; and Lady Margaret, seeing how her false and artful representations had worked upon the best feelings of an inexperienced heart, lost no opportunity of improving and increasing their effect.

These repeated attempts to move Calantha to a determination, which was held out to her as a virtuous and honourable sacrifice made to duty and to justice, were not long before they were attended with success. Urged on all sides continually, and worked upon by those she loved, she at last yielded with becoming inconsistency; and one evening, when she saw her father somewhat indisposed, she approached him, and whispered in his ear, that she had thought better of her conduct, and would be most happy in fulfilling his commands in every respect. 'Now you are a heroine, indeed,' said Lady Margaret, who had overheard the promise: 'you have shewn that true courage which I expected from you – you have gained a victory over yourself, and I cannot but feel proud of you.' 'Aye,' thought Calantha, 'flattery is the chain that will bind me; gild it but bright enough, and be secure of its strength: you have found, at last, the clue; now make use of it to my ruin.'

'She consents,' said Lady Margaret; 'it is sufficient; let there be no delay; let us dazzle her imagination, and awakenᶜ her ambition, and gratify her vanity by the most splendid presents and preparations!' /

CHAPTER. XIV.

CALANTHA'S jewels and costly attire – her equipages and attendants, were now the constant topic of conversation. Every rich gift was ostentatiously exhibited; while congratulations, were on all sides, poured forth, upon[a] the youthful bride. Lady Margaret, eagerly displaying the splendid store to Calantha,[b] asked her if she were not happy. – 'Do not,' she replied[c] addressing her aunt, 'do not fancy that I am weak enough to value these baubles: – My heart at least is free from a folly like this: – I despise this mockery of riches.' 'You despise it!' repeated Lady Margaret, with an incredulous smile: – 'you despise grandeur and vanity! Child,[d] believe one who knows you well, you worship them;[e] they are your idols; and while your simple voice sings forth romantic praises of simplicity and retirement, you have been cradled in luxury, and you cannot exist without it.'

Buchanan was now daily, nay even hourly expected: – Lady Margaret,[f] awaited him with anxious hope; Calantha[g] with encreasing[h] fear. Having one morning ridden out to divert her mind from the dreadful suspense under which she laboured, and meeting with Sir Everard, she enquired of him respecting her former favourite: 'Miss Elinor,' said the doctor, 'is still with her aunt, the abbess of Glenaa; and, her noviciate being over, she will soon, I fancy, take the veil. You cannot see her; but if your Ladyship will step from your horse, and enter into my humble abode, I will shew you a portrait of St. Clara, for so we now call her, she being indeed a saint; and sure you will admire it.' Calantha accompanied the doctor, and was struck with the singular beauty of the portrait. 'Happy St. Clara,' she said, and sighed: – 'your heart, dedicated thus early to Heaven, will escape the struggles and temptations to which mine is already exposed. Oh! that I too, might follow your example; and, far from a world for which I am not formed, pass my days in piety and peace.'

That evening, as the Duke of Altamonte led his daughter through the crowded apartments, presenting her to every one previous to her marriage, she was suddenly informed that Buchanan was arrived. Her forced spirits,[i] and assumed courage at once forsook her; she fled to her room; and there giving vent to her real feelings, wept bitterly. – 'Yet why should I grieve thus?' she said: – 'What though he be here to claim me? my hand is yet free: – I will not give it against the feelings of my heart.' – Mrs.ª Seymour had observed her precipitate flight, and following, insisted upon being admitted. She endeavoured to calm her; but it was too late.

From that day, Calantha sickened: – the aid of the physician, and the care of her friends were vain: – an alarming illness seized upon her mind, and affected her whole frame. In the paroxysm of her fever, she called repeatedly upon Lord Avondale's name, which confirmed those around her in the opinion they entertained, that her malady had been occasioned by the violent effort she had made, and the continual dread under which she had existed for some time past, of Buchanan's return. Her father bitterly reproached himself for his conduct; watched by her bed in anxious suspence; and under the impression of the deepest alarm, wrote to his old friend the admiral, informing him of his daughter's danger, and imploring him to urge Lord Avondale to forget what had passed[b] and to hasten again to Castle Delaval. – He stated that, to satisfy his sister's ambition, the greater part of his fortune should be settled upon Buchanan, to whom his title descended; and if, after this arrangement, Lord Avondale still continued the same as when he had parted from Calantha, he only requested his forgiveness of his former apparent harshness, and earnestly besought his return without a moment's loss of time.

His sister,[c] he strove in vain to appease: – Lady Margaret was in no temper of mind to admit of his excuses. Her son had arrived and again left the castle, without even seeing Calautha; and when the Duke attempted to pacify Lady Margaret, she turned indignantly from him, declaring that[d] if he had the weakness to yield to the arts and stratagems of a spoiled and wayward child, she would instantly depart from under his roof, and never see him more. No one event could have grieved him so much, as this open rupture with his sister. Yet his child's continued danger turned his thoughts from this,[e] and every other consideration: – he yielded to her wishes: – he could not endure the sight of her misery: – he had from infancy[f] never refused her slightest request: – and could he now, on so momentous an occasion, could he now force her inclinations and constrain her choice.

The kind intentions of the Duke were however[g] defeated. Stung to the soul, Calantha would not hear of marriage with Lord Avondale: – pride, a far stronger feeling than love, at that early period, disdained to receive concessions even from a father: – and[h] a certain moroseness began to mark her character, as she slowly recovered from her illness, which never had been observed in it before. She became austere and reserved; read nothing but books of theology and controversy; seemed even to indulge an inclination for a monastic life; was often with Miss St. Clare; and estranged herself from all other society.

'Let her have her will,' said Lady Margaret, 'it is the only means of curing her of this new fancy.' – The Duke however[i] thought otherwise: he was greatly alarmed at the turn her disposition seemed to have taken, and tried every means in his power to remedy and counteract it. – A[a] year passed thus away; and the names of Buchanan and Lord Avondale were rarely or never[b] mentioned at the castle; when one evening, suddenly and unexpectedly, the latter appeared there to answer in person, a message which the Duke had addressed to him, through[c] the Admiral, during his daughter's illness.

Lord Avondale had been abroad since last he had parted from Calantha; he had gained the approbation of the army in which he served; and[d] what was better, he knew that he deserved it. His uncle's letter had reached him when still upon service. He had acted upon the staff;[e] he now returned to join his own regiment[f] which was quartered at Leitrim;[35] and his first care, before he proceeded upon the duties of his profession, was to seek the Duke, and to claim, with diminished fortune and expectations, the bride his early fancy had chosen.[36] – 'I will not marry him – I will not see him:' – These were the only words Calantha pronounced, as they led her into the room where he was conversing with her father.

When she saw him, however, her feelings changed. Every heart which has ever known[g] what it is to meet after a long estrangement, the object of its first, of its sole, of its entire devotion, can picture to itself the scene which followed. Neither pride, nor monastic vows, nor natural bashfulness, repressed the full flow of her happiness at the moment,[h] when Lord Avondale rushed forward to embrace her, and[i] calling her his own Calantha, mingled his tears with hers. – The Duke, greatly affected, looked upon them both. 'Take her,' he said, addressing Lord Avondale, 'and be assured, whatever her faults, she is my heart's pride – my treasure. Be kind to her: – that I know you will be, whilst the enthusiasm of passion lasts: but ever be kind to her, even when it has subsided: – remember[j] she has yet to learn what it is to be controuled.' 'She shall never learn it,' said Lord Avondale, again embracing Calantha: 'by day, by night,[k] I have lived but in this hope: – she[l] shall never repent her choice.' 'The God of Heaven vouchsafe his blessing upon you,' said the Duke. – 'My sister may call this weakness; but the smile on my child's countenance is a sufficient reward.' /

CHAPTER XV.

WHAT Lord Avondale had said was true.[a] – One image had pursued him in every change of situation, since he had parted from Calantha; and though he had scarcely permitted his mind to dwell on hope; yet he felt that, without her, there was no happiness for him on earth; and he thought that once united to her, he was beyond the power of sorrow or misfortune. So chaste, even in thought, she seemed – so frank and so affectionate, could he be otherwise than happy with such a companion? How then was he astonished, when, as soon as they were alone, she informed him that, although she adored him, she was averse to the fetters he was so eager to impose. How was he struck to find that all the chimerical, romantic absurdities, which he most despised, were tenaciously cherished by her; to be told that dear as he was, her freedom was even dearer; that she thought it a crime to renounce her vows, her virgin vows; and that she never would become a slave and a wife; – he must not expect it.

Unhappy Avondale! even such an avowal did not open his eyes, or deter him from his pursuit. Love blinds the wisest: and fierce passion domineers over reason. The dread of another separation inspired him with alarm. Agitated – furious – he now combatted every objection, ventured every promise, and loved even with greater fondness from the encreasing[b] dread of again losing what he had hoped was already his own. – 'Men of the world are without religion,' said Calantha with tears; 'Women of the world are without principle. Truth is regarded by none. I love and honour[c] my God, even more than I love you; and truth is dearer to me than life. I am not like those I see: – my education, my habits, my feelings are different; I am like one uncivilized and savage; and if you place me in society, you will have to blush every hour for the faults I shall involuntarily commit. Besides this objection, my temper – I am more violent – Oh that it were not so;[d] but can I, ought I, to deceive you.'....[e] 'You are all that is noble, frank[f] and generous: you shall guide me,' said Lord Avondale;[g] 'and I will protect you. Be mine: – fear me not: – your principles, I venerate; your religion I will study – will learn – will believe in. – What more?'[h]

Lord Avondale sought,[i] and won that strange uncertain being, for whom he was about to sacrifice so much. He considered not the lengthened journey of life – the varied scenes through which they were to pass; where all the qualities in which she was wholly deficient would be so often and so absolutely required – discretion, prudence, firm and steady principle, obedience, humility. – But[a] to all her confessions and remonstrances, he replied: – 'I[b] love, and you return my passion: – can[c] we be otherwise than blest! You are the dearest object of my affection, my life, my hope, my joy. If you can live without me, which I do not believe, I cannot without you;[d] and that is sufficient. Sorrows must come on all;[e] but united together we can brave them. – My Calantha you torture me,[f] but to try me. Were I to renounce you –[g]were I to take you at your word, you, you would be the first to regret and to reproach me.' – 'It[h] is but the name of wife I hate,' replied the spoiled and wayward child. –'I must command: – my will.' – 'Your will, shall be my law,'[i] said Lord Avondale, as he knelt before her: 'you shall be my mistress – my guide – my monitress – and I, a willing slave.' –[j] So spoke the man, who, like the girl he addressed, had died sooner than have yielded up his freedom,[k] or his independence to another; who, high and proud, had no conception of even the slightest interference with his conduct or opposition to his wishes; and who[l] at the very moment that in words he yielded up his liberty, sought only the fulfilment of his own desire, and the attainment of an object upon which he had fixed his mind.

The day arrived. A trembling bride, and an impassioned lover faintly articulated the awful vow. Lord Avondale thought himself the happiest of men; and Calantha, though miserable at the moment, felt that, on earth, she loved but him. In the presence of her assembled family, they uttered the solemn engagement, which bound them through existence to each other; and though Calantha was deeply affected, she did not regret the sacred promise she had made.

When Lord Avondale, however, approached to take her from her father's arms – when she heard that the carriages awaited,[m] which were to bear them to another residence, nor love, nor force prevailed. 'This is my home,' she cried: 'these are my parents. Share all I have – dwell with me where I have ever dwelt; but think not that I can quit them thus.' No spirit of coquetry – no petty airs, learned or imagined, suggested this violent and reiterated exclamation –[n] 'I will not go.' I will not – was sufficient[o] as she imagined, to change the most determined character; and when she found that force was opposed to her violence, terror, nay[p] abhorrence took possession of her mind; and it was with shrieks of despair she was torn from her father's bosom.[37]

'Unhappy Avondale!' said Sophia, as she saw her thus borne away, 'may that violent spirit grow tame,[q] and tractable, and may Calantha at length prove worthy of such a husband!' This exclamation was uttered with a feeling which mere interest for her cousin could not have created. In very truth, Sophia loved Lord Avondale. And Alice Mac Allain, who heard the prayer with surprise and indignation, added fervently: –[r] 'that he may make her happy –[s] that he may know the value of the treasure he possesses –[t] this is all I ask of heaven.[u] – Oh! my mistress – my protectress – my Calantha – what is there left me on earth to love, now thou art gone? Whatever they may say of thy errors[v] even those errors are dearer to my heart,[w] than all the virtues thou has left behind.' /

CHAPTER XVI.

It was at Allanwater, a small villa amidst the mountains, in the county of Leitrim, that Lord and Lady Avondale passed the first months of their marriage. This estate had been settled upon Sir Richard Mowbray,[a] during his lifetime, by his brother, the late Earl of Avondale. It was cheerful, though retired; and to Calantha's enchanted eyes,[b] appeared all that was most romantic and beautiful upon earth. What indeed had not appeared beautiful to her in the company of the man she loved! Every one fancies that there exists in the object of their peculiar admiration a superiority over others. Calantha perhaps[c] was fully justified in this opinion. Lord Avondale displayed even in his countenance the sensibility of a warm, ardent[d] and generous character. He had a distinguished and prepossessing manner, entirely free from all affectation. It is seldom that this can be said of any man, and more seldom of one possessed of such singular beauty of person. He appeared indeed wholly to forget himself; and was ever more eager in the interests of others than his own. Many there are, who, though endowed with the best understandings, have yet an inertness, an insensibility to all that is brilliant and accomplished; and who, though correct in their observations, yet fatigue in the long intercourse of life by the sameness of their thoughts. Lord Avondale's understanding, however, fraught as it was with knowledge, was illumined by the splendid light of genius, yet not overthrown by its force. Of[e] his mind, it might be truly said, that it[f] did not cherish one base, one doubtful or worldly feeling. He was so sincere that, even in conversation, he never mis-stated, or exaggerated a fact. He saw at a glance the faults of others; but his extreme good nature and benevolence prevented his taking umbrage at them. He was, it is true, of a hot and passionate temper, and if once justly offended, firm in his resolve, and not very readily appeased; but he was too generous to injure or to hate even those who might deserve it. When he loved, and he never really loved but one, it was with so violent, so blind a passion, that he might be said to doat upon the very errors of the girl to whom he was thus attached. To the society of women he had been early accustomed; but had suffered too much from their arts, and felt too often the effects of their caprices, to be easily made again their dupe and instrument. Of beauty he had ofttimes been the willing slave. Strong passion, opportunity, and entire liberty of conduct, had, at an early period, thrown him into its power. His profession, and the general laxity of morals, prevented his viewing his former conduct in the light in which it appeared to his astonished bride; but when she sighed, because she feared that she was not the first who had subdued his affections, he smilingly assured her, that she should be the last – that no other should ever be dear to him again.

Calantha, in manner, in appearance, in every feeling, was but a child. At one hour, she would look entranced upon Avondale, and breathe vows of love and tenderness:[a] at another, hide from his gaze, and weep for the home she had left. At one time she would talk with him and laugh from the excess of gaiety she felt; at another, she would stamp her foot upon the ground in a fit of childish impatience, and exclaiming, 'You must not contradict me in any thing,' she would menace to return to her father, and never see him more.

If Lord Avondale had a defect, it was too great good nature, so that he suffered his vain and frivolous partner, to command, and guide, and arrange all things around him, as she pleased, nor foresaw the consequence of her imprudence, though too often carried to excess. With all his knowledge, he knew not how to restrain; and he had not the experience necessary to guide one of her character: – he could only idolize; he left it to others to censure and admonish.

It was also for Calantha's misfortune, that Lord Avondale's religious opinions[38] were different from those in which she had been early educated.[b] It was perhaps to shew him the utility of stricter doctrines, both of faith and morality,[c] that heaven permitted one so good and whole,[d] as he was, to be united with one so frail and weak. Those doctrines which he loved to discuss, and support in speculation, she eagerly seized upon, and carried into practice; thus proving to him too clearly,[e] their dangerous and pernicious tendency. Eager to oppose and conquer those opinions in his wife, which savoured as he thought of bigotry and prudish reserve,[f] he tore the veil at once from her eyes, and opened hastily her wondering mind to a world before unknown. He foresaw not the peril to which he exposed her:[39] – he heeded not the rapid progress of her thoughts – the boundless views of an over-heated imagination. At first she shrunk with pain and horror, from every feeling which to her mind appeared less chaste,[g] less pure, than those to which she had long been accustomed; but when her principles, or rather her prejudices, yielded to the power of love, she broke from a restraint too rigid,[h] into a liberty the most dangerous from its novelty, its wildness and its uncertainty.[40]

The monastic severity which she had imposed upon herself, from exaggerated sentiments of piety and devotion, gave way with the rest of her former maxims – She knew not where to pause, or rest; her eyes were dazzled, her understanding bewildered; and she viewed the world, and the new form which it wore before her, with strange and unknown feelings, which she could neither define, nor command.

Before this period, her eyes had never even glanced upon the numerous pages which have unfortunately been traced by the hand of profaneness and impurity;^a even the more innocent fictions of romance had been withheld from her; and her mother's precepts had, in this respect, been attended to by her with sacred care. Books of every description were now, without advice, without selection, thrown open before her;^b horror and astonishment at first retarded the course of curiosity and interest: – Lord Avondale smiled; and soon the alarm^c of innocence was converted into admiration at the wit,^d and beauty with which some of these works abounded. Care is taken when the blind are cured, that the strong light of day should not fall too suddenly upon the eye; but no caution was observed in at once removing from Calantha's mind, the shackles, the superstition, the reserve, the restrictions which overstrained^e notions of purity and piety had imposed.

Calantha's lover had become her master; and he could not tear himself one moment from his pupil. He laughed at every artless or shrewd remark, and pleased himself with contemplating the first workings of a mind, not unapt in learning, though till then exclusively wrapt up in the mysteries of religion, the feats of heroes, the poetry of classic bards, and the history of nations the most ancient and the most removed. – 'Where have you existed, my Calantha?' he continually said: – 'who have been your companions?' 'I had none,' she replied; 'but wherever I heard of cruelty, vice, or irreligion, I turned away.' 'Ah, do so still, my best beloved,' said Lord Avondale, with a sigh. 'Be ever as chaste, as frank, as innocent, as now.' 'I cannot,' said Calantha, confused and grieved. 'I thought it the greatest of all crimes to love: – no ceremony of marriage – no doctrines,^f men have invented, can quiet my conscience: – I know no longer what to believe, or what to doubt: – hide me in your bosom: – let us live far from a world which you say is full of evil: – and never part from my side; for you are – Henry you are, all that is left me now. I look no more for the protection of Heaven, or the guidance of parents; – you are my only hope: – do you preserve and bless me; for I have left every thing for you.'^g /

CHAPTER XVII.

THERE is nothing so difficult to describe as happiness. Whether some feeling of envy enters into the mind upon hearing of it, or whether it is so calm, so unassuming, so little ostentatious in itself, that words give an imperfect idea of it, I know not.[a] It is easier to enjoy it,[b] than to define it. It springs in the heart, and shews itself on the countenance; but it shuns all display; and is oftener found at home, when home has not been embittered by dissensions, suspicions[c] and guilt, than any where else upon earth. Yes, it is in home[d] and in those who watch there for us. Miserable is the being,[e] who turns elsewhere for consolation! Desolate is the heart which has broken the ties that bound it there.

Calantha was happy; her home was blessed; and in Lord Avondale's society every hour brought her joy. Perhaps the feelings which,[f] at this time united them,[g] were too violent – too tumultuous. Few can bear to be thus loved – thus indulged: very few minds are strong enough to resist it. Calantha was utterly enervated by it; and when the cares of life first aroused Lord Avondale, and called him from her, she found herself unfit for the new situation she was immediately[h] required to fill. When for a few hours he left her, she waited with trembling anxiety for his return; and though she murmured not at the necessary change, her days were spent in tears, and her nights in restless agitation.[i] He more than shared in her distress: he even encouraged the excess of sensibility which gave rise to it; for men, whilst they love, think every new caprice and weakness in the object of it but a new charm; and whilst Calantha could make him grave or merry – or angry or pleased, just as it suited her, he pardoned every omission – he forgave every fault.

Used to be indulged and obeyed, she was not surprised to find him a willing slave; but she had no conception that the chains he now permitted to be laid upon him, were ever to be broken; and tears and smiles, she thought, must, at all times, have the power over his heart which they now possessed. She was not mistaken: – Lord Avondale was of too fine a character to trifle with the affections he had won; and Calantha had too much sense and spirit to wrong him. He looked to his home therefore for comfort and enjoyment. He folded to his bosom the only being upon earth, for whom he felt one sentiment of passion or of love. Calantha had not a thought that he did not know, and share: his heart was as entirely open,ᵃ as her own.

Was it possible to be more happy? It was;ᵇ and that blessing too, was granted. Lady Avondale became a mother: – She gave to Avondale, the dearest gift a wife can offer – a boy, lovely in all the grace of childhood – whose rosy smiles, and whose infant caresses, seemed even more than ever to unite them together. He was dear to both; but they were far dearer to each other. At Allenwater,ᶜ⁴¹ in the fine evenings of summer, they wandered out upon the mountains, and saw not in the countenance of the villagers half the tenderness and happiness they felt themselves. They uttered thereforeᵈ no exclamations upon the superior joy of honest industry: – a cottage offered nothing to their view, which could excite either envy or regret: – theyᵉ gave to all, and were loved by all; but in all respects they felt themselves as innocent, and more happy than those who surrounded them.

In truth, the greater refinement, the greater polish the mind and manner receive, the more exquisite must be the enjoyment the heart is capable of obtaining.ᶠ Few know how to love: – it is a word which many misuse; but they who have felt it, know that there is nothing to compare with it upon earth. It cannot however exist if in unionᵍ with guilt. If ever it doʰ spring up in a perverted heart, it constitutes the misery that heart deserves: – it consumes and tortures,ⁱ till it expires. Even, however, when lawful and virtuous, it may be too violent: – it may render those who are subject to it,ʲ negligent of other duties, and careless of other affections: this in some measure was the case of Lord and Lady Avondale.

From Allenwater,ᵏ Lord and Lady Avondale proceeded to Monteith,⁴² an estate of Lord Avondale's, where his Aunt Lady Mowbrayˡ and his only sister Lady Elizabeth Mowbrayᵐ resided. Sir Richard and Lady Mowbray had never had any children, but Elizabeth and Lord Avondale were as dear to them, and perhaps dearerⁿ than if they had been their own. The society at Monteith was large. There pleasure and gaiety and talent were chiefly prisedᵒ and sought after, while a strong party spirit prevailed. Lady Monteith,⁴³ a woman of an acute and penetrating mind, had warmly espoused the cause of the ministry of the day. Possessed of every quality that could most delight in society, – brilliant, beautifulᵖ and of a truly masculine understanding, she was accurate in judgment, and at a glance could penetrate the secrets of others; yet was she easily herself deceived. She had a nobleness of mindᑫ which the intercourse with the worldʳ and exposure to every temptation,ˢ had not been able to destroy. Bigotted and prejudiced in opinions which early habit had consecrated, she was sometimes too severe in her censures of others.ᵗ

At Castle Delaval, the society was even too refined; and a slight tinge of affectation might, by those who were inclined to censure, be imputed to it. Though ease was not wanting, there was a polish in manner, perhaps in thought, which removed the general tone somewhat too far from the simplicity of nature; sentiment, and all the romance of virtue, was encouraged.

At Monteith, on the contrary, this over refinement was the constant topic of ridicule. Every thought was there uttered, and every feeling expressed: – there was neither shyness, nor reserve, nor affectation. Talent opposed itself to talent with all the force of argument. – The[a] loud laugh that pointed out any new folly, or hailed any new occasion of mirth, was different from the subdued smile, and gentle hint to which Calantha had been accustomed. Opinions were there liberally discussed; characters stripped of their pretences; and satire mingled with the good humour, and jovial mirth, which on every side abounded.

She[b] heard and saw every thing with surprise; and though she loved and admired the individuals, she felt herself unfit to live among them. There was a liberality of opinion and a satiric turn which she could not at once comprehend; and she said to herself, daily, as she considered those around her – [c] 'They are different from me. – I[d] can never assimilate myself to them:[e] I was every thing in my own family;[f] and I am nothing here.' What talents she had,[g] were of a sort they could not appreciate; and all the[h] defects were those which they most despised. The refinement, the romance, the sentiment she had imbibed, appeared in their eyes assumed and unnatural; her strict opinions[i] perfectly ridiculous; her enthusiasm[j] absolute insanity; and the violence of her temper, if contradicted or opposed, the pettishness of a spoiled and wayward child. Yet too indulgent, too kind to reject her, they loved her, they caressed her, they bore with her petulance and mistakes. It was, however, as a child they considered her: – they treated her as one not arrived at maturity of judgment. /

Her reason by degrees became convinced by the arguments which she continually heard; and all that was spoken at random, she treasured up as truth: even whilst vehemently contending and disputing in defence of her favourite tenets, she became of another opinion. So dangerous is a little knowledge – so unstable is violence. Her soul's immortal hopes seemed to be shaken by the unguarded jests of the profane,[k] who casually visited at Monteith, or whom she met with elsewhere: – she read till she confounded truth and falsehood, nor knew any longer what to believe: – she[l] heard folly censured[m] till she took it to be criminal; but crime she saw tolerated[n] if well concealed. The names she had set in[o] her very heart as pure and spotless, she heard traduced and vilified: –[p] indignantly she defended them with all the warmth of ardent youth: – they were proved guilty; she wept in agony, she loved them not less, but she thought less favourably of those who had undeceived her.

The change in Calantha's mind was constant – was daily: it never ceased – it[q] never paused; and none marked its progress, or checked her career. In emancipating herself from much that was no doubt useless, she stripped herself by degrees of all, till she neither feared, nor cared, nor knew any longer what was, from what was not.

Nothing gives greater umbrage than a misconception and mistaken application of tenets and opinions which were never meant to be thus understood and acted upon. Lady Mowbray,[a] a strict adherent to all customs and etiquettes, saw with astonishment in Calantha a total disregard of them; and her high temper could ill brook such a defect.[b] Accustomed to the gentleness of Elizabeth, she saw with indignation the liberty her niece had assumed. It was not for her to check her; but rigidity, vehemence in dispute, and harsh truths, at times too bitterly expressed on both sides, gave an appearance of disunion between them, which happily was very far from being real, as Calantha loved and admired Lady Mowbray[c] with the warmest affection.

Lord Avondale, in the mean time, solely devoted to his wife, blinded himself to her danger. He saw not the change a few months had made, or he imputed it alone to her enthusiasm for himself. He thought others harsh to what he regarded as the mere thoughtlessness of youth; and, surrendering himself wholly to her guidance, he chided, caressed and laughed[d] with her in turn. 'I see how it is Henry,'[e] said Sir Richard, before he left Ireland, –[f] 'you are a lost man; I shall leave you another year to amuse yourself; and I fancy by that time all this nonsense will be over. I love you the better for it, however, my dear boy; –[g] a soldier never looks so well, to my mind, as when kneeling to a pretty woman, provided he does his duty abroad,[h] as well as at home, and that praise every one must give you. /

CHAPTER XVIII.

THE threatening storm of rebellion[44] now darkened around. – Acts[a] of daily rapine and outrage alarmed the inhabitants of Ireland, both in the capital and in the country: all the military forces were increased;[b] Lord Avondale's regiment, then at Leitrim, was ordered out on actual service; and the business of his profession employed every moment of his time. The vigorous measures pursued, soon produced a favorable change; tranquillity was apparently restored; and the face of things resumed its former appearance; but the individual minds that[c] had been aroused to action were not so easily[d] quieted, and the charms of an active life were not so readily[e] laid aside. Lord Avondale was still much abroad – much[f] occupied; and the time hanging heavy upon Calantha's hands, she was not sorry to hear that they were going to spend[g] the ensuing winter in London.

In the autumn, previous to their departure for England, they passed a few weeks at Castle Delaval, chiefly for the purpose of meeting Lady Margaret Buchanan who had till then[h] studiously avoided every occasion of meeting Lady Avondale. Buchanan had neither seen her nor sent her one soothing message since that event,[i] so angry he affected to be, at what, in reality, gave him the sincerest delight.

Count Gondimar had returned from Italy, and was now at the castle. He had brought letters from Viviani to Lady Margaret, who said at once when she had read them: 'You wish to deceive me. These letters are dated from Naples, but our young friend is here – here even in Ireland.' 'And his vengeance,' said Gondimar, laughing. Lady Margaret affected, also, to smile: – 'Oh, his vengeance!' she said, 'is yet to come: – save me from his love now; and I will defend myself from the rest.'

Lord and Lady Dartford were, likewise, at the castle. He appeared cold and careless. In his pretty inoffensive wife, he found not those attractions, those splendid talents which had enthralled him for so long a period with Lady Margaret. He still pined for the tyranny of caprice, provided the load of responsibility and exertion were removed: and the price of his slavery were that exemption from the petty cares of life, for which he felt an insurmountable disgust. From indolence, it seemed he had fallen again into the snare which was spread for his ruin; and having, a second time, submitted to the chain, he had lost all desire of ever again attempting to shake it.[j] Lady Dartford, too innocent to see her danger, lamented the coldness of her husband, and loved him with even fonder attachment, for the doubt she entertained of his affection. She was spoken of by all with pity and praise: her conduct was considered as examplary,[a] when, in fact,[b] it was purely the effect of nature; for every hope of her heart was centered in one object, and the fervent constancy of her affection arose, perhaps, in some measure from the uncertainty of its being returned. Lady Margaret continued to see the young Count Viviani in secret: – he had now been in Ireland for some months: – his manner to Lady Margaret was, however, totally changed: – he had accosted her,[c] upon his arrival, with the most distant civility, the most studied coldness: – he affected ever that marked indifference which proved him but still too much in her power; and, while his heart burned with the scorching flames of jealousy, he waited for some opportunity of venting his desire of vengeance, which, from its magnitude, might[d] effectually satisfy his rage.

Lord Dartford saw him once as he was retiring in haste from Lady Margaret's apartment; and he enquired of her eagerly who he was. – 'A young musician,[45] a friend of Gondimar's, an Italian,' said Lady Margaret. 'He has not an Italian countenance,' said Lord Dartford, thoughtfully. 'I wish I had not seen him: – it is a face which makes a deep and even an unpleasant impression. You call him Viviani, do you? – whilst I live, I never shall forget Viviani!'

Cards, billiards and music, were the usual nightly occupations. Sir Everard St. Clare and the Count Gondimar sometimes entered into the most tedious and vehement political disputes, unless when Calantha could influence the latter enough to make him sing,[e] which he did in an agreeable, though not in an unaffected manner. At these times, Mrs. Seymour, with Sophia and Frances, unheeding either the noise or the gaiety,[f] eternally embroidered fancy muslins, or, with persevering industry, painted upon velvet. Calantha mocked at these innocent recreations. 'Unlike music, drawing and reading, which fill the mind,' she said; – 'unlike even to dancing which, though accounted an absurd mode of passing away time, is active and appears natural to the human form and constitution.'[46]

'Tell me Avondale,' Calantha would say, 'can any thing be more tedious than that incessant irritation of the fingers – that plebian, thrifty and useless mode of increasing in women a love of dress – a selfish desire of adorning their own persons? – I ever loathed it. – There is a sort of self-satisfaction about these ingenious working ladies, which is perfectly disgusting. It gratifies all the little errors of a narrow mind, under the appearance of a notable and domestic turn. At times, when every feeling of the heart should have been called forth, I have seen Sophia examining the patterns of a new gown, and curiously noting every fold of a strangers[g] dress. Because a woman who, like a mechanic, has turned her understanding, and hopes, and energies, into this course, remains uninjured by the storms around her, is she to be admired? – must she be exalted?'[h] 'It is not their occupation, but their character, you censure: – I fear, Calantha, it is their very virtue you despise.' 'Oh no!' she replied,[i] indignantly: 'when real virtue, struggling with temptations of which these senseless, passionless creatures have no conception, clinging for support to Heaven, yet preserves itself uncorrupted amidst the vicious and the base, it deserves a crown of glory, and the praise and admiration of every heart. Not so these spiritless immaculate prejudiced sticklers for propriety. I do not love Sophia: –ᵃ no, though she ever affords me a cold extenuation for my faults – though through life she considers me as a sort of friend whom fate has imposed upon her through the ties of consanguinity. I did not – could not – cannot love her; but there are some, far better than herself, noble ardent characters, unsullied by a taint of evil; and I think, Avondale, without flattery, you are in the list, that I would die to save; that Iᵇ would bear every torture and ignominy, to support and render happy.' – 'Try then my Calantha,' said Lord Avondale, 'to render them so; for, believe me, there is no agony so great as to remember that we have caused one moment's pang to such as have been kind and good to us.' 'You are right,' said Calantha, looking upon him with affection.

Oh! if there be a pang of heart too terrible to endure and to imagine, it would be the consideration that we have returned unexampled kindness,ᶜ by ingratitude, and betrayed the generous noble confidence that trusted every thing to our honour and our love. Calantha had not, however, this heavy charge to answer for at the time in which she spoke, and her thoughts were gay, and all those around seemed to share in the happiness she felt.

Lord Avondale one day reproved Calantha for her excessive love of music. – 'You have censured work,' he said, 'imputedᵈ to it every evil, the cold and the passionless can fall into: – I now retort your satire upon music.' Some may smile at this; but had not Lord Avondale's observation more weight than at first it may appear. Lady Avondale often rode to Glenaa to hear Miss St. Clare sing. Gondimar sung not like her; and his love breathingᵉ ditties went not to the heart, like the hymns of the lovely recluse. But for the deep flushes which now and then overspead St. Clara's cheeks, and the fire which at times animated her bright dark eye, some might have fancied her a being of a purer nature than our own – one incapable of feeling any of the fierce passions that disturb mankind; but her voice was such as to shake every fibre of the heart, and might soon have betrayed to an experienced observer the empassionedᶠ violence of her real character.

Sir Everard, who had one day accompanied Calantha to the convent, asked his niece in a half serious, half jesting manner, concerning her gift of prophecy. 'Have not all this praying and fasting, cured you of it, my little Sybel?'ᵍ he said. – 'No,' replied the girl; 'but that which you are so proud of, makes me sad: – it is this alone which keeps me from the sports which delight my companions: – it is this which makes me weep when the sun shines bright in the clear heavens, and the bosom of the sea is calm.' – 'Will you shew us a specimen of your art?' said Sir Everard, eagerly. – Miss St. Clare coloured, and smiling archly at him, 'The inspiration is not on me now,ʰ uncle,' she said; 'when it is, I will send and let you know.' – Calantha embraced her, and returned from her visit more and more enchanted with her singular acquaintance. /

CHAPTER XIX.

As soon as Lord and Lady Avondale had quitted Castle Delaval, they returned to Allanwater, previous to their departure for England. Buchanan, as if to mark his still-continued resentment against Calantha,[a] arrived at Castle Delaval, accompanied by some of his London acquaintance[b] almost as soon as she had quitted it. He soon distinguished himself in that circle by his bold libertine manners, his daring opinions[c] and his overbearing temper. He declared himself at utter enmity with all refinement, and professed his distaste for what is termed good society. It was not long, however, before Lady Margaret observed a strange and sudden alteration in her son's manners and deportment: – he entered into every amusement proposed; he became more than usually condescending; and Alice Mac Allain, it was supposed, was the sole cause of his reform.

Alice was credulous; and when she was first told that she was as fair[d] as the opening rose, and soft and balmy as the summer breeze, she listened with delight to the flattering strain, and looked in the mirror to see if all she heard,[e] were true. She beheld there a face, lovely as youth and glowing health could paint it, dimpling with ever-varying smiles, while hair, like threads of gold, curled in untaught ringlets over eyes of the lighest blue; and when she heard that she was loved, she could not bring herself to mistrust those vows which her own bosom was but too well prepared to receive. She had, perhaps, been won by the first who had attempted to gain her affections; but she fell into hands where falsehood had twined itself around the very heart's core: – she learned to love in no common school, and one by one every principle and every thought was perverted; but it was not Buchanan who had to answer for her fall! She sunk into infamy, it is true, and ruin irreparable; but she passed through all the glowing course of passion and romance; nor awoke, till too late, from the dream which had deluded her.

Her old father, Gerald Mac Allain, had, with the Duke's permission, promised her hand in marriage to a young man in the neighbourhood, much esteemed for his good character. Linden had long considered himself as an approved suitor. When, therefore, he was first informed of the change which had occurred in her sentiments, and, more than all, when he was told with every aggravation of her misconduct and duplicity, he listened to the charge with incredulity, until the report of it was confirmed from her own lips, by an avowal, that she thought herself no longer worthy of accepting his generous offer,[a] – that to be plain, she loved another, and wished never more to see him, or to hear the reproaches which she acknowledged were her due. 'I will offer you no reproaches,' said Linden, in the only interview he had with her; 'but remember, Miss Mac Allain, when I am far away, that if ever those who, under the name of friend,[b] have beguiled and misled you, should prove false and fail you, – remember, that[c] whilst Linden lives, there is one left who would[d] gladly lay down his life to defend and preserve you, and[e] who, being forced to quit you, never will reproach you: no, Alice – never.'[f]

'Gerald,' said Lady Margaret, on the morning when Alice was sent in disgrace from the castle, 'I will have no private communication between yourself and your daughter. She will be placed at present in a respectable family; and her future conduct will decide in what manner she will be disposed of hereafter.' The old man bent to the ground in silent grief; for the sins of children rise up in judgment against their parents. 'Oh let me not be sent from hence in disgrace,' said the weeping girl; 'drive me not to the commission of crime. – I am yet innocent. – Pardon a first offence.'[g] 'Talk not of innocence,' said Lady Margaret, sternly: 'those guilty looks betray you. – Your[h] nocturnal rambles, your daily visits to the western cliff, your altered manner,[i] – all have been observed by me and Buchanan'– 'Oh[j] say not, at least, that he accuses me. Whatever my crime, I am guiltless, at least, towards him.'[k] 'Guiltless or not, you must quit our family immediately; and to-morrow, at an early hour, see that you are prepared.'

It was to Sir Everard's house that Alice was conveyed. There were many reasons which rendered this abode more convenient to Lady Margaret than any other. The Doctor was timid and subservient, and Count Gondimar was already a great favourite of the youngest daughter,[l] so that the whole family were[m] in some measure, in Lady Margaret's power. Her ladyship accordingly insisted upon conveying Alice, herself, to Lady St. Clare's house; and having safely lodged her in her new apartment, returned to the castle, in haste, and appeared at dinner, pleased with her morning's adventure;[n] her beauty more radiant from success.

It is said that nothing gives a brighter glow to the complexion, or makes the eyes of a beautiful woman sparkle so intensely, as triumph over another. Is this, however, the case with respect to women alone? Buchanan's florid cheek was dimpled with smiles; no sleepless night had dimmed the lustre of his eye; he talked incessantly, and with unusual affability addressed himself to all, except to his mother; while a look of gratified vanity was observable whenever the absence of Alice was alluded to. He had been pleased with being the cause of ruin to any woman; but his next dearest gratification was the having it supposed that he was so. He was much attacked upon this occasion, and much laughing and whispering was heard. The sufferings of love are esteemed lightly till they are felt;[o] and there were, on this occasion, few at the Duke's table, if any, who had ever really known them. /

CHAPTER XX.

TIME[a] which passes swiftly and thoughtlessly for the rich and the gay, treads ever with leaden foot, for those who are miserable and deserted. Bright prospects carry the thoughts onward; but for the mourning heart, it is the direct reverse:[b] – it lives on the memory of the past;[c] traces ever the same dull round; and loses itself in vain regrets,[d] and useless retrospections. No joyous morn now rose to break the slumbers of the once innocent and happy Alice: peace of mind was gone, like the lover who had first won her affections only, it seemed,[e] to abandon her to shame and remorse.

At Sir Everard's, Alice was treated with impertinent curiosity, tedious advice[f] and unwise severity. 'I hate people in the clouds,' cried the Doctor, as he led her to her new apartment. 'Who would walk in a stubble field with their eyes gazing upon the stars? – You would perhaps, and then[g] let me say, nobody would pity you, Miss, if you tumbled into the mire.'[h] 'But kind people would help me up again, and the unkind alone would mock at me, and pass on.'[i] 'There are so many misfortunes in this life, Miss Mac Allain, which come unexpectedly upon us, that, for my life, I have not a tear to spare for those who bring them on themselves.' 'Yet, perhaps, sir, they are[j] of all others, the most unfortunate.' 'Miss Alice, mark me, I cannot enter into arguments, or rather[k] shall not, for we do not always think proper to do what we can. Conscious rectitude is certainly a valuable feeling, and I am anxious to preserve it now: therefore, as I have taken charge of you, Miss, which is not what I am particularly fond of doing, I must execute what I think my duty. Please then[l] to give over weeping, as it is a thing in a woman which never excites commiseration in me. Women and children cry out of spite: I have noticed them by the hour: therefore, dry your eyes; think less of love, more of your duty; and recollect[m] that people who step out of their sphere are apt to tumble downwards till the end of their days, as nothing is so disagreeable as presumption in a woman. I hate presumption, do I not Lady St. Clare? So no more heroics, young Miss,' continued he, smiling triumphantly, and shaking his head: –[n] 'no more heroics, if you value my opinion. I hate romance and fooleries in women:[o] do I not, Lady St. Clare? – and heaven be praised, since the absence of my poor mad brother, we have not a grain of it in our house. We are all downright people,ᵃ not afraid of being called vulgar, because we are of the old school;ᵇ and when you have lived a little time with us, Miss, we shall, I hope, teach you a little sound common sense – a very valuable commodity let me tell you, though youᶜ fine people hold it in disrepute.'

In this manner, Miss Mac Allain's mornings were spent, and her evenings even more tediously; for the Doctor, alarmed at the republican principles which he observed fast spreading, was constantly employed in writing pamphlets in favour of government, which he read aloud to his family, when not at the castle, before he committed them to the Dublin press. Two weeks were thus passed, by Alice,ᵈ with resignation; a third, it seemsᵉ was beyond her endurance; for one morning Sir Everard's daughters entering in haste, informed their father and mother that she was gone. 'Gone,' cried Lady St. Clare! 'the thing is impossible.' 'Gone,' cried Sir Everard! 'and where? and how?'ᶠ The maids were called, and one Charley Wright, who served for footman, coachmanᵍ and every thing else upon occasion, was dispatched to seek her, while the doctorʰ without waiting to hear his wife's surmises,ⁱ or his daughter's lamentations, seized his hat and stick and walked in haste to the castle.

His body erect, his cane still under his arm, the brogue stronger than everʲ from inward agitation, he immediately addressed himself to the Duke and Lady Margaret and soon converted their smiles into fear and anger, by informing them that Alice Mac Allain had eloped.

Orders were given, that every enquiry should be made for the fugitive; and the company at the castle being informed one by one of the event, lost themselves in conjectures upon it. Lady Margaret had no doubt herself, that her son was deeply implicated in the affair, and in consequenceᵏ every search was set on foot, but, as it proved in the event, without the least success. Mr. Buchanan had left Castle Delaval the week before, which confirmed the suspicions already entertained on his account.

Lady Avondale was in London when she was informed of this event. Her grief for Alice's fate was very sincere, and her anxiety for her even greater; but Lord Avondale participated in her sorrow – he endeavoured to sooth her agitation; and how could he fail in his attempt: even misery is lightened, if it is shared; and one look, one word, from a heart which seems to comprehend our suffering, alleviates the bitterness.

Though Lady Avondale had not seen Buchanan since her marriage, and had heard that he was offended with her, she wrote to him immediately upon hearing of Alice's fate, and urged him by every tie,ˡ she thought most sacred and dear – by every impression most likely to awaken his compassion, to restore the unfortunate girl to her suffering father, or at least to confide her,ᵐ to her care, that she might if possible protect and save her from further misfortune. –ⁿ To her extreme astonishment, she received an answer to this letterᵒ with a positive assurance from him^a that he had no concern,^b whatever in Miss Mac Allain's departure; that he was as ignorant as herself,^c whither she could be gone; and that it might be recollected he had left Castle Delaval some days previous to that event.

Lady Dartford who had returned to London^d and sometimes corresponded with Sophia, now corroborated Buchanan's statement, and assured her that she had no reason to believe Buchanan concerned in this dark affair, as she had seen him several times and he utterly denied it. Lady Dartford was however too innocent,^e and inexperienced to know how men of the world can deceive; she was even ignorant of her husband's conduct; and though she liked not Lady Margaret, she doubted not that she was her friend: – who indeed doubts till they learn by bitter experience the weakness of confiding! /

CHAPTER XXI.

THE whole party, at Castle Delaval,ª now proceeded to London for the winter, where Lord and Lady Avondale were already established in the Duke's mansion in ...... Square.

A slight cold and fever, added to the anxiety and grief Lady Avondale had felt for her unhappy friend, had confined her entirely to her own apartment; and since her arrival in town, Count Gondimar was almost the only person who had been hitherto admitted to her presence.

He and Viviani now lodged in the same house; but the latter still concealed himself and never was admitted to Lady Margaret's presence except secretlyᵇ and with caution. He often enquired after Calantha; and one evening the following conversation took place respecting her between himself and the Count:

'You remember her,' said Gondimar, 'a wild and wayward girl. Is she less, do you suppose, an object of attraction now in the more endearing character of mother and of wife – so gentle,ᶜ so young she seems, so pure, and yet so passionately attached to her husband and infant boy, that I think even you Vivianiᵈ would feel convinced of her integrity. She seems indeedᵉ one born alone to love, and to be loved, if love itself might exist in a creature whom purity,ᶠ and every modest feeling seem continually to surround.'

Viviani smiled in scorn. 'Gondimar, this Calantha, this fair and spotless flower is a woman, and, as such, she must be frail. Besides, I know that she is so in a thousand instances, though as yet too innocent to see her danger,ᵍ or to mistrust our sex. You have often described to me her excessive fondness for music. What think you of it? She does not hear it as the Miss Seymours hear it, you tell me. She does not admire it, as one of the lovers of harmony might. Oh no; she feels it in her very soul – it awakens every sensibility – it plays upon the chords of her overheated imagination – it fills her eyes with tears, and strengthens and excites the passions,ʰ which it appears to soothe and to compose. There is nothing which the power of music cannot effect, when it is thus heard. Your Calantha feels it to a dangerous excess. Let me see her, and I will sing to her till the chaste veil of every modest feeling is thrown aside, and thoughts of fire dart into her bosom, and loosen every principle therein. Oh Iⁱ would trust every thing to the power of melody.ᵃ Calantha is fond of dancing too,ᵇ I hear; and dancing is the order of the night. This is well; and once, though she saw me not amidstᶜ the crowd, I marked her, as she lightly bounded the gayest in the circle, from the mere excess of the animal spirits of youth. Now Miss Seymour dances; but it is with modest dignity: her sister Frances dances also, and it is with much skill and grace, her sidelong glance searching for admiration as she passes by; but Calantha sees not, thinks not, when she dances: –ᵈ her heart beats with joyous pleasure – her countenance irradiates – and almost wild with delight, she forgets every thing but the moment she enjoys.⁴⁷ Let Viviani but for one night be her partner, and you shall see how pure is this Calantha. She boasts tooᵉ of the most unclouded happiness, you tell me, and of the most perfect state of security and bliss; theyᶠ who soar above others, on the wings of romance, will fall. Ohᵍ surely they will fall. Let her butʰ continue in her present illusion a fewⁱ short years – let her but take the common chances of the life she will be called upon to lead; and you, or I, or any man, may possess her affections, nor boast greatly of the conquest. In one word, she is now in London. Give but Viviani one opportunity of beholding her: it is all I ask.'

Gondimar listened to his young friend with regret. 'There are women enough, Viviani,' he said mournfully; 'spare this one. I have an interest in her safety.' –ʲ 'I shall not seek her,' replied Viviani proudly: 'please your own fancy: I care not for these triflers – not I.' /

CHAPTER XXII.

To that heartless mass of affectation, to that compound of every new and every old absurdity, to that subservient spiritless[a] world of fashion, Lady Avondale was now for the first time introduced. It burst at once upon her delighted view, like a new paradise of unenjoyed sweets – like a fairy kingdom peopled with ideal inhabitants. Whilst she resided at Monteith and Castle Delaval, she had felt an eager desire to improve her mind; study of every sort was her delight, for he who instructed her was her lover – her husband; one smile, from[b] him could awaken every energy – one frown, repress every feeling of gaiety,[c] for every word he uttered amused and pleased;[d] she learned with more aptness than a school-boy:[e] and he who wondered at the quickness of his pupil, forgot to ascribe her exertions and success to the power which alone occasioned them – a power which conquers every difficulty and endures every trial.

Arrived in that gay city, that fair mart where pleasure and amusement gather around their votaries, –[f] where incessant hurry after novelty employs every energy, and desire of gaiety fills every hour, every feeling and every thought, Calantha hailed every new acquaintance – every new amusement; and her mind[g] unpolished and ignorant, opened with admiration and wonder upon so new, so diversified a scene. To the language of praise and affection,[h] she had been used; to unlimited indulgence and liberty, she was accustomed; but the soft breathing voice of flattery,[i] sounded to her ear far sweeter,[j] than any other more familiar strain; though often, in the midst of its blandishments, she turned away to seek for Lord Avondale's approbation. /

Calantha was happy before; but now it was like a dream of enchantment; and her only regret was that her husband seemed not to partake as much,[k] as she could have wished in her delight. Yet he knew the innocence of her heart, the austerity with which she shrunk from the bare thought of evil;[l] and he had trusted her even in the lion's den, so certain was he of her virtue,[m] and attachment. Indeed, Lord Avondale, though neither puffed with vanity, nor overbearing with pride, could not but be conscious, as he looked around, that both in beauty of person, in nobility of parentage, and more than these, in the impassioned feelings of an uncorrupted heart, and the rich gifts of a mind enlightened by wisdom and study, –ᵃ none were his superiors, and very few his equals; and if his Calantha could have preferred the effeminate and frivolous beings who surrounded her, to his sincere and strong attachment, would she be worthy, in such case, of a single sigh of regretᵇ or the smallest struggle to retain her! – No: – he was convinced that she would not; and, as in word and deed,ᶜ he was faithful to her, he feared not to let her take the course which others trod, or enjoy the smiles of fortune, while youth and happiness were in her possession.

The steed that never has felt the curb, as it flies lightly and wildlyᵈ proud of its liberty among its native hills and valleys, may toss its head and plunge as it snuffs the air and rejoices in its existence, while the tame and goaded hack trots along the beaten road, starting from the lash under which it tremblesᵉ and stumbling and falling, if not constantly upheld. – Now see the goal before her. Calantha starts for the race. Nor curb, nor reinᶠ have ever fettered the pupil of nature – the proud, the daring votress of liberty and love. What though she quit the common path, if honour and praise accompany her steps, and crown her with success, shall he who owns her despise her? or must he, can he, mistrust her? He did not; and the high spirits of uncurbed youth were in future her only guide – the gayest therefore, where all were gay – the kindest, for excess of happiness renders every heart kind. In a few months after Lady Avondale's arrival in London, she was surrounded, as it appeared, by friends who would have sacrificed their lives and fortunes to give her pleasure. Friends! – it was a name she was in the habit of giving to the first who happened to please her fancy. This even was not required: the frowns of the world were sufficient to endear the objects it censuresᵍ to her affection; and they who had not a friend, and deserved not to have one, were sure, without other recommendationʰ to find one in Calantha. All looked fresh, beautiful and new to her eyes; every person she met appeared kind, honourableⁱ and sincere; and every party brilliant; for her heart, blest in itselfʲ reflected its own sunshine around. /

Mrs. Seymour, after her arrival in townᵏ was pleased to see Calantha so happy. No gloomy fear obtruded itself; she saw all things with the unclouded eye of virtue; yet when she considered how many faults, how many imprudences, her thoughtless spirits might lead her to commit, she trembled for her; and onceˡ when Calantha boasted of the extacy she enjoyed – 'long may that innocent heart feel thus,' she said, 'my only, my beloved niece; but whilst the little bark is decked with flowers, and sails gaily in a tranquil sea, steer it steadily, remembering that rough gales may comeᵐ and we should ever be prepared.' She spoke with an air of melancholy: she had perhaps,ⁿ herself, suffered from the goodness and openness of her heart; but whatever the faults and sorrows into which she had fallen, no purer mind ever existed than hersº – no heart ever felt more strongly.

The affectation of generosity is common; the reality is so rare, that its constant and silent course passes along unperceived, whilst prodigality and ostentation bear away the praise of mankind. –[a] Calantha was esteemed generous; yet indifference for what others valued, and thoughtless profusion were the only qualities she possessed. It is true that the sufferings of others melted a young and ardent heart into the performance of many actions which would never have occurred to those of a colder and more prudent nature. But was there any self-denial practised; and was not she, who bestowed,[b] possessed of every luxury and comfort,[c] her varying and fanciful caprices could desire! Never did she resist the smallest impulse or temptation. If to give had been a crime, she had committed it; for it gave her pain to refuse, and she knew not how to deprive herself of any gratification. She lavished, therefore, all she had, regardless of every consequence; but happily[d] for her, she was placed in a situation which prevented her from suffering as severely for her faults,[e] as probably she deserved.

Two friends now appeared to bless her further, as she thought, by their affection and confidence – Lady Mandeville,[f] and Lady Augusta Selwyn.[48] The former she loved; the latter she admired. Lord Avondale observed her intimacy with Lady Mandeville with regret; and once, though with much gentleness, reproved her for it. 'Henry,' she replied, 'say not one word against my beautiful, though perhaps unfortunate friend: spare Lady Mandeville; and I will give you up Lady Augusta Selwyn; but remember the former is unprotected and unhappy.'

Mrs. Seymour was present when Lord Avondale had thus ventured to hint his disapprobation of Calantha's new acquaintance. – 'Say at once, that Calantha shall not see any more of one whom you disapprove: – her own character is not established. Grace and manner are prepossessing qualities; but it is decorum and a rational adherence to propriety which alone can secure esteem. Tell me not of misfortunes,' continued Mrs. Seymour, with increasing zeal in the good cause, and turning from Lord Avondale to Calantha. 'A woman[g] who breaks through the lesser rules which custom and public opinion have established, deserves to lose all claim to respect; and they who shrink not at your age,[h] from even the appearance of guilt, because they dread being called severe and prudish, too generally follow the steps of the victims their[i] false sentiments of pity have induced them to support. Lord Avondale'[j] continued she, with more of warmth than it was her custom to shew – 'you will lament, when it is too late, the ruin of this child. Those who now smile at Calantha's follies will soon be the first to frown upon her faults. She is on the road to perdition; and now is the moment, the only moment perhaps, in which to check her course. You advise: – I command. My girls at least,[k] shall not associate with Lady Mandeville, whom no one visits. Lady Avondale of course is her own mistress.'

Piqued at Mrs. Seymour's manner, Calantha appealed to her husband: 'and shall I give up my friend, because she has none but me to defend her? Shall my friendship –' 'Alas[l] Calantha,' said Lord Avondale, 'you treat the noblest sentiment of the heart as a toy[a] which is to be purchased to-day, and thrown aside to-morrow.

Believe me, friendship is not to be acquired by a few morning visits:[b] nor is it to be found, though I fear it is too often lost, in the crowd of fashion.' He spoke this mournfully. The ready tears trembled in Lady Avondale's eyes. – 'I will see no more of her, if it gives you pain. I will never visit her again.' – Lord Avondale could not bear to grieve her.

A servant entered with a note, whilst they were yet together: – a crimson blush suffused Calantha's cheeks. 'I see[c] said Lord Avondale smiling, as if fearful of losing her confidence, –[d] 'it is from your new friend.' It was so: – she had sent her carriage[e] with a request that Lady Avondale would immediately call upon her. – She hesitated; looked eagerly for a permission, which was too soon granted; and, without[f] making any excuse, for she had not yet[g] learned the art, she hastened from the lowering eyes of the deeply offended Mrs. Seymour. /

CHAPTER XXIII.

LONG as she had now been known to Lady Mandeville, she had only once before seen her at her own house. She now found her reclining upon a sofa in an apartment more prettily than magnificently ornamented: – a shawl was thrown gracefully over her; and her hair, in dark auburn ringlets, half concealed her languishing blue eyes. Lady Mandeville was at this time no longer in the very prime of youth. Her air and manner had not that high polish, which at first sight seduces and wins. On the contrary, it rather was the reverse, and a certain pedantry took off much from the charm of her conversation. Yet something there was about her, which attracted.[49] She seemed sincere too, and had less of that studied self-satisfied air, than most women, who affect to be well informed.

'I am glad you are come, my loved[a] friend,' she said, extending her hand to Calantha when she entered. 'I have just been translating an Ode of Pindar: –[b] his poetry is sublime: it nerves the soul and raises it above vulgar cares; – but you do not understand Greek, do you?[50] Indeed to you it would be a superfluous acquisition, married as you are, and to such a man.' – Lady Avondale, rather puzzled as to the connection between domestic happiness, and the Greek language, listened for further explanation; – but with a deep sigh, her lovely acquaintance talked of her fate, and referred to scenes and times long passed, and utterly unknown to her. She talked much too of injured innocence, of the malignity of the world, of her contempt[c] for her own sex, and of the superiority of men.

Children as fair, and more innocent than their mother, entered whilst she was yet venting her complaints. A husband she had not; – but lovers. What man was there who could see her, and not, at all events wish himself of the number! Yet she assured Lady Avondale, who believed her, that she despised them all; that moreover she was miserable, but[d] vicious;[51] that her very openness and frankness ought to prove that there was nothing to conceal. The thought of guilt entered not at that time into Calantha's heart; and when a woman affirmed[e] that she was innocent, it excited in her no other surprise, than that she should, for one moment, suppose her so barbarous, and so malevolent,[f] as to think otherwise.[g] Indeed there seemed to her as great a gulph between those she loved, and vice, as that which separates the two extremes of wickedness and virtue; nor had she yet learned to comprehend the language of hypocrisy and deceit.

Though the presence of the children had not made any difference, the entrance of three gentlemen, whom Lady Mandeville introduced to Lady Avondale, as her lovers, gave a new turn to the conversation; and here it should be explained, that the term lover, when Lady Mandeville used it, was intended to convey no other idea than that of an humble attendant,[a] – a bearer of shawls, a writer of sonnets, and a caller of carriages. 'With Lord Dallas you are already acquainted,' she said, sighing gently. 'I wish now to introduce to you Mr. Clarendon,[b] a poet: and Mr. Tremore,[c] what are you? speak for yourself; for I hardly know in what manner to describe you.' 'I am anything, and everything that Lady Mandeville pleases,' said Mr. Tremore,[d] bowing to the ground, and smiling languidly upon her. Mr. Tremore[e] was one of the most unsightly lovers that ever aspired to bear the name.[52] He was of a huge circumference, and what is unusual in persons of that make, he was a mass of rancour and malevolence – gifted however with a wit so keen and deadly, that with its razor edge, he cut to the heart most of his enemies, and all his friends. Lord Dallas, diminutive and conceited, had a brilliant wit, spoke seldom, and studied deeply every sentence which he uttered. He affected to be absent; but in fact no one ever forgot himself so seldom. His voice, untuned and harsh, repeated with a forced emphasis certain jests and bon mots which had been previously made, and adapted for certain conversations.[53] Mr. Clarendon alone seemed gifted with every kind of merit: – he[f] had an open ingenuous countenance, expressive eyes, and a strong and powerful mind.

The conversation alternately touched upon the nature of love, the use and beauty of the greek[g] language, the pleasures of maternal affection, and the insipidity of all English society. It was rather metaphorical at times: – there was generally in it a want of nature – an attempt at display: but to Calantha it appeared too singular, and too attractive to wish it otherwise. She had been used, however, to a manner rather more refined – more highly polished than any she found out of her own circle and family. A thousand things shocked her at first, which afterwards she not only tolerated,[h] but adopted. There was a want of ease, too, in many societies, to which she could not yet accustom herself; and she knew not exactly what it was which chilled and depressed her when in the presence of many who were, upon a nearer acquaintance, amiable and agreeable. Perhaps too anxious a desire to please, too great a regard for trifles, a sort of selfishness, which never loses sight of its own identity, occasions this coldness among these votaries of fashion. The dread of not having that air, that dress, that refinement which they value so much, prevents their obtaining it; and a degree of vulgarity steals unperceived amidst the higher classes in England, from the very apprehension they feel of falling into it. Even those, who are natural, do not entirely appear so.

Calantha's life was like a feverish dream: – so crowded, so varied, so swift in its transitions, that she had little time to reflect; and when she did, the memory of the past was so agreeable and so brillant, that it gave her pleasure to think of it again and again. If Lord Avondale was with her, every place appeared even more than usually delightful; but, when absent, her letters, no longer filled with lamentations on her lonely situation, breathed from a vain heart[a] the lightness, and satisfaction it enjoyed.

It may be supposed that one so frivolous and so thoughtless, committed every possible fault and folly which opportunity and time allowed. It may also be supposed, that such imprudence met with its just reward; and that every tongue was busy in its censure, and every gossip in exaggerating the extraordinary feats of such a trifler. Yet Calantha, upon the whole, was treated with only too much kindness; and the world, though sometimes called severe, seemed willing to pause ere it would condemn, and was intent alone to spare – to reclaim[b] a young offender.[c] /

CHAPTER XXIV.

How different from the animated discussion at Lady Mandeville's, was the loud laugh and boisterous tone of Lady Augusta Selwyn, whom Calantha found, on her return, at that very moment stepping from her carriage, and enquiring for her. 'Ah, my dear sweet friend,' she cried, flying towards Calantha, and shaking her painfully by the hand, 'this fortuitous concurrence of atoms, fills my soul with rapture. But I was resolved to see you. I have promised and vowed three things in your name; therefore, consider me as your sponsor, and indeed I am old enough to be such. In the first place, you must come to me to-night, for I have a little supper, and all my guests attend only in the hope of meeting you. You are the bribe I have held out – you are to stand me in lieu of a good house, good cook, agreeable husband, and pretty face,[a] – in all of which I am most unfortunately deficient. Having confessed thus much, it would be barbarous, it would be inhuman you know to refuse me. Now for the second favour,' continued this energetic lady: – 'come alone; for though I have a great respect for Mrs. and Miss Seymour, yet I never know what I am about when their very sensible eyes are fixed upon me.' – 'Oh you need not fear, Sophia would not come if I wished it; and Mrs. Seymour' – 'I have something else to suggest,' interrupted Lady Augusta: –[b] 'introduce me immediately to your husband: he is divine, I hear – perfectly divine!' 'I cannot at this moment; but' – 'By the bye, why were you not at the ball last night. I can tell you there were some who expected you there. Yes, I assure you, a pair of languid blue eyes watching for you – a fascinating new friend waiting to take you home to a *petit souper très-bien assorti*.'[c54] I went myself. It was monstrously dull at the ball: – insupportable, I assure you; perfectly so. Mrs. Turner and her nine daughters! It is quite a public calamity, Mrs. Turner being so very prolific – the produce so frightful. Amongst other animals,[d] when they commit such blunders, the brood is drowned; but we christians are suffered to grow up till the land is overrun.' 'Heigho.' 'What is the matter? You look so *triste* to-day, not even my wit can enliven you. – Is'nt it well, love? or has its husband been plaguing it? Now I have it: –[e] you have, perchance, been translating an Ode of Pindar. I was there myself this morning; and it gave me the vapours for ten minutes; but I am used to these things you know child, and you are a novice. By the bye, where is your cousin, *le beau capitaine, le chef des brigands*?[55] I was quite *frappé*[56] with his appearance.' 'You may think it strange,' said Calantha, 'but I have not seen him these eight years

– not since he was quite a child.' 'Oh, what an interview there will be then,' said Lady Augusta: 'he is a perfect ruffian.'

'Are youᵃ aware that we have three sets of men now muchᵇ in request? – There are these ruffians, who affect to be desperate, who game, who drink, who fight, who will captivate you, I am sure of it. Theyᶜ are always just going to be destroyed, or rather talk as if they were; and every thing they do, they must do it to desperation. Then come the exquisites. Lord Dallas is one, a sort of refined *petit maître*,[57] quite thorough bred, though fullᵈ of conceit. As to the third set, your useful men, who know how to read and write, in which class critics, reviewers, politicians and poets stand, you may always know them by their slovenly appearance. But you are freezing, *mon enfant*.[58] What can be the matter? I will release you in a moment from my visitation. Iᵉ have ten thousand things to say. – Will you come to my opera box Tuesday? Are you going to the masked ball Thursday? Has Mrs. Churchill sent to you for her *déjeûné paré*.[59] I know she wishes, more than I can express, to have you. Perhaps you will let me drive you there. My ponies are beautiful arabians: have you seen them? Oh, by the bye, why were you not at your aunt Lady Margaret's concert? I believe it was a concert: – thereᶠ was a melancholy noise in one of the rooms; but I did not attend to it.' – 'Do you not like music?' – 'I do;ᵍ but I must own I am not one who profess to be all enchantment at the scraping of a fiddle, because some old philharmonic plays on it; nor can I admire the gurgling and groaning of a number of foreigners, because it is called singing.

'They tell meʰ you think of nothing but love and poetry. I dare say you write sonnets to the moon – the chaste moon, and your husband. How sentimental!' 'And you,' – 'No, my dear, I thank heavenⁱ I never could make a rhyme in my life. – Farewell – adieu – remember to-night,ʲ – bring Lord Avondale – that divine Henry: though beware too; for many a lady has to mourn the loss of her husband, as soon as she has introduced him into the society of *fascinating* friends.' 'He is out of town.' 'Then so much the better. After all, a wife is only pleasant when her husband is out of the way. She must either be in love, or out of love with him. If the latter, they wrangle; and if the former, it is ten times worse. Lovers are at all times insufferable; but when the holy laws of matrimony give them a lawful right to be so amazingly fond and affectionate, it makes one sick.' 'Which are you, in love or out of love with Mr. Selwyn?' – 'Neither,ᵏ my child, neither. He never molests me, never intrudes his dear dull personage on my society. He is the bestˡ of his race, and only married me out of pure benevolence. We were fourteen raw Scotch girls – all hideous, and no chance of being got rid of, either by marriage,ᵐ or death – so healthy and ugly. I believe we are all alive and flourishing somewhereⁿ or other now. Think then of dear good Mr. Selwyn, who took me for his mate, because I let him play at cards whenever he pleased. Heᵒ is so fond of cheating, he never can get any one but me to play with him. Farewell. – *A revoir*. – I shall expect you at ten. – *Adieu, chère petite*.' Saying which Lady Augusta left Calantha.ᵖ /

CHAPTER XXV.

CALANTHA imagined,ª and was repeatedly assured, that her husband neglected her:⁶⁰ the thought gave her pain: she contrasted his apparent coldness and gravity with the kindness and flattery of others. Even Count Gondimar was more anxious for her safety,ᵇ and latterly she observed that he watched her with increasing solicitude. At a masked ball, in particular, the Italian Count followed her till she was half offended. 'Why do you thus persecute me as to the frivolity and vanity of my manner? Why do you seem so infinitely more solicitous concerning me than my husband and my relations?' she said, suddenly turningᶜ and looking earnestly at him. 'What is it to you with whom I may chance to converse? How is it possible that you can see imperfections in me, when others tell me I am faultless and delightful?' 'And do you believe that the gay troop of flatterers who now follow you,' said a mask,ᵈ who was standing near the Count, 'do you believe that they feel any other sentiment for you than indifference?' 'Indifference!' repeated Calantha, 'what can you mean? I am secure of their affection; and I have found more friends in London since I first arrived there, than I have made in the whole previous course of my life.' 'You are their jest and their derision,' said the same mask. –ᵉ 'Am I,' she said, turning eagerly round to her partner, Lord Trelawny,⁶¹ 'am I your jest,ᶠ and your derision?' 'You are all that is amiable and adorable,' he whispered. 'Speak louder,' said Lady Avondale, 'tell this Italian Count, and his discourteous friend, what you think of me; or will they wait to hear,ᵍ what we all think of them.'ʰ Gondimar, offended, left her; and she passed the night at the ball;ⁱ but felt uneasy at what she had said.

Monteagle house,ʲ at which the masquerade was given, was large and magnificent. The folding doors opened into fine apartments, each decorated with flowers, and filled with masks. Her young friends, Sophia and Lady Dartford, in the first bloom and freshness of youth, attracted much admiration. Their dress was alike, and while seeming simplicity was its greatest charm, every fold, every turnᵏ was adapted to exhibit their figure, and add to their natural grace. If vanity can give happiness to the heart, how must theirs have exulted; for encomium and flattery was the only language they heard.

Lady Avondale, in the mean time, fatigued with the ceremonious insipidity of their conversation, and delighted at having for once escaped from Count Gondimar, sought in vain to draw her companions into the illuminated gardens, and not succeeding, wandered into them alone, followed by some masks in the disguise of gipsies, by whom she was soon surrounded; and one of them whom she now recognised[a] to be the same who had spoken to her with Gondimar, now under[b] the pretence of telling her fortune, said to her every thing that was most severe. 'What,' said he, turning to one of his companions, 'do you think of the line in this lady's hand? It is a very strange one: I augur no good from it.' The dress of the mask who spoke was that of a friar, his voice was soft and mournful. 'Caprice'[c] said the young man, whom he addressed: 'I read no worse fault. Come, I will tell her fortune. – Lady, you were born under a favoured planet,' – 'Aaron,' – interrupted the first gipsey,[d 62] 'you are a flatterer, and it is my privilege to speak without disguise. Give me the hand, and I will shew her destiny.' After pausing a moment, he fixed his dark eyes upon Calantha, the rest of his face being covered by a cowl, and in a voice like music, so soft and plaintive begun. –

> The task to tell thy fate,[e] be mine,
> To guard against its ills,[f] be thine;
> For heavy treads the foot of care[g]
> On those who are so young and fair.
>
> The star, that on thy birth shone bright,
> Now casts a dim uncertain light:
> A threatening sky obscures its rays,[h]
> And shadows o'er thy future days.
>
> In fashion's magic circle bound,
> Thy steps shall tread her mazy round,
> While pleasure, flattery[i] and art,
> Shall captivate thy fickle heart.
>
> The transient favorite of a day,
> Of folly and of fools the prey;
> Insatiate vanity shall pine
> As honour, and as health decline,[j]
> Till reft of fame, without a friend,
> Thou'lt meet, unwept, an early end.

Lady Avondale coloured; and the young man who had accused her of caprice, watching her countenance, and seeing the pain these acrimonious lines had given her, reproved the friar. 'No, no' he cried[k] 'if she must hear her destiny, let me reveal it.'

> The task to tell thy fate,[a] be mine,
> And every bliss I wish thee, thine.

> So heavenly fair, so pure, so blest,
>   Admired by all, by all carest,
> The ills of life thou ne'er shalt know,
> Or weep alone for others woe.[b]

'For the honour of our tribe, cease Aaron' said a female gipsey advancing:[c] 'positively I will not hear any more of this flat parody. The friar's malice I could endure; but this will mar all.' – Whatever[d] the female gipsey might say, Aaron had a certain figure, and countenance[e] which were sufficiently commanding and attractive. He had disengaged himself from his companions; and now approached Calantha, and asked her to allow him to take care of her through the crowd. 'This is abominable treachery,' said the female gipsey: – 'this conduct is unpardonable: good faith and good fellowship were ever our characteristics.' 'You should not exert your power'[f] answered the young man, 'against those who seem so little willing to use the same weapons in return. I will answer for it[g] that, though under a thousand masks, the lady you have attacked,[h] would never say an ill natured thing.'[i] 'Take care of her goodnature[j] then,' said the gipsey archly: [k] – 'it may be more fatal.'

The gipsey[l] then went off, with the rest of her party;[m] but Aaron remained, and, as if much pleased with the gentleness of Lady Avondale's behaviour, followed her. 'Who are you?' said she.[n] 'I will not take the arm of one who is ashamed of his name'[o] – 'And yet it is only thus unknown, I can hope to find favour.'[p] 'Did I ever see you before?' 'I[q] have often had the happiness of seeing you: – but[r] am I then really so altered?' said he turning to her, and looking full in her face, 'that you cannot even guess my name?' 'Had[s] I ever beheld you before,' answered Lady Avondale, 'I could not have forgotten it.' He bowed with a look of conceit, and Lady Avondale coloured at his comprehending the compliment, she had sufficiently intended to make. Smiling at her confusion, he assured her he had a right to her attention – '*Stesso sangue, Stessa sorte*' – said he[t] in a low voice.

Calantha could hardly believe it possible: – the words he pronounced were those inscribed on her bracelet. 'And are you my cousin?' said she:[u] 'is it indeed so? no: I cannot believe it.' Buchanan bowed again. 'Yes,' said he;[v] 'and a pretty cousin you have proved yourself to me. I had vowed never to forgive you; but you are much too lovely and too dear for me to wish to keep my oath.' A thousand remembrances now crowded on her mind – the days of her infancy – the amusements and occupations of her childhood;[w] and she looked vainly in Buchanan's face,[x] for the smallest traces of the boy she had known so well. Delighted with her evening's adventure, and solely occupied with her companion, the masquerade, the heat and all other annoyances were forgotten, till Lady Dartford being fatigued, entreated her to retire.

She had conversed during the greater part of the evening[a] with Lord Dartford. The female gipsey to whose party he belonged, and who had attacked Lady

Avondale, was Lady Margaret Buchanan. He had asked Lady Dartford many questions about himself, to all of which she had answered with a reserve that had pleased him, and with a praise so unaffected, so heartfelt, and so little deserved, that he could not but deeply feel his own demerit. He did not make himself known, but suffered Lady Margaret to rally and torment his unoffending wife; asking her repeatedly, why so pretty, and so young, Lord Dartford permitted her to go to a masquerade without a protector. 'It is,' replied Lady Dartford innocently, 'that he dislikes this sort of amusement, and knows well, that those who appear unprotected, are sure of finding friends.' At this speech Lady Margaret laughed prodigiously; and turning to the Friar,[b] who, much disguised, still followed her, asked him,[c] if he had never seen Lord Dartford at a masquerade, giving it as her opinion, that he was very fond of this sort of amusement, and was probably there at that very moment.

In the mean time, Calantha continued to talk with Buchanan, and eagerly enquired of him who it was who, thus disguised,[d63] had with so much acrimony attacked her. 'I do not know the young man,' he answered: –[e] 'my mother calls him Viviani: – he is much with her; but he ever wears a disguise, I think; for no one sees him;[f] and, except Gondimar, he seems not to have another acquaintance in England.' /

It has been said that the weak-minded are alone attracted by the eye; and they who say this,[g] best know what they mean. To Calantha it appeared that the eye was given her[h] for no other purpose than to admire all that was fair and beautiful. Certain it is, she made that use of her's;[i] and whether the object of such admiration was man, woman, or child, horse or flower, if excellent in its kind, she ever gave them the trifling homage of her approbation. Her new-found cousin was therefore[j] hailed by her with the most encouraging smile; and how long she might have listened to the account he was giving her of his exploits, is unknown, had not Frances approached her in a hasty manner, and said, 'Do come away: – the strangest thing possible has happened to me: – Lord[k] Trelawney has proposed to me, and I – I have accepted his offer.' 'Accepted[l] his offer!' Calantha exclaimed, with a look of horror. 'Oh, pray,[m] keep my secret till we get home,' said Frances. 'I dare not tell Sophia; but you must break it to my mother.'

Lord Trelawney was a silly florid young man, who laughed very heartily and good humouredly, without the least reason. He wore the dress, and had been received in that class of men, whom Lady Augusta called the exquisites. He had professed the most extravagant adoration for Lady Avondale, so that she was quite astonished at his having attached himself so suddenly to Frances; but not being of a jealous turn, she wished her joy most cordially, and when she did the same by him, –[n] 'Could not help what I've done,' he said, looking tenderly at her through a spying-glass: –[a] 'total dearth of something else to say: – can never affection her much: – but she's your cousin, you know:' – and then he laughed.

Lady Avondale prevailed on Frances to keep this important secret from her mother till morning,[b] as that good lady had not long been in bed,[c] and to arouse her with such unexpected news at five o'clock[d] had been cruel and useless. The next morning, long before Lady Avondale had arisen, every one knew the secret; and very soon after, preparations for the marriage were made. The young bride received presents and congratulations: her spirits were exuberant; and her lover, perfect and delightful. Even Lady Avondale beheld him with new eyes, and the whole family, whenever he was mentioned, spoke of him as a remarkably sensible young man, extremely well informed, and possessed of every quality best adapted to ensure the happiness of domestic life. /

CHAPTER XXVI.

From the night of the masquerade, Lady Avondale dared hardly confess to herself, how entirely she found her thoughts engrossed by Buchanan. She met him again at a ball. He entreated her to let him call on her the ensuing day: – he said he had much to tell her: – his manner was peculiar; and his eyes, though not full of meaning in general, had a certain look of interest that gratified the vainest of human hearts. 'I shall be at home till two,' said Calantha.ᵃ 'I shall be with you at twelve,' he answered. – Late as the hour of rest might appear to some, Calantha was up, and attired with no ordinary care to receive him, at the time he had appointed. Yet no Buchanan came. –ᵇ Oh! could the petty triflers in vanity and vice, know the power they gain, and the effect they produce by these arts, they would contemn the facility of their own triumph. It is ridiculous to acknowledge it, but this disappointment encreasedᶜ Calantha's anxiety to see him to the greatest possible degree: she scarce could disguise the interest it created.

Gondimar unfortunately called at the moment when Calantha was most impatient and irritable. 'You expected another,' he said sarcastically; 'but I care not. I came not here in the hope of pleasing Lady Avondale. I came to inform her.' –ᵈ 'I cannot attend now.'ᵉ 'Read this letter,' said Gondimar. Calantha looked carelessly upon it – it was from himself: – it contained an avowal of attachment and of interest for her; in proof of which he asked permission to offer her a gift, which he said he was commissioned to bring her from Italy. Lady Avondale returned the the letter coldly, and with littleᶠ affectation of dignity, declined the intended present. It is so easy to behave well, when it is our pleasure to do so,ᵍ as well as our duty. Gondimar, however, gave her but little credit for her conduct. 'You like me not?' he said. 'Do you doubt my virtue?' she replied eagerly. 'Aye, Lady –ʰ or, at all events, your power of preserving it.'

Whilst Gondimar yet spoke, Buchanan gallopped by the window, and stopped at the door of the house. His hands were decorated with rings, and a gold chain and half-concealed picture hung around his neck: –ⁱ his height, his mustachios, the hussar trappings of his horse, the high colour in his cheek, and his dark flowing locks, gave an air of savage wildness to his countenance and figure, which much delighted Calantha.⁶⁴ He entered with familiar ease; talked much of himself, and more of some of his military friends; stared at Gondimar, and then shook hands with him. After which, he began a vehement explanation of his conduct respecting Alice; assuring Calantha upon his honour – upon his soul, that he had no hand in her elopement. He then talked of Ireland; described the dreadful, the exaggerated accounts of what had occurred there; and ended by assuring Gondimar[a] that the young Glenarvon was not dead, but was at this time at Belfont, concealed there with no other view than that of heading the rebels. The accounts which the Duke of Altamonte had received in part corroborated Buchanan's statement.

Calantha listened, however, with more interest to the accounts Buchanan now gave; and[b] as he said he was but just returned from Dublin, even Gondimar thought the news which he brought worthy of some attention. 'Send that damned Italian away,' said Buchanan in a loud whisper –[c] 'I have a million of things to tell you. If you keep him here, I shall go: – my remaining will be of no use.' Unaccustomed to curb herself in the least wish, Calantha now whispered to Gondimar, that she wished him to leave her, as she had something very particular to say to her cousin; but he only smiled contemptuously upon him, and sternly asking her, since when this amazing intimacy had arisen[d] – placed himself near the piano-forte, striking[e] its chords with accompaniments till the annoyance was past bearing.

Buchanan consoled himself by talking of his dogs and horses; and having given Calantha a list of the names of each, began enumerating to her the invitations he had received for the ensuing week. Fortunately, at this moment, a servant entered with a note for Gondimar. 'Does the bearer wait?' he exclaimed with much agitation upon reading it; and immediately left the room.

Upon returning home, Count Gondimar perceived with surprise, in the place of the person he had expected, one of the attendants of the late Countess of Glenarvon,[f] – a man whose countenance and person he well remembered from its peculiarly harsh and unpleasant expression. – 'Is my young Lord alive?' said the man in a stern manner. Count Gondimar replied in the negative. 'Then, Sir, I must trouble you with those affairs which most nearly concern him.' 'Your name, I think is Macpherson?' said Count Gondimar. 'You lived with the Countess of Glenarvon.' The man bowed, and giving a letter into the hands of the Count, 'I am come from Italy at this time,' he replied, 'in search of my late master – La Crusca and myself.' 'Is La Crusca with you?' said Gondimar[g] starting. 'The letter will inform you of every particular,' replied the man with some gravity. 'I shall wait for the child, or[h] your farther orders.' Saying this, he left the Count's apartment; and returned into the anti-chamber, where a beautiful little boy was waiting for him. /

On that very evening, after a long conversation with Macpherson, Count Gondimar again sought Calantha at her father's house, where, upon enquiring for her, he was immediately admitted. After some little hesitation, he told her that he had brought her the present of which he had made mention in his letter; that if she had the unkindness to refuse it, some other perhaps would take charge of it: – it^a was a gift which, however unworthy he was to offer it, he thought would be dearer in her estimation than the finest jewels, and the most costly apparel: – it was a fair young boy, he said, fitted to be a Lady's page, and trained in every cunning art his tender years could learn. 'He will be a play mate;'^b he said^c smiling, 'for your son, and when,' added he in a lower voice, 'the little Mowbrey[65] can speak, he will learn to lisp in that language which alone expresses all that the heart would utter – all that in a barbarous dialect it dares not – must not say.' /

As he yet spoke, he took the hat from off Zerbellini's head, and gently pushing him towards Calantha, asked him to sue for her protection. The child immediately approached, hiding himself with singular fear from the caresses of the Count. 'Zerbellini,' said Gondimar in Italian, 'will you love that lady?' 'In my heart;'^d replied the boy, shrinking back to Calantha, as if to a late found^e but only friend. Sophia was called, and joined in the general interest and admiration the child excited. Frances shewed him to Lord Trelawney, who laughed excessively at beholding him. Lady Margaret, who was present, looking upon him stedfastly, shrunk as if she had seen a serpent in her way, and then recovering herself, held her hand out towards him. Zerbellini fixed his eyes on Calantha, as if watching in her countenance for the only commands which he was to obey; and when she drew him towards her aunt, he knelt to her, and kissed her hand with the customary grace and courtesy of an Italian.

From that day^f Calantha thought of nothing but Zerbellini.[66] He was a new object of interest: – to dress him, to amuse him, to shew him about, was her great delight. Wherever she went he must accompany her: in whatever she did or said, Zerbellini must bear a part. The Duke of Myrtlegrove[67] advised her to make him her page; and for this purpose he ordered him the dress of an Eastern slave. Buchanan gave him a chain with a large turquoise heart; and as he placed it around the boy, he glanced his eye on Calantha. Presents, however, even more magnificent were in return immediately dispatched by her to the Duke,^g and to Buchanan:

Count Gondimar read the letters Calantha had written with the gifts; for she had left them, as was her custom, open upon the table. All she wrote, or received, were thus left; not from ostentation, but indifference and carelessness. 'Are you mad,' said the Italian^h 'or worse than mad?' 'I affect it not,' replied Lady Avondale. 'I conclude, thereforeⁱ that it is real.' Indeed^j there was a strange compound in Calantha's mind. She felt but little accountable for her actions,^k and she often had observed that if ever she had^l the misfortune to reflect^m and consequently to resolve against any particular mode of conduct, the result was that she ever fell into the error she had determined to avoid. She might indeed have said that the spirit was willingⁿ but the flesh was weak; for whatever she resolved, upon the slightest temptation to the contrary, she failed to execute. /

CHAPTER XXVII.

'I am astonished my dear Gondimar,' said Viviani one day, addressing him, 'at the description which you gave me of Lady Avondale. I have seen her since we conversed together^a about her, more than once; and there is not, I think, much trace left of that excessive timidity of manner – that monastic rigidity in her opinions and conduct, of which you made mention in one of your letters from Castle Delaval.' 'I was wrong, utterly wrong,' said Gondimar, 'and you may now rank this model of purity, this paragon of wives, this pupil of nature, whom I have so often praised to you, on a level with the rest of her fellow mortals.' 'Not on a level – not on a level,' replied Viviani with gravity; 'but falling as I fear, far beneath it.' /

The Count then repeated in a solemn tone the description of Rome[b] which Lucian has placed in the mouth of Nigrinus[c68] applying the enumeration of vices, temptations[d] and corruptions, attributed to the fairest capital of the world, to London; and then asked of Gondimar, if it were possible for one like Calantha[e] to sojourn long amidst such scenes, without in some measure acquiring the manners, if not falling into the errors to which the eyes and ears were every hour accustomed? He spoke of her with regret, as he thus pronounced her on the verge of ruin: – 'a prey,' he said indignantly, 'for the spoiler – the weak and willing victim of vanity.' 'The courts of her father are overrun with petitioners and mendicants,' said Gondimar: 'her apartments are filled with flatterers[f] who feed upon her credulity: she is in love with ruin: it stalks about in every possible shape, and in every shape,[g] she hails it: – woe is it;[h] victim of prosperity, luxury and self indulgence.'[i]

'And Avondale,' said Viviani. 'Lord Avondale,' replied the Count, 'knows not, thinks not, comprehends not her danger or his own. But the hour of perdition approaches; the first years of peace and love are past; folly succeeds; and vice is the after game. These are the three stages in woman's life. Calantha is swiftly passing through the second: – the third will succeed. The days and months once glided away in a dream of joy, dangerous and illusive – in a dream, I repeat; for all that depends on the excess and durability of any violent passion must be called a dream. Such passion, even though sanctioned by the most sacred ties, if it engrossess every thought, is not innocent – cannot be lawful. It plants the seeds of corruption[a] which flourish and gain strength hereafter. This is the climate in which they will soonest ripen: – this is the garden and soil,[b] where they take the most rapid, and the deepest root.' 'And think you,[c] that Calantha and Avondale,[d] are already weary of each other? that the warm and vivid imagination of youthful love is satiated with excess? or that disappointment has followed upon a nearer view?' 'All passion,' replied Gondimar – falling back[e] and impressively raising his hand – 'all passion is founded on . . . . ' 'Friend,' said Viviani, 'thy prate is unmercifully tedious,' – 'I half believe that thou art thyself in love with this Calantha; but for an explanation and detail of that master passion, I know not why I applied to you:[f] Calantha is the object of your pursuit not mine.' 'Of my pursuit! in truth I believe you feel more interest in her conduct than I do,[g] I am old and weary of these follies; life is just opening upon you; Calantha is your idol.' 'No,' replied Viviani, with a smile of scorn.[h] 'It is not that party coloured[i] butterfly, which ranges ever from flower to flower, spreading its light pinions in the summer breeze, or basking in the smiles of fortune, for which my life is consumed, my soul is scorched with living fire, and my mind is impaired and lost! Oh would to heaven that it were! No arts, no crimes were then required to win and to enjoy. The pulse of passion beats high within her, and pleads for the lover who dares to ask.[j] Wild fancy, stimulated by keen sensibility and restless activity of mind, without employment, render her easy to be approached, and easy to be influenced and worked upon. Love is the nature of these favourites of fortune: from earliest infancy –[k] they feel its power! and their souls[l] enervated, live but upon its honied vows. Chaste – pure! What are these terms? The solitary recluse is not chaste, as I have heard; and these, never – never.'[m] [69]

'Yet Lady Margaret you say[n] is unmoved.' 'What of Lady Margaret?' interrupted Viviani, while bitter smiles quivered upon his lip. 'Do you mark the pavement of stone upon which you tread? Do you see the steel of which this sabre is composed – once heated by the flames, now hard and insensible? – so cold,[o] – so petrified is the heart, when it has once given full vent to passion. Marble is that heart[p] which only beats for my destruction. The time is not yet arrived, but I will dash the cup of joy from her lips; then drink the dregs myself, and die.' 'Mere jealous threats,' said Gondimar. 'The curse of innocent blood is on her,' replied Viviani, as his livid cheeks and lips resumed a purple dye. 'Name her no more.' 'Explain yourself,' cried his astonished friend. 'You frequently allude to scenes of deeper guilt and horror, than I dare even suffer myself to imagine possible.' 'The heart of man is unfathomable,' replied Viviani; – 'that which seems, is not: – that which is, seems not: we should neither trust our eyes nor ears,[q] in a world like this. But time, which ripens all things, shall disclose the secrets even of the dead.'

A short time after this conversation with Gondimar, Viviani took leave of him. He informed him fully of his projects; and Lady Margaret was also consulted upon the occasion. 'What is become of your menaced vengeance,'ᵃ she said, smiling upon him, in their last parting interview. He laughed at the remembrance of his words. 'Am I the object now of your abhorrence,'ᵇ she said, placing her white hand carelessly upon his head. 'Not absolutely,' replied the young Count, shrinking, however, from the pressure of that hand. 'Touch me not,' he whispered more earnestly, 'it thrills through my soul. – Keep those endearments for Dartford: leave me in peace.' Immediately after this he left London; and by the first letter Lady Margaret received from him, she found that he was preparing to embark.

CHAPTER XXVIII.

Frances Seymour's marriage with Lord Trelawny[a] was now celebrated, after which the whole family left London for Ireland.

Sophia, previous to her departure, reproved Calantha for her obstinacy, as she called it, in remaining in town. 'I leave you with pain,' she said: 'forgive me if I say it, for I see you have no conception of the folly of your conduct. Ever in extremes, you have acted as I little expected from the wife of Lord Avondale; but I blame him equally for giving you such unbounded freedom: – only the very wise and the very good know how to use it.' 'Sophia,' replied Calantha, 'I wish not for reproaches: – have confidence in me: – we cannot all be exactly alike. You are a pattern of propriety and virtue, and verily you have your reward: –[b] I act otherwise, and am prepared for censures: – even yours cannot offend me. Lord Avondale talks of soon returning to Ireland: I shall then leave this dear delightful London without regret; and you shall find me when we all meet for the spring at Castle Delaval, just the same, as when I entered[c] it.' Never the same, thought Sophia, who marked, with astonishment, the change a few months had made.

They were yet speaking, and taking a cold farewell of each other, when a thundering rap at the door interrupted them, and before Sophia could retreat, Mr. Fremore,[70] Count Gondimar and Lady Mandeville were ushered in. A frozen courtesy, and an austere frown, were the only signs of animation Sophia gave, as she vanished from their view; for she seemed hardly to have energy sufficient left, to walk out of the room in an ordinary manner.[d] /

'You have been ill,' said Lady Mandeville, accosting Calantha. 'It is a week since I have seen you. Think not, however, that I am come to intrude upon your time: I only called,[e] as I passed your door, to enquire after you. Mr. Fremore tells me you are about to visit the Princess of Madagascar.[71] Is this true? for I never believe any thing I hear?' 'For once,' said Calantha, 'you may do so; and on this very evening, my introduction is to take place.' 'It is with regret I hear it,' said Lady Mandeville with a sigh: 'we shall never more see any thing of you. Besides, she is not my friend.' Calantha assured Lady Mandeville her attachment could endure all sorts of trials; and laughingly enquired of her respecting her lovers, Apollonius, and the Greek Lexicon she was employed in translating. Lady Mandeville answered her with some indifference on these subjects; and having said all that she could in order to dissuade her against visiting the Princess, took her leave.

That evening, at the hour of ten, Lord Avondale and Mr. Fremore being in readiness, Calantha drove according to appointment to visit the wife of the great Nabob,[72] the Princess of Madagascar. Now who is so ignorant as not to know that this Lady resides in an old-fashioned gothic building, called Barbary House,[73] three miles beyond the turnpike? and who is so ignorant as not to be aware that her highness would not have favoured Lady Avondale with an audience, had she been otherwise than extremely well with the world, as the phrase is – for she was no patroness of the fallen! the caresses and *petits mots obligeants*[a][74] which dropt from her during this her first interview, raised Lady Avondale in her own opinion; but that was unnecessary. What was more to the purpose, it won her entirely towards the Princess.

Calantha now, for the first time, conversed with the learned of the land: – she heard new opinions started, and old ones refuted;[b] and she gazed unhurt, but not unawed, upon reviewers, poets, critics, and politicians. At the end of a long gallery, two thick wax tapers,[c] rendering 'darkness visible,'[75] the princess was seated. A poet of an emaciated and sallow complexion stood beside her; of him it was affirmed that in apparently the kindest and most engaging manner, he, at all times, said precisely that which was most unpleasant to the person he appeared to praise. This yellow hyena[76] had, however, a heart noble, magnanimous and generous; and even his friends, could they but escape from his smile and his tongue, had no reason to complain.[d] Few events, if any, were ever known to move the Princess[e] from her position. Her pages – her foreign attire, but genuine English manners, voice and complexion, attracted universal admiration. She was beautiful too, and had a smile it was difficult to learn to hate or to mistrust. She spoke of her own country with contempt; and, even in her dress, which was magnificent, attempted to prove the superiority of every other over it. Her morals were simple and uncorrupt, and in matters of religious faith she entirely surrendered herself to the guidance of Hoiaouskim.[77] She inclined her head a little upon seeing Lady Avondale; the *dead*, I mean the sick poet, did the same;[f] and Hoiaouskim, her high priest, cast his eyes, with unassuming civility, upon Calantha, thus welcoming her to Barbary House.

The princess then spoke a little sentence – just enough to shew how much she intended to protect Lady Avondale. She addressed herself, besides, in many dialects, to an outlandish set of menials; appointing every one in the room some trifling task, which was performed in a moment by young and old, with surprising alacrity. Such is the force of fashion and power, when skilfully applied. After this, she called Calantha: a slight exordium followed then a wily pointed catechism; her Highness nodding at intervals, and dropping short epigrammatic sentences, when necessary, to such as were in attendance around her. 'Is she acting?' said

Calantha, at length, in a whisper, addressing the sallow complexioned Poet,[a] who stood sneering and simpering behind her chair. 'Is she acting, or is this reality?' 'It is the only reality you will ever find in the Princess,' returned her friend. She acts the Princess of Madagascar from morning till night, and from night till morning. You may fall from favour,[b] but you are now at the height: no one ever advanced further – none ever continued there long.'

'But why,' said Lady Avondale, 'do the great Nabob, and all the other Lords in waiting, with that black hord of savages' – 'Reviewers, you mean, and men of talents.' 'Well, whatever they are, tell me quickly why they wear collars, and chains around their necks at Barbary House?' 'It is the fashion,' replied the poet.[c] 'This fashion is unbecoming your race,' said Lady Avondale: 'I would die sooner than be thus enchained.' 'The great Nabob,' quoth Mr. Fremore, joining in the discourse,[d] 'is the best, the kindest, the cleverest man I know; but,[e] like some philosophers, he would sacrifice much for a peaceable life. The Princess is fond of inflicting these lesser tyrannies:[f] she is so helplessly attached to these trifles – so overweaningly fond of exerting her powers, it were a pity to thwart her. For my own part,[g] I could willingly bend to the yoke, provided the duration were not eternal; for observe that the chains are well gilded; that the tables are well stored; and those who bend the lowest are ever the best received.' 'And if I also bow my neck,' said Calantha, 'will she be grateful? May I depend upon her seeming kindness?' The Poet's[h] naturally pale complexion turned to a bluish green at this enquiry.

Cold Princess! where are your boasted professions now? You taught Calantha to love you, by every petty art of which your sex is mistress. She heard, from your lips, the sugared poisons you were pleased to lavish upon her. You laughed at her follies, courted her confidence, and flattered her into a belief that you loved her.[i] Loved her! – it is a feeling you never felt. She fell into the mire; the arrows of your precious crew were shot at her – like hissing snakes hot and sharpened with malice and venomed fire; and you, yes – you were the first to scorn her: – you,[j] by whom she had stood faithfully and firmly amidst a host of foes – aye, amidst the fawning rabble, who still crowd your doors, and laugh at and despise you. Thanks for the helping hand of friendship in the time of need – the mud and the mire have been washed from Calantha; the arrows have been drawn from a bleeding bosom; the heart is still sound, and beats to disdain you. The sun may shine fairly again upon her; but never, whilst existence is prolonged, will she set foot in[k] the gates of the Palace of the great Nabob, or trust to the smiles and professions of the Princess of Madagascar.[78] /

CHAPTER XXIX.

'AND what detains you in town?' said Gondimar, on the eve of Mrs. Seymour and Sophia's departure. 'Will this love of gaiety never subside. Tell me, Lady Avondale, do you believe all that the Duke of Myrtlegrove, and your more warlike cousin have said to you? – What means the blush on your indignant cheek?'[a] The young duke is more enamoured of the lustre of his diamond ring and broach, than of the brightest eyes that ever gazed on him; and though the words glory and renown drop from the mouth of Buchanan, love, I think, has lost his time in aiming arrows at his heart. Has he one? – I think not?' 'But[b] who has one in London?' 'You[c] have not assuredly,' said the Count: 'and, if you knew the censures that are every where passed upon you, I think, for Lord Avondale's sake, you would regret it.' 'I do; but indeed –'[d]

The entrance of Buchanan put a stop to this conversation. 'Are you ready?' he cried. 'Ready! I have waited for you three hours: it is five, and you promised to come before two.'[e] 'You would excuse me, I am sure, if you knew how excessively ill I have been. I am but this moment out of bed. That accursed hazard[79] kept me up till ten this morning. Once, I sat two days and nights at it: but it's no matter.' 'You[f] take no care of yourself. – I[g] wish for my sake you would.' The manner in which Calantha said this, was most particularly flattering and kind: it was, indeed, ever so; but the return she met with (like the lady who loved the swine – 'Honey,' quoth she, 'thou shalt in silver salvers dine:' 'Humph,' quoth he)[h] [80] was most uncourteous. 'Truly[i] I care not if I am knocked on the head to-morrow,' replied Buchanan. 'There is nothing worth living for in life: every thing annoys me: I am sick of all society, Love,[j] sentiment, is my abhorrence.'[k] 'But driving, dearest Buchanan, – riding, – your mother – your – your cousin[l].' 'Oh, d. . .n it; don't talk about it. It's all a great bore.'

'And can Lady Avondale endure this jargon?'[m] 'What is that Italian here again?' whispered Buchanan. 'But come, let's go. My horses must not wait, they are quite unbroke; and the boy can't hold them. Little Jem yesterday had his ribs broke; and this youngster's no hand. Where shall we drive?' 'To perdition,' whispered Gondimar. 'Can't wait,' said Buchanan, impatiently: and Calantha hurried away.

The curricle was beautiful;[81] the horses fiery; Buchanan in high spirits; and Calantha – ah[a] must it be confessed? – more elated with this exhibition through the crowded streets, than she could have been at the most glorious achievement. /

'Drive faster,[b] – faster still,' she continually said,[c] to shew her courage. Alas! real courage delights not in parade; but anything[d] that had the appearance of risk or danger, delighted Calantha. 'Damn it, how Alice pulls.'[e] 'Alice!' said Calantha. 'Oh hang it; don't[f] talk of that. Here's Will Rattle, let me speak to him; and Dick, the boxer's son. Do you mind stopping?'[g] 'Not in the least.' Saying which they pulled in, as Buchanan termed it;[h] and a conversation ensued, which amused Calantha extremely. 'How soon shall you be off?' said Will Rattle, as they prepared to drive on. – 'It's a devilish bore staying in London now,' replied Buchanan: 'only I've been commanded to stay,' saying which he smiled, and turned to Lady Avondale, 'or I should have been with my regiment before this. The moment I am released, however, I shall go there. – Hope to see you to-night, Will. Mind and bring Charles Turner. – There's a new play. /

Oh[i] I forgot: – perhaps I shan't be let off; shall I?' 'No,' replied Calantha, extremely pleased at this flattering appeal. Will bowed with conceit, and off they galloped, Buchanan repeating as they went, 'A damned strange fellow that – cleverer than half the people though, who make such a noise. I saved his life once in an engagement. Poor Will,[j] he's so grateful, he would give all he has for me,[k] – I'll be d...d if he would not.' Let[l] this suffice. The drive was not very long; and, the danger of being overturned excepted, utterly devoid of interest.

Lady Dartford had returned to town. Perhaps no one ever heard that she had left it: like the rose leaf upon the glass full of water, her innocent presence made not the slightest difference, nor was her absence at any time observed. She, however,[m] called upon Calantha, a few moments after Buchanan had taken her home. Lady Avondale was with her lord, in the library[n] when she came. 'Why did you let her in?' she said rather crossly to the servant; when another loud rap at the door announced Lady Mandeville and Lady Augusta Selwyn. Calantha was writing a letter; and Lord Avondale was talking to her of the arrangements for their departure. 'I wish I ever could[o] see you one moment alone,' he said,[p] 'Say I am coming – or shall not come,' she replied; and during the time she remained to finish the conversation with her husband, she could not help amusing herself with the thought of Lady Dartford's alarm,[q] at finding herself in the presence of Lady Mandeville, whom she did not visit. 'You do not attend at all,' said Lord Avondale; 'you are of no use whatever;'[r] Alas! he had already found[s] that the mistress of his momentary passion, was not the friend and companion of his more serious thoughts. Calantha was of no use to any one. She began to feel the bitterness of this certainty, but she fled from the reflection with pain.[t]

Eager to amuse Lady Dartford, Lady Augusta, who knew her well, entertained her till Lady Avondale joined them, with a variety of anecdotes of all that had

taken place since her departure; and, having soon exhausted other subjects, began upon Calantha herself. 'She is positively in love with Captain Buchanan,' said she.
ᵃ 'At every ball he dances with her; at every supper he is by her side; all London is talking of it. Only think too how strange, just as he was said to haveᵇ proposed to Miss Macvicker – a fortune – twenty thousand a year – a nice girl, who really looks unhappy. Poor thing,ᶜ it is very hard on her. –ᵈ I always feel for girls.' 'Come,' said Lady Mandeville, 'last night you know, they did not interchange a word: he talked the whole evening to that young lady with the singular name. How I detest gossiping and scandal. Calantha deserves not this.' 'Bless us,ᵉ how innocent we are all of a sudden,'ᶠ interrupted Lady Augusta!ᵍ 'have you any pretentions, dearest lady, to that innoxious[82] quality? Now are you not aware that this is the very perfection of the art of making love – this not speaking? But this is what always comes of those who are so mighty fond of their husbands. Heavens,ʰ how sick I have been of all the stories of their romantic attachment. There is nothing, my dear, like Miss Seymour,ⁱ for making one sick. She always gives me the vapours.'

'Where do you go to-night?' said Lady Dartford, wishing to interrupt a conversation which gave her but little pleasure. 'Oh, to fifty places; but I came here partly too in the hope of engaging Lady Avondale to come to me tonight. She is a dear soul, and I do not like her the worse for shewing a little spirit.'ʲ 'I cannot,' said Lady Mandeville, 'think there is much in this; a mere caprice, founded on both sides in a little vanity. After seeing Lord Avondale, I cannot believe there is the smallest danger for her. Good heavens,ᵏ if I had possessed such a husband!'ˡ 'Oh, now for sentiment,' said Augusta:ᵐ 'and God knows, if I had possessed a dozen such, I should have felt as I do at this moment. Variety – variety! Better change for the worse than always see the same object.'ⁿ 'Well, if you do not allow the merit of Henry Avondale to outweigh this love of variety, what say you to Mr. Buchanan, being her cousin, brought up with her from a child.'ᵒ 'Thanks for the hint – you remember the song of

> 'Nous nous aimions dés l'enfance
> Tête-à-Tête-à chaque instant.'

and I am certain, my dear sentimental friend, that

> 'A notre place
> Vous en auriez fait autant.'[83] /

Then going up to the glassᵖ Lady Augusta bitterly inveighed against perverse nature, who with such a warm heart,ᑫ had given her such an ugly face. 'Do you know,' she said, still gazing upon her uncouth features, addressing herself to Lady Dartford – 'do you know that I have fallen in love myself,ʳ since I saw you; – and with whom do you think?' 'I think I can guess, and shall take great credit to myself, if I am right. Is not the happy man an author?' said Lady Dartford.

– 'You have him, upon my honour – Mr. Clarendon, by all that is wonderful: – he is positively the cleverest man about town. – Well I am glad to see my affairs also make some little noise in the world.' – 'I can tell you however,' said Lady Mandeville, 'that he is already engaged; – and Lady Mounteagle occupies every thought of his heart.'

'Good gracious, my dear, living and loving have done but little for you; and the dead languages prevent your judging of living objects.ᵃ – Engaged! you talk of falling in love,ᵇ as if it were a matrimonial contract for life. Now dontᶜ you know that every thing in nature is subject to change: – it rains to dayᵈ – it shines to-morrow; – we laugh, – we cry:ᵉ – and the thermometer of love rises and falls, like the weather glass, from the state of the atmosphere: – one while it is at freezing point; – another it is at fever heat. – How then should the only imaginary thing in the whole affair – the object I mean which is *always purely ideal* – how should that remain the same?'

Lady Mandeville smiled a little, and turning her languid blue eyes upon Lady Dartford, asked her if she were of the christianᶠ persuasion? Lady Dartford was perfectly confounded: – she hesitatingly answered in the affirmative. Upon which, Lady Augusta fell back in her chair, and laughed immoderately; but fearful of offending her newly made acquaintance, observed to her, that she wore the prettiest hat she had ever seen. 'Where did you get it?' said she. – The question was a master key to Lady Dartford's thoughts: – caps, hatsᵍ and works of every description were as much a solace to her, in the absence of her husband, as the greekʰ language, or the pagan philosophy could ever haveⁱ been to Lady Mandeville, under any of her misfortunes. – 'I got it,' said she, brightening up with a grateful look, at the only enquiry she had heard, that was at all adapted to her understanding, 'at Madame de la Roche's: – it is the cheapest thing you can conceive: – I only gave twenty guineas for it: – and you know I am not reckoned very clever at making bargains.'ʲ 'I should think not,' answered Lady Augusta, adverting only to the first part of the sentence.

Calantha entered at this moment.ᵏ 'Oh my sweet soul,' said Lady Augustaˡ, embracing her, 'I began to despair of seeing you. – But what was the matter with you last night? I had just been saying that you looked so very grave. Notwithstanding which, Lord Dallas could think, and talk only of you. He says your chevelure[84] is perfectly grecianᵐ – the black ringlets upon the white skin; but I never listen to any compliment that is not paid directly or indirectly to myself. He is quite adorable: – do you not think so, hey? – noⁿ – I see he is too full of admiration for you – too refined. Lady Avondale's heart must be won in a far different manner: – insult – rudeness – is the way to it. –ᵒ What! blush so deeply! Is the affair, then, too serious for a jest? Why, *mon enfant*, you look like Miss Macvicker this morning. – And is it true she will soon be united to you by the ties of blood, as she now seems to be by those of sympathy and congeniality of soul?'

The eternal Count Gondimar, and afterwards Buchanan[a] interrupted Lady Augusta's attack. New topics of discourse were discussed: – it will be needless to detail them: – time presses. Balls, assemblies, follow: – every day exhibited a new scene of frivolity and extravagance; – every[b] night was passed in the same vortex of fashionable dissipation. /

CHAPTER XXX.

THE spring was far advanced. Calantha's health required the sea air; but her situation rendered a long journey hazardous. Lord Avondale resolved to await her confinement in England. The birth of a daughter was an additional source of happiness: Anabel was the name given to the little infant.[85] Harry Mowbray[a] was now in his second year. The accounts from Ireland were more satisfactory. Mrs. Seymour wrote constantly to Calantha[b] regretting her absence. Weeks, however, flew by,[c] in the same thoughtless vanities: months passed away without regret or care. –[d] Autumn was gone: – winter again approached. –[e] London, though deserted,[f] by the crowd, was still gay. Calantha lived much with her Aunt[g] Margaret, Lady Mandeville, and the Princess of Madagascar. The parks and streets, but lately so thronged with carriages, were now comparatively lonely and deserted. Like the swallows at the appointed hour, the gay tribe of fashionable idlers had vanished; and a new set of people appeared in their place: – whence, or why, nobody could guess.

One day Zerbellini, Calantha's little page, had just returned with a note from Buchanan; a french hair dresser was cutting her hair; milliners and jewellers were displaying upon every table new dresses – caps – chains – rings –[h] for the ensuing winter; and Calantha's eye was dazzled – her ear was charmed – when her aunt Margaret entered. – 'God bless your Ladyship, God preserve you,' said a woman half starved, who was waiting for an answer to her petition. – '*Mi Lady; ne prendra-t-elle pas ce petit bonnet?*'[86] said Madame la Roche. 'Yes, every thing, any thing,' she answered impatiently, as she got up to receive her aunt. – She was unusually grave. Calantha trembled; for she thought she was prepared to speak to her about Buchanan. She was extremely relieved when she found that her censures turned solely upon her page. 'Why keep that little foreign minion?' she said, indignantly. 'Is the Count Viviani so very dear, that any present of his must be thus treasured up and valued?' 'The Count Viviani?'[i] said Calantha astonished: 'who is he?' – 'Well, then, Gondimar,' replied Lady Margaret. 'Calantha – as a favour, I request you send[j] back that boy.' – Lady Avondale's prayers were at first her sole reply; and like Titania,[k] in her second, when Oberon demanded the trusty Henchman, she boldly refused.[87] Lady Margaret left her immediately:

– she was calm, but offended. She was then going to Castle Delaval. Calantha told her they should join her there in the course of the next month. She only smiled,ᵃ with a look of incredulity and contempt;ᵇ asking her, if her beloved Henry would really be so cruel as to tear her away at last from London? and saying this she took leave.

Lord Avondale and Calantha had been conversing on this very subject in the morning. He was surprised at her ready acquiescence in his wish to return to Ireland. 'You are then still the same,' he said affectionately. – 'I am the same,' she replied rather fretfully;ᶜ 'but you are changed: – every one tells me you neglect me.' 'And have they who tell you so,' said he with a sigh, 'any very good motive in thus endeavouring to injure me in your opinion? If I attended to what every one said, Calanthaᵈ perhaps I too should have some reason to complain. – Business of importance has alone enengaged my attention. You know I am not one who assume much; and if I say that I have been employed, you may depend on its being the case. I hope, then, I am not wrong when I have confided myself, and every thing that is dearest to me, to your honour and your love.' – 'Ahᵉ no: – you are not wrong,' she answered; 'but perhaps if you confided less, and saw more of me, it would be better. Before marriage, a woman has her daily occupations: she looks for the approving smile of her parents: – she has friends who cheer her – who take interest in her affairs. But when we marry, Henry, we detach ourselves from all, to follow one guide. For the first years, we are the constant object of your solicitude: – you watch over us with even a tenderer care than those whom we have left, and then you leave us – leave us too,ᶠ among the amiable and agreeable, yet reprove us, if we confide in them, or love them. Marriage is the annihilation of love.'

'The error is in human nature,' said Lord Avondale smiling – 'We always see perfection in that which we cannot approach: – there is a majesty in distance and rarity, which every day's intercourse wears off. Besides, love delights in gazing upon that which is superior: – whilst we believe you angels, we kneel to you, we are your slaves; – we awake and find women, and expect obedience: – and is it not what you were made for?' – 'Henry, we are made your idols too – too long, to bear this sad reverse: – you should speak to us in the language of truth from the first, or never. – Obey –ᵍ is a fearful word to those who have lived without hearing it; and truth from lips which have accustomed us to a dearer language, sounds harsh and discordant. We have renounced society, and all the dear ties of early friendship, to form one strong engagement,ʰ and if that fails, what are we in the world?ⁱ – beings without hope,ʲ or interest – dependants – encumbrances – shadows of former joys – solitary wanderers in quest of false pleasures – or lonely recluses, unblessing and unblest.'

Calantha had talked herself into tears, at the conclusion of this sentence; and Lord Avondale, smiling at a description she had given, so little according with the gay being who stood before him, pressed her fondly to his bosom; and said he would positively hear no more. 'You treat me like a child – a fool,' –ᵃ she said: – 'you forget that I am a reasonable creature.' 'I do, indeed, Calantha: – youᵇ so seldom do any thing to remind me of it.' 'Well, Henry, one day you shall find your error. I feel that within, which tells me that I could be superior – aye –ᶜ very superior to those who cavil at my faults, and first encourage and then ridicule me for them. I love –ᵈ I honour you, Henry. You never flatter me. Even if you neglect me, you have confidence in me – and, thank God, my heart is still worthy of some affection.ᵉ It is yet time to amend.' Calantha –ᶠ thought it had been – as she took in haste a review of her former conduct – of time, how neglected! – friends, how estrangedᵍ – money lavished in vain! – and health impaired by the excess of late hours, and endless, ceaseless dissipation.

London had still attractions for Calantha;ʰ but the thought of fresh air, and green fields recurring, she was soon prepared for the journey. She passed the intervening days before her departure in taking leave of her friends. Lady Mandeville, in bidding adieu to her, affirmed that the interchange of ideas between congenial souls,ⁱ would never be lessened, nor interrupted by absence. She would write to her, she said, and she would think of her; and, seeing Calantha was really sorry to part with her, 'You have none of the philosophy,' she said, 'which your cousin and your aunt possess, and every trifle, therefore, has power to afflict you: – you scarcely know me, and yet you are grieved to leave me. Promise ever to judge of me by what you see yourself, and not through the medium of others; for the world, which I despise from my soul, has long sought to crush me, because I had pride of character enough to think for myself.'

If any thing had been wanting to strengthen Calantha's regard, this boast had been sure of its effect; for it was one of her favourite opinions, not indeed that the world should be despised, but that persons should dare to think, and act for themselves, even though against its judgments. She was not then,ʲ aware how this cant phrase is ever in the mouths of the veriest slaves to prejudice, – how little real independence of character is found amongst those who have lost sight of virtue. Like spendthrifts,ᵏ who boast of liberality, they are forced to stoop to arts and means, which those whom they affect to contemn,ˡ would blush even to think of. Virtue alone can hope to stand firm and unawed above the multitude. When vice assumes this fearless character, it is either unblushing effrontery and callous indifference to the opinion of the wise and good, or at best,ᵐ but overweening pride, which supports the culprit, and conceals from the eyes of others, the gnawing tortures he endures – the bitter agonizing consciousness of self-reproach. /

CHAPTER XXXI.

Lord Avondale was desirous of passing the winter with his family at Monteith, and in the spring he had promised the Duke of Altamonte to accompany Lady Avondale to Castle Delaval. Lady Mandeville and Lady Augusta Selwyn were invited to meet them there at that time. The wish of pleasing Calantha, of indulging even her very weaknesses, seemed to be the general failing of all who surrounded her: – yet what return did she make? – each day new follies engrossed her thoughts; – her levity and extravagance continually increased; and whilst with all the ostentation of generosity[a] she wasted the fortune of her husband upon the worthless and the base, –[b] he denied himself every amusement, secretly and kindly to repair the ruin – the misery –[c] the injustice her imprudence and wanton prodigality had caused.

During a long and melancholy journey, and after her arrival at Monteith, Calantha, with some astonishment, considered the difference of Lord Avondale's views, character[d] and even talents for society and conversation, as compared with those of her former companions. Lord Avondale had no love of ostentation – no effort – a perfect manliness of conduct and character, a real, and not feigned, indifference to the opinion and applause of the vain and the foolish; yet with all this, he was happy, chearful,[e] ready to enter into every amusement or occupation which gave others pleasure. He had not one selfish feeling. It was impossible not to be forcibly struck with the comparison.

Calantha, with her usual inconsistency, now made all those sensible and judicious remarks[f] which people always make,[g] when they have lived a life of folly, and suddenly return to a more tranquil course. She compared the false gaiety which arises from incessant hurry and vanity,[h] with that which is produced by nature and health. She looked upon the blue sky and the green fields; watched the first peeping snow-drop and crocus; and entered with delight into all the little innocent pleasures of a rural life: nor did even a slight restlessness prevail, nor any erring thoughts steal back to revisit the gay scenes she had left. In very truth[i] she was more adapted, she said, to her present course of life than to any other; and, however guilty of imprudence, she thanked God she had not heavier sins to answer for; nor was there a thought of her heart,[j] she would not have wished her husband to know, unless from the fear of either giving him pain[a] or betraying others.

At length, however, and by degrees, something of disquiet began to steal in upon the serenity of her thoughts: – her mind became agitated, and sought an object: – study, nay, labour[b] she had preferred to this total want of interest. While politics and military movements engaged Lord Avondale almost wholly, and the rest of the family seemed to exist happily enough in the usual course, she longed for she knew not what. There was a change in her sentiments, but she could not define it. It was not as it had been once: yet there was no cause for complaint. She was happy, but her heart seemed not to partake of her happiness: regret[c] mingled at times with her enjoyments.

Lady Mowbray[d] spoke with some asperity of her late conduct; Lady Elizabeth enquired laughingly[e] if all she heard were true;[f] for every folly, every fault, exaggerated and misrepresented, had flown before her: she found that all which she had considered as merely harmless, now appeared in a new and more unpleasing light. Censures at home and flattery abroad are a severe trial to the vain and the proud. She thought her real friends austere; and cast one longing glance back upon the scene which had been so lately illumined by the gaiety, the smiles, the kindness and courtesy of her new acquaintance.

Whilst the first and only care of Lord Avondale, every place was alike delightful to Calantha:[g] for in his society she enjoyed all that she desired; but now that she saw him estranged, absent, involved[h] in deeper interests, she considered, with some feelings of alarm, the loneliness of her own situation. In the midst of hundreds,[i] she had no real friends: –[j] those of her childhood were estranged from her by her marriage; and those her marriage had united her with, seemed to perceive only her faults, nor appreciated the merits she possessed. To dress well, to talk well, to write with ease and perspicuity, had never been her turn. Unused to the arts and amusements of social intercourse, she had formerly felt interest in poetry, in music, in what had ceased to be, or never had existed; but now the same amusements, the same books, had lost their charm: she knew more of the world, and saw and felt their emptiness and fallacy. In the society of the generality of women and men she could find amusement when any amusement was to be found; but, day after day, to hear sentiments she could not think just, and to lose sight of all for which she once had felt reverence and enthusiasm, was hard. If she named one she loved, that one was instantly considered as worthless: if she expressed much eagerness for the success of any project, that eagerness was the subject of ridicule.[k]

Oh I am changed, she continually thought;[l] I have repressed and conquered every warm and eager feeling; I love and admire nothing;[m] yet am I not heartless and cold enough for the world in which I live. What is it that makes me miserable? There is a fire burns within my soul; and all those whom I see and hear are insensible. Avondale alone feels as I do; but[n] alas! it is no longer for me. Were I dead, what difference would it make to any one? I am the object of momentary amusement or censure to thousands; but,ª of love, to none. I am as a child, as a mistress to my husband; but never his friend, his companion. Oh for a heart's friend, in whom I could confide every thought and feeling;ᵇ who would share and sympathize with my joy or sorrow;ᶜ to whom I could say, 'you love me – you require my presence;' and for whom in returnᵈ I would give up every other enjoyment. Such friend was once Lord Avondale. By what means have I lost him?

Often when in tears she thus expressed herself. Her husband would suddenly enter; laugh with her without penetrating her feelings; or, deeply interested in the cares of business, seek her only as a momentary solace and amusement. Such, however, he seldom now found her; for she cherished a discontented spirit within her;ᵉ and though too proud and stubborn to complain, she lived but on the memory of the past.

Calantha'sᶠ principles had received a shock, the force and effect of which was greatly augmented by a year of vanity and folly;ᵍ her health too was impaired from late hours and an enervating life; she could not walk or ride as formerly; and her great occupation was the indulgence of a useless and visionary train of thinking. She imagined that which was not, and lost sight of reality; – pictured ideal virtues, and saw not the world as it is. Her heart beat with all the fervour of enthusiasm; but the turn it took was erroneous. She heard the conversation of others; took a mistaken survey of society; and withdrew herself imperceptibly from all just and reasonable views. Ill motives were imputed to her, for what she considered harmless imprudence;ʰ she felt the injustice of these opinions; and, instead of endeavouring to correct those appearances which had caused such severe animadversion, in absolute disgust she steeled herself against all remonstrances. Every one smiles on me and seems to love me – the world befriends me – she continually thought;ⁱ yet I am censured and misrepresented. My relations – the only enemies I have – are those who profess to be my friends. Convincedʲ of this, she became lonely. She had thoughts which once she would have mentioned as they occurred, but which she now concealed and kept solely to herself. She became dearer in her own estimation, as she detached herself from others, and began to feel coldly, even towards those whom she had once loved. /

CHAPTER XXXII.

IT is dangerous to begin life by surrendering every feeling of the mind and the heart to any violent passion –[a] Calantha had loved and been loved to such an excess, that all which followed it appeared insipid. Vanity might fill the space for a moment,[b] or friendship, or charity, or benevolence; but still there was something gone[c] which, had it never existed, had never been missed and required. Lord Avondale was perhaps more indulgent and more affectionate now, than at first; for a lover ever plays the tyrant; but even this indulgence was different; and that look of adoration – that blind devotion – that ardent, constant solicitude, when, without a single profession, one may feel certain of being the first object in life to the person thus attached,[d] – all this was past.

Such love is not depravity. To have felt it, and to feel it no more, is like being deprived of the light of the sun, and seeing the same scenes, which we once viewed brilliant beneath its beams, dark, clouded and cheerless. –[e] Calantha had given up her heart too entirely to its power, ever more to endure existence without it. Her home was a desert; her thoughts were heavy and dull; her spirits and her health were gone; and even the desire of pleasing, so natural to the vain, had ceased. Whom was she to wish to please, since Avondale was indifferent? or[f] what to her was the same, absent and preoccupied.

Such depression continued during the gloomy wintry months; but with the first warm breeze of spring, they left her;[g] and in the month of May, she prepared to join the splendid party which was expected at Castle Delaval – as gay in heart herself as if she had never moralized upon the perishableness[h] of all human happiness.

Upon a cool and some what dreary morning in the month of May, Calantha[i] left Monteith, and sleeping one night at Allenwater,[j] hastened to Castle Delaval, where blazing hearths and joyous countenances, gave her[k] a cheering welcome. Lady Mandeville and Lady Augusta had, according to promise, arrived there a week before, to the utter consternation of Mrs. Seymour. Calantha perceived in one moment,[l] that she was not extremely well with her or with her cousins upon this account. Indeed the former scarcely offered her her hand, such a long detail of petty offences had been registered against her,[m] since they had last parted. It was also justly imputed to Calantha that Lady Mandeville had been invited to the

Castle.ᵃ A stately dignity was therefore assumed by Sophia and Mrs. Seymour on this occasion:ᵇ they scarce permitted themselves to smile during the whole time Lady Mandeville remained, for fear, as Calantha concluded,ᶜ that Satan, taking advantage of a moment of levity, should lead them into further evil. The being compelled to live in company with one of her character, was more than enough.

'I am enraptured at your arrival,' said Lady Augusta, flying towards Calantha,ᵈ the moment she perceived her. 'You are come at the happiest time: you will be diverted here in no ordinary manner: the days of romance,ᵉ are once again displayed to our wondering view.'ᶠ 'Yes,' said Lady Trelawney,⁸⁸ 'not a day passes without an adventure.' Before Calantha enquired into the meaning of this, she advanced to Lady Mandeville, who, languidly reclining upon a couch, smiled sweetly on seeing her. Secure of the impression she had made, she waited to be sought, and throwing her arm around her, gave her kisses so soft and so tender, that she could not immediately extricate herself from her embrace.

Lady Augusta, eager to talk, exclaimed – 'Did you meet any of the patrole?' 'I was reading the address to the united Irishmen,' said Calantha, who could hear and think of nothing else.ᵍ 'Are you aware who is the author?' 'No; but it is so eloquent, so animated, I was quite alarmed when I thought how it must affect the people.' 'You shock me, Calantha,' said Mrs. Seymour. 'The absurd rhapsody you mean, is neither eloquent nor animating: it is a despicable attempt to subvert the government, a libel upon the English, and a poor piece of flattery to delude the infatuated malcontents in Ireland.' Lady Augusta winked at Calantha, as if informing her that she touched upon a sore subject. 'The author,' said Lady Trelawney, who affected to be an enthusiast, 'is Lord Glenarvon.'

'I wishʰ Frances,' said Mrs. Seymour, 'you would call people by their right names. The young man you call Lord Glenarvon,ⁱ has no claim to that title;⁸⁹ his grandfather was a traitor; his father was a poor miserable exile, who was obliged to enter the Navyʲ by way of gaining a livelihood; his mother was a woman of very doubtful character (as she said this she looked towards Lady Mandeville); and this young man, educated nobody knows how, having passed his time in a foreign country, nobody knows where, from whence he was driven it seems by his crimes, is now unfortunately arrived here to pervert and mislead others, to disseminate his wicked doctrines amongst an innocent but weak people, and to spread the flames of rebellion, already kindled in other parts of the Island.ᵏ Oh, he is a dishonour to his sex;ˡ and it makes me mad to see how you all run after him, and forget both dignity and modesty, to catch a glimpse of him.'

'What sort of looking man is he, dear aunt?' said Calantha. 'Frightful – mean,' said Mrs. Seymour. 'His stature is small,' said Lady Mandeville; 'but his eye is keen and his voice is sweet and tunable. Lady Avondale believe me, he is possessed of that persuasive language, which never fails to gain upon its hearers. Take heed to your heart: remember my words,ᵃ – beware of the young

Glenarvon.' Gondimar, after the first salutation upon entering the room, joined in the conversation; but he spoke with bitterness of the young Lord; and upon Lady Trelawney's attempting to say a few words in his favour, 'Hear Sir Everard on this subject,' said the Count – 'only hear what he thinks of him.' 'I fear,' said Sophia, 'that all these animadversions will prevent our going to-morrow, as we proposed, to see the Priory.' 'Nothing shall prevent me,' replied Lady Augusta. 'I only beg,' said Mrs. Seymour 'that I may not be of the party, as the tales of horror I have heard concerning the inhabitants of St. Alvin Priory, from old Lord de Ruthven, at Belfont Abbey, prevent my having the smallest wish or curiosity to enter its gates.'

Count Gondimar, now coming towards Calantha, enquired after Zerbellini. At the request of every one present, he was sent for. Calantha saw a visible change in Lady Margaret's countenance, as he entered the room, 'He is the living image' – she murmured, in a low hollow tone – 'Of whom?' said Calantha eagerly. – She seemed agitated and retired. Gondimar in the evening, took Calantha apart,[b] and said these extraordinary words to her, 'Zerbellini is Lady Margaret and Lord Dartford's son: treat him according to his birth; but remember, she would see him a slave sooner than betray herself: she abhors, yet loves him. Mark her; but never disclose the secret with which I entrust you.' Astonished, confounded, Calantha now looked upon the boy with different eyes. Immediately his resemblance to the family of Delaval struck her – his likeness to herself – his manner so superior to that of a child in his situation. The long concealed truth, at once flashed upon her. A thousand times she was tempted to speak upon the subject. She had not promised to conceal it from Lord Avondale: she was in the habit of telling him every thing: however she was now for the first time silent, and there is no more fatal symptom than when an open communicative disposition grows reserved.

END OF VOL. I.
LONDON: PRINTED BY SCHULZE AND DEAN, 13, POLAND STREET.

GLENARVON.

IN THREE VOLUMES.

VOL. II.

LONDON:
PRINTED FOR HENRY COLBURN,
1816

GLENARVON.

VOL. II.

Mon plaisir me coute la vie!

GLENARVON.

Disperato dolor, che il cor mi preme
Gia pur pensando, pria che ne favelle.[1]

VOL. II. /

GLENARVON.

CHAPTER I.

In the morning Calantha beheld crowds of discontented catholics who thronged the outer courts waiting to see her father.² Petitions for redress were thrown in at the windows; and whilst they were at breakfast, Sir Everard entering, without even waiting to see who was present, asked eagerly if the Duke was^a at home: he, at the same moment gave a huge paper closely written, into the hands of one of the servants, desiring it to be instantly delivered to the Duke; 'and tell him, sir,' vociferated the doctor, 'it is my case written out clear, as he commanded – the one^b I had the honour to present to him t'other day, when he had not leisure to look upon it:' then turning round, / and seeing Calantha, 'By my soul,' he exclaimed, 'if here ain't my own dear Lady Calantha; and God be praised Madam, you are come amongst us; for the devil and all is broke loose since you've been away. Let's look at you: well, and you are as tall and handsome as ever; but I – Oh! Lady Calantha Delaval, begging your pardon, what a miserable wretch am I become. Lord help me, and deliver me. Lord help us all, in unmerited affliction.'

Calantha had not heard of Sir Everard's misfortunes; and was really afraid to ask him what had occurred. He held her hand, and wept so audibly, that she already saw some of those present turning away, for fear^c they should not be able to conceal their laughter: his strange gestures were indeed a hard trial. 'Be pacified, calm yourself my good Doctor,' said Mrs. Seymour, giving him a chair: 'Heaven forfend,' said Sir Everard: 'Nature, Madam, will have a vent. I am the most / miserable man alive: I am undone, you well know; but Lord! this dear child knows little if any thing about it. Oh! I am a mere nothing now in the universe.' Gondimar, with a smile, assured Sir Everard that could never be the case, whilst he retained, unimpaired, that full rotundity of form. 'Sir, are you here?' cried the Doctor,^d fiercely: 'but it is of small importance. I am no longer the soft phlegmatic being you left me. I am a wild beast, Sir – a dangerous animal. – Away with your scoffs. – I will fight, Sir – murder, Sir – aye, and 'smile whilst I murder.'³

There was something in these words which turned Lady Margaret's cheeks to a deadly pale; but the Doctor, who had sought for forcible expressions alone, without the least heeding the application, continued to storm and to rage. 'I'm a man,' he cried, 'accustomed to sufferings and to insult. Would you credit it, dear

Lady Calantha: can you comprehend / it? – that lawless gang – those licentious democrats – those rebellious libertines, have imposed on the inordinate folly of my wife and daughters, who, struck mad, like Agave in the orgies of Bacchus,[4] are running wild about the country, their hair dishevelled, their heads ornamented with green cockades, and Lady St. Clare, to the shame of her sex and me, the property of a recruiting serjeant, employed by one of that nest of serpents at the abbey, to delude others, and all,[a] I believe, occasioned by that arch fiend, Glenarvon.'

'Oh!' cried Gerald Mac Allain, who was in attendance at the breakfast table, 'saving your honour's pardon,[b] the young Lord of Glenarvon has been the cause of my two brave boys being saved from the gallows. I will rather lose my life, than stand to hear him called an arch fiend.' 'He is one, old Gerald, whether you or I call him so or no. Witness how, the other night, he set the rabble with their / torches to burning Mr. O'Flarney's barns, and stealing his sheep and oxen and all his goods.' 'Och it's my belief the rector of Belfont, when he comes, will speak a word for him thoft,'[5] returned Gerald Mac Allain; 'for, save the presence of the Duke, who is not here to hear me, he has been our guard and defence all the while his grace's honour has been out of the kingdom.' 'Curses light upon him and his gang,' cried Sir Everard, furiously. 'Are not Miss Laura and Miss Jessica after him at this very time, and my pretty niece, my young, my dear Elinor, and Lady St. Clare, more crazy than all, is not she following him about as if he were some god?'

'The whole country are after him,' cried Gerald Mac Allain, enthusiastically: 'its[c] a rage, a fashion.' 'Its[d] a phrenzy,' returned the Doctor, – 'a pestilence which has fallen on the land, and all, it's[e] my belief, because the stripling has not one christian principle, or habit in him: / he's[f] a heathen.' 'If it is the young Glenarvon,' said Gondimar, approaching the irritated Doctor, 'he is my friend.' 'Don't bring[g] any of your knock me down arguments to me, Sir. His being your friend, only gives a blacker shade to his character, in my opinion.'[h] 'Sir, I hate personal attacks.' 'A blow that hits, Count, and a cap that fits, are sure to make a[i] sufferer look foolish, excessively foolish: not but what you did so before.[j] I never believed in baseness and malignity till I knew the Count Gondimar.' 'Nor I in arrogance and stupidity, till I knew Sir Everard.' 'Count, you are the object of my astonishment.' 'And you, Sir, of my derision.' 'Italian, I despise you.' 'I should only feel mortified, if Sir Everard did otherwise.' 'The contempt, Sir, of the meanest, cannot be a matter of triumph.' 'It is a mark of wisdom, to be proud of the scorn of fools.' 'Passion makes me mad.' 'Sir, you were that before.' / 'I shall forget myself.' 'I wish you would permit me to do so.'

'A truce to these quarrels, good doctor,' said the Duke, who had entered the room during the latter part of the discussion. 'I have been reading some papers of a very serious nature; and I am sorry to say it appears from them that Sir Everard has very great cause for his present irritation of mind: he is an aggrieved man. This Lord Glenarvon, or whatever the young gentleman styles himself, has acted in a manner not only unjustifiable, but such as I am afraid will ultimately lead to his entire ruin. Count Gondimar, I have often heard you speak of this unfortunate young man, with more than common interest. Could not you make use of your friendship and intimacy with him, to warn him of the danger of his present conduct, and lead him from the society of his worthless associates. He seems to be acting under the influence of a mad infatnation.' Gondimar / assured the Duke,[a] that he had no sort of influence with the young Lord. 'Read these papers, at your leisure,' said the Duke: 'they are statements, you will find, of a number of outrages committed by himself and his followers, on people highly respectable and utterly defenceless. For the common follies of youth, there is much excuse; but nothing can palliate repeated acts of licentious wickedness and unprovoked cruelty. I am inclined to believe these accounts are much exaggerated; but the list of grievances is large; and the petitioners for redress are many of them my most worthy and long-tried servants, at the head of whom O'Flarney's name is to be found.'

'No, my Lord, – mine is at the head of the list,' cried the doctor; 'and in every other part of it, no injuries can be equal to mine. What are barns, pigs, firearms, compared to a father's wrongs – a husband's injuries. Ah, consider my case first. Restore Miss St. Clare, and I'll[b] / be pacified. Why do I raise laughter by my cry? It is my niece, my favourite child, who has been taken from me.' 'Pray explain to me seriously, Sir,' said Lady Augusta, approaching the doctor, with much appearance of interest, 'how came your family to fall into the unfortunate situation to which you allude?' 'How came they,' said the Count? 'can you ask,[c] when you see Sir Everard at the head of it?' 'Madam,' said the Doctor with equal solemnity, 'this momentous crisis has been approaching some time. St. Clara, as we called her, my most lovely and interesting Elinor's affections have long been seduced. We all knew, lamented and concealed the circumstance. The old lady's conduct, however, was quite an unexpected blow. But since they took to their nocturnal rambles to St. Mary's, St. Alvin's, and all the saints around, their sanctity has not been much mended that I see, and their wits are fairly overset. / As to my girls, I really feel for them: my[d] own disgrace I can easily support: but oh my Elinor!

'What nocturnal meetings have taken place at St. Mary's and St. Alvin's?' said Lady Trelawney, with a face of eager curiosity. 'The discontented flock together in shoals,' said the Doctor, indignantly, 'till by their machinations, they will overturn the State. At Belfont, opposite my very window, – aye, even in that great square house which Mr. Ochallavan built, on purpose to obstruct Lady St. Clare's view, have they not set up a library? The Lord help me. And was it not there I first saw that accursed pamphlet Lord Glenarvon wrote; which rhapsody did not I myself immediately answer? Lady Calantha, strange things have occurred since your departure. Captain[e] Kennedy, commander of the district, can't[f] keep his men. Cattle walk out of the paddocks of themselves: women, children, pigs, wander after Glenarvon; / and Miss Elinor, forgetful of her old father, my dear mad brother, her aunt, her religion, and all else, to the scandal of every one in their senses, heads the rabble. They have meetings under ground, and over ground; out at sea, and in the caverns: no one can stop the infection; the poison in[a] the fountain of life; and our very lives[b] and estates are no longer in safety. You know not, you cannot know, what work we have had since you last left us.' Sir Everard paused, and then taking a couple of pamphlets from his pocket, entreated Calantha to peruse them. 'Cast your eye over these,' he said: 'I wrote them in haste; they are mere sketches of my sentiments; but I am going to publish. Oh! when you see what I am now going to publish. It is intituled[6] a refutation of all that has or may be said by the disaffected, in or out of the kingdom.' /

CHAPTER II.

THE party at the castle had postponed their visit to St. Alvin Priory till the feast of St. Kathereen and St. Mary, which in that neighbourhood was always celebrated with much observance. A fair was held upon the downs,[a] in honour of these two martyrs. The rocks near which the ruins of the convent stood, were called the Black Sisters, and it was there,[b] and in the Wizzard's[c] Glen, which stretched from the top to the foot of the mountain, that the meetings of the discontented had been held. The day proved fair; and at an early hour the carriages and horses were in attendance. Mrs. Seymour and many others declined being of the party; but Lady Margaret took Gondimar's arm with a smile of good humour, which she could at times put on. / Buchanan drove Calantha in his barouche.[7] Sir Everard rode by Calantha's side on a lowly white palfrey, as if to protect her. Lady Mandeville was with her; and Lady Trelawney took Sophia and Lady Augusta Selwyn in her carriage. The rest of the gentlemen were some on horseback and some in curricles.

The whole country smiled around. There were ringers, and pipers, and hurlers upon the down. The cliff, towards the sea, was covered with booths and tents. Flocks, herds and horses had been brought from far for sale, ornamented with ribbands;[8] green being the favourite colour. Scarcely ever was witnessed a scene more gay. This, and the vessels laden with fish, crowding into the harbour below, and the high mountains beyond, struck even the Italian, whose eyes had been accustomed to all that nature can produce of picturesque and majestic. The beauty of the girls, with their long blue mantles thrown aside / from their shoulders, their dark hair fastened behind with a knot of ribband, was the subject of discussion. Comparisons of the difference of form between one nation and another arose. All descended from their carriages and horses. Lady Mandeville repeated poetry; Gondimar became sentimental; Buchanan looked at the horses, enquired their prices, and soon joined the hurlers, in whose combat he grew so much interested, that no one could draw him from thence until the moment when they left the fair, where they had remained[d] till they were all much fatigued.

'What are you laughing at so immensely?' cried Lady Augusta Selwyn, approaching Lord Trelawney, who was nearly enclosed in a circle of some hundreds. The moment Lady Augusta approached; with a courtesy seldom seen but in Ireland, the crowd made way for her. 'I am listening,' said he, 'to a preacher – a most capital preacher, whom / they call Cowdel O'Kelly. Only observe him: what a rogue it is, with that hypocrite^a mildness of manner, that straight^b black hair, that presbyterian stiffness and simplicity.' 'But what is he saying?' enquired Lady Augusta. The preacher, standing upon a cart, was delivering an exhortation in a very emphatic manner, to a vast concourse of attentive hearers. The presence of the party from the Castle had no effect upon him: he was inveighing against the insolence of his superiors in rank, and pleading in favour of the rights of man.

When he had concluded his discourse, the crowd dispersed, some laughing at him, and some much edified[c] by his discourse. O'Kelly looked after them: – 'That is the way of the world,' he said: 'it gets all it can from a man, and then it leaves him; but all that is, is for the best; therefore, amen, your honours; so be it.' Lord Trelawney laughed to an excess. 'Your name,' said he,[d] 'I take it, it is Cowdel / O'Kelly.' 'If you take it to be my name, your honour can't be any ways wrong in calling me by it; but I call myself citizen Wailman.' 'And why the devil, my honest friend, do you call yourself so?' 'To please myself, and trick my master.' 'And pray who is your master?' 'When I know that,[e] I'll let you know.' 'What! not know your master?' 'Why what master knows his servant? There's nothing extraordinary in that, my Lord.' 'But pray, my good citizen Wailman, where do you live, and where does your master live?' – [f] 'I live where I can, your honour; and as to my master, every one knows he lives under ground, in the family vault.'

'Is he dead then, or what can he be doing under ground?' said Lady Trelawney. 'Looking for friends, Miss, I believe; for he has none, that I see, above board.' 'I am sure this is a rebel in disguise,' whispered Lady [g] Trelawney. Her Lord laughed. /

A beautiful little boy now pushing his way through the crowd, plainly pronounced the words, 'O'Kelly come home; I am very tired.' The man, hastily descending from the cart, called him his young prince – his treasure; and lifted him up in his arms. 'He is about the same age as Henry Mowbray,'[h] said Calantha, 'and very like him.[i] What is your name, my pretty child?' 'Clare of Costally,'[j] said the boy; 'and it should by rights be Lord Clare – should it not, O'Kelly?' As he spoke, he smiled and put his little rosy hands to O'Kelly's mouth, who kissed them, and making a slight bow,[k] would have retired. 'What, are you going? will you not stay a moment?' 'I fear I intrude too much on your honour's time.' 'Not in the least – not in the least, good Mister Wailman; pray stay a little longer.' 'Why, fair and honest, if I don't intrude too much on your time, my lord,[l] you do on mine; and so your servant.' /

'I really believe he belongs to the abbey,' said Lady Trelawney, who had reentered her barouche, and was driving with the rest of the party,[m] towards St. Alvin Priory. 'See how he steals along by the cliff,[n] in the same direction we are going.' 'It was a lovely child,' said Lady Augusta;[o] 'but to be sure no more like Harry; only Lady Avondale is always in the seventh heaven of romance.' 'Look, pray look,' interrupted Frances: 'I assure you that is Sir Everard St. Clare's wife, and Lauriana and Jessica are with her. I am certain of it,' she continued, throwing herself nearly out of the carriage to gaze upon them. Lord Trelawney was extremely diverted. 'And there is the recruiting serjeant: only observe the manner in which they are habited.' The two unhappy girls, drest in the most flaunting attire, singing in chorus the song of liberty, covered[a] with green ribbands, were walking in company with a vast number of young / men, most of them intoxicated, and all talking and laughing loudly. Calantha begged Buchanan to stop the carriage, that she also might see them pass;[b] which they did, marching to the sound of the drum and fife: but her heart sickened when she saw the beautiful recluse of Glenaa amongst them. Elinor came near: she raised her full black eye, and gazed with fearless effrontery upon Calantha.

It was the same face she had seen a few years back at the convent: but alas, how changed; – the rich and vivid crimson of her cheek, the deep dark brown of the wild ringlets which waved above her brow, the bold masculine manners and dress she had assumed, contrasting[c] with the slender beauty of her upright form. She was drest in uniform, and walked by the side of a young man, whose pale,[d] thoughtful countenance struck every one. Elinor appeared desperate and utterly hardened: her presence / inspired Calantha with a mixed feeling of horror and commiseration, which Lady St. Clare's ludicrous figure, and Jessica and Lauriana's huge and clumsy personages turned into disgust.

'Oh did you behold her? – did you see my poor deluded Elinor?' cried Sir Everard, riding up to Calantha, as she still gazed from the open carriage upon the procession: 'did you see my unfortunate girls?' 'I did, indeed,' said Lady Avondale, the tears springing into her eyes: 'I saw them and stopped; for it occurred to me, that, perhaps, I might speak to them – might yet save them.' 'And would you have condescended so much? Oh! this is more than I dared ask[e] or hope.' Saying which, the Doctor wept, as was his custom, and Buchanan laughed. 'You are so good,' continued he:[f] 'you were in tears when you saw your former playmates disgracing themselves, and their sex; but in the rest of the carriages I heard / nothing but jesting, and loud laughter. And oh! would you credit it, can you believe it, Lady St. Clare had the audacity to drop me a courtesy as she passed.'

'Was the tall young man, who was walking by the side of Elinor, Cyrel Linden?' 'It was the same,' cried the Doctor – 'gone mad like the rest, though they tell me it is all for the love of Miss Alice; and that since her loss, he is grown desperate, and cares not what becomes of him. They'll be hanged, however;[g] that is one consolation – Lady St. Clare, as well as the rest. Indeed,' cried he, drawing closer, 'I am credibly informed that the officers of justice have an eye upon them, and wait only to obtain[h] further evidence of their treasonable practices, to take them up.'[i] During this discourse, the carriage drove slowly up the hill; but soon proceeding at a brisker pace, the doctor[j] was obliged to draw in his steed and retire. The party now entered the park. /

CHAPTER III.

BELFONT Abbey and St. Alvin's ruined Priory appeared in view. The ivy climbed around the turrets;^a and the grass grew upon the paved courts, where desolation and long neglect prevailed. At a distance from the convent, a ruin, a lonely pile stood upon the cliff in solitary grandeur. Not a tree, nor any appearance of cultivation was seen around: barren moors, the distant mountains, and the vast ocean, every where filled the eye. The servants rang at the bell of the outer gate: it resounded through the vaulted passages with a long repeated echo. – A boy immediately answered the summons:^b with a look of stupid astonishment, he waited^c in expectation of their commands.

Buchanan enquired of the boy, if they / might see the Priory. 'I suppose so,' was his reply. And without further preamble, they alighted. 'It must be rather melancholy to live here during the winter months,' said Calantha to the boy, as she passed him. 'And summer too,' he answered. 'We are told,' said Frances, 'that this Priory is haunted by ghosts: have you ever seen any?' He shook his head. 'I hears them sometimes, an' please your honour,' he said; 'but^d I never meddle^e with them, so they never comes after me as I see.' 'Are^f you going to shew us the house?' cried Sir Everard advancing; 'or, if not, why do you keep us waiting in this dark passage? go on; we are in haste.' The boy, proceeding towards an inner apartment, knocked at the door, calling to the housekeeper, and telling her that there was company below who wished to take the round of the castle. The old dame courtesying low in a mysterious manner^g / led the way: the boy immediately retreated.

Calantha was much tired; her spirits had undergone a severe shock; and the sight of Linden and St. Clara, as she was still called, made an impression upon her she scarcely could account for. The gaiety of the dresses, the fineness of the evening, the chorus of voices laughing and singing as they marched along, indifferent apparently to their future fate – perhaps^h hardened and insensible to it – all made an impression which it is impossible the description of the scene can give; but long it dwelt in her remembrance. Unused to check herself in any feeling, she insisted upon remaining in front of the Castle, whilst the rest of the party explored its secret mysteries and recesses. 'I am sure you are frightened,'ⁱ

said Lord Trelawney; 'but perhaps you will have more cause than we: it looks very gloomy without, as well as within.'

They went, and she remained upon the / cliff, watching the calm sea, and the boats at a distance, as they passed and repassed from the fair.ª 'And can a few short years thus harden the heart?' she exclaimed, 'was St. Clara innocent, happy, virtuous? can^b one moment of error thus have changed her? Oh^c it is not possible. Long before the opportunity for evil presented itself, her uncontrouled passions must have misled her, and her imagination, wild and lawless, must have depraved her heart. Alice was innocent; he who first seduced her from peace, deceived her; but St. Clara was not of this character. I understand – I think I understand the feelings which impelled her to evil. Her image haunts me.^d I tremble with apprehension. Something within seems to warn me, and to say that, if I wander from virtue^e like her, nothing will check my course – all^f the barriers, that others fear to overstep, are nothing before me. God preserve me from sin! the sight of St. Clara fills me with alarm. Avondale. / where art thou? save me. My course is but just begun: who knows whither the path I follow leads? my will – my ungoverned will, has been hitherto, my only law.'

Upon the air at that moment she heard the soft notes of a flute. She listened attentively: – it ceased. There are times when the spirit is troubled –^g when the mind, after the tumult of dissipated and active life, requires rest and seeks to be alone. Then thoughts crowd in upon us so fast, that we hardly know how to bear them; conscience reflects upon every former action; and the heart within trembles, as if in dread of approaching evil. The scene around was calculated to inspire every serious reflection. The awful majesty of the ruined building, ill accorded with the loud laugh and the jests of the merry party now entering its walls. Once those walls had been, perhaps inhabited by beings thoughtless and gay.^h Where were they now? had they / memoryⁱ of the past? Knowledge of the present? or were^j they cold, silent, insensible as those deserted scenes? how perishable is human happiness! what recollection has the mind of any former state? in the eye of a creator can a mite, scarce^k visible, be worth either solicitude or anger? 'Vain the presumptuous hope,' said Calantha to herself. 'Our actions are unobserved by any but ourselves; let us enjoy what we can whilst we are here; death only returns us to the dust from whence we sprung; all hopes, all interests, all occupations, are vain: to forget is the first great science; and to enjoy, the only real object of life. What happiness is here^l below, but in love.'

So reasoned the unhappy victim of a false judgment and strong passion. I was blest; I am so no more. The world is a wilderness to me; and all that is in it, vanity and vexation of spirit.... Whilst yet indulging these fallacious opinions – whilst gazing on the western / turret, and watching the shadows as they varied on the walls, she again heard the soft notes of music. It seemed like the strains of other times, awakening in the heart remembrances of some former state long passed and changed. Hope, love and fond regret, answered alternately to the call. It was in the season of the year when the flowers bloomed: it was on a spot immortalized in ancient story, for deeds of prowess and of fame. Calantha turned her eyes upwards and beheld the blue vault of heaven without a cloud. The sea was of that glossy^a transparency – that shining brightness, the air of that serene calm that, had it been during the wintry^b months, some might have thought the halcyon was watching upon her nest, and breathing her soft and melancholy minstrelsy through the air.

Calantha endeavoured to rouse herself. She felt as if in a dream, and, hastily advancing to the spot from whence the sounds proceeded, she there beheld a / youth, for he had not the form or the look of manhood, leaning against the trunk of a tree, playing at intervals upon a flute, or breathing, as if from a suffering heart, the sweet melody of his untaught song. He started not when she approached: – he neither saw nor heard her – so light was her airy step, so fixed were his eyes and thoughts. She gazed for one moment^c upon his countenance – she^d marked it. It was one of those faces which, having once beheld, we never afterwards forget. It seemed as if the soul of passion had been stamped and printed upon every feature. The eye beamed into life as it threw up its dark ardent gaze, with a look nearly of inspiration, while the proud curl of the upper lip expressed haughtiness and bitter contempt; yet, even mixed with these fierce characteristic feelings, an air of melancholy and dejection shaded^e and softened every harsher expression. Such a^f countenance / spoke to the heart, and filled it with one vague yet powerful interest – so strong, so undefinable, that it could not easily be overcome.⁹

Calantha felt the power, not then alone, but evermore. She felt the empire, the charm, the peculiar charm, those features –^g that being must have for her. She could have knelt and prayed to heaven to realize the dreams,^h to bless the fallen angel in whose presence she at that moment stood, to give peace to that soul, upon which was plainly stamped the heavenly image of sensibility and genius. The air he had played was wild and plaintive: he changed it to one more harsh. She now distinctly heard the words he sung: –ⁱ

> This heart has never stoop'd its pride
>   To slavish love, or woman's wile;
> But, steel'd by war, has oft defy'd
>   Her craftiest art and brightest smile. /
>
> This mind has trac'd its own career,
>   Nor follow'd blind, where others trod;
> Nor, mov'd by love, or hope or fear,
>   E'er bent to man, or worshipp'd God.
>
> Then hope not now to touch with love,
>   Or in its chains a heart to draw,
> All earthly spells have fail'd to move;
>   And heav'n's whole terrors cannot awe:

> A heart, that like some mountain vast,
>   And cold with never-melting snow,
> Sees nought above, nor deigns to cast
>   A look away on aught below.

An emotion of interest – something she could not define, even to herself, had impelled Calantha to remain till the song was ended: a different feeling now prompted her to retire in haste. She fled; nor stopped, till she again found herself opposite the castle gate, where she had been left by her companions.

While yet dwelling in thought upon the singular being she had one moment / beheld[a] – whilst asking herself what meant this new,[b] this strange emotion, she found another personage by her side, and recognized, through a new disguise, her morning's acquaintance, Wailman the preacher, otherwise called Cowdel O'Kelly. This rencontre[c] gave an immediate turn to her thoughts.[d] She enquired of him if he were an inhabitant of Belfont Abbey? 'No, madam,' he answered, 'but of St. Alvin Priory.' She desired him to inform her,[e] whether any one resided there who sung in the manner she then described. 'Sure, then, I sing myself in that manner,' said the man, 'if that's all; and beside me, there be some who howl and wail, the like you never heard. Mayhap it is he you fell in with; if so, it must have moved your heart[f] to tears.'

'Explain yourself,' said Calantha eagerly. 'If he is unhappy, it is the same I have seen and heard. Tell me what sorrows have befallen him?' 'Sorrows! why enough too, to plague any / man. Has he not got the distemper?' 'The distemper!' 'Aye, Lady;[g] for did he not catch it sleeping in our dog-kennel, as he stood petrified there one night, kilt by the cold? When my Lord found him, he had not a house to his head then, it's[h] my belief; but now indeed he's got one, he's no wiser, having, as I think, no head to his house.' 'Och! it would surprise you how he howls and barks, whenever the moon shines bright. But here be those who fell on me at the fair. In truth I believe they be searching for the like of you.' /

CHAPTER IV.

The party from the castle now joined Calantha. They were in evident discomfiture. Their adventures had been rather less romantic than Lady Avondale's, and consequently had not given them such refined pleasure; for while she was attending to a strain of such enchanting sweetness, they had been forcibly detained in an apartment of the priory, unwillingly listening to very different music.

The housekeeper having led them through the galleries, the ladies, escorted by Count Gondimar, Lord Trelawney and Sir Everard, turned to examine some of the portraits, fretted cornices and high casements, till the dame who led the way, calling to them, shewed them a large dreary apartment hung with tapestry, and requested them to observe the / view from the window. 'It is here,' she said, 'in this chamber, that John de Ruthven drank hot blood from the skull of his enemy and died.' A loud groan, at that moment, proceeded from an inner chamber.[a] 'That must be the ghost,' said Lord Trelawney. His Lady shrieked. The dame, terrified at Lady Trelawney's terror, returned the shriek by a piercing yell, rushed from the room,[b] closing the heavy door in haste, which fastened with a spring lock, and left the company not a little disconcerted.

'We are a good number, however,' cried Frances, taking fast hold of her Lord, who smiled vacantly upon her. 'We certainly can match the ghost in point of strength: but it is rather unpleasant to be confined here till the old[c] woman recovers her senses.' Groans most piteous and terrible interrupted this remark – groans uttered as if in the agony of a soul ill at rest. Sophia grasped Sir Everard St. Clare's hand. Sir Everard / looked at Lady Margaret. Lady Margaret disdainfully returned the glance. 'I fear not,' she said; 'but we will assuredly have this affair examined. I shall speak to my brother the moment I return: there is possibly some evil concealed which requires investigation.' 'Hark! I hear a step,' said Frances. 'If I were not afraid of seeing a ghost,' cried Lord Trelawney, 'faith, I would climb up to that small grated window.'

'I fear no ghosts,' replied Count Gondimar, smiling. 'The sun has not set, therefore I defy them thus. – Only take care and hold the stool upon the table, that I may not break my neck.' 'What do you see?' 'A large room lighted by two candles: – would it were but a lamp.' 'Truly this is a fair beginning. – What is the matter now? – why what the devil is the matter? – If you come down so precipitately I cannot support you. Help! the Count is literally fainting.' It was true. 'A sudden dizziness – a palpitation' / – He only uttered these words and fell; a ghastly paleness overspread his face; the cold damps stood upon his forehead.

'This is the most unfortunate confirmation of the effects of terror upon an evil conscience,' exclaimed Sir Everard, 'that ever I beheld. I'll be bound there is not an Irish or English man here, that would have been so frightened.' 'It's[a] a dizziness, a mere fainting fit,' said Gondimar. 'Let me feel his pulse,' cried Sir Everard. 'Well, doctor?'[b] 'Well, sir he has no pulse left: – give him air.'[c] 'I am better now,' said Gondimar, with a smile,[d] as he revived. 'Was I ill enough for this?' – Sir[e] Everard called in. Lord Trelawney's curiosity engaged him to climb to the grated window; but the candles had been extinguished, probably, for all beyond the window was utter darkness.

Whilst some were assisting the Count, the rest had been vainly endeavouring to / open the door. A key was now heard on the outside; and the solemn boy entering, said to Lady Margaret, 'I am come to tell your honour,[f] that our dame being taken with the qualms and stericks, is no ways able of shewing you any further into the Priory.' 'I trust, however, that you will immediately shew us out of it, Sir,' said Gondimar. 'It not being her fault, but her extrame weakness,' continued the boy: 'she desires me to hope your honours will excuse her.' 'We will certainly excuse her; but,' added Lady Margaret, 'I must insist upon knowing from her, or from some of you, the cause of the groans we heard, and what all those absurd stories of ghosts can arise from. I shall send an order for the house to undergo an immediate examination, so you had better tell all you know.'

'Then, indeed, there be no mischief in them groans,' said the boy, who appeared indifferent whether the house were / examined or not. 'Its[g] only that gentleman as howls so, who makes them queer noises. I thought ye'd heard something stranger than that. There be more singular noises than he makes, many's the time.' 'Sirrah, inform me who inhabits this d – d Priory?' said Count Gondimar. 'What, you're recovered from your qualms and stericks, I perceive, though the old dame is so ill with them?' 'No jesting, Sir Everard. I must sift this affair to the bottom. Come, Sir, answer straightly, who inhabits this Priory?' 'Sure, Sir, indeed none as can get a bed in the Abbey.' 'You evade, young one: you evade my enquiry: to the point;[h] be plain.' 'That he can't help being,' said Lord Trelawney. 'Proceed, Sir, lead us as fast as possible out of these cold damp galleries; but talk as you go.' 'Like the cuckoo.' 'Lord Trelawney, your jests are mighty pleasant; but I have peculiar reasons for my enquiries.' 'And I for my jokes.' 'Come, / Sirrah, proceed: I shall say no more at present.' 'Do you like being here?' said Lady Trelawney, taking up the question. 'Well enough,' returned the stupid boy. 'I hear,' continued Frances, 'there are some who play upon the harp in the night, and sing so, that the country people round, say they are spell-bound.' 'Oh musha! there be strange things heard in these here old houses: one must not always believe all one hears.'

Count Gondimar and Lady Margaret, were engaged in deep discourse. 'I can hardly believe it,' said she.ª 'It is most true – most terribly true,' said Gondimar. 'I will question the boy myself,' she cried; 'he is subtle with all that appearance of clownish simplicity; but we shall gather something from him. Now, Lady Trelawney, give me leave to speak, and do you lead these gentlemen and ladies into the fresh air. Lady Augusta says she longs to behold living objects and day-light. I shall soon overtake / you. Come here.ᵇ I think, from what I have gathered, that St. Alvin Priory has not been inhabited by any of the Glenarvon family since the year ****: in that case, who has had charge of it?' 'None but Mr. Mackenzie and Dame since the old Lord de Ruthven's and his son the young Colonel's time. There's been no quality in these parts till now; but about three years and better, the young Lord sent some of his friends here, he being in Italy; and as they only asked for the ouldᶜ ruin, and did not wish to meddle with the castle, they have done their will there. The steward lets them bide.'

'Have they been here above three years?' 'Indeed then, that they've not, your honour; for sometimes they've all been here, and sometimes there's not a soul alive: but since last Michaelmas, there's been no peace for them.' 'Can you tell me any of their names?' 'All, I believe; for isn't there one calls himself Citizen Costolly, whom we take to be the / master, the real Lord; but he cares not to have it thought: only he's such a manner with him, one can't but think it. Then there's Mister O'Kelly, he as calls himself Citizen Wailman – the wallet; and there's another as sings, but has no name, a female;ᵈ and there's a gentleman cries and sobs, and takes care of a baby; and his name, I think, is Macpherson; then there's the old one as howls; and Mrs. Kellyᵉ O'Grady; and St. Clara, the prophetess; besides many more as come to feast and revel here.' 'And what right have they to be here?' 'Why to be sure, then, they've not any right at all; that's what we are all talking of; except them letters from my Lord; and they all live a strange wicked life under ground, the like of thaves; and whatever's the reason, for some time past, that young gentleman as was, is disappeared: nothing's known as to what's gone with him – only he's gone; and the child – och! the young master's here, and the / only one of 'em, indeed, as looks like a christian.' 'Is his name Clare of Costolly?' 'Ah! sure your honour knows him.'

Having reached the front porch, by the time the boy had gone through his examination, Lady Margaret perceiving O'Kelly, sent for him, and tried, vainly, to make him answer her enquiries more satisfactorily; which not being able to accomplish, she set forth to return home, in an extreme ill humour. Lord Trelawney rallied her about the ghost. Casting an angry glance at him, she refused positively to return home in either of the carriages; saying, she was resolved to walk back across the cliff, the short way. Some of the gentlemen proposed escorting her; but she haughtily refused them, and desired permission to be a few moments left to herself. They, therefore, re-entered their carriages, and returned without any further event.

Calantha was tired and grave during / the drive home; and, what may perhaps appear strange, she named not her adventure. 'It is himself – it must be,' 'Who?' said Lady Mandeville. Confused at having betrayed her own thoughts, – 'Young Linden,' she cried, looking out of the carriage; and then feigned sleep, that she might think over again and again on that countenance,[a] that voice, that being, she had one moment seen. /

CHAPTER V.

LADY MARGARET walking hastily off, had arrived near the Convent of St. Mary, as the last ray of the setting sun blazed in the west, and threw its golden light over the horizon. Close to the convent, is built the chapel where the young Marquis and all the family of Altamonte are interred. It stands upon a high barren cliff, separated by a branch of the sea from the village of Belfont, to which any one may pass by means of the ferry below. To the north of the chapel, as far as the eye can trace, barren heaths and moors, and the distant view of Belfont and St. Alvin Priory, present a cheerless aspect; while the other side displays the rich valley of Delaval, its groves, gardens and lake, with the adjacent wood. /

At this spot Lady Margaret arrived, as has been said, at sun-set. She thought she had been alone; but she heard a step closely following her: she turned round, and, to[a] her extreme surprize, beheld a man pursuing[b] her, and, just at that moment, on the point of attaining her. His black brows and eyes were contrasted with his grizzly hair; his laugh was hollow; his dress wild and tawdry. If she stopped for a moment to take breath, he stopped at the same time; if she advanced rapidly, he followed. She heard his steps behind, till passing near the convent he paused, rending the air with his groans, and his clenched fist repeatedly striking his forehead, with all the appearance of maniac fury, whilst with his voice he imitated the howling of the wind.

Terrified, fatigued and oppressed, Lady Margaret fled into the thickest part of the wood, and waited till she conceived the cause of her terror was removed. She soon / perceived, however, that the tall figure behind her was waiting for her reappearance. She determined to try the swiftness of her foot, and sought with speed to gain the ferry: – she durst not look behind:[c] – the heavy steps of her pursuer gained upon her: – suddenly she felt his hand upon her shoulder, as, with a shrill voice and loud laugh, he triumphed at having overtaken her. She uttered a piercing shriek; for on turning round she beheld. . . .

His name I cannot at present declare; yet this I will say:[d] [10] it was terrible to her to gaze upon that eye – so hollow, so wild, so fearful was its glance. From the sepulchre, the dead appeared to have arisen to affright her; and, scarce recovering from the dreadful vision, with a faltering step, and beating heart, she broke from that grasp – that cold hand – that dim-fixed eye – and gained with difficulty the hut of the fisherman, who placed her in safety on the other side of the cliff.

The castle bell had already summoned / the family; dinner awaited; and the duke having repeatedly enquired for Lady Margaret, was surprised to hear that she had returned home alone and after dusk. The servant, who informed him of this circumstance, said that her ladyship appeared extremely faint and tired; that her women attendants had been called; that they apprehended she was more ill than she would acknowledge. He was yet speaking, when,[a] with a blaze of beauty and even more than her usual magnificence of dress, she entered, apologised for the lateness of her appearance, said the walk was longer than she had apprehended, and, taking her brother's arm, led the way into the dining room. But soon the effort she had made, proved too great: – her colour changed repeatedly; she complained that the noise distracted her; she scarcely took any part in the conversation; and retiring early, sought a few hour's repose.

Mrs. Seymour accompanied her out,[b] / whilst the rest of those whose curiosity had been much excited in the morning, narrated their morning adventures[c] and enquired eagerly concerning Lord Glenarvon's character and mode of life. At the mention of his name, the colour rushed into Calantha's face. Was it himself she had seen? – She was convinced it was. That countenance verified all that she had heard against him: it was a full contradiction to all that Lady Trelawney had spoken in his favour; it expressed a capability of evil – a subtlety that led the eye of a stranger to distrust; but, with all, it was not easily forgotten. The address to the people of Ireland[d] which Lady Avondale had read before with enthusiasm, she read now with a new, an[e] undefinable sensation. She drew also those features – that countenance; and remembered the air he had sung and the tones of his voice. – She seemed to dive into the feelings of a heart utterly different from what she had ever yet observed:[f] a sort of / instinct gave her power at once to penetrate into its most secret recesses; nor was she mistaken. She heard,[g] with eager curiosity, every[h] anecdote narrated of him by the country esquires and gentry who dined at the castle; but she felt not surprised at the inconsistencies and absurdities repeated.[i] Others discredited what was said: she believed the worst; yet still the interest she felt was undiminished. It is strange: she loved not – she admired not that countenance; yet, by day, by night, it pursued her. She could not rest, nor write, nor read; and the fear of again seeing it,[j] was greater than the desire of doing so. She felt assured that it was Lord Glenarvon: – there was not a doubt left upon her mind respecting this circumstance. Mrs. Seymour saw that Calantha was pre-occupied: she thought that she was acquainted with the secret which disturbed Lady Margaret –[k] that horrid secret which maddened and destroyed her: / for, since her adventure at the Priory, Lady Margaret had been ill.

It was[a] not till after some days retirement, that she sent for Calantha, and when she visited her in her own apartment, she found her silent and trembling. 'Where is your boy?' she said.[b] 'He sleeps: would you that I should bring him you?' 'I do not mean your son: I mean that minion – that gaudy thing, you dress up for your amusement – that fawning insect[c] Zerbellini.' Calantha shuddered; for she knew that a mother could not thus speak of her child without suffering acutely. 'Has my pretty Zerbellini done any thing to deserve such unkind words from you? If so, I will chide him for it. Why do you frown? Zerbellini haste here: make your obeisance to Lady Margaret.' The boy approached: Lady Margaret fixed her eyes steadily upon him: the colour rushed into her cheek,[d] then left her pale, as the hue of death. '*Oimè si muoja!*' exclaimed / Zerbellini: '*Eccelenza si muoja;*'[11] and he leant forward to support her; but Lady Margaret moved not.

Many moments passed in entire silence. At last, starting as if from deep reflection, 'Calantha' she said[e] 'I know your heart too well to doubt its kindness: – the presence of this child,[f] will cause the misery of your father.' 'Of my father!' 'Do you not guess wherefore? I read his feelings yesterday: and can you my child[g] be less quick in penetrating the sentiments of those you love? do you not perceive that Zerbellini is of the very age and size – your lost – and – lamented brother would have been? ... and certainly not unlike the duchess.' She hesitated – paused – recovered herself. 'I would not for the world have you suggest this to a human being. I would not appear to have said – what you, out of an affectionate regard might – should – have considered.' – 'I am astonished: you quite amaze me,' replied Calantha; yet she too well guessed her feelings. /

You heard your father yesterday[h] say, how necessary it was for him to attend the general meeting at Belfast: he flies us to avoid this boy – the likeness – in short, oblige me, place him at the garden cottage, or at the Rector of Belfont's – he will attend to him. I am told you mean to leave your children with Mr. Challoner: if so, he might likewise keep this boy. His strong resemblance – his age – his manner – have given me already the acutest pain. – My brother will never demand any sacrifice of you; – but I, Lady Avondale, – I solicit it. –Shall be refused'? 'Dearest aunt, can you ask this? Zerbellini shall be immediately sent from the castle.' 'Oh no: such precipitate removal would excite curiosity.' 'Well then, allow me to place him, as you say, under the care of the Rector of Belfont and his wife – or – But how strange – why – did you never observe this before?'

'Calantha,' said Lady Margaret,[i] in / a hollow tone, 'it is the common talk: every one observes it: every eye fixes itself upon him, and seems to – to – to – reproach – to-morrow – morn – to-morrow morning, I must quit this place – business of importance calls me away – I hope to see you shortly: I shall return as soon as possible – perhaps I shall not go. – The trifle I now suggest, is solely for my brother's sake. – If you mention one word of this to any one, the sacrifice

I ask will lose its value. Above all, if the Count Gondimar is made a confidant.'
'Fear not: I shall request as of myself, that Zerbellini may be placed with my little son: but you cannot think how much you surprise me. My father has seen the boy so often; has spoken so frequently with him; has appeared so perfectly at his ease.'

'The boy,' said Lady Margaret, 'is the living picture of – in short I have dreamt a dreadful dream. Shall I confess my weakness, Calantha: I dreamt last night, / that I was sitting^a with a numerous and brilliant assembly, even in this very castle; and of a sudden, robed in the white vestments of an angel, that boy appeared – I saw his hand closely stealing behind – he had a dagger in it – oh it made me sick –^b and coming towards me – I mean towards your father – he stabbed him. – These^c phantasies shew an ill constitution – but, for a short time, send the child away, and do not expose my weakness – do not love.^d I have many sorrows –^e my nerves are shattered – bear with me –^f you know not, and God forbid you should ever know, what it is to labour under the pressure of guilt – guilt? aye,^g – and such as that brow of innocence, that guileless generous heart, never can comprehend. 'My aunt, for God sake, explain yourself.' Lady Margaret smiled. 'Oh not such guilt either, as to excite such looks as these: only I have suffered my heart to wander, child; and I have been punished.' /

Calantha was less surprised at this conversation, from remembering the secret Gondimar had communicated, than she otherwise must have been; but she could not understand what had given rise to this paroxysm of despair at that^h particular moment. A singular circumstance now occurred, which occasioned infinite conjecture to all around. Every morning, as soon as it was light, and every evening at dusk, a tall old man in a tattered garb, with a wild and terrible air, seated himself in front of the castleⁱ windows, making the most lamentable groans, and crying out in an almost unintelligible voice, 'Woe, on woe, to the family of Altamonte.' The Duke was no sooner apprised of this circumstance, than he ordered the supposed maniac to be taken up;^j but Lady Margaret implored, entreated and even menaced, till she obtained permission from her brother to give this wretched object his liberty.

Such an unusual excess of charity – / such sudden, and violent commiseration of^k a being who appeared to have no other view than the persecution and annoyance of her whole family, was deemed strange; but when they no longer were molested by the presence of the fanatic, who had denounced their ruin, they ceased to converse about him, and soon the whole affair was forgotten. Calantha indeed remembered it; but a thousand new thoughts diverted her attention, and a stronger interest led her from it. /

CHAPTER VI.

The Rector of Belfont had willingly permitted the little Zerbellini to be place under his wife's care. The distance from thence to the castle was short; and Calantha had already sent her children there for the benefit of sea-bathing. On returning one day thence,[a] she called upon Gerald Mac Allain, who had absented himself from the castle, ever since Mr. Buchanan had appeared there. She found him mournfully employed in looking over some papers and drawings, which he had removed to his own habitation. Upon seeing Lady Avondale he arose, and pointing[b] to the drawings, which she recognized: 'Poor Alice,' he said, 'these little remembrances tell me of happier days, and make me sad; but when I see you, my Lady, I forget my sorrows.' / Linden's cottage was at a very little[c] distance from Gerald Mac Allain's. Calantha now informed him that she had met young Linden at the fair, and had wished to speak to him;[d] but that she did not immediately remember him, he was so altered. Gerald said 'it was no use for her to speak to him, or for any one else, he was so desperate-like;[e] and,' added he, 'Alice's misconduct has broke all our hearts: we never meet now as formerly; we scarce dare look at each other as we pass.'

'Tell me, Gerald,' said Calantha, 'since you have spoken to me on this melancholy subject, what is the general opinion about Alice? Has Linden no idea of what has become of her? – had he no suspicion, no doubt of her, till the moment when she fled?' 'Oh yes, my Lady,' said the old man, 'my poor girl estranged herself from him latterly; and when Linden was obliged to leave her to go to the county of Leitrim[f] for Mr. / O'Flarney, during his absence, which lasted six weeks, he received a letter from her, expressing her sorrow that she never could belong to him. Upon his return he found her utterly changed; and in a few weeks after, she declined his further visits; only once again consenting to see him. It was on the very morning before my Lady Margaret conveyed her away from the castle.'

'But did you never suspect that things were going on ill before? – did Linden make no attempt to see her at the Doctor's? It seems strange that no measures should have been taken before it was too late.' 'Alas! my dear young lady, you do not know how difficult it is to suspect and chide what we love dearly. I had given up my child into other hands; she was removed entirely from my humble sphere;

and whilst I saw her happy, I could not but think her deserving; and when she became otherwise, she was miserable, and it was not the moment to / shew her any severity. Indeed, indeed, it was impossible for me to mistrust or chide one so above me as my Alice.ª As to young Linden, it turned his mind. I walked to his father's house, ill as I was, just to shake hands with him and see him, as soon as I was told of what had passed. The old gentleman, Cyrel'sᵇ father, could not speak. The mother wept as soon as she beheld me; but there was not one bitter word fell from either, though they knew it would prove the ruin of the young man, their son, and perhaps his death.'

'From that time,ᶜ till the present,' continued Gerald, 'I seldom see Linden; he always avoids me. He altered very much, and took to hard drinking and bad company; his mind was a little shaken; he grew very slack at his duty; and listed, we suppose, with that same gang, which seduced my two poor boys from their allegiance and duty. He was reprimanded and punished by his commander; / but it seems all one,ᵈ for Mr. Challoner was telling me, only a few days since, that in the last business there with Squire O'Flarney,ᵉ Linden was taken notice of by the justice. There's no one can save him, he seems so determined-like on his own ruin; and they say,ᶠ its the cause why the old father is on his death-bed at this present time.ᵍ There is no bitterness of heart like that which comes from thankless children. They never find out, till it is too late, how parents loved them: – but it was not her fault – no – I don't blame her – (he knit his brow) – no – I don't blame her. – Mr. Buchanan is no child of our own house, though he fills the place of that gracious infant which it pleased the Lord to take to himself. Mr. Buchanan is the son of a strange father: – I cannot consider him as one of our own –ʰ so arbitrary: – but that's not the thing.'

'Gerald,' said Calantha, 'you are not sure that Buchanan is the culprit: we / should be cautious in our judgments.' 'Oh, but I am sure, and I care not to look on him; and Linden, they say, menaces to revenge on the young lord, my wrongs and his own; but his old father begs him for God's sake to be peaceable. Perhaps, my Lady, you will look on the poor gentleman: what though 'tis a dying man – you'll be gratified to see him, there is such a calm upon his countenance.' 'Must he die?' 'Why, he's very precarious-like: – but your noble husband, the young Lord Avondale, is very good to him – he has done all a man and a soldier could do to save him.' 'I too will call,' said Calantha, to hide from Gerald how much she was affected; 'and, as to you, I must entreat as a favour, that you will return to the castle: to-morrow is Harry's birth-day:ⁱ and it will not be a holiday, my father says, if you are not, as you were wont to be, at the head of the table with all the tenants.' 'I will come,' said Gerald, 'if it were only on / account of my Lord's remembering me;ʲ and all the blessings of the land go with him, and you, and his noble house, till the end of time, and with the young Lord of Glenarvon beside, who saved Roy and Conal from a shameful death – that he did.'

'But you forget,' said Calantha, smiling, 'that, by your own account, he was the first to bring them there.'ª 'By my heart, but he's a noble spirit for all that;ᵇ and he has my good wishes, and those of many beside.' As he spoke, his eye kindled with enthusiasm. Calantha's heart beat high: she listened with eager interest. 'He's as generous as our own,' continued he;ᶜ 'and if he lets his followers take a pig or two from that rogue there, Squire Flarney, does not he give half he has to those in distress? If I could ever meet him face to face, I'd tell him the same; but we never know when he's among us; for sure, there'sᵈ St. Clara the prophetess, he wentᵉ to see her once, they say, and she / left her aunt the Abbess, and the convent, and all the nuns, and went off after him, as mad as the rest. Och! you'd bless yourself to see how the folks crowd about him at the season, but they're all gone from these parts now, in hopes of saving Linden,ᶠ I'm told; for you know, I suppose,ᵍ that he's missing, and if he's deserted, its said they are sureʰ to shoot him on account of the troubles.'

'Three times there have been meetings in that cleft there,' continued Gerald, pointing towards the Wizzard'sⁱ Glen: 'it was that was the first undoing of Miss St. Clare: they tell me she's all for our being delivered from our tyrants; and she prophecies so, it would do you good to hear her. Oh, they move along, a thousand at a time,ʲ in a silence would surprise you – just in the still night, and you can scarce hear them tread as they pass; but I know wellᵏ when they're coming, and there is not oneˡ of us who live here about the town, would betray / them,ᵐ though the reward offered is very stupendous.'

'But see, here are some of the military coming'ⁿ ... 'That officer is General Kennedy,' said Lady Avondale, approaching towards him: 'he is not a tyrant at least.' Asᵒ she said this, she bowed to him, for she knew him well. He often dined at the Castle.ᵖ He was saying a few words to her upon common uninteresting topics, when, a soldier beckoning to him, two horsemen appeared. – 'He's found,'ᑫ said one: 'there is no doubt of his guilt; and twenty other names are on the list.' 'I trust in God it is not Linden, of whom you are speaking,' said Calantha. General Kennedy made no answer: he only bowed to her, as if to excuse himself; and retired.

Calantha observed a vast number of people assembled on the road, close to the village. Gerald Mac Allain could scarcely support himself. She enquired / what they were waiting for. 'To see the deserters,' they answered. It was women, children, parents who spoke: some wept aloud; others stood in silent anguish; many repeated the name of him in whom they took deepest interest, asking if his wasʳ of the number. Linden's she heard most frequently. 'Ill luck to the monsters! – ill luck to the men of blood!' was vociferated the whole way she went. 'This will kill the old man,' said Gerald: 'it will be his death: he has been all night fearing it, ever since Linden has been missing.'

The crowd, seeing Calantha, approached in all directions. 'Oh beg our king, your father, to save them,' said one: 'Jesus reward you:' and they knelt and prayed to her. She was too much affected to answer. Some of the officers approached her, and advised her to retire. 'The crowd will be immense,' they said: 'your Ladyship had / better not remain to witness this heart-breaking scene.'ᵃ "Twenty names are on the list,' continued the officer, 'all deserted, as soon as Linden did. Mercy, in this instance, will be weakness: too much has already been shewn.' /

CHAPTER VII.

CALANTHA returned home with a heavy heart; and spoke to Lord Avondale and her father. They both intreated her not to interfere. The moment indeed was alarming and eventful; whatever measures were necessary, it was not for her to judge; and while enthusiasm in the cause of liberty beguiled some, it was, she felt it was, the duty of a woman to try and soften[a] and conciliate every thing.[b] Linden's fate was peculiarly unfortunate, and Lord[c] Avondale generously interested himself for him. Had money been able to purchase his release, there was no sum he would not have offered. They heard with[d] the deepest regret, that it was a case where mercy could not be shewn, without apprehending the most fatal effects from it. Linden and Seaford had together entered / the militia not above three years back. Linden, an only son, was now in his twentieth year, and Seaford, was scarce eighteen. Their example was deemed the more necessary for the general safety, as so many in the same regiment had deserted upon hearing of their disaffection. In the month of December last, they had all taken the treasonable oaths; and their rash conduct and riotous proceedings had already more than once incurred[e] the severity of the law.

Linden and two others had been accused, and afterwards pardoned on a former occasion: their names had been likewise erased from the list of offenders. This second breach of faith was deemed unpardonable. Mercy, it was supposed, would but appear like weakness and alarm; all intercessions[f] were utterly fruitless; they were tried, found guilty and condemned. Linden was so much beloved by his companions, that several attempts were made, even by his fellow-soldiers and comrades, to rescue[g] him from / the hands of justice; but he disdained to be so released; and when he heard of the tumult his condemnation had excited, he asked his captain's permission to be spared the last bitter conflict of walking through his own native town. The request was denied him.

On the 18th of May, at the hour of four, the time appointed to assemble, twenty-three men, who had taken part in the riot, were called out. The regiment, after this, slowly advanced in solemn procession through the town, followed by the cavalry, and all the horse artillery. The streets were thronged – the windows were crowded – not a word was spoken; but the sobs and cries of friends, parents and old acqaintance, who came out to take a last farewell, were heard. After passing through Belfont, they turned to the high road, and continued the march until they reached the plains above[a] Inis Tara, about two miles from the town. /

Linden and Seaford were then brought forward with a strong escort. They continued silent and firm to the last. Just as the pause was made, before the command was given that they should kneel, the mother of Linden, supported by Mac Allain, forced her way through the crowd, and implored permission to take a last farewell of her son. The officer desired that she might pass; but the crowd was so great that it was with difficulty she could arrive at the spot: – when there, she only once shook hands with the young man, and said she had brought him his father's blessing: – he made no answer, but appeared very deeply affected. He had shewn the most deliberate courage till that hour. It now forsook him, and he trembled excessively.

'Thank God I am spared this,' said his companion: 'I have no mother left.' The signal was immediately given to fire; and the party prepared to do their duty. A troop of horse at that moment, in the / green uniform of the national guards, appeared from an ambush, and a desperate struggle ensued. The mutineers set up a terrible yell during the combat. The inhabitants, both of the town and country, joined them in every direction. Lord Avondale and many other officers present came up to the assistance of General Kennedy's small force, and soon restored order. The party of horse were put to flight. The colonel of the regiment immediately ordered a court-martial; and three prisoners, who were taken with[b] Seaford and Linden, were executed[c] on the spot.

In the skirmish, the young man who headed the party of the horse, and exposed[d] himself most eagerly to rescue Linden, was wounded in the left arm: his person was described; the circumstance was mentioned; and a high reward was offered for his head. It was supposed by many that he was Lord Glenarvon.

The severity of these proceedings / struck an immediate panic throughout the disaffected. The inhabitants of the town of Belfont arrayed themselves in black. A long and mournful silence succeeded; and few there were who penetrated, under[e] the veil of submissive acquiescence, the spirit of rebellion and vengeance, which was preparing to burst forth. Gerald Mac Allain, forgetful of his wrongs, appeared at the castle; Lady St. Clare wrote the most penitent letter[f] to Sir Everard; and with her two daughters Jessica and Laura, entreated permission to return. Every one of the tradesmen and farmers of any respectability took[g] their names from the new club, opposite[h] Sir Everard's house; and a sort of mournful tranquillity and terror seemed to reign throughout.

A few days after this melancholy transaction, Linden's mother died; and as Calantha was returning from Belfont, she met the crowd who had followed her to the grave. They all passed her in silence, / nor gave her one salutation, or smile of acknowledgment, as on other occasions; yet they were her father's own tenants, and most of their countenances she remembered from childhood. When she mentioned this circumstance at the castle, she was informed that Lord Avondale's having taken an active part against the party who had come forward to save the deserters, was the cause of this.ᵃ

To such heights,ᵇ at this time, was the spirit of party carried. The whole kingdom, indeed,ᶜ was in a state of ferment and disorder. Complaints were made, redress was claimed, and the people were everywhere mutinous and discontented. Even the few of their own countrymen, who possessed the power, refused to attend to the grievances and burthens of which the nation generally complained, and sold themselves for hire, to the English government. Numerous absenteesᵈ had drawn great part of the money out / of the country; oppressive taxes were continued; land was let and sub-let to bankers and stewards of estates,ᵉ to the utter ruin of the tenants; and all this caused the greatest discontent.ᶠ

Some concessions were now granted in haste – some assurances of relief made;ᵍ but the popular spirit of indignation, once excited, was not to be allayed by the same means which had, perhaps, prevented its first rise. The time for conciliation was past. A foreign enemy lost no opportunity of adding to the increasing inward discontent. The friends of government had the power of the sword and the weight of influence on their side; but the enemies were more numerous, more desperate, more enthusiastic. The institution of political clubs, the combination of the United Irishmen, for the purpose of forwarding a brotherhood of affection, a communion of rights, amongst those of every different persuasion, even aʰ military force was now attempted; / and the constant cry of all the inhabitants of either town or country was a total repeal of the penal statutes, the elective franchise, reform of parliament, and commutation of tythes.¹²

Whilst, however, the more moderate with sincerity imagined, that they were upholding the cause of liberty and religion; the more violent,ⁱ who had emancipated their minds from every restraint of prejudice or principle, did not conceal that the equalization of property, and the destruction of rank and titles was their real object. The revolutionary spirit was fast spreading, and since the appearance of Lord Glenarvon, at Belfont, the whole of the county around was inʲ a state of actual rebellion. /

CHAPTER VIII.

GLENARVON seemed, however, to differ in practice from his principles; for whilst many of those who had adopted the same language had voluntarily thrown off their titles, and divided their property amongst their partizans, he made a formal claim for the titles[a] his grandfather had forfeited; and though he had received no positive assurance that his claim would be considered,[b] he called himself by that name alone, and insisted upon[c] his followers addressing him in no other manner.[13] This singular personage,[d] of whom so many, for a long period, had heard the strangest reports, whom many[e] imagined to be dead, and who seemed, whenever he appeared, to make no light impression upon all those with whom he conversed, had passed his youth in a foreign country, / and had only twice visited the abode of his ancestors until the present year.

It was amidst the ruins of ancient[f] architecture, and the wild beauties of Italian scenery, that his splendid genius and uncommon faculties were first developed. Melancholy, unsocial, without a guide, he had centered upon[g] himself every strong interest, and every aspiring hope. Dwelling ever in the brilliant regions of fancy, his soul turned with antipathy from the ordinary cares of life. He deeply felt the stigma that[h] had been cast upon his family in the person of his grandfather, who, from the favourite of a changing prince,[i] had become the secret accomplice of a bloody conspiracy. The proofs of his guilt were clear; his death was a death of shame; and the name of traitor was handed down with the coronet to which his only surviving heir so eagerly aspired.

By his nearest friends he was now / called Glenarvon; and so jealous did he appear of his rank, that he preferred disguise, straits and difficulties, to a return to his own country without those titles, and that fortune, which he considered as his due. One object of interest succeeded another; a life of suspense was preferred to apathy; and the dark counsels of unprincipled associates, soon led one, already disloyal in heart, to the very brink of destruction. Flushed with the glow of intemperate heat, or pale with the weariness of secret woe, he vainly sought in a career of pleasure, for that happiness which his restless mind prevented him from enjoying.[j]

Glenarvon[k] had embraced his father's profession, wherein he had distinguished himself by his courage and talent; but to obey another was irksome; and the length of time which must elapse before he could obtain the command of a ship, soon disgusted him with the service. He / plunged, therefore, into all the tumults of dissipation, to which a return to Rome and Florence invited him.

He gave[a] up his days and nights to every fierce excess; and soon the high spirit of genius was darkened, the lofty feelings of honor were debased, and the frame and character sunk equally dejected under the fatigue of vigils and revels, in which reason and virtue had no share. Intervals of gloom succeeded, till, stimulated again, his fallen countenance betrayed a disappointed heart; and he fled from unjoyous feasts and feverish hopes to lowliness and sullen despair. He had been wronged, and he knew not how to pardon: he had been deceived, and he existed henceforward, but to mislead others. His vengeance was dark and sudden – it was terrible. His mind, from that hour, turned from the self-approving hope, the peace of a heart at rest.[b]

The victim of his unfortunate[c] attachment / had fallen a prey to the revengeful jealousy of an incensed husband; but her death was not more sudden, more secret, than that of the tyrant who had destroyed her. Every one knew by whose hand the fair and lovely Fiorabella had perished; but no eye bore witness against the assassin, who, in the depths of night had immediately revenged her loss. The murderer and the murdered were both alike involved in the impenetrable veil of mystery. The proud and noble family who had been injured, had neither the power, nor the inclination to seek redress. Lord Glenarvon was seen no more at Florence: he had been the cause of this tragic scene. It afflicted his generous heart when he reflected upon the misery he had occasioned; but not even his bitterest enemy could have suspected him of deeper guilt. His youth was untainted by the suspicion of crime, and the death of Giardini, with[d] / greater show of justice, was affixed[e] to another, and a more dangerous hand.

Fascinated with the romantic splendour of ideal liberty, and intent upon flying from the tortures of remembrance, which the death of his mistress, and the unpleasant circumstances attending Giardini's murder must naturally excite, he[f] had visited Ireland in the spring of the year . . . . , and had remained there some months, unknown even to his adherents, who flocked around him, attracted by his eloquence, and easily won[g] by his address. One only victim returned with him in his voluntary exile,[h] from his native land. One only miserable enthusiast devoted herself to his fortunes, and accompanied him in his flight. O'Kelly, the son of a tenant of his father's[i] recognized his youthful lord, and early ingratiated himself into his favour.

With this sole attendant, and the unhappy girl who had renounced her country / and her virtue for his sake, he departed,[j] nor was seen again at St. Alvin Priory till the present year.

Indeed the report of his death was so often affirmed;[k] that when he again presented himself, so changed in manner and in form, before his adherents, they questioned one with another whether he was in reality their lord. 'I am not what I seem,' he would frequently say; 'I am not him whom you take me for.'

Strange things were rumoured concerning this Glenarvon.ᵃ There was a man in his service who had returned with him, who spoke to none, who answered no enquiries, who had never before been seen with him in his former visits. It was said that he knew many things if he durst but utter them. All feared and avoided this man. His name was Macpherson, the same whom Gondimar had seen in town; but all felt irresistably attracted by his youthful master. / Glenarvon's projects – his intentions were now but too generally suspected; – it was a critical moment; and his presence at that particular time, in Ireland, occasioned many conjectures.ᵇ /

CHAPTER IX.

In this his second visit to his native country, Glenarvon desired his servant, O'Kelly, to find a person of respectability who would take charge of a child, then only in his second year. Clare of Costolly was his name; but whether the boy was the son of Lord Glenarvon, or some little favourite who, for the moment, had obtained his interest, none knew, or[a] durst enquire.

Indeed, the impenetrable mystery which surrounded Lord Glenarvon was involved in a deeper shade of concealment at this time, than[b] at any former period; for scarce had he set foot in his new habitation,[c] when a singular and terrific inmate appeared also at the Priory – a maniac! who was however welcomed[d] with the rest of the strange assemblage, and a room / immediately allotted for his reception. In vain the affrighted nurse remonstrated; the maniac's eyes were fixed upon the child, with frantic wildness; and Glenarvon, deaf to her entreaties, permitted Clare to attend upon the unwelcome stranger and saw him in his arms without alarm.

Even in his most dreadful paroxysms, when all others were afraid of approaching him, Glenarvon would calmly enter into his chamber, would hear his threats unawed, – would gaze on him, as if it gave him delight to watch the violence of misguided passion; to hear the hollow laugh of ideotsy, or fix the convulsed eye of raving insanity.

That which was disgusting or terrific to man's nature, had no power over Glenarvon. He had looked upon the dying and the dead; had seen the tear of agony without emotion; had heard the shriek of despair, and felt the hot blood as it flowed from the heart of a murdered / enemy, nor turned from the sickening sight – Even the storms of nature could not move Glenarvon. In the dark night, when the tempest raged around and the stormy ocean beat against the high impending cliffs, he would venture forth, would listen to the roaring thunder without fear, and watch the forked lightning as it flashed along the sky.

The rushing winds but seemed to sooth his perturbed spirit; and the calm of his brow remained unaltered in every changing scene. Yet it was the calm of hopeless despair, when passion, too violent to shew itself by common means, concentrates itself at once around the heart, and steels it against every sentiment of mercy.

Who had dared to enquire of that eye the meaning of its glance? or who had trusted to the music of that soft voice, when it breathed forth vows of tenderness and love? or who, believing in the light / of life which beamed upon that countenance, had considered the sportive jests of fancy – the brilliant sallies of that keen wit as the overflowing testimony of a heart at rest? None – none believed or trusted in Glenarvon. – Yet thousands flocked around and flattered him; amidst this band of ruffians, this lawless unprincipled gang, the recluse of Glenaa – the lovely, but misguided Elinor was now too often seen. She was the spirit and soul of the merry[a] party: her wit enlivened; her presence countenanced; her matchless beauty attracted. Scarce in her sixteenth year, the pride of her family, the wonder and ornament of the whole country, she forsook her solitude and hopes of heaven – she left the aunt, who had fostered and cherished her from childhood, to become avowedly the mistress of Glenarvon. On horse, or on foot, she accompanied him. In the attire of a boy she unblushingly followed / his steps! his former favourites were never even named, or alluded to – his present mistress occupied all his attention.

When St. Clara described the sufferings of her country, every heart melted to compassion, or burned with indignation; but when her master, when Glenarvon played upon her harp, or sung the minstrelsy of the bards of other times, he inspired the passions which he felt, and inflamed the imagination of his hearers to deeds of madness – to acts of the most extravagant absurdity.[b] Crowds followed upon his steps;[c] yet it was melancholy to see them pass – so fair, so young and yet so utterly hardened and perverted. Who could behold her,[d] and not compassionate her fate? What was to become of her when Glenarvon had ceased to love; and did he love? – Never: in the midst of conquests, his heart was desolate; in the fond embrace of mutual affection, he despised the victim of his art. /

Of all the friends, flatterers and followers, he had gained by his kindness, and lost by his caprice, not one remained to fill, in his bosom, that craving void which he himself had made. Wherever he appeared, new beauty attracted his worship, and yielded to his power;[e] yet he valued not the transient possession, even whilst smiling upon the credulous being who had believed in his momentary affection. Even whilst soothing her with promises and vows, which he meant not for one hour to perform, he was seeking the means of extricating himself from her power – he was planning his escape from the thraldom of her charms? Was he generous? Aye, and prodigal by nature; but there was a part of his character which ill accorded with the rest;[f] it was a spirit of malignity if wounded, which never rested[g] till it had satisfied its vengeance. An enemy, he could have pardoned and have loved; but he knew not how to bear with or forgive a friend. /

His actions appeared the immediate result of impulse; but his passions were all subject to his controul, and there was a systematic consistency even in his most irregular conduct. To create illusions, and raise affection in the breasts of others, has been the delight of many: to dispel the interest he had created was Glenarvon's care. Love he had studied as an art: he knew it in all its shades and gradations; for he had traced its progress in his own and many another breast.[a] Of knowledge and wisdom, he had drank deep at the fountain head, nor wanted aught that could give liveliness and variety to his discourse.

He was, besides, a skilful flatterer, and knew in what weak part, he best might apply his power. But the sweetness of his praise, could only be exceeded by the bitterness of his contempt – the venomed lash of his deadly wit.

That in which Glenarvon most prided himself – that in which he most excelled, / was the art of dissembling. He could turn and twine so near the truth, with[b] more than Machiavelian subtlety, that none could readily detect his falsehood; and when he most appeared frank and unguarded, then he most deceived. Falsehood and craft were stamped upon his countenance, written upon his brow, marked in his words, and scarce concealed beneath the winning smile which often-times[c] played upon his lips.

'If I could but see him once,' said Lady Augusta, 'I should be satisfied; but to hear his name from morning till night – to have every fault, folly, nay even crime attributed to him by one party, and every virtue, charm and fascination given him by the other, – it is enough to distract women in general, and me in particular. Is there no mercy for curiosity? I feel I shall do something absurd, extremely absurd, if an interview is not contrived.' 'Nothing can be more easy,' said the Duke: 'you shall / dine with him, at the next public day. I have already sent him a card of invitation.' 'Under what title?' 'To Captain de Ruthven.' 'He will assuredly not come,' said Lady Trelawney. 'That I think probable,' said the Duke, laughing. 'The malicious affirm that his arm is in a sling; and if so, his appearance just at present would be unwise.' The conversation soon took another turn; and Lord Avondale entering, informed Calantha that he had a letter from Sir Richard, and must immediately[d] join him at Cork. /

CHAPTER X.

ADMIRAL Buchanan and Sir Richard Mowbray[a] had, in the month of January, returned to England, where they had received the thanks of the Lower House for their distinguished conduct and assistance[b] on the memorable 4th[c] of June. The ships had been now ordered into harbour to undergo some trifling repairs, and the Admirals had been commanded to take their station at Cork.[d] The enthusiasm with which the heroes were greeted on their return, did honour to the feelings of the Irish nation. They were invited to every house in the neighbourhood; and *fêtes* and balls were given to shew them respect. The Duke and Lord Avondale went forward to receive them.

Commodore Emmet, an old acquaintance[e] who resided at Cork, sent to offer / his house, not only to them, but to the whole party at Castle Delaval; if they could make up their minds[f] to accept Sir George's invitation, and dine on board the Royal William on the 4th[g] of June, in commemoration of that day and its success. There were few, if any, of those invited who refused; but none accepted the invitation with so much enthusiasm as Calantha. The letter from Sir George Buchanan to Lady Margaret,[h] was as follows: –

'Cork, June 1st,[i] 1796.

'My dear Lady Margaret,

'In answer to a letter which I received this morning, dated May 29th, ult.[j] I request the honour of your Ladyship's company on board the Royal William, now in harbour at the Cove. The Duke and the rest of his family and party have already promised me this favour, and I am not prepared to accept from yourself any denial on account of those circumstances / to which you allude, and which, I entreat you sincerely to believe are, on my part, utterly forgotten. Let me request you, then, to banish from your memory every trifling disagreement, and to meet me, upon an occasion so flattering as is the present to my feelings and those of our friends, with the good-will and kindness you will ever find in the heart of your Ladyship's most obedient and affectionate brother and servant.

'GEORGE BUCHANAN.'

In consequence of this invitation, Lady Margaret and the rest of the Duke's family set out on the morning of the 3rd,ᵃ and arrived about the hour of dinner at Commodore Emmet's – a large brick building about a quarter of a mile beyond the town of Cork. The Duke and Lord Avondale, and their loquacious host, had been waiting some time, it appeared, in much anxiety.[b] The latter gave to each the / most cordial welcome; boasted that he could lodge them all; talked incessantly, as he shewed them to their apartments; entreated them not to dress, as dinner awaited; and left them, assuring each[c] that they were the exact image of the Duke, whom he concluded to be, like the Patriarchs of old, the father of the whole company. His voice murmured on as he descended the stairs, whilst Cassandra and Eloise,[d] his daughters, appeared to offer their services in his place.

The dining-room was small; the guests were numerous; the table was crowded with huge pieces of meat: the Commodore talked incessantly; his children, his servants, his brother, seemed all gifted alike with the same spirit of activity: it was incessant bustle, hurry, noise and contrivance. Music, cards, and tricks of every kind were displayed during the evening; and in the morning, long before the sun had arisen, carpenters, / mechanics, ship-builders,[e] and cooks, awoke the guests by the noise of their respective pursuits.

Sir George Buchanan had sent to request the Duke's company at an early hour on the morrow. The day proved fair, the boats were ready, and they set forth on their expedition in high spirits. Many ships and smaller vessels were spread over the harbour; and bands of music played as they passed. The beauty of the cove[f] of Cork, the trees bending to the water side, the fortress, and the animated picture which a mercantile city presents, – delighted all. But feelings of enthusiasm kindled, in every heart, when they approached the Royal William, and beheld its venerable commander. The sea was rough, and the spray of the waves was at times blown over the boat. The Miss Emmets thought of their new dresses; Sophia of danger; and Calantha of the glory of thus proudly riding over the billowy ocean. /

Lady Margaret, though silent, was more deeply agitated: – her mind recurred in thought to scenes long past. She was now to behold, after a lapse of many years, her husband's brother, whom she had treated with the most marked indignity, and for whom she had vainly attempted to feel contempt. He had ever conducted himself towards her with courteous, though distant civility; but had yet shewn the most decided disapprobation of her conduct. When she had last beheld him, she was in the full splendour of youth and beauty, surrounded by an admiring world, and triumphant in the possession of every earthly enjoyment. Time had but little changed the majesty of her form; but something worse than time had stamped upon her countenance an expression never to be effaced; while her marked brow assumed an air of sullen pride and haughty reserve:[g] as she ascended from the boat into the ship,[h] she gazed upon the long forgotten features of / her brother; and she seemed to be deeply affected. Age had bleached his once dark locks; but he was still unimpaired in mind and form. He bent lowly down to receive her: she felt him clasp her to his bosom; and,ª overcome by this unexpected kindness, her tears streamed upon his hand: – he, too, could have wept; but,ᵇ recovering himself, with a commanding air, he came forward to receive his other guests.

The ship was in the highest order; the feast prepared was magnificent; and when the Duke stood up and bowed with grace to drink the Admiral's health, the sailors cheered, and the toast was repeated from the heart by every individual. But he, though greatly affected and pleased at the homage shewn him, bowed to the Duke, returning him the compliment; and afterwards, drinking the health of Sir Richard Mowbray,ᶜ said, that he owed every thing to his assistance – that, in the glorious action of the 4th,ᵈ his ship / had conferred new honours on the British Navy, and he had received the commendation of Admiral Howe.ᵉ

At that name, every individual arose. The name of Howe was repeated from mouth to mouth with an expression of exalted admiration; his applauses were spokenᶠ by every tongue; and many an eye that had never shewn weakness, till that moment, filled with tears at the name of their venerable, their dear commander. Captain Emmet, during this scene, was employed in eating voraciously of whatever he could lay hands on. Miss Emmet, who thought it a great honor to converse with a lord, had seated herself by the side of Lord Avondale, narrating her own adventures, freely stating her own opinions, and pleased with herself and every one present; while her father likewise talked at the other end of the table, and Admiral Buchanan laughed heartily, but good humouredly at his friend's oppressive eloquence. /

Suddenly Lord Avondale turned to Calantha and asked her if she were ill? She knew not, she could not define the sort of pain and joy she felt at that moment. Her eyes had long been fixed upon one who took no part in this convivial scene – whose pale cheek and brow expressed much of disappointed hope, or of joyless indifference. He had that youthful, nay boyish air, which renderedᵍ this melancholy the more singular. – It was not affected, though his manner had in it nothing of nature;ʰ but the affectation was rather that of assumed respect for those he cared not for, and assumed interest in topics to which he hardly attended, than the reverse. He even affected gaiety; but the heart's laugh never vibrated from his lips; and, if he uttered a sentence, his eye seemed to despise the being who listened with avidity to his observation. It was the same, – oh! yes, it was, indeed, the same, whom Calantha had one moment beheld at St. Alvin Priory. /

His face, his features, were the same, it is true;ⁱ but a deeper shade of sadness now overspread them; and sorrow and disappointment had changed the glow of boyish health to a more pallid hue. What! in a month? it will be said. – A day might, perhaps, have done it. However, in the present instance, it was not as if some sudden and defined misfortune had opprest the soul by a single blow: it was rather as if every early hope had long been blighted; and every aspiring energy had been destroyed. There was nothing pleasing to gaze upon: it was mournful; but it excited not[a] sympathy, nor confidence. The arm was in a sling – the left arm. There could be no doubt that he was the hero who had risked his life to save young Linden. Was it, indeed, Lord Glenarvon whom Calantha beheld? Yes, it was himself. – Face to face she[b] stood before him, and gazed with eager curiosity upon him. /

Never did the hand of the sculptor, in the full power of his art, produce a form and face more finely wrought, so full of soul, so ever-varying in expression. Was it possible to behold him unmoved? Oh! was it in woman's nature to hear him, and not to cherish every word he uttered? And, having heard him, was it in the human heart ever again to forget those accents, which awakened every interest, and quieted,[c] every apprehension? The day, the hour, that very moment of time was marked and destined. It was Glenarvon – it was that spirit of evil whom she beheld; and her soul trembled within her, and felt its danger.

Calantha was struck suddenly, forcibly struck; yet the impression made upon her, was not in Glenarvon's[d] favour. The eye of the rattle-snake, it has been said, once fixed upon its victim, overpowers it with terror and alarm: the bird, thus charmed, dares not attempt its escape; it sings its last sweet lay; flutters its little / pinions in the air; then falls like a shot[e] before its destroyer, unable to fly from his fascination. Calantha bowed, therefore with the rest, pierced to the heart at once by the maddening power that destroys alike the high and low; but she liked not the wily turn of his eye, the contemptuous sneer of his curling lip, the soft passionless tones of his voice;[f] – it was not nature, or if it was nature,[g] not that to which she had been accustomed; – not the open, artless expression of a guileless heart.

Starting from the kind of dream in which she had for one moment been wrapped, she now looked around her. The affectation with which she veiled the interest she felt, is scarce accountable.[h]

Lord Glenarvon was the real object of her thoughts, yet she appeared alone to be occupied with every other. She laughed with Lord Trelawney; talked to the Miss Emmets; examined with interest every part of the ship, carelessly / approaching the very edge of it; yet once she met that glance, which none ever[i] who had seen, could forget, and she stopped as if rivetted to the earth. – He smiled; but whether it was a smile of approbation, or of scorn, she could not discover: the upper lip was curled, as if in derision; but the hand that was stretched out to save her, as she stood on the brink of the vessel, and the soft silvery voice which gently admonished her to beware, lest one false step should plunge her headlong into the gulph below, soon re-assured her.

It was late before the Duke took leave of the admiral, who promised to breakfast with the Commodore the ensuing day. The guns once more were fired; the band played as for their arrival; but the music now seemed to breathe a sadder strain; for it was heard,ᵃ softened by distance, and every stroke of the oars rendered the sounds more and more imperfect. The sun was setting, and cast its lustre on the / still waves: even the loquacity of the Emmets was for a few moments suspended; it was a moment which impressed the heart with awe; it was a scene never to be forgotten. The splendour of conquest, the tumult of enthusiasm, the aged veteran, and more than all, perhaps, that being who seemed early wrecked in the full tide of misfortune, were all fixed indelibly in Calantha's memory. Future times might bring new interests and events; magnificence might display every wonderful variety; but the impression of that sceneᵇ never can be effaced. /

CHAPTER XI.

CALANTHA could not speak one word during the evening; but while Miss Emmets sung – indifferently, she listened and even wept at what never before excited or interest, or melancholy. At night, when in sleep, one image pursued her, – it was all lovely – all bright: it seemed to be clothed in the white garments of an angel; it was too resplendent for eyes to gaze on; – she awoke. Lord Avondale slept in the inner room; she arose and looked upon him, whilst he reposed. How long, how fondly she had loved those features – that form. What grace, what majesty, what beauty was there! But when those eyes awake, she said, they will not look for me. That heart is at peace, and thou canst sleep, Henry, and my sorrows are not known / or heeded by thee. Happy Avondale: – Miserable, guilty Calantha!ᵃ

At an early hour the ensuing day, Captain Emmet proposed a drive to Donallan Park, which he said was a fair domain, fully deserving the attention of the Duke of Altamonte. Cassandra and Heloisa[b] [14] clamorously seconded this proposal. In this energetic family, Mrs. Emmet alone gave the eye and the ear a little repose. Stretched upon a couch in languid[c] listless inactivity, she gazed upon the bustling scene before her, as if entirely unconnected with it;[d] nor seemed to know of greater suffering than when called[e] from her reveries, by the acute voices of her family, to the bustle and hurry of common life. To the question of whether she would accompany them to Donallan Park, she answered faintly, that she would not go. A fat and friendly lieutenant, who fondly hung over her, urged her to relent, and with / some difficulty, at length, persuaded her to do so.[f]

Every one appeared much pleased with their excursion, or possibly with some incident during their drive, which had made any excursion agreeable. Of Donallan Park, however, Calantha remembered little: this alone, she noted, that as they walked through a shrubbery, Lord Glenarvon suddenly disengaging himself from Miss Emmet, who had monopolized[g] his arm, gathered a rose – the only rose in bloom (it being early in the summer) and turning back, offered it to Calantha. She felt confused – flattered perhaps; but if she were flattered by his giving it to her, she had reason to be mortified by the remark which accompanied the gift. 'I offer it to you,' he said, 'because the rose at this season is rare, and all that is new or rare has for a moment, I believe, some value in your estimation.'¹⁵ She understood his meaning: / her eye had been fixed upon him with more than common interest; and all that others said and Miss Emmet affected, he thought, perhaps, that she could feel.¹⁶ There was no proof she gave of this, more unequivocal, than her silence. Her spirits were gone; a strange fear of offending had come upon her; and when Lady Trelawney rallied her for this change, 'I am not well,' she said; 'I wish I had never come to Cork.'

On the ensuing morning[a] they returned to Castle Delaval. Previous to their departure, Admiral Buchanan had a long interview with Lady Margaret, during which time Lord Glenarvon walked along the beach with Calantha and Sophia. 'Shall you be at Belfont again this year?' said Miss Seymour. 'I shall be at Castle Delaval in a few days,' he answered, smiling rather archly at Calantha, she knew not wherefore. But she turned coldly from him, as if fearing to meet / his eyes. Yet not so was it her custom to behave towards those whom she sought to please, and what woman upon earth exists, who had not wished to please Glenarvon? Possibly she felt offended at what he had said when giving her the rose in Donallan's gardens;[b] or it may be that her mind, hitherto so enthusiastic, so readily attracted, was grown callous and indifferent, and felt not those charms and the splendour of those talents which dazzled and misled every other heart.

Yet is it unflattering to fly,[c] to feel embarrassed, to scarcely dare to look upon the person who addresses us? Is this so very marked a sign[d] of indifference? It is not probable that Lord Glenarvon thought so. He appeared not to hate the being who was thus confused in his presence, but to think that he felt what he inspired were presumption. With all the wild eagerness of enthusiasm, her infatuated spirit felt what, with all the art / of well dissembled vanity, he feigned. She quitted him with a strong feeling of interest. She, however, first heard him accept her father's invitation, and agree to accompany Sir George Buchanan in his promised visit to Castle Delaval. /

CHAPTER XII.

On their return thither, they found the guests they had left in a lamentable state of dullness. Lord Glenarvon was the first subject of enquiry. Is he arrived? – have you seen him? – do you like him? – were repeated on all sides. 'Who? – who?' 'There can be but one – Lord Glenarvon!' 'We all like him quite sufficiently[a] be assured of that,' said Sophia, glancing her eye somewhat sarcastically upon Calantha. 'He is a very strange personage,' said Lady Margaret. 'My curiosity to see him had been highly excited: I am now perfectly satisfied. He certainly has a slight resemblance to his mother.' 'He has the same winning smile,' said Gondimar; 'but there all comparison ceases.' 'What says my Calantha?' said Lady / Mandeville, 'does her silence denote praise?' 'Oh! the greatest,' she replied in haste, 'I hope, my dear girls,' said Mrs. Seymour, rather seriously addressing her daughters, 'that you will neither of you form any very marked intimacy with a person of so singular a character as is this young lord. I was rather sorry when, by your letter, I found he was invited here.' 'Oh, there is no need of caution for us!' replied Lady Trelawny, laughing: 'perhaps others may need these counsels, but not we: we are safe enough; are we not, Sophia?'

Lord Glenarvon, the object of discussion, soon appeared at the castle, to silence both praise and censure. There was a studied courtesy in his manner – a proud humility, mingled with a certain cold reserve, which amazed and repressed the enthusiasm his youth and misfortunes had excited. The end was as usual: – all were immediately won by this unexpected / manner:[b] – some more, some less, and Mrs. Seymour the last. But, to Calantha's infinite amusement, she heard her speaking in his defence a few hours after his arrival; and the person she addressed, upon this occasion, was Sir Everard St. Clare, who vehemently asseverated, though only in a whisper, that the Duke must be mad to permit such a person to remain at the castle in times like the present.

Sir Everard then stated, that Lady St. Clare and her daughters were returned to Belfont, and so eager to be again received into society, that if they dared hope that any of the Duke's family would accept their invitation, they intended to give a concert on the night of the great illumination for the Admiral's arrival at Belfont. Mrs. Seymour smiled in scorn; but Lady Margaret kindly promised to go there;ᵃ and as soon as Mrs. Seymour heard that it was merely in a political light they were to countenance / them, she was satisfied. For the present terror of all the party, on the government side, was lest the rebels should get the better, and murder them for their tenets.ᵇ

I will not sayᶜ what Lord Glenarvon said to Calantha very shortly after his arrival at the castle; it was not of a nature to repeat;ᵈ it was made up of a thousand nothings; yet they were so different from what others had said: it shewed her a mark of preference; at least it seemed so;ᵉ but it was not a preference that could alarm the most wary, or offend the most scrupulous. Such as it was, however, it flattered and it pleased; it gave a new interest to her life,ᶠ and obliterated from her memory every long cherished feeling of bitterness or regret.

It chanced one day, that, when seated at dinner, by Mrs. Seymour, to whom he paid no little attention, he enquired of her concerning Mac Allain, who waited upon that occasion behind the Duke's / chair. 'Why looks he so miserable?' he said. 'Why turn his eyes so incessantly towards Mr. Buchanan?' Mrs. Seymour hesitated, as if fearing to allude to a transaction which she never thought of without horror and dislike; but she no sooner pronounced the name of Mac Allain, than Lord Glenarvon's countenance altered: he started! and, watching Buchanan with a look of loathing antipathy, exhibited such a variety of malevolent passions, in the space of a few moments, that Sophia, who sat near Calantha on the opposite side of the table, asked her, as she read countenances so well, to tell her what her new friend's expressed at that instant. She raised her eyes; but met Glenarvon's. He saw;ᵍ he was the object of attention: he smiled; and,ʰ the sweetness of that smile alone being considered: 'I know not,' she said, in some confusion; 'but this I believe, that the hand of Heaven never impressed on man a countenance so / beautiful, so glorious!' 'Calantha!' said Sophia, looking at her. Calantha sighed. 'What is it even so? – Heaven defend us!' somewhat confused, Calantha turned to the Count Gondimar; and, talking with affected spirits, soon appeared to have forgotten both the smile and the sigh.

'You once, when in London, gave me permission to warn you,' said the Count, who observed every thing that was passing, 'when I thought you in danger. Now,' continued he, – 'now is the moment. It was not when dancing with Mr. Clarendon, or playing the coquette with Buchanan and the Duke of Myrtlegrove, that I trembled for you. Lord Avondale was still dear, even in those days – but now – O! the inconstancy of the human heart. You, even you, are changed.' 'Not me,'ⁱ she replied; 'but alas! that time is arrived which you predicted: he cares no more for me; but I can never forget him. / See,' she continued, 'how utterly indifferent he appears, yet I would die for him.' 'That will be of little service: you will prove his ruin and misery. Mark my words, Lady Avondale; and, when too late, remember what I have dared to say!'ʲ

'Every woman complains,' she continued, smiling, 'therefore, let me prove an exception. I have no reproaches to make Lord Avondale; and, except in your suspicious mind, there is no evil to apprehend.' 'Tell me, candidly; if the trial were made, if the hour of temptation were to come, could you, do you think – could you have strength and courage to resist it?' 'Could I! Can you ask! It will not be accounted presumption to affirm, that I feel secure. But possibly this arises from my conviction, that there can be no temptation for me: I love my husband:[a] there is no merit then in being true to what we love.'

As she yet spoke, Zerbellini approached / and asked her, in Italian, to read a note Lord Glenarvon had sent her. It was written with a pencil, and contained but few words: it requested her to speak no more with the Count Gondimar. He saw the manner in which the paper was delivered, and guessed from whom it came. 'I told you so,' he cried. 'Alas! shall I affect to offer you advice, when so many nearer and dearer friends are silent – shall I pretend to greater wisdom – greater penetration? Is it not inordinate vanity to hope, that any thing I can suggest will be of use?' 'Speak,' said Calantha; for the subject was interesting to her; 'at all events I shall not be offended.' 'The serpent that is cherished in the bosom,' said Gondimar, fiercely, 'will bite with deadly venom – the flame that brightly dazzles the little wanton butterfly, will destroy it. The heart of a libertine is iron: it softens when heated with the fires of lust;[b] but it is cold and hard in itself. The whirlwinds / of passions[c] are strong and irresistible; but when they subside, the calm of insensibility will succeed. Remember the friend of thy youth; though he appear unkind, his seeming neglect is better worth than the vows and adulation of all beside. Oh! Lady Avondale, let one that is lovely, and blest as you are, continue chaste[d] even in thought.'[17]

Calantha looked up, and met Gondimar's eyes: the fire in them convinced her that love alone dictated this sage advice; and none ever can conceive how much that feeling had been encreased by thus seeing a rival before him, whom he could not hope to render odious or ridiculous.

That day Lord Glenarvon had passed at the castle. On the following, he took his leave.[e] The Duke appeared desirous of conciliating him; Lady Margaret was more than ordinarily[f] brilliant and agreeable; Mrs. Seymour relaxed something of her frigidity; and the rest / of the ladies were enthusiastic in their admiration.[g]

Calantha[h] spoke much and often apart with Gondimar. Every thought of her heart seemed concentrated on the sudden in one dark interest; yet it was not love that she felt: it could not be. By day, by night, one image pursued her;[i] yet to save, to reclaim, to lead back from crime to virtue – from misery to peace, was, as she then apprehended, her sole desire.[j] Were not all around alike infatuated? Was not the idol of her fancy a being to whom all alike paid the insense[k] of flattery – the most lowly –[l] the most abject?

'Let them pursue,' she cried: 'let them follow after,ª and be favoured in turn. I alone, self-exiled, will fly, will hide myself beneath every concealment. He shall hear their words,ᵇ and believe in their adulation; but never, whilst existence is allowed me, shall he know the interest with which he has inspired / me.' Resolved upon this, and dreading her own thoughts, she danced, she rode, she sang, she talked to every one, sought every amusement, and seemed alone to dread one instant of repose – one single moment of time devoted to self examination and reflection. Ceaseless hurry, joyless mirth, endless desire of amusement varied the days as they flitted by. 'Oh, pause to reflect!' said Gondimar. But it was vain: new scenes of interest succeeded each other;ᶜ till suddenly she started as if shuddering on the very edge of perdition, in the dark labyrinth of sin – on the fathomless chasmᵈ which opened before her feet. /

CHAPTER XIII.

Lord Glenarvon was now considered as^a a favoured guest at the castle. He came –^b he went, as it suited his convenience or his humour. – But every time he appeared,^c the secret interest he had excited,^d was strengthened; and every time he went, he left apparently deeper marks of regret.

Sir Richard Mowbrey and Sir George Buchanan,^e were at this time also at the castle. Sir Everard, forgetful of his wrongs, and his Lady of her projects for the emancipation of her countrymen, kept open house during their stay; Lady St. Clare, in pursuance of her plan of restoring herself to society, assisted herself with her daughters, at a concert in the great assembly rooms^f at Belfont, given in honour of the Admiral's arrival. / On this eventful^g evening, the whole party at the castle resolved to make a most wonderful *éclat*,[18] by their brilliant appearance and condescension.^h The Duke addressed himself to every individual with his accustomed affability. Lord Avondale attended solely to his Uncle,ⁱ who amused himself by walking up and down that part of the room which was prepared for the dancers, bowing to all, shaking hands with all, and receiving those compliments which his brave conduct deserved. Pale, trembling, and scarcely heeding the scene, Calantha watched with breathless anxiety for one alone; and that one, for what cause she knew not, spoke not to her.

'Where is he?' – 'which^j is he?' – Was whispered now from mouth to mouth. The Admiral, the Duke, the concert were forgotten. One object appeared suddenly to engage the most boundless curiosity. 'Is that really Lord Glenarvon?' said a pretty little woman / pushing her way towards him. 'Oh let me but have the happiness of speaking one word to him: – let me but say, when I return to my home, that I have seen him, and I shall be overjoyed.' Calantha made room for the enthusiastic Lady: – she approached – she offered her hand to the deliverer of his Country as she called him: – he^k accepted it with grace, but some embarrassment. The rush was then general: every one would see – would speak to their Lord – their King; and the fashionable reserve which affectation had, for a moment, taught the good people of Belfont to assume, soon vanished, when nature spoke in their bosoms: so that had not the performers of the grand *concerto* called to order, Lord Glenarvon had been absolutely obliged to make his retreat. The mystery in which his fate appeared involved, his youth, his misfortunes, his brave conduct, and perhaps even his errors awakened this interest in such as beheld him. But he turned / from^a the gaze of strangers with bitterness.

'Will you allow me to seat myself near you?' he said, approaching Calantha's chair. 'Can you ask?' 'Without asking, I would not. You may possibly stay till late: I shall go early. My only inducement in coming here was you.' 'Was me! Do^b not say, what I am well assured is not true.' 'I never say what I do not feel. Your presence here alone makes me endure all this fulsome flattery, noise, display. If you dance – that is, when you dance, I shall retire.'

The concert now began with frequent bursts of applause. All were silent: – suddenly^c a general murmur proclaimed some new and unexpected event: – a young performer appeared. Was it a boy! Such grace – such beauty, soon betrayed her: it was Miss St. Clare. She could not hope for admittance in her own character; yet, under a feigned name, she had promised to assist at the performance; / and the known popularity of her songs, and the superior sweetness of her voice, prevented the professors from enquiring too much into the propriety of such an arrangement.

Messieurs John Maclane and Creighton had just been singing in Italian, an opera buffa. The noise they had made was such, that even the most courteous had been much discountenanced. A moment's pause ensued; when, without one blush of modest diffidence,^d but, on the contrary, with an air of dauntless and even contemptuous effrontery, the youthful performer seized her harp – Glenarvon's harp – and singing, whilst her dark brilliant eyes were fixed upon him alone, she gave vent to the emotions of her own bosom, and drew tears of sympathy from many another. The words were evidently made at the moment; and breathed from the heart. She studied not the composition, but the air was popular, and for that cause it had effect.^{e 19}/

The admiration for the young enthusiast was checked by the extreme disgust her shameless ill conduct had occasioned. The tears, too, of Sir Everard, who was present, and audibly called upon his cruel ungrateful niece, extorted a stronger feeling of sympathy than her lawless and guilty love.^f She retired the moment she had ended her song, and the commotion her presence had excited subsided with her departure.

The heiress of Delaval, decked in splendid jewels, had not lost by comparison^g with the deserted Elinor. She was the reigning favourite of the moment: every one observed it, and smiled upon her the more on that account. To be the favourite of the favoured was too much. The adulation paid to her during the evening;^h and the caresses lavished upon her had possibly turned a wiser head than her's; but alas! a deeper interest employed her thoughts, and Glenarvon's attention was her sole object. /

Calantha had felt agitated and serious during Miss St. Clare's performance. Lord Glenarvon had conversed with his customary ease; yet something had wounded her. Perhaps she saw, in the gaze of strangers, that this extreme and sudden intimacy was observed; or possibly her heart reproached her. She felt that not vanity alone, nor even enthusiasm, was the cause of her present emotion. She knew not, nor could imagine the cause;[a] but, with seeming inconsistency, after refusing positively to dance, she sent for Buchanan and joined in that delectable amusement;[b] and, as if the desire of exercise had superseded every other, she danced on with an energy and perseverance, which excited the warmest approbation in all. 'What spirits Lady Avondale has!' said one. 'How charming she is!' cried another. She herself only sighed.

'Have you ever read a tragedy of Ford's?' whispered Lady Augusta to Calantha, / as soon as she had ceased to exhibit – 'a tragedy entitled *The Broken Heart*.'[20] 'No,' she replied, half vexed, half offended. 'At this moment you put me vastly in mind of it. You look most woefully. Come, tell me truly, is not your heart in torture? and, like your namesake Calantha, while lightly dancing the gayest in the ring, has not the shaft already been struck, and shall you not die ere you attain the goal?' She indeed felt nearly ready to do so; and fanning herself excessively, declared, that it was dreadfully hot – that she should absolutely expire of the heat: yet while talking and laughing with those who surrounded her, her eye looked cautiously round, eager to behold the resentment and expected frowns of him whom she had sought to offend; but there was no frown on Lord Glenarvon's brow – no look of resentment.

'And are you happy?' he said, approaching her with gentleness. 'Perhaps / so, since some can rejoice in the sufferings of others. Yet I forgive you, because I know you are not yourself. I see you are acting from pique;[c] but you have no cause; for did you know my heart, and could you feel what it suffers on your account, your doubts would give way to far more alarming suspicions.' He paused, for she turned abruptly from him. 'Dance on then, Lady Avondale,' he continued, 'the admiration of those for whose society you were formed – the easy prey of every coxcomb to whom that ready hand is so continually offered, and which I have never once dared to approach. Such is the respect which will ever be shewn to the object of real admiration, interest and regard, although that object seems willing to forget that it is her due. But,' added he, assuming that air of gaiety he had one moment laid aside, 'I detain you, do I not? See Colonel Donallan and the Italian Count await you.' 'You[d] mistake me,' she said gravely; 'I could / not presume to imagine that my dancing would be heeded by you: –[e] I could have no motive –'[f] 'None but the dear delight of tormenting,' said he,[g] 'which gave a surprising elasticity to your step, I can assure you. Indubitably had not that impulse assisted, you could not thus have excelled yourself.' 'If you knew,' she said, 'what I suffer at this moment you would spare me. Why do you deride me?'

'Because, oh Lady Avondale, I dare not – I cannot speak to you more seriously. I feel that I have no right – no claim on you. I dread offending; but to-morrow I shall expiate all; for I leave you to-morrow. – Yes, it must be so. I am going from Ireland. Indeed I was going before I had the misery of believing that I should leave any thing[a] in it I could ever regret.' What Calantha felt, when he said this, cannot be described.

'Will you dance the two next dances with me?' said Colonel Donallan, now approaching. 'I am tired: will you excuse / me? I believe our carriages are ordered.' 'Oh surely you will not go away before supper.' 'Ask Lady Mandeville what she means to do.' 'Lady Trelawney and Miss Seymour stay.' 'Then[b] perhaps I shall.' The Colonel bowed and retired. – 'Give me the rose you wear,' said Glenarvon in a low voice, 'in return for the one I presented you at Donallan Park.' 'Must I?' 'You must,' said he,[c] smiling. With some hesitation, she obeyed; yet she looked around in hopes no vigilant eye might observe her. She took it from her bosom, and gave it tremblingly into his hands. A large pier glass reflected the scene to the whole company. The rose thus given, was received with transport. It said more, thus offered, than a thousand words: – it was taken and pressed to a lover's lips, till all its blushing beauties were gone, then it was cast down on the earth to be trampled upon by many. And had Calantha wished it, she might have read in the / history of the flower, the fate that ever attends on guilty love.

And was it love she felt so soon – so strongly! – It is not possible. Alarmed, grieved, flattered at his altered manner, she turned aside to conceal the violent, the undefinable emotions, to which she had become a prey: – a dream of ecstasy for one moment fluttered in her heart; but the recollection of Lord Avondale recurring, she started with horror from herself – from him; and, abruptly taking leave, retired.

'Are you going?' said Glenarvon. 'I am ill,' she answered. 'Will you suffer me to accompany you?' he said, as he assisted her into her carriage; 'or possibly it is not the custom in this country: – you mistrust me – you think it wrong.' – 'No,' she answered with embarrassment; and he seated himself by her side. The distance to the castle was short. Lord Glenarvon was more respectful, more reserved, more silent than / before he had entered the carriage. On quitting it alone,[d] he pressed her hand to his heart, and bade her feel for the agony she had implanted there. None, perhaps, ever before felt what she did at this instant. . . . . . /

CHAPTER XIV.

IF any indifferent person approach us, it either is disagreeable, or at least unimportant; but when it is a person we love, it thrills through the heart, and we are unable to speak or to think. Could she have imagined,ᵃ that Lord Glenarvon felt for her, she had been lost. But that was impossible;ᵇ and yet his manner; – it was so marked, there could be no doubt. She was inexperienced, we may add, innocent; though no doubt sufficientlyᶜ prepared to become every thing that was the reverse. Yet in a moment she felt her own danger, and resolved to guard against it. How then can so many affirm, when they know that they are loved, that it is a mere harmless friendship! how can they, in palliation of their errors, bring forward the perpetually repeated excuse,ᵈ / that they were beguiled! The heart that is chaste and pure will shrink the soonest from the very feeling that would pollute it: – in vain it would attempt to deceive itself: the very moment we love, or are loved, something within us points out the danger: – even when we fly from him, to whom we could attach ourselves, we feel a certain embarrassment – an emotion, which is not to be mistaken; and, in a lover's looks, are there not a thousand assurances and confessions which no denial of words can affect to disguise?ᵉ

Lord Glenarvon had denied to Calantha the possibility of his ever again feeling attachment. This had not deceived her; but she was herself too deeply and suddenly struck to the heart to venture to hope for a return. Besides, she did not think of this as possible: – he seemed to her so far above her – so far above everything. She considered him as entirely different from all others; and, if not superior, at least dissimilar and consequently / not to be judged of by the same criterion.

It is difficult to explain Calantha's peculiar situation with respect to Lord Avondale. Yet it is necessary briefly to state in what manner they were situated at this particular period; for otherwise, all that is related must appear like a mere fable, improbable and false.ᶠ They were dearer to each other perhaps, than any two who had been so long united in marriage. They loved each other with more passion, more enthusiasm than is often retained; but they were, from a thousand circumstances, utterly estranged at this time; and that apparently by mutual consent – like two violent spirits which had fretted and chafed and opposed each other, till both were sore and irritated.

In the course of years, they had said every thing that was most galling and bitter; and though the ardent attachment they really felt, had ever followed those momentary bursts of fury, the veil had / been torn aside – that courtesy, which none should ever suffer themselves to forget, had been broken through, and they had yielded too frequently to the sudden impulse of passion, ever to feel secure that the ensuing moment might not produce a scene of discord.

A calm, a deliberate tyrant,[a] had vanquished Calantha; a violent one[b] could not. When provoked, Lord Avondale was too severe; and when he saw her miserable and oppressed, it gave him more suffering than if he had himself been subdued. There are few spirits which cannot be overcome if dexterously attacked; but with the fierce and daring, force and violence[c] will generally be found useless. It should be remembered that, like madness, these disturbed[d] characters see not things as they are; and, like martyrs and fanatics, they attach a degree of glory to every privation and punishment in the noble cause of opposition to what they conceive is unjust authority. / Such a character is open and guileless; but unhappily, the very circumstance that makes it sincere, renders it also, if misturned, desperate and hardened.[e]

During the first years of their marriage, these tumultuous scenes but strengthened the attachment they felt for each other; but when Lord Avondale's profession absorbed his mind, he dreaded a recurrence of what had once so fully[f] engrossed his thoughts. He left Calantha, therefore, to the guidance of that will, which she had so long and pertinaciously indulged. Absent, pre-occupied, he saw not, he heard not, the misuse she made of her entire liberty. Some trifle, perhaps, at times, reached his ear; a scene of discord ensued; much bitterness on both sides followed: and the conviction that they no longer loved each other, added considerably to the violence of recrimination. They knew not how deeply rooted affection such as they had once felt, must ever / be – how the very ties that compelled them to belong to each other, strengthened, in fact, the attachment which inclination and love had first inspired; but, with all the petulance and violence of character natural to each, they fled estranged and offended from each other's society.

Lord Avondale sought, in an active and manly profession, for some newer interest, in which every feeling of ambition could have part; and she, surrendering her soul to the illusive dream of a mad and guilty attachment, boasted that she had found again the happiness[g] she had lost; and contrasted even[h] the indifference of her husband, to[i] the ardour, the devotion, the refined attention of a newly acquired friend. /

CHAPTER XV.

O BETTER had it been to die than to see and hear Glenarvon. When he smiled, it was like the light radiance[a] of heaven; and when he spoke, his voice was more soothing in its sweetness than music. He was so gentle in his manners, that it was in vain even to affect to be offended; and, though he said he never again could love, he would describe how some had died, and others maddened, under the power of that fierce passion – how every tie that binds us, and every principle and law, must be broken through, as secondary considerations, by its victims: –[b] he would speak home to the heart; for he knew it in all its turnings and windings; and, at his will, he could rouze[c] or tame the varying passions of those over whom he sought to exercise dominion. Yet, when by every / art and talent he had raised the scorching flames[d] of love, tearing himself from his victim, he would leave her, then[e] weep for the agony of grief by which he saw her destroyed.

Had he betrayed in his manner to Calantha that freedom, that familiarity so offensive in men, but yet so frequent amongst them, she would yet have shuddered. But what was she to fly? Not from the gross adulation, or the easy flippant protestations to which all women are soon or late accustomed;[f] but from a respect, at once refined and flattering – an attention devoted even to her least wishes, yet without appearing subservient – a gentleness and sweetness, as rare as they were fascinating; and these combined with all the powers of imagination, vigour of intellect, and brilliancy of wit, which none ever before possessed in so eminent[g] a degree; and none ever since have even presumed to rival. Could she fly from a being unlike all others – sought / for by every one, yet, by his own confession, wholly and entirely devoted to herself.

How cold,[h] compared with Glenarvon[i] was the regard her family and friends affected! Was it confidence in her honour, or indifference? Lord Glenarvon asked Calantha repeatedly, which it most resembled – he appealed to her vanity even, whether strong affection could thus neglect[j] and leave the object of its solicitude? Yet, had she done nothing to chill a husband and parent's affection – had she not herself lessened the regard they had so faithfully cherished?

Calantha thought she had sufficient honour and spirit to tell her husband at once the danger to which she was exposed; but when she considered more seriously her situation, it appeared to her almost ridiculous to fancy that it was so imminent. If upon some occasion, Lord Glenarvon's manner was ardent, the ensuing morning she found him cold, distant / and pre-occupied, and she felt ashamed of the weakness which for one moment^a could have made her imagine she was the object of his thoughts. Indeed, he often took an opportunity of stating, generally, that he never could feel either interest or love for any thing on earth; that once he had felt too deeply and had suffered bitterly from it; and that now his sole regret was in the certainty that he never again could be so deceived.

He spoke with decision^b of leaving Ireland, and more than once repeated, emphatically to the Duke, 'I shall never forget the kindness which prompted you to seek me out, when under very unpleasant circumstances; I shall immediately withdraw my name from the club;^c my sentiments I cannot change:^d but you have already convinced me of the folly of spreading them amongst the unenlightened multitude.'

Sir Everard, who was present, lifted up / his hands at such discourse. 'He is a convert of mine, I verily believe,' he cried; 'and Elinor' – 'Miss St. Clare,' whispered Glenarvon, turning to the Doctor, 'has long been admonished by me, to return to an indulgent uncle, and throw herself on your mercy.' 'My mercy!' said Sir Everard, bursting into tears, – 'my gratitude. Oh! my child, my darling.' 'And believe me,' continued Lord Glenarvon, with an air which seemed haughtily to claim belief, 'I return her as innocent as she came to me. Her imagination may have bewildered and beguiled her; but her principles are uncorrupted.' 'Generous young nobleman!' exclaimed Sir Everard, ready to kneel before him – 'noble, mighty, grand young gentleman! wonder of our age!' Lord Glenarvon literally smiled through his tears; for the ridicule of Sir Everard did not prevent his excellent and warm feelings from affecting those who knew him well. 'And will she / return to her poor uncle?' 'I know not,' said Lord Glenarvon, gravely: 'I fear not; but I have even implored her to do so.' 'Oh, if you fail who are so fair and so persuasive, who can hope to move her?' 'She may hear a parent's voice,' said Glenarvon, 'even though deaf to a lover's prayer. 'And are you indeed a lover to my poor deluded Elinor?' 'I was,' said Lord Glenarvon, proudly; 'but her strange conduct, and stubborn spirit have most effectually cured me; and I must own, Sir Everard, I do not think I ever again can even affect a feeling of that sort:^e after all, it is a useless way of passing life.' 'You are right,' said the Doctor; 'quite right; and it injures the health; there is nothing creates bile, and hurts the constitution more, than suspense and fretting: – I know it by myself.'

They were standing in the library during this discourse. Lady Avondale entered now;^f Lord Glenarvon approached / her. They were for a few moments alone: – he lent^g over her; she held a book in her hand; he read a few lines: it is not possible to describe how well he read them. The poetry he read was beautiful as his own:^h it affected him. He read more; he became animated; Calantha looked up; he fixed his eyes on hers; he forgot the poem; his hand touched hers, as he replaced the book before her; she drew away her hand; he took it and put[a] it to his lips. 'Pardon me,' he said, 'I am miserable: but I will never injure you. Fly me, Lady Avondale: I deserve not either interest or regard; and to look upon me is in itself pollution to one like you.' He then said a few words expressive of his admiration for her husband: – 'He is as superior to me,' he said, 'as Hyperion to a satyr:[21] – and you love him, do you not?' continued he, smiling. 'Can you ask?' 'He seems most attached, too, to you.' 'Far, far more than I deserve.' /

'I can never love again,' said Glenarvon, still holding her hand: 'never. There will be no danger in my friendship,' he said after a moments[b] thought: 'none; for I am cold as the grave – as death; and all here,' he said pressing her hand upon his heart, 'is chilled, lost, absorbed. They will speak ill of me,' he continued rather mournfully; 'and you will learn to hate me.' 'I! never, never. I will defend you, if abused; I will hate those who hate you; I –' He smiled: 'How infatuated you are,' he said, 'poor little thing that seeks to destroy itself. Have you not then heard what I have done?' 'I have heard much' said Calantha, 'but I know – I feel it is false.' 'It is all too true,' said Lord Glenarvon carelessly: – 'all quite true; and there is much worse yet: – But it is no matter,' he continued; 'the never dying worm feeds upon my heart:[c] I am like death, Lady Avondale; and all beneath is seared.' /

Whilst the conscience wakes, and the blush of confused and trembling guilt yet varies the complexion, the sin is not of long standing, or of deep root; but when the mind seeks to disguise from itself its danger,[d] – when, playing upon the edge of the precipice, the victim willingly deludes itself, and appears hard and callous to every admonitory caution, then is the moment for alarm; and that moment now appeared to realize Calantha's fears.

Attacked with some asperity by her numerous friends, for her imprudent conduct, she now boldly avowed her friendship for Glenarvon, and disclaimed the possibility of its exceeding the bounds which the strictest propriety had rendered necessary.[e] She even gloried in his attachment; and said that there was not one of those who were admonishing her to beware who would not readily, nay, even gladly fill her place. Calantha had seen their letters to him: she had marked / their advances – too fatal symptom of the maddining disease! she really imagined that all others like herself, were enamoured with the same idol;[f] and in this instance she was right: – the infatuation was general: he was termed the leader of the people, the liberator of his country, the defender of the rights of Ireland. If he wandered forth through Belfont, he was followed by admiring crowds; and whilst he affected to disdain the transient homage, she could not[g] but perceive that he lost no opportunity by every petty artifice of encreasing the illusion. /

CHAPTER XVI.

At this crisis the whole party at the castle were disturbed by the unexpected arrival of the Princess of Madagascar at Dublin. A small fleet had been seen approaching the coast: it was rumoured that the French in open boats[a] were preparing to invade Ireland;[22] but it proved, though it may sound rather ludicrous to say so, only the great Nabob and the Princess of Madagascar. Their immense retinue and baggage, which the common people took for the heavy artillery, arrived without incident or accident at Belfont; and the couriers having prepared the Duke for the reception of his illustrious guest, they awaited her arrival with considerable impatience.

During the bustle and noise[b] this little event occasioned, Lord Glenarvon came / to Lady Avondale and whispered in her ear, 'I shall walk this evening: contrive to do so[c] as I have something of importance to tell you.' As he spoke, he pretended to pick up a ring.[23] 'Is this yours?' he said. 'No.' 'It is,' he whispered; and placed it himself upon her finger.[d] It was an emerald with an harp[e] engraved upon it – the armorial bearing of Ireland: 'let us be firm and united,' was written under. 'I mean it merely politically,' he said smiling. 'Even were you a Clarissa, you need not be alarmed: I am no Lovelace,[24] I promise you.'

The princess was now announced, fifty-three attendants and twenty-four domestic friends, were her small and conscientious establishment, besides a cook, confectioner and laundress, to the total discomfiture of Irish hospitality. The high priest in the dress of the greek church,[f] ever attended her, and eagerly sought to gain adherents to the only true established / church, at whatever house he occasionally rested. The simplicity of Hoiouskim, his eagerness, his abilities and information, added an agreeable variety[g] at Castle Delaval.

But neither the presence of the Nabob nor the caresses of the princess[h] who cast many a gentle glance upon Glenarvon[i] could for one moment detach his thoughts from Calantha. On the contrary he answered her with distant reserve and appeared eager to shew to every one the marked distinction he felt for the woman he loved. Oh! he is really sincere,[j] she thought as he left them all to attend to her. 'I amuse –[k] I soothe him,' the hope rendered her blest and she felt indifferent to every consequence.

'You are not as pretty^a as Sophia,' said Glenarvon^b looking on her; 'but I admire you more. Your errors are such as you have frankly confessed; but you have others which you wished me not to perceive. Few have so many / faults,^c yet how is it that you have wound yourself already around^d this cold, this selfish heart, which had resolved never again to admit any.^e You love your husband^f Lady Avondale: I respect you too well to attempt to change your affection; but if I wished it, your eyes already tell me what power I have gained: – I could do what I would.' 'No, no,' she answered. 'You are too vain.' 'None ever yet resisted me,' said Glenarvon: 'do you think you could?' Calantha scarce knew how to answer; but while she assured him she could resist any one and had no fear for herself, she felt the contrary; and trembled with mixed apprehensions of joy and sorrow at her boast – when others approached, he did not change his manner to Calantha: he discontinued his conversation; but he still looked the same: he was not fearful as some would have been, or servile, or full of what might be said: – he^g seemed in all respects careless or desperate. / He laughed, but his laugh was not the heart's laugh: his wit enlivened and dazzled others; but it seemed not the effect of exuberant^h spirits.

It was not unfrequently the custom at Castle Delaval, during the fine summer evenings, to walk after dinner, before cards or music. The flower gardens, and shrubbery were the most usual places of resort. Lady Augusta smilingly observed to Lady Mandeville and Sophia, that, for some evenings past, Lady Avondale had taken more extensive rambles, and that Lord Glenarvon and she were oftentimes absent till supper was announced. The Count Gondimar, who overheard the remark, affected to think it malignant, and asked with a sarcastic sneer, whether Lord Avondale were with her on these evening excursions? 'Little Mowbrayⁱ seems a great favorite of Lord Glenarvon's,' said Lady Augusta; 'but I do not fancy his father is often of the party, or that his being Lady Avondale's child / is the cause of it:^j the boy has a sprightly wit. We must not draw unfair conclusions: last year Mr. Buchanan gave us alarm; and now,^k it is quite natural we should all fall in love with Lord Glenarvon. I have myself; only he will not return my advances. Did you observe what an eye I made him at breakfast? . . . but that never was a love making meal. Place me but near him at supper, and you shall see what I can do.'

Gondimar suddenly left Lady Augusta, who was walking on the terrace. He had caught a glimpse of Calantha as she wandered slowly by the banks of Elle: – he hastened to the spot; he saw her; he penetrated her feelings; and he returned thoughtful and irritated to the Castle. Snatching a pen, he wrote for some time. Lady Trelawney and Lady Augusta, observing him, approached and insisted upon being made acquainted with his studies. 'It is an ode you are inditing, I am certain,' said the latter, 'I saw you / struck by the God as you darted from me.' 'You are right,' cried Gondimar, 'I am composing a song.' 'In English too, I perceive.' What, if it be English? you know one of my talents,^l can write even in that d – d^a language: so criticise my rhapsody if you dare. At all events,^b Lady Avondale will admire it; for it is about a rose and love – most sentimental. And where is she? for till her return, I will not shew it you.'

If that question,^c where is Lady Avondale? must be answered, it is with sorrow and regret that such answer will be made: – she was walking slowly, as Gondimar had seen her, by the banks of the river Elle: she was silent, too, and mournful; her spirits were gone; her air was that of one who is deeply interested in all she hears. She was not alone – Lord Glenarvon was by her side. It was their custom thus to walk: they met daily; they took every opportunity of meeting; and when in their morning and evening rambles she pointed out the beautiful / views around, the ranging mountains,^d and the distant ocean, – he would describe,^e in glowing language, the far more magnificent and romantic scenery of the countries through which he had passed – countries teaming with rich fruits, vinyards^f and olive groves; luxuriant vales and mountains, soaring above the clouds, whose summits were white with snow, while a rich and ceaseless vegetation adorned the valleys beneath. He told her that he hated these cold northern climes, and the bottle green of the Atlantic; – that could she see the dark blue of the Mediterranean, whose clear wave reflected the cloudless sky, she would never be able to endure those scenes in which she now took such delight. And soon those scenes lost all their charms for Calantha; for that peace of mind which gave them charms was fast departing; and she sighed for that beautiful land to which his thoughts reverted, and those Italian climes, to which he said, he so soon must return. /

CHAPTER XVII.

It was upon this evening that, having walked for a considerable time^a Lady Avondale felt fatigued and rested for a moment near the banks of Elle. She pointed to the roses which grew luxuriently^b around. 'They are no longer rare,' she said^c alluding to the one he had given her upon their first acquaintance at Donallan: 'but are they the less prized?' He understood her allusion, and pulling a bud from the mossy bank on which it grew, he kissed it, and putting it gently to her lips asked her, if the perfume were sweet, and which she preferred of the two roses which he had offered her? She knew not what she answered; and she afterwards wished she could forget what she had then felt.^d

Gondimar passed by them at that moment: – / He observed her confusion; he retired as if fearful of encreasing it; and, but too conscious that such conversation was wrong, Calantha attempted once to change it. 'I will shew you the new lodge,' she said turning up a large gravel walk, out of the shrubbery. 'Shew me!' Glenarvon answered smiling. 'Trust me, I know every lodge and walk here better than yourself;' and he amused himself with her surprise. Some thought, however, occurred, which checked his merriment – some remembrances made this boast of his acquaintance with the place painful to him. There was one, whom he had formerly seen and admired, who was no longer present and whom every one but himself appeared to have forgotton – one who^e lovely in the first bloom of spotless youth;^f had felt for him all that even his heart could require. She was lost – he should never see her more.

A momentary gloom darkened his countenance at this recollection. He / looked upon Calantha and she trembled; for his manner was much altered. Her cheeks kindled as he^g spoke: – her eye dared no longer encounter his. If she looked up for a moment, she withdrew in haste, unable to sustain the ardent glance: her step tremblingly advanced, lingering, but yet not willingly retreating^h Her heart beat in tumult, or swelled with passion, as he whispered to her that, which she ought never to have heard. She hastened towards the castle: – he did not attempt to detain her.

It was late: the rest of the company were gone home. Thither she hastened; and hurrying to the most crowded part of the room, flushed with her walk, she complained of the heat, and thought that every eye was fixed upon her with looks of strong disapprobation. Was it indeed so? or was it a guilty conscience which made her think so?

Lady Mandeville,[a] observing her distress, informed her that Count Gondimar, / had been composing a song, but would not sing it till she was present. She eagerly desired to hear it. 'It is about a rose,' said Gondimar, significantly glancing his eye upon the one in Calantha's bosom. The colour in her cheeks became redder far than the rose.[b] 'Sing it,' she said, 'or rather let me read it ... or ... but wherefore are you not dancing, or at billiards? How dull it must be for Clara and Charlotte' (these were two of Lady Mandeville's children). 'You never thought of Lady Mandeville's beautiful children, and our state of dullness, while you were walking,' cried Lady Augusta, 'and last night you recollect that when you made every one dance, you sat apart indulging vain phantasies and idle reveries. However, they are all gone into the ball-room, if dancing is the order of the night; but as for me, I shall not stir from this spot, till I hear Count Gondimar's song.'

'I will sing it you, Lady Avondale,' / said the Count, smiling at her distress, 'the first evening that you remain at your balcony alone, watching the clouds as they flit across the moon, and listening, I conclude, to the strains of the nightingale.' 'Then,' she said, affecting unconcern, 'I claim your promise for tomorrow night, punctually at nine.' He approached the piano-forte. 'Ah[c] not now – I am engaged, – I must dance.' 'Now or never,' said the Count. 'Never then, never,' she answered, almost crying, though she affected to laugh. Lady Augusta entreated for the song, and the Count, after a short prelude, placed the manuscript paper before him, and in a low tone of voice began: –

(To the air of *Ils ne sont plus.*')

> Waters of Elle! thy limpid streams are flowing,
>   Smooth and untroubled, through the flow'ry vale:
> O'er thy green banks once more, the wild rose blowing,
>   Greets the young spring, and scents the passing gale. /
>
> Here 'twas at eve, near yonder tree reposing,
>   One still too dear, first breath'd his vows to thee:
> Wear this, he cried, his guileful love disclosing,
>   Near to thy heart, in memory of me.
>
> Love's cherished gift, the rose he gave, is faded;
>   Love's blighted flower, can never bloom again.
> Weep for thy fault – in heart – in mind degraded;
>   Weep, if thy tears can wash away the stain.
>
> Call back the vows, that once to heaven were plighted,
>   Vows full of love, of innocence and truth.
> Call back the scenes in which thy soul delighted:
>   Call back the dream that blest thy early youth.

Flow silver stream, tho' threatening tempests lower,
   Bright, mild and clear, thy gentle waters flow;
Round thy green banks, the spring's young blossoms flower;
   O'er thy soft waves the balmy zephyrs blow.

– Yet, all in vain; for never spring arraying
   Nature in charms, to thee can make it fair.
Ill fated love, clouds all thy path, pourtraying
   Years past of bliss, and future of despair.

Gondimar seemed affected whilst he sung; and Calantha felt nearly suffocated with every sort of feeling. Lady Augusta / pretended not to understand it, and hastened with Calantha into the adjoining room. Lord Glenarvon followed and approached Lady Avondale: 'Remember me in your prayers, my gentlest friend,' he whispered. 'Even in the still night let some remembrance of Glenarvon occur. Think of me, for I am jealous even of thy dreams.' The angry glance of Gondimar interrupted the conference.

Calantha could not sleep that night. A thousand fears and hopes rushed upon her mind. She retired to her room:^a at one time seized a pen, and wrote, in all the agony of despair, a full confession of her guilty feelings to her husband; the next she tore the dreadful testimony of her^b erring heart, and addressed herself to heaven for mercy. But vain the struggle. From childhood's earliest day she never had^c refused herself one wish, one prayer.^d She knew not^e on the sudden how to curb^f the fierce and maddening fever that / raged within. 'I am lost,' she cried, 'I love – I worship. To live without him will be death – worse, worse than death. One look, one smile from Glenarvon, is dearer than aught^g else that heaven has to offer. Then let me not attempt, what I have not power to effect. Oh, as his friend, let me still behold him. His love, some happier, some better heart shall possess.' Again she started with horror from herself. 'His love!' she cried, 'and can I think of him in so criminal – so guilty a manner! I who am a wife, and more^h – a mother! Let me crush such feelings even now in their birth. Let me fly him, whilst yet it is possible; nor imagine the grief, he says my absence will cause,ⁱ can exceed the misery my dishonourable attachment will bring upon both! And did he dare to tell me that he loved me? Was not this in itself a proof that he esteemed me no longer? Miserable, wretched Calantha; / where shall I fly to hide my shame? How conceal from a lover's searching eyes that he is too dear?'

With such thoughts she attempted to close her eyes; but dreadful dreams disturbed her fancy; and the image of Glenarvon pursued her even in sleep. She saw him – not kneeling at her feet, in all the impassioned transports of love; not radiant with hope, nor even mournful with despondency and fear; but pale, deadly, and cold: his hand was ice,^j and as he placed it upon hers, she shrunk as from the grasp of death, and awoke oppressed with terror. /

CHAPTER XVIII.

No one had apparently observed Lady Avondale's feigned indisposition that evening – feigned, indeed, it was not; no one soothed her during her sleepless night; and in the morning when she awoke, at an early hour, Lord Avondale asked her not the cause of her disquiet.ª She arose and descended upon the terrace: – her steps involuntarily led her to the banks of the Elle. The flowers, fresh with dew, sparkled in the sunshine, and scented the soft morning air. She hurried on, regardless of the distance. The rose he had given her was faded;ᵇ but its leaves were preserved by her with fondest care.

Whilst yet she walked, at a little distance she perceived Gondimar, and was in consequence / preparing to return, when he abruptly accosted her; and with a manner too little respectful, rudely seized her hand. 'Have you not slept?' he cried, 'my charming, my adored young friend, that you are thus early in your walk; or did you imagine that others, beside myselfᶜ would wander upon these banks, and await your fairy step? O suffer one who admires – who loves, to open his heart to you – to seize this opportunity.' 'Leave me –ᵈ approach me not. What have I done to deserve this from you?' she exclaimed. 'Why seize my hand by force? Why press it – oh God!ᵉ to those detested lips? Leave me, Count Gondimar: forget not the respect due to every woman.' 'Of virtue!' he replied, with a scornful smile. 'But tell me, has Lady Avondale never suffered such insults from some who have no better claim? Has she still a right to this amazing mockery of respect? Ah! trust me, we cannot / command our love.' 'Neither can we command our abhorrence – our disgust,' she exclaimed, breaking from his grasp and hastening away.

As Calantha re-entered the Castle, she met Lady Margaret and Glenarvon, who appeared surprised and disconcerted at seeing her. 'Has Count Gondimar been speaking to you upon any subject of importance?' said Lady Margaret in a whisper, trying to conceal a look of suspicion, and some embarrassment. Before Calantha could answer, he had joined them; and explaining fully that their meeting had been entirely accidental, they both walked offᶠ together apparentlyᵍ in earnest discourse, leaving Lord Glenarvon and Lady Avondale together. Calantha's heart was full, she could not speak, she therefore left him in haste and when alone she wept. Had she not reason; for every indignity and grief was falling fast upon her. She / could not tell what had occurred to Lord Avondale – he had a fierce[a] and dangerous spirit; and to Glenarvon she would not,[b] upon every account. Glenarvon awaited her return with anxiety. 'I was surprised to see you with my aunt,' she said, 'what could you be saying[c] to her.' He evaded the question, and tenderly enquired of her the cause of her uneasiness and tears. He loved beyond a doubt – at least he convinced Calantha that he did so.

Confused, perturbed, she, more than ever felt the danger of her situation: trembling she met his eyes, fearing lest he should penetrate her secret. Confident in her own strength: 'I will fly,' she said, 'though it be to the utmost extremity of the earth; but I will never yield – never betray myself. My fate is sealed – misery must, in future, be my portion; but no eye shall penetrate into the recesses of my heart.[d] – none shall share my distress, or counsel / me in my calamity.' Thus she reasoned;[e] and struggling as she thought, against her guilty passion, by attempting to deceive the object of her devotion, she in reality yielded herself entirely to his power, self deluded and without controul.

How new to her mind appeared the fever of her distracted thoughts! Love she had felt – unhappy love, she had once for a time experienced; but no taint of guilt was mingled with the feeling; and the approach to vice she started from with horror and alarm. Lord Glenarvon had succeeded too well – she had seen him – she had heard him too often; she fled in vain: he read his empire in the varying colour of her cheeks; he traced his power in every faltering[f] word, in every struggling sigh: that strange silence, that timid air, that dread of beholding him – all confirmed, and all tempted him forward to pursue his easy / prey. 'She is mine,' he cried exultingly,[g] – 'mine, too, without a struggle, –[h] this fond wife, this chaste and pure Calantha. Wherever I turn, new victims fall before me – they await not to be courted.'

But Lord Glenarvon had oftentimes said, that he never again could feel affection for any woman. How then was the interest he shewed Calantha to be accounted for? What name was he to give it? It was the attachment of a brother to the sister whom he loved:[i] it was all devotion – all purity; he would never cherish a thought that might not be heard in heaven, or harbour one wish detrimental to the happiness of his friend. This was said, as it often has been said: both felt that it was false; but both continued to repeat, what they wished to believe possible. His health and spirits had much declined; he looked as if sorrows, which he durst not utter, afflicted / his heart; and though, in the presence of others he affected gaiety, when alone with Calantha he did not disguise his sadness. She sought to console him: she was grave – she was gentle, she could be both; and the occasion seemed to call for her utmost kindness.

He spoke much to her; and sometimes read as Lord Avondale once had done; and none ever but Lord Avondale read as well.[25] His tears flowed for the sorrows of those whose poetry and history he repeated. Calantha wept also; but it was for Glenarvon, that she mourned. When he^a had ended the tale of love and sorrow, his eyes met hers and they spoke more – far more than words. Perhaps he generously resolved to contend against his own feelings; even at times he warned her of her danger. – But, when he bade her fly him, he held her hand, as if to detain her; and when he said the / passion he cherished would cause the misery of both, he acknowledged that her presence alleviated his sufferings, and that he could not bear to see her less. /

CHAPTER XIX.

THERE are scenes of guilt it would be horrible to paint – there are hours of agony it is impossible to describe! All sympathy recedes from triumphant vice[a] and the kindest heart burns with indignation at the bare recital of unpunished crime. By night, by day, the tortures of remorse pursued Lady Avondale. In a husband's presence, she trembled; from a parent's tenderness she turned with affected coldness; her children, she durst not look upon. To the throne of heaven, she no longer offered up one prayer;[b] upon a sleepless bed, visions of horror distracted her fancy; and when, at break of day, a deep and heavy slumber fell on her, instead of relieving a weary spirit, feverish dreams and maddening apprehensions disturbed her rest. Glenarvon had entirely / possessed himself of her imagination.

Glenarvon had said, there was a horrid secret, which weighed upon his mind. He would start at times, and gaze on vacancy; then turn to Calantha, and ask her what she had heard and seen. His gestures, his menaces were terrific. He would talk to the air; then laugh with convulsive horror; and gazing wildly around, enquire of her, if there were[c] not blood upon the earth, and if the ghosts of departed men had not been seen by some.

Calantha thought that madness had fallen upon his mind, and wept to think that talents such as his were darkened and shrouded over by so heavy a calamity. But when the fierce moment was passed, tears would force their way into his eyes,[d] and placing her hand upon his burning head, he would call her his sole comforter, the only hope that was left him upon earth; his dearest, his only friend; / and he would talk to her of happier times; of virtues that had been early blighted; of hopes that his own rashness and errors had destroyed.

It was one day, one dark and fatal day, when passion raging in his bosom, and time and opportunity at hand, he suddenly approached her, and seizing her with violence, asked her if she returned his love. 'My friendship is ruin,' he cried; 'all alliance with me must cast disgrace upon the object of my regard. But, Calantha, you must be mine! May I not even now call you thus? Shall they ever persuade you to abandon me? Vain is all attempt at disguise,' he continued; 'I love you to madness and to distraction – you know it too well. Why then suffer me to feel the tortures I endure, when a word – a look from you could relieve me. You are not indifferent: say then that you are not – thou, who alone canst save me. Here even, in the presence of heaven, I will open my whole / heart before you – that heart is seered[26] with guilt; it is bleeding with venomed wounds, incurable and deadly. A few short years, I have perhaps yet to linger;[a] thou mayest accelerate my fate, and plunge me still lower, whilst I cling to thee for mercy; but will you do it, because you have the power?'

Calantha scarce could support herself. After a moment's pause, he continued; 'You shall hear me. – Never, since the hour of my birth, never – I make no exception of either the living, or, what is far dearer and more sacred to me, the dead – never did I love with such mad and frantic violence as now. O seek not to disguise it; that love is returned. I read it even now in thine eyes, thy lips; and whilst, with assumed and barbarous coldness, you would drive me from you, your own heart pleads for me; and, like myself, you love.'

Faint and trembling, Calantha now leant for support upon that arm which / surrounded her, and from which she, in vain, attempted to shrink. It was a dreadful moment. Glenarvon, who never yet had sued in vain, marked every varying turn of her countenance which too well expressed his empire and her own weakness. 'I cannot live without you. – mine you are mine[b] you shall ever be,' he said, 'whilst this heart beats with life.' Then with a smile of exultation, he seized her in his arms.

Starting however[c] with all the terror which the first approach to guilt must ever cause, 'Spare me,' she cried, terrified and trembling: 'even though my heart should break in the struggle, let me not act so basely by him to whom I am bound.' – 'Say only, that you do not hate me – say only,' he continued, with more gentleness, and pressing her hand to his lips – 'say only, that you share the tortures of agony you have inflicted – say that which I know and see – that I am loved to adoration – even as I love you.' /

With tears she besought him to spare her. 'I feel your power too much,' she said. 'All that I ought not – must not say, I think and feel. Be satisfied; your empire is complete. Spare me – save me; I have not power to feign.' Her tears fell now unrestrained. 'There is no need of this,' he said, recovering himself; 'you have sealed my fate. A moment of passion beguiled me: I am calm now, as when first I met you – calm and cold, even as yourself. Since it is your wish, and since my presence makes your misery, let us part. – I go, as I have often said; but it shall be alone. My country I leave without regret; for the chain of tyranny has encompassed it: friends, I have none; and thou, who wert as an angel of light to me – to whom I knelt for safety and for peace – mayst thou be blest: this is all I ask of heaven. As for me, nothing can increase the misery I feel. I wish you not to believe it, or to share it. This is no lover's despondency – no sudden and violent paroxysm occasioned / by disappointed passion. It is uttered,' he continued, 'in the hopelessness of despair: it is the confession, not the repining of a heart that was early blighted and destroyed.'

Calantha now interrupted him. 'I alone am guilty,' she replied, 'talk not of leaving me; we may still be friends – we must never be more.' 'Oh! promise that we shall never be less.' Glenarvon looked on her with kindness. 'Let no fears dissuade you until I shew myself unworthy of the trust. Forsake not him, whose only happiness is in your affection. I was joyless and without hope, when first I met you; but the return, to loneliness and misery, is hard to bear. Be virtuous, and, if it may be so, be happy.' 'That I never more can be,' she answered. 'You are young in sin yet,' said Glenarvon; 'you know not its dangers, its pleasures, or its bitterness. All this, ere long, will be forgotten.' 'Never forgotten,' she replied, 'oh never!' /

CHAPTER XX.

GLENARVON[27] wandered forth every evening[a] by the pale moon, and no one knew whither he went, and no one marked but Calantha how late was his return. And when the rain fell heavy and chill, he would bare his forehead to the storm; and faint and weary wander forth, and often he smiled on others and appeard calm, whilst the burning fever of his blood continued to rage within.

Once Calantha followed him, it was at sunset, and he shewed when he beheld her, no mark of surprise or joy. She followed him to the rocks called the Black Sisters, and the cleft in the mountain called the Wizzard's Glen; there was a lonely cottage near the cleft where St. Clara, it was said, had taken up her abode. He knocked; but she was from / home: he called; but no one replied from within. Her harp was left at the entrance of a bower: a few books and a table were also there. Glenarvon approached the harp and leaning upon it, fixed his eyes mournfully and stedfastly[b] upon Calantha. 'Others who formerly felt or feigned interest for me,' he said[c] 'were either unhappy in their marriage, or in their situation; but you brave every thing for me. Unhappy Calantha! how little do you know the heart for which you are preparing to sacrifice so much.'

The place upon which they stood was wild and romantic; the sea murmured beneath them; distant sounds reached them from the caverns; and the boats passed to and fro within the harbour. The descent was rugged and dangerous. Calantha looked first upon the scene, and then upon Glenarvon: still he leant upon the harp, and seemed to be lost in melancholy remembrances.

'Sing once again,' she said, at length / interrupting him – 'Ah! sing as I first heard you: – those notes reached the heart.' 'Did they?' he cried, approaching her, as his lips pressed, upon hers, one ardent kiss. The blood rushed from her heart in alarm and agitation: – she trembled and turned from him. 'There is no cause,' he said, gently following her: – 'it is the first kiss of love, sweet one; the last alone[d] is full of bitterness.'

'Sing to me' she said, confused and terrified, 'for God's sake,[e] approach me not[28] – I am alone – I fear you.' 'I will[f] sing,' he said, 'and check those fears,' saying which he began. It was not like a song, but a sort of soft low murmur, with an air of such expression and empassioned feeling, that every note said more than words: it vibrated to the soul.

'Farewell.'ª
Ah! frown not thus – nor turn from me,
    I must not – dare not – look on thee;
    Too well thou know'st how dear thou art,
    'Tis hard but yet 'tis best to part:
    I wish thee not to share my grief,
    It seeks, it hopes, for no relief. /
'Farewell.'
    Come give thy hand, what though we part,
    Thy name is fixed, within my heart;
    I shall not change, nor break the vow
    I made before and plight thee now;
    For since thou may'st not live for me,
    'Tis sweeter far to die for thee.
'Farewell'
    Thou'lt think of me when I am gone[b]
    None shall undo, what I have done;
    Yet even thy love I would resign
    To save thee from remorse like mine;
    Thy tears shall fall upon my grave:
    They still may bless – they cannot save.

'Sing no more,' said Calantha, 'let us return home. I know not what I say, or do. Judge not of my feelings by those which predominate in your presence. I may be weak, I acknowledge your power, I am lost irretrievably if you are resolved upon it.' 'Calantha', said Lord Glenarvon firmly, 'you may trust implicitly to my honor. – These are the last guilty words, I will ever suffer to pass my lips. Henceforward consider me only as your friend – as such accept my hand.'[c] /

At that moment,[d] they were interrupted; a bark from Inis Tara approached the shore, and O'Kelly, Lord Glenarvon's servant, and two other men lighted.[f] 'To avoid observation, I will join my friends one moment,' he said, 'if you will walk gently home, I can overtake you, – but, perhaps you will await my return.' 'I will go home: it is late,' said Calantha. He appeared much vexed; 'well then[e] I will await your return,' saying this Calantha descended with him the rugged path down the cliff, and watched the lessening bark, and heard the distant shouts from some of his followers who were assembled in the cavern, as they hailed his approach to land: after which a long silence prevailed, alone interrupted by the rippling of the waves. The meeting was apparently over: there were whole parties returning from below, in different directions.

Whilst yet awaiting Lord Glenarvon's return, Calantha heard the same air repeated,[g] / which he had so lately played. It seemed as if the wind, as it blew

along the wooded shores[a] had struck upon the chords.[29] It was strange; for Glenarvon was gone. She turned in haste, and from above beheld a young man. Ah no – it was St. Clara. Too soon she saw that it was her. Her ear had caught the last murmurs of Glenarvon's song, and her hand feebly repeated the strain. But, soon perceiving Calantha, she gazed with wild alarm one moment upon her, then,[b] throwing the plumed hat aside, with a grace and ease peculiar to herself, she struck the full chords, and her clear voice ascended upon the air in soft impassioned numbers. Lady Avondale heard the words of her song as it murmured along the breeze.

(To the air of, *'Hear me swear how much I love.'*)

> By that smile which made me blest,
> And left me soon the wretch you see –
> By that heart I once possest,
> Which now, they say, is given to thee –
> By St. Clara's wrongs and woes –
> Trust not young Glenarvon's vows. /
>
> By those lays which breathe around
> A poet's great and matchless art –
> By that voice whose silver sound
> Can soothe to peace th' imprisoned heart –
> By every bitter pang I prove –
> Trust not young Glenarvon's love.
>
> Each brighter, kinder hope forsaking,
> Bereft of all that made life dear[c]
> My health impaired, my spirit breaking,
> Yet still too proud to shed one tear:
> Oh lady, by my wrongs and woes,
> Trust not young Glenarvon's vows.
>
> And when at length the hand of death
> Shall bid St. Clara's heart be still –
> When struggling with its[d] latest breath,
> His image shall her fancy fill,
> Ah trust to one whose death shall prove
> What fate attends Glenarvon's love.[30]

Lady Avondale eagerly attempted to approach[e] her. 'Beautiful[f] unhappy St. Clara, I will be your friend – will protect you.'[g] She ran forward, and climbed the steep ascent with ease;[h] but the youthful harper arose – her dark sunny ringlets waving over her flushed cheek and eyes: she slightly bowed to Calantha as if in / derision; and laughing,[i] as she upheld a chain with an emerald ring, bounded over the rocks with an activity, which long habit had rendered familiar.

Calantha beheld her no more: but the distant shouts of applause re-echoed as at first among the caverns and mountains; and the bark with Lord Glenarvon soon reappeared[a] in sight. She awaited his return. As he approached the beach, a loud murmur of voices from behind the rock continued. He joined her in a moment. His countenance was lighted with the ray of enthusiasm: – his altered manner shewed the success his efforts had obtained. He told Calantha of his projects; he described to her the meetings which he had held by night and day; and he spoke with sanguine hope of future success – the freedom of Ireland, and the deathless renown of such as supported her fallen rights. 'Some day you must follow me,' he cried: 'let me shew you the cavern beneath the rock, where I / have appointed our meeting for the ensuing week.'

'I will walk no more with you to Inis Tara: – the harp sounds mournfully on those high cliffs: – I wish never more to hear it.' 'Have you seen St. Clara?' he said, without surprise. 'She sings and plays well, does she not? But she is not dear to me: think not of her. I could hate her, but that I pity her. Young as she is, she is cruelly hardened and vindictive.' – 'I cannot fear her: she is too young and too beautiful to be as abandoned as you would make me think.' – 'It is those who are young and beautiful you should fear most,' said he, approaching her more nearly. – 'I may fear them,' she replied, 'but can you teach me to fly them?'

It was now late: very little else[b] passed: they returned home, where they were received with considerable coldness. But Lady Mandeville, perceiving the state of suffering to which Calantha had reduced / herself, generously came forward to sooth and to assist her. She appeared really attached to her; and at this time more even than at any former period, shewed her sincere and disinterested friendship. And yet she was the person Mrs. Seymour distrusted; and even Glenarvon spoke of her with asperity and disdain. 'Adelaide! though an envious world may forsake thee, a grateful friend shall stand firm by thee to the last.' Such were Calantha's thoughts,[c] as Lady Mandeville, languidly throwing her rounded arm over her, pressed her to her bosom, and sighed to think of the misery she was preparing for herself. – 'Yet, when I see how he loves thee,' she continued, 'I cannot blame, I will not judge thee.'

That evening Glenarvon wrote to Lady Avondale. His letter repeated all he had before said; it was ardent: it was unguarded. She had scarce received it, scarce placed it in her bosom, when Lady Margaret attacked her. 'You / think,' she said, 'that you have made a conquest. Silly child, Lord Glenarvon is merely playing upon your vanity.' Lady Augusta whispered congratulations: Sophia hoped she was pleased with her morning walk; Sir Everard coldly asked her if she had beheld[d] his niece, and then, with a sneer at Lord Glenarvon, said it was vastly pleasant to depend upon certain people's promises.

All this time Calantha felt not grieved: Glenarvon had said he loved her: it was enough: his attachment was worth all else beside; and Lord Avondale's increasing neglect and coldness steeled her heart against the crime of inconstancy.

Before supper, Glenarvon took an opportunity of speaking to her. 'If you accept my friendship,' he said frowning, 'I must be obeyed: – you will find me a master – a tyrant perhaps; not a slave. If I once love, it is with fervor – with madness. I must have no trifling, no rivals. The being I worship must be / pure even in thought; and, if I spare her, think not that it is to let others approach her. No, Lady Avondale; not even what appears most innocent to you, shall be endured by me. I shall be jealous of every look, word, thought. There must be no shaking of hands, no wearing of chains[a] but such as I bestow, and you must write all you think and feel without reserve or fear. Now, mark me, fly if you have the power; but if you remain, you already know your fate.

Calantha resolved to fly: yes;[b] she felt the necessity. To-morrow, she said, she would go. That to-morrow came, and she had not strength. Glenarvon wrote constantly: she replied with the same openness. 'Your letters chill me,' he said, 'call me your friend, your lover: call me Glenarvon – Clarence if you will. All these forms, these regulations are odious amongst those who are attached. Say that you love, beloved Calantha: my own heart's friend, say it; / for I see it, and know it.' There is no greater crime in writing it than in feeling it. Calantha said it too soon – too soon she wrote it. 'My dearest Clarence, my friend, my comforter:' such were the terms she used. Shame to the pen, the hand that dared to trace them. Days, and days passed, and soon Glenarvon was all on earth to her; and the love he felt or feigned, the only hope and happiness of her existence. /

CHAPTER XXI.

Lord Avondale[a] now looked more and more coldly on Calantha;[b] but all others courted and flattered her. The Princess and many others had departed. Mrs. Seymour alone appeared to watch her with anxiety. In vain Calantha affected the most thoughtless gaiety: remorse and suspense alternately agitated her mind. One evening she observed Lord Glenarvon and her aunt, Mrs. Seymour, in earnest discourse – she knew not then that she herself was the subject. 'She is pure, she is innocent,' said Mrs. Seymour: 'her spirits wild and thoughtless, may have led her into a thousand follies; but worse, never – never.' – 'Fierce passion burns in her eye,' said Glenarvon, scornfully: 'the colour in her cheeks varies. – I love her as well as you / can,' he continued, laughing; 'but do you think she does not love me a little in return?' – 'Oh! even in jest, do not talk thus of Calantha,' said Mrs. Seymour: 'you alarm me.' – 'There is no occasion,' replied Glenarvon: 'calm yourself. I only said, that were I to attempt it I could succeed; she should be ready to leave you, and Lord Avondale, her dear husband and her babes, and her retinue, and all else; and I could make her follow me as St. Clara did:[c] aye verily; but, in truth, I will not.' Mrs. Seymour was angry; she coloured; she was hurt. 'You could not,' she replied with warmth.[d] 'O I know her well,[e] and know you could not. Whatever her faults, she is so pure, so chaste even in thought.' – 'She loves me.' – 'It is false[f] said Mrs. Seymour, still more eagerly. 'Even if she had any foolish romantic liking to another than her husband, Buchanan is the favourite'[g] – 'Buchanan!' said Lord Glenarvon with a sneer. 'I will make her heart ache for this,' after which he retired.

Calantha knew not then one word of what had passed. The morning after[h] she was informed by Mrs. Seymour that Lord Glenarvon was gone. 'Gone! where?' she said rather in surprise, and agitated. 'I know not,' replied Mrs. Seymour, coldly enough. 'I conclude to Belfont: his uncle Lord de Ruthven[i] is arrived there. But, indeed, I am glad he is gone: – you have not conducted yourself well. I, your aunt, have no doubt of you; but others,[j] who know you less, Calantha,[k] blame you more.'

A letter was now delivered to Mrs. Seymour: she opened it: it was from Glenarvon; she was dreadfully agitated upon reading it. It contained these words:

– 'As you seem to doubt the confidence and attachment with which your niece, the[a] Countess of Avondale, has honoured me, I enclose you one of her own letters, that you may see my vanity alone did not authorise me in the conclusion that she was attached to me. Her duplicity to me can scarcely justify the means I take of / opening an aunt's eyes; but the peculiar circumstances of my situation will, I hope, excuse it. Your most obedient servant. GLENARVON.'

This letter enclosed one of Lady Avondale's – one which, however, she had not blushed to write. She read it with terror when Mrs. Seymour placed it in her hands. Cruel Glenarvon! could he have the heart thus to betray me – to my own aunt too. Oh![b] had that aunt been less indulgent, less kind, what had been my fate?

'You are innocent yet, my child,' said Mrs. Seymour, placing her arms around her; 'and the early conviction of the meanness and wickedness of him for whom you were preparing to sacrifice so much, will render it easy to reclaim yourself from your present errors, and look with less confidence in future.'[c] – 'Never, never, will I pardon him,' cried / Calantha, with supprest indignation.[d] 'I will not hate; that were too flattering to his vanity: I will not fly; that were a proof that there was cause for it: but, lowered to the dust as I ought to feel – humbled to the earth (and whilst she spoke, she looked and felt more proudly, more vainly than ever), even I can despise him. What are superior talents, if he who possesses them can act thus? Oh! I would[e] rather die in torture, than ever pardon this.'

'Be less violent,' said Mrs. Seymour, with a look of heart-broken tenderness and affection: 'that stubborn spirit must be subdued.' – 'I will revenge –––' 'Be calm, Calantha: think what you are saying: how unfeminine and how puerile! Put off these frowns and this idle rage, and look reasonably upon your own conduct, not upon his.' – 'Shall you ever permit him to enter these doors again?' – 'Had I the power, assuredly never.' – 'Oh, let him return; I care / not; I can see him with the scorn, with the indifference he deserves. Do not look thus, my dearest aunt: dry your tears: I am not worth one single tear now; but I will act in future so as to silence even these too just reproaches.'

'Do you repent, Calantha?' – 'Do not talk of repentance: I cannot feel it: my sin is light compared with his.' – 'Towards your husband.' – 'Oh! Lord Avondale, he is happy enough: he cares not.' – 'Indeed he does, my child. I tremble for you: every hour of your life is a continual warfare and peril. One danger no sooner ends than another arises. Will you never consider the duties of your situation, or the character you have to form and to preserve?' – 'Who is more loved than I am? On whom does even the world smile with greater kindness? Beauties, wits, the virtuous – can they cope with me? I am every one's friend, and every one loves, even though they blame Calantha.' As / she said this, she smiled,[f] and threw herself on her aunt's bosom.

But all this Calantha did but to cheer her aunt. Though not false, she dreaded any one's seeing the real state of her mind: at this moment,ª she thought Mrs. Seymour too gentle, and of too tender a nature to bear the violence of her headstrong character: –ᵇ she knew it would cause her misery were she to read her heart's secret, and she smiled therefore and spoke with levity, whilst her soul was in torture. But the very moment Mrs. Seymour had left her, Calantha gave way to the rage of fury, and the despondency she felt. To have lost Glenarvon, was at this time the real source of her regret; – to speculate upon the cause of his sudden cruelty and treachery her sole occupation.

At the hour of dinner Mrs. Seymour again entered her room; but without a single reproach. She had been crying – her eyes were swollen and red; but she / affected scarcely to remember what had passed, and urged Calantha to accompany her to dinner, as her absence on the day Lord Glenarvon was from home,ᶜ might appear strange. But Lady Avondale stubbornly refused, and would not speak. She even appeared sullen, that her aunt might not see she was miserable. She even affected more anger, more violence than she felt against Glenarvon, that she might disguise from herself and her aunt the pang his loss had given her. She relented however when she saw her aunt's grief; and, struggling with tears which never come till passion is over, and which she thought it weak to display, she dressed and appeared at dinner. It was alone to please Mrs. Seymour she had done so; and, solely engrossed with the past, and utterly indifferent to the mortifying remarks her melancholy and silence occasioned, Calantha hated those who had the unkindness to censure and judge her, and looked not upon herself with one sentiment of condemnation.ᵈ /

Towards evening Lord Avondale came to her, and said kindly enough that she looked ill. Then her heart smote her, and affecting a pettish ill temper, which she did not, could not feel, she replied that she was well, and took up a book, as if to read. May none ever experience the torture Calantha felt, when, instead of being offended, he gently pressed her hand. She had rather he had struck a dagger into her heart.

Upon retiring to rest, Lady Avondale sent for Zerbellini, and asked him respecting Lord Glenarvon. The boy was a constant favourite and playmate of his;ᵉ he carried notes and flowers, from each to the other; and artless as he was, he already felt delight in the eager interest so much mystery and secresyᶠ required. – He told Lady Avondale a thousand anecdotes of Glenarvon; but he had told them so often that they failed to please. He then showed her the presents he had received from those who formerly professed to like her. 'And did you ever shew / them to Lord Glenarvon?' said Lady Avondale?ᵍ The thought occurring that this might have offended. 'I did,' said Zerbellini, with a shrewd smile. – 'And was he angry?' – 'Oh, not in the least: only the more kind; and he did question me so:' and then the boy repeated a thousand things that he had asked, which shewed Calantha,ª too well, how eager he was to ascertain, from other lips than her's, every minute detail of follies and errors she had committed. There was no need for this.

Lady Avondale felt indignant; for there was not a thought of her heart[b] she desired to conceal from him.[c] What she had done wrong, she herself had confessed without reserve; and to be thus cross-examined and distrusted,[d] deeply grieved her. She thought,[e] too, it lessened her regard; it gave her a worse opinion of Glenarvon; and this god – this idol, to whom she had bowed so low, sunk at once from the throne of glory upon which her imagination / had raised him. 'If I pardon this,' she cried, as she sent Zerbellini away, and hastened to bed, – 'if ever I waste a tear, or sigh, or thought, on him[f] again, may I suffer what I deserve. – But the thing is impossible.'

Lady Mandeville at this time was all kindness to Lady Avondale. She was going from the castle; and, as she parted, she gave her this advice.[g] 'Never place yourself in the power of any man: love of this sort is apt to terminate in a wreck; and whoever puts most to stake[h] will be the sufferer.' Lady Augusta also departed. /

CHAPTER XXII.

From that day, Lady Avondale grew more calm;[a] a degree of offended pride supported her; and she resolved, cost what it might, to continue firm. She saw, that private communications were taking place between Lady Margaret, her Father,[b] and even her Aunt[c] and Glenarvon. He had already contrived to interest every individual in the castle in his affairs. – Lord Avondale often spoke of him with praise; Sir Richard, though he said he was a comical personage, admired him, and the female part of the society were all eager and enthusiastic about him.[d]

Lady Avondale experienced every feeling that can be imagined during this short period; and received the half concealed taunts of her acquaintance with / becoming fortitude – even their commiseration for his having left her. She heard their boasts too of what he had written to them, without once repining; but envy, rancour, malice, hatred, rage and regret – all, more or less, arose and subsided in her breast, till she heard one morning, with a sort of trepidation, that Lord Glenarvon was in the adjoining room. Mrs. Seymour immediately came to her. 'Tell me truly,' she said, 'have you any objection to his dining here?' 'Quite the contrary,' said Calantha, with indifference; and she waited till she heard the sound of the horses galloping from the outer court; she then looked from the window, and her heart told her too well that she was not yet entirely recovered from her infatuation.

At dinner they were to expect him; and 'till dinner Lady Avondale could think of nothing else. Mrs. Seymour watched her with anxiety. – She affected all things,[e] to disguise what she felt, and / she did it[f] better than before, for habit now rendered the effort less painful. But Lady Margaret, laughing at her,[g] whispered maliciously in her ear, that every thought and feeling,[h] was more strongly exhibited by her, with all her attempts to hide them than by most others, when they wished them to be seen. 'And I know,' she added, unkindly enough, 'you would give any thing on earth to be friends with him again.' 'With who?'[i] 'See he appears,' she said, 'shall I name him?'

Lady Avondale had resolved to be firm. There is a degree of dignity, which every proud mind can assume. To have forgiven so much treachery and cruelty, had been contemptible. She felt it, and prepared for the encounter. 'He will do every thing to regain you,' said Mrs. Seymour, 'but I have confidence in your present feelings. Shew him, that you are not what he imagines; and prove to me, that I may still be proud of my / child.'³¹ Lady Avondale had taken Glenarvon's ring from her finger, she had placed upon her neck a row of pearls her husband had given her, upon the eve of her marriage, and thus decorated, she thought her heart had likewise returned to its ancient allegiance.

Lady Avondale^a entered the dining-room. Lord Glenarvon passed her at the moment; he was in earnest conversation with Lady Margaret, and slightly bowed to her. She was surprised, she had expected kindness and contrition. She was, however, resolved to act up to the very strictest bounds which decorum prescribed. With some haughtiness, some appearance at least of dignity, she seated herself as far from him as he could desire, and by addressing herself calmly but entirely to others, she sought to attain that look of unconcern, which he had so readily assumed.

Dinner was no sooner over than unable any longer to conceal her vexation, / Lady Avondale[b] retired to her room to compose herself. Upon returning, the large society were employed either with billiards, cards, or work – except a few of the men, amongst whom she perceived Lord Glenarvon. Had he refrained from speaking to her, she could have borne it, – had he even looked as grave, as ill as usual; but an unusual flow of spirits – a peculiar appearance of health, had taken place of that customary languor,[c] to which he was at times subject.

The evening and the supper passed without his saying one word in apology for his unkindness, or in the least attending to her increasing irritation. Lady Avondale[d] affected unconcern as well as she could, but it looked like any thing else; and in the morning she awoke but to suffer new humiliations. She saw him smile as he named her in a whisper to Lady Trelawney. She heard him talk to others upon subjects he had once spoken of only to herself. Immediately / upon this apparent rupture, new hopes arose; new claims were considered; and that competition for his favour, which had ceased, began again. Lady Trelawney laughed and talked with him; at times turning her eye triumphantly towards Calantha. Sophia confided her opinions to his breast; affected to praise him for his present conduct, and the tear of agony, which fell from Calantha's eye, excited the indignation it deserved.[e]

'I have sacrificed too much for one who is heartless,' she said; 'but, thank God[f] it is yet time for amendment.' Alas! Lady Avondale knew not, as she uttered these words, that there is no moment in which it is so difficult to act with becoming dignity and firmness, as that in which we are piqued and trampled upon by the object of our devotion. Glenarvon well knew this, and smiled at the pang he inflicted, as it proved his power, and exhibited its effects to all. Lady / Avondale summoned to her aid even her faults – the spirit, the pride of her character, her very vanity; and rested her hopes of firmness upon her contempt for weakness, her abhorrence of vice. She looked upon him, and saw his attempts to wound, to humiliate, to grieve; and she despised the man who could have recourse to every petty art to torture one for whom he had professed so much. If he wished to expose her weakness to every eye, too well he had succeeded. /

CHAPTER XXIII.

FEW women know how to conceal successful love, but none can conceal their doubt, resentment and jealousy. Men can do both, and both without a struggle. They feel less, and fear more. But this was not the case with Lord Glenarvon, nor did he wish to appear indifferent; he only wished Calantha to feel his power, and he delighted in the exhibition of it. In vain she had formed the best resolutions, they were now all rendered useless. Lord Glenarvon had forestalled her wise intention, no coldness – no indifference she could assume, had equalled that, which he either affected or felt.

Upon the bosom of Mrs. Seymour, Calantha wept for her fault; it was infatuation, she said, she was cured: the / lesson, though somewhat harsh, had not been fruitless. Again, she made every promise, which affection and repentance could suggest. She heard the name of her husband pronounced, and longed to throw herself before him, and commend herself to his mercy. I do repent, indeed I do, said Calantha, repeatedly in the course of the day; and she thought her penitence had been sincere. Humbled now, and gentle, she thought only of pleasing her aunt, Lord Avondale, and her friends. She was desired to play during the evening: to shew her ready obedience[a] she immediately obeyed. Lord Glenarvon was in an adjoining room; he entered when she began: springing up, Lady Avondale left the harp; then, seeing Lord Avondale surprised, she prepared to tune it.

Lord Glenarvon approached, and offered her his hand, she refused it. 'Will you play?' he said – and she turned the key with so much force that it broke the / chords asunder. 'You have wound them too tight, and played upon them too often,' he said. 'Trifle not with me thus – I cannot play now,' she replied. 'Leave me, I entreat you.' 'You know not what you have done,' he replied. 'All I ask – all I implore is, that you will neither come near me, nor speak to me more, for I am mad.' 'Women always recover from these paroxysms,' said he, gaily. Calantha attempted to play, and did so extremely ill, after which she went to bed, happier, it must be owned, for she had seen in Lord Glenarvon's manner that he was not indifferent, and this rendered it more easy for her to appear so.

The next morning Lady Avondale went out immediately after breakfast, without speaking to Lord Glenarvon. He twice attempted it, but with real anger, she refused to hear him. It was late in the day, when, having sought for her before dinner, he at length found her / alone. His voice faultered, his eyes were filled with tears. 'Lady Avondale – Calantha,' he said, approaching her, 'forgive me. – I ask it of you, and more, if you require it, I will kneel – will sue for it. You can make me what you please – I am wholly in your power.' 'There is no need for this,' she said coldly.

'I will not rise till you forgive me. If you knew all – if ... but can you indeed believe me indifferent, or cold? Look at me once: raise your eyes and behold him, who lives but in you.' 'All this is useless, you have grieved me; but I do not mean to reproach,[a] the idle complainings of a woman are ever useless. 'To think that she suffers,' said Glenarvon, 'is enough. Look once – once only, look upon me.' 'Let us part in peace,' she replied: 'I have no complaint to make, I have nothing to forgive,' 'raise[b] your eyes, and look – Calantha look once on me.' /

She turned to him, she saw that face whose every feature was engraved deep in her very heart – that smile of sweetness – that calm serenity, she had not power to speak – to think; and yet recovering from this strange enchantment, – 'How could you betray me?' she said. 'I judge you not, but I can never feel either interest, or friendship again.' 'Yet,' said Glenarvon gravely, 'I need both at this time, for I am miserable and ill too, only I do not wish to excite your compassion by these arts, and I had rather die unforgiven, than use any towards you.'

'Wherefore did you betray me?' 'Can you ask? I was deeply wounded. It is not enough for me that you love me, all must, and shall know it. I will make every sacrifice for you – run every risk; but every risk and every sacrifice must be shared.' 'Whatever my feelings may be,' she answered coldly, 'you shall never subdue me again. I may be / infatuated, but I will never be criminal – You may torture me as you please, if you have the power over me which you imagine, but I can bear torture, and none ever yet subdued me.'

'Calantha,' said Lord Glenarvon, taking her hand firmly, and smiling half scornfully, 'you shall be my slave. I will mould you as I like; teach you to think but with my thoughts, to act but with my feelings, you shall wait nor murmur – suffer, nor dare complain – ask, and be rejected – and all this, I will do, and you know it, for your heart is already mine.' 'If I forgive you,' she cried. 'If you do not' he said, approaching nearer. 'I never will.' 'And 'till you do, though your whole family should enter, I will kneel here – here, even at your feet.' 'You think to menace me.' 'I know my empire. Take off those ornaments: replace what I have given you: this too you shall wear,' he said, throwing a chain around her,[c] / 'Turn from me if you can: the heart that I have won, you cannot reclaim,[d] and though the hand be thus denied me, this, this is mine.' Saying this, he pressed her lips to his, a strange feeling thrilled to her heart as she attempted vainly to hate him, or extricate herself from his embrace. 'I love you to madness,'ᵃ he said, 'and you distract me. Trust yourself entirely to me, it is the only means of safety left. Yes, Calantha, I will do for you, what no man ever did before. If it destroy me, I will never lead you to guilt, only rely upon me, be guided by me.' 'You ran the risk' she said, 'of our being separated for ever, of making my aunt miserable. Of – – –' 'Nonsenseᵇ child, I never risk any thing, it was necessary your aunt should know,ᶜ and the fear of losing you entirely will make her readily consent to my seeing you more than ever.' 'Oh God! what guilt.ᵈ Think not that my attachment is such as to bear it.' 'It shall bear all / things,' said Glenarvon; 'but if you sacrifice what I desire, I will conquer every wrong feeling for your sake?ᵉ Our friendship will then be innocent.' 'Not absolutely . . . . . . indeed I fear it; and if – – – .' 'Ah! leave these gloomy thoughts. If love should triumph – if you feel half for me, what I feel from my soul for you, then you shall accompany me from hence. Avondale may easily find another wife, but the world contains for me but one Calantha.'

Lady Avondale felt happy. – Shame on the guilty heart that dared to feel so! but alas, whilst Glenarvon thus addressed her,ᶠ she did feel most happy. In a moment, the gloom that had overshadowed her future hopes, was dispelled. She saw her lover – her friendᵍ more than ever united to her. He consented even to respect what remaining virtue she had left, and from his gentle, his courteous words, it was not her wish to escape. Yet still she resolved to leave him. Now, / that peace was again restored, that her irritated mind was calm, that her vanity was flattered, and her pride satisfied, now the admonitions of her aunt recurred,ʰ and even while her heart beat fondest for him, she pronounced her own doom, and declared to him that she would tear herself away from him for ever. 'Perhaps this must be,' he said, after a moment's pause; 'but not yet, Calantha, ahⁱ not yet.' As he spoke, he again pressed her to his bosom,³² and his tears fell over her.ʲ Oh! had he not thus wept, Calantha had not loved him. Struggling with his feelings for her, he generously resolved to save, to spare her. 'Remember this,' he said, 'when they condemn me. – Remember,ᵏ Calantha, what I have done for you; how I have respected you; and let not their idle clamours prevail.'

Lady Avondale was too happy to feel vain. Glenarvon loved, as she never had been loved before, every hour – / every moment of each passing day he seemed alone intent, and occupied with her; he wrote his minutest thoughts; he counselled, he did not command. He saw that power, ambition, was her ruling passion, and by affecting to be ruled, he completely mastered her – in word, in look, in thought, he was devoted to her. Other men think only of themselves; Glenarvon conquered himself a thousand times for her.³³ What is a momentary, a degrading passion to the enjoyment she felt in his society? It only lowers the object of its fancy, he sought to raise her even in her own esteem. 'Forgive her, pity us,' he said, addressing Mrs. Seymour, who saw in a moment, with alarm, their reconciliation. 'Drive us not to despair, I will respect her – will preserve her, if you do not attempt to tear her from me, but dread the violence of madness, if you reduce us to the last rash step. Oh dread / the violence of a mad and incurable attachment.

Calantha's sole attention was now to hide from those it might grieve, the change which a few days had again wrought. She appeared at dinner, she seated herself opposite to Glenarvon. There was no look of exultation in his countenance, his eyes met her's mournfully. The diamond bracelets that adorned her arms, had been given her by him; the chain and locket, which contained his dark hair, had been placed around her neck in token of his regard; the clasp that fastened the band around her waist, was composed of richest jewels brought by him from distant countries; and the heart that was thus girt round and encircled with his gifts, beat only for him, regardless of every other tie. 'Oh my child! my child!' said Mrs. Seymour, gazing on her in agony. 'I will never reproach you, but do not break my / heart. You are ill in mind and health, you know not what you say or do; God forgive and pardon you, my unhappy Calantha!'ᵃ 'Bear with me a few moments,'ᵇ said Lady Avondale much agitated: 'I will part from him; only give me time. Fear me not: I will neither leave you nor act wickedly,ᶜ but if you seek too hastily to sever us, oh my aunt, you may be the means of driving two desperate minds to misery and madness.'ᵈ /

CHAPTER XXIV.

A FEW days previous to this quarrel and reconciliation, Sir Everard St. Clare had been thrown from his horse in consequence of a tumult, in which[a] having beheld his niece and a dimness coming over his eyes,[b] he was no longer able to support himself. The fall was said to have[c] injured his spine. He was confined to his own room; but no one could prevail upon him to lie upon his bed, or admit Lady St. Clare, who sat continually sobbing at his door, lamenting her conduct and imploring his pardon.

Whatever were the sufferings of Lady Avondale's mind at this time, she yet resolved to visit this afflicted family, as she had a real regard for the doctor in spite of his singularities. She was preparing therefore the ensuing day, to call upon / him, when a servant informed her that a young gentleman below desired to speak with her. Her heart beat upon hearing the name Clarence of Costolly: but upon entering the room she soon discovered, in the personage before her, the doctor's unhappy niece, Elinor, upon whom every counsel was lost – every menace and punishment powerless.

Elinor had entered the castle with a look of bold defiance; yet her lips trembled, as she twice vainly attempted to address Lady Avondale, who moved forward to enquire the cause of her visit. 'I am come,' said Miss St. Clare with haughty insolence, 'to ask a favour of you – tell me shall it be granted? my[d] uncle is ill: he has sent to see me. This may be a mere feint to draw me into his power. I will trust myself with no one but you: – if you will engage for me, that I shall not be detained, I will go to him; if not, come what will, I will never more set foot into his house.' 'Your / having listened to the prayers of Sir Everard, answered Lady Avondale eagerly, 'is a proof to me that you have a kind heart, and you are so young, that I feel sure, oh most sure, that you will return to a more virtuous course.' 'To virtue!' said Elinor with a smile of scorn 'never – never.'

As she spoke, a letter dropped from her bosom. Lady Avondale saw from the superscription – the name of Glenarvon. Her heart sickened at the sight; she tried to conceal her emotion; but she had not yet learned sufficiently how to dissemble. Elinor, with ill suppressed rage, watched Lady Avondale: she could scarcely stand the fury of her glance, when in a voice, nearly choked with passion, 'take it,'[e] she said, throwing the letter to her. 'Yes, you shall give it him – give it to your lover. I would have hated you, I would have injured you; but I cannot.

No wonder he admires you: I could myself; but I am miserable.' / Lady Avondale raised her eyes: every fierce expression had left Elinor's countenance: with a subdued,ᵃ and mournful air, she turned aside as if ashamed of the weakness she had shewn; then, taking a little miniature and chain from her neck, 'heᵇ sent for this too,' she cried. 'He sent for all he gave me, to offer to his new idol. Take it then, lady; and tell himᶜ I obeyed his last command.'

A tear dimmed for a moment her eye;ᵈ recovering herself, 'heᵉ has not power,' she cried, 'to break a heart like mine. 'Tis such as you, may die for love – I have yet many years to live.' Lady Avondale sprang forward to return the picture – the letter; but St. Clare, with a precipitancy she was not prepared for, had left her; Lady Avondale arrived at the door of the Castle only in time to see her gallop off.

While she was yet holding the letter and picture in her hand, Glenarvon was announced. He looked at both without exhibiting any symptom of surprise, and having read the letter, shewed it to Calantha. It greatly shocked her. 'I am so used,' said heᶠ smiling, 'to these scenes, that they have lost all power with me.' 'Unhappy Elinor'ᵍ said Lady Avondale. 'In good truth' said Glenarvonʰ 'you may spare your pity, Calantha: the lady has spirit enough: it is her lover who ought to claim compassion. Now do not frown,' said he, 'orⁱ reproach, or torment me about her. I know it was wrong first to take her with me – it was wrong to see her since; but never more, you may rely upon it, shall I transgress; and if you knew all, you would not blame me. She absolutely forced herself upon me. She sat at my door, and wept when I urged her to return home. What could I do:ʲ I might have resisted. – Calantha, when passion is burning in every vein – when opportunity is kind – and when those who from the modesty / of their sex ought to stand above us and force us from them, forget their dignity and sue and follow us, it is not in man's nature to resist. Is it in woman's?' he continued smiling archly.

'I blame you not,' she replied; 'but I pity her. Yet wherefore not shew her some little kindness!'ᵏ 'A look, a word would bring her back to me. She misrepresents every thing: she deceives herself.' 'Love is ever apt to do so.' 'Oh! my adored Calantha, look not thus on me. You are not like this wretched girl: there is nothing feminine, or soft, or attractive in her; in you there is every charm.' 'You loved her once,'ˡ said Calantha. 'It was passion, phrenzy, it was not love – not what I feel for my Calantha.' 'As you regard me, be kind to her.' 'I was very kind once, was I not?' 'Oh not in that manner – not so.' 'How thenᵐ my soul? explain yourself; you shall instruct me.' 'Counsel her to repent.' 'From the / lips that first taught her to err, how will such counsel prevail?' 'Why take your picture from her?' 'To give it to the only friend I have left.' 'I shall send it her again.' 'She will only laugh at you.' 'I had rather be the cause of her laughter, than of her tears.' 'Fear not: she is not prone to weeping; but perhaps,' he continued in a tone of pique, 'you would wish to give *me* back also, as well as the portrait.' 'Oh never – never.' This was Lady Avondale's answer; and Lord Glenarvon was satisfied. /

CHAPTER XXV.

LADY Avondale sent the portrait to Miss St. Clare, and vainly endeavoured to restore her to her uncle's protection. She again spoke of her to Glenarvon.

'Cannot I yet save her?' she said; 'Cannot I take her home, and sooth her mind, and bring her back to virtue and to peace?' 'Never more,' he replied: 'it is past: her heart is perverted.' 'Is there no recall from such perversion?' 'None, none, my friend.' His countenance, whilst he spoke, assumed much of bitterness. 'Oh there is no recall from guilty love. The very nature of it precludes amendment, as these beautiful, these emphatic lines express, written by the Scottish bard,[34] who had felt their truth:'[a] – /

> 'The sacred lowe o'weel-plac'd love,
>   Luxuriantly indulge it;
> But never tempt th'illicit rove,
>   Tho' naething should divulge it:
> I wave the quantum o' the sin,
>   The hazard of concealing;
> But och! it hardens a' within,
>   And petrifies the feeling.'[35]

'Is it indeed so?[b] Alas! then, what will become of me?' 'Calantha, your destiny is fixed,' he cried, suddenly starting as if from deep thought; 'there is a gulph before you, into which you are preparing to plunge. I would have saved you – I tried; but cannot. You know not how to save yourself. Do you think a momentary pause, a trifling turn, will prevent the fall? Will you now fly me? now that you are bound to me, and the fearful forfeiture is paid? Oh turn not thus away: – look back at the journey you have taken from innocence and peace: and fear to tread the up-hill path / of repentance and reformation alone. Remember when a word or look were regarded by you as a crime – how you shuddered at the bare idea of guilt. Now you can hear its language with interest: it has lost its horror: Ah soon it shall be the only language your heart will like[c] Shrink not, start not, Calantha:[d] the road you pursue is that which I have followed. See and acknowledge then, the power I hold over your heart; and yield to what is already destined. You imagine, when I speak of guilt, that you can shrink from me, that you can hate me; but you have lost the power, and let me add, the right: you are become a sharer in that iniquity – you must be a sharer in my fate. The actual commission of crime still excites horror; but do you remember when you shuddered at every approach to it? And cannot he who has triumphed thus far gain all, think you, if it were his desire? Yes, you are mine – a being wholly relying upon a wish, a breath, which I may / chuse to kindle. Avondale's peace – your honour, are in my hands. If I resign you, my heart will break in the struggle; but if I give way . . . . .'

'Oh then,' she cried, 'then are we ruined for ever and for ever. Do not, even were I to consent, O! do not lead me to wrong. What shall ever remunerate us for the loss of self-approbation? He smiled bitterly. 'It is,' he said, 'a possession, I never yet cared greatly to retain.' 'And is self-approbation the greatest of all earthly enjoyments? Is man so independent, so solitary a being, that the consciousness of right will suffice to him, when all around brand him with iniquity, and suspect him of guilt?' He paused, and laughed. 'Let us be that which we are thought,' he cried, in a more animated tone. 'The worst is thought; and that worst we will become. Let us live on earth but for each other: another country will hide us from the censures of the prejudiced; and / our very dependence upon each other, will endear us more and more.' Calantha withdrew her hand – she looked upon him with fear; but she loved, and she forgot her alarm. /

CHAPTER XXVI.[36]

STRANGE as it may appear, a husband, unless his eyes are opened by the confession of his guilty partner, is the last to believe in her misconduct; and when the world has justly stamped disgrace upon her name, he shares in his wife's dishonour, for he is supposed by all to know, and to connive at her crime. But though this be a painful truth, experience every day confirms, that a noble and confiding husband is too often, and too easily deceived. In the marriage state there is little love,[a] and much habitual confidence. We see neglect and severity on the part of the man; and all the petty arts and cunning wiles on the side of his more frail and cowardly partner. Indifference first occasions this blindness; infatuation increases it; and in proportion as all interest / is lost for the object who so deceives, such husband lives the dupe of the wife, who despises him for his blindness and dies in the same happy illusion, in whch he has so long passed away his life. He even presses to his heart, as he leaves them his possessions, the children of some deceitful friend, who, under the plea[b] of amity to himself, has fed upon his fortunes, and seduced the affections of his wife.

Disgusting as such picture may be thought, is it not, unhappily for us, daily exhibited to the public view? and shall they who tolerate and see it, and smile in scorn at its continued and increasing success, affect to start with horror from Calantha's tale? or to discredit that Avondale was yet ignorant of her guilt? He was ofttimes[c] engaged with the duties of his profession – nor thought that whilst risking his life in the service of his country, the woman he loved and confided in, had betrayed him.[d] /

His cheeks were red with the hue of health; his eyes shone bright with sparkling intelligence; he laughed the loud heart's laugh at every merry jest, and slept with unbroken slumbers, the sleep of the righteous and the just. Calantha looked upon him as we look afar off upon some distant scene where we once dwelt, and from which we have long departed. It awakens in our memory former pains and pleasures; but we turn from it with bitterness; for the sight is distressing to us.

Harry Mowbray[e] loved his father and followed him; the baby Anabel held out her arms to him when he passed; but Calantha assumed a stern coldness in his presence, and replied to his few enquiries with all the apparent insensibility of a proud and offended mind: yet such is the imperfection of human nature, that it is possible Lord Avondale cherished her the more for her very faults. Certain it is, that he felt proud of her, and / every casual praise which, even from the lips of strangers, was bestowed on Calantha, gave him more delight than any profession, however flattering, that could have been made to himself. To see her blest was his sole desire; and when he observed the change in her manner and spirits, it grieved, it tortured him: – he sought, but in vain, to remove it. At length business of importance called him from her. 'Write,' he said, at parting, 'write, as you once used. My presence has given but little satisfaction to you; I dare not hope my absence will create pain.' 'Farewell,' said Lady Avondale, with assumed coldness. 'There are false hearts in this world, and crimes are enacted, Henry, at home ofttimes, as well as abroad. Confide in no one. Believe not what your own eyes perceive. Life is but as the shadow of a dream. All here is illusion. We know not whom we love.'

How happy some may imagine – how happy Calantha must have felt now that / Lord Avondale was gone. Far from it. She for the first time felt remorse.^a His departure filled her with gloom: – it^b was as if her last hope of safety were cut off; as if her good angel had for ever abandoned her; and with a reserve and prudence, which in his presence, she had failed to assume, she now turned with momentary horror from the near approach of vice.^c The thought of leaving her home and Lord Avondale, had not indeed ever seriously occurred, although she constantly listened to the proposal of doing so, and acted so as to render such a step^d necessary. She had seen Lord Avondale satisfied, and whilst Lord Glenarvon was near her, no remorse^e obtruded – no fear^f occurred – she formed no view for the future. To die with him, or to live but for that moment of time, which seemed to concentrate every possible degree of happiness, this was the only desire of which she had felt capable. But now, she shuddered – she paused: – the baseness / of betraying a noble, confiding husband, struck her mind, and filled it with alarm; but such alarm appeared only to accelerate her doom. 'If I can resist and remain without deeper guilt, I will continue here,' she cried; 'and if I fail in the struggle, I will fly with Glenarvon.' – This false reasoning consoled her. A calm, more dangerous than the preceding agitation, followed this resolve.

Glenarvon had changed entirely in his manner, in his character; all art, all attempt at wounding or tormenting was passed. He seemed himself the sufferer, and Calantha, the being upon whose attachment he relied, he was as fearful of vexing her, as she was of losing him. On earth he appeared to have no thought but her; and when again and again he repeated, 'I never loved as I do now, – oh never.' It may be doubted whether that heart exists which could have disbelieved him. Others who affect only, / are ever thoughtful of^g themselves; and some plan, some wary and prudential contrivance frequently appears, even in the very height of their passion. The enjoyment of the moment alone, and not the future continuance of attachment, employs their hopes. But Glenarvon seemed more anxious to win every affection of her heart; to fix every hope of her soul upon himself; to study every feeling as it arose, sift every motive, and secure his empire upon all that was most durable, than to win her in the usual acceptation of the word. And even though jealous that she should be ready to sacrifice every principle of honour and virtue, should he demand it, he had a pride in saving her from that guilt into which she was now voluntarily preparing to plunge.

Day by day, the thought of leaving all for him appeared more necessary and certain. – She no longer shuddered at the mention of it. She heard him describe / their future life – the countries they should visit; and it even pleased her to see that he was sincere in his intentions. No disguise was now required: he called not the fire that burnt in his heart by the name of friendship and of interest: 'it is love,' he cried, '– most guilty – most unconquerable. Hear it, mark it, and yet remain without alarm. Ah! think not that to share it alone is required: your soul must exult, that it has renounced every hope beyond; and Glenarvon's love must entirely fill your affections. Nay more, you shall sue for the sacrifice which is demanded of others. Yourself shall wish it; for I will never wrest from you that which, unless freely given, is little worth. Perhaps, even when you desire to be mine, I, even I shall spare you, till maddening with the fierce fires that devour us, you abandon all for me.'

He now opened to her the dark recesses / of his heart; deeds of guilt concealed from other eyes, he now dwelt upon to Calantha with horrid pleasure. 'Shrink not, start not,' he exclaimed, when she trembled at each new confession.[37] 'Proud, even of my crimes, shalt thou become, poor victim of thy mad infatuation; this is the man for whom thou leavest Avondale! Mark me[a] Calantha, – view me as I am, nor say hereafter that Glenarvon could deceive.' 'And do you never feel remorse?' she said. – 'Never.' 'Do you believe?' – His countenance for one moment altered. 'I know not,' he said, and he was grave. 'Oh must I become as hardened as wicked'[b] she said, bursting into tears. He pressed her mournfully to his bosom. 'Weep,' he replied, 'I like to see your tears; they are the last tears of expiring virtue. Henceforward you will shed no more.'

Those who have given way to the violence of any uncontrouled passion know / that during its influence, all other considerations vanish. It is of little use to upbraid or admonish the victim who pursues his course: the fires that goad[c] him on to his ruin, prevent his return. A kind word, an endearing smile, may excite one contrite tear; but he never pauses to reflect, or turns his eyes from the object of his pursuit. In vain the cold looks of an offended world, the heavy censures, and the pointed, bitter sarcasms of friends and dependants. Misfortunes, poverty, pain, even to the rack, are nothing if he obtain his view. It is a madness that falls upon the brain and heart. All is at stake for that one throw; and he who dares all, is desperate, and cannot fear. It was phrenzy, not love, that raged in Calantha's bosom.

To the prayers of a heart-broken parent, Lady Avondale opposed the agonizing threats of a distempered mind. 'I will leave you all, if you take him / from me. On earth there is nothing left me but Glenarvon. – Oh name not virtue and religion to me. – What are its hopes, its promises, if I lose him.' The fever of her mind was such, that she could not for one hour rest: he saw the dreadful power he had gained, and he lost no opportunity of encreasing it. Ah did he share it? In language the sweetest, and the most persuasive, he worked upon her passions, till he inflamed them beyond endurance.

'This, this is sin,' he cried, as he held her to his bosom, and breathed vows of ardent,[a] burning love. 'This is what moralists rail at, and account degrading. Now tell them, Calantha, thou who didst affect to be so pure – so chaste, whether the human heart can resist it? Religion bids thee fly me,' he cried: 'every hope of heaven and hereafter warns thee from my bosom. Glenarvon is the hell thou art to shun: – this is the hour of trial. Christians must resist. Calantha arise, / and fly me; leave me alone, as before I found thee. Desert me, and thy father and relations shall bless thee for the sacrifice: and thy God, who redeemed thee, shall mark thee for his own.' With bitter taunts he smiled as he thus spoke: then clasping her nearer to his heart, 'Tell both priests and parents,' he said exultingly, 'that one kiss from the lips of those we love, is dearer than every future hope.'[b]

All day, – every hour in the day, – every instant of passing time Glenarvon thought but of Calantha. It was not love, it was distraction.[c] When near him, she felt ecstacy: but if separated, though but[d] for one moment, she was sullen and desponding. At night she seldom slept; a burning fever quickened every pulse: the heart heat as if with approaching dissolution, – delirium fell upon her brain. No longer innocent, her fancy painted but visions of love; and to be / his alone, was all she now wished for, or desired on earth. He felt,[e] he saw, that the peace of her mind, her life itself were gone[f] for ever, and he rejoiced in the thought. /

CHAPTER XXVII.[38]

ONE night, as she retired to her room, Gondimar met her in the passage, leading from Mrs. Seymour's apartment. 'Lost woman,' he cried, fiercely seizing her, 'you know not what you love; – look to his hand, there is blood on it!' . . . . That night was a horrid night to Calantha; she slept, and the dream that oppressed her, left her feeble and disordered. The ensuing day she walked by the shores of the sea: she bared her forehead to the balmy gales. She looked upon every cheerful countenance in hopes of imbibing happiness from the smile that brightened their's,[a] but it was vain.

Upon returning, she met Glenarvon. They walked together to the mountains; they conversed; and half in jest she asked him for his hand, – 'not that hand,' / she said, 'give me your right hand: I wish to look upon it.' 'I believe I must refuse you, your manner is so strange,' he replied. 'Do if you please, for the reason I wish to see it is more so. It was a dream, a horrid dream, which made me ill last night. The effect, perhaps of what you told me yesterday.' 'I should like to hear it. Are you superstitious?' 'No; but there are visions unlike all others, that impress us deeply, and this was one. I almost fear to tell it you.' 'I too have dreamt,' said he, 'but my dream, sweet one, brought only to my fancy, the dearest wishes of my heart. Oh would to God that I might live to realize a dream like that, which blest me yesternight. Shall I repeat it?'[b] 'Not now, I am too sad for it;[c] but mine, if indeed you wish it, you may hear.'

'I dreamt (but it is absurd to repeat it) that I was in some far distant country. I was standing by the sea, and the fresh / air blew gently upon me, even as it does now; but[d] . . . . . . it was night. There was a dirge sung as in monasteries, and friars passed to and fro, in long procession before me. Their torches now and then lighted the vaults, and the chaunt was mournful, and repeatedly interrupted – all this was confused. – That which was more striking, I remember better. A monk in black stood before me; and whilst he gazed upon me, he grew to a height unusual and monstrous: he seemed to possess some authority over me, and he questioned me as to my conduct and affections. I tried to disguise from him many thoughts which disturbed me; I spoke in a hurried manner of others; I named you not. He shook his head; and then looking fiercely at me, bade me beware of Clarence de Ruthven (for so he called you). I never can forget his voice. 'All others you may see, you may converse with; but, Calantha, beware, 'he said, 'of Clarence / de Rutheven: he is a .... he is a ....' 'A what?' enquired Glenarvon eagerly. 'I dare not continue.'

Glenarvon, however, insisted upon hearing this. 'I never, never can tell,' said Calantha, for you look so much offended – so serious. –ᵃ After all, what nonsense it is thus to repeat a dream.' 'That which seems to have made no little impression upon Lady Avondale's mind, cannot fail of awakening some interest in mine. It is a very strange vision,' continued he,ᵇ fixing his eyes on her. 'These idle phantasies are but repetitions of the secret workings of the mind. Your own suspicions have coloured this. Go on, let me hear all.' 'Indeed I forget; – it was confused. I seemed in my dream to doubt his words. Only this I remember: – he bade me ask you for your hand – your right hand; he said there was a stain of blood on it; and in a low solemn tone, he added, "he will not give it you; there is a mark / upon it: he dare not give it you;" and I awoke.'

'To think me every thingᶜ however bad, that your monk may chuse to make me out. Well foolish dreamer, look at my hand: say, is there a mark on it?' The laugh which accompanied this question was forced. Calantha started back, as she againᵈ observed that almost demoniac smile. His eyes glared upon her with fierce malignity; his livid cheeks became pale; and over his forehead, an air of deep distress struggled with the violence of passion, till all again was calm, cold, and solemn, as before. She was surprised at his manner; for although he made light of it, he was certainly displeased, and much moved by this foolish occurrence.

Glenarvon continued absent and irritable during the whole of the walk; nor ceased enquiring oftentimes, that day,ᵉ respecting what she had said. It appeared to her less extraordinary, when she / remembered the circumstances concerning Linden;ᶠ yet he had so often acknowledged that event to her, – so often spoke of him with pity and regret, that had he merely thought she alluded to such transaction, he had been proud of the effort he had made to save him, and of the blood he had shed upon that account. Whatever then occasioned this strange perturbation; – however far imagination might wander, even though it pictured crimes unutterable, – under Glenarvon's formᵍ all might be forgiven. Passion, perhaps, had misled its victim, and who can condemn another when maddening under its trying influence! It was not for Calantha to judge him. It was her misfortune to feel every thing with such acute and morbid sensibility, that what in others had occasioned a mere moment of irritation, shook every fibre around her heart. The death of a bird, if it had once been dear, made her miserable; and the slightest insult, as she termed it, / rendered her furious. Severity but caused a desperate resistance, and kindness alone softened or subdued her. Glenarvon played upon every passion to the utmost; and when he beheld her, lost beyond all recall,ʰ he seemed to love her most.

How vain were it^a to attempt to paint the struggles, the pangs, the doubts, the fears, the endless unceasing irritation of a mind disordered by guilty love. Remorse had but little part in the disease; passion absorbed^b every feeling, every hope; and to retain Glenarvon was there any thing his weak and erring victim had refused? Alas! the hour came, when even to leave all and follow him appeared incumbent. The very ruin such conduct must occasion to Calantha, engaged her more eagerly to agree to the proposal.

Lady Margaret was now at times^c engaged with him in secret discourses, which occasioned much apparent dissention between them; but Calantha was not the subject. 'He has the heart of a fiend.' / Lady Margaret would often exclaim, as she left him; and Calantha could perceive that, with all her power of dissimulation,^d she was more moved^e more irritated by him, than she ever had been before by any other. He also spoke of Lady Margaret with bitterness, and the asperity between them grew to such a height, that Calantha apprehended the most fatal effects from it. Still, however, the Duke wished to conciliate a dangerous and malignant foe; and though his visits to the castle were short, compared with what they had been, they were as frequent as ever. /

CHAPTER XXVIII.

It happened one morning that Calantha, having been walking with Lord Glenarvon, upon her return entered the library rather unexpectedly, and perceived Zerbellini with the Count Gondimar and Lady Margaret. They all seemed in some confusion at her entrance. She was however too deeply occupied with other thoughts to enquire into their strange embarrassment; and looking at Glenarvon, she watched the varying expression of his countenance with anxious solicitude. At dinner that day[a] he seated himself near her. Mrs. Seymour's eyes were filled with tears. 'It is too late,' he said, in a low whisper: 'be firm: it makes me mad to see the arts that are used to separate us. Speak only to me – think only of me. What avail their frowns. / their reproaches? I am dearer, am I not than all?'

Dinner being over, Calantha avoided her aunt's presence. She perceived it, and approaching her, 'My child,' she said, 'do not fly me. My unhappy Calantha,[b] you will break my heart,[c] if you act thus.' At that moment Lady Margaret joined them:[d] 'Ask Calantha,' she said, 'now ask her about the pearl necklace.'

The pearl necklace in question was one which Lord Avondale had given Calantha[e] on the eve of her marriage. She was now accused of having given it to Lord Glenarvon. It is true that she had placed in his hands all the jewels of which she was mistress, that his presents might not exceed in value such as she had power to offer; they had been too magnificent otherwise for her to receive; and though only dear because they were his gifts, yet to have taken them without return had been more pain than pleasure: / one smile of his were worth them all – one approving look, far dearer. This gift of Lord Avondale's, however, she had considered as sacred, and neither Lord Glenarvon's love, nor her own perversion, had led her to touch it. She had received it when innocent and true; it was pain to her even to look upon it now; and when she heard the accusation made against her, she denied it with considerable warmth; for guilt but irritates the mind, and renders the perpetrator impatient of accusation. 'This indignation is rather ill-timed however,' said Lady Margaret, sarcastically: 'there are things more sacred than pearls thrown away; and if the necklace has not been given, it is, I believe, the only thing, that has been retained.'[f]

Such unpleasant conversation was now interrupted by Sophia, who entered the room. – 'The necklace is found,' she said:[a] 'and who do you think had taken it?' 'I care not,' said Calantha / proud and offended at their former suspicions. 'Zerbellini!' 'Oh impossible!' 'Some of Lady Margaret's servants first suggested the possibility,' said Sophia. 'His desk and wardrobe were consequently examined, and scarce giving credit to the testimony of their sight, the lost prize was discovered in his silken vest.' Calantha indignantly resisted the general belief that the boy was the real culprit. Every one left the room, and eagerly enquired into the whole affair. 'If ocular proof be necessary to convince you,' said Lady Margaret, returning to Calantha and leading her from the billiard room, accompanied by many others, 'you shall now have it; and see,' she cried, pausing as she entered the boy's apartment, 'how soundly criminals can sleep!' 'Aye, and how tranquil and innocent they can appear,' continued Gondimar smiling as he stood by the side of the page's bed. Glenarvon's countenance, rendered more terrible by / the glimmering of the lamp, changed at these words.

There, sleeping in unsuspicious peace, lay the youthful Zerbellini, his cheeks blooming, his rich auburn hair flowing in clusters about his face, his arms thrown over his head with infantine and playful grace. 'If he be guilty,' said Calantha, looking earnestly at him, 'Great God, how[b] much one may be deceived!' 'How much one may be deceived!' said the Duke turning back and glancing his eye on the trembling form of his daughter. The necklace was produced: but a look of doubt was still seen on every countenance, and Lord Glenarvon, sternly approaching Gondimar, asked him whether some villain might not have placed it there, to screen himself and to ruin the boy? 'I should be loath,' replied the Italian, with an affectation of humility, 'very loath to imagine that such a wretch could exist.' A glance of bitter scorn, was the only reply vouchsafed. /

'We can see the boy, alone, in the morning,' said Sophia in a low whisper to Calantha; 'there is more in this than we know of. Be calm; fear not, and tomorrow, we can with caution discover all.' 'Do not talk of to-morrow,' replied Calantha angrily: 'an hour, a moment is too long to bear injustice. I will plead with my father.' So saying, she followed him, urging him to hear her. 'Consider the youth of the child,' she said, 'even if guilty, remember he is but young.' 'His youth but aggravates the crime,' said the Duke, haughtily repulsing her. 'When the young can act basely, it shews that the heart's core is black. Plead not for him: look to yourself, child,' he fiercely cried, and left her. The time was past when a prayer of Calantha's was never breathed in vain; and struggling with a thousand strong emotions, she fled to her own room, and gave vent to the contending / passions, by which she was so greatly agitated.

That night,[c] Lord Glenarvon slept not at the Castle. Zerbellini's guilt was now considered as certain. The Duke himself awakening the child, asked him if he had taken the necklace. He coloured extremely; hid his face, and then acknowledged the offence. He was questioned respecting his motive; but he evaded, and would not answer. His doom was fixed.ᵃ 'I will take him from hence,' said Gondimar. 'He must not remain here a single hour; but no severity shall be shewn to so youthful an offender.'

It was at that dark still hour of the night, when spirits that are troubled wake, and calmer eyes are closed in sleep, that Lady Margaret and Count Gondimar, entering Zerbellini's room, asked him if he were prepared. 'For what?' exclaimed the boy, clasping his hands together. '*Oimè! eccelenza che vuoi!* Save me,' he cried, appealing to Lady / Margaret. 'I will not, cannot go. Willᵇ no one pity me? Oh Gondimar! are these your promises – your kindnesses?' 'Help me to bear him away,' said Gondimar to Lady Margaret. 'If Glenarvon should hear us?ᶜ and force was used to bear the struggling boy from the Castle?'ᵈ

In the morning Calantha was informed, by Lady Margaret, of the whole transaction. She said, however, that on account of his youth, no other notice would be taken of his fault, than that of his being immediately sent back to his parents at Florence.

Calantha was unquiet and restless the whole of the day. 'The absence of your page,' said Lady Margaret sarcastically, as she passed her, 'seems to have caused you some little uneasiness. Do you expect to find him in any of these rooms? Have you not been to Craig Allen Bay, or the Wizzard's glen? Has the Chapel been examined thoroughly?' /

A loud noise and murmur interrupted her. The entrance of the Count Gondimar, pale and trembling, supported by Lord Glenarvon and a servant, gave a general alarm. – 'Ruffians,' said Gondimar, fiercely glancing his eyes around, 'attacked our carriage, and forced the child from my grasp.' 'Where? – how?' 'About twenty miles hence,' said the Italian. 'Curse on the darkness, which prevented my defending myself as I ought.' 'Those honorable wounds,' said Glenarvon, 'prove sufficiently that the Count wrongs himself.' 'Trelawny,' whispered Gondimar, 'do me a favour. Fly to the stables; view well Glenarvon's steed; mark if it bear any appearance of recent service: I strongly suspect him: and but for his presence at these gates, so calm, so cleanly accoutred, I could have staked my soul it was by his arm I received these wounds.'

'The horse,' said Lord Trelawny, when he returned, 'is sleakᵉ and far different / from the reeking steeds that followed with your carriage.' Glenarvon smiled scornfully on the officious Lord: then fixing his eye sternly upon Gondimar, 'I read your suspicions,' said heᶠ in a low voice, as he passed: 'they are just. Now, serpent, do thy worst: thou art at my mercy.' 'Not at thine,' replied Gondimar, grinding his teeth. 'By the murdered . . . . .' 'Say no more,' said Glenarvon, violently agitated, while every trembling nerve attested the agony he endured. 'For God's sake be silent. I will meet you at St. Alvin's to-night: you shall investigate the whole of my conduct, and you will not find in it aught to give you just offence.' 'The ground upon which you stand has a crimsoned dye,' said Gondimar, with a malicious smile: 'look at your hand, my lord . . . . ' Glenarvon, faint and exhausted, scarce appeared to support himself any longer; but suddenly collecting all his forces together, with a / struggle, which nature seemed scarcely equal to endure, he sprung upon the Italian, and asked him fiercely the meaning of his words. Gondimar now, in his turn, trembled; Lord Trelawney interposed; and peace was apparently restored. /

CHAPTER XXIX.

THE scene of the morning had caused considerable speculation. The count, though slightly indisposed – appeared at dinner; after which Lord Glenarvon took a hasty leave. It need not be said what Calantha's feelings were. Gondimar and Lady Margaret talked much together, during the evening. Calantha wrote in anxiety to Glenarvon. No one was now near to comfort her. As she retired slowly and sadly to her room in dreadful suspense, O'Kelly, Glenarvon's servant, passed her on the stairs. The sight of his countenance was joy to her. 'My lord waits to see you, at the back door on the terrace,' he said, as he affected to hasten away with a portmanteau on his shoulder. She heard and marked the words, and watching an opportunity hastened to the / door. It was locked; but O'Kelly awaited her and opened it. To be in the power of this man was nothing: he was Glenarvon's long tried and faithful servant; yet she felt confused when she met his eyes; and thought it an indignity that her secret had been betrayed to him. Glenarvon, however, had commanded her to trust him; and every command of his she too readily obeyed. 'My lord is going,' said the man. 'Where?' she cried; in the utmost agony. 'From Ireland,' said O'Kelly. 'But he waits for you by yonder tree,' she hastened forward.

'Ah speak to me,' she said, upon seeing him: 'my heart is tortured; confide at least in me: let me have the comforts[a] of believing that I contribute to the happiness of one human being upon earth; I who cause the misery of so many.' Glenarvon turned from her to weep.[b] 'Tell me the cause of your distress.' 'They will tear you from me,' he said.[c] 'Never, never,' / she answered. 'Look not on me, frail fading flowret,' he said, in a hollow mournful tone – 'ah look not on me, nor thus waste thy sweets upon a whited sepulchre, full of depravity,[d] and death. Could'st thou read my heart – see how[e] it is seared, thou would'st tremble and start back with horror.' 'I have bound myself to you,' she replied, 'I am prepared for the worst: it cannot be worse than the crime of which I am guilty; grieve not then for me, I am calm,[f] and happy – oh most happy, when I am thus with you.'

There is a look of anguish, such as a slave might give when he betrays his master – such as a murderer in thought might shew previous to the commission of the bloody act, in presence of his victim: – such a look, so sad, so terrible, impressed a momentary gloom over the beautuful countenance of Glenarvon. Yes, when she said that she was happy, at that very time he shrunk from the joy she / professed; for he knew that he had led her to that which would blast all peace in her heart for ever.

'Calantha' at length Glenarvon said, 'before I explain myself, let me press thee once more to my heart –ᵃ let me pour out the agonies of my soul, to my only friend. I have promised your aunt to leave you: yes; for thy dear sake, I will go; and none shall hereafter say of me, that I led you to share my ruined fortunes, or cast disgrace upon your name! Whatever my wrongs and injuries, to others, let one woman exist to thank me for her preservation. It will break my heart; but I will do it. You will hear dreadful things of me, when I am away: you will learn to hate, to curse me.' 'Oh never, Glenarvon, never.' 'I believe you love me,' he continued; 'and ere we part, ere we forget every vow given and received – every cherished hope, now blighted so cruelly for me, give me some proof of your sincerity. Others perhaps have been my / victims; I, alas! am your's. You do not know, you cannot know what I feel, you have made me insensible to every other pursuit. I seem to exist alone in you, and for you, and can you, can you then abandon me? goᵇ if it be your pleasure, receive the applause of the world, of friends, of those who affect the name; and when they hear that Glenarvon has fled, a voluntary exile from his country without one being to share his sorrows, perishing by slow degrees of a cruel and dangerous malady, which long has preyed upon his constitution, then let your husband and your aunt triumph in the reflection, that they have hastened his doom. And you, wretched victim, remember that,ᶜ having brightened for a few short hours my weary path, you have left me at the last more lonely, more deserted even than when first you appeared before me. Oh Calantha, let others mock at my agony, and doubt the truth of one who has but too well deserved their suspicions; but do not you / refuse to believe me. Young as I appear, I have made many miserable: but none more so than myself; and, having cast away every bright hope of dawning fame and honor, I renounce even now the only being who stands like a guardian angel between myself and eternal perdition. Oh canst thou doubt such love? and yet believing it, wilt thou consent that I should thus abandon thee? I have sacrificed for thee the strong passions that, like vultures, prey upon my heart – fortune, honor, every hope, even beyond the grave, for thy happiness – for thy love! Ah say canst thou – wilt thou now abandon me?'

'Glenarvon,' Lady Avondale replied, weeping bitterly. 'I am much more miserable than you can be; I have more love for you than it is possible you can feel for me. I am not worth half what you inspire. I never will consent to part,ᵈ 'Then you must accompany me,' he said, looking her full in the face. 'Alas! if I do / thus, how will yourself despise me. When society, and those whose opinion you value, brand her name with infamy who leaves all for you, where shall we fly from dishonor? how will you bear up under my disgrace?' 'I will bear you in my arms from the country that condemns you – in my heart, your name shall continue spotless as purity,' he replied, – 'sacred as truth, I will resist every opposition, and slay every one who shall dare to breathe one thought against you. For you I could renounce and despise the world; and I will teach you that love is in itself such ecstacy, that all we leave for it is nothing to it.'

'How can I resist you?' she answered. 'Allow me to hear and yet forget the lessons which you teach – let me look on you, yet doubt you – let me die for you, but not see you thus suffer.'[a] 'Come with me now – even now,' said Glenarvon fiercely,[b] – 'I must make you mine before we part: then I will trust you; but not / till then.' He looked upon her with scorn, as she struggled from his grasp. 'Calantha, you affect to feel more than I do,' he cried; 'but your heart could not exist under what I endure. You love! – Oh you do not know how to love;' 'do[c] not be so cruel to me: look not so fierce Glenarvon. For you, for you, I have tempted the dangers of guilt; for you, I have trembled and wept; and, believe it, for you I will bear to die.' 'Then give yourself to me: this very hour be mine.' 'And I am your's for ever:' 'but it must be your own free act and deed.'[39] Fear not; Lady Margaret is in my power; I am appointed to an interview with her to-morrow; and your aunt dares not refuse you, if you say that you will see me. It is on your firmness I rely: be prudent: it is but of late I counsel it. Deceit is indeed foreign to my nature; but what disguise would I not assume to see you?'

O'Kelly interrupted this conference by whispering something in his ear. – / 'I will attend her instantly.' 'Whom?' said Calantha. 'Oh no one.' 'Ah speak truly: tell me what mean those words – those mysterious looks: you smile: that moon bears witness against you; tell me all.' 'I will trust you,' said Glenarvon. 'Oh, my Lord, for God's[d] sake,' said O'Kelly interfering[e] 'remember your vows, I humbly entreat.' 'Hear me,' said Glenarvon, in an authoritative tone, repulsing him. 'What are you all without me? Tremble then at daring to advise, or to offend me. Lady Avondale is mine; we are but one, and she shall know my secret, though I were on the hour betrayed.' 'My Lady you are lost,' said the man, 'if you do not hasten home; you are watched;[f] I do implore you to return to the castle.' Lord Glenarvon reluctantly permitted her to leave him; he promised to see her on the following morning; and she hastened home. /

CHAPTER XXX.

UNABLE to rest, Calantha wrote during the whole of the night; and in the morning, she heard that the Duke was in possession of her letter. Lady Margaret entered, and informed her of this.

She also stated that the note would soon be returned into her own hands, and that this might convince her that^a although much might be suspected from its contents, neither herself nor the Duke were of opinion that Lord Avondale should at present be informed of the transaction. While Lady Margaret was yet speaking, the Duke, opening the door, with a severe countenance approached Calantha, and placing the letter to Lord Glenarvon upon the table, assured her, with coldness, that he considered her as her own mistress, and should not interfere. Lady Margaret / without a word^b being uttered on her part, left the room.

As soon as she was gone, the Duke approached his daughter. 'This is going too far,' he said, pointing to the letter: 'there is no excuse for you.' She asked him, with some vivacity, why he had broken the seal, and wherefore it was not delivered as it was addressed. With coldness he apologized to her for the liberty he had taken, which even a father's right over an only child, he observed, could scarcely authorise. 'But,' continued he, 'duty has of late been so much sacrificed to inclination, that we must have charity for each other. As I came, however, by your letter somewhat unfairly, I shall make no comments upon it, nor describe the feelings that it excited in my mind – only observe, I will have this end here; and my commands, like your's, shall be obeyed.' He then reproached her for her behaviour of late.^c 'I have seen you give way,' he said, 'to exceeding low / spirits, and I am desirous of knowing why this grief has suddenly been changed to ill-timed gaiety and shameless effrontery? Will nothing cure you of this love of merriment? Will an angry father, an offended husband, and a contemning world but add to and encrease it? Shall I say happy Calantha, or shall I weep over the hardness of a heart,^d that is insensible to the grief of others, and has ceased to feel for itself? Alas! I looked upon you as my comfort and delight; but you are now to me, a heavy care – a never ceasing reproach; and if you persist in this line of conduct, the sooner you quit this roof, which rings with your disgrace, the better it will be for us all. Those who are made early sacrifices to ambition and interest may plead some excuse; but you,ª Calantha, what can you say to palliate your conduct? A father's blessing accompanied the choice your own heart made; and was not Avondale a noble choice? What quality is there, / whether of person or of mind, in which he is deficient? I think of him with feelings of pride.' – 'I do so, too, my father.' – 'Go, poor deluded child,' he continued, in an offended tone, 'fly to the arms of your new lover, and seek with him that happiness of which you have robbed me for ever, and which I fear you yourself never more will know. Do not answer me, or by those proud looks attempt to hide your disgrace. I am aware of all you would urge; but am not to be swayed by the sophistry you would make use of.ᵇ This is no innocent friendship. Beware to incense me by uttering one word in its defence. Are you not taught that God, who sees the heart, looks not at the deed, but at the motive? In his eye the murderer who has made up his mind to kill, has already perpetrated the deed; and the adultress who....' – 'Ah, call me not by that name, my father: I am your only child. No proud looks shall now shew themselves, or support / me; but on my knees here, even here, I humble myself before you. Speak not so harshly to me: I am very miserable.'

'Consent to see him no more. Say it, my child, and all shall be forgotten – I will forgive you.' – 'I must see him once more – ah! once more; and if he consents, I will obey.' – 'Good God! do I live to hear such words? It is then to Lord Glenarvon's mercy, and to no effort of your own, that I am to owe your amendment? See him then, but do it in defiance of my positive commands: – see him, Calantha; but the vengeanceᶜ of an offended God, the malediction of a father fall on thee for thy disobedience: – see him if it be thy mad resolve; but meet my eyes no more. A lover may be found at any time; but a father, once offended, is lost for ever: his will should be sacred; and the God of Heaven may see fit to withdraw his mercy from a disobedient child.' The Duke, as he spoke these words, tremblingᵈ / with passion, and darting an angry eye upon Calantha, left her. The door closed. She stood suspended – uncertain how to act. –

At length recovering, she seized a pen, and wrote to Glenarvon. – 'I am miserable;ᵉ but let me, at all events, spare you. Come not to the Castle. Write to me: it is all I ask. I must quit you for ever. Oh, Glenarvon, I must indeed see you no more; or involve all whom I love, and yourself who art far dearer, in my disgrace. Let me hear from you immediately. You must decide for me: I have no will on earth but your's – no hope but in the continuance of your love. Do not call me weak. Write to me: say you approve; for if you do not, I cannot obey.'

Having sent her letter with some fear, she went to Mrs. Seymour, who was far from well, and had been some days confined to her room. She endeavoured to conceal from her what had passed in the / morning respecting her father. Mrs. Seymour spoke but little to her, she seemed unequal to the task imposed upon her by others, of telling Calantha that which she knew would cause her pain.

She was dreadfully agitated, and, holding[a] her niece's hand, seemed desirous she should not leave her for any length of time.

Towards noon, Calantha went out for a few moments, and near the Elm wood met Glenarvon. 'Oh, for Heaven's sake,' she cried, 'do not come here: some one may see you.' – 'And if they do,' he said calmly, 'what of that?' – 'I cannot stay now: – for your sake I cannot:' – 'Meet me to-night.' – 'Where?[b] How?' – 'At the Chapel.' – 'At what hour?' – 'At twelve.' – 'That is too early.' – 'At three.' – 'I dare not come.' – 'Then farewell.' – 'Glenarvon!' He turned back. 'I cannot be thus trifled with,' he said. 'You have given yourself to me: I was not prepared for this wavering and caprice.' – 'Oh, you know not what / has passed.' – 'I know all.' – 'My aunt is ill.' He smiled contemptuously. 'Act as you think right,' he said; 'but do not be the dupe of these machinations.' – 'She is really ill;[c] she is incapable of art.' – 'Go to her, then.' – 'And you – shall I see you no more?' – 'Never.' – 'I shall come to-night.' – 'As you please.' – 'At all events, I shall be there, Glenarvon. – Oh look not thus on me. You know, you well know your power: do not lead me to infamy and ruin.'

Glenarvon seized Calantha's hand, which he wrung with violence. Passion in him was very terrible: it forced no fierce words from his lips; no rush of blood suffused his cheeks and forehead; but the livid pale of suppressed rage spread itself over every feature: even his hands bore testimony to the convulsive effort which the blood receding to his heart[d] occasioned. Thus pale, thus fierce, he gazed on Calantha with disdain. – 'Weak, timid being, is it for this I have renounced so much? – Is it for such as you that / I have consented to live? How different from her I once loved. Go to the parents for whom I am sacrificed; call back the husband who is so preferred to me; note well his virtues and live upon his caresses: – the world will admire you[e] and praise you. I knew how it would be and am satisfied.' Then with a rapid change of countenance from malice to bitter anguish, he gazed on her, till his eyes were filled with tears: his lips[f] faltered as he said farewell. Calantha approached too near: he pressed her to his heart. 'I am yours,' she said, half suffocated. 'Nor parents, nor husband, nor fear of man or God[g] shall ever cause me to leave you.' – 'You will meet me tonight then.' – 'I will.' – 'You will not play upon my irritated feelings by penitential letters and excuses – you are decided, are you? Say either yes or no; but be firm to either.' – 'I will come then, let death or disgrace[h] be the consequence. /

CHAPTER XXXI.

In the course of the day, Glenarvon wrote to Calantha. 'I have never sought to win you to me after the manner other men might desire,' he said. 'I have respected your opinions; and I have resisted more than woman's feelings can conceive. But Calantha you have shared the struggle. I have marked in your eye the fire of passion, in the quivering of your lip and changing complexion, the fierce power which destroyed you. When in the soft language of poetry, I have read to you, or spoken with the warmth I knew not how to feign, you have turned from me[a] it is true; but pride more than virtue, inclined your firm resistance. Every principle in your heart is shaken; every tie that ought to bind thee most, is broken; and I who should / triumph at my success, weep only for thy fall. I found thee innocent, confiding and sincere: I leave thee – but, oh God! wilt thou thus be left? wilt thou now that thy soul itself partakes in thy guilt, wilt thou forsake me?' 'Upon[b] this night,' continued Glenarvon, 'you have given me a solemn promise to meet me in secret: it is the first time concealment has been rendered necessary. I know your nature too well, not to be convinced that you are already preparing to retract. Do so, if it be your will: – I wish you not to take one step without fully appreciating its consequences, and the crime incurred. I have never disguised to you the guilt of our attachment since the moment in which I felt assured of my own sentiments. I wished you to feel the sacrifice you were making: how otherwise could I consider it as any? my love is worth some risk. Every one knows my weakness; and did you feel half what you inspire, you would be / proud, you would glory in what you now attempt to hide. The woman I love, must see, must hear, must[c] believe and confide in no other but me. I renounce every other for you[d] – And, now that I claim you as my own, expect[e] the fulfilment of your many professions. Shew me that you can be firm and true: give yourself to me entirely: you are mine; and you must prove it. I am prefered[f] before every earthly being in my Calantha's heart – my dearest, my only friend. Of this indeed I have long ceased to entertain a single doubt; but now I require more. Even in religious faith – even in hopes, in reliance upon the mercy of God.[g] I cannot bear a competitor and a rival.

'There is a rite accounted infamous amongst christians: – there is an oath which it is terrible to take. By this, by this alone, I will have you bound to me – not here alone, but if there be a long hereafter then shall we evermore be linked together: then shall you be mine / far more, far dearer than either mistress or bride. It is, I own, a mere mockery of superstition;[a] but what on earth deserves a higher name? Every varying custom and every long-established form, whether in our own land, or those far distant tracts which the foot of man has rarely traversed, deserves no higher name. The customs of our forefathers – the habit of years, give a venerable and sacred appearance to many rites; but all is a dream, the mere colouring of fancy, the frail perishable attempts of human invention. Even the love we feel, Calantha – the beaming fires which now stimulate our hearts, and raise us above others is but illusion – like the bright exhalations which appear to mislead, then vanish and leave us more gloomy than before.'

Calantha's eyes were fixed; her hand was cold; no varying colour, no trepidation shewed either life or vigour; there was a struggle in her mind; and / a voice seemed to call to her from her inmost soul: 'For the last time, Calantha, it seemed to say, I warn thee, for the last time I warn thee. Oh hear the voice of conscience as it cries to thee for the last time:[b] – go not to thy ruin;[c] plunge not thy soul into the pit of hell; hurl not destruction upon thy head. What is this sin against thy religion? How canst thou throw off thy faith and reliance upon thy God? It is a mere mockery of words; a jealous desire to possess every avenue of thy heart's affections, to snatch thee from every feeling of remorse and virtue; to plunge thee in[d] eternal perdition. Hear me: by thy mother's name I call; go not to thy soul's ruin and shame' . . . . 'Am I mad, or wherefore is my soul distracted? Oh Glenarvon, come again to me: my comforter – my heart's friend, oh leave me not. By every tie thou art bound to me: never, never will I forsake thee. What are the reproaches of conscience – what the fancied pangs of remorse, / to the glory, the ecstacy of being thine! Low as I am fallen; despised, perhaps, by all who hear my fate, I have lived one hour of joy, worth every calamity I may be called upon to endure. Return Glenarvon, adored, beloved. Thy words are like the joys of Heaven:[e] Thy presence is the light of life: existence without thee would not be worth the purchase. – Come all the woes that may, upon me, never will I forsake Glenarvon.'

The nurse entered Calantha's room, bearing her boy in her arms. She would not look on him: – 'take[f] him away,' she said; 'take him to my aunt.' The child wished to stay: – for the first time he hung about her with affection; for he was not of that character, and seldom shewed his love by infantine fondness and caresses. She started from his gentle grasp, as if from something terrible: 'take[g] him away,' she shrieked to the affrighted woman, 'and never let him come near me more.' /

I know there are some[h] whose eyes may glance upon these pages, who will regard with indignation the confession here made respecting the character of Calantha. But it is as if those who had never known sickness and agony mocked at its power

– as if those who had never witnessed the delirious ravings of fever or insanity reasoned upon its excess: –ᵃ they must not judge who cannot understand.

Driven to despair – guilty in all but the last black deed that brands the name and character with eternal infamy, Calantha resolved to follow Glenarvon. How indeed could she remain! To her every domestic joy was forever blasted; and a false estimate of honour inclined her to believe, that it was right in her to go. – But not to-nightᵇ she said. Oh not like a culprit and a thief in the midst of the night, will I quit my father's house, or leave my aunt sick and ill to grieve herself almost to death for my sake. /

Preserving, during the evening, a sullen silence, an affectation of offended pride, Calantha retired early; looked once upon the portraits of her husband and mother; and then turned from them in agony. 'He was all kindness to me – all goodness: he deserved a happier fate. Happier! alas he is blest: I alone suffer – I alone am miserable; never, never can I behold him more.' These were the last words Calantha uttered, as she prepared for an interview she dreaded. It was now but twelve o'clock: she threw herself upon her bed, and waited in trepidation and alarm for the hour of three. A knock at the door aroused her. It was O'Kelly; but he waited not one instant: he left a gold casket with a ring, within was a letter: 'My beloved,' it said, 'I wait for thee. Oh repent not thy promise.'ᶜ Nothing else was written. The hand she well knew: the signature was. 'Ever and thine alone, Glenarvon.' /

CHAPTER XXXII.

It was past three o'clock, when Calantha opened the cabinet where the page's clothes were formerly kept, and drew from thence his mantle and plumed hat; and, thus disguised, prepared herself for the interview. She slowly descended the stairs: the noisy revels of the servants might still at intervals be heard: in a moment she glided through the apartments and passages, till she found herself at the door which led to the terrace. It opened heavily, and closed again with a loud noise, Alarmed, lest she should be discovered, she flew with rapidity over the terrace and lawn, till she approached the wood, and then she paused to take breath, and to listen if all were silent.

Calantha[a] walked fearfully onwards. The first night on which she had met / Glenarvon the moon was bright and full, and the whole scene was lighted by its rays; but now, it was on the wane – the silver crescent shone alone, and the clouds continually passing over it, cast fearful shadows upon the grass. She found herself in the thickest part of the wood. She heard a hollow murmur: – it was but the alders, waving in the wind, which made a tremulous noise[b] like voices whispering at a distance. She passed on, and the recollection that it was to Glenarvon that she was hastening, and that it was probably for the last time, made her indifferent to her fate, and rendered her fearless. Besides, the desperate and the guilty never fear: a deeper feeling renders them callous to all beside – a spirit of defiance deadens in them the very edge of apprehension. She proceeded to the appointed place. The sea dashed against the cliff below; and the bleak wind whistled through the ruined chapel as it came in hollow blasts over the heath. /

Calantha perceived Glenarvon. He was leaning upon one of the broken rocks: he viewed, unawed, the melancholy scene before him. No superstitious terrors had[c] power to shake his soul: misery had done its utmost to subdue him. Nor ray of hope,[d] nor prosperity, could afford him comfort, or remove his dejection. In the first transports of joy at seeing him, she darted towards him; but when she marked the paleness of his cheeks, and the stillness of his attitude, she started back, and advanced slowly: for she feared to disturb him.

The evening breeze had blown back his dark locks, and bared his pale forehead, upon which the light of the moonbeam fell. She gazed upon him; and while she contemplated the beautiful majesty of his figure, his fixed and mournful eyes, his countenance so fraught with feeling, she approached him. 'My friend, my lover,' she said. 'Ah! my / little trembling page, my Zerbellini, welcome to my heart,' he answered: 'I knew you would not fail; but I have waited for you till every bright illusion of hope has been changed into visions of despondency and fear. We meet now: but is it indeed to part no more! Glenarvon is your's, and shall never be severed from you.'

'Ah! triumph over yourself and me,' she cried, clasping her hands in agony.^a 'Ask any sacrifice but this. Do not make me contemptible to you and to myself.' Calantha, the time for safety is past: it is too late now. I have linked my soul to your's; I love you in defiance of myself; I know it to be guilt, and to be death; but it must be. We follow but the dark destiny that involves us:^b we cannot escape from fate. For you alone I live: – be now but mine. They tell you of misery, of inconstancy, of lovers'^c perjuries, from the olden time; but you shall prove them false. You leave much, it is / true – rank, fame and friends, a home and the dearest ties of a mother's heart – children; but have you not embittered all that you relinquish?^d Say that I yield you up and fly, – to what fate shall I then consign you?^e to what endless repining, unjoyous solitary hours – remorse, regret, the bitter taunt of friends, the insulting scorn of strangers, and, worse than all – O! worse than all the recoiling heart can endure, the unsuspicious confidence and caresses of an injured husband, of him you have already betrayed. O Calantha, turn from these to a lover's bosom; seek for comfort here; and now, even now, accompany me in my flight . . . .'^f

'I will leave all for you: – I love but you: be you my master.' Scarce had she uttered the impious oath which bound her to him, when her heart, convulsed with terror, ceased to beat. ''Tis but in words – oh God! 'tis but in words, that thy guilty servant has offended. No – / even in the delirium of passion, even in the transports of love,^{g 40} the fear of thy vengeance spake terrors into her soul, and ingratitude for all thy favours was not to be numbered with her sins.' But the oath which she had taken was terrible. She considered herself as no longer under the protection of her God. She^h trembled exceedingly; and fear for one moment overpowered her. Lord Glenarvon looked upon her, mournfully, as if sorry for the sin which he had cast upon her soul. 'Now,' he said, 'you will look back upon these moments, and you will consider me with abhorrence. I have led you with me to ruin and remorse.' 'On me – on me, be the sin; let it fall upon me alone,' she replied; but if, after this, you forsake me, then shall the vengeance of Godⁱ be satisfied – the measure of my crime be at its full. It is not in my power – I cannot forsake you now: I will go with you, Glenarvon, if it were to certain death and ruin. I am your's^j alone. / But this night I must return home,' she said. 'I will not leave my father thus – I will not cause my aunt's death.' 'If you leave me now I shall lose you.' 'O Glenarvon, let me return; and after seeing them once again, I will follow you firm until death.'

He placed a ring upon her finger. 'It is a marriage bond,' he said; 'and if there be a God, let him now bear witness to my vows: – I here, uncompelled by menace, unsolicited by entreaty, do bind myself through life to you. No other, in word or thought, shall ever hold influence or power over my heart. This is no lover's oath – no profession which the intoxication of passion may extort: it is the free and solemn purpose of a soul conquered and enchained by you. Oh Calantha, beloved, adored, look upon me, and say that you believe me. Lean not upon a lover's bosom, but upon a friend, a guardian and protector, a being wholly relying on your mercy and / kindness. My love, my soul, look yet once upon me.'[41]

'Why fall our tears? Is it in terror of approaching evil, or in regret for involuntary error? My bosom's comfort, my soul's idol, look not thus coldly on me; for I deserve it not. Your will is mine: lead me as it delights your fancy: I am a willing slave.' 'If you abandon me,' said Calantha, in tears. 'May the curse of God burn my heart and consume me! may every malediction and horror fall tenfold upon my head! may phrenzy[a] and madness come upon my senses! and tortures in this world and the next be my portion, if ever I change my sentiments[b] towards you!'

With words like these, Glenarvon silenced her as she returned to the castle; and, strange as it may seem, untroubled sleep – such sleep as in better days she once enjoyed, fell upon all her senses, quieted every passion, and obliterated, for a few hours, the scenes of guilt which tortured her with their remembrance. /

CHAPTER XXXIII.

To wake is terrible when the heaviness of sin is upon us! – to wake, and see every object around us the same as before; but to feel that we are utterly changed! I am still in a father's house, she thought, as late the ensuing morning she opened her eyes.[a] 'My name is not yet branded with disgrace; but I belong alone upon earth to Glenarvon. Mrs. Seymour sent for her: the nurse entered with the children. But Calantha looked upon the ring,[b] and trembled.'

Lady Avondale ordered her horses, and, dressing in haste, entered Mrs. Seymour's room. Never had she found it easy to deceive till that moment. To tell her the truth had been to kill her: she feigned therefore with ease, for her aunt's life required it, and she herself was desperate. / 'Have you kept your resolution, my Calantha?' – 'Yes,' she replied, nor blushed at affirming it. 'Two days, and you have not seen Glenarvon?' she said, with a faint smile!^c Is this possible? – 'I thought one had killed me,' replied Calantha; but I look well; do I not?' and she hurried from her presence.

Calantha's[d] horses awaited: she rode out the whole of the day: it seemed to her as if a moment's pause or rest would have been agony unutterable. And yet, when the spirit is heavy there is something unpleasant in the velocity of motion: throwing, therefore, the reins upon her well-trained steed, she paced slowly over the mountain's side, lost in reflections which it had been pain to interrupt.

Suddenly a horse and rider, in full speed, darting along the moor, approached and crossed upon her path. 'Whither ride you lady,[e] so slow?' said Miss St. Clara,[f] whom she now recognized, scarce reining in her swift footed charger. 'And / whither ride you, Lady, so fast?' said Calantha, courteously returning her salute. 'To perdition,' cried Elinor; 'and they that wish to follow must ride apace.' The hat and plume of sacred green, the emerald clasp, the gift of Glenarvon, were all but too well observed by Calantha. Deeply she blushed, as St. Clara, fixing her dark eyes upon her, asked her respecting him. 'Is thy young lover well?' she said;[g] 'and wilt thou be one of us? He slept last night at Belfont: he could not rest: didst thou?' Saying which, she smiled, and rode away.

Oppressed with many bitter doubts, Calantha returned to the Castle; and what is strange, she felt coldly towards Glenarvon. On her return, she found letters from him for the most ardent, the most impassioned she had yet received. He spoke with grief of her unkindness: he urged her by every tie most dear, most sacred, to see him,ª and fly with him. Yet, that night, she went not to meet / him; she wrote not kindly; she loved not. She retired early; and her thoughts were painful and terrible. But such is the inconsistency of the human heart; her coldness seemed but to encrease his ardour. She received that night, the warmest,ᵇ the most unguarded letters; she even now dreaded the violence of his attachment. Remorse, she felt, had taken the place of passion in her own heart: for all within was chilled, was changed.

As she thus sat in sullen silence, unwilling to think – unable to forget, she heard a step stealing along the passage; and in a moment Glenarvon entered her apartment. 'We are lost,' she cried. 'I care not,' he said, 'so that I but see you.' – 'For God'sᶜ sake, leave me.' – 'Speak lower,' he said, approaching her: 'be calm, for think you that when you have risked so much for me, I dare not share the danger. After all, what is it? Whoever enters must do it at their peril: their life shall pay the forfeit: I / am armed.' – 'Good God!ᵈ how terrible are your looks: I love you; but I fear you.'

'Do you remember,' said Glenarvon,ᵉ 'that day when I first told you of my love? You blushed then, and wept: did you not? But you have forgotten to do either now. Why, then, this strange confusion?' – 'I am sick at heart. Leave me.' – 'Never! O most loved, most dear of all earthly beings, turn not thus away from me; look not as if you feared to meet me; feel not regret; for if it be a crime, that be on me, Calantha – on me alone. I know how men of the world can swear and forswear: I know, too, how much will be attempted to sever you from me: but by that Godᶠ in whose sacred eye we stand; by all that the human heart and soul can believe and cherish, I am not one of that base kind, who would ever betray the woman that trusted in me. Even were you unfaithful to me, I could not change. You are all on earth / that I love, and, perhaps what is better worth, that I esteem and respect – that I honor as above every other in goodness, purity and generousᵍ noble feelings. O! think not so humbly of yourself: say not that you are degraded. My admiration of you shall excuse your error: myʰ faithful attachment whilst existence is given to either of us shall atone for all. Look on me, my only friend; dry up the tears that fall for an involuntary fault; and consider me as your protector, your lover, your husband.

There required not many words, not many protestations. Calantha wept bitterly; but she felt happy. 'If you change now,' she said, 'what will become of me? Let me go with you, Glenarvon, from this country: I ask not for other ties than those that already bind us. Yet I once more repeat it, I know you must despise me.' – 'What are words and vows, my heart's life, my soul's idol, what are they? The false, the vain, the worldlyminded / have made use of them; but I must have recourse to them, Calantha, since you can look at me, and yet mistrust me. No villany that ever yet existed, can exceed that which my falsehood to you would now evince. This is no common worldly attachment: no momentary intoxication of passion. Often I have loved: many I have seen; but none ever sacrified for me what you have done; and for none upon earth did I ever feel what I do for you. I might have made you mine long ago: perhaps I might have abused the confidence shewn me, and the interest and enthusiasm I had created; but, alas! you would then have despised me. I conquered myself; but it was to secure you more entirely. I am your's only: consent therefore to fly with me, make any trial you please of my truth. What I speak I have written: my letters you may shew, my actions you may observe and sift. I have not one thought that is unknown to you – one wish, one / hope of which you are not the first and sole object. Many disbelieve that I am serious in my desire that you should accompany me in my flight. They know me not: I have no views, no projects. Men of the world look alone to fortune, fame, or interest; but what am I? The sacrifice is solely on your part: I would to God[a] it were on mine. If even you refuse to follow me, I will not make this a plea for abandoning you: I will hover around, will protect, will watch over you. Your love makes my happiness: it is my sole hope in life. Even were you to change to me, I could not but be true to you.'

Did Glenarvon really wish Calantha to accompany him: he risked much; and seemed to desire it. But there is no understanding the guileful heart; and he who had deceived many, could assuredly deceive her. Yet it appears, that he urged her more than ever to fly with him; and that when, at length she said that her resolution was fixed – that / she would go, his eyes in triumph gloried in the assurance;[b] and with a fervour he could not have feigned he called her his. Hitherto, some virtuous, some religious hopes,[c] had still sustained her:[d] now all ceased; perversion led the way to crime, and hardness of heart and insensibility followed.

One by one, Glenarvon repeated to her confessions of former scenes. One by one, he betrayed to her the confidence others had reposed in his honour. She saw the wiles and windings of his mind, nor abhorred them: she heard his mockery of all that is good and noble; nor turned from him. Is it the[e] nature of guilty love thus to pervert the very soul? Or what in so short a period could have operated so great a change? Till now[f] the hope of saving, of guarding, of reclaiming, had led her on: now frantic and perverted passion absorbed all other hopes; and the crime he had commended, whatever had been its drift, she had not feared to commit.[g] /

Calantha had read of love, and felt it; she had laughed at the sickening rhapsodies of sentiment, and turned with disgust from the inflamatory[h] pages of looser pens; but, alas! her own heart now presented every feeling she most[i] abhorred; and it was in herself,[j] she found the reality of all that during[k] her whole existence, she had looked upon with contempt and disgust.[l] Every remaining scruple left her; she still urged delay; but to accompany her master and lover,[m] was now her firm resolve. /

CHAPTER XXXIV.

GLENARVON had retired unperceived by any, on the evening he had visited her, in her apartment. The following day be appeared at the castle; they both avoided each other: she indeed trembled at beholding him. 'Meet me at the chapel to night,' he whispered. Alas! she obeyed too well.

They were returning through the wood: she paused one moment to look upon the sea: it was calm; and the air blew soft and fresh upon her burning forehead. – What dreadful sight is that ... a female figure,[a] passing through the thicket behind, with a hasty step approached them, and knelt down as if imploring for mercy. Her looks were wild; famine had stamped its hollow prints in furrows on her cheeks;[b] she clasped her / hands together; and fixing her eyes wildly upon Glenarvon, remained in silence.

Terrified, Calantha threw herself for safety at his feet; and he clasping her closely to his bosom saw but her. 'Oh[c] Glenarvon,' she cried, 'look, look; it is not a human form: it is some dreadful vision, sent to us by the power of God,[d] to warn us.' 'My soul, my Calantha, fear not: no power shall harm you.'

Turning from her, Glenarvon now gazed for one moment on the thin and ghastly form, that had occasioned her terror. 'God bless you,' cried[e] the supplicant. He started at the hollow sound. It seemed to him indeed that the awful blessing was a melancholy reproach for his broken faith. He started:[f] for in that emaciated form, in that wild and haggard eye, he thought he recognized some traces of one whom he had once taken spotless as innocence to his heart, – then left a prey to remorse and disappointment. For the sake of that resemblance,[g 42] he offered money / to the wretch who implored his mercy, and turned away, not to behold again so piteous, so melancholy a spectacle.

Intently gazing upon him, she uttered a convulsive groan, and sunk extended on the earth. Calantha and Glenarvon both flew forward to raise her. But the poor victim was no more: her spirit had burst from the slight bonds that yet retained it in a world of pain and sorrow. She had gazed for the last time upon her lover,[h] who had robbed her of all happiness through life; and the same look, which had first awakened love in her bosom, now quenched the feeling[i] and with it life itself. The last wish of her heart, was a blessing, not a curse for[j] him who had abandoned her: and the tear that he shed unconsciously over a form so altered, that he did not know her, was the only tear that blessed the last hour of Calantha's once favorite companion Alice Mac Allain.

Oh! need a scene which occasioned / her every bitter pang be repeated? – need it be said that, regardless of themselves or any conclusions which their being together at such an hour might have occasioned: they carried the unconscious girl to the door of the castle, where O'Kelly was waiting to receive them. Every one had retired to rest; it was late; and one of Calantha's maids and O'Kelly alone remained in fearful anxiety watching for their return.

Terrified at the haggard looks, and lifeless form before her, Calantha turned to Glenarvon. But his countanance was changed; his eyes were fixed. 'It is herself,' he cried; and unable to bear the sight, a faintness came over him: – the name of Alice was pronounced by him. O'Kelly understood his master. 'Is it possible,' he exclaimed, and seizing the girl in his arms, he promised Calantha to do all in his power to restore her, and only implored her to retire to her own apartment: 'For my master's sake, / dear Lady, be persuaded,' he said. He was indeed no longer the same subservient strange being, he had shewn himself hitherto; he seemed to assume a new character, on an occasion which called for his utmost exertion;ª he was all activity and forethought, commanding every thing that was to be done, and awakening Lord Glenarvon and Calantha to a sense of their situation.

Although Lady Avondale was at last persuaded to retire, it may be supposed that she did not attempt to rest; and being obliged in some measure to inform her attendant of what had passed, she sent her frequently with messages to O'Kelly to inquire concerning her unhappy friend. At last she returned with a few lines, written by Lord Glenarvon. 'Calantha,' he said, 'You will now learn to shudder at my name, and look upon me with horror and execration. Prepare yourself for the worst: – It is Alice whom we beheld. She came to / take one last look at the wretch who had seduced, and then abandoned her: – She is no more. Think not, that to screen myself, I have lost[b] the means of preserving her. – Think me not base enough for this; but be assured that all care and assistance have been administered. The aid of the physician, however has been[c] vain. Calm yourself Calantha: I am very calm.'

The maid, as she gave this note, told Calantha that the young woman whom Mr. O'Kelly,[d] had discovered at the door of the castle, was poor Miss Alice – so altered, that her own father, she was sure[e] would not know her. 'Did you see her?' 'O yes, my Lady: Mr. O'Kelly took me to see her, when I carried the message to him: and there I saw my Lord Glenarvon so good, so kind, doing every thing that was needed to assist her, so that it would have moved the heart of any one to have seen him.' While the attendant thus continued to talk, / her young mistress wept, and[f] having at length dismissed her, she opened the door,[g] listening with suspense to every distant noise.

It was six in the morning, when a loud commotion upon the stairs,ª aroused her. Hurrying down, she beheld a number of servants carrying some one for air, into one of the outer courts. It was not the lifeless corpse of Alice. From the glimpse Calantha caught, it appeared a larger form, and, upon approaching still nearer, her heart sickened at perceiving that it was the old man, Gerald Mac Allain, who having arisen to enquire into the cause of the disquiet he heard in the house[b] had been abruptly informed by some of the servants, that his daughter had been discovered without any signs of life, at the gates of the castle. O'Kelly and the other attendants had pressed forward to assist him.

Calantha now leaving him in their hands, walked in trembling alarm, / through the hall, once more to look upon her unhappy friend. There leaning against one of the high black marble pillars, pale, as the lifeless being whom, stretched before him, he still continued to contemplate, she perceived Glenarvon. His eyes were fixed: in his look there was all the bitterness of death; his cheek was hollow: and in that noble form, the wreck of all that is great might be traced. 'Look not thus,' she said, 'Oh Glenarvon: it pierces my heart to see you thus: grief must not fall on one like you.' He took her hand, and pressed it to his heart; but he could not speak. He only pointed to the pale and famished form before him; and Calantha perceiving it, knelt down by its side and wept in agony,[c] 'There was a time,' said he,[d] 'when I could have feared to cast this sin upon my soul, or rewarded so much tenderness and affection, as I have done. But I have grown callous to all;[e] and now my only, my dearest friend, I will tear myself / away from you for ever. I will not say God bless you: – I must not bless thee, who have brought thee to so much misery. Weep not for one unworthy of you: – I am not what you think, my Calantha. Unblessed myself, I can but give misery to all who approach me. All that follow after me come to this pass; for my love is death, and this is the reward of constancy. Poor Alice, but still more unhappy Calantha, my heart bleeds for you: for myself, I am indifferent.

Gerald now returned, supported by O'Kelly. The other servants, by his desire, had retired; and when he approached the spot were his child was laid, he requested even O'Kelly to leave him. He did so; and Mac Allain advanced towards Lord Glenarvon. 'Forgive a poor old man,' he said in a faltering voice: 'I spoke too severely, my lord: a father's curse in the agony of his first despair,[f] shall not be heard. Oh Lady Calantha,' said the old man, turning / to her, 'Lord Glenarvon has been very noble and good to me; my sons had debts, and he paid all they owed: they had transgressed and he got them pardoned. You know not what I owe to my lord; and yet when he told me, this night, as I upbraided the wretch that had undone my child and was the cause of her dishonor and death, that it was himself had taken her from my heart; I knelt down and cursed him. Oh God, Oh God! pardon the agony of a wretched father, a poor old man who has lived too long.'

Calantha could no longer master her feelings; her sobs, her cries were bitter and terrible. They wished to bear her forcibly away. O'Kelly insisted upon the necessity of her assuming at least some self command; and whispering to her, that[a] if she betrayed any violent agitation, the whole affair must be made public: he promised himself to bring her word of every minute particular, if she would for a few hours at least remain tranquil. 'I / shall see you again,' she said, recovering herself and approaching Lord Glenarvon before she retired: 'You are not going?' 'Going!' said he:[b] 'undoubtedly I shall not leave the castle at this moment; it would look like fear; but after this, my dearest friend, I do not deceive myself, you cannot, you ought not more to think of me.' 'I share your sorrows,' she said: 'you are most miserable; think not then, that I can be otherwise.' 'And can you still feel any interest for one like me? If I could believe this, even in the bitterness of affliction, I should still feel comfort: –[c] but, you will learn to hate me.' 'Never. Oh would to God[d] I could; but it is too late now. I love you, Glenarvon, more than ever,[e] even were it to death.[f] Depend on me.' Glenarvon pressed her hand,[g] in silence; then following her 'for[h] your dear sake, I will live,' he said. 'You are my only hope now. Oh Calantha![i] how from my soul I honour you.' /

Calantha threw herself upon her bed; but her agitation was too great to allow of her recurring in thought to the past, and fatigue once again occasioned her taking a few moment's rest. /

CHAPTER XXXV.

WHEN Lady Avondale awoke from her slumbers^a she found the whole castle in a state of confusion. Lady Margaret had twice sent for her. Every one was occupied with this extraordinary event. Her name, and Lord Glenarvon's were mentioned together, and conjectures, concerning the whole scene, were made by every individual.

At Gerald Mac Allain's earnest entreaties, the body of Alice was conveyed to his own house, near the Garden Cottage. He wished no one to be informed of the particulars of her melancholy fate. He came, however, a few days after her removal, to ask for Calantha. She was ill; but immediately admitted him.^b They talked together upon all that had occurred. He gave her a letter, and a broach, which / had been found upon the body. It^c was addressed to Lord Glenarvon. There was also a lock of hair, which seemed, from the fineness of its texture, to belong to a child. The letter was a mournful congratulation on his supposed marriage with a lady in England, written at some former period; it wished him every happiness, and contained no one reproach. The broach consisted of a heart's ease, which she entreated him sometimes to wear in remembrance of one, who had loved him truly. 'Heart's ease to you – *mais triste pensée pour moi*,'[43] was engraved upon it. 'You must yourself deliver these,' said Mac Allain looking wistfully at Calantha. She promised to do so.

Mac Allain then drew forth a larger packet which was addressed to himself. 'I have not yet read it,' he said, 'I am not able to see for my tears; but it is the narration of my child's sorrows; and when I have ended it, I will give it to you, my dear lady,^d and to any other / whom you may wish. 'Oh Mac Allain!' said Lady Avondale, 'by every tie of gratitude and affection which you profess, and have shewn our family, do not let any one read this but myself: – do not betray Lord Glenarvon. He feels your sufferings: he more than shares them. For my sake I ask you this. Keep this transaction secret; and, whatever may be suspected, let none know the truth. – Say: may I ask it?'

Calantha's agitation moved him greatly. He wept in bitter anguish. 'The destroyer of my child,' he said, 'will lead my benefactress into misery. Ah! my dear young lady,^e how my heart bleeds for you.' Impatiently, she turned away.

'Will you hear my entreaties,' she said. 'You may command; but the news of my child's death is spread: many are talking of it already: I cannot keep it secret.' 'Only let not Lord Glenarvon's name appear.' Mac Allain promised to do all in his power[a] to silence / every rumour; and, with the help of O'Kelly, he, in some measure succeeded. The story believed was, that Mr. Buchanan first had carried her[b] with him to England, where she had fallen into poverty and vice. No further enquiry was made; but Lord Glenarvon himself confided to many, the secret which Calantha was so eager to conceal.

The narrative of Alice's sufferings may be omitted by those who wish not to peruse it. Lord Glenarvon desired to read it when Calantha had ended it. He also took the broach, and pressing it to his lips, appeared very deeply affected. After this,[c] for a short time he absented himself from the castle. The following pages, written by Alice, were addressed to her only surviving parent. No comment is made on them; no apology offered for their insertion. If passion has once subdued the power of reason, the misery and example of others never avails, even[d] / were we certain of a similar fate. If every calamity we may perhaps deserve, were placed in view before us, we should not pause – we should not avert[e] our steps. To love, in defiance of virtue is insanity, not guilt. To attempt the safety of its victims, were a generous but useless effort of unavailable[f] interference. It is like a raging fever, or the tempest's fury – far beyond human aid to quell.[g] Calantha read, however, the history of her friend, and wept her fate.

ALICE'S NARRATIVE.

'My dear and honoured father,

'To you I venture to address this short history of my unhappy life, and if sufferings and pain can in part atone for my misconduct, I surely shall be forgiven by you; but never, while existence, however miserable, is prolonged, never shall I forgive myself. Perhaps even now, the rumour of my disgrace has reached you, / and added still severer pangs to those you before endured. But oh! my father, I have,[h] in part, expiated my offences. Long and severe sorrows have followed me, since I left your roof, and none more heart rending – oh! none to compare with the agony of being abandoned by him, for whom I left so much. You remember, my dear father, that, during the last year, which I passed at the castle, the attention which Mr. Buchanan had paid me, was so marked, that it occasioned the most serious apprehensions in Lady Margaret, on his account. Alas! I concealed from every one, the true cause of my encreasing melancholy; and felt happy that the suspicions of my friends and protectors were thus unintentionally misled. I parted with Linden, nor told him my secret. I suffered the severest menaces and[i] reproofs, without a murmur; for I knew myself guilty, though not of the crime with which I was charged. At Sir Everard St. Clare's I found means to / make my escape, or rather, the mad attachment of one far above me, removed every obstacle, which opposed his wishes and my own.

'But it is time more particularly to acquaint you, my dear father, by what accident I first met with Lord Glevarvon, to whom my fate was linked – whose attachment once made me blessed – whose inconstancy has deprived me of every earthly hope. Do you remember once, when I obtained leave to pass the day with you, that my brother, Garlace, took me with him in his boat, down the river Allan, and Roy and yourself were talking eagerly of the late affray which had taken place in our village. I then pointed out to you the ruins of St. Alvin's[a] Priory, and asked you the history of its unhappy owners. My father, that evening,[b] when yourself and Roy were gone on shore, my brother Garlace fixing the sail, returned with me down the current with the wind: and as we passed near the banks from behind / the rocks, we heard soft low notes, such as they say spirits sing over the dead; and as we turned by the winding shore, we soon perceived a youth who was throwing pebbles into the stream, and ever whilst he threw them, he continued singing in that soft, sweet manner I have said. He spoke with us, and the melancholy sound of his voice, attracted us towards him. We landed close by the place near which he stood. He accompanied us to the front of the castle; but then entreating us to excuse his proceeding further, he retired; nor told us who he was. From that day, I met him in secret. Oh! that I had died before I had met with one so young, so beautiful, but yet so utterly lost. Nothing could save him: my feeble help could not reclaim him: it was like one who clasped a drowning man, and fell with him in the struggle: he had cast sin and misery upon his soul. Never will I soil these pages with the record of what he uttered; / his secrets shall be buried as in a sepulchre; and soon, most soon shall I perish with them' . . . .

Calantha paused in the narrative; she gasped for breath; and wiping away the tears which struggled in her eyes: 'If he treated my friend with unkindness,' she said, 'dear as he has hitherto been to me, I will never behold him more.' She then proceeded.

'All enjoyment of life has ceased: – I am sick at heart. The rest of my story is but a record of evil. To exhibit the struggles of guilty love, is but adding to the crime already committed. I accuse him of no arts to allure: he did but follow the impulse of his feelings: he sought to save – he would have spared me: but he had not strength. O my father, you know Lord Glenarvon – you have felt for him, all that the most grateful enthusiasm could feel; and for the sake of the son whom he restored to you, you must forgive him the ruin of an ungrateful child, who / rushed forward herself to meet it. Unused to disguise my sentiments, I did not attempt even to conceal them from him; and when he told me I was dear, I too soon shewed him, how much more so he was to me. For when the moment of parting forever[c] came, when I saw my Lord, as I thought, for the last time, you must not judge me – you cannot even in fancy imagine, all I at that hour endured – I left my country, my home – I gave up every hope on earth or heaven for him. Oh God[a] in mercy pardon me, for I have suffered cruelly; and you, my father, when you read these pages, bless me, forgive me. Turn not from me, for you know not the struggles of my heart – you can never know what I have endured.'

Calantha breathed with greater difficulty; and paused again. She paced to and fro within her chamber, in strong agitation of mind. She then eagerly returned to peruse the few remaining pages, / written by her miserable, her infatuated friend. – 'She was not guilty,' she cried. 'The God of Heaven will not, does not condemn her. Oh she was spotless as innocence compared with me.'

'There were many amongst Lord Glenarvon's servants who were acquainted with my secret. Through every trouble and some danger I followed him; nor boast much of having felt no woman's fear; for who that loves can fear. I will not dwell upon these moments of my life: they were the only hours of joy, which brightened over a career of misery and gloom. Whilst loved by the object of one's entire devotion – whilst surrounded by gaiety and amusement, the voice of conscience is seldom heard; and, I will confess it, at this time I fancied myself happy. I was Glenarvon's mistress; and I knew not another wish upon earth. In the course of the three years, passed with him in England and in Italy, I became mother of a child, and Clare, / my little son, was dear to his father. But after his birth, he forsook me.'

We were in England at the time, at the house of one of his friends, when he first intimated to me the necessity of his leaving me. He had resolved, he said, to return to Florence, and I was in too weak a state of health to permit[b] my accompanying him. I entreated, I implored for permission to make the attempt. He paused for some time, and then, as if unable to refuse me, he consented – reluctantly, I will own it; but still he said that I should go. He never appeared more fond, more kind than the evening before his departure. That evening, I supped with him and his friends. He seemed tired; and asked me more than once if I would not go to rest. His servant, a countryman of ours, by name O'Kelly, brought me a glass with something in it, which he bade me drink; but I would not. Lord Glenarvon came to me, and bade me take it. 'If it were poison,'. / I said,[c] fondly, 'I would take it from your hands, so that I might but die upon your bosom.' 'It is not poison,' he said, 'Alice, but what many a fine lady in London cannot rest without. You will need repose; you are going a long journey[d] to-morrow; drink it love; and mayest thou sleep in peace.' I took the draught and slumbered, even while reposing in his arms . . . .

'Oh my father, he left me. – I awoke to hear that he was gone – to feel a misery I never can describe. From that day, I fell into a dangerous illness. I knew not what I said or did. I heard,[e] on recovering, that my lord had taken another mistress, and was about to marry; that he had provided for me with money; that he had left me my child. I resolved to follow:[a] – I recovered in that hope alone. I went over to Ireland: – the gates of the abbey were shut against me. Mr. Hard Head, a friend of my lord's whom I once named to you, met me as I stood an helpless / outcast, in my own country; he spoke to me of love; I shuddered at the words. – The well known sound of kindness. 'Never, never,' I said, as I madly[b] sought to enter the gates which were closed against me. – O'Kelly passed me: – I knelt to him. Was he man – had he human feelings? In mercy oh my God,[c] in mercy hear me, let me behold him again. I wrote, I know not what I wrote. My letters, my threats, my supplications were answered with insult – every thing was refused me. . . . .

'It was at night, in the dark night, my father, that they took my boy – my Clare, and tore him from my bosom . . . . Yes, my sleeping boy was torn by ruffian hands from my bosom. Oh! take my life, but not my child. Villains! by what anthority do you rob me of my treasure? Say, in whose name you do this cruel deed. "It is by order of our master, Lord Glenarvon." I heard no more; yet in the convulsive grasp of / agony, I clasped the boy[d] to my breast. "Now tear him from his mother," I cried, "if you have the heart;" and my strength was such that they seemed astonished at my power of resistance. They knew not the force of terror, when the heart's pulse beats in every throb, for more than life. The boy clung to me for support. "Save, save me," he cried. I knelt before the barbarians – my shrieks were vain – they tore him from me. – I felt the last pressure of his little arms – my Clare – my child – my boy. – Never, oh never, shall I see him again. Oh wretched mother! my boy, my hope is gone. – How often have I watched those bright beaming eyes, when care and despondency had sunk me into misery! – how oft that radiant smile has cheered when thy father cruelly had torn my heart! now never, never, shall I behold him more. . . . .
. . . .

'Linden had heard of my disgrace and / misery; he had written to me, but he knew not where I was. . . . .

'I will sail to-morrow, if I but reach Cork. – I have proved the ruin of a whole family. – I hear Linden has enlisted with the rioters. A friend of his met me and spoke to me of him, and of you my father. He promised to keep my secret: yet if he betrays me, I shall be far away before you hear of my fate. – I grieve for the troubles of my country. – All the malcontents flock together from every side to Belfont. Lord Glenarvon hears their grievances: – his house is the asylum of the unfortunate: – I alone am excluded from its walls. – Farewell to Ireland, and to my dear father. – I saw my brother Garlace pass; he went throught the court to St. Alvin, with many other young men. They talked loudly and gaily: he little thought that the wretch who hid her face from them was his sister – his own – his only sister, of whom he was once so fond. I saw Miss St. Clare too; but I never saw Glenarvon. . . . . /

'From my miserable Lodging, Cork, Thursday Night.

'The measure of my calamity is at its full. The last pang of a breaking heart is over – My father forgive me. – We sailed;ª a storm has driven us back. I shall leave Ireland no more. The object of my voyage is over: I am returned to die . . . . . . what more is left me. . . . . . .I cannot write. . . . I have lost every thing.'

'Sunday.

'I have been very ill. – When I sleep fires consumes me: I heard sweet music, such as angels sing over the dead: – there was one voice clear,ᵇ and soft as a lute sounding at a distance on the water: – itᶜ was familiar to me; but he fled when I followed. . . . . Every one talks of Lord Glenarvon. – Yes, he is come back – he is come back to his own country covered with glory. – a bride awaits him, I was told.ᵈ – He is happy; and I shall not grieve, if I see / him – yes, if I see him once more before I die: – it is all I ask.ᵉ I am so weak I can scarcely write; but my father, my dear Father,ᶠ I wish to tell you all. – I will watch for him among the crowd. . . . .

'Tuesday Night, Belfont.

'I walked to Belfont; – and now the bitterness of death is passed. – I have seen that angel face once again – I have heard that sweetest voice, and I can lie down,ᵍ and die; for I am happy now. – He passed me; but oh! bitter bitterʰ sight to me, he turned from me, and looked upon another. – Theyⁱ tell me it was my preserver and benefactress: they say it was Lady Avondale. He looked proud of her, and happy in himself. – I am glad he looked happy; but yet I thought he turned his eyes on me, and gazed upon me once so sadly, as if in this mournful countenance and altered form, he traced the features of her whom he had once loved so well. – But no – it could not be: / – he did not know me; and I will see him again. If he will but say, "Alice: God bless you," I shall die satisfied. – And if my child still lives, and comes again to you, so cold, so pale – take him to your heart, dear father, and forgive his mother – I am ill, and cannot write. They watch me; my pencil is almost worn out, and they will give me no other. – I have one favor to ask, and it is this: – when I came to Dublin, I gave all the money I had to buy this broach – take it to Lady Avondale. They say she is very good, and perhaps, when she hears how ill I am, she will pardon my faults, and give it for me to Lord Glenarvon. – I shall wait for him every day in the same wood, and who knows but I may see him again'. . . . .

And Alice did see him again; – and she did kneel to him; – and she received from his hands the relief he thought she craved; – and the unexpected kindness broke her heart. – She died; – and she / was buried in the church near Belfont. There was a white stone placed upon her grave, and her old father went daily there and wept; and he had the tree that now grows there planted; and it was railed around, that the cattle and wild-goats, might not destroy it.'

'Take the band from my head,' said Calantha. 'Give me air. This kills me.......' She visited the grave of Alice: she met Mac Allain returning from it, they uttered not one word as they passed each other. The silence was more terrible than a thousand lamentations.... Lady Margaret sent for Calantha. She looked ill, and was much agitated. 'It is time,' said Lady Margaret, to speak to you. 'The folly of your conduct,' – 'Oh it is past folly,' said Calantha weeping. Lady Margaret looked upon her with contempt. 'How weak, and how absurd is this. Whatever your errors, need you thus confess them? and / whatever your feelings, wherefore betray them to the senseless crowd?

'Calantha,' said Lady Margaret in a hollow tone, 'I can feel as deeply as yourself. Nature implanted passions in me, which are not common to all; but mark the difference between us: – a strong mind dares at least conceal the ravages the tempest of its fury makes. It assumes that character to the vulgar herd which it knows is alone capable of imposing restraint upon it. Every one suspects me, but none dare reproach me. You, on the contrary, are the butt against which every censure is levelled: they know that your easy nature can pardon malignity,[a] and the hand that insults you to-day will crave your kindness to-morrow. When you are offended, with puerile impotence and passionate violence, you exhibit the effects of your momentary rage; and by breaking of tables, or by idle words, shew your own weakness. Thus you are ever subdued by the / very exhibition of your passions. And now that you love, instead of rendering him you love your captive, you throw yourself entirely in his power, and will deeply rue the confidence you have shewn. Has he not already betrayed you. You know not Glenarvon. His heart, black as it is, I have read and studied. Whatever his imagination idolizes, becomes with him a sole and entire interest. At this moment he would fly with you to the extremity of the earth, and when he awakes,[b] from his dream, he will laugh at you, and at himself for his absurdity. Trust not that malignant and venomed tongue. The adder that slumbers in the bosom of him who saved it, recovers, and bites to the heart the fool that trusted it. Warned on all sides, beware! and if nothing else can save you, learn at least who this Glenarvon is, what he has done. He is......'

'Lord Glenarvon,' said a servant: at that very instant the door opened, and he / entered. He started at seeing Calantha, who, greatly embarrassed, durst not meet his eyes. It seemed to her, that to have heard him spoken of with unkindness was a sort of treachery to an attachment like their's. Lady Margaret's words had wounded and grieved her; but they had not shaken her trust; and when she looked upon him and saw that beautiful countenance, every doubt left her. Before she quitted the room, she observed however, with surprise, the smile of enchanting sweetness, the air of kindness, even of interest, with which Lady Margaret received him; and one jealous fear crossing her fancy, she lingered as if reproachfully enquiring what meant these frequent visits to her Aunt. Glenarvon, in a moment, read the doubt: – 'yes,'ª he cried, following her, 'you are right: if ever I have loved another with idolatry it was thy Aunt; but be assured I loved in vain. And now Calantha, I would agree, whilst existence were prolonged, / to see her no more, sooner than cause you one hour's uneasiness. Be satisfied at least, that she abhors me.'

'None of this whispering,' said Lady Margaret, smiling gently, 'at least in my presence.' 'I never loved before as now,' said Glenarvon, aloud. 'Never,' said Lady Margaret, with an incredulous and scornful smile. 'No,' said Glenarvon, still gazing on Calantha; 'all is candour, innocence, frankness in that heart; the one I idolized, too long, was like my own – utterly corrupted.' 'You wrong the lady,' said Lady Margaret carelessly. 'She had her errors, I acknowledge; but the coldness of Glenarvon's heart, its duplicity, its malignity, is unrivalled.' Calantha, deeply interested and agitated, could not quit the room. Glenarvon had seized her hand; his eyes, fixed upon her, seemed alone intent on penetrating her feelings: she burst into tears: he approached and kissed her.[b] 'You shall not tear her from me,' he said, to Lady Margaret, / 'She goes with me by God:[c] she is bound to me by the most sacred oaths: we are married:[d] are we not dearest?' 'Have you confessed to her,' said Lady Margaret, contemptuously. 'Everything.'

'She loves you no doubt the better for your crimes.' 'She loves me, I do believe it,[e] said Glenarvon, in an impassioned tone,' and may the whole world,' if she wishes it, know that by every art, by every power I possess, I have sought her: provided they also know,' he continued with a sneer, 'that I have won her. She may despise me; – you may teach her to hate; but of this be assured – you cannot change me. Never, never was I so enslaved. Calantha, my soul, look on me. – Glenarvon kneels to you. I would even appear humble – weak,[f] if it but gratify your vanity; for humility to you is now my glory – my pride.'

'Calantha,' said Lady Margaret, in a protecting tone, 'are you not vain?' / 'This Glenarvon has been the lover of many hundreds; to be thus preferred is flattering. Shall I tell you, my dear niece, in what consists your superiority? You are not as fair as these; you are not perhaps as chaste;[g] but you are loved more because your ruin will make the misery of a whole family, and your disgrace will cast a shade upon the only man whom Glenarvon ever acknowledged as superior to himself – superior both in mind and person. This, child, is your potent charm – your sole claim to his admiration. Shew him some crime of greater magnitude, point out to him an object more worth the trouble and pain of rendering more[h] miserable, and he will immediately abandon you.'

Glenarvon cast his eyes fiercely upon Lady Margaret. The disdain of that glance silenced her, she even came forward with a view to conciliate: and affecting an air of playful humility – 'I spoke but from mere jealousy,' she said. 'What woman of my age could bear to / see another so praised, so worshipped in her presence. It is as if the future heir of his kingdom were extolled in presence of the reigning sovereign. Pardon me, Glenarvon. I know, I see you love her.' 'By my soul I do; and look,' he cried exultingly, 'with what furious rage the little tygress gazes on you. She will harm you, I fear,' he continued laughing, 'if I do not carry her from your presence. Come then Calantha: *we* shall meet again,' he said, turning back and pausing as they quitted Lady Margaret's apartment. The tone of his voice, and his look, as he said this was peculiar: nor did he for some moments regain his composure.

Lady Margaret spoke a few words to Calantha that evening. 'I am in the power of this man,' she said, 'and you soon will be. He is cold, hard and cruel. Do any thing: but, if you have one[a] regard for yourself, go not with him,'[b] 'I know his history, his errors,' said Calantha; / 'but he feels deeply.' 'You know him,' said Lady Margaret, with a look of scornful superiority: 'as he wishes you to believe him, he even may exaggerate, were that possible, his crimes, the more to interest and surprise. You know him, Calantha, as one infatuated and madly in love can imagine the idol of its devotion. But there will come a time when you will draw his character with darker shades, and taking from it all the romance and mystery of guilt, see him, as I do, a cold malignant heart, which the light of genius, self-love and passion, have warmed at intervals; but which, in all the detail of every-day life, sinks into hypocrisy and baseness. Crimes have been perpetrated in the heat of passion, even by noble minds; but Glenarvon is little, contemptible and mean. He unites the malice and petty vices of a woman, to the perfidy and villany of a man. You do not know him as I do.'[44]

'From this hour.' said Calantha, indignation / burning in her bosom, 'we never more, Lady Margaret, will interchange one word with each other. I renounce you entirely; and think you[c] all that you have dared to say against my loved, my adored Glenarvon.'

Lady Margaret sought Calantha before she retired for the night, and laughed at her for her conduct. 'Your rage, your absurdity but excite my contempt. Calantha, how puerile this violence appears to me; above all, how useless. Now, from the earliest day of my remembrance, can any one say of me that they beheld me forgetful of my own dignity, from the violence of my passions. Yet I feel, think you not, and have made others feel. Your childish petulance but operates against yourself. What are threats, blows and mighty words from a woman. When I am offended, I smile; and when I stab deepest, then I can look as if I had forgiven. Your friends talk of you with kindness or unkindness as it suits their / fancy: some love; some pity, but none fear Calantha. Your very servants, though you boast of their attachment, despise and laugh at you. Your husband caresses you as a mistress, but of your conduct he takes not even heed. What is the affection of the crowd? what the love of man? make yourself feared! Then, if you are not esteemed, at least you are out-wardly honoured, and that reserve, that self-countroul, which you never sought even to obtain, keeps ordinary minds in alarm. Many hate me; but who dares even name me without respect. Yourself, Calantha, even at this moment, are ready to fall upon my bosom and weep, because I have offended you. Come child – your hand. I fain would save you, but you must hear much that pains you, before I can hope even to succeed. Only remember: '*si vous vous faites brebis le loup vous mangera.*'[45] She smiled as she said this, and Calantha, half offended, gave her the hand for which she solicited. /

CHAPTER XXXVI.⁴⁶

Mrs. Seymour was now extremely unwell, the least agitation was dreaded for her. Calantha was constantly enquiring after her; but could not bear to remain long in her presence. Yet at night she watched by her, when she did not know of it; and though she had ceased to pray for herself, she prayed for her. Could it be supposed that, at such a moment, any personal feelings would engage Calantha to add to her uneasiness. Alas! she sought in the last resources of guilt to alleviate every apprehension she might cherish; she feigned a calm she felt not; she made every promise she meant not to fulfil; she even spoke of Glenarvon with some severity for his conduct[a] to Alice; and when Mrs. Seymour rejoiced at her escape, she pressed her hand and / wept. Lady Margaret, from the day of their quarrel, cold and stern, ever arose to leave the room when Calantha entered it, and Mrs. Seymour seeing resentment kindling in her niece's eye, in the gentlest manner urged her to bear with her aunt's humour.

Lord Glenarvon had not written to Calantha for some days;[b] he had left the castle;[c] and she laboured under the most painful suspense. The narrative of Alice's sufferings was still in her possession. At length he sent for it. 'My Calantha,' he said, in a letter she received from him, 'My Calantha, I have not heard from you, and my misery is the greater, as I fear that you are resolved to see me no more. I wish for the narrative in your possession; I know the impression it must make; and strange as it may appear, I almost rejoice at it. It will spare you much future sorrow; and it can scarce add one pang to what I already suffer. Had you accompanied me, it / was, I will now acknowledge, my firm resolve to have devoted every moment of my life to your happiness – to have seen, to have thought, to have lived, but for you alone. I had then dared to presume, that the excess of my attachment would remunerate you, for all the sacrifices you might be compelled to make; that the fame of Glenarvon would hide, from the eyes of a censorious world, the stigma of disgrace, which must, I fear, involve you; and that, at all events, in some other country, we might live alone for each other. – The dream is past; you have undeceived me; your friends require it: be it, as you and as they desire. I am about to quit Ireland. If you would see me before I go, it must be on the instant. What are the wrongs of my country to me? Let others, who have wealth and power, defend her: – let her look to English policy for protection; to English justice for liberty and redress. Without a friend, even as I first set foot upon these shores, I now abandon them.' /

'Farewell, Calantha. Thou art the last link which yet binds me to life. It was for thy sake – for thine alone, that I yet forbore. It is to save thee, that I now rush onward to meet my fate: grieve not for me. I stood a solitary being till I knew you. I can encounter evils when I feel that I alone shall suffer. Let me not think that I have destroyed you. But for me, you then[a] might have flourished happy and secure. O why would you tempt the fate of a ruined man? – I entreat you to send the papers in your possession. I am prepared for the worst. But if you could bring yourself to believe the agony of my mind at this moment, you would still feel for me, even though in all else chilled and changed. – Farewell, dearest of all earthly beings – my soul's comforter and hope, farewell.' 'I will go with thee Glenarvon, even should my fate exceed Alice's in misery – I never will forsake thee.'

Calantha's[b] servant entered at that moment, / and told her that Lord Glenarvon was below – waiting for the answer. 'Take these papers,' said Calantha, and with them she enclosed a ring which had been found upon Alice: 'Give them yourself to Lord Glenarvon: I cannot see him. – You may betray me, if it is your inclination; I am in your power; but to save is not. Therefore, for God's sake,[c] do not attempt it....' The attendant had no difficult task in executing this errand. She met Lord Glenarvon himself, at the door of the library.

Upon alighting from his horse, he had enquired for Lady Margaret Buchanan; before she was prepared to receive him, the papers were delivered into his hands; he gave them to O'Kelly; and after paying a shorter visit to Lady Magaret than at first he had intended, he returned to the inn at Belfont, to peruse them. First however he looked upon the broach, and taking up the ring, he pressed it to his lips and sighed, for he remembered it / and her to whom it had been given. Upon this emerald ring, the words: '*Eterna fede*,'[47] had been inscribed. He had placed it upon his little favourite's hand, in token of his fidelity, when first he had told her of his love; time had worn off and defaced the first impression; and '*Eterno dolor*,'[48] had been engraved by her in its place – thus telling in few words the whole history of love – the[d] immensity of its promises – the cruelty of its disappointment.[e]

Calantha was preparing to answer Glenarvon's letter: her whole soul was absorbed in grief, when Sophia entered and informed her that the Admiral was arrived. It was, she knew, his custom to come and go without much ceremony; but his sudden presence, and at such a moment, overpowered her. Perhaps too, her husband might be with him! she fell: Sophia called for assistance. 'Good God!'[f] what is the matter?' she said, 'You have just kilt my lady,' said the / nurse; 'but she'll be better presently: let her take her way – let her take her way.' And before Calantha could compose herself, Sir Richard was in her room. She soon saw by his hearty open countenance, that he was perfectly ignorant of all that had occurred; and to keep him so, was now her earnest endeavour. But she was unused to deceit: all her attempts at it were forced: it was not in her nature; and pride alone, not better feeling prevented its existence. /

CHAPTER XXXVII.

Sir Richard apologized for his abrupt appearance; and told Calantha that he had been with Lord Avondale to visit his relations at Monteith, where he had left him employed, as he said, from morning till night, with his troops in quelling disturbances and administering justice, which he performed but ill, having[a] as he expressed it, too kind a heart. He then assured her that her husband had promised to meet him[b] the present day at the castle, and enquired of her if she knew wherefore his return had been delayed. She in reply informed him, that he had no intention of joining them, and even produced his last cold letter, in which he told her that she might visit him at Allenwater, at the end of the month, with the children, if all continued tranquil in / those quarters. She spoke this in an embarrassed manner; her colour changed repeatedly; and her whole appearance was so dissimilar from that to which the Admiral had been accustomed, that he could not but observe it.

Sir Richard, having with seeming carelessness, repeated the words, 'He'll be here this week that's certain,' now addressed himself to the children, telling Harry Mowbray[c] the same, 'And perhaps he'll bring you toys.' 'He'll bring himself,' said the child, 'and that's better.'[d] 'Right, my gallant boy,' returned the Admiral; 'and you are a fine little fellow for saying so.' Thus encouraged, the child continued to prattle. 'I want no toys now, uncle Richard. See I have a sword, and a seal too. Will you look at the impression: – the harp means Ireland: "Independence" is the motto; we have no crown; we want no kings.' 'And who gave you this seal?' said Sir Richard, fiercely. 'Clarence / Glenarvon,' replied the boy, with a smile of proud exultation. 'D – n your sword and your seal,' said the Admiral. 'I like no rebel chiefs, not I;' and he turned away. 'Are you angry with me, uncle Richard?' 'No, I am sick, child – I have the head ache.' The Admiral had observed Calantha's agitation, and noted the boy's answers; for he left the room abruptly, and was cold and cross the rest of the day.

Colonel Donallan having invited the whole family and party, to his seat at Cork, Lady Trelawny[e] and the rest of the guests now left the castle. It was possibly owing to this circumstance that the Admiral, who was not a remarkably keen observer, had opportunity and leisure to watch Calantha's conduct. In a moment she perceived the suspicion that occurred; but as he was neither very refined, nor very sentimental, it occurred without one doubt of her actual guilt, or one desire to save her from / its consequences: – it occurred with horror, abhorrence,ª and contempt. Unable to conceal the least thing,ᵇ or to moderate his indignation, he resolved, without delay, to seize the first opportunity of taxing her with her ill conduct. In the meantimeᶜ she felt hardened and indifferent;ᵈ and, instead of attempting to conciliate, by haughty looks and a spirit of defiance, she rendered herself hateful to every observer. That compassion, which is sometimes felt and cherished for a young offender, could not be felt for her; nor did she wish to inspire it. Desperate and insensible, she gloried in the cause of her degradation; and the dread of causing her aunt's death, and casting disgrace upon her husband's name, alone retained her one hour from Glenarvon.

On the very day of the Admiral's arrival, he heard enough concerning Calantha to excite his most vehement indignation; and at the hour of dinner, therefore, as he passed her,ᵉ he called her by a name / too horrible to repeat. Stung to the soul, she refused to enter the dining-room; and, hastening with fury to her own apartment, gave vent to the storm of passion by which she was wholly overpowered. There, unhappily, she found a letter from her lover – all kindness, all warmth. 'One still there is,' she said, 'who loves, who feels for the guilty, the fallen Calantha.' Every word she read, and compared with the cold neglect of others, or their severity and contempt. There was none to fold her to their bosom, and draw her back from certain perdition. She even began to think with Glenarvon, that they wished her gone. Some feelings of false honor, too, inclined her to thinkᶠ she ought to leave a situation, for which she now must consider herself wholly unfit.

But there was one voice which still recalled her: – it was her child's. 'My boy will awake, and find me gone – he shall never have to reproach his mother.' And / she stood uncertain how to act. Mrs. Seymour, to her extreme astonishment, was the only person who interrupted these reflections. She was the last she had expected to do so. She had read in the well-known lineaments of Calantha's face: – that face which, as a book, she had perused from infancy, some desperate project: – the irritation, the passionate exhibition of grief was past – she was calm. Sophia, at Mrs. Seymour's request, had therefore written to Calantha. She now gave her the letter. But it was received with sullen pride: – 'Read this, Lady Avondale,' she said, and left the room. Calantha never looked at her, or she might have seen that she was agitated; but the words – 'Read this, Lady Avondale,' repressed all emotion in her. It was long before she could bring herself to open Sophia's letter. A servant entered with dinner for her. 'The Admiral begs you will drink a glass of wine,' he said. She made no answer; but desired her maid to take it / away, and leave her. She did not even perceive that Mac Allain, who was the bearer of this message, was in tears.

Sophia's letter was full of commonplace truisms, and sounding periods – a sort of treatise upon vice, beginning with a retrospect of Calantha's past life, and ending with a cold jargon of worldly considerations. A few words, written in another hand, at the conclusion, affected her more: – they were from her aunt, Mrs. Seymour. 'You talk of leaving us, of braving misfortunes, Lady Avondale,' she said: 'you do not contemplate, you cannot conceive, the evils you thus deride. I know; – yes, well I know, you will not be able to bear up under them. Ah! believe me, Calantha, guilt will make the proudest spirit sink, and your courage will fail you at the moment of trial. Why then seek it? – My child, time flies rapidly, and it may no longer be permitted you to return and repent. You now fly from reflection; but it will overtake you / when too late to recall the emotions of virtue. Ah! remember the days of your childhood; recollect the high ideas you had conceived of honor, purity and virtue:ª – what disdain you felt for those who willingly deviated from the line of duty: – how true, how noble, how just were all your feelings. You have forsaken all; and you began by forsaking him who created and protected you! What wonder, then, that having left your religion and your God, you have abandoned every other tie that held you back from evil! Say, where do you mean to stop?ᵇ Are you already guilty in more than thought? – No, no; I will never believe it; but yet, even if this were so, pause before you cast public dishonor upon your husband and innocent children. Oh! repent, repent, it is not yet too late.'

'It is too late,' said Calantha, springing up, and tearing the letter: 'it is too late;' and nearly suffocated with the / agony of her passionate grief. She gasped for breath. 'Oh! that it were not. I cannot – I dare not stay to meet the eyes of an injured husband, to see him unsuspicious, and know that I have betrayed him. This is too hard to bear: – a death of torture is preferable to a continuance of this; and then to part, my aunt knows not, nor cannot even conceive, the torture of that word. She never felt what I do – she knows not what it is to love, and leave. . . . These words comprise every thing, the extremes of ecstacy and agony. Oh! who can endure it. They may tear my heart to pieces; but never hope that I will consent to leave Glenarvon.'

The consciousness of these feelings, the agitation of her mind, and the dread of Lord Avondale's return, made her meet Sophia, who now entered her apartment with some coldness. The scene that followed need not be repeated. All that a cold and common-place friend can urge, / to upbraid, villifyᶜ and humiliate, was uttered by Miss Seymour; and all in vain. She left her,ᵈ therefore, with much indignation; and, seeing that her mother was preparing to enter the apartment she had quitted: 'O! go not to her,' she said; 'you will find only a hardened sinner; you had best leave her to herself. My friendship and patience are tired out at last; I have forborne much; but I can endure no more. Oh! she is quite lost.'

'She is not lost, she is not hardened,' said Mrs. Seymour, much agitated. 'She is my own sister's child:ᵃ she will yet hear me.'

'Calantha,' said Mrs. Seymour, advancing, 'my child;' and she claspedᵇ her to her bosom. She would have turned from her, but she could not. 'I am not come to speak to you on any unpleasant subject,' she said. 'I cannot speak myself,'ᶜ answered Calantha, hiding her face, not to behold her aunt: 'all I ask of you is not to hate me; and God / reward you for your kindness to me: I can say no more; but I feel much.' 'You will not leave us, dear child?' 'Never, never, unless I am driven from you – unless I am thought unworthy of remaining here.' 'You will be kind to your husband, when he returns – you will not grieve him.' 'Oh! no, no: I alone will suffer; I will never inflict it upon him; but I cannot see him again; he must not return: you must keep him from me. I never...' 'Pause, my Calantha: make no rash resolves. I came here not to agitate, or to reproach. I ask but one promise, no other will I ever exact: – you will not leave us.' This change of manner in her aunt produced the deepest impression upon Lady Avondale. She looked, too, so like her mother, at the moment, that Calantha thought it had been her. She gave her her hand: she could not speak. 'And did they tell me she was hardened?' said Mrs. Seymour. / 'I knew it could not be: my child, my own Calantha, will never act with cruelty towards those who love her. Say only the single words: 'I will not leave you,' and I will trust you without one fear.' 'I will not leave you!' said Calantha, weeping bitterly, and throwing herself upon her aunt's bosom. 'If it break my heart, I will never leave you, unless driven from these doors!' Little more was said by either of them. Mrs. Seymour was deeply affected, and so was Calantha.

After she had quitted her, not an hour had elapsed, when Sir Richard, without preparation, entered. His presence stifled every good emotion – froze up every tear. Calantha stood before him with a look of contempt and defiance, he could not bear. Happily for her, he was called away, and she retired early to bed. 'That wife of Avondale's has the greatest share of impudence,' said the Admiral, addressing the / company, at large, when he returned from her room, 'that ever it was my fortune to meet. One would think, to see her, that she was the person injured; and that we were all the agressors. Why, she has the spirit of the very devil in her! but I will break it, I warrant you.' /

CHAPTER XXXVIII.

THE next morning, regardless of the presence of the nurses and the children, who were in Lady Avondale's apartment – regardless indeed[a] of any consideration, but that which rage and indignation had justly excited, the Admiral again entered Calantha's room, and in a high exulting tone, informed her that he had written to hasten her husband's return. 'As to Avondale, d'ye see,' he continued 'he is a d – d fine fellow, with none of your German sentiments,[49] not he;[b] and he will no more put up with these goings on, than I shall; nor shall you pallaver him over: for depend upon it, I will open his eyes, unless from this very moment you change your conduct. Yes, my Lady Calantha, you look a little surprised, I see, at hearing good English spoken to you; but I am / not one who can talk all that jargon of sensibility, they prate round me here. You have the road open; you are young, and may mend yet; and if you do, I will think no more of the past. And as to you, Mrs. Nurse, see that these green ribbands be doffed. I prohibit Lord Mowbray[c] and Lady Annabel from wearing them. I hate these rebellious party colours. I am for the King, and old England; and a plague on the Irish marauders, and my Lord Glenarvon at the head of them – who will not take ye, let me tell you, Lady[d] fair, for all your advances. I heard him say so myself, aye, and laugh too, when the Duke told him to be off, which he did, though it was in a round about way; for they like here, to press much talk into what might be said in a score of words. So you need not look so mighty proud; for I shall not let you stir from these apartments, do you see, till my nephew comes; and, then, God mend you, or take you;[e] for we will not / bear with these proceedings, not we of the navy, whatever your land folks may do.'

'Sir Richard,' said Calantha, 'you may spare yourself and me this unkindness, – I leave this house immediately, – I leave your family from this hour; and I will die in the very streets sooner than remain here. Take this,' she said throwing the marriage ring from her hand; 'and tell your nephew I never will see him more: – tell him[f] if it is your pleasure[g] that I love another, and had rather be a slave in his service, than Lord Avondale's wife. I ever hated that name, and now I consider it with abhorrence.' 'Your Ladyship's words are big and mighty,' cried Sir Richard; 'but while this goodly arm has a sinew and this most excellent door has a key you

shall not stir from hence.' As he yet spoke, he advanced to the door; but she, darting before him, with a celerity he had not expected, left him, exclaiming as she / went, 'you have driven me to this: tell them you have done it' ....
....

In vain the Admiral urged every one he met to pursue Calantha. The moment had been seized, and no power can withstand, no after attempt can regain the one favourable moment that is thus snatched from fate. The castle presented a scene of the utmost confusion and distress. Miss Seymour was indignant; the servants were in commotion; the greatest publicity was given to the event from the ill judged indiscretion of the Admiral. Mrs. Seymour alone,[a] was kept in ignorance; the Duke coldly, in reply to the enquiry of what was to be done, affirmed that no step should be taken[b] unless, of herself, the unhappy Calantha returned to seek the pardon and protection of those friends whom she had so rashly abandoned, and so cruelly misused. Yet, not withstanding the prohibition[c] / every place was searched, every measure to save was thought of, and all without success.

Sir Richard then set[d] down with Annabel in his arms, and the little boy by his side, crying more piteously than the nurse who stood opposite encreasing the general disturbance, by her loud and ill-timed lameutations. 'If my Lord had not been the best of husbands, there would have been some excuse for my Lady.' 'None Nurse[e] – none whatever;' sobbed forth Sir Richard, in a voice scarcely audible, between passion and vexation. 'She was a good mother, poor Lady: that I will say for her.' 'She was a d – d wife though,' cried Sir Richard; 'and that I must say for her.' After which, the children joining, the cries and sobs were renewed by the nurse, and Sir Richard, with more violence than at first. 'I never thought it would have come to this,' said the nurse, first recovering. / 'Lord[f] ma'am, I knew it would end ill, when I saw those d – d green ribbands'. . . . 'Who[g] would have thought such a pretty looking gentleman would have turned out such a villain!' 'He is no gentleman at all,' said Sir Richard angrily. 'He is a rebel, an outcast. Shame upon him.' And then again the nurse's cries checked his anger, and he wept more audibly than before.

'Would you believe it, after all your kindness,' said Sophia, entering her mother's room[h] 'Calantha is gone.' At the words 'she's[i] gone,' Mrs. Seymour fainted; nor did she for some time recover; but with returning sense, when she saw not Calantha, when asking repeatedly for her, she received evasive answers; terror again overcame her – she was deeply and violently agitated. She sent for the children; she clasped them to her bosom. They smiled upon her; and that look, was a pang beyond all others of bitterness. / The Admiral, in tears, approached her; lamented his interference; yet spoke with just severity of the offender. 'If I know her heart, she will yet return,' said Mrs. Seymour. 'She will never more return,' replied Sophia. 'How indeed will she dare appear, after such a public avowal of her sentiments – such a flagrant breach of every sacred duty. Oh, there is no excuse for the mother who thus abandons her children – for the wife who stamps dishonour on a husband's fame – for the child that dares to disobey a father's sacred will?' 'Sophia[a] beware. Judge not of others – judge not; for the hour of temptation may come to all. Oh judge her not,' said Mrs. Seymour, weeping bitterly; 'for she will yet return.'

Towards evening Mrs. Seymour again enquired for Calantha. They told her she had not been heard of; her agitation proved too well the doubt she entertained. / 'Send again,' she continually said, and her hand, which Lady Margaret held in hers, became cold and trembling. They endeavoured to comfort her; but what comfort was there left.[b] They tried to detain her in her own apartment; but the agony of her sufferings was too great; – her feeble frame – her wasted form[c] could ill endure so great a shock. The Duke, affected beyond measure, endeavoured to support her. 'Pardon her, receive her with kindness,' said Mrs. Seymour, looking at him. 'I know she will not leave you thus: I feel that she must return.' 'We will receive her without one reproach,' said the Duke. 'I, too, feel secure that she will return.' 'I know her heart: she can never leave us thus. Go yourself, Altamonte,' said Lady Margaret: – 'let[d] me go.' 'Where would you seek her?' 'At Lord Glenarvon's,' said Mrs. Seymour, faintly. 'Oh! she is not there,' said the Duke, / 'She never will act in a manner we must not pardon.' Mrs. Seymour trembled at these words – she was ill, most ill; and they laid her upon her bed, and watched in silence and agony around her.

The Duke repeated sternly –[e] I trust she is not gone to Lord Glenarvon – *all* else I can forgive.

END OF VOL. II.
LONDON: PRINTED BY SCHULZE AND DEAN, 13,
POLAND STREET, OXFORD STREET.

GLENARVON.

IN THREE VOLUMES

VOL. III.

LONDON:

PRINTED FOR HENRY COLBURN. 1816.

GLENARVON.

VOL. III.

Il n'est plus temps.

GLENARVON.

Dísperato dolor, chè il cor mi preme
Gìa pur pensando, pria che ne favelle.[1]

VOL. III. /

GLENARVON.

CHAPTER I.

Love, though, when guilty, the parent of every crime, springs forth in the noblest hearts, and dwells ever with the generous and the high-minded. The flame that is kindled by Heaven burns brightly and steadily to the last, its object great and superior, sustained by principle, and incapable of change. But, when the flame is unsupported[a] by these pure feelings, it rages and consumes us, burns up and destroys every noble hope, perverts the mind, and fills with craft and falsehood every avenue to the heart. Then that which was a paradise, becomes a hell;[b] and the victim of its power,[c] a maniac and a fiend. They know not the force / of passion, who have not felt it – they know not the agony of guilt, who have not plunged into its burning gulf, and trembled there. O! when the rigorous and the just turn with abhorrence from the fearful sight – when, like the pharisee, in the pride of their unpolluted hearts, they bless their God that they are not as this sinner –[d] let them beware; for the hour of trial may come to all; and that alone is the test of superior strength. When man, reposing upon himself, disdains the humility of acknowledging his offences and his weakness before his Creator, on the sudden that angry God sees fit to punish him in his wrath, and he who has appeared invulnerable till that hour, falls prostrate at once before the blow; perhaps then, for the first time, he relents; and, whilst he sinks himself, feels for the sinner whom, in the pride and presumption of his happier day, he had mocked at and despised. There are trials, which human frailty / cannot resist – there are passions implanted in the heart's core, which reason cannot subdue; and God himself compassionates, when a fellow-creature refuses to extend to us his mercy or forgiveness.[e] [2]

Fallen, miserable Calantha! where now are the promises of thy youth – the bright prospects of thy happiness? Where is that unclouded brow – that joyous look of innocence which once bespoke a heart at ease? Is it the same, who, with an air of fixed and sullen despondency, flying from a father's house, from a husband's protection, for one moment resolved to seek the lover whom she adored, and follow him, regardless of every other tie? Even[f] in that hour of passion and of guilt, the remembrance of her husband, of her sacred promise to her aunt, and of that gentle supplicating look with which it was received, recurred. A moment's reflection changed the rash resolve; and hastening forward, / she knew not where^a – she cared not to what fate – she found herself^b after a long and weary walk^c at the vicar's house, near Kelladon – a safe asylum and retreat.

The boat which had conveyed her from the shore^d returned; and a few hours after brought Glenarvon to the other side of the rocks, known in the country by the name of the Wizzard's^e Glen, and ofttimes the scene of tumult and rebellious meeting. Calantha little expected to see him. He met her towards evening, as weary and trembling she stood, uncertain where to fly, or what to do.^f The moment of meeting was terrible to both; but that which followed was more agonizing still. A servant of her father's had discovered her after a long search. He informed her of her aunt's illness and terror. He^g humbly, but firmly, urged her instantly to return.

Calantha had resolved never to do so; but, lost as she was, the voice of her / aunt still had power to reach her heart – 'Is she very ill?' 'Very dangerously ill,'^h said the man; and without a moments^i delay, she immediately consented to return. She resolved to part from him she adored; and Glenarvon generously agreed to restore her to her aunt, whose sufferings had affected his heart – whose prayers had moved him, as he said, to the greatest sacrifice he ever was called upon to make. Yet still he upbraided her for her flight, and affirmed, that had she but confided herself in him,^j she had long before this have been^k far away from scenes so terrible to witness, and been spared a state of suspense so barbarous to endure. Whilst he spoke, he gazed upon her with much sadness.

'I will leave you,' he said; 'but the time may come when you will repent, and call in vain for me. They may tear my heart from out my breast – they may tear thee from me, if it is their mad desire. I shall^l or die, or recover, or forget thee. / But oh! miserable victim – what^m shall become of thee? Do they hope their morality will unteach the lessons I have given;^n or pluck my image from that heart? Thou art mine,^o wedded to me, sold to me; and no after-time can undo for thee,^p what I have done. Go; for I can relinquish thee. But have they taught thee,^q what it is to part from him you love? never again to hear his voice – never again to meet those eyes, whose every turn and glance you have learned to read and understand?'

Calantha could not answer. 'You will write kindly and constantly to me,' at length she said. 'May God destroy me in his vengeance,' cried Glenarvon eagerly, 'if, though absent, I do not daily, nay, hourly think of thee, write to thee, live for thee! Fear not, thou loved one. There was a time when inconstancy had been a venial error – when insecure of thy affections, and yet innocent, to fly thee had been a / duty,^r to save thee had been an angel's act of mercy and of virtue; – but now when thou art mine;^s when, sacrificing the feelings of thy heart for others, thou dost leave me –^t can you believe that I would add to your grief and increase my own.^u Can you believe him you love so base as this? Oh! yes, Calantha, I have acted the part of such a villain to your lost friend, that even you mistrust me.' She reassured him:^v 'I have given my very soul to you, O! Glenarvon. I believe in you,^w as I once did in Heaven. I had rather doubt myself and every thing than you.'

She now expressed an anxiety to return and see her aunt. 'Yet, Calantha, it may perhaps be said that you have fled to me. The stain then is indelible. Think of it, my beloved; and think, if I myself conduct you back, how the malevolent, who are ever taunting you, will say that I wished not to retain you. They know me not; they guess not / what I feel; and the world, ever apt to judge by circumstances imperfectly related, will imagine' . . . . 'At such a moment,' said Calantha, impatiently, 'it is of little importance what is thought. When the heart suffers keenly, not[a] all the sayings of others are of weight.[b] Let them think the worst, and utter what they think. When we fall, as I have done, we are far beyond their power:[c] the venomed shaft of malice cannot wound; for the blow under which we sink is alone heeded. I feel now but this, that I am going to part from you.'

Glenarvon looked at her, and the tears filled his eyes. 'Thy love,' he said, 'was the last light of Heaven,[d] that beamed upon my weary pilgrimage: thy presence recalled me from error: thy soft voice stilled every furious passion. It is all past now – I[e] care not what becomes of me.' As he spoke, they approached the boat, and entering it, sailed with a gentle breeze across the bay. Not a / wave rippled over the sea[f] – not a cloud obscured the brightness of the setting sun. 'How tranquil and lovely is the evening!' said Glenarvon, as the bark floated upon the smooth surface. 'It is very calm now,' she replied, as she observed the serenity of his countenance. 'But, ah! who knows how soon the dreadful storms may arise, and tear[g] us to destruction.'

The boat now touched[h] the shore, where a crowd of spectators were assembled – some watching from the top of the high cliff, and others idly gazing upon the sea. The figure of Elinor distinctly appeared amongst the former, as bending forward, she eagerly watched for Glenarvon. Her hat and plume distinguished her from the crowd; and the harp, her constant companion, sounded at intervals on the breeze,[i] in long and melancholy cadences. Her dark wild eye fixed itself upon him as he approached. 'It is my false lover,' / she said, and shrieked. 'Hasten, dearest Calantha,' he cried, 'from this spot, where we are so much observed. That wretched girl may, perhaps, follow us. Hasten; for see with what rapidity she advances.' 'Let her come,' replied Calantha. 'I am too miserable myself to turn from those that[j] are unhappy.' Elinor approached:[k] she gazed on them as they passed:[l] she strained her eyes to catch one last glimpse of Glenarvon as he turned the path.

Many of his friends, retainers[m] and followers were near. He bowed to all with gracious courtesy; but upon Elinor he never cast his eyes. 'He's gone!' she cried, shouting loudly, and addressing herself to her lawless associates, in the language they admired. 'He is gone;[n] and peace be with him; for he is the leader of the brave.' They now[o] passed on in silence to the castle; but Elinor, returning to her harp, struck the chords with enthusiasm, whilst the caverns of the / mountains re-echoed to the strain. The crowd who had followed loudly applauded, joining in the chorus to the well-known sound of 'Erin m'avourneen – Erin go brah.'[3] /

CHAPTER II.

THE moment of enthusiasm was past; the setting sun warned every straggler and passenger to return. Some had a far distant home to seek; others had left their wives or their children. Elinor turned from the golden light which illuminated the west, and gazed in agony upon the gloomy battlements of St. Alvin Priory, yet resplendent with the last parting ray. Of all who followed her, few only now remained to watch her steps. She bade them meet her at the cavern at the accustomed hour. She[a] was weary, and feigned that till then she would sleep. This she did to disembarrass herself of them.

Upon raising herself after a little time, they were gone. It was dark – it was / lonely. She sat and mused upon the cliff, till the pale moon broke through the clouds, and tipped every wave with its soft and silvery light. – 'The moon shines bright and fair,' she said: 'the shadows pass over it. Will my lover come again to me? It is thy voice, Glenarvon, which sings sweetly and mournfully in the soft breeze of night.

> My heart's fit to break, yet no tear fills my eye,
> As I gaze on the moon, and the clouds that flit by.
> The moon shines so fair, it reminds me of thee;
> But the clouds that obscure it, are emblems of me.
> They will pass like the dream of our pleasures and youth;
> They will pass like the promise of honor and truth;
> And bright thou shalt shine, when these shadows are gone,
> All radiant – serene – unobscur'd; but alone.

'And did he pass me so coldly by? And did he not once look on me?' she said, 'But I will not weep: he shall not break my spirit and heart. Let him / do so to the tame doves for whom he has forsaken me. Let such as Alice and Calantha die for his love: I will not.' – She took her harp: her voice was tired and feeble. She faintly murmured the feelings of her troubled soul. It sounded like the wind, as it whispered through the trees, of the mournful echo of some far distant flute.

> SONG.
> And can'st thou bid my heart forget[b]
> What once it lov'd so well;
> That look – that smile, when first we met;

That last – that sad farewell?

Ah! no: by ev'ry pang I've prov'd,
By ev'ry fond regret,
I feel, though I no more am lov'd,
I never – can forget.

I wish'd to see that face again,
Although 'twere chang'd to me:
I thought it not such madd'ning pain
As ne'er to look on thee. /

But, oh! 'twas torture to my breast,
To meet thine alter'd eye,
To see thee smile on all the rest,
Yet coldly pass me by.

Even now, when ev'ry hope is o'er
To which I. . . . .

'Are these poetical effusions ended?' said a soft voice from behind. – She started; and turning round, beheld the figure of a man enveloped[a] in a dark military cloak, waiting for her upon the cliff. – 'What a night it is! not a wave on the calm sea: not a cloud in the Heavens. See how the mountain is tinged with the bright moonshine. Are you not chill'd – are[b] you not weary; wandering thus alone?' 'I am prepared to follow you,' said Elinor, 'though not as a mistress, yet as a slave.' 'I do not love you,' said the man, approaching her. 'Oh, even if you were to hang about and kneel to me as once, I cannot love you! Yet it once was pleasant to be so loved; was it / not?' I think not of it now,' said Elinor, while a proud blush burned on her cheek. 'This is no time for retrospection.' 'Let us hasten forwards, by the light of the moon: I perceive that we are late. – Have you forgiven me?' 'There are injuries, Glenarvon, too great to be forgiven: speak not of the past: let us journey on.'

The lashing of the waves against the rocks, alone disturbed the silence of this scene.[c] They walked in haste by each others side, till they passed Craig Allen Point, and turned into the mouth of a deep cavern. Whispers were then heard from every side – the confusion of strange voices, the jargon of a foreign dialect, the yells and cries of the mutineers and discontented. 'Strike a light,' said Elinor's companion, in a commanding tone, as he advanced to the mouth of the rock. – In a moment, a thousand torches blazed around, whilst shouts of joy proclaimed a welcome to the visitor, / who was accosted with every mark of the most obsequious devotion.

'How many have taken the oath tonight?' said a stout ill-looking man, advancing to the front line. 'Sure, Citizen Conner,[d] fifty as brave boys as ever suck'd whiskey from the mother country,' answered O'Kelly from within. The ferocious band of rebels were now ordered forward, and stood before their leader; some much intoxicated, and all exhibiting strange marks of lawless and riotous insubordination. 'We'll pay no tythes to the parsons,' said one. 'We'll go to mass, that we will, our own way.' 'We'll be entirely free.' 'There shall be no laws amongst us.' 'We'll reform every thing, won't we?' 'And turn all intruders out with the tyrants.' 'Here's to the Emerald Isle! Old Ireland for ever! Erin for ever!' 'Come, my brave boys,' shouted forth one Citizen Cobb, 'this night get yourselves pikes – make yourselves arms. Beg,[a] buy, / or steal, and bring them here privately at the next meeting. We'll send your names in to[b] the directory. Fear nothing,[c] we will protect you:[d] we'll consider your grievances. Only[e] go home peaceably, some one way, and some another – by twos, by threes.[f] Let us be orderly as the king's men are. We are free men; and indeed free men can make as good soldiers.'

'I would fain speak a few words, citizen, before we part to-night. The hour is not yet ripe; but you have been all much wronged. My heart bleeds for your wrongs. Every tear that falls from an Irishman is like a drop of the heart's best blood:[g] is't not so, gentlemen? Ye have been much aggrieved; but there is one whom ye have for your leader, who feels for your misfortunes; who will not live among you to see you wronged:[h] and who, though having nothing left for himself, is willing to divide his property amongst you all to the last shilling. See / there, indeed, he stands amongst us. Say, shall be speak to you?' 'Long life to him – let him speak to us.' 'Hear him.' 'Let there be silence as profound as death.' 'Sure and indeed we'll follow him to the grave.' 'Och, he's a proper man!' A thousand voices having thus commanded silence:

'Irishmen,' said Glenarvon, throwing his dark mantle off, and standing amidst the grotesque and ferocious rabble, like some God[i] from a higher world – 'Irishmen, our country shall soon be free: – you are about to be avenged. That vile government, which has so long, and so cruelly oppressed you, shall soon be no more! The national flag – the sacred green, shall fly over the ruins of despotism; and that fair capital, which has too long witnessed the debauchery, the plots, the crimes of your tyrants, shall soon be the citadel of triumphant patriotism and virtue. Even if we fail, let us die defending the rights of man[4] – / the independence of Ireland. Let us remember that as mortals we are liable to the contingencies of failure; but that an unalterable manliness of mind, under all circumstances, is erect and unsubdued. If you are not superior to your antagonist in experience and skill, be so in intrepidity. Art, unsupported by skill, can perform no service. Against their superior practice, array your superior daring; for on the coward, who forgets his duty in the hour of danger, instant punishment shall fall; but the brave, who risk their lives for the general cause, shall receive immediate distinction and reward. – Arise then, united sons of Ireland – arise like a great and powerful people, determined to live free or die.'[5]

Shouts of applause for a moment interrupted Glenarvon. Then, as if inspired with renewed enthusiasm, he proceeded: 'Citizens, or rather shall I not say, my friends; for such you have proved yourselves to me, my own and / dear countrymen; for though an exile, whom misfortune from infancy has pursued, I was born amongst you, and first opened my delighted eyes amidst these rocks and mountains, where it is my hope and ambition yet to dwell. The hour of independence approaches. Let us snap the fetters by which tyrants have encompassed us around: let us arouse all the energies of our souls; call forth all the merit and abilities, which a vicious government has long consigned to obscurity; and under the conduct of great and chosen leaders, march with a steady step to victory.'[6]

Here Glenarvon was again interrupted by the loud and repeated bursts of applause. Elinor then springing forward, in a voice that pierced through the hearts of each, and was echoed back from cave to cave – 'Heard ye the words of your leader?' she cried: 'and is there one amongst you base enough to desert him?' 'None, none.' 'Then arm / yourselves, my countrymen:[a] arm yourselves by every means in your power:[b] and rush like lions on your foes. Let every heart unite, as if struck at once by the same manly impulse; and Ireland shall itself arise to defend its independence; for in the cause of liberty, inaction is cowardice: and may every coward forfeit the property he has not the courage to protect! Heed not the glare of hired soldiery, or aristocratic yeomanry: they cannot stand the vigorous shock of freedom. Their trappings and their arms will soon be your's. Attack the tyrants in every direction, by day and by night. – To war – to war! Vengeance on the detested government of England! What faith shall you keep with them? What faith have they ever kept with you? Ireland can exist independent. O! let not the chain of slavery encompass us around. – Health to the Emerald isle! Glenarvon and Ireland for ever!' /

CHAPTER III.

THE cry of joy[a] has ceased. Elinor and her companion have quitted the cavern. Before she parted for the night, she asked him respecting one he loved. 'Where is Calantha?' she said. 'In yon dreary prison,' he replied, pointing to Castle Delaval: – 'like a rose torn from the parent stem, left to perish in all its sweetness – gathered by the hand of the spoiler, and then abandoned. I have left her.'[7] 'You look miserable, my Lord.' 'My countenance is truer to my feelings than I could have supposed.' 'Alice dead – Calantha discarded! I heard the tale, but it left no credit with me. – Can there be hearts so weak as thus to die for love? 'Tis but a month ago, I think, you said you never would leave her; that this was / different from all other attachments; that you would bear her hence.' 'I have changed my intention: is that sufficient?' 'Will she die, think you?' 'Your uncle will, if you continue thus,' replied Glenarvon. 'I am sick at heart, Elinor, when I look on you.' 'Old men, my Lord, will seek the grave; and death can strike young hearts, when vain men think it their doing. I must leave you.' 'Wherefore in such haste?' 'A younger and truer lover awaits my coming: I am his, to follow and obey him.' 'Oh, Elinor, I tremble at the sight of so much cold depravity – so young and so abandoned. How changed from the hour in which I first met you at Glenaa! Can it be possible?' 'Aye, my good Lord; so apt a scholar, for so great a master.'

Glenarvon attempted to seize her hand. 'Do you dare to detain me? Touch me not. I fear you.' . . . . 'Elinor[b] to what perdition are you hastening? I adjure / you by your former love, by Clare of Costoly, the boy for whom you affect such fondness, who still remains the favorite of my heart, return to your uncle. I will myself conduct you.' 'Leave your hold, Glenarvon: force me not to shriek for succour. – Now that you have left me, I will speak calmly. Are you prepared to hear me?' 'Speak.' 'Do you see those turrets which stand alone, as if defying future storms? Do you behold that bleak and barren mountain, my own native mountain, which gave me the high thoughts and feelings I possess; which rears its head, hiding it only in the clouds? Look above: see the pale moon, that moon which has often witnessed our mutual vows, which has shone upon our parting tears, and which still appears to light us on our guilty way: by these, by thyself, thy glorious self, I swear I never will return to virtue: /

> For the heart that has once been estrang'd,
> With some newer affection may burn,
> It may change, as it ever has chang'd,
> But, oh! it can never return.'

'By these eyes, which you have termed bright and dear; by these dark shining locks, which your hands have oft entwined; by these lips, which, prest by your's have felt the rapturous fire and tenderness of love – virtue and I are forsworn: and in me, whatever I may appear, henceforward know that I am your enemy. Yes, Glenarvon, I am another's now.' 'You can never love another as you have loved me: you will find no other like me.' 'He is as fair and dear, therefore detain me not. I would rather toil for bread, or beg from strangers, than ever more owe to you one single, one solitary favour. Farewell – How I have adored, you know: how I have been requited, think – when sorrows as acute as those you have inflicted visit / you. Alice, it is said, blest you with her dying breath. Calantha is of the same soft mould; but there are deeds of horror, and hearts of fire: – the tygress has been known to devour her young; and lions, having tasted blood, have fed upon the bowels of their masters.'

St. Clare, as she spoke, stood upon the edge of the high cliff to which they had ascended. The moon shone brightly on her light figure, which seemed to spring from the earth, as if impelled forward by the strength of passion. The belt of gold which surrounded her slender waist burst, as if unable longer to contain the proud swelling of her heart: she threw the mantle from her shoulders; and raising the hat and plume from her head, waved it high in the air: then darting forward, she fled hastily from the grasp of Glenarvon, who watched her lessening form till it appeared like a single speck in the distance, scarce visible to the eye. /

CHAPTER IV.

Before Glenarvon had met Elinor upon the clift,[a] he had conducted Lady Avondale to her father's house. The first person who came forward to meet them was Sir Richard. 'My dear child,' he said, 'what could have induced you to take in such a serious manner what was meant in jest? There is your aunt dying in one room; and every one in fits or mad in different parts of the house. The whole thing will be known all over the country; and the worst of it is, when people talk, they never know what they say, and add, and add, till it makes a terrible story. But come in, do; for if the world speak ill of you, I will protect you: and as to my Lord Glenarvon / there, why it seems after all he is a very good sort of fellow; and had no mind to have you; which is what I hinted at before you set out, and might have saved you a long walk, if you would only have listened to reason. But come in, do; for all the people are staring at you, as if they had never seen a woman before. Not but what I must say, such a comical one, so hot and hasty, I never happened to meet with; which is my fault, and not your's. Therefore, come in; for I hate people to do any thing that excites observation. There now; did not I tell you so? Here are all your relations perfectly crazy: and we shall have a scene in the great hall, if you don't make haste and get up stairs before they meet you.' 'Where is she? where is she?' said Mrs. Seymour; and she wept at beholding her. But Calantha could not weep: her heart seemed like ice within her: she could neither weep nor speak. 'My child, my Calantha,' / said Mrs. Seymour, 'welcome back.' Then turning to Glenarvon, whose tears flowed fast, 'receive my prayers, my thanks for this,' she exclaimed. 'God reward[b] you for restoring my child to me.'

'Take her,' said Lord Glenarvon, placing Calantha in Mrs. Seymour's arms; 'and be assured, I give to you what is dearer to me, far dearer than existence. I do for your sake what I would not for any other: I give up that which I sought, and won, and would have died to retain – that which would have made life dear, and which, being taken from me, leaves me again to a dull blank, and dreary void. Oh! feel for what I have resisted; and forgive the past.' 'I cannot utter my thanks,' said Mrs. Seymour. 'Generous Glenarvon! God reward you for it, and bless you.' She gave him her hand.

Glenarvon received the applauses of all; and he parted with an agitation so / violent, and apparently so unfeigned, that even the duke, following, said, 'We shall see you, perhaps, to-morrow: we shall ever, I'm sure, see you with delight.' Calantha alone shared not in these transports; for the agony of her soul[a] was beyond endurance. Oh, that she too could have thought Glenarvon sincere and generous; that she too, in parting from him, could have said, a moment of passion and my own errors have misled him! – but he has a noble nature. Had he taken her by the hand, and said – Calantha, we both of us have erred; but it is time to pause and repent: stay with a husband who adores you: live to atone for the crime you have committed: – she had done so. But he reproached her for her weakness; scorned her for the contrition he said she only affected to feel; and exultingly enquired of her whether, in the presence of her husband, she should ever regret the lover she had lost. /

When we love, if that which we love is noble and superior, we contract a resemblance to the object of our passion; but if that to which we have bound ourselves is base, the contagion spreads swiftly, and the very soul becomes black with crime. Woe be to those who have ever loved Glenarvon! Lady Avondale's heart was hardened; her mind utterly perverted; and that face of beauty, that voice of softness, all, alas! that yet could influence her. She was, indeed, insensible to every other consideration. When, therefore, he spoke of leaving her,[b] – of restoring her to her husband, she heard him not with belief; but she stood suspended, as if waiting for the explanation such expressions needed. – It came at length. 'Have I acted it to the life?' he whispered, ere he quitted her. ''Tis[c] but to keep them quiet. Calm yourself. I will see you again to-morrow.'

That night Calantha slept not; but she watched for the approaching morrow. / It came: – Glenarvon came, as he had promised: he asked permission to see her one moment alone;[d] he was not denied. He entered, and chided her for her tears; then pressing her to his bosom,[e] he inquired if she really thought that he would leave her: 'What now – now that we are united by every tie; that[f] every secret of my soul is your's? Look at me, thou dear one: look again upon your master, and never acknowledge another.' 'God bless and protect you,' she answered. 'Thanks, sweet, for your prayer; but the kiss I have snatched from your lips is sweeter far for me. Oh, for another, given thus warm from the heart! It has entranced – it has made me mad.[g] What fire burns in your eye? What ecstasy is it thus to call you mine? Oh, tear from your mind every remaining scruple! – shrink not. The fatal plunge into guilt is taken: what matter how deep the fall. You weep, love; and for what? Once you were pure and spotless; / and then, indeed, was the time for tears; but now that fierce passions have betrayed you – now that every principle is renounced, and every feeling perverted, let us enjoy the fruits of guilt.[h]

'They talk to us of parting: – we will not part. Though contempt may brand my name, I will return and tear thee from them when the time is fit; and you shall drink deep of the draught of joy, though death and ignominy may be mingled with it. Let them see you again – let the ties strengthen that I have broken. That which has strayed from the flock,ᵃ will become even dearer than before; and when most dear, most prized: a second time I will return, and a second time break through every tie, every resolve. Dost shudder, sweet one? To whom are you united? Remember the oaths – the ring; and however estranged – whatever you may hear, remember that you belong to me, to me alone. And even,' continued he, smiling / with malicious triumph, 'even though the gallant soldier, the once loved Avondale return, can he find again the heart he has lost? If he clasp thee thus, 'tisᵇ but a shadow he can attempt to bind. The heart, the soul, are mine. O! Calantha, you know not what you feel, nor half what you would feel, were I in reality to leave you. There's a fire burns in thee, fierce as in myself:ᶜ you are bound to me now; fear neither man nor God.ᵈ I will return and claim you.'

As he spoke, he placed around her neck a chain of gold, with a locket of diamonds, containing his hair; saying as he fastened it:ᵉ 'Remember the ring:ᶠ this, too, is a marriage bond between us;' and, kneeling solemnly, 'I call your God,' said he, 'I call him now to witness, while that I breathe, I will consider you as my wife, my mistress; the friend of my best affections. Never, Calantha, will I abandon, or forget thee:ᵍ – / never, by Heaven! shalt thou regret thy attachment or my own.'

'Glenarvon,' said Calantha, and she was much agitated, 'I have no will but your's; but I am not so lost as to wish, or to expect you to remain faithful to oneʰ you must no longer see:ⁱ – only, when you marry –' 'May the wrath of Heaven blast me,' interrupted he,ʲ 'if ever I call any woman mine but you, my adored, my sweetest friend. I will be faithful; but you – you must return to Avondale: and shall he teach you to forget me? No, Calantha, never shall you forget the lessons I have given:ᵏ my triumph is secure. Think of me when I am away:ˡ dream of me in the night, as that dear cheek slumbers upon its pillow; and, when you wake, fancy yourself in Glenarvon's arms.ᵐ Our's has been but a short-tried friendship,' he said; 'butⁿ the pupils of Glenarvon never can forget their master. Better they had lived for years in folly and vice / with thousands of common lovers,ᵒ than one hour in the presence of such as I am. Do you repent, love? It is impossible. Look back to the time that is gone; count over the hours of solitude and social life; bear in your memory every picture of fancied bliss, and tell me truly if they can be compared to the transport, the ecstasy of being loved.⁸

'Oh! there is Heaven in the language of adoration; and one hour thus snatched from eternity is cheaply purchased by an age of woe. My love, my soul, look not thus. Now is the season of youth. Whilstᵖ fresh and balmy as the rose in summer,ᑫ dead to remorse, and burning with hidden fires, dash all fear and all repentance from you; leave repinings to the weak and the old, and taste the consolation love alone can offer. What can heal its injuries? What remove its

regrets? What shews^a you its vanity and illusion but itself? This hour we enjoy /
its transports, and to-morrow, sweet, we must live upon its remembrance.

'Farewell, beloved. Upon thy burning lips receive a parting kiss; and never let or father, or husband, take it thence.^b Dissemble well, however; for they say the conquering hero returns – Avondale. Oh! if thou shouldst – but it is impossible – I feel that you dare not forget me.^c We must appear to give way: we have been too unguarded: we have betrayed ourselves: but, my life, my love is your's. Be true to me. You need not have one doubt of me: I never, never will forsake you. Heed not what I say to others:^d I do it but to keep all tranquil, and to quiet suspicion. Trust all to one who has never deceived thee. I might have assumed a character to you more worthy, more captivating. But have you not read the black secrets of my heart – aye, read, and shuddered, and yet forgiven me?' /

CHAPTER V.

THE repetition of a lover's promises is perhaps as irksome to those who may coldly peruse them, as the remembrance is delightful to those who have known the rapture of receiving them. I cannot, however, think that to describe them is either erroneous or unprofitable.ᵃ It may indeed be held immoral to exhibit, in glowing language, scenes which ought never to have been at all; but when every day, and every hour of the day – at all times, and in all places, and in all countries alike, man is gaining possession of his victim by similar arts, to paint the portrait to the life, to display his base intentions, and their mournful consequences, is to hold out a warning and admonition to innocence and virtue:ᵇ / this cannot be wrong. All deceive themselves. At this very instant of time, what thousands of beguiled and credulous beings are saying to themselves in the pride of their hearts, 'I am not like thisᶜ Calantha,' or, 'thank God,ᵈ the idol of my fancy is not a Glenarvon.' They deem themselves virtuous, because they are yet only upon the verge of ruin:ᵉ they think themselves secure, because they know not yet the heart of him who would mislead them. But the hour of trial is at hand; and the smile of scorn may soon give place to the bitter tear of remorse.ᶠ

'Many can deceive,' said Glenarvon, mournfully gazing on Calantha whilst she wept; 'but is your lover like the common herd? Oh! we have loved, Calantha,ᵍ better than they know how: we have dared the utmost: your mind and mine must not even be compared with their's. Let the vulgar dissemble and fear – let them talk idly in the unmeaning jargon / they admire: they never felt what we have felt; they never dared what we have done: to win, and to betray, is with them an air – a fancy: and fit is the delight for the beings who can enjoy it. Such as these, a smile or a frown may gain or lose in a moment. But tell me, Calantha, have we felt nothing more? I who could command you, am your slave: every tear you shed is answered not by my eyes alone, but in my heartʰ of hearts; and is there that on earth I would not, will not sacrifice for you?

'I know they will wound you, and frown on you because of me; but if once I shew myself again, the rabble must shrink at last:ⁱ they dare not stand before Glenarvon. Heaven, or hell, I care not which, have cast a ray so bright around my brow, that not all the perfidy of a heart as lost as mine, of a heart loaded, as you know too well, with crimes man shudders even to imagine – not all the envy and malice of those whom my / contempt has stung, can lower me to their level. And you, Calantha, do you think you will ever learn to hate me, even were I to leave, and to betray you? Poor blighted flower, which I have cherished in my bosom, when scorned and trampled on, because you have done what they had gladly done^a if I had so but willed it! Were I to subject you to the racking trial of frantic jealousy, and should you ever be driven by fury and vengeance to betray me, you would but harm yourself. To thy last wretched hour, thou wouldst pine in unavailing recollection and regret; as Clytie,[9] though bound and fettered to the earth, still fixes her uplifted eyes upon her own sun, who passes over, regardless in his course, nor deigns to cast a look below.'

It was at a late hour that night, when after again receiving the thanks of a whole family – when after hearing himself called the preserver of the wretch who scarcely dared to encounter his eyes, / Lord Glenarvon took a last and faltering leave of Calantha. Twice he returned and paused;^b he knew not how to say farewell: it seemed as if his lips trembled beneath the meaning of that fearful word – as if he durst not utter a knell to so much love – a death to every long cherished^c hope. At length, in a slow and solemn voice, 'Farewell, Calantha,' he said. 'God forgive us both, and bless you.' Lady Avondale for one instant ventured to look upon him;^d it was but to impress upon her memory every feature, every lineament, and trace of that image, which had reigned so powerfully over her heart. Had thousands been present, she had seen but that one: – had every danger menaced him, he had not moved. Thus in the agony of regret they parted:^e but that regret was shared; and as he glanced his eye for the last time on her, he pointed to the chain which he wore with her resemblance / near his heart; and he bade her take comfort in the thought that absence could never tear that image from him. /

CHAPTER VI.

AND now the glowing picture of guilt is at an end;[a] the sword of justice hangs over the head of a devoted criminal; and the tortures of remorse are alone left me to describe. But no: remorse came not yet:[b] absence but drew Calantha nearer to the object of her attachment. They never love so well,[c] who have never been estranged. Who is there that in absence clings not with increasing fondness to the object of its idolatry, watches not every post, and trembling with alarm, anxiety[d] and suspense, reads not again and again every line that the hand of love has traced? Is there a fault that is not pardoned in absence? Is there a doubt that is not harboured and believed, however agonizing? Yet, though believed, is / it not at once forgiven? Every feeling but one is extinct in absence; every idea but one image is banished as profane. Lady Avondale had sacrificed herself and Glenarvon, as she then thought, for others:[e] but she could not bring herself to endure the pang she had voluntarily inflicted.

She lived therefore but upon the letters she daily received from him; for those letters were filled with lamentations for her loss, and with the hope of a speedy return. Calantha[f] felt no horror at her conduct. She deceived herself: conscience itself had ceased to reprove a heart so absorbed, so lost in the labyrinth of guilt. Lord Avondale wrote to her but seldom: she heard however with uneasiness that his present situation was one that exposed him to much danger; and after a skirmish with the rebels, when she was informed that he was safe, she knelt down,[g] and said, 'Thank God for it!' as if he had still been dear. / His letters, however, were repulsive and cold. Glenarvon's, on the other hand, breathed the life and soul of love.

In one of these letters, Glenarvon informed her, that he was going to England, to meet at Mortanville Priory several of his friends. Lady Mandeville, Lady Augusta Selwyn, and Lady Trelawney, were to be of the party. 'I care not,' he said, 'who may be there. This[h] I know too well, that my Calantha will not.' He spoke of Lady Mowbrey and Lady Elizabeth with praise. 'Oh! if your Avondale be like his sister, whom I have met with since we parted, what indeed have you not sacrificed for me?' He confided to her, that Lady Mandeville had entreated him to visit her in London: 'But what delight can I find in her society?' he said:[i] 'it will only remind me of one I have lost.'

His letter, after his arrival in England, ended thus: 'I will bear this separation as long as I can, my Calantha; but my / health is consumed by my regret; and, whatever you may do, I live alone – entirely alone. We may be alone in the midst of crowds; and if indifference, nay, almost dislike to others, is a proof of attachment to you, you will be secure and satisfied. I had a stormy passage from Ireland. Is it ominous of future trouble? Vain is this separation.

'I will bear with it for a short period;[a] but in the spring, when the soft winds prepare to waft us, fly to me; and we will traverse the dark blue seas, secure, through thousand storms, in each others devotion. Were you ever at sea? How does the roar of the mighty winds, and the rushing of waters, accord with you – the whistling of the breeze, the sparkling of the waves by night, and the rippling of the foam against the sides of that single plank which divides you from eternity? Fear you, Calantha? Oh, not if your lover were by your side, your head reclining on his bosom, your heart / freed from every other tie, and linked alone by the dearest and the tenderest to his fate! Can you fancy yourself there, about the middle watch? How many knots does she make? How often have they heaved the log?[10] Does she sail with the speed of thought, when that thought is dictated by love? Perhaps it is a calm. Heed it not: towards morn it will freshen: a breeze will spring up; and by to-morrow even, we shall be at anchor. Wilt thou sail? "They that go down into the great deep; they see the wonders of the Lord."[11] That thou may'st see as few as possible of his terrific wonders, is, my beloved, the prayer of him who liveth alone for thee!

'The prettiest and most perilous navigation for large ships is the Archipelago. There we will go; and there thou shalt see the brightest of moons, shining over the headlands of green Asia, or the isles,[b] upon the bluest of all waves – the most beautiful, but the most treacherous. / Oh, Calantha! what ecstasy were it to sail together, or to travel in those pleasant lands I have often described to you – freed from the gloom and the forebodings this heavy, noisome atmosphere engenders!^c – Dearest! I write folly and nonsense: – do I not? But even this, is it not a proof of love?'

After his arrival at Mortanville Priory, Glenarvon wrote to Calantha a minute account of every one there. He seemed to detail to her his inmost thoughts. He thus expressed himself concerning Miss Monmouth:[12] – 'Do you remember how often we have talked together of Miss Monmouth? You will hear, perhaps, that I have seen much of her of late. Remember she is thy relative; but, oh! how unlike my own, my beloved Calantha! Yet she pleases me well enough. They will, perhaps, tell you that I have shewn her some little attention. Possibly this is true; but, God[d] be my witness, I never for one moment even have / thought seriously about her.' Lady Trelawney, in writing to her sister, thought rather differently. It was thus that she expressed herself upon that subject. 'However strange you may think it,' she said in her letter to Sophia, 'Lord Glenarvon has made a proposal of marriage to Miss Monmouth. I do not believe what you tell me of his continuing to write to Calantha. If he does, it is only by way of keeping her quiet; for I assure you he is most serious in his intentions. Miss Monmouth admires, indeed I think loves him; yet she has not accepted his offer. Want of knowledge of his character, and some fear of his principles, have made her for the present decline it. But their newly made friendship is to continue; and any one may see how it will end. In the mean time, Lord Glenarvon has already consoled himself for her refusal – but I will explain all this when we meet.

'Remember to[a] say nothing of this to / Calantha, unless she hears of it from others; and advise her not to write so often. It is most absurd, believe me. Nothing, I think, can be more wanting in dignity,[b] than a woman's continuing to persecute a man who is evidently tired of her. He ever avoids all conversation on this topic; but with me, in private, I have heard a great deal, which makes me think extremely well of him. You know how violent Calantha is in all things: – it seems,[c] in the present instance, that her love is of so mad and absurd a nature, that it is all he can do to prevent her coming after him. Such things, too, as she has told him! A woman must have a depraved mind, even to name such subjects.

'Now, I know you will disbelieve all this; but at once to silence you, I have seen some passages of her letters; and more forward and guilty professions none ever assuredly ventured to make. Her gifts too! – he is quite loaded with them; / and while, as he laughingly observed, one little remembrance from a friend is dear, to be almost bought thus is unbecoming, both in him to receive, and herself to offer. As to Lord Glenarvon, I like him more than ever. He has, indeed, the errors of youth; but his mind is superior, and his heart full of sensibility and feeling.' /

CHAPTER VII.

IF Glenarvon's letters had given joy to Calantha[a] in more prosperous and happier days, when surrounded by friends, what must they have appeared to her now, when bereft of all? They were as the light of Heaven to one immersed in darkness:[b] they were as health to the wretch who has pined in sickness: they were as riches to the poor, and joy to the suffering heart. What then must have been her feelings when they suddenly and entirely ceased! At first, she thought the wind was contrary, and the mails irregular. Of one thing she felt secure – Glenarvon could not mean to deceive her. His last letter, too, was kinder than any other; and the words with which he concluded it[c] were such as to / inspire her with confidence. 'If, by any chance, however improbable,' he said, 'my letters fail to reach you, impute the delay to any cause whatever;[d] but do me enough justice not for one moment to doubt of me. I will comply with every request of your's; and from you I require in return nothing but remembrance – the remembrance of one who has forgotten himself, the world, fame, hope, ambition – all here, and all hereafter, but you.'

Every one perhaps has felt the tortures of suspense: every one knows its lengthened pangs: it is not necessary[e] here to paint them. Weeks now passed, instead of days, and still not one line, one word from Glenarvon. Then it was that Lady Avondale thus addressed him:

'It is in vain, my dearest friend, that I attempt to deceive myself. It is now two weeks since I have watched, with incessant anxiety, for one of those dear, / those kind letters, which had power to still the voice of conscience, and to make one, even as unworthy as I am, comparatively blest. You accused me of coldness; yet I have written since, I fear, with only too much warmth. Alas! I have forgotten all the modesty and dignity due to my sex and situation, to implore for one line, one little line, which might inform me you were well, and not offended. Lord Avondale's return, I told you, had been delayed. His absence, his indifference, are now my only comfort in life. Were it otherwise, how could I support the unmeasured guilt I have heaped upon my soul? The friends of my youth are estranged by my repeated errors and long neglect. I am as lonely, as miserable in your absence as you can wish.

'Glenarvon, I do not reproach you: I never will. But your sudden, your unexpected silence, has given me more anguish than I can express. I will not / doubt you: I will follow your last injunctions, and believe every thing sooner than that you will thus abandon me. If that time is indeed arrived – and I know how frail a possession guilty love must ever be – how much it is weakened by security – how much it is cooled by absence: do not give yourself the pain of deceiving me: there is no use in deceit. Say with kindness that another has gained your affections; but let them never incline you to treat me with cruelty. Oh, fear not, Glenarvon, that I shall intrude, or reproach you. I shall bear every affliction, if you but soften the pang to me by one soothing word.

'Now, possibly, when you receive this, you will laugh at me for my fears: you will say I but echo back those which you indulged. But so sudden is the silence, so long the period of torturing suspense, that I must tremble till I receive one line from your dearest hand – one line to say that you are not offended / with me. Remember that you are all on earth to me; and if I lose that for which I have paid so terrible a price, what then will be my fate!

'I dread that you should have involved yourself seriously. Alas! I dread for you a thousand things that[a] I dare not say. My friend, we have been very wicked. It is myself alone I blame. On me, on me be the crime; but if my life could save you, how gladly would I give it up! Oh, cannot we yet repent! Act well, Glenarvon: be not in love with crime: indeed, indeed, I tremble for you. It is not inconstancy that I fear. Whatever your errors may be, whatever fate be mine, my heart cannot be severed from you. I shall, as you have often said, never cease to love; but, were I to see your ruin, ah, believe me, it would grieve me more than my own. I am nothing, a mere cypher: you might be all that is great and superior. Act rightly, then, my friend; and / hear this counsel, though it comes from one as fallen as I am. Think not that I wish to repine, or that I lament the past. You have rendered me happy: it is not you that I accuse. But, now that you are gone, I look with horror upon my situation; and my crimes by night and by day appear unvarnished before me.

'I am frightened, Glenarvon: we have dared too much. I have followed you into a dark abyss; and now that you, my guide, my protector, have left my side, my former weakness returns, and all[b] that one smile of your's could make me forget, oppresses and confounds me. The eye of God[c] has marked me, and I sink at once. You will abandon me: that thought comprises all things in it. Therein lies the punishment of my crime; and God, they say, is just. The[d] portrait which you have left with me has a stern look. Some have said that the likeness of a friend is preferable to himself, for that it ever smiles upon us; but / with me it is the reverse. I never saw Glenarvon's eyes gaze coldly on me till now. Farewell.

'Ever with respect and love,
'Your grateful, but unhappy friend,
'Calantha.'

Lady Avondale was more calm when she had thus written. The next morning a letter was placed in her hand. Her heart beat high. It was from Mortanville Priory: – but it was from Lady Trelawney, in answer to one she had sent her, and not from Glenarvon.

'Dearest cousin,' said Lady Trelawney, 'I have not had time to write to you one word before. Of all the places I ever was at, this is the most perfectly delightful. Had I a spice in me of romance, I would attempt to describe it; but, in truth, I cannot. Tell Sophia we expect her for certain next week; and, if you wish to be diverted from all black / thoughts, join our party. I received your gloomy letter after dinner.[a] I was sitting on a couch by ––– , shall I tell you by whom? – by Lord Glenarvon himself. At the moment in which it was delivered, for the post comes in here at nine in the evening, he smiled a little as he recognized the hand; and, when I told him you were ill, that smile became an incredulous laugh; for he knows well enough people are never so ill as they say. Witness himself: he is wonderfully recovered: indeed, he is grown perfectly delightful. I thought him uncommonly stupid all this summer, which I attribute now to you; for you encouraged him in his whims and woes. Here, at least, he is all life and good humour. Lady Augusta says he is not the same man; but sentiment, she affirms, undermines any constitution; and you are rather too much in that style.

'After all, my dear cousin, it is silly to make yourself unhappy about any / man. I dare say you thought Lord Glenarvon very amiable: so do I: – and you fancied he was in love with you, as they call it;[b] and I could fancy the same: and there is one here, I am sure, may fancy it as well as any of us: but it is so absurd to take these things seriously. It is his manner; and he owns himself that a *grande passion* bores him to death; and that if you will but leave him alone, he finds a little absence has entirely restored his senses.

'By the bye, did you give him .... but that is a secret. Only I much suspect that he has made over all that you have given him to another. Do the same by him, therefore; and have enough pride to shew him that you are not so weak and so much in his power as he imagines. I shall be quite provoked if you write any more to him. He shews all your letters: I tell you this as a friend: only, now, pray do not get me into a scrape, or repeat it. /

'Do tell me when Lord Avondale returns. They say there has been a real rising in the north: but Trelawney thinks people make a great deal of nothing at all: he says, for his part, he believes it it all talk and nonsense. We are going to London, where I hope you will meet us. Good bye to you, dear coz. Write merrily, and as you used. My motto, you know, is, laugh whilst you can, and be grave when you must. I have written a long letter to my mother and Sophia; but do not ask to see it. Indeed, I would tell you all, if I were not afraid you'd be so foolish as to vex yourself about what cannot be helped.'

Lady Avondale[a] did vex herself; and this letter from Frances made her mad. The punishment of crime was then at hand: – Glenarvon had betrayed, had abandoned her. Yet was it possible, or was it not the malice of Frances who wished to vex her? Calantha could not / believe him false. He had not been to her as a common lover: – he was true: she felt assured he was;[b] yet her agitation was very great. Perhaps he had been misled, and he feared to tell her. Could she be offended, because he had been weak? Oh, no! he knew she could not: he would never betray her secrets; he would never abandon her, because a newer favourite employed his momentary thoughts. She felt secure he would not, and she was calm.

Lady Avondale walked to Belfont. She called upon[c] many of her former friends; but they received her coldly.[d] She returned to the castle; but every eye that met her's appeared to view her with new marks of disapprobation. Guilt, when bereft of support, is ever reprobated; but see it decked in splendour and success, and where are they who shrink from its approach? Calantha's name was the theme of just censure, but in Glenarvon's presence, who had / discovered that she was thus worthless and degraded? And did they think she did not feel[e] their meanness. The proud heart is the first to sink before contempt – it feels the wound more keenly than any other can.

O, there is nothing in language that can express the deep humiliation of being received with coldness, when kindness is expected – of seeing the look, but half concealed, of strong disapprobation from such as we have cause to feel beneath us, not alone in vigour of mind and spirit, but even in virtue and truth. The weak, the base, the hypocrite, are the first to turn with indignation from their fellow mortals in disgrace; and, whilst the really chaste and pure suspect with caution, and censure with mildness, these traffickers in petty sins, who plume themselves upon their immaculate conduct, sound the alarum bell at the approach of guilt, and clamour their anathemas / upon their unwary and cowering prey.

For once they felt justly;[f] and in this instance their conduct was received without resentment. There was a darker shade on the brow, an assumed distance of manner, a certain studied civility, which seemed to say, that, by favour, Lady Avondale was excused much; that the laws of society would still admit her; that her youth, her rank and high connexions, were considerations which averted from her that stigmatising brand, her inexcusable behaviour otherwise had drawn down: but still the mark was set upon her, and she felt its bitterness the more, because she knew how much it had been deserved.

Yet of what avail were the reproving looks of friends, the bitter taunts of companions, whom long habit had rendered familiar, the ill-timed menaces and rough reproaches of some, and the innuendoes / and scornful jests of others? They only tended to harden a mind rendered fierce by strong passion, and strengthen the natural violence of a character which had set all opposition at defiance, and staked every thing upon one throw – which had been unused to refuse itself the smallest gratification, and knew not how to endure the first trial to which it ever had been exposed. Kindness had been the only remaining hope; and kindness, such as the human heart can scarce believe in, was shewn in vain. Yet the words which are so spoken seldom fail to sooth. Even when on the verge of ruin, the devoted wretch will turn and listen to the accents which pity and benevolence vouchsafe to utter; and though they may come too late, her last looks and words may bless the hand that was thus stretched out to save her.

It was with such looks of grateful affection that Lady Avondale turned to Mrs. Seymour, when she marked the / haughty frowns of Lady Margaret, and the cold repulsive glance with which many others received her. Yet still she lived upon the morrow; and, with an anguish that destroyed her, watched, vainly watched, for every returning post. Daily she walked to that accustomed spot – that dear, that well known spot, where often and often she had seen and heard the man who then would have given his very existence to please;[a] and the remembrance of his love, of his promises, in some measure re-assured her.

One evening, is she wandered there, she met St. Clara, who passed her in haste, whilst a smile of exulting triumph lighted her countenance. Lady Avondale sighed, and seated herself upon the fragment of a rock; but took no other notice of her. There was a blaze of glorious light diffused over the calm scene, and the gloomy battlements of Belfont Priory yet shone with the departing ray. When Calantha arose to depart, she / turned from the golden light which illuminated the west, and gazed in agony upon the spot where it was her custom to meet her lover. The vessels passed to and fro upon the dark blue sea; the sailors cheerfully followed their nightly work; and the peasants, returning from the mountains with their flocks, sung cheerfully as they approached their homes. Calantha had no home to return to;[b] no approving eye to bid her welcome: her heart was desolate. She met with an aged man, whose white locks flowed, and whose air was that of deep distress. He looked upon her. He asked charity of her as he passed: he said that he was friendless, and alone in the world. His name she asked: he replied, 'Camioli.' 'If gold can give you peace, take this,' she said. He blessed her: he called her all goodness – all loveliness; and he prayed for her to his God. 'Oh, God of mercy!'[c] / said Calantha, 'hear the prayer of the petitioner: grant me the blessing he has asked for me. I never more can pray. He little knows the pang he gave. He[d] calls me good: alas! that name and Calantha's are parted for ever.

> Poor wretch! who hast nothing to hope for in, life,
> But the mercy of hearts long success has made hard.
> No parent hast thou, no fond children, no wife,
> Thine age from distress and misfortune to guard.

Yet the trifle I gave, little worth thy possessing,
Has call'd forth in thee, what I cannot repay:
Thou hast ask'd of thy God for his favour and blessing;
Thou hast pray'd for the sinner, who never must pray.

Old man, if those locks, which are silver'd by time,
Have ne'er been dishonor'd by guilt or excess;
If when tempted to wrong, thou hast fled from the crime;
By passion unmov'd, unappall'd by distress: /

If through life thou hast follow'd the course that is fair,
And much hast perform'd, though of little possess'd;
Then the God of thy fathers shall favour the prayer,
And a blessing be sent to a heart now unblest. /

CHAPTER VIII.

Lady Avondale wrote again and again to Glenarvon. All that a woman would repress, all that she once feared to utter, the now ventured to write. 'Glenarvon,' she said, 'if I have displeased you, let me at least be told my fault by you: you who have had power to lead me to wrong, need not doubt your influence if you would now but advise me to return to my duty. Say it but gently – speak but kindly to me, and I will obey every wish of your's. But perhaps that dreaded moment is arrived, and you are no longer coustant and true. Ah! fear not one reproach from me. I told you how it must end; and I will never think the worse of you for being as all men are. But do not add cruelty / to inconstancy. Let me hear from your own lips that you are changed. I but repeat your words, when once my letters failed to reach you – suspense, you then said, was torture: and will you now expose me to those sufferings which you even knew not how to endure? Let no one persuade you to treat her with cruelty, who, whatever your conduct may be, will never cease to honour and to love you.

'Forgive, if too presumptuous, I have written with flippant gaiety, or thoughtless folly. Say I have been to blame; but do not you, Glenarvon, do not you be my accuser. You are surrounded by those who possess beauty and talents, far, far above any which I can boast; but all I had it in my power to give, I offered you; and, however little worth, no one can bear to have that all rejected with contempt and ingratitude. And are they endeavouring to blacken me in your opinion? and do they call this acting / honourably and fairly? Lady Trelawney perhaps – ah! no, I will not believe it. Besides, had they the inclination, have they the power to engage you to renounce me thus?

'Glenarvon, my misery is at the utmost. If you could but know what I suffer at this moment, you would pity me. O leave me not thus: I cannot bear it. Expose me not to every eye: drive me not to desperation. This suspense is agonizing: this sudden, this protracted silence is too hard to bear. Every one does, every one must, despise me: the good opinion of the wise and just, I have lost for ever; but do not you abandon me, or if you must, oh let it be from your own mouth at least that I read my doom. Say that you love another – say it, if indeed it is already so; and I will learn to bear it. Write it but kindly. Tell me I shall still be your friend. I will not upbraid you: no grief of mine shall make me forget your former kindness. / Oh no, I will never learn to hate or reproach you, however you may think fit to trample upon me. I will bless your name with my last breath – call you[a] even from the grave, where you have sent me – only turn one look, one last dear look to me.'

Such was her letter. At another time she thus again addressed him:

'Glenarvon, my only hope in life, drive me not at once to desperation. Alas! why do I write thus? You are ill perhaps?[b] or my friends surrounding you, have urged you to this?[c] In such case, remember my situation. Say but kindly that my letters are no longer a solace to you, and I will of myself cease to write; but do not hurl me at once from adoration to contempt and hate. Do not throw me off, and doom me to sudden, to certain perdition. Glenarvon, have mercy. Let compassion, if love has ceased, impel you to show me some humanity. I knew it is degrading thus to write. I ought to / be silent, and to feel that if you have the heart to treat me with harshness, it is lowering myself still further thus to sue. But oh! my God, it is no longer time to think of dignity – to speak of what is right. I have fallen to the lowest depth. You, you are the first to teach me how low, how miserably I am fallen. I forsook every thing for you. I would have followed you; and you know it. But for your's and other's sake, I would have sacrificed all – all to you. Alas! I have already done so.

'If you should likewise turn against me – if you[d] for whom so much is lost, should be the first to despise me, how can I bear up under it. Dread the violence of my feelings – the agonizing pang, the despair of a heart so lost, and so betrayed. Oh, write but one line to me. Say that another has engaged you to forsake me – that you will love me no more; but that as a friend you will still feel some affection, some interest for me. / I am ill, Glenarvon. God knows I do not affect it, to touch you. Such guilt as mine, and so much bitter misery! – how can I bear up under it? Oh pity the dread, the suspense I endure. You know not what a woman feels when remorse, despair[e] and the sudden loss of him she loves, assail her at once.

'I have seen, I have heard of cruelty, and falsehood;[f] but you, Glenarvon – oh you who are so young, so beautiful, can you be inhuman? It breaks my heart to think so. Why have you not the looks, as well as the heart of a villain? Oh why take such pains, such care, to lull me into security, to dispel every natural fear and suspicion, a heart that loves must harbour, only to plunge me deeper in agony – to destroy me with more refined and barbarous cruelty? Jest not with my sufferings. God knows they are acute and real. I feel even for myself when I consider what I am going to endure. Oh spare one victim at least. / Generously save me: I ask you not to love me. Only break to me yourself this sudden change – tell me my fate, from that dear mouth which has so often sworn never, never to abandon me.' /

CHAPTER IX.

Days again passed in fruitless expectation; nights, in unceasing wakefulness and grief. At length one morning, a letter was put into Lady Avondale's hands. It was from Glenarvon. It is impossible to describe the joy, the transport of that moment; nor how, pressing it to her lips, she returned thanks to God[a] for receiving, what it was a crime against that Being[b] thus to value. She glanced her eye over the superscription; but she durst not open it. She dreaded lest some cause should be assigned for so long a silence, which might appear less kind than what she could easily endure. The seal was not his seal; and the black wax, so constantly his custom to use, was exchanged for red. The motto upon the / seal (for lovers attend to all) was not that which at all times he made use of when addressing Calantha. It was a seal she knew too well. A strange foreboding that he was changed, filled her mind. She was prepared for the worst, as she apprehended. At last she broke the seal; but she was not prepared for the following words written by his own hand, and thus addressed to her. Oh! had he the heart to write them?

Mortanville Priory, November the 9th.

Lady Avondale,

 I am no longer your lover; and since you oblige me to confess it, by this truly unfeminine persecution, – learn, that I am attached to another; whose name it would of course be dishonourable to mention. I shall ever remember with gratitude the many instances I have received of the predilection you have shewn in my favour. I shall ever continue your friend, if your ladyship will permit me so to / style myself; and, as a first proof of my regard, I offer you this advice, correct your vanity, which is ridiculous; exert your absurd caprices upon others; and leave me in peace.[13]

Your most obedient servant,
Glenarvon.

This letter was sealed and directed by Lady Mandeville; but the hand that wrote it was Lord Glenarvon's; and therefore it had its full effect. Yes; it went as it was intended, to the very heart; and the wound thus given, was as deep as the most cruel enemy could have desired. The grief of a mother for the loss of her child has been described, though the hand of the painter fails ever in expressing the agonies of that moment. The sorrows of a mistress when losing the lover she adores, has been[a] the theme of every age. Poetry and painting, have exhausted the expression of her despair, and painted to the life, that which themselves could conceive – could / feel and understand. Every one can sympathise with their sufferings; and that which others commiserate, is felt with less agony by ourselves. But who can sympathize with guilt, or who lament the just reward of crime?

There is a pang, beyond all others – a grief, which happily for human nature few have been called upon to encounter. It is when an erring but not hardened heart, worked up to excess of passion, idolized and flattered into security, madly betraying every sacred trust, receives all unlooked for, from the hand it adores, the dreadful punishment which its crime deserves. And, if there can be a degree still greater of agony, shew to the wretch who sinks beneath the unexpected blow – shew her, in the person of her only remaining friend and protector, the husband she has betrayed – the lover of her youth! Oh shew him unsuspicious, faithful, kind; and do not judge her, if at such moment, the dream dispelled, frantic violence impelling her / to acts of desperation and madness, lead her rash hand to attempt her miserable life. Where, but in death can such outcast seek refuge from shame, remorse[b] and all the bitterness of despair? Where but in death? Oh, God; it is no coward's act![c] The strength of momentary passion may nerve the arm for so rash a deed; but faint hearts will sicken at the thought.

Calantha durst not – no, she durst not strike the blow. She seized the sharp edged knife, and tried its force. It was not pain she feared. Pain, even to extremity, she already felt. But one single blow – one instant, and all to be at an end. A trembling horror seized upon her limbs: the life-blood chilled around her heart. She feared to die. Pain, even to agony, were better than thus to brave Omnipotence – to rush forward uncalled into that state of which no certain end is known: to snatch destiny into our own power, and draw upon ourselves, / in one instant of time, terrors and punishments above the boundless apprehension even of an evil imagination to conceive.

Calantha's eye, convulsed and fixed, perceived not the objects which surrounded her. Her thoughts, quick as the delirious dream of fever, varied with new and dreadful pictures of calamity. It was the last struggle of nature. – The spirit within her trembled at approaching dissolution. – The shock was too great for mortal reason to resist. Glenarvon – Glenarvon! that form – that look alone appeared to awaken her recollection, but all else was confusion and pain.[14]

It was a scene of horror. May it for ever be blotted from the remembrance of the human heart! It claims no sympathy: it was the dreadful exhibition of a mind which passion had misled, and reason had ceased to guide. Calantha bowed not before that Being who had seen fit to punish her in his wrath. She sought nor vengeance, nor future hope. / All was lost for her; and with Glenarvon, every desire in life, every aspiring energy vanished. Overpowered, annihilated, she called for mercy and release. She felt that mortal passion domineered over reason; and, after one desperate struggle for mastery, had conquered and destroyed her.

Her father watched over and spoke to her. Mrs. Seymour endeavored to awaken her to some sense of her situation: – she spoke to her of her husband. Calantha! when reason had ceased to guide thee, she called to sooth, to warn thee, but thou couldst not hear. That voice of conscience, that voice of truth, which in life's happier day thou had'st rejected, now spoke in vain; and thy rash steps hurried on to seek the termination of thy mad career. /

CHAPTER X.

When the very soul is annihilated^a by some sudden and unexpected evil, the outward frame is calm – no appearance of emotion, of tears, of repining, gives notice of the approaching evil. Calantha^b motionless, re-perused Glenarvon's letter, and spoke with gentleness to those who addressed her. Oh! did the aunt that loved her, as she read that barbarous letter, exhibit equal marks of fortitude? No: in tears, in reproaches, she vented her indignation: but still Calantha moved not.

There is a disease which it is terrible to name. Ah, see you not its symptoms in the wild eye of your child. Dread, dread the violence of her uncurbed passions, / of an imagination disordered and overpowered. Madness to frenzy has fallen upon her. What tumult, what horror, reigns^c in that mind: how piercing were the shrieks she uttered: how hollow the cry that echoed Glenarvon's name! Lady Margaret held her to her bosom, and folded her arms around her. No stern looks upbraided her for her crimes: all was kindness unutterable – goodness that stabbed to the heart. And did she turn from such indulgence – did her perverted passions still conquer every better feeling, as even on a bed of death her last hope was love – her last words Glenarvon!

Sophia approached Calantha with words of kindness and religion;^d but the words of religion offered no balm to a mind estranged and utterly perverted. Her cheeks were pale, and her hollow eyes, glazed and fixed, turned from the voice of comfort. Mrs. Seymour placed her children near her; but with tears of / remorse she heard them speak, and shrunk from their caresses. And still it was upon Glenarvon that she called. Yet when certain death was expected, or far worse, entire loss of reason, she by slow degrees recovered.

There is a recovery from disease which is worse than death; and it was her destiny to prove it. She loved her own sorrow too well: she cherished every sad remembrance: she became morose, absorbed, and irritated to frenzy, if intruded upon. All virtue is blighted in such a bosom – all principle gone. It feeds upon its own calamity. Hope nothing from the miserable: a^e broken heart¹⁵ is a sepulchre in which the ruin of every thing that is noble and fair is enshrined.^f

That which causes the tragic end of a woman's life, is often but a moment of amusement and folly in the history of a man. Women, like toys, are sought after,^g

and trifled with, and then thrown / by with every varying caprice. Another, and another still succeed; but to each thus cast away, the pang has been beyond thought, the stain indelible, and the wound mortal. Glenarvon had offered his heart to another. He had given the love gifts[a] – the chains and the rings which he had received from Calantha, to his new favourite. Her letters he had shewn; her secrets he had betrayed;[b] to an enemy's bosom he had betrayed the struggles of a guilty heart, tortured with remorse, and yet at that time at least but too true, and faithful to him. 'T was[c] the letters written in confidence which be shewed! It was[d] the secret thoughts of a soul he had torn from virtue and duty to follow him, that[e] he betrayed!

And to whom did he thus expose her errors? – To[f] the near relations of her husband, to the friends, and companions of her youth; and instead of throwing a veil upon the weakness he himself had caused, when / doubt, remorse[g] and terror had driven her to acts of desperation. Instead[h] of dropping one tear of pity over a bleeding, breaking-heart,[i] he committed those testimonies of her guilt, and his own treachery, into the hands of incensed and injured friends. They were human: they saw but what he would have them see:[j] they knew but what he wished them to know: they censured her already, and rather believed his plausible and gentle words, than the frantic rhapsodies of guilt and passion. They read the passages but half communicated; they heard the insidious remarks; they saw the letters in which themselves were misrepresented and unkindly named; nor knew the arts which had been made use of to alienate Calantha. They espoused the cause of Glenarvon, and turned with anger and contempt against one whom they now justly despised. Even Sophia, whom the terror of despair had one moment softened – even Sophia,[k] had not / long been in the society of Glenarvon after her arrival in England, when she also changed; so powerful were the arguments which he used to persuade her; or so easily tranquillized is resentment when we ourselves are not sufferers from the injury. /

CHAPTER XI.

On quitting Castle Delaval, Lord Glenarvon went as he had promised, to Mr. Monmouth's seat[a] in Wales, by name, Mortanville Priory. There, in a large and brilliant society, he soon forgot Calantha. Lady Augusta rallied him for his caprice; Lady Mandeville sought to obtain his confidence: tears[b] and reproaches are ever irksome; and the confidence that had once been placed in a former mistress, now suddenly withdrawn, was wholly given to her. A petitioner is at all times intrusive; and sorrow at a distance but serves to encrease the coldness and inconstancy it upbraids. The contrast is great between smiling and triumphant beauty, and remorse, misery[c] and disgrace. And, if / every reason here enumerated were insufficient,[d] to account for a lover's inconstancy, it is enough in one word to say, that Lady Avondale was absent; for Lord Glenarvon was of a disposition to attend so wholly to those, in whose presence he took delight, that he failed to remember those to whom he had once been attached; so that like the wheels of a watch, the chains[e] of his affections might be said to unwind from the absent, in proportion as they twined themselves around the favorite of the moment; and being extreme in all things, he could not sufficiently devote himself to the one, without taking from the other all that he had given.

'T were[f] vain to detail the petty instances of barbarity he made use of.[g] The web was fine enough, and wove with a skilful hand. He even consulted with Lady Mandeville in what manner to make his inhuman triumph more poignant – more galling; and when he heard / that Calantha was irritated even unto madness, and grieved almost unto death, he only mocked at her for her folly, and despised her for her[h] still remaining attachment to himself. 'Indeed she is ill,' said Sophia, in answer to his insulting enquiry, soon after her arrival at Mortanville Priory. 'She is even dangerously ill.' 'And pray may I ask of what malady?' he replied, with a smile of scorn. 'Of one, Lord Glenarvon,' she answered with equal irony, 'which never will[i] endanger your health – of a broken heart.' He laughed. 'Of deep remorse,' she continued. 'And no regret?' said he, looking archly at her. 'Do not jest,' she retorted: 'the misery which an unhallowed attachment must in itself inflict, is sufficient, I should think, without adding derision to every other feeling.' 'Does Miss Seymour speak from experience or conjecture?'

Before Miss Seymour could answer, Lady Mandeville, who was present, / whispered something to Glenarvon; and he laughed. Sophia asked eagerly what she was saying. 'It is a secret,' said Glenarvon[a] significantly. 'How happy must Lady Mandeville be at this moment!' said Lady Augusta, 'for every one knows that the greatest enjoyment the human mind can feel, is when we are in the act of betraying a secret confided to us by a friend, or informing an enemy of something upon which the life and safety of another depends.' 'Come,' said Lady Mandeville, 'you are very severe; but I was only urging Lord Glenarvon to listen to Miss Seymour's admonitions in a less public circle. Miss Monmouth may be displeased if she hears of all this whispering.' So saying, she took Glenarvon's arm, and they walked out of the room together.

'After all, he is a glorious creature,' said Lady Trelawney. 'I wish I had a glorious creature to walk with me this morning,' said Lady Augusta with a / sneer;[b] 'but how can I hope for support, when Calantha, who had once thousands to defend her, and whom I left the gayest where all were gay, is now dying alone, upbraided, despised, and deserted. Where are her friends?' 'She fell by her own fault entirely,' said Lord Trelawney. 'Her life has been one course of absurdity. A crime here and there are[c] nothing, I well know,' said Lady Augusta; 'but imprudence and folly, who can pardon?' 'She has a kind heart,' said Frances. 'Kind enough to some,' said her lord; 'but talk not of her, for I feel indignant at her very name.' 'There is nothing excites our indignation so strongly,' said Lady Augusta, 'as misfortune. Whilst our friends are healthy, rich, happy, and, above all, well dressed and gaily attended, they are delightful, adorable. After all, your sensible judicious people on the long run are the best: they keep a good eye to their own interest; and / these flighty ones are sure to get into scrapes. When they do, we flatterers have an awkward part to play: we must either turn short about, as is the case now, or stand up in a bad cause, for which none of us have heart or spirit.' 'There is no excuse for Calantha,' said Miss Seymour. 'God forbid I should look for one,' said Lady Augusta. 'I am like a deer, and ever fly with the herd;[d] there is no excuse, Miss Seymour, ever, for those who are wounded and bleeding and trodden upon. I could tell you – but here come these glorious creatures! Are you aware, that when Lady Avondale sent a few days since for her lover's portrait, and a lock of his hair,[e] Lady Mandeville yesterday in an envelope enclosed a braid of her own.[16] *C'est piquant cela: j'admire!*'[17] 'How illnatured the world is!' said Miss Monmouth, who had heard the latter part of this discourse. 'Not ill natured or wicked, my dear,' / said Lady Augusta; 'only weak, cowardly[f] and inordinately stupid.' 'With what self-satisfaction every one triumphs at the fall of those whose talents or situation raise them a little into observation!' said Miss Monmouth. 'Common sense is so pleased,' said Lady Augusta, 'when it sees of how little use any other sense is in this life, that one must forgive its triumph; and its old saws and wholesome truisms come out with such an increase of length and weight, when the enemy to its peace has tumbled down before it, that it were vain to attempt a defence of the culprit condemned. I know the world too well to break through any of the lesser rules and customs imposed, but you, my dear, know nothing yet:[a] therefore I cannot talk to you.'

Miss Monmouth was the only child of the Honorable Mr. Monmouth, a near relation of Lady Mowbrey's. Her youth, her innocence, a certain charm of manner / and of person, rare and pleasing, had already, apparently,[b] made some impression upon Glenarvon. He had secretly paid her every most marked attention. He had even made her repeatedly the most honourable offers. At first, trembling and suspicious, she repulsed the man of whom rumour had spoken much, which her firm principles and noble generous heart disapproved; but soon attracted and subdued by the same all splendid talents, she heard him with more favourable inclinations. She was, herself, rich in the possession of every virtue and grace;[c] but, alas! too soon she was over-reached by the same fascination and disguise which had imposed upon every other.

Amongst the many suitors who at this time appeared to claim Miss Monmouth's hand, Buchanan was the most distinguished. Lady Margaret eagerly desired this marriage. She put every engine to work in a moment to defeat Glenarvon's / views, and secure the prize for her son. She even left Ireland upon hearing of his increasing influence, and joined for a few weeks the party at Mortanville Priory. The parents of Miss Monmouth were as eager for Buchanan, as the young lady[d] was averse. Glenarvon saw with bitterness the success his rival had obtained, and hated the friends and parents of Miss Monmouth for their mistrust of him. By day, by night, he assailed an innocent heart, not with gross flattery, not with vain professions. He had a mask for every distinct character he wished to play; and in each character he acted to the very life.

In this instance,[e] he threw himself upon the generous mercy of one who already was but too well inclined to favour him. He candidly acknowledged his errors; but he cast a veil over their magnitude; and confessed only what he wished should be known. Miss Monmouth, he said, should reform him; her gentle voice / should recall his heart from perversion; her virtues should win upon a mind, which, the errors of youth, the world and opportunity had misled.

Miss Monmouth was the idol of her family. She was pure herself, and therefore unsuspicious. Talents and judgment had been given her with no sparing hand; but to these, she added the warmest, the most generous heart, the strongest feelings, and a high and noble character. To save, to reclaim one, whose genius she admired, whose beauty attracted, was a task too delightful to be rejected. Thousands daily sacrifice their hearts to mercenary and ambitious views; thousands coldly, without one feeling of enthusiasm or love, sell themselves for a splendid name; and can there be a mind so cold, so corrupted, as to censure the girl, who, having rejected a Buchanan, gave her hand and heart, and all that she possessed, to save, to bless, and to reclaim a Glenarvon. /

CHAPTER XII.

HAPPILY for Miss Monmouth, at the very moment her consent was given, Lady Margaret placed a letter in Glenarvon's hands, which threw him into the deepest agitation, and obliged him instantly, and for a short time, to hasten to England. He went there[a] in company with Lady Margaret; and strange as it may appear, the love, the idolatry, he had professed for so many, seemed now with greater vehemence than for others transferred to herself. Whether from artifice or caprice, it is unnecessary to say, but Lady Margaret at least made shew of a return. She never lost sight of him for one moment. She read with him; she talked with him; she chided him with all the wit and grace of which she / was mistress; and he, as if maddening in her presence, gazed on her with wild delight; and seemed inclined to abandon every thing for her sake.

Lady Margaret applied to her numerous friends for the ship which had long been promised to Lord Glenarvon, as a reward for his former services. She wrote to Sir George Buchanan for[b] his appointment; she spoke with eloquence of his misfortunes; and whether from her representations, or some other cause, his titles and estates were at length restored to him.[18] Thanking her for the zeal she had shewn, he proposed to return with her immediately to Italy.

She now hesitated. Her brother had written to her: these were the words of his letter: 'Buchanan is desirous that his marriage should be celebrated in this place. Miss Monmouth, I fear, has been compelled to accept his hand; and I should pity her, if such force did not / save her from a far worse fate. I mean a marriage with Glenarvon.'

Glenarvon was by Lady Margaret's side when this letter was received. He held one of Lady Margaret's white hands in his: he was looking upon the rings she wore, and laughingly asking her if they were the gifts of Dartford. 'Look at me, my beautiful mistress,' he said, with the triumph of one secure. She carelessly placed the letter before his eyes. 'Correct your vanity,' she said, whilst he was perusing it, alluding to the words he had written to Calantha; 'exert your caprices upon others more willing to bear them; and leave me in peace.'

Stung to the soul, Glenarvon started; and gazed on her with malignant rage;[c] then grinding his teeth with all the horror of supprest rage, 'I am not a fly to be trodden upon, but a viper that shall sting thee to the heart. Farewell for ever,' he cried, rushing from her. Then / returning one moment with calmness, and smiling on her, 'you have not grieved me,' he said gently: 'I am not angry, my fair mistress. We shall meet again: fear not we shall meet again.' 'Now I am lost,' said Lady Margaret, when he was gone. 'I know by that smile that my fate is sealed.'

There is nothing so uncongenial to the sorrowing heart as gaiety and mirth; yet Calantha was at this time condemned to witness it. No sickness, no sufferings of its owners, prevented extraordinary festivities at the castle. Upon the evening of the celebration of Buchanan's marriage, there were revels and merry-making as in happier times; and the peasantry and tenants, forgetful of their cabals and wrongs, all appeared to partake in the general festivity. The ribband of green was concealed beneath large bouquets of flowers; and healths and toasts went round with tumults of applause, regardless of the sorrows of the owners of the / castle.[a] The lawn was covered with dancers. It was a cheerful scene; and even Calantha smiled, as she leant upon her father's arm, and gazed upon the joyful countenances which surrounded her; but it was the smile of one whose heart was breaking,[b] and every tenant as he passed by and greeted her looked upon the father and the child, and sighed at the change which had taken place in the appearance of both.

Suddenly, amidst the dancers, with a light foot, as if springing from the earth, there appeared, lovely in beauty and in youth, the fairest flower of Belfont. It was Miss St. Clare. No longer enveloped in her dark flowing mantle, she danced amidst the village maidens, the gayest there. She danced with all the skill of art, and all the grace of nature. Her dress was simple and light as the web of the gossamer;[c] her ringlets, shining in the bright sun-beams, sported with the wind: red was her cheek as the first / blush of love, or the rose of summer, when it opens to the sun.

Upon the lake the boats, adorned with many coloured ribbands, sailed with the breeze. Bands of music played underneath[d] the tents which were erected for refreshments. The evening was bright and cloudless. Elinor was the first and latest in the dance – the life and spirit of the joyous scene. Some shrunk back it is true at first, when they beheld her; but when they saw her smile, and that look of winning candour, which even innocence at times forgets to wear, that playful[e] youthful manner, re-assured them. 'Can it be possible!' said Calantha, when the music ceased, and the villagers dispersed – 'can you indeed affect this gaiety, or do you feel it, St. Clare?' 'I feel it,' cried the girl, laughing archly. 'The shafts of love shall never pierce me; and sorrows, though they fall thicker than the rain of Heaven, shall never break my heart.' 'Oh! teach / me to endure afflictions thus. Is it religion that supports you?' 'Religion!' St. Clare sighed.

'Yon bright heaven,' she said, up-lifting her eyes, 'is not for me. The time has been, when, like you, I could have wept, and bowed beneath the chastening rod of adversity; but it is past. Turn you, and repent[a] lady; for you are but young in sin, and the heart alone has wandered. Turn to that God of mercy, and he will yet receive and reclaim you.' A tear started into her eyes, as she spoke. 'I must journey on;[b] for the time allowed me is short. Death walks among us even now. Look at yon lordly mansion – your father's house. Is it well defended from within? Are there bold hearts ready to stand forth in the time of need? Where is the heir of Delaval: – look to him: – even now they tear him from you. The fiends, the fiends are abroad: – look to your husband, lady – the gallant Earl of Avondale: / red is the uniform he wears; black is the charger upon which he rides; but the blood of his heart shall flow. It is a bloody war we are going to: this is the year of horror!!! Better it were never to have been born, than to have lived in an age like this.'

'Unhappy maniac,' said a voice from behind. It was the voice of the Bard Camioli: 'unhappy St. Clare!' he said. She turned; but he was gone. Every one now surrounded Miss St. Clare, requesting her to sing. 'Oh I cannot sing,' she replied, with tears, appealing to Calantha; then added lower – 'my soul is in torture. That was a father's voice, risen from the grave to chide me.'

Calantha took her hand with tenderness; but Miss St. Clare shrunk from her. 'Fly me,' she said, 'for that which thou thinkest sweet has lost its savour. Oh[c] listen not to the voice of the charmer, charm she ever so sweetly.[d] [19] Yet ere we part, my young and dear protectress, / take with you my heart's warm thanks and blessings; for thou hast been kind to the friendless – thou hast been merciful to the heart that was injured, and in pain. I would not wish to harm thee. May the journey of thy life be in the sunshine and smiles of fortune. May soft breezes waft thy gilded bark upon a smooth sea, to a guileless peaceful shore. May thy footsteps tread upon the green grass, and the violet and the rose spring up under thy feet.' Calantha's pale cheeks and falling tears were her only answer to this prayer. /

CHAPTER XIII.

CAMIOLI had been some time concealed in Ireland. He now entered his Brother Sir Everard's door. Upon that night he was seized with illness, before he had time to explain his intentions. He had placed a bag of gold in the hands of his brother; and now, in the paroxysm of his fever, he called upon his daughter; he urged those who attended on him to send for her, that he might once again behold her. 'I am come to die in the land of my father,'[a] he said. 'I have wandered on these shores to find if all I heard were true. Alas! it is true; and I wish once more to see my unhappy child – before I die.'

They wrote to Elinor; they told her of her father's words. They said: 'Oh, Elinor, return; ungrateful child – haste / thee to return. Thy father is taken dangerously ill. I think some of the wretches around us have administered poison to him. I know not where to find thee. He has called thrice for thee; and now he raves. Oh hasten; for in the frantic agony of his soul, he has cursed thee; and if thou dost not obey the summons, with the last breath of departing life, he will bequeath thee his malediction. O, Elinor, once the pride and joy of thy father's heart, whom myself dedicated as a spotless offering before the throne of Heaven, as being too fair, too good for such a lowly one as me – return ere it be too late, and kneel by the bed of thy dying father. This is thy house. It is a parent calls, however unworthy; still it is one who loves thee; and should pride incline thee not to hear him, O how thou wilt regret it when too late – Ever, my child, thy affectionate, but most unhappy uncle,

EVERARD ST. CLARE.' /

She received not the summons – she was far distant when the letter was sent for her to the mountains. She received it not till noon; and the bard's last hour was at hand.

Miss Lauriana St. Clare then addressed her – 'If any feeling of mercy yet warms your stubborn heart, come home to us and see your father, ere he breathe his last. 'Tis a fearful sight to see him: he raves for you, and calls you his darling and his favourite – his lost lamb, who has strayed from the flock, but was[b] dearer than all the rest. Miss Elinor, I have little hopes of stirring your compassion; for in the days of babyhood you were hard Oh^a listen not to the voice of the charmer, charm she ever so sweetly. and unyielding, taking your own way, and disdaining the counsel of such as were older and wiser than you. Go too, child; you have played the wanton with your fortune, and the hour of shame approaches.'^b

Miss St. Clare heard not the summons – upon her horse she rode swiftly over / the moors – it came too late – Camioli had sickened in the morning, and ere night, he had died.

They wrote again: 'Your father's spirit has forsaken him: there is no recall from the grave. With his last words he bequeathed his curse to the favourite of his heart; and death has set its seal upon the legacy. The malediction of a father rests^c upon an ungrateful child!'

Elinor stood upon the cliff near Craig Allen Bay, when her father's corpse was carried to the grave. She heard the knell and the melancholy dirge: she saw the procession as it passed: she stopped its progress, and was told that her father in his last hour had left her his malediction. Many were near her, and flattered her at the time; but she heard them not.

Elinor stood on the barren cliff, to feel, as she said, the morning dew and fresh mountain air on her parched forehead. 'My brain beats as if to madden me: – the fires of hell consume me: – it is a / father's curse:'^d she cried; and her voice, in one loud and dreadful shriek, rent the air. 'Oh it is a father's curse;' then pausing with a fixed and horrid^e eye: 'Bear it, winds of heaven, and dews of earth,' she cried: 'bear it to false Glenarvon: – hear it, fallen angel, in the dull night, when the hollow wind shakes your battlements and your towers, and shrieks as it passes by, till it affrights your slumbers: – hear it in the morn, when the sun breaks through the clouds, and gilds with its beams of gold the eastern heavens: – hear it when the warbling skylark, soaring to the skies, thrills with its pipe, and every note of joy sound in thy ear as the cry of woe. The old man is dead, and gone: he will be laid low in the sepulchre: his bones shall be whiter than his grey hairs. He left his malediction upon his child. May it rest with thee, false Glenarvon.^f Angel of beauty, light, and delight of the soul, thou paradise of joys unutterable / from which my heart is banished, thou God whom I have worshipped with sacrilegious incense, hear it and tremble. Amidst revels and feastings, in the hour of love, when passion beats in every pulse, when flatterers kneel, and tell thee thou art great, when a servile world bowing before thee weaves the laurel wreath of glory around thy brows, when old men forget their age and dignity to worship thee, and kings and princes tremble before the scourge of thy wit – think on the cry of the afflicted – the last piercing cry of agonizing and desperate despair. Hear it, as it shrieks in the voice of the tempest, or bellows from the vast fathomless ocean; and when they tell thee thou art great, when they tell thee thou art good, remember thy falsehood, thy treachery. Oh remember it and shudder, and say to thyself thou art worthless, and laugh at the flatterers that would deny it.' /

CHAPTER XIV.

Nothing is more mistaken than to suppose that unkindness and severity are the means of reclaiming an offender. There is no moment in which we are more insensible to our own errors than when we smart under apparent injustice. Calantha saw Glenarvon triumphant, and herself deserted. The world, it is true, still befriended her; but her nearest relatives[a] and friends supported him. Taunted with her errors, betrayed, scorned, and trampled upon, the high spirit of her character arose in proportion as every hope was cut off. She became violent, overbearing, untractable even to her attendants, demanding a more than ordinary degree of respect, from the suspicion that it might no longer be paid. Every / error of her life was now canvassed, and brought forth against her. Follies and absurdities long forgotten, were produced to view, to aggravate her present disgrace; and the severity which an offended world forbore to shew, Sophia, Frances, the Princess of Madagascar, Lady Mandeville, and Lord Glenarvon, were eager to evince.

But, even at this hour, Calantha had reason to acknowledge the kindness and generosity of some; and the poor remembered her in their prayers. Those whom she had once protected, flew forward to support her; and even strangers addressed her with looks, if not words[b] of consolation. It was not the gay, the professing, the vain[c] that shewed compassion in a moment of need – it was not the imprudent and vicious whom Calantha had stood firm by and defended: these were the first to desert her. But it was the good, the pious, the benevolent, who came to her, and even courted an acquaintance / they once had shunned; for their hope was now to reclaim.

Humbled, not yet sufficiently, but miserable, her fair name blasted, the jest of fools, the theme of triumphant malice, Calantha still gave vent to every furious passion, and openly rebelled against those who had abandoned her. She refused to see any one, to hear any admonitions, and, sickening at every contradiction to her authority, insisted upon doing things the most ill judged[d] and unreasonable, to shew her power, or her indignation. Struck with horror at her conduct, every one now wrote to inform Lord Avondale of the absolute necessity of his parting from her. Hints were not only given, but facts were held up to view, and a life of folly, concluding in crime,ᵃ was painted with every aggravation. Calantha knew not at this time the eager zeal that some had shewn,ᵇ to hurl just vengeance upon a self-devoted victim. She was informed therefore of Lord Avondale's expected / return, and prepared to receive him with hardened and desperate indifference.

She feared not pain, nor death: the harshest words occasioned her no humiliation: the scorn, the abhorrence of companions and friends, excited no other sentiment in her mind than disgust. Menaced by every one, she still forbore to yield, and boldly imploringᶜ if she were guilty, to be tried by the laws of her country – laws, which thoughᵈ she had transgressed, she revered, and would submit to, she defied the insolence, and malice of private interference.

From this state, Calantha was at length aroused by the return of Lord Avondale. It has been said, that the severest pang to one not wholly hardened, is the unsuspicious confidence of the friend whom we have betrayed, the look of radiant health and joy which we never more must share, that eye of unclouded virtue, that smile of a heart at rest, and, worse than all perhaps, the soft confiding words / and fond caresses offered after long absence. Cruel is such suffering. Such a pangᵉ Calantha had already once endured, when last she had parted from her lord; and for such meeting she was again prepared. She had been ill, and no one had read the secret of her soul. She had been lonely, and no one comfortedᶠ her in her hours of solitude: she had once loved Lord Avondale, but absence and neglect had entirely changed her. She prepared therefore for the interview with cold indifference, and her pride disdained to crave his forgiveness, or to acknowledge itself undeserving in his presence. 'He is no longer my husband,' she repeated daily to herself. 'My heart and his are at variance – severed by inclination, though unhappily for both united by circumstances. Let him send me from him: I am desperate and care not.'

None sufficiently consider, when they describe the hateful picture of crime, how every step taken in its / mazy road, perverts, and petrifies the feeling. Calantha, in long retrospect over her former life, thought only of the neglect and severity of him she had abandoned. She dwelt with pleasure upon the remembrance of every momentary act of violence, and thought of his gaiety and merriment, as of a sure testimony that he was not injured by her ill conduct. 'He left me first,' she said. 'He loves me not; he is happy; I alone suffer.' And the consolation she derived from such reflections steeled her against every kindlier sentiment.

Lord Avondale returned. There was no look of joy in his countenance – no radiant heartfelt smile which bounding spirits and youthful ardour once had raised. His hollow eye betokened deep anxiety; his wasted form, the suffering he had endured. Oh, can it be said that the greatest pang to a heart, not yet entirely hardened, is unsuspicious confidence? Oh, can the momentary selfish pang a / cold dissembling hypocrite may feel, be compared to the unutterable agony of such a meeting? Conscience itself must shrink beneath the torture of every glance. There is the record of crime – there, in every altered lineament of that well known face. How pale the withered cheek – how faint the smile that tries to make light and conceal the evil under which the soul is writhing.

And could Calantha see it, and yet live? Could she behold him kind, compassionating, mournful, and yet survive it? No – no frenzy of despair, no racking pains of ill requited love; no, not all that sentiment and romance can paint or fancy, were ever equal to that moment. Before severity, she had not bowed – before contempt, she had not shed one tear – against every menace, she felt hardened; but,[a] in the presence of that pale and altered brow, she sunk at once. With grave but gentle earnestness, he raised her from the earth. She / durst not look upon him. She could not stand the reproachful glances of that eye, that dark eye which sometimes softened into love, then flamed again into the fire of resentment. She knelt not for mercy: she prayed not for pardon: a gloomy pride supported her;[b] and the dark frown that lowered over his features was answered by the calm of fixed despair.

They were alone. Lord Avondale, upon arriving, had sought her in her own apartment: he had heard of her illness. The duke had repeatedly implored him to return; he had at length tardily obeyed the summons. After a silence of some moments: 'Have I deserved this?' he cried. 'Oh Calantha, have I indeed deserved it?' She made no answer to this appeal. 'There was a time,' he said, 'when I knew how to address you – when the few cares and vexations, that ever intruded themselves, were lightened by your presence; and forgotten in / the kindness and sweetness of your conversation. You were my comfort and my solace;[c] your wishes were what I most consulted; your opinions and inclinations were the rule of all my actions. But I wish not to grieve you by reminding you of a state of mutual confidence and happiness which we never more can enjoy.

'If you have a heart,' he continued, looking at her mournfully, 'it must already be deeply wounded by the remembrance of your behaviour to me, and can need no reproaches. The greatest to a feeling mind is the knowledge that it has acted unworthily; that it has abused the confidence reposed in it, and blasted the hopes of one, who relied solely upon its affection. You have betrayed me. Oh! Calantha, had you the heart? I will not tell you how by degrees suspicion first entered my mind, till being more plainly informed of the cruel truth, I attempted, but in vain, to banish every / trace of you from my affections. I have not succeeded – I cannot succeed. Triumph at hearing this if you will. The habit of years is strong. Your image and that of crime and dishonour, can never enter my mind together. Put me not then to the agony of speaking to you in a manner you could not bear, and I should repent. They say you are not yet guilty; and that the man for whom I was abandoned has generously saved you . . . . but[d] consider the magnitude of those injuries which I have received;ª and think me not harsh, if I pronounce this doom upon myself and you: – Calantha, we must part.'

The stern brow gave way before these words; and the paleness of death overspread her form. Scarce could she support herself. He continued: 'Whatever it may cost me, and much no doubt I shall suffer, I can be firm. No importunity from others, no stratagems shall prevail. I came, because I would not / shrink from the one painful trial I had imposed upon myself. For your's and other's sakes, I came, because I thought it best to break to you myself my irrevocable determination. Too long I have felt your power: too dearly I loved you, to cast dishonour upon your as yet unsullied name. The world may pardon, and friends will still surround you. I will give you half of all that I possess on earth;[b] and I will see that you are supported and treated with respect. You will be loved and honoured; and, more than this, our children, Calantha, even those precious and dear ties which should have reminded you of your duty to them, if not to me, – yes, even our children, I will not take from you, as long as your future conduct may authorize me in leaving them under your care.[20] I will not tear you from every remaining hope; nor by severity,[c] plunge you into further guilt; but as for him, say / only that he for whom I am abandoned was unworthy.'

As he uttered these words, the frenzy of passion for one moment shook his frame. Calantha in terror snatched his hand. 'Oh, hear me, hear me, and be merciful!' she cried, throwing herself before his feet. – 'For God's sake hear me.' 'The injury was great,' he cried: 'the villain was masked; but the remembrance of it is deep and eternal.'

He struggled to extricate his hand from her grasp: it was cold, and trembling.... 'Calm[d] yourself,' he at length said, recovering his composure: 'these scenes may break my heart, but they cannot alter its purpose. I may see your tears, and while under the influence of a woman I have loved too well, be moved to my own dishonour. I may behold you humble, penitent, wretched, and being man, not have strength of mind to resist.' /

'And is there no hope, Avondale?' 'None for me,' he replied mournfully: 'you have stabbed here even to my very heart[e] of hearts.' 'Oh, hear me! look upon me.' 'Grant that I yield, wretched woman; say that I forgive you – that you make use of my attachment[f] to mislead my feelings – Calantha, can you picture to yourself the scene that must ensue? Can you look onward into after life, and trace the progress of our melancholy journey through it? Can you do this, and yet attempt to realize, what I shudder even at contemplating? Unblest in each other, solitary, suspicious, irritated, and deeply injured – if we live alone, we shall curse the hours as they pass, and if we rush for consolation into society, misrepresented, pointed at, derided, – oh, how shall we bear it?'

Her shrieks, her tears, now overpowered every other feeling. 'Then it is for the last time we meet. You come / to tell me this. You think I can endure it?' 'We will not endure it,' he cried fiercely, breaking from her. 'I wish not to speak with severity; but beware, for my whole soul is in agony, and fierce passion domineers: tempt me not to harm you, my beloved: return to your father: I will write – I will see you again.'..... 'Oh!ª leave me not – yet hear me. – I am not guilty – I am innocent – Henry, I am innocent.'

Calantha knelt before him, as she spoke: – her tears choaked her voice. 'Yet hear me; look at me once; see, see in this face if it bear traces of guilt. Look, Henry. You will not leave me.' She fell before him; and knelt at his feet. 'Do you remember how you once loved me?' she said, clasping his hand in her's. 'Think how dear we have been to each other: and will you now abandon me? Henry, my husband, have you forgotten me? Look at the boy. Is it not your's? Am I not its / mother? Will you cause her death who gave him life? Will you cast disgrace upon the mother of your child? Can you abandon me – can you, have you the heart?.... Haveᵇ mercy, oh my God! have mercy.... Iᶜ am innocent.' /

CHAPTER XV.

THE convulsive sobs of real agony, the eloquence which despair and affection create in all, the pleadings of his own kind and generous heart were vain. He raised her senseless from the earth; he placed her upon a couch; and without daring to look upon her, as he extricated his hand from the strong grasp of terror, he fled from her apartment.

Mrs. Seymour had waited to see him; and, when he had quitted her niece's room, she arrested him as he would have hastened by her, at the head of the stairs. Her ill state of health, and deep anxiety, had enfeebled her too much to endure the shock of hearing his irrevocable intention. He knew this, and wished to break it to her gently. She pressed his / hand; she looked upon his countenance. All a mother's heart spoke in those looks. Was there a hope yet left for her unhappy niece? 'Oh, if there yet be hope, speak, Lord Avondale; spare the feelings of one who never injured you;[a] look in that face and have mercy, for in it there is all the bitterness of despair.' He sought for expressions that might soften the pang – he wished to give her hope; but too much agitated himself to know what he then said: 'I am resolved – I am going immediately,' he said, and passed her by in haste. He saw not the effect of his words – he heard not the smothered shriek of a heart-broken parent.

As he rushed forward, he met the duke, who in one moment marked, in the altered manner of Lord Avondale – the perfect calm – the chilling proud reserve he had assumed, that there was no hope of reconciliation. He offered him his hand: he was himself much moved. / 'I can never ask, or expect you to forgive her,' he said,[b] in a low broken voice. 'Your generous forbearance has been fully appreciated by me. I number it amongst the heaviest of my calamities, that I can only greet you on your return with my sincere condolements, Alas! I gave you as an inheritage a bitter portion. You are at liberty to resent as a man, a conduct, which not even a father can expect, or ask you to forgive.' Lord Avondale turned abruptly from the duke: 'Are my horses put to the carriage?' he said impatiently to a servant. 'All is in readiness.' 'You will not go?' 'I must: my uncle waits for me at the inn at Belfont; he would scarcely permit me. . . .'

The shrieks of women from an adjoining apartment interrupted Lord Avondale. The duke hastened to the spot. Lord Avondale reluctantly followed. 'Lady

Avondale is dead,' said one: 'the barbarian has murdered her.' – / Lord Avondale flew forward. The violence of her feelings had been tried too far. That irrevocable sentence, that assumed sternness, had struck upon a heart, already breaking. Calantha was with some difficulty brought to herself. 'Is he gone?' were[21] the first words she uttered. 'Oh! let him not leave me yet.'

Sir Richard, having waited at Belfont till his patience was wholly exhausted, had entered the castle, and seeing how matters were likely to terminate, urged his nephew with extreme severity to be firm. 'This is all art,' he said: 'be not moved by it.' Lord Avondale waited to hear that Calantha was better, then entered the carriage, and drove off. 'I will stay awhile,' said Sir Richard, 'and see how she is; but if you wait for me at Kelly Cross, I will overtake you there. Be firm: this is all subterfuge, and what might have been expected.' /

Calantha[a] upon recovering, sought Sir Richard. Her looks were haggard and wild: despair had given them a dreadful expression. 'Have mercy – have mercy. I command, I do not implore you to grant me one request,' she said – 'to give me yet one chance, however, undeserved. Let me see him, cruel man: let me kneel to him.' 'Kneel to him!' cried Sir Richard, with indignation: 'never, You have used your arts long enough to make a fool, and a slave, of a noble,[b] confiding husband. There is some justice in Heaven:[c] I thank God his eyes are open at last. He has acted like a man. Had he pardoned an adultress – had he heard her, and suffered his reason to be beguiled – had he taken again to his heart the wanton who has sacrificed his honour, his happiness, and every tie, I would have renounced him for ever. No, no, he shall not return: by God, he shall not see you again.' /

'Have mercy,' still repeated Lady Avondale; but it was but faintly. 'I'll never have mercy for one like you, serpent, who[d] having been fondled in his bosom, bit him to the heart. Are you not ashamed to look at me?' Calantha's tears had flowed in the presence of her husband; but now they ceased. Sir Richard softened in his manner. 'Our chances in life are as in a lottery,' he said; 'and if one who draws the highest prize of all, throws it away in very wantonness, and then sits down to mourn for it, who will be so great a hypocrite, or so base a flatterer, as to affect compassion? You had no pity for him: you ought not to be forgiven.'

'Can you answer it to yourself to refuse me one interview? Can you have the heart to speak with such severity to one already fallen?' 'Madam, why do you appeal to me? What are you approaching me for? What can I do?'

'Oh, there will be curses on your / head, Sir Richard, for this; but I will follow him. There is no hope for me but in seeing him myself.' 'There is no hope at all, madam,' said Sir Richard, triumphantly: 'he's my own nephew; and he acts as he ought. Lady Avondale, he desires you may be treated with every possible respect. Your children will be left with you, as long as your conduct –' 'Will he see me?' 'Never.' /

CHAPTER XVI.

Sir Richard ordered his carriage at twelve that evening, and did not even tell Lady Avondale that he was going from the castle. Calantha, fatigued with the exertions of the day, too ill and too agitated to leave her room, threw herself upon the bed near her little son. Mac Allain and the nurse spoke with her; promised to perform her last injunctions; then left her to herself.

The soft breathing of Harry Mowbrey, who slept undisturbed beside her, soothed and composed her mind. Her thoughts now travelled back with rapidity over the varied scenes of her early and happier days: her life appeared before her like a momentary trance – like a dream that leaves a feverish and indistinct / alarm upon the mind. The span of existence recurred in memory to her view, and with it all its hopes, its illusions, and its fears. She started with abhorrence at every remembrance of her former conduct, her infidelity and neglect to[a] the best and kindest of husbands – her disobedience to an honoured parent's commands. Tears[b] of agonizing remorse streamed from her eyes.

In that name of husband the full horror of her guilt appeared. Every event had conspired together to blast his rising fortunes, and his dawning fame. His generous forbearance to herself, was, in fact, a sacrifice of every worldly hope; for, of all sentiments, severe and just resentment from one deeply injured, is that which excites the strongest sympathy; while a contrary mode of conduct, however founded upon the highest and best qualities of a noble mind, is rarely appreciated. The cry of justice is alone supported; and the husband who / spares and protects an erring wife, sacrifices his future hopes of fame and exalted reputation at the shrine of mercy and of love. She suddenly started with alarm. 'What then will become of me?' she cried. 'The measure of my iniquity is at its full.'

Calantha's tears fell upon her sleeping boy. He awoke, and he beheld his mother; but he could not discern the agitation of her mind. He looked on her, therefore, with that radiant look of happiness which brightens the smile of childhood; nor knew, as he snatched one kiss in haste, that it was the last, the last kiss from a mother, which ever through life should bless him with its pressure.

It was now near the hour of twelve; and Mrs. Seymour cautiously approached Calantha's bed. 'Is it time?' 'Not yet, my child.' 'Is Sir Richard gone?' 'No;ᵃ he is still in his own apartment. I have written a few lines,' said Mrs. Seymour tenderly; 'but if you fail, / what hope is there that anything I can say will avail?' 'Had my mother lived,' said Calantha, 'she had acted as you have done. You look so like her at this moment, that it breaks my heart.[22] Thank God, she does not live, to see her child's disgrace.' As she spoke, Calantha burst into tears, and threw her arms around her aunt's neck.

'Calm yourself, my child.' 'Hear me,' said Lady Avondale. 'Perhaps I shall never more see you. I have drawn down such misery upon myself, that I cannot bear up under it. If I should die, – and there is a degree of grief that kills – take care of my children. Hide from them their mother's errors. Oh, my dear aunt, at such a moment as this, how all that attracted in life, all that appeared brilliant, fades away. What is it I have sought for? Not real happiness – not virtue, but vanity, and far worse.' 'Calantha,' said Mrs. Seymour, as she wept over her / niece, 'there is much to say in palliation of thy errors. The heart is sometimes tried by prosperity; and it is in my belief the most difficult of all trials to resist. Who then shall dare to say, that there was not one single pretext, or excuse, for thy ill conduct? No wish, no desire of thine was ever ungratified. This in itself is some palliation. Speak, Calantha: fear not; for who shall plead for thee, if thou thyself art silent?'

'From the deep recesses of a guilty, yet not humble heart, in the agony and the hopelessness of despair,' said Calantha, 'I acknowledge before God and before man, that for me there is no excuse. I have felt, I have enjoyed every happiness, every delight, the earth can offer. Its vanities, its pleasures, its transports have been mine; and in all instances I have misused the power with which I have been too much and too long entrusted. Oh, may the God of worlds innumerable, who scatters his / blessings upon all and maketh his rain to fall upon the sinner, as upon the righteous, extend his mercy even unto me.'

'Can I do any thing for you, my child?' said Mrs. Seymour. 'Speak for me to Sophia and Frances,' said Calantha, 'and say one word for me to the good and the kind; for indeed I have ever found the really virtuous most kind. As to the rest, if any of those with whom I passed my happier days remember me, tell them, that even in this last sad hour I think with affection of them; and say, that when I look back even now with melancholy pleasure upon a career, which, though short, was gay and brilliant – upon happiness, which though too soon misused and thrown away, was real and great, it is the remembrance of my friends, and companions – it is the thought of their affection and kindness, which adds to and imbitters every regret – for that kindness was lavished in vain. Tell them / I do not hope that my example can amend them: they will not turn from one wrong pursuit for me; they will not compare themselves with Calantha; they have not an Avondale to leave and to betray. Yet when they read my history – if amidst the severity of justice which such a narrative must excite, some feelings of forgiveness and pity should arise, perhaps the prayer of one, who has suffered much, may ascend for them, and the thanks of a broken heart be accepted in return.'

Mrs. Seymour wept, and promised to perform Calantha's wishes. She was still with her, when Mac Allain knocked at the door, and whispered, that all was in readiness. 'Explain every thing to my father,' said Calantha, again embracing her aunt; 'and now farewell.' /

CHAPTER XVII.

'Sure what a stormy night it is! Lard[a] help us, Mr. Mac Allain,' said the nurse, as she wrapped her thick cloth mantle over the sweet slumberer that fondled in her bosom, and got into a post-chaise and four[23] with much trepidation and difficulty. 'I never saw the like! there's wind enough to blow us into the sea, and sea enough to deluge the land. The Holy Virgin, and all the saints protect us!' Gerald Mac Allain having with some trouble secured the reluctant and loquacious matron, now returned for another and a dearer charge, who, trembling and penitent, followed him to the carriage. 'Farewell, my kind preserver,' said Calantha, her voice scarcely audible. 'God bless, God protect you, / dear lady,' said the old man in bitter grief. 'Take care of Henry.[b] Tell my father that I have been led to this step by utter despair. Let no one suspect your friendly aid. Lord Avondale, though he may refuse to see me, will not be offended with the kind hearts that had pity on my misfortunes.' 'God bless you, dear lady,' again reiterated the old man, as the carriage drove swiftly from the gates.

But the blessing of God was not with Lady Avondale; she had renounced his favour and protection in the hour of prosperity; and she durst not even implore his mercy or his pardon in her present affliction. Thoughts of bitterness crowded together: she could no longer weep – the pressure upon her heart and brain would not permit it.

'Eh! dear heart, how the carriage rowls!' was the first exclamation which awoke her to a remembrance of her situation. 'We are ascending the mountain. / Fear not, good nurse. Your kindness in accompanying me shall never be forgotten.' 'Och musha, what a piteous night it is! – I did not reckon upon it.' 'You shall be rewarded and doubly rewarded for your goodness. I shall never forget it. Lord Avondale will reward you.' 'Hey sure you make me weep to hear you; but I wish you'd tell the cattle not to drive so uncommon brisk up the precipice. Lord have mercy, if there ain't shrouds flying over the mountains!' 'It is only the flakes of snow driven by the tempest.'

'Do not fret yourself thus,' continued Lady Avondale. 'I will take care of you, good nurse.' 'I have heard say, and sure I hope it's no sin to mention it again, my lady, that the wind's nothing more than the souls of bad christians, who can't get into Heaven, driven onward, alacks the pity! and shrieking as they pass.' 'I have heard the same,' / replied Calantha mournfully. 'Och lard!ª my lady, I hope not: I'm^b sure its a horrid thought. I hope, my lady,^c you don't believe it. But how terrible your dear ladyship looks, by the light of the moon. I trust in all the saints, the robbers have not heard of our journey. – Hark what a shriek!' 'It is nothing but the wind rushing over the vast body of the sea. You most not give way to terror. See how the child sleeps: they say one may go in safety the world over, with such a cherub: Heaven protects it. Sing it to rest, nurse, or tell it some merry tale.'

The carriage proceeded over the rocky path, for it could scarce be termed a road; the wind whistled in at the windows; and the snow drifting, covered every object. 'There it comes again,' said the affrighted nurse. 'What comes?' 'The shroud with the death's head peeping out of it. It was just such a night as this, last Friday night as ever / came, when the doctor's brother, the prophet Camioli, on his death bed, sent for his ungrateful daughter, and she would not come. I never shall forget that night. Well, if I did not hear the shriek of the dear departed two full hours after he gave up the ghost. The lord help us in life, as in death, and defend us from wicked children. I hope your dear ladyship does'nt remember that it was just on this very spot at the crossing, that Drax O'Morven was murdered by his son: and is'nt there the cross, as I live, just placed right over against the road to warn passengers of their danger. – Oh!'. . . .^d

'What is the matter, nurse? For God^e sake speak.' 'Oh!'. . . . 'Stop^f the carriage. In the name of his Grace the Duke of Altamonte, I desire you to stop,' cried a voice from behind. 'Drive on, boys, for your life. Drive on in mercy. We are just at Baron's Down: – I see the lights of the village, at the bottom / of the hill. Drive for your life: a guinea for every mile you go.'^g The nurse shrieked:^h the carriage flew; jolts, ruts, and rocks, were unheeded by Calantha. 'We are pursued. Rush on: – reach Baron's Down: – gallop your horses. Fear not. I value not life, if you but reach the inn – if you but save me from this pursuit.' 'Stop,' cried a voice of thunder. 'Fear not,' 'Drive Johnny Carl,' screamed the nurse. 'Drive Johnny Carl,' repeated the servant.

The horses flew; the post boys clashed their whips; the carriage wheels scarce appeared to touch the ground. A yell from behind seemed only to redouble their exertions. They arrive: Baron's Down appears in sight: lights are seen at the windows of the inn. The postboys ring and call: the doors are open: Lady Avondale flew from the carriage: – a servant of the duke's arrested her progress. 'I am sorry to make so bold; / but I come with letters from his grace your father. Your Ladyship may remain at Baron's Down to-night; but tomorrow I must see you safe to the castle. Pardon my apparent boldness: it is unwillingly that I presume to address you thus. My commands are positive.'

'Sure there's not the laist room at all for the ladies; nor any baists to be had, all the way round Baron's Down; nor ever so much as a boy to be fetched,ᵃ as can take care of the cattle over the mountain,' said the master of the inn, now joining in the conversation. 'What will become of us?' cried the nurse. 'Dear, dear lady, be prevailed on: give up your wild enterprise:ᵇ return to your father. Lady Anabel will be quite kilt with the fatigue. Beᶜ prevailed upon: give up this hopeless journey.' '*You* may return, if it is your pleasure: I never will.' 'Your ladyship will excuse me,' said the servant, producing some letters;ᵈ 'but I must entreat your / perusal of these, before you attempt to proceed.'

'You had better give my lady your best accommodations,' said the nurse in confidence to the landlord: 'she is a near connexion of the Duke of Altamonte's. You may repent any neglect you may shew to a traveller of such high rank.' 'There's nae rank will make room,' retorted the landlord. 'Were she the late duchess herself, I could only give her my bed, and go without one. But indeed couldn't a trifle prevail with the baists as brought you, to step over the mountains as far as Killy Cross?' 'There's nae trifle,' said a man, much wrapped up, who had been watching Lady Avondale – 'there's nae trifle shall get ye to Killy Cross, make ye what haste ye can, but what we'll be there before ye.' Calantha shuddered at the meaning of this threat, which she did not understand; but the nurse informed her it was a servant of Sir Richard Mowbrey's. /

CHAPTER XVIII.

THE letters from her father, Lady Avondale refused to read. Many remonstrances passed between herself and the duke's servant. The result was a slow journey in the dark night, over a part of the country which was said to be infested by the marauders. No terror alarmed Lady Avondale, save that of losing a last, an only opportunity of once more seeing her husband – of throwing herself upon his mercy – of imploring him to return to his family, even though she were exiled from it. 'Yet, I will not kneel to him, or ask it. If when he sees me, he has the heart to refuse me,' she cried, 'I will only shew him my child; and if he can look upon it, and kill its mother, let him do it. I think in that / case – yes, I do feel certain that I can encounter death, without a fear, or a murmur.'

The carriage was at this time turning down a steep descent, when some horsemen gallopping past, bade them make way for Sir Richard Mowbrey. Calantha recognized the voice of the servant: it was the same who had occasioned her so much alarm at the inn near Baron Moor. But the nurse exclaimed in terror that it was one of the rebels: she knew him, she said, by his white uniform;[a] and the presence alone of the admiral, in the duke's carriage, convinced her of her mistake. 'Thanks be to heaven,' cried she the moment she beheld him, 'it is in rail[b] earnest the old gentleman.' 'Thanks be to heaven,' said Calantha, 'he either did not recognize me, or cares not to prevent my journey.' 'Well, if it isn't himself,' said the nurse, 'and the saints above only know why he rides for pleasure, / this dismal night, over these murderous mountains; but at all events he is well guarded. Alack! we are friendless.'

Lady Avondale sighed as the nurse in a tremulous voice ejaculated these observations; for the truth of the last remark gave it much weight. But little did she know at the[c] moment, when the admiral passed, how entirely her fate depended on him.

It was not till morning they arrived at Kelly Cross, 'Bless my heart, how terrible you look. What's the matter, sweet heart?' said the nurse as they alighted from the carriage. – 'Look up, dear. – What is the matter?' – 'Nurse, there is a pressure upon my brain, like an iron hand; and my eyes see nothing but dimness. Oh God![d] where am I! Send, oh nurse, send my aunt Seymour – Call my – my husband – tell Lord Avondale to come – is he still here? – There's[a] death on me: I feel it here – here.' – 'Look up, sweet dear: – cheer yourself: / – you'll be better presently.' 'Never more, nurse – never more. There is death on me, even as it came straight upon my mother. Oh God!'[b] – 'Where is the pain?' 'It came like ice upon my heart, and my limbs feel chilled and numbed. – Avondale – Avondale.'

Calantha was carried to a small room, and laid upon a bed. The waiter said that Lord Avondale was still at the inn. The nurse hastened to call him. He was surprised; but not displeased when he heard that Lady Avondale was arrived. He rushed towards her apartment. Sir Richard was with him. 'By G – d, Avondale, if you forgive her, I will never see you more. Whilst I live, she shall never dwell in my house.' 'Then mine shall shelter her,' said Lord Avondale, breaking from Sir Richard's grasp: 'this is too much;' and with an air of kindness, with a manner gentle and affectionate, Lord Avondale now entered, and approached his wife. 'Calantha,' / he said, 'do not thus give way to the violence of your feelings. I wish not to appear stern. . . . [c] My God! what is the matter?' 'Your poor lady[d] is dying,' said the nurse. 'For the love of mercy, speak one gracious word to her.' 'I will, I do,' said Lord Avondale, alarmed. 'Calantha,' he whispered, without one reproach, 'whatever have been your errors, turn here for shelter to a husband's bosom. I will never leave you.[e] Come here, thou lost one. Thou hast strayed from thy guide and friend. But were it to seal my ruin, I must, I do pardon thee.[f] Oh! come again, unhappy, lost Calantha. Heaven[g] forgive you, as I do, from my soul. – What means this silence – this agonizing suspense?'

'She faints,' cried the nurse. 'May God have mercy!' said Lady Avondale. 'There is something on my mind. I wish to speak – to tell – your kindness kills me. I repent all. – Oh, is it too / late?' – It was. – For amendment, for return from error, for repentance it was too late. Death struck her at that moment. One piercing shriek proclaimed his power, as casting up her eyes with bitterness and horror, she fixed them upon Lord Avondale.

That piercing shriek had escaped from a broken heart. It was the last chord of nature, stretched to the utmost till it broke. A cold chill spread itself over her limbs. In the struggle of death, she had thrown her arms around her husband's neck; and when her tongue cleaved to her mouth, and her lips were cold and powerless, her eyes yet bright with departing life had fixed themselves earnestly upon him, as if imploring pardon for the past.

Oh, resist not that look, Avondale! it is the last. Forgive her – pity her: and if they call it weakness in thee thus to weep, tell them that man is weak, / and death dissolves the keenest enmities. Oh! tell them, that there is something in a last look from those whom we have once loved, to which the human soul can never be insensible. But when that look is such as was Calantha's, and when the last prayer her dying lips expressed was for mercy, who shall dare to refuse and to resist it? It might have rent a harder bosom than thine. It may ascend and plead before the throne of mercy.ª It was the prayer of a dying penitent: – it was the agonizing look of a breaking heart.

Weep then, too generous Avondale, for that frail being who lies so pale so cold in death before thee. Weep: for thou wilt never find again another like her. She was the sole mistress of thy affections, and could wind and turn thee at her will. She knew and felt her power, and trifled with it to a dangerous excess. Others may be fairer, and more / accomplished in the arts which mortals prize, and more cunning in devices and concealment of their thoughts; but none can ever be so dear to Avondale's heart as was Calantha.ᵇ /

CHAPTER XIX.

Sir Richard wished to say one word to console Lord Avondale; but he could not. He burst into tears; and knelt down by the side of Calantha. 'I am an old man,' he said. 'You thought me severe; but I would have died, child, to save you. Look up and get well. I can't bear to see this: – no, I can't bear it.' He now reproached himself. 'I have acted rightly perhaps, and as she deserved; but what of that: if God were to act by us all as we deserve, where should we be? Look up, child – open your eyes again – I'd give all I have on earth to see you smile once on me – to feel even that little hand press mine in token of forgiveness.' 'Uncle,' said Lord Avondale, in a faltering[a] voice, / whatever Calantha's faults, she forgave every one, however they had injured her;[b] and she loved you.' 'That makes it all the worse,' said the admiral. 'I can't believe she's dead.'

Sir Richard's sorrow, whether just or otherwise, came too late. Those who act with rigid justice here below – those who take upon themselves to punish the sinner whom God for inscrutable purposes one moment spares, should sometimes consider that the object against whom their resentment is excited will soon be no more. Short-lived is the enjoyment even of successful guilt. An hour's triumph has perhaps been purchased by misery so keen, that were we to know all, we should only commiserate the wretch we now seek to subdue and to punish. The name of Christians[c] we have assumed; the doctrine of our religion, we have failed to study. How often when passion and rancour move us to shew our zeal in the cause of virtue, / by oppressing and driving to ruin unutterable, what we call successful villainy, the next hour brings us the news that the object of our indignation is dead. – That soul is gone, however polluted, to answer before another throne for its offences. Ah! who can say that our very severity to such offender may not turn back upon ourselves, and be registered in the Heaven we look forward to with such presumption, to exclude us for ever from it.

Sir Richard gazed sadly now upon his nephew. 'Don't make yourself ill, Henry,' he said. 'Bear up under this shock. If it makes you ill, it will be my death.' 'I know you are too generous,' said Lord Avondale, 'not to feel for me.' 'I can't stay any longer here,' said Sir Richard, weeping. 'You look at me in a manner to break my heart. I will return to the castle; tell them all that has happened;

and then bring the children to you at Allenwater. I will go / and fetch Henry to you.' 'I can't see him now,' said Lord Avondale: 'he is so like her.' 'Can I do any thing else for you?' said Sir Richard. 'Uncle,' said Lord Avondale mournfully, 'go to the castle, and tell them I ask that every respect should be shewn in the last rites they offer to – ' 'Oh, I understand you,' said Sir Richard, crying: 'there will be no need to say that – she's lov'd enough.' 'Aye[a] that she was,' said the nurse; 'and whatever her faults, there's many a-one prays for her at this hour; for since the day of her birth, did she ever[b] turn away from those who were miserable or in distress?'[c] 'She betrayed her husband,' said Sir Richard. 'She had the kindest, noblest heart,' replied Lord Avondale. 'I know her faults: her merits few like to remember. Uncle, I cannot but feel with bitterness the zeal that some have shewn against her.' 'Do sot speak thus, Henry,' said Sir Richard. 'I / would have stood by her to the last, had she lived; but she never would appear penitent and humble. I thought her wanting in feeling. She braved every one; and did so many things that....'[d] 'She is dead,' said Lord Avondale, greatly agitated. 'Oh, by the affection you profess for me, spare her memory.' 'You loved her then even – .' 'I loved her better than any thing in life.'

Sir Richard wept bitterly. 'My dear boy, take care of yourself,' he said. 'Let me hear from you.' 'You shall hear of me,' said Lord Avondale. The admiral then took his leave; and Lord Avondale returned into Calantha's apartment. The nurse followed. Affected at seeing his little girl, he prest[e] her to his heart, and desired she might immediately be sent to Allenwater. Then ordering every one from the room, he turned to look for the last time upon Calantha. There was not the faintest tint of colour on her pale transparent / cheek. The dark lashes of her eye shaded its soft blue lustre from his mournful gaze. There was a silence around. It was the calm – the stillness of the grave.

Lord Avondale pressed her lips to his. 'God bless, and pardon thee, Calantha,' he cried. 'Now even I can look upon thee and weep. O, how could'st thou betray me! 'It is not an open enemy that hath done me this dishonour, for then I could have borne it: neither was it mine adversary that did magnify himself against me; for then peradventure I would have hid myself from him: but it was even thou, my companion, my guide, and mine own familiar friend.' – We took sweet counsel together[24].... farewell!'[f] It was myself who led thee to[g] thy ruin. I loved thee more than man should love so frail a being, and then I left thee to thyself. I could not bear to grieve thee; I could not bear to curb thee; and thou hast lost / me and thyself. Farewell. Thy death has left me free to act.[h] Thou had'st a strange power over my heart, and thou[i] did'st misuse it.'

As he uttered these words, while yet in presence of the lifeless form of his departed, his guilty wife, he prepared to leave the mournful scene. 'Send the children to Allenwater, if you have mercy.' These were the last words he addrest to the nurse as he hurried from her presence.

O man, how weak and impotent is thy nature! Thou can'st hate, and love, and kiss the lips of thy enemy, and strike thy dagger into the bosom of a friend. Thou can'st command thousands, and govern empires; but thou can'st not rule thy stormy passions, nor alter the destiny that leads thee on. And could Avondale thus weep for an ungrateful wife? Let those who live long enough in this cold world to feel its heartlessness, answer such enquiry.[a] Whatever she had / been, Calantha was still his friend. Together they had tried the joys and ills of life; the same interests united them: and the children as they turned to their father, pleaded for the mother whom they resembled. – Nothing, however, fair or estimable, can replace the loss of an early friend. Nothing that after-life can offer will influence us in the same degree. It has been said, that although our feelings are less acute in maturer age than in youth, yet the young mind will soonest recover from the blow that falls heaviest upon it. In that season of our life, we have it in our power, it is said, in a measure to repair the losses which we have sustained. But these are the opinions of the aged, whose pulse beats low – whose reasoning powers can pause, and weigh and measure out the affections of others. In youth these losses affect the very seat of life and reason, chill the warm blood in its rapid current, unnerve every fibre / of the frame, and cause the phrenzy of despair.

The duke was calm; but Lord Avondale felt with bitterness his injury and his loss. The sovereign who has set his seal to the sentence of death passed upon the traitor who had betrayed him, ofttimes in after-life has turned to regret the friend, the companion he has lost. 'She was consigned to me when pure and better than those who now upbraid her. I had the guidance of her; and I led her myself into temptation and ruin.[b] Can a few years have thus spoiled and hardened a noble nature! Where are the friends and flatterers, Calantha, who surrounded thee in an happier hour? I was abandoned for them: where are they now? Is there not one to turn and plead for thee – not one! They are gone in quest of new amusement. Some other is the favourite of the day. The fallen are remembered only by their faults.' /

CHAPTER XX.

Lord Avondale wrote to Glenarvon, desiring an immediate interview. He followed him to England; and it was some months before he could find where he was. He sought him in every place of public resort, amidst the gay troop of companions who were accustomed to surround him, and in the haunts of his most lonely retirement. At length he heard that he was expected to return to Ireland, after a short cruize. Lord Avondale waited the moment of his arrival; watched on the eve of his return, and traced him to the very spot, where, alas! he had so often met his erring partner.

It was the last evening in June, Glenarvon stood upon the high cliff; / and Lord Avondale approached and passed him twice, 'Glenarvon,' at length he cried, 'do you know me, or are you resolved to appear ignorant of my intentions?' 'I presume that it is Lord Avondale whom I have the honour of addressing.' 'You see a wretch before you, who has neither title, nor country, nor fame, nor parentage.[a] You know my wrongs. My heart is bleeding. Defend yourself; for one of us must die.' 'Avondale,' said Lord Glenarvon, 'I will never defend myself against you. You are the only man who dares with impunity address me in this tone and language. I accept not this challenge. Remember that I stand before you defenceless. My arm shall never be raised against your's.'

'Take this, and defend yourself,' cried Lord Avondale in violent agitation. 'I know you a traitor to every feeling of manly principle, honour and integrity. I know you; and your mock generosity, / and lofty language shall not save you.' 'Is it come to this?' said Glenarvon, smiling with bitterness. 'Then take thy will. I stand prepared. 'Tis well to risk so much for such a virtuous wife! She is an honourable lady – a most chaste and loving wife. I hope she greeted thee on thy return with much tenderness: I counselled her so to do; and when we have settled this affair, after the most approved fashion, then bear from me my best remembrances and love. Aye, my love, Avondale: 'tis a light charge to carry,[b] and will not burthen thee.'

'Defend yourself,' cried Lord Avondale fiercely. 'If it is thy mad wish, then be it so, and now stand off.' Saying this, Glenarvon accepted the pistol, and at the same moment that Lord Avondale discharged his, he fired in the air. 'This shall not save you,' cried Lord Avondale, in desperation. 'Treat me not like a child. Glenarvon, prepare. / One of us shall die. – Traitor! – villain!' 'Madman,' said Glenarvon scornfully, 'take your desire; and if one of us indeed must fall, be it you.' As he spoke, his livid countenance betrayed the malignity of his soul. He discharged his pistol full at his adversary's breast. Lord Avondale staggered for a moment. Then, with a sudden effort, 'The wound is trifling,' he cried, and, flying from the proffered assistance of Glenarvon, mounted his horse, and gallopped from the place.

No seconds, no witnesses, attended this dreadful scene. It took place upon the bleak moors behind Inis Tara's heights, just at the hour of the setting sun. 'I could have loved that man,' said Glenarvon, as he watched him in the distance.[a] 'He has nobleness, generosity, sincerity. I only assume the appearance of those virtues. My heart and his must never be compared: therefore I am compelled to hate him: – but / O![b] not so much as I abhor myself.' Thus saying, he turned with bitterness from the steep, and descended[c] with a firm step by the side of the mountain.

Glenarvon[d] stopped not for the rugged pathway; but he paused to look again upon the stream of Elle, as it came rushing down the valley:[e] and he paused to cast one glance of welcome upon Inis Tara, Glenarvon bay,[f] and the harbour terminating the wide extended prospect. The myrtles and arbutus[25] grew luxuriantly, intermixed with larch and firs. The air was hot: the ground was parched and dry. The hollow sound of the forests; the murmuring noise of the waves of the sea; the tinkling bell that at a distance sounded from the scattered flocks – all filled his heart with vague remembrances of happier days, and sad forebodings of future sorrow. As he approached the park of Castle Delaval, he met with some of the tenantry, who informed him of Calantha's death. /

Miss St. Clare stood before him. Perhaps at that moment his heart was softened by what he had just heard: I know not; but approaching her,[g] 'St. Clare,' he cried, 'give me your hand: it is for the last time I ask it. I have been absent for some months. I have heard that which afflicts me. Do not you also greet me unkindly. Pardon the past. I may have had errors; but to save, to reclaim you, is there any thing I would not do?' St. Clare made no answer. 'You may have discomforts of which I know not. Perhaps you are poor and unprotected. All that I possess, I would give you, if that would render you more happy.' Still she made no reply. 'You know not, I fancy, that my castles have been restored to me, and a gallant ship given me by the English court. I have sailed, St. Clare:[26] I only now return for a few weeks, before I am called hence for ever. Accept some mark of my regard; / and pardon an involuntary fault. Give me your hand.' – 'Never,' she replied;[h] 'all others, upon this new accession of good fortune, shall greet and receive you with delight. The world shall smile upon you, Glenarvon; but I never. I forgave you my own injuries, but not Calantha's[i] and my country's.'

'Is it possible, that one so young as you are, and this too but a first fault, is it possible you can be so unrelenting?' – 'A first fault, Glenarvon! The lessons you have taught were not in vain: they have been since repeated; but my crimes be on you!' – 'Is it not for your sake, miserable outcast, alone, that I asked you to forgive me? What is your forgiveness to me? I am wealthy, and protected: am I not? Tell me, wretched girl, what are you?' – 'Solitary, poor, abandoned, degraded,' said Miss St. Clare: 'why do you ask? you know it.' – 'And yet when I offer all things / to you, cannot you bring that stubborn heart to pardon?'ª – 'No: were it in the hour of death, I could not.' – 'Oh, Elinor, do not curse me at that hour. I am miserable enough.' – 'The curse of a broken heart is terrible,' said Miss St. Clare, as she left him; 'but it is already given. Vain is that youthful air; vain, my lord, your courtesy, and smiles, and fair endowments: – the curse of a broken heart is on you: and, by night and by day, it cries to you as from the grave. Farewell, Glenarvon: we shall meet no more.'

Glenarvon descended by the glen: his followers passed him in the well known haunt; but each as they passed him muttered unintelligible sounds of discontent: though the words, 'ill luck to you,' not unfrequently fell upon his ear. /

CHAPTER XXI.

From[a] Kelly Cross to Allenwater, the road passes through mountains which, rough and craggy, exhibit a terrific grandeur. The inhabitants in this part of the country are uncivilized and ferocious. Their appearance strongly betokens oppression, poverty, and neglect. A herd of goats may be seen browzing upon the tops of the broken cliffs; but no other cattle, nor green herbage. A desolate cabin here and there; inactivity, silence, and despondency, every where prevail. The night was sultry, and the tired horse of Lord Avondale hung back to the village he had left, and slowly ascended the craggy steep. When he had attained the summit of the mountain, / he paused to rest, exhausted by the burning pain of his wound.

Lord Avondale then looked back at the scenes he had left.

Before his eyes appeared in one extensive view the bright silver surface of Glenarvon bay,[b] breaking through the dark shades of distant wood, under the heights of Inis Tara and Heremon, upon whose lofty summits the light of the moonbeam fell. To the right, the Dartland hills arose in majestic grandeur; and far onwards, stretching to the clouds, his own native hills, the black mountains of Morne; while the river Allan, winding its way through limestone rocks and woody glens, rapidly approached towards the sea.

Whilst yet pausing to gaze upon these fair prospects, on a night so clear and serene, that every star shone forth to light him on his way, yells terrible and disorderly broke upon the sacred stillness, / and a party of the rebels rushed upon him. He drew his sword, and called loudly to them to desist. Collingwood, an attendant who had waited for him at the inn, and had since accompanied him, exclaimed: 'Will you murder your master, will you attack your lord, for that he is returning amongst you?' – 'He wears the English uniform,' cried one. 'Sure he's one of the butchers sent to destroy us. We'll have no masters, no lords;[c] he must give up his commission, and his titles, or not expect to pass.' – 'Never,' said Lord Avondale, indignantly: 'had I no commission, no title to defend, still as a man, free and independent, I would protect the laws and rights of my insulted country. Attempt not by force to oppose yourselves to my passage. I will pass without asking or receiving your permission.'

'It is Avondale, the lord's son,' cried one: 'I know him by his spirit. / Long life to you! and glory, and pleasure attend you' – 'Long life to your honour!' exclaimed one and all; and in a moment the enthusiasm in his favour was as great, as general, as had been at first the execration and violence against him. The attachment they bore to their lord was still strong. 'Fickle, senseless beings!' he said, with bitter contempt, as he heard their loyal cry. 'These are the creatures we would take to govern us: this is the voice of the people;[a] these are the rights of man.' – 'Sure but you'll pity us, and forgive us; and you'll be our king again, and live amongst us; and the young master's just gone to the mansion; and didn't we draw him into his own courts? and ain't we returning to our cabins after seeing the dear creature safe: and, for all the world, didn't we indade take ye for one of the murderers in the uniform, come to kill us, and make us slaves? Long life to your honour!' /

All the time they thus spoke, they kept running after Lord Avondale, who urged on his horse to escape from their persecution. A thousand pangs at this instant tortured his mind. This was the retreat in which he and Calantha had passed the first, and happiest year of their marriage. The approach to it was agony. The fever on his mind augmented. The sight of his children, whom he had ordered to be conveyed thither, would be terrible: – he dreaded, yet he longed to clasp them once more to his bosom. The people had named but one, and that was Harry Mowbrey. Was Anabel also there? Would she look on him, and remind him of Calantha? These were enquiries[b] he hardly durst suggest to himself.

Lord Avondale hastened on. And now the road passed winding by the banks of the rapid and beautiful Allan, till it led to the glen, where a small villa, adorned with flower gardens, wood and / lawn, broke upon his sight. His heart was cheerless,[c] in the midst of joy: he was poor, whilst abundance surrounded him. Collingwood rang at the bell. The crowd had reached the door, and many a heart,[d] and many a voice, welcomed home the brave Lord Avondale. He passed them in gloom and silence. 'Are the children arrived?' he said, in a voice of bitterness, to the old steward, whose glistening eyes he wished not to encounter. 'They came, God bless them, last night. They are not yet awakened.' 'Leave me,' said Lord Avondale. 'I too require rest;' and he locked himself into the room prepared for his reception; whilst Collingwood informed the astonished gazers that their lord was ill, and required to be alone. 'He was not used,' they said, as they mournfully retired, 'to greet us thus. But whatever he thinks of his own people, we would one and all gladly lay down our lives to serve him.' /

CHAPTER XXII.

Upon that night when the meeting between Lord Glenarvon and Lord Avondale had taken place, the great procession in honour of St. Katharine passed through the town of Belfont. Miss St. Clare, having waited during the whole of the day to see it, rode to St. Mary's church, and returned by the shores of the sea, at a late hour. As she passed and repassed before her uncle's house, she turned her dark eye upwards, and saw that many visitors and guests were there. They had met together to behold the procession.

Lauriana and Jessica stood in their mother's bay[a] window. Tyrone, Carter, Grey, and Verny,[b] spoke to them concerning their cousin. 'See where she rides / by, in defiance,' said one. 'Miss St. Clare, fie upon this humour,' cried another[c] 'the very stones cry shame on you, and our modest maidens turn from their windows, that they may not blush to see you.' 'Then are there few enough of that quality in Belfont,' said St. Clare smiling; 'for when I pass, the windows are thronged, and every eye is fixed upon me.' 'What weight has the opinion of others with you?' 'None.' 'What your own conscience?' 'None.' 'Do you believe in the religion of your fathers?' 'It were presumption to believe: I doubt all things.' 'You have read this;[d] and it is folly in you to repeat it;[e] for wherein has Miss Elinor a right to be wiser than the rest of us?' 'It is contemptible in fools to affect superior wisdom.' 'Better believe that which is false, than dare to differ from the just and the wise: the opinion of ages should be sacred: the religion and laws of our forefathers / must be supported.' 'Preach to the winds, Jessica: they'll bear your murmurs far, and my course is ended.'

The evening was still: no breeze was felt; and the swelling billows of the sea were like a smooth sheet of glass, so quiet, so clear. Lauriana played upon the harp, and flatterers told her that she played better than St. Clare. She struck the chords to a warlike air, and a voice, sweet as a seraph angel's, sung from below. 'St. Clare, is it you? Well I know that silver-sounding voice. The day has been hot, and you have ridden far: dismount, and enter here. An aunt and relations yet live to receive and shelter thee. What, though all the world scorn, and censure thee, still this is thy home. Enter here, and you shall be at peace.' 'Peace and my heart are at variance. I have ridden far, as you say, and I am weary;[f] yet I must journey to the mountains, before I rest. Let me ride on in haste. My course will soon / be o'er.' 'By Glenarvon's name I arrest you,' said Lauriana. 'Oh, not that name: all but that I can bear to hear.'

Cormac O'Leary, and Carter, and Tyrone, now come[a] down, and assisted in persuading her to alight. 'Sing to us,' they cried. 'What hand can strike the harp like thine? What master taught thee this heavenly harmony?' 'Oh, had you heard his song who taught me, then had you wept in pity for my loss. What does life present that's worth even a prayer? What can Heaven offer, having taken from me all that my soul adored? Why name Glenarvon? It is like raising a spirit from the grave; or giving life again to the heart that is dead: it is as if a ray of the sun's glorious light shone upon these cold senseless rocks; or as if a garden of paradise were raised in the midst of a desert: birds of prey and sea-fowl alone inhabit here. They should be something like Glenarvon who dare / to name him.' 'Was he all this indeed?' said Niel Carter incredulously.

'When he spoke, it was like the soft sound of music. The wild impassioned strains of his lyre awakened in the soul every emotion: it was with a master-hand that he struck the chords;[27] and all the fire of genius and poetry accompanied the sound. When Heaven itself has shed its glory upon the favourite of his creation, shall mortal beings turn insensible from the splendid ray? You have maddened me: you have pronounced a name I consider sacred.' 'This prodigy of Heaven, however,' said Cormac O'Leary, 'behaves but scurvily to man. Glenarvon it seems has left his followers, as he has his mistress. Have you heard, that in consequence of his services, he is reinstated in his father's possessions, a ship is given to him, and a fair and lovely lady has accepted his hand? Eves now, he sails with the / English admiral and Sir Richard Mowbrey.'[28]

The rich crimson glow faded from Elinor's cheek. She smiled, but it was to conceal the bitterness of her heart. She knew the tale was true; but she cared not to repeat it. She mounted her horse, and desiring Cormac O'Leary, Niel Carter, and others, to meet her that night at Inis Tara, she rode away, with more appearance of gaiety than many a lighter heart. /

CHAPTER XXIII.

Elinor rode not to the mountains; she appeared not again at Belfont; but turning her horse towards the convent of Glenaa, she entered there, and asked if her aunt the abbess were yet alive. 'She is alive,' said one of those who remembered Miss St. Clare; 'but she is much changed since she last beheld you. Grieving for you has brought her to this pass.'

What the nun had said was true. The abbess was much changed in appearance; but through the decay, and wrinkles of age, the serenity and benevolence of a kind and pious heart remained. She started back at first, when she saw Miss St. Clare, that unfeminine attire inspired her with feelings of disgust: all / she had heard too of her abandoned conduct chilled her interest; and that compassion which she had willingly extended to the creeping worm, she reluctantly afforded to an impenitent, proud, and hardened sinner.

'The flowers bloom around your garden, my good aunt; the sun shines ever on these walls: it is summer here when it is winter in every other place. I think God's blessing is with you.' The abbess turned aside to conceal her tears;[a] then rising, asked wherefore her privacy was intruded upon in so unaccustomed a manner. 'I am come,' said Elinor, 'to ask a favour at your hands, and if you deny me, at least add not unnecessary harshness to your refusal. I have a father's curse on me, and it weighs me to the earth. When they tell you I am no more, say, will you pray for my soul? The God of Heaven dares not refuse the prayer of a saint like you.'

'This is strange language, Miss St. / Clare; but if indeed my prayers have the efficacy you think for, they shall be made now, even now that your heart may be turned from its wickedness to repentance.' – 'The favour I have to ask is of great moment: there will be a child left at your doors;[b] and ere long it will crave your protection; for it is an orphan boy, and the hand that now protects it will soon be no more. Look not thus at me: it is not mine. The boy has noble blood in his veins; but he is the pledge of misfortune and crime.'

The abbess raised herself to take a nearer view of the person with whom she was conversing. The plumed hat and dark flowing mantle, the emerald clasp and chain, had little attraction for one of her age and character; but the sunny ringlets which fell in profusion over a skin of alabaster, the soft smile of enchantment blended with the assumed fierceness of a military air, the deep expressive glance of passion and sensibility, / the youthful air of boyish playfulness, and that blush which years of crime had not entirely banished, all, all awakened the affection of age;[a] and, with more of warmth, more of interest than she had wished to shew to one so depraved, she pressed the unhappy wanderer to her heart. 'What treacherous fiends have decoyed, and brought thee to this, my child? What dæmons have had the barbarous cruelty to impose upon one so young, so fair?'

'Alas! good aunt, there is not in the deep recesses of my inmost heart,[b] a recollection of any whom I can with justice accuse but myself. That God who made me, must bear witness, that he implanted in my breast, even from the tenderest age, passions fiercer than I had power to curb. The wild tygress who roams amongst the mountains – the young lion who roars for its prey amidst its native woods – the fierce eagle who soars above all others, and cannot brook a rival in its flight, were tame and tractable / compared with me. Nature formed me fierce, and your authority was not strong enough to curb and conquer me. I was a darling and an only child. My words were idolized as they sprung warm from my heart; and my heart was worth some attachment, for it could love with passionate excess. In my happier days, I thought too highly of myself; and forgive me, Madam, if, fallen as I am, I still think the same. I cannot be humble.[29] When they tell me I am base, I acknowledge it: pride leads me to confess what others dare not; but I think them more base who delight in telling me of my faults: and when I see around me hypocrisy and all the petty arts of fashionable vice, I too can blush for others, and smile in triumph at those who would trample on me. It is not before such things[c] as these, such canting cowards, that I can feel disgrace; but before such as you are – so good, so pure, and yet so merciful, I stand at once confounded.' /

'The God of Heaven pardon thee!' said the abbess. 'You were once my delight and pride. I never could have suspected ill of you.' 'I too was once unsuspicious,' said St. Clare. 'My heart believed in nothing but innocence. I know the world better now. Were it their interest, would they thus deride me? When the mistress of Glenarvon, did they thus neglect, and turn from me? I was not profligate, abandoned, hardened, then! I was lovely, irresistible! My crime was excused. My open defiance was accounted the mere folly and wantonness of a child. I have a high spirit yet, which they shall not break. I am deserted, it is true; but my mind is a world in itself, which I have peopled with my own creatures. Take only from me a father's curse, and to the last I will smile, even though my heart is breaking.'

'And are you unhappy,'[d] said the abbess, kindly. 'Can you ask it, / Madam? Amidst the scorn and hatred of hundreds, do I not appear the gayest of all? Who rides so fast over the down? Who dances more lightly at the ball? And if I cannot sleep upon my bed, need the world be told of it? The virtuous suffer, do they not? And what is this dream of life if it must cease so soon? We know not what we are: let us doubt all things – all but the curse of a father, which lies heavy on me. Oh take it from me to-night! Give me your blessing; and the time is coming when I shall need your prayers.'

'Can such a mind find delight in vice?' said the abbess, mildly gazing upon the kneeling girl. 'Why do you turn your eyes to Heaven, admiring its greatness, and trembling at its power, if you yet suffer your heart to yield to the delusions of wickedness?' 'Will such a venial fault as love be accounted infamous in Heaven?' 'Guilty love is the / parent of every vice. Oh, what could mislead a mind like your's, my child?' 'Madam, there are some born with a perversion of intellect, a depravity of feeling, nothing can cure. Can we straighten deformity, or change the rough features of ugliness into beauty?' 'We may do much.' 'Nothing, good lady, nothing; though man would boast that it is possible. Let the ignorant teach the wise; let the sinner venture to instruct the saint; we cannot alter nature. We may learn to dissemble; but the stamp is imprest with life, and with life alone it is erased.'

'God bless, forgive, and amend thee!' said the abbess. 'The sun is set, the hour is late: thy words have moved, but do not convince me.' 'Rise, daughter, kneel not to me: there is one above, to whom alone that posture is due.' As St. Clare rode from the convent, she placed a mark upon the wicket of the / little garden, and raising her voice, 'Let him be accursed,' she cried, 'who takes from hence this badge of thy security: though rivers of blood shall gush around, not a hair of these holy and just saints shall be touched.' /

CHAPTER XXIV.

THE preparations made this year by France, in conjunction with her allies,[a] and the great events which took place in consequence of her enterprizes, belong solely to the province of the historian. It is sufficient to state, that the armament which had been fitted out on the part of the Batavian Republic, sailed at a later period of the same year, under the command of Admiral de Winter, with the intention of joining the French fleet at Brest, and proceeded[b] from thence to Ireland, where the discontents and disaffection were daily increasing, and all seemed ripe for immediate insurrection.

Lord Glenarvon was at St. Alvin Priory, when he was summoned to take / the command of his frigate, and join Sir George Buchanan and Admiral Duncan at the Texel.[30] Not a moment's time was to be lost: he had already exceeded the leave of absence he had obtained. The charms of a new mistress, the death of Calantha, the uncertain state of his affairs, and the jealous eye with which he regarded the measures taken by his uncle and cousin de Ruthven, had detained him till the last possible moment; but the command from Sir George was peremptory, and he was never tardy in obeying orders which led him from apathy and idleness to a life of glory.

Glenarvon prepared, therefore, to depart, as it seemed, without further delay, leaving a paper in the hands of one of his friends, commissioning him to announce at the next meeting at Inis Tara the change which had taken place in his opinions, and entire disapprobation of the lawless measures which had been recently adopted by the disaffected. He / took his name from out the directory; and though he preserved a faithful silence respecting others, he acknowledged his own errors, and abjured the desperate cause in which he had once so zealously engaged.

The morning before he quitted Ireland, he sent for his cousin Charles de Ruthven, to whom he had already consigned the care of his castles and estates. 'If I live to return,' he said gaily, 'I shall mend my morals, grow marvellous virtuous, marry something better than myself, and live in all the innocent pleasures of connubial felicity. In which case, you will be what you are now, a keen expectant of what never can be your's. If I die, in the natural course of events, all this will fall to your share. Take it now then into consideration: sell, buy, make whatever is for your advantage; but as a draw-back upon the estate, gentle cousin, I bequeath also to your care two children – the one, my trusty Henchman, a love / gift, as you well know, who must he liberally provided for – the other, mark me Charles! – a strange tale rests upon that other: keep him carefully: there are enemies who watch for his life: befriend him, and shelter him, and, if reduced to extremities, give these papers to the duke. They will unfold all that I know; and no danger can accrue to you from the disclosure. I had cause for silence.'

It was in the month of August, when Lord Glenarvon prepared to depart from Belfont. The morning was dark and misty. A grey circle along the horizon shewed the range of dark dreary mountains; and far above the clouds one bright pink streak marked the top of Inis Tara, already lighted by the sun, which had not risen sufficiently to cast its rays upon aught beside this lofty landmark. Horsemen, and carriages, were seen driving over the moors; but the silent loneliness / of Castle Delaval continued undisturbed till a later hour.

It was there that Lady Margaret, who had returned from England, awaited with anxiety the promised visit of Glenarvon. Suddenly a servant entered, and informed her that a stranger, much disguised, waited to speak with her. – His name was Viviani. – He was shewn into Lady Margaret's apartment. A long and animated conversation passed. One shriek was heard. The stranger hurried from the castle. Lady Margaret's attendants found her cold, pale, and almost insensible. When she recovered, 'Is he gone?' she said eagerly. 'The stranger is gone,' they replied. Lady Margaret continued deeply agitated; she wrote to Count Gondimar, who was absent; and she endeavoured to conceal from Mrs. Seymour and the duke the dreadful alarm of her mind. She appeared at the hour of dinner, and talked even as usual of the daily news. /

'Lord Glenarvon sailed this morning,' said Mrs. Seymour. 'I heard the same,' said Lady Margaret. 'Young De Ruthven is, I understand –' 'What?' said Lady Margaret, looking eagerly at her brother – 'appointed to the care of Lord Glenarvon's affairs. You know, I conclude, that he has taken his name out of the directory, and done every thing to atone for his former errors.' 'Has he?' said Lady Margaret, faintly. 'Poor Calantha,' said Mrs Seymour, 'on her death-bed spoke of him with kindness. He was not in fault,' she said. 'She bade me even plead for him, when others censured him too severely.' 'It is well that the dead bear record of his virtues,' said Lady Margaret. 'He has the heart of. . . .'

'Mr. Buchanan,' said a servant, entering abruptly, and, all in haste, Mr. Buchanan suddenly stood before his mother. There was no need of explanation. In one moment, Lady Margaret read in / the countenance of her son, that the dreadful menace of Viviani had been fulfilled; that his absence at this period was but too effectually explained; that all was known. Buchanan, that cold relentless son, who never yet had shewn or affection, or feeling – whose indifference had seldom yielded to any stronger emotion than that of vanity, now stood before her, as calm as ever, in outward show; but the horror of his look, when he turned it upon her, convinced her that he had heard the dreadful truth. Mrs. Seymour and the duke perceiving that something important had occurred, retired.

Lady Margaret and her son were, therefore, left to themselves. A moment's pause ensued, Lady Margaret first endeavoured to break it: 'I have not seen you,' she said at length, affecting calmness, 'since a most melancholy scene – I mean the death of Calantha.'

'True,' he cried, fixing her with / wild horror; 'and I have not seen you since. ... Do you know Viviani?' – 'Remember,' said Lady Margaret, rising in agitation, 'that I am your mother, Buchanan; and this strange manner agitates, alarms, terrifies me.' 'And me,' he replied. 'Is it true,' at length he cried, seizing both her hands with violence – 'Say, is it true?' 'False as the villain who framed it,' said Lady Margaret. 'Kneel down there, wretched woman, and swear that it is false,' said Buchanan; 'and remember that it is before your only son that you forswear yourself – before your God, that you deny the dreadful fact.'

Lady Margaret knelt with calm dignity, and upraising her eyes as if to heaven, prepared to take the terrible oath Buchanan had required. 'Pause,' he cried: 'I know it is true, and you shall not perjure yourself for me.' 'The story is invented for my ruin,' said Lady Margaret, eagerly. 'Believe your mother, / oh, Buchanan, and not the monster who would delude you. I can prove his words false. Will you only allow me time to do so? Who is this Viviani? Will you believe a wretch who dares not appear before me? Send for him: let him be confronted with me instantly: I fear not Viviani. To connect murder with the name of a parent is terrible – to see an executioner in an only son is worse.' 'There are fearful witnesses against you.' 'I dare oppose them all.' 'Oh, my mother, beware.' 'Hear me, Buchanan. Leave me not. It is a mother kneels before you. Whatever my crime before God, do you have compassion. I am innocent – Viviani is. . . .' 'Is what?' 'Is false. I am innocent. Look at me, my son. Oh, leave me not thus. See, see if there is murder in this countenance. Oh, hear me, my boy, my William. It is the voice of a mother calls to you, as from the grave.' /

Buchanan was inexorable. He left her. – He fled. – She followed, clinging to him, to the door. – She held his hand to her bosom: she clasped it in agony. He fled: and she fell senseless before him. Still he paused not; but rushing from her presence, sought Viviani, who had promised to meet him in the forest. To his infinite surprise, in his place he met Glenarvon. 'The Italian will not venture here,' said the latter; 'but I know all. Has she confessed?' 'She denies every syllable of the accusation,' said Buchanan; 'and in a manner so firm, so convincing, that it has made me doubt. If what he has written is false, this monster, this Viviani, shall deeply answer for it. I must have proof – instant, positive proof. Who is this Viviani?[a] Wherefore did he seek me by mysterious letters and messages, if he dares not meet me face to face? I will have proof.' 'It will be difficult to obtain positive proof,' said Glenarvon. / 'La Crusca, who alone knows, besides myself and Viviani, this horrid secret[a] is under the protection of my cousin de Ruthven. How far he is acquainted with the murder I know not; but he fears me, and he dares not openly oppose me. Lady Margaret has proved her innocence to him likewise,' he continued smiling bitterly; 'but there is yet one other witness.' – 'Who, where?' 'The boy himself.' 'Perhaps this is all a plot to ruin my wretched mother,' said Buchanan. 'I shall have it brought to light.' 'And your mother publicly exposed?' 'If she is guilty, let her be brought to shame.' 'And yourself to ruin,' said Glenarvon. 'To ruin unutterable.'

They arrived at Belfont, whilst thus conversing. The evening was dark. They had taken a room at the inn. Glenarvon enquired of some around him, if Colonel St. Alvin were at the abbey. He was informed that he was / at Colwood Bay. 'Ask them now,' said Glenarvon in a whisper, 'concerning me.' Buchanan did so, and heard that Lord Glenarvon had taken ship for England that morning, had abandoned his followers, and received a bribe for his treachery from the English court. The people spoke of him with much execration. Glenarvon smiling at their warmth: 'This was your idol yesterday: to-morrow,' he continued, 'I will give you another.' As soon as Buchanan had retired to his room, as he said, to repose himself, for he had not closed his eyes since he had left England, his companion, wrapping himself within his cloak, stole out unperceived from the inn, and walked to St. Alvin Priory. /

CHAPTER XXV.

SHORTLY after Buchanan's departure, Lady Margaret had recovered from her indisposition. She was tranquil, and had retired early to rest. The next morning she was in her brother's apartment, when a servant entered with a letter. 'There is a gentleman below who wishes to speak with your grace.' 'What is his name?' 'I know not, my lord; he would not inform me.' The duke opened the letter. It was from M. De Ruthven,[a] who entreated permission to have a few moments conversation with the duke, as a secret of the utmost importance had been communicated to him that night:[b] but it was of the most serious consequence that Lady Margaret Buchanan should be kept in ignorance / of the appeal. The name was written in large characters, as if to place particular emphasis upon it; and as unfortunately she was in her brother's apartment at the moment the letter was delivered, it was extremely difficult for him to conceal from her its contents, or the agitation so singular and mysterious a communication had caused him.

Lady Margaret's penetrating eye observed in a moment that something unusual had occurred; but whilst yet commanding herself, that she might not shew her suspicions to her brother, Mac Allain entered, and giving the duke a small packet, whispered to him that the gentleman could not wait, but begged his grace would peruse those papers, and he would call again. 'Sister,' said the duke, rising, 'you will excuse. Good God! what do I see? What is the matter?' Lady Margaret had arisen from her seat: – the hue of death had overspread her lips and cheeks: – yet calm in the midst / of the most agonizing suspense, she gave no other sign of the terror under which she laboured. Kindly approaching, he took her hand.

'That packet of letters is for me,' she said in a firm low voice. 'The superscription bears my name,' said the duke, hesitating. 'Yet if – if by any mistake – any negligence –' – 'There is no mistake, my lord,' said the servant advancing. 'Leave us,' cried Lady Margaret, with a voice that resounded throughout the apartment; and then again faltering, and fainting at the effort, she continued: 'Those letters are mine: – my enemy and your's has betrayed them: – Viviani may exhibit the weakness and folly of a woman's heart to gratify his revenge; but a generous brother should disdain to make himself the instrument of his barbarous, his unmanly cruelty.' 'Take them, 'said the duke, with gentleness: 'I would not read them for the world's worth. / That heart is noble and generous, whatever its errors; and no letters could ever make me think ill of my sister.'

Lady Margaret trembled exceedingly. 'They wish to ruin me,' she cried – 'to tear me from your affection – to make you think me black – to accuse me, not of weakness, brother, but of crimes.' – 'Were they to bring such evidences, that the very eye itself could see their testimony, I would disbelieve my senses, before I could mistrust you. Look then calm and happy, my sister. We have all of us faults; the best of us is no miracle of worth; and the gallantries of one, as fair, as young, as early exposed to temptation as you were, deserve no such severity. Come, take the detested packet, and throw it into the flames.' – 'It is of no gallantry that I am accused; no weakness, Altamonte; it is of murder!' The duke started. 'Aye, brother, of the murder of an infant.' He smiled, 'Smile too, when I say further – of the / murder of your child.' – 'Of Calantha!' he cried in agitation. 'Of an infant, I tell you; of the heir of Delaval.'

'Great God! have I lived to hear that wretches exist, barbarous, atrocious enough, thus to accuse you? Name them, that my arm may avenge you – name them, dearest Margaret; and, by heavens, I will stand your defender, and at once silence them.' 'Oh, more than this: they have produced an impostor – a child, brother – an Italian boy, whose likeness to your family I have often marked.' 'Zerbellini?' 'The same.' 'Poor contrivance to vent their rage and malice! But did I not ever tell you, my dearest Margaret, that Gondimar, and that mysterious Viviani, whom you protected, bore an ill character. They were men unknown, without family, without principle, or honour.' 'Brother,' said Lady Margaret, 'give me your hand: swear to me that you know / and love me enough to discredit at once the whole of this: swear to me, Altamonte, that without proving their falsehood, you despise the wretches who have resolved to ruin your sister.'

The duke now took a solemn oath, laying his hand upon her's, that he never could, never would harbour one thought of such a nature. He even smiled at its absurdity; and he refused to see either the stranger, or to read the packet – when Lady Margaret, falling back in a hollow and hysteric laugh, bade him tear from his heart the fond, the doating simplicity that beguiled him: – 'They utter that which is true,' she cried. 'I am that which they have said.' She then rushed from the room.

The duke, amazed, uncertain what to believe or doubt, opened the packet of letters, and read as follows: –

'My gracious and much injured patron, Lord Glenarvon's departure, / whilst it leaves me again unprotected, leaves me also at liberty to act as I think right. Supported by the kindness of Colonel de Ruthven, I am emboldened now to ask an immediate audience with the Duke of Altamonte. Circumstances preclude my venturing to the castle: – the enemy of my life is in wait for me[a] – The Count Viviani and his agents watch for me by night and by day. Lady Margaret Buchanan, with Lord Glenarvon's assistance, has rescued the young Marquis of Delaval from his perfidious hands; but we have been long obliged to keep him a close prisoner at Belfont Abbey, in order to preserve him from his persecutors. My Lord Glenarvon sailed yesternoon, and commended myself and the marquis to the colonel's care. We were removed last night from St. Alvin's to Colwood Bay, where we await in anxious hope of being admitted into the Duke of Altamonte's presence. / This is written by the most guilty and miserable servant of the Duke of Altamonte.

'ANDREW MACPHERSON.'

'Thanks be to God,' cried the duke, 'my sister is innocent; and the meaning of this will be soon explained.' The remainder of the packet consisted of letters – many of them in the hand-writing of Lady Margaret, many in that of Glenarvon: some were dated Naples, and consisted of violent professions of love: the letters of a later date contained for the most part asseverations of innocence, and entreaties for secrecy and silence: and though worded with caution, continually alluded to some youthful boy, and to injuries and cruelties with which the duke was entirely unacquainted. In addition to these extraordinary papers, there were many of a treasonable nature, signed by the most considerable landholders and tenantry in the country. / But that which most of all excited the duke's curiosity, was a paper addressed to himself in Italian, imploring him, as he valued the prosperity of his family, and every future hope, not to attend to the words of Macpherson, who was in the pay of Lord Glenarvon, and acting under his commands; but to hasten to St. Alvin's Priory, when a tale of horror should be disclosed to his wondering ears, and a treasure of inconceivable value be replaced in his hands. /

CHAPTER XXVI.

So many strange asseverations, and so many inconsistencies, could only excite doubt, astonishment, and suspicion; when Lady Margaret, re-entering the apartment, asked her brother in a voice of excessive agitation, whether he would go with Colonel de Ruthven, who had called for him? And without leaving him time to answer, implored that he would not. 'Your earnestness to dissuade me is somewhat precipitate – your looks – your agitation....' 'Oh, Altamonte, the time is past for concealment, go not to your enemies to hear a tale of falsehood and horror. I, whom you have loved, sheltered, and protected, I, your own, your only sister, have told it you – will tell it you further; but before I make / my brother loathe me – oh, God! before I open my heart's black secrets to your eyes, give me your hand. Let me look at you once more. Can I have strength to endure it? Yes, sooner than suffer these vile slanderers to triumph, what dare I not endure!

'I am about to unfold a dreadful mystery, which may no longer be concealed. I come to accuse myself of the blackest of crimes.' 'This is no time for explanation,' said the duke. 'Yet hear me; for I require, I expect no mercy at your hands. You have been to me the best of brothers – the kindest of friends. Learn by the confession I am now going to make, in what manner I have requited you.' Lady Margaret rose from her chair at these words, and shewed strong signs of the deep agitation of mind under which she laboured. Endeavouring not to meet the eyes of the duke, 'You received me,' she continued, in a hurried manner, 'when my character was lost / and I appeared but as a foul blot to sully the innocence and purity of one who ever considered me and treated me as a sister. My son, for whom I sacrificed every natural feeling – my son you received as your child, and bade me look upon as your heir. Tremble as I communicate the rest.

'An unwelcome stranger appeared in a little time to supplant him. Ambition and envy, moving me to the dreadful deed, I thought by one blow to crush his hopes, and to place my own beyond the power of fortune.' 'Oh, Margaret! pause – do not, do not continue – I was not prepared for this. Give me a moments time – I cannot bear it now.' Lady Margaret, unmoved, continued. 'To die is the fate of all; and I would to God that some ruffian hand had extinguished my existence at the same tender age. But think not, Altamonte, that these hands are soiled with your / infant's blood. I only wished the deed – I durst not do it.

'I will not dwell upon a horrid scene which you remember full well. There is but one on earth capable of executing such a crime: he loved your sister; and to possess this heart, he destroyed your child. – How he destroyed him I know not. We saw the boy, cold, even in death – we wept over him: and now, upon plea of some petty vengeance, because I will not permit him to draw me further into his base purposes, he is resolved to make this scene of blood and iniquity public to the world. He has already betrayed me to a relentless son; and he now means to bring forward an impostor in the place of your murdered infant!' – 'Who will do this?' – 'Viviani; Viviani himself will produce him before your eyes.' 'Would to God that he might do so!' cried the duke, gazing with pity and horror on the fine / but fallen creature who stood before him.

'I have not that strength,' he continued, 'you, of all living mortals, seem alone to possess. – My thoughts are disturbed. – I know not what to think, or how to act. You overwhelm me at once: and your very presence takes from me all power of reflection. Leave me, therefore.' 'Never, till I have your promise. I fear you: I know by your look, that you are resolved to see my enemy – to hear.' 'Margaret, I will hear you to-morrow.' 'No to-morrow shall ever see us two again together.' 'In an hour I will speak with you again – one word.' – As he said this, the duke arose: and seizing her fiercely by the arm: 'Answer but this – do you believe the boy this Viviani will produce?[a] – do you think it possible?[b] – answer me, Margaret, and I will pardon all – do you think the boy is my long lost child?' 'Have no such hope; he is dead. Did / we not ourselves behold him? Did we not look upon his cold and lifeless corpse?' 'Too true, my sister.' 'Then fear not: Buchanan shall not be defrauded.' 'It is not for Buchanan that I speak: he is lost to me: I have no son.' 'But I would not have you fall a prey to the miserable arts of this wretch. Beware of Viviani – remember that still I am your sister: and now, for the last time, I warn you, go not to Colwood Bay; for if you do. . . .' 'What then?' 'You seal your sister's death.' As she uttered these words. Lady Margaret looked upon the duke in agony, and retired. /

CHAPTER XXVII.

THE duke continued many moments on the spot where she had left him, without lifting his eyes from the ground – without moving, or speaking, or giving the smallest sign of the deep feelings by which he was overpowered; when suddenly Lord Glenarvon was announced.

The duke started back: – he would have denied him his presence. It was too late: – Glenarvon was already in the room. The cold dews stood upon his forehead; his eye was fixed; his air was wild. 'I am come to restore your son,' he said, addressing the duke. 'Are you prepared for my visit? Has Lady Margaret obeyed my command, and confessed?' 'I thought,' said the duke, 'that you had left Ireland. For your / presence at this moment, my lord, I was not prepared.' 'Whom does Lady Margaret accuse?' said Lord Glenarvon tremulously. 'One whom I know not,' said the duke – 'Viviani.' Glenarvon's countenance changed, as with a look of exultation and malice he repeated: – 'Yes, it is Viviani.' He then briefly stated that Count Gondimar, having accompanied Lady Margaret from Italy to Ireland in the year – had concealed under a variety of disguises a young Italian, by name Viviani. To him the charge of murdering the heir of Delaval was assigned; but he disdained an act so horrible and base. La Crusca, a wretch trained in Viviani's service, could answer for himself as to the means he took to deceive the family. Lord Glenarvon knew nothing of his proceedings: he alone knew, he said, that the real Marquis of Delaval was taken to Italy, whence Gondimar, by order of Viviani some years afterwards, brought him to England, presenting / him to Lady Avondale as her page.

In corroboration of these facts, he was ready to appeal to Gondimar, and some others, who knew of the transaction. Gondimar, however, Lord Glenarvon acknowledged, was but a partial witness, having been kept in ignorance as to the material part of this affair, and having been informed by Lady Margaret that Zerbellini, the page, was in reality her son. It was upon this account that, in the spring of the year,[a] suddenly mistrusting Viviani, Lady Margaret entreated Count Gondimar to take the boy back with him to Italy; and not being able to succeed in her stratagems, on account of himself (Glenarvon) being watchful of her, she had basely worked upon the child's feelings, making him suppose he was serving Calantha by hiding her necklace from his (Lord Glenarvon's) pursuit. On which false accusation of / theft, they had got the boy sent^a from the castle.

Lord Glenarvon then briefly stated, that he had rescued him from Gondimar's hands, with the assistance of a servant named Macpherson, and some of his followers; and that ever since he had kept him concealed at the priory. 'And where is he at this time?' said the duke. – 'He was with Lord Glenarvon's cousin, Colonel de Ruthven, at Colwood Bay.' – 'And when could the duke speak with Viviani?' – 'When it was his pleasure.' 'That night?' – 'Yes, even on that very night.' – 'What witness could Lord Glenarvon bring, as to the truth of this account, besides Viviani?' – 'La Crusca, an Italian, from whom Macpherson had received the child when in Italy – La Crusca the guilty instrument of Viviani's crimes.' – 'And where was La Crusca?' – 'Madness had fallen on him after the child had been taken from him / by Viviani's orders: he had returned in company with Macpherson to Ireland. Lord Glenarvon had offered him an asylum at his castle. Lady Margaret one day had beheld him; and Gondimar had even fainted upon seeing him suddenly, having repeatedly been assured that he was dead.' – 'By whom was he informed that he was dead?' – 'By Lady Margaret and Viviani.' – 'Was Gondimar then aware of this secret?' – 'No; but of other secrets, in which La Crusca and Viviani were concerned, equally horrible perhaps, but not material now to name.'

This conversation having ended, the duke ordered his carriage, and prepared to drive to Colwood Bay. Lord Glenarvon promised in a few hours to meet him there, and bring with him Viviani. 'If he restore my child, and confesses every thing,' said the duke, before he left Lord Glenarvon, 'pray inform him, that I will promise him a pardon.' 'He values not such promise,' said Glenarvon / scornfully. 'Lady Margaret's life and honour are in his power. Viviani can confer favours, but not receive them.' The duke started, and looked full in the face of Glenarvon. 'Who is this Viviani?' he said, in a tone of voice loud and terrible. 'An idol,' replied Glenarvon, 'whom the multitude have set up for themselves, and worshipped, forsaking their true faith, to follow after a false light – a man who is in love with crime and baseness – one, of whom it has been said, that he hath an imagination of fire playing around a heart of ice – one whom the never-dying worm feeds on by night and day – a hypocrite,'[31] continued Glenarvon, with a smile of bitterness, 'who wears a mask to his friends, and defeats his enemies by his unexpected sincerity – a coward, with more of bravery than some who fear nothing; for, even in his utmost terror, he defies that which he fears.' 'And where is this wretch?' said the / duke: 'what dungeon is black enough to hold him? What rack has been prepared to punish him for his crimes?' 'He is as I have said,' replied Glenarvon triumphantly, 'the idol of the fair, and the great. Is it virtue that women prize? Is it honour and renown they worship? Throw but the dazzling light of genius upon baseness, and corruption, and every crime will be to them but an additional charm.'

'Glenarvon,' said the duke gravely,[a] 'you have done me much wrong; but I mean not now to reproach you. If the story which you have told me is true, I must still remember that I owe my son's safety to you. Spare Lady Margaret; keep the promise you have solemnly given me; and at the hour you have mentioned, meet me with the Italian and this boy at Colwood Bay.' Glenarvon left the presence of the duke immediately, bowing in token of assent. The Duke then rang the bell, and ordered / his carriage. It was about four in the afternoon when he left the castle: he sent a message to Lady Margaret and Mrs. Seymour, to say that he had ordered dinner to await his return at seven. /

CHAPTER XXVIII.

No sooner had the duke, accompanied by Macpherson, who waited for him, left the castle, than Mrs. Seymour sought Lady Margaret in her apartment. The door was fastened from within: – it was in vain she endeavoured by repeated calls to obtain an answer,[a] – a strange fear occurred to her mind. – There were rumours abroad, of which she was not wholly ignorant. Was it credible that a sudden paroxysm of despair had led her to the last desperate measure of frantic woe? The God of mercy forbid! Still she felt greatly alarmed. The duke returned not, as he had promised: the silence of the castle was mournful; and terror seemed to have spread itself amongst all the inhabitants. Mac Allain / entered repeatedly, asking Mrs. Seymour if the duke were not to have returned at the hour of dinner; and whether it was true that he was gone out alone. Eight, nine, and ten sounded; but he came not.

Mac Allain was yet speaking, when shrieks, long and repeated, were heard. The doors burst open; servants affrighted entered; confusion and terror were apparent in all. 'They are come, they are come!' exclaimed one. 'We are going to be murdered. The rebels have broken into the park and gardens: we hear their cry. Oh, save us – save us from their fury! See, see, through the casement you may behold them: with their pikes and their bayonets, they are destroying every thing they approach.' Mac Allain threw up the sash of the window: the servants crowded towards it. The men had seized whatever arms they could find: the women wept aloud. By the light of the moon, crowds were / seen advancing through the wood and park, giving the alarm by one loud and terrific yell. They repeated one word more frequently than any other. As they approached, it was plainly distinguished: – murder! murder! was the cry; and the inhabitants of the castle heard it as a summons to instant death. The Count Viviani's name and Lady Margaret's were then wildly repeated. The doors were in vain barricadoed and defended from within. The outer courts were so tumultuously crowded, that it became dangerous to pass. Loud cries for the duke to appear were heard.

A rumour that the heir of Delaval was alive had been circulated – that blood had been spilt. 'Let us see our young lord, long life to him!' was shouted in transports of ecstasy by the crowd; whilst yells of execration mingled against his persecutor and oppressor. 'Return: shew yourself to your own people: no ruffian hand shall dare to harm you. / Long life to our prince, and our king!' – Suddenly a bugle horn from a distance sounded. Three times it sounded; and the silence became as general as the tumult previously had been. In the space of a few moments, the whole of the crowd dispersed; and the castle was again left to loneliness and terror.

The inhabitants scarcely ventured to draw their breath. The melancholy howling of the watch-dogs alone was heard. Mrs. Seymour, who had shewn a calm fortitude in the hour of danger, now sickened with despondency. 'Some direful calamity has fallen upon this house. The hand of God is heavy upon us.' She prayed to that Being who alone can give support: and calm and resigned, she awaited the event. It was past three, and no news of the Duke. She then summoned Mac Allain, and proposing to him that he should arm himself and some others, she sent them forth in quest of their master. They / went; and till their return, she remained in dreadful suspense. Lady Margaret's door being still locked, she had it forced; but no one was there. It appeared she had gone out alone, possibly in quest of her brother. /

CHAPTER XXIX.

WHEN the duke arrived at Colwood Bay, he found Colonel de Ruthven prepared to receive him; but was surprised and alarmed at hearing that Lord Glenarvon had that very morning sent for Zerbellini, and neither himself nor the boy had been seen since. The duke then informed the colonel that Lord Glenarvon had been at the castle about an hour since; but this only made the circumstance of his having taken away the child more extraordinary. It was also singular that Lord Glenarvon had paid for his passage[a] the night before, and had taken leave of his friends, as if at that moment preparing to sail: his presence at the castle was, however, a full answer to the latter report: and whilst every / enquiry was set on foot to trace whither he could be gone, the duke requested permission of the colonel himself to examine the maniac La Crusca and Macpherson: the former was still at St. Alvin Priory – the latter immediately obeyed the summons, and prepared to answer every question that was put to him.

The duke first enquired of this man his name, and the principal events of his life. Macpherson, in answer to these interrogations, affirmed, that he was a native of Ireland; that he had been taken a boy into the service of the late Countess of Glenarvon, and had been one of the few who had followed her into Italy; that after this he had accompanied her son, the young earl, through many changes of life and fortune; but having been suddenly dismissed from his service, be had lost sight of him for above a year; during which time he had taken into his pay a desperado, named La / Crusca, who had continued with him whilst be resided at Florence.

After this, Macpherson hesitated, evaded, and appeared confused; but suddenly recollecting himself: 'I then became acquainted,' he said, 'with the Count Viviani, a young Venetian, who took me immediately into his service, and who, residing for the most part in the palace belonging to Lady Margaret at Naples, passed his time in every excess of dissipation and amusement which that town afforded. In the spring of the year, the count accompanied Lady Margaret secretly to Ireland, and, after much conversation with me, and many remonstrances on my part, gave me a positive command to carry off the infant Marquis of Delaval, but to spare his life. He menaced me with employing La Crusca in a more bloody work, if I hesitated; and, having offered an immense bribe, interest, affection for himself, and fear, / induced me to obey. My daughter,' continued Macpherson, 'was in the power of the count: – she had listened too readily to his suit. "I will expose her to the world – I will send her forth unprovided," he said, "if you betray me, or refuse to obey."'

'No excuses,' cried the duke, fiercely: 'proceed. It is sufficient you willed the crime. Now tell me how amongst you you achieved it.' 'I must be circumstantial in my narrative,' said Macpherson; 'and since your grace has the condescension to hear me, you must hear all with patience; and first, the Count Viviani did not slay the Lord of Delaval: he did not employ me in that horrid act. I think no bribe or menace could have engaged me to perform it: but a strange, a wild idea, occurred to him as he passed with me through Wales, in our journey hither; and months and months succeeded, before it was in my power to execute his commands. / He sent me on a fruitless search,[a] to discover an infant who in any degree might resemble the little marquis. Having given up the pursuit as impossible, I returned to inform the count of the failure of his project. A double reward was proffered, and I set forth again, scarce knowing the extent of his wishes, scarce daring to think upon the crime I was about to commit.

'It is useless to detail my adventures, but they are true. I can bring many undoubted witnesses of their truth: and there yet lives an unhappy mother, a lonely widow, to recount them. It was one accursed night, when the dæmons of hell thought fit to assist their agent – after having travelled far, I stopt[b] at an inn by the road-side, in the village[c] of Maryvale, in the County of Tyrone. I called for a horse; my own was worn out with fatigue: I alighted, and drank deep of the spirits that were brought me, for they drove away all disturbing thoughts: / – but, as I lifted the cup a second time to my lips, my eyes fixed themselves upon a child; and I trembled with agitation, for I saw my prey before me. The woman of the house spoke but little English; but she approached me, and expressed her fear that I was not well. Sensible that my emotion had betrayed me, I affected to be in pain, offered her money, and abruptly took leave. There was a wood not far from the town.

'On a subsequent evening I allured her to it: the baby was at her breast. I asked her its name. – 'Billy Kendal,'[32] she answered, 'for the love of its father who fights now for us at a distance.' 'I will be its father,' I said. But she chid me from her, and was angrily about to leave me: striking her to the earth, I seized the child. The age, the size – every thing corresponded. I had bartered my soul for gold, and difficulties and failures had not shaken me. I had made every necessary preparation; and / all being ready and secure, I fled; nor stopped, nor staid, nor spoke to man, nor shewed myself in village or in town, till I arrived at my journey's end.'

I arrived in the neighbourhood of Castle Delaval, and continued to see my master, without being recognized by any other. He appeared much agitated when he first beheld me. I cannot forget his smile. He desired me to keep the boy with me out at sea that night; and directing me to climb from the wherry[33] up the steep path of the western cliff (where but yesterday I stood when the colonel sent for me), he promised to place food, and all that was requisite for us, near the chapel. 'But trust no one with your secret,' he said: 'let not the eye of man glance upon you. Meet me in the night, in the forest near the moor, and bring the child. Mind that *you* do not utter one word, and let *it* not have the power of disturbing us. Do you understand me?' / 'Yes,' I said, and shuddered because I did so. My master saw me shrink, and reminded me of the reward. I undertook punctually to fulfil every injunction: it was now too late to repent. But, oh, my lord! when I think of that night, that accursed night, what horror comes over me!

'It was past twelve o'clock when I took the boy up from a sweet sleep, and fastening the wherry near the foot of the rock, with one hand I climbed the steep ascent, while with the other I carefully held the child. In one part the cliff is almost perpendicular: my foot slipped, and I was in danger of falling; but I recovered myself with much exertion. There was no moon; and the wind whistled loud and shrilly through the churchyard. It is, I believe, two miles from thence to the castle; but through the thick wood I now and then caught a glimpse of its lighted portico; and, remembering its former gaiety, 'you rejoice / to-night,' I thought, 'with music and dancing, regardless of my sorrows, or the hardships of others, even more wretched than I: but to-morrow, the black foot of care shall tread heavy even upon you.'

'The wind rustled among the trees. This was the spot in which I was to meet my employer. I heard a step; it approached; and I pressed the child nearer to my bosom. 'Some mother is weeping for you surely,[a] little boy,' I said; 'and would give all she is worth to see that pretty face again. She little dreams of your hard fate, or into what rough hands her treasure has fallen; but I will not harm thee, boy. Hard must be the heart that could.' Such were my thoughts: God be witness, such were my intentions at that moment. I now saw La Crusca; and well I knew by the villain's countenance his horrible intentions: the lantern he carried glimmered / through the trees;[b] his eyes glared as in a low voice he enquired for the boy: and, as he was still concealed from him under my cloak, he seized me by the arm, and asked me why I trembled. He urged me instantly to deliver the child to him; but finding that I hesitated, he rudely grasped him; and the boy waking suddenly, cried aloud. 'Did not our master tell you to prevent this?' said the Italian, enraged, as, bidding the child be at peace, he abruptly fled with it. I heard not long after one piteous shriek, and then all was silent.

'I returned to the boat. All there looked desolate. The little companion who had cheered the lonely hours was no more. The mantle remained. I threw myself upon it. Suddenly, upon the waves I thought I saw the figure of the child. I heard its last cry. I ever hear that piteous cry. The night was dark: the[c] winds blew chilly over the vast water: / my own name was pronounced in a low voice from the cliff.

'It was my lord who spoke, – my master[a] – the Count Viviani. He had returned to give me further instructions. I ascended the fearful steep, and listened in silence; but, before he left me, I ventured to ask after the boy, 'Leave him to me,' said the count, in an angry tone. 'He is safe: he shall sleep well tonight.' Saying this, he laughed. 'O! can you jest?' I said. 'Aye, that I can. This is the season of jesting,' he answered; 'for, mark my words, Macpherson, we have done a deed shall mar our future merriment, and stifle the heart's laugh for ever. Such deeds as these bleach the hair white before its time, give fearful tremblings to the limbs, and make man turn from the voice of comfort on the bed of death. We have sent a cherub thither,' continued the count, pointing up to heaven, 'to / stand a fearful testimony against us, and exclude us for ever from its courts.'

'Saying which, he bade me hasten to some distant country. He entrusted the Lord of Delaval to my care,[34] repeated his instructions, and for the second time that night departed. The morning sun, when it rose, all glorious, and lighted the eastern sky with its beams, found me still motionless upon the cliff. My eye involuntarily fixed upon the great land-mark, the mountains which extend behind yon beautiful valley; but, starting at the thought of the crime I had committed, I turned for ever from them. I thought never again to behold a prospect so little in unison with my feelings. It is many years since I have seen it; but now I can gaze on nothing else. My eyes are dim with looking upon the scene, and with it upon the memory of the past.'

Macpherson paused: – He turned to see what impression his narrative had made on the duke: he was utterly / silent. – Macpherson therefore continued: 'So far we had succeeded but too well in our black attempt; but the fair boy intrusted to me sickened under the hardships to which I was obliged to expose him. The price agreed on was paid me. La Crusca joined me; and together we reared the child in a foreign country, so as I hope to do him honour. But a dark malady at times had fallen upon La Crusca. He would see visions of horror; and the sight of a mother and a child threw him into frenzy, till it became necessary to confine him. I had not heard for some time from my master. I wished to bring my young charge back to his own country, before I died. I wrote; but no one answered my letters.[b] I applied to the Count Gondimar; but he refused to hear me.

'In the dead of night, however, even when I slept, the child was torn from me. I was at Florence, when some villain seized the boy. I had[c] assumed / another name:[d] I lived apparently in happiness and affluence. I think it was the Count Gondimar who rifled my treasure. But he denied it.[e35]

'Accompanied by La Crusca, I returned first to England and then to Ireland. I sought Count Gondimar; but he evaded my enquiries; and having taken the child from me, insisted upon my silence, and dispatched me to Ireland with letters for the Lord Glenarvon, who immediately recognized and received me.' 'Where?' cried the duke. Macpherson hesitated. – 'At the priory, where he then resided, and where he remained; concealed: La Crusca was likewise permitted to dwell there; but of this story my lord was ignorant till now.' 'That is false,' said the duke. 'One morning La Crusca beheld Lady Margaret even as in a vision, on that spot to which I every day returned; but he had not power to speak. Madness, phrenzy[a] had fallen on him. Lord Glenarvon protected him. His / house was also my only refuge. He gathered from me much of the truth of what I have related, but I never told him all. I durst not speak till now. He was deeply moved with the wrongs of the injured boy; he vowed to revenge them; but he has forgotten his promise; he has left us, he has forsaken us. I am now in the service of another: this gentleman will befriend me; and the Duke of Altamonte will not turn from the voice of his miserable servant.'

'Where?' said the duke starting, 'where did you say Viviani, that damned Italian, had once concealed the child? He is there now perhaps! there, there let us seek him.' – 'In the chapel,' said Macpherson hesitating, 'there is a vault, of which he retains the key; and there is a chamber in the ruined turret, where I have oft-times passed the night.' 'Let us hasten there this instant,' said the duke. – 'What hour is it?' 'Nine.' 'Oh! that it may not be too late! that he / may not already have taken advantage of the darkness of evening to escape!' Saying this, the duke and Colonel de Ruthven having previously given orders to the servants to watch Macpherson carefully, drove with all possible haste to the chapel, near the Abbey of Belfont. But still they hoped that Viviani was their friend – He could have no motive in concealing the child: his only wish was probably to restore him, and by this means make terms for himself. With such thoughts they proceeded to the appointed spot. And it is there that for some moments we must leave them. The duke was convinced in his own mind who his real and sole enemy was; he was also firmly resolved not to let him escape.[b36] /

CHAPTER XXX.

Viviani had long and repeatedly menaced Lady Margaret with vengeance. In every moment of resentment, on every new interview, at every parting scene, revenge, immediate and desperate, was the cry; but it had been so often repeated, and so often had proved a harmless threat, that it had at length lost all effect upon her. She considered him as a depraved and weak character – base enough to attempt the worst; but too cowardly to carry his project into effect. She knew him not. That strong, that maddening passion which had taken such deep root in his soul, still at times continued to plead for her; and whilst hope, however fallacious, could be cherished by him, he would not at once crush her beyond / recovery. A lesser vengeance had not gratified the rage of his bosom; and the certainty that the menaced blow when it fell would overwhelm them both in one fate, gave him malignant consolation.

Her renewed intercourse with Lord Dartford, he had endured. Lord Dartford had prior claims to himself; and though it tortured him to see them in each other's society, he still forbore: but when he saw that he was the mere object of her hate, of her ridicule, of her contempt, his fury was beyond all controul. He wrote to her, he menaced her; he left her, he returned; but he felt his own little importance in the unprovoked calm with which she at all times received him: and maddening beyond endurance, 'This is the moment,' he cried: 'now, now I have strength to execute my threats, and nothing shall change me.'

It was in London that Count Viviani, having left Lady Margaret in anger, addressed / Buchanan by letter. 'Leave your steeds, and your gaming tables, and your libertine associates,' he said. 'Senseless and heartless man, awake at last. Oh! you who have never felt, whose pulse has never risen with the burning fires of passion, whose life, unvaried and even, has ever flowed the same – awake now to the bitterness of horror, and learn that you are in my power.' Buchanan heard the tale with incredulity; but when obliged to credit it, he felt with all the poignancy of real misery. The scene that took place between himself and his mother had left him yet one doubt: upon that doubt he rested. It was her solemn asseveration of innocence. But the heart that is utterly corrupted fears not to perjure itself; and he continued in suspense; for he believed her guilty.

Such was the state of things, when Viviani, having by fraud again possessed himself of Zerbellini, sought Lady Margaret, / and found her a few moments after the duke had left the castle. He well knew whither he was gone; he well knew also, that it was now too late to recall the vengeance he had decreed; yet one hope for Lady Margaret and himself remained: – would she fly with him upon that hour. *All* was prepared for flight in case he needed it; and with her, what perils would he not encounter. He entered the castle, much disguised: he made her the proposal; but she received it with disdain. One thing alone she wished to know; and that she solemnly enjoined him to confess to her: was Zerbellini the real heir of Delaval? – was she guiltless of the murder of her brother's child? 'You shall see him, speak with him,' said Viviani, 'if you will follow me as soon as the night is dark. I will conduct you to him, and your own eyes and ears shall be convinced.'

So saying, he left her to all the horrors / of her own black imagination; but, returning at the time appointed, he led her to the wood, telling her that the boy was concealed in an apartment of the turret, close to the chapel. Suddenly pausing, as he followed the path: – 'This is the very tree,' he cried, turning round, and looking upon her fiercely; 'yes, this is the spot upon which La Crusca shed the blood of an innocent for you.' 'Then the boy was really and inhumanly murdered,' said Lady Margaret, pale with horror at the thought, but still unappalled for herself. 'Yes, lady, and his blood be on your soul! Do you hope for mercy?' he cried, seizing her by the arm. 'Not from you.' 'Dare you appeal to heaven?' She would not answer. 'I must embrace thee here, lady, before we for ever part.' 'Monster!' said Lady Margaret, seeing[37] the dagger in his hand, as he placed his arm around her neck. 'I have already resolved that I will never survive public / infamy; therefore I fear you not; neither will I endure your menaces, nor your insulting and barbarous caresses. Trifle not with one who knows herself above you – who defies and derides your power. I dare to die.' And she gazed unawed at his closely locked fist. 'Stab here – stab to this heart, which, however lost and perverted, yet exists to execrate thy crimes, and to lament its own.' 'Die then – thus – thus,' said her enraged, her inhuman lover, as he struck the dagger, without daring to look where his too certain hand had plunged it. Lady Margaret shrunk not from the blow; but fixing her dying eyes reproachfully upon him, closed them not, even when the spirit of life was gone.

Her murderer stood before her, as if astonished at what he had dared to do. 'Lie there, thou bleeding victim,' he said, at length pausing to contemplate his bloody work. 'Thou hast thought it no wrong to violate thy faith – to make / a jest of the most sacred ties.[a] Men have been thy victims: now take the due reward of all thy wickedness. What art thou, that I should have idolized and gazed with rapture on that form? – something even more treacherous and perverted than myself. Upon thee, traitress, I revenge the wrongs of many; and when hereafter, creatures like thee, as fair, as false, advance into the world, prepared even from childhood to make a system of the arts of love, let them, amidst the new conquests upon which they are feeding their growing vanity, hear of thy fate and tremble.'

Saying these words, and flying with a rapid step, his dagger yet reeking with the blood of his victim, he entered the town of Belfont, at the entrance of which he met St. Clare, and a crowd of followers, returning from the last meeting at Inis Tara. 'Hasten to the castle,' he cried, addressing all who surrounded him; 'sound there the alarum; for / the heir of Altamonte is found; Lady Margaret Buchanan is murdered. – Hasten there, and call for the presence of the duke; then return and meet me at the chapel, and I will restore to your gaze your long forgotten and much injured lord.' The people in shouts re-echoed the mysterious words, but the darkness of evening prevented their seeing the horrid countenance of the wretch who addressed them. St. Clare alone recognised the murderer, and fled. Viviani then returned alone to the chapel. /

CHAPTER XXXI.

The carriage which had conveyed the Duke of Altamonte and Colonel De Ruthven from Colwood Bay could not proceed along that narrow path which led across the wood to the chapel; they were therefore compelled to alight; and, hastening on along the road with torches and attendants, they enquired repeatedly concerning the loud shouts and yells which echoed in every direction around them.

They were some[a] little distance from the chapel, when the duke paused in horror. – The moonlight shone upon the bank, at the entrance of the beech trees; and he there beheld the figure of a female as she lay extended upon the ground, covered with blood. Her own rash / hand, he thought, had perhaps destroyed her. He approached, – it was Lady Margaret! That proud spirit, which had so long supported itself, had burst its fetters. He gazed on her in surprise. – He stood a few moments in silence, as if it were some tragic representation he were called to look upon, in which he himself bore no part – some scene of horror, to which he had not been previously worked up, and which consequently had not power to affect him. Her face was scarce paler than usual; but there was a look of horror in her countenance, which disturbed its natural expression. In one hand, she had grasped the turf, as if the agony she had endured had caused a convulsive motion; the other was stained with blood, which had flowed with much violence. It was strange that the wound was between her right shoulder and her throat, and not immediately perceivable, as she had fallen back upon it: – it was more than strange, for it admitted little / doubt that the blow had not been inflicted by herself. Yet, if inhumanly murdered, where was he who had dared the deed? The duke knelt beside her: – he called to her; but all mortal aid was ineffectual.

The moon-beam played amidst the foliage of the trees, and lighted the plains around: – no trace of the assassin could be observed: – the loneliness of the scene was uninterrupted. A dark shadow now became visible upon the smooth surface of the green – was it the reflection of the tree – or was it a human form? It lengthened – it advanced from the thicket. The shapeless form advanced; and the heart of man sunk before its approach; for there is none who has looked upon the murderer of his kind without a feeling of alarm beyond that which fear creates. That black shapeless mass – that guilty trembling being, who, starting at his own shadow, slowly crept forward, then paused to listen – then advanced / with haste, and paused again, – now, standing upon the plain between the beech wood and the chapel, appeared like one dark solitary spot in the lonely scene.

The duke had concealed himself; but the indignant spirit within prompted him to follow the figure, indifferent to the fate that might await on his temerity. Much he thought that he knew him by his air and Italian cloak; but as his disguise had entirely shrouded his features, he could alone indulge his suspicions; and it was his interest to watch him unperceived. He, therefore, made sign to his attendants to conceal themselves in the wood; and alone, accompanied by Colonel De Ruthven, he followed towards the chapel. There the figure paused, and seemed to breathe with difficulty, slowly turning around to gaze if all were safe: – then, throwing his dark mantle back, shewed to the face of Heaven the grim and sallow visage of / despair – the glazed sunken eye of guilt – the bent cowering form of fear. – 'Zerbellini,' he cried, 'Zerbellini, come down. – Think me not your enemy – I am your real friend, your preserver. – Come down, my child. With all but a brother's tenderness, I wait for you.'

Arouzed by this signal, a window was opened from an apartment adjoining the cloister; and a boy, lovely in youth, mournfully answered the summons. 'O! my kind protector!' he said, 'I thought you had resolved to leave me to perish here. If, indeed, I am all you tell me – if you do not a second time deceive me, will you act by me as you ought? Will you restore me to my father?' The voice, though soft and melodious, sounded so tremulously sad, that it immediately awakened the deepest compassion, the strongest interest in the duke. He eagerly advanced forward. Colonel De Ruthven entreated him to remain a few moments longer concealed. He / wished to know Viviani's intention; and they were near enough to seize him at any time, if he attempted to escape.

They were concealed behind the projecting arch of the chapel; and whilst they beheld the scene, it was scarce possible that the Italian should so turn himself as to discover them. By the strong light of the moon, which stood all glorious and cloudless in the Heavens, and shone upon the agitated waves of the sea, the duke, though he could not yet see the face of the Italian, whose back was turned, beheld the features of Zerbellini – that countenance which had often excited a strange emotion in his bosom, and which now appealed forcibly to his heart, as claiming an alliance with him. Let then the ecstasy of his feelings be imagined, whilst still dubious, still involved in uncertainty and surprise. Viviani, having clasped the boy to his bosom, said in an impassioned voice these words: – 'Much injured child, / thou loveliest blossom, early nipped in the very spring-time of thy life, pardon thy murderer. Thou art the heir and lord of all that the pride of man can devise; yet victim to the ambition of a false and cruel woman, thou hast experienced the chastening rod of adversity, and art now prepared for the fate that awaits thee.

'Albert,' he continued, 'let me be the first to address thee by that name, canst thou forgive, say, canst thou forgive me?' 'I know as yet but imperfectly,' said the boy, 'what your conduct to me has been. At times I have trusted you as a friend, and considered you as a master.' 'This is no time, my dear boy, for explanations – are you prepared? At least, embrace the wretch who has betrayed you. Let these tainted and polluted lips impress one last fond kiss upon thy cheek of rose, fair opening blossom, whose young heart, spotless as that of cherubims on high, has early felt / the pressure of calamity. Smile yet once on me, even as in sleep I saw thee smile, when, cradled in princely luxury, the world before thee, I hurled thee from the vanities of life, and saved thy soul. Boy of my fondest interest, come to my heart, and with thy angel purity snatch the fell murderer from perdition. Then, when we sleep thus clasped together, in the bands of death, ascend, fair and unpolluted soul, ascend in white-robed innocence to Heaven, and ask for mercy of thy God for me!'

'Wretch!' cried the duke, rushing forward: – but in vain his haste. With the strength of desperate guilt, the Italian had grasped the boy, and bearing him in sudden haste to the edge of the frightful chasm, he was on the point of throwing himself and the child from the top of it, when the duke, with a strong grasp, seizing him by the cloak, forcibly detained him. – 'Wretch,' he cried, 'live to feel a father's vengeance! – live to....' / 'To restore your son,' said Glenarvon, with a hypocritical smile, turning round and gazing on the duke. 'Ha, whom do I behold! no Italian, no Viviani, but Glenarvon.' 'Yes, and to me, to me alone, you owe the safety of your child. Your sister decreed his death – I sav'd him. Now strike this bosom if you will.' – 'What are you? Who are you?' said the duke. 'Is it now alone that you know Glenarvon?' he replied with a sneer. 'I suspected this; but that name shall not save you.' – 'Nothing can save me,' said Glenarvon, mournfully. 'All hell is raging in my bosom. My brain is on fire. *You* cannot add to my calamities.' 'Why a second time attempt the life of my child?' 'Despair prompted me to the deed,' said Glenarvon, putting his hand to his head: 'all is not right here – madness has fallen on me.' 'Live, miserable sinner,' said the duke, looking upon him with contempt: 'you are too base / to die – I dare not raise my arm against you.' 'Yet I am defenceless,' said Glenarvon, with a bitter smile, throwing the dagger to the ground. 'Depart for ever from me,' said the duke – 'your presence here is terrible to all.'

Zerbellini now knelt before his father, who, straining him closely to his bosom, wept over him. – In a moment, yells and cries were heard; and a thousand torches illumined the wood. Some stood in horror to contemplate the murdered form of Lady Margaret; others, with shouts of triumph, conveyed the heir of Delaval to his home. Mrs. Seymour, Mac Allain, and others, received with transport the long lost boy: shouts of delight and cheers, long and repeated, proclaimed his return. The rumour of these events spread far and wide; the concourse of people who crowded around to hear and inquire, and see their young lord, was immense.

A mournful silence succeeded. Lady / Margaret's body was conveyed to the castle. Buchanan followed in hopeless grief: he prest the duke's hand; then rushed from his presence. He sought St. Clare. 'Where is Glenarvon?' he cried. 'In his blood, in his blood, I must revenge my own wrongs and a mother's death.' Glenarvon was gone. One only attendant had followed him, O'Kelly, who had prepared every thing for his flight. Upon that night they had made their escape, O'Kelly, either ignorant of his master's crimes, or willing to appear so, tried severely but faithful to the last. They sailed: they reached the English shore; and before the rumour of these events could have had time to spread, Glenarvon had taken the command of his ship, following with intent to join the British fleet, far away from his enemies and his friends.

Macpherson was immediately seized. He acknowledged that Lord Glenarvon, driven to the necessity of concealing / himself, had, with Lady Margaret and Count Gondimar's assistance, assumed the name of Viviani, until the time when he appeared in his own character at St. Alvin's[a] Priory. The rest of the confession he had privately made concerning the child was found to be true. Witnesses were called. The mother of Billy Kendall and La Crusca corroborated the fact. La Crusca and Macpherson received sentence of death. /

CHAPTER XXXII.

THE heart sometimes swells with a forethought of approaching dissolution; and Glenarvon, as he had cast many a homeward glance upon his own native mountains, knew that he beheld them for the last time. Turning with sadness towards them, 'Farewell to Ireland,' he cried; 'and may better hearts support her rights, and revenge her wrongs! I must away.' Arrived in England, he travelled in haste; nor paused till he gained the port in which his ship was stationed. He sailed in a fair frigate with a gallant crew, and no spirit amongst them was so light, and no heart appeared more brave. Yet he was ill in health; and some observed that he drank much, and oft, and that he started from his own thoughts; / then laughed and talked with eagerness, as if desirous to forget them. 'I shall die in this engagement,' he said, addressing his first lieutenant. 'Hardhead, I shall die; but I care not. Only this remember – whatever other ships may do, let the Emerald be first and last in action. This is Glenarvon's command. – Say, shall it be obeyed?'[38] – Upon the night[39] after Lord Glenarvon had made his escape from Ireland, and the heir of Delaval had been restored to his father, a stranger stood in the outer gates of St. Alvin Priory – It was the maniac La Crusca, denouncing woe, and woe upon Glenarvon. St. Clare marked him as she returned to the Wizzard's Glen, and, deeply agitated, prepared to meet her followers. It was late when the company were assembled. A flash of agony darted from her eyes, whilst with a forced smile, she informed them that Lord Glenarvon had disgraced himself for ever; and, lastly, had abandoned his country's cause. / 'Shame on the dastard!' exclaimed one. 'We'll burn his castle,' cried another. 'Let us delay no longer,' was murmured by all. 'There are false friends among us. This is the night for action. To-morrow – who can look beyond to-morrow?' 'Where is Cormac O'Leary?' said St. Clare. 'He has been bribed to forsake us.' 'Where is Cobb O'Connor?' 'He is appointed to a commission in the militia, but will serve us at the moment.'[a] 'Trust not the faithless varlet: they who take bribes deserve no trust.'

'Oh, God!' cried St. Clare indignantly; have I lived to see my country bleeding; and is there not one of her children firm by her to the last?' 'We are all united, all ready to stand, and die, for our liberty,' replied her eager followers. 'Lead on: the hour is at hand. At the given signal, hundreds, nay, thousands, in every part of the kingdom, shall rush at once to arms, and fight gallantly / for the rights of man. The blast of the horn shall echo through the mountains, and, like the lava in torrents of fire, we will pour down upon the tyrants who oppress us. Lead on, St. Clare: hearts of iron attend you. One soul unites us – one spirit actuates our desires: from the boundaries of the north, to the last southern point of the island, all await the signal.' 'Hear it kings and oppressors of the earth,' said St. Clare: 'hear it, and tremble on your thrones. It is the voice of the people, the voice of children you have trampled upon, and betrayed. What enemy is so deadly as an injured friend?'

Saying this, and rushing from the applause with which this meeting concluded, she turned to the topmost heights of Inis Tara, and gazed with melancholy upon the turrets of Belfont. Splendid was the setting ray of the sun upon the western wave: calm was the scene before her: and the evening breeze blew softly / around. Then placing herself near her harp, she struck for the last time its chords. Niel Carter and Tyrone had followed her. Buchanan, and de Ruthven, Glenarvon's cousin, stood by her side. 'Play again on thy harp the sweet sounds that are dear to me. Sing the songs[a] of other days,' he said 'Oh, look not sad, St. Clare: I never will abandon thee.' 'My name is branded with infamy,' she cried: 'dishonour and reproach assail me on every side. Black are the portals of hell – black are the fiends that await to seize my soul – but more black is the heart of iron that has betrayed me. Yet I will sing the song of the wild harper. I will sing for you the song of my own native land, of peace and joy, which never more must be mine.'

'Hark! what shriek of agony is that?' – 'I hear nothing.' 'It was his dying groan. – What means your altered brow, that hurried[b] look?' It was the / sudden inspiration of despair. Her eye fixed itself on distant space in wild alarm – her hair streamed – as in a low and hurried tone she thus exclaimed, whilst gazing on the blue vault of heaven:

> 'Curs'd be the fiend's detested art,
> Impress'd upon this breaking heart.
> Visions dark and dread I see.
> Chill'd is the life-blood in my breast.
> I cannot pause – I may not rest:
> I gaze upon futurity.
>
> 'My span of life is past, and gone:
> My breath is spent, my course is done.
> Oh! sound my lyre, one last sad strain!
> This hand shall wake thy chords no more.
> Thy sweetest notes were breath'd in vain:
> The spell that gave them power is o'er'.

'Dearest, what visions affright you?' said de Ruthven. 'When shall the wishes of the people be gratified? What sudden gloom darkens over your countenance?' said her astonished followers. 'Say, prophetess, what woe do you denounce / against the traitor?' In a low murmuring voice, turning to them, she answered:

> 'When turf and faggots crackling blaze;
> When fire and torch-lights dimly burn;
> When kine at morn refuse to graze,
> And the green leaf begins to turn;
> Then shall pain and sickness come,
> Storms abroad, and woes at home.
> When cocks are heard to crow at ev'n,
> And swallows slowly ply their wing;
> When home-bound ships from port are driv'n,
> And dolphins roll, and mermaids sing;
> Then shall pain and sickness come,
> Storms abroad, and woes at home.
> When the black ox shall tread with his foot
> On the green growing saplin's tender root;
> Then a stranger shall stand in Glenarvon's hall,
> And his portals shall blaze and his turrets shall fall.
> Glenarvon, the day of thy glory is o'er;
> Thou shalt sail from hence, but return no more.
> Sound mournfully, my harp; oh, breath a strain,
> More sad than that which Sion's daughters sung,
> When on the willow boughs their harps they hung,
> And wept for lost Jerusalem! A train
> More sorrowful before my eyes appear:
> They come, in chains they come! The hour of fate is near. /
> Erin, the heart's best blood shall flow for thee.
> It is thy groans I hear – it is thy wounds I see.
> Cold sleep thy heroes in their silent grave:
> The leopard lords it o'er their last retreat.
> O'er hearts that once were free and brave,
> See the red banners proudly wave.
> They croach, they fall before a tyrant's feet.
> The star of freedom sets, to rise no more.
> Quench'd is the immortal spark in endless night:
> Never again shall ray so fair, so bright,
> Arise o'er Erin's desolated shore.'

No sooner had St. Clare ended, than Buchanan, joining with her and the rest of the rebels, gave signal for the long expected revolt. 'Burn his castle – destroy his land,' said St. Clare. Her followers prepared to obey: with curses loud and repeated, they vented their execration. Glenarvon, the idol they had once adored, they now[a] with greater show of justice despised. 'Were he only a villain,' said one, 'I, for my part, would pardon him: but he is a coward and a hypocrite: when he commits a wrong he turns it upon another: he is a / smooth dissembler, and while he smiles he stabs.' All his ill deeds were now collected together from far and near, to strengthen the violence of resentment and hate. Some looked upon the lonely grave of Alice, and sighed as they passed. That white stone was placed over a broken heart, they said: another turned to the more splendid tomb of Calantha, and cursed him for his barbarity to their lady: 'It was an ill return to so much love – we do not excuse her, but we must upbraid him.' Then came they to the wood, and Buchanan, trembling with horror, spoke of his murdered mother. 'Burn his castles,' they cried, 'and execrate his memory from father to son in Belfont.' St. Clare suddenly arose in the midst of the increasing crowd, and thus, to inforce her purpose, again addressed her followers: –

'England,[b] thou hast destroyed thy sister country,' she cried.[40] 'The despot before whom you bow has cast slavery / and ruin upon us. O man – or rather less, O king, drest in a little brief authority, beware, beware! The hour of retribution is at hand. Give back the properties that thy nation has wrested from a suffering people. Thy fate is decreed; thy impositions are detected; thy word passes not current among us: beware! the hour is ripe. Woe to the tyrant who has betrayed his trust!' – These were the words which Elinor uttered as she gave the signal of revolt to her deluded followers. It was even during the dead of night, in the caverns of Inis Tara, where pikes and bayonets glittered by the light of the torch, and crowds on crowds assembled, while yells and cries reiterated their bursts of applause.

The sound of voices and steps approached. Buchanan, de Ruthven, and St. Clare, parted from each other. 'It will be a dreadful spectacle to see the slaughter that shall follow,' said St. Clare. 'Brothers and fathers shall / fight against each other. The gathering storm has burst from within: it shall overwhelm the land. One desperate effort shall be made for freedom. Hands and hearts shall unite firm to shake off the shackles of tyranny – to support the rights of man – the glorious cause of independence. What though in vain we struggle – what though the sun that rose so bright in promise may set in darkness – the splendid hope was conceived – the daring effort was made; and many a brave heart shall die in the sacred cause. What though our successors be slaves, aye, willing slaves, shall not the proud survivor exult in the memory of the past! Fate itself cannot snatch from us that which once has been. The storms of contention may cease – the goaded victims may bear every repeated lash; and in apathy and misery may kneel before the feet of the tyrants who forget / their vow. But the spirit of liberty once flourished at least; and every name that perishes in its cause shall stand emblazoned in eternal splendour – glorious in brightness, though not immortal in success.' /

CHAPTER XXXIII.

'Hark!' said the prophetess: "tis the screams of despair and agony: – my countrymen are defeated: – they fall: – but they do not fly. No human soul can endure this suspense: – all is dark and terrible: the distant roar of artillery; the noise of conflict; the wild tumultuous cries of war; the ceaseless deafening fire. – Behold the rolling volumes of smoke, as they issue from the glen! – What troop of horse comes riding over the down? – I too have fought. This hand has dyed itself in the blood of a human being; this breast is pierced; but the pang I feel is not from the wound of the bayonet. – Hark! how the trumpet echoes from afar beyond the mountains. – They halt – they obey my last commands / – they light the beacons on the hill! Belfont and St. Alvin shall blaze; the seat of his fathers shall fall; and with their ashes, mine shall not mingle! Glenarvon, farewell! Even in death I have not forgiven thee! – Come, tardy steed, bear me once again; and then both horse and rider shall rest in peace for ever.'

It was about the second hour of night when St. Clare reached Inis Tara, and stood suspended between terror and exultation, as she watched the clouds of smoke and fire which burst from the turrets of Belfont. The ranks were every where broken: soldiers in pursuit were seen in detached parties, scouring over every part of the country: the valley of Altamonte rang with the savage contest, as horse to horse, and man to man, opposed each other. The pike and bayonet glittered in the moon-beam; and the distant discharge of musketry, with the yell of triumph, and the groans of despair, / echoed mournfully upon the blast. Elinor rose upon her panting steed to gaze with eager eyes towards Belfont.

It was not the reflection of the kindling fires that spread so deathlike a hue over her lips and face. She was bleeding to death from her wounds, while her eye darted forth, as if intently watching, with alternate hope and terror, that which none but herself could see – it was a man and horse advancing with furious haste from the smoke and flames, in which he had appeared involved. He bore a lovely burthen in his arms, and shewing her Clare of Costolly as he passed. 'I have fulfilled your desire, proud woman,' he cried: 'the castle shall burn to the earth: the blood of every enemy to his country shall be spilt. I have saved the son of Glenarvon; and when I have placed him in safety, shall de Ruthven be as dear?' 'Take my thanks,' said Elinor faintly, as the blood continued to flow from her wounds. / 'Bear that boy to my aunt, the Abbess of Glenaa: tell her to cherish him for my sake. Sometimes speak to him of St. Clare.

'Now, see the flame of vengeance how it rises upon my view. Burn, fire; burn. Let the flames ascend, even to the Heavens. So fierce and bright are the last fires of love, now quenched, for ever and for ever. The seat of his ancestors shall fall to the lowest earth – dust to dust – earth to earth. What is the pride of man? – The dream of life is past; the song of the wild harper has ceased; famine, war, and slavery, shall encompass my country.

> 'But yet all its fond recollections suppressing,
> One last dying wish this sad bosom shall draw:
> O, Erin, an exile bequeaths thee his blessing;
> Land of my forefathers, Erin go brah.'[41]

As she sung the last strain of the song, which the sons of freedom had learned, she tore the green mantle from her breast, / and throwing it around the head of her steed, so that he could not perceive any external object, she pressed the spur into his sides, and gallopped in haste to the edge of the cliff, from which she beheld, like a sheet of fire reddening the heavens, the blazing turrets of Belfont. She heard the crash: she gazed in triumph, as millions of sparks lighted the blue vault of the heavens; and volumes of smoke, curling form the ruins, half concealed the ravages of the insatiate flame. Then she drew the horn from her side, and sounding it loud and shrill from Heremon cliff, heard it answered from mountain to mountain, by all her armed confederates. The waves of the foaming billows now reflected a blood-red light from the scorching flames........

Three hundred and sixty feet was the cliff perpendicular from the vast fathomless ocean. 'Glenarvon, hurah! Peace to the broken hearts! Nay, start not, Clarence:[42] to horse, to horse! Thus charge; / it is for life and honour.' The affrighted steed saw not the fearful chasm into which, goaded on by his rider, he involuntarily plunged. But de Ruthven heard the piercing shriek he gave, as he sunk headlong into the rushing waters, which in a moment overwhelming both horse and rider, concealed them from the view of man. /

CHAPTER XXXIV.

SHORT is the sequel of the history which is now to be related. The strong arm of power soon suppressed this partial rebellion. Buchanan was found stretched in death upon the field of battle, lovely in form even in that hour.

The Marquis of Delaval, restored to his family and fortune, soon forgot the lesson adversity had taught. In the same follies and the same vanities his predecessors had passed their days, he likewise endeavoured to enjoy the remainder of his. The Duke of Altamonte lived long enough to learn the mournful truth, which pride had once forborne to teach,[a] the perishableness of all human strength, the littleness of all human greatness, and the vanity of every enjoyment this world can offer. Of Sophia, of Frances, of / Lady Dartford, what is there to relate? They passed joyfully[b] with the thousands that sail daily along the stream of folly, uncensured and uncommended. Youth, beauty, and vanity, were their's: they enjoyed and suffered all the little pleasures, and all the little pains of life, and resisted all its little temptations. Lady Mandeville and Lady Augusta Selwyn fluttered away likewise each pleasureable moment as frivolously, though perhaps less innocently; then turned to weep for the errors into which they had been drawn, more humble in themselves when sorrow had chastened them. Then it was that they called to the flatterers of their prosperous days; but they were silent and cold: then it was that they looked for the friends who had encircled them once; but they were not to be found: and they learned, like the sinner they had despised, all that terror dreams of on its sick bed, and all that misery in its worst moments can conceive. Mrs. Seymour, in acts / of piety and benevolence, retired to the Garden Cottage, a small estate the Duke of Altamonte had settled on her; and she found that religion and virtue, even in this world, have their reward. The coldness, the prejudice, which, in the presumption of her heart had once given her an appearance of austerity, softened in the decline of life; and when she considered the frailty of human nature, the misery and uncertainty of existence, she turned not from the penitent wanderer who had left the right road, and spoke with severity alone of hardened and triumphant guilt. Her life was one fair course of virtue; and when she died, thousands of those whom she had reclaimed or befriended followed her to the grave.

As to the Princess of Madagascar, she lived to a good old age, though death repeatedly gave her warning of his approach. 'Can any humiliation, any sacrifice avail?' she cried, in helpless alarm, seeing his continual advances. 'Can I yet be saved?' she said, addressing / Hoiouskim, who often by a bold attempt had hurried away this grim king of terrors. 'If we were to sacrifice the great nabob, and all our party, and our followers – can fasting, praying, avail? shall the reviewers be poisoned in an emince![43] shall –' It was hinted to the princess at length, though in the gentlest manner possible, that this time, nor sacrifice, nor spell, would save her. Death stood broad and unveiled before her. 'If then I must die,' she cried, weeping bitterly at the necessity, 'send with haste for the dignitaries of the church. I would not enter upon the new world without a passport; I, who have so scrupulously courted favour every where in this. As to confession of sins, what have I to confess, Hoiouskim? I appeal to you: is there a scribbler, however contemptible, whose pen I feared might one day be turned against me, that I have not silenced by the grossest flattery? Is there a man or woman of note in any kingdom that I have not crammed / with dinners, and little attentions, and presents, in hopes of gaining them over to my side? And is there, unless the helpless, the fallen, and the idiot, appear against me, any one whom it was my interest to befriend that I have not sought for and won? What minion of fashion, what dandy in distress, what woman of intrigue, who had learned to deceive with ease, have I not assisted? Oh, say, what then are my sins, Hoiouskim? Even if self-denial be a virtue, though I have not practised it myself, have I not made you and others daily and hourly do so?' Hoiouskim bowed assent. Death now approached too near for further colloquy. The princess, pinching her attendants, that they might feel for what she suffered, fainted: yet with her dying breath again invoking the high priest: 'Hoiouskim,' she cried, 'obey my last command: send all my attendants after me, my eider down quilts, my coffee pots, my carriages, my confectioner: and tell the cook –' As she uttered that short / but comprehensive monosyllable, she expired. Peace to her memory! I wish not to reproach her: a friend more false, a foe more timid yet insulting, a princess more fond of power, never before or since appeared in Europe. Hoiouskim wept beside her, yet, when he recovered (and your philosophers seldom die of sorrow) it is said he retired to his own country, and shrunk from every woman he afterwards beheld, for fear they should remind him of her he loved so well, and prove another Princess of Madagascar. The dead, or yellow poet was twice carried by mistake to the grave.[44] It is further said,[a] that all the reviewers, who had bartered their independence for the comforts and flattery of Barbary House, died in the same year as the princess, of an epidemic disorder; but of this, who can be secure? Perhaps, alas! one yet remains to punish the flippant tongue, that dared to assert they were no more. But to return from this digression. /

CHAPTER XXXV.

At Allenwater the roses were yet in bloom: and the clematis and honeysuckle twined beneath the latticed windows, whilst through the flower gardens the stream of Allen flowed smooth and clear. Every object around breathed the fragrance of plants – the charms and sweets of nature. The heat of summer had not parched its verdant meads, and autumn's yellow tints had but just touched the shadowy leaf. Wearied with scenes of woe, Lord Avondale, having broken from society and friends, had retired to this retreat – a prey to the fever of disappointment and regret – wounded by the hand of his adversary, but still more effectually destroyed by the unkindness and inconstancy of his friend. /

Sir Richard, before the last engagement, in which he lost his life,[a] called at Allenwater. – 'How is your master?' he said, in a hurried manner. 'He is ill,' said James Collingwood. 'He will rise from his bed no more.' Sir Richard pressed forward; and trembling exceedingly, entered Lord Avondale's room. – 'Who weeps so sadly by a dying father's bed?' 'It is Harry Mowbrey, Calantha's child, the little comforter of many a dreary hour. The apt remark of enquiring youth, the joyous laugh of childhood, have ceased. The lesson repeated daily to an anxious parent has been learned with more than accustomed assiduity: but in vain. Nature at last has given way: – the pale emaciated form – the hand which the damps of death have chilled, feebly caresses the weeping boy.'

James Collingwood stood by his master's side, his sorrowful countenance / contrasting sadly with that military air which seemed to disdain all exhibition of weakness; and with him, the sole other attendant of his sufferings, Cairn of Coleraine, who once in this same spot had welcomed Calantha, then a fair and lovely bride, spotless in vestal purity, and dearer to his master's heart than the very life-blood that gave it vigour. He now poured some opiate drops into a glass, and placed it in the feeble hand which was stretched forth to receive it. 'Ah! father, do not leave me,' said his little son, pressing towards him. 'My mother looked as you do before she left me: and will you go also? What then will become of me?' Tears gushed into Lord Avondale's eyes, and trickled down his faded cheeks. 'God will bless and protect my boy,' he said, endeavouring to raise himself sufficiently to press his little cherub lips. It was like a blushing rose, placed by the hand of affection / upon a lifeless corpse – so healthful bloomed the child, so pale the parent stem!

'How feeble you are, dear father,' said Harry: 'your arms tremble when you attempt to raise me. I will kneel by you all this night, and pray to God to give you strength. You say there is none loves you. I love you; and Collingwood loves you; and many, many more. So do not leave us.' – 'And I love you too, dear, dear Harry,' cried Sir Richard, his voice nearly suffocated by his grief; 'and all who knew you honoured and loved you; and curse be on those who utter one word against him. He is the noblest fellow that ever lived.' 'Uncle Richard, don't cry,' said the boy: 'it grieves him so to see you. Don't look so sad, dear father. Why is your hand so cold: can nothing warm it?' 'Nothing, Harry.' – 'Do not weep so bitterly, dear uncle. I have suffered agony. Now, all is peace, – God bless / you and my children.' 'Open your dear eyes once again, father, to look on me. Oh! Collingwood, see they are closed: – Will he not look on me ever again? My sister Annabel shall speak to him. – My dear mamma is gone, or she would sooth him. – Oh, father, if you must leave me too, why should I linger here? How silent he is!' – 'He sleeps, Sir,' – 'I think he does not sleep, Collingwood. I think this dreadful stillness is what every one calls death. Oh! father, look at me once more. Speak one dear word only to say you love me still.' 'I can't bear this,' said Sir Richard, hurrying from the room, 'I can't bear it.'

The hour was that in which the setting sun had veiled its last bright ray in the western wave: – it was the evening of the tenth of October!!!

On the evening of the tenth of October, Glenarvon had reached the coast of Holland, and joined the British squadron under Admiral Duncan. The Dutch / were not yet in sight; but it was known that they were awaiting the attack at a few miles distance from shore, between Camperdown and Egmont. It was so still that evening that not a breath of air rippled upon the glassy waters. It was at that very instant of time, when Avondale, stretched upon his bed, far from those scenes of glory and renown in which his earlier years had been distinguished, had breathed his last; that Glenarvon, whilst walking the deck, even in the light of departing day, laughingly addressed his companions: 'Fear you to die?' he cried, to one upon whose shoulder he was leaning. 'I cannot fear. But as it may be the fate of all, Hardhead,' he said, still addressing his lieutenant, 'if I die do you present my last remembrance to my friends. – Ha! have I any? – Not I, i'faith.

> 'Now fill up a bowl, that I may pledge / you; and let him whose conscience trembles, shrink. I cannot fear;
> 'For, come he slow, or come he fast,
> It is but Death that comes at last.'

He said, and smiled – that smile so gentle and persuasive, that only to behold it was to love. Suddenly he beheld before him on the smooth wave a form so pale, so changed, that, but for the sternness of that brow, the fixed and hollow gaze of that dark eye, he had not recognized, in the fearful spectre, the form of Lord Avondale. 'Speak your reproaches as a man would utter them,' he said. 'Ask of me the satisfaction due for injuries; but stand not thus before me, like a dream, in the glare of day – like a grim vision of the night, in the presence of thousands.' – The stern glazed eye moved not: the palpable form continued. Lord Glenarvon gazed till his eyes were strained with the effort, and every faculty was benumbed and overpowered. /

Then fell a drowsiness over his senses which he could not conquer; and he said to those who addressed him, 'I am ill: – watch by me whilst I sleep.' He threw himself upon his cloak, listless and fatigued, and sunk into a heavy sleep. But his slumbers were broken and disturbed; and he could not recover from the unusual depression of his spirits. Every event of his short life crowded fast upon his memory: – scenes long forgotten recurred: – he thought of broken vows, of hearts betrayed, and of all the perjuries and treacheries of a life given up to love, But reproaches and bitterness saddened over every dear remembrance, and he participated, when too late, in the sufferings he had inflicted.

All was now profoundly still: the third watch sounded. The lashing of the waves against the sides of the ship – the gentle undulating motion, again lulled a weary and perturbed spirit to repose. Suddenly upon the air he heard a fluttering, like / the noise of wings, which fanned him while he slept. Gazing intently, he fancied he beheld a fleeting shadow pass up and down before him, as if the air, thickening into substance, became visible to the eye, till it produced a form clothed in angelic beauty and unearthly brightness. It was some moments before he could bring to his remembrance whom it resembled, – till a smile, all cheering, and a look of one he had seen in happier days, told him it was Calantha. Her hair flowed loosely on her shoulders, while a cloud of resplendent white supported her in the air, and covered her partly from his view. Her eyes shone with serene lustre; and her cheeks glowed with the freshness of health: – not as when impaired by sickness and disease, he had seen her last – not as when disappointment and the sorrows of the world had worn her youthful form – but renovated, young, and bright, with superior glory she now met his ardent / gaze; and, in a voice more sweet than music, thus addressed him:

'Glenarvon,' she said, 'I come not to reproach you. It is Calantha's spirit hovers round you. Away with dread; for I come to warn and to save you. Awake – arise, before it be too late. Let the memory of the past fade from before you: live to be all you still may be – a country's pride, a nation's glory! Ah, sully not with ill deeds the bright promise of a life of fame.' As she spoke, a light as from heaven irradiated her countenance, and, pointing with her hand to the east, he saw the sun burst from the clouds which had gathered round it, and shine forth in all its lustre. 'Are you happy?' cried Glenarvon, stretching out his arms to catch the vision, which hovered near. – 'Calantha, speak to me: am I still loved? Is Glenarvon dear even thus in death?'

The celestial ray which had lighted up the face of the angel, passed from before / it at these words; and he beheld the form of Calantha, pale and ghastly, as when last they had parted. In seeming answer to his question, she pressed her hands to her bosom in silence, and casting upon him a look so mournful that it pierced his heart, she faded from before his sight, dissolving like the silvery cloud into thin air. At that moment, as he looked around, the bright sun which had risen with such glorious promise, was seen to sink in mists of darkness, and with its setting ray, seemed to tell him that his hour was come, that the light of his genius was darkened, that the splendour of his promise was set for ever: but he met the awful warning without fear.

And now again he slept; and it seemed to him that he was wandering in a smooth vale, far from the haunts of men. The place was familiar to his memory: – it was such as he had often seen amidst the green plains of his native country, in the beautiful season of spring; and ever / and anon upon his ear he heard the church-bell sounding from afar off, while the breeze, lately risen, rustled among the new leaves and long grass. Fear even touched a heart that never yet had known its power. The shadows varied on the plain before him, and threw a melancholy gloom on the surrounding prospect. Again the church-bell tolled; but it was not the merry sound of some village festival, nor yet the more sober bell that calls the passenger to prayer. No, it was that long and pausing knell, which, as it strikes the saddened ear, tells of some fellow-creature's eternal departure from this lower world: and ever while it tolled, the dreary cry of woe lengthened upon the breeze, mourning a spirit fled. Glenarvon thought he heard a step slowly stealing towards him; he even felt the breath of some one near; and raising his eye in haste, he perceived the thin form of a woman close beside him. In her arms she held a child, more wan than / herself. At her approach, a sudden chill seemed to freeze the life-blood in his heart.

He gazed again. 'Is it Calantha?' said he. 'Ah, no! it was the form of Alice.'[45] She appeared as one returned from the grave, to which long mourning and untimely woes had brought her. – 'Clarence,' she said in a piercing voice, 'since you have abandoned me I have known many sorrows. The God of Mercy deal not with you as you have dealt with me!' She spoke no more; but gazing in agony upon an infant which lay at her bosom, she looked up to Heaven, from whence her eyes slowly descended upon Glenarvon. She then approached, and taking the babe from her breast, laid it cold and lifeless on his heart. It was the chill of death which he felt – when, uttering a deep groan, he started up with affright.

The drops stood upon his forehead – his hands shook – he looked round him, / but no image like the one he had beheld was near. The whiteness of the eastern sky foretold the approach of day. The noise and bustle in the ship, the signal songs of the sailors,[a] and the busy din around, told him that he had slept enough. The Dutch squadron now appeared at a distance upon the sea: every thing was ready for attack.

That day Lord Glenarvon fought with more than his usual bravery. He was the soul and spirit which actuated and moved every other. At twelve the engagement became general, every ship coming into action with its opponent. It was about four in the afternoon, when the victory was clearly decided in favour of the British flag. The splendid success was obtained by unequalled courage, and heroic valour. The result it is not for me to tell. Many received the thanks of their brave commander on that day; many returned in triumph to the country, / and friends who proudly awaited them. The Emerald frigate, and its gallant captain, prepared likewise to return; but Glenarvon, after the action, was taken ill. He desired to be carried upon deck: and, placing his hand upon his head, while his eyes were fixed, he enquired of those around if they did not hear a signal of distress, as if from the open sea. He then ordered the frigate to approach the spot whence the guns were fired. A fresh breeze had arisen: the Emerald sailed before the wind. To his disturbed imagination the same solemn sound was repeated in the same direction. – No sail appeared – still the light frigate pursued. 'Visions of death and horror persecute me,'[46] cried Glenarvon. 'What now do I behold – a ship astern! It is singular. Do others see the same, or am I doomed to be the sport of these absurd fancies? Is it that famed Dutch merchantman,[b] condemned through all eternity to sail / before the wind,[47] which seamen view with terror, whose existence until this hour I discredited?' He asked this of his companions; but the smile with which Glenarvon spoke these words, gave[c] place to strong feelings of surprise and alarm. – Foreign was the make of that ship; sable were its sails; sable was the garb of its crew; but ghastly white and motionless were the countenances of all. Upon the deck there stood a man of great height and size, habited in the apparel of a friar. His cowl concealed his face; but his crossed hands and uplifted attitude announced his profession. He was in prayer: – he prayed much, and earnestly – it was for the souls of his crew. Minute guns were fired at every pause; after which a slow solemn chaunt began; and the smoke of incense ascended till it partially concealed the dark figures of the men.

Glenarvon watched the motions of that vessel in speechless horror; and now before / his wondering eyes new forms arose, as if created by delirium's power to augment the strangeness of the scene. At the feet of the friar there knelt a form so beautiful – so young, that, but for the foreign garb and well remembered look, he had thought her like the vision of his sleep, a pitying angel sent to watch and save him. – 'O Fiorabella,' he cried; 'first, dearest, and sole object of my devoted love, why now appear to wake the sleeping dæmons in my breast – to madden me with many a bitter recollection?' The friar at that moment, with relentless hand, dashed the fair fragile being, yet clinging round him for mercy, into the deep dark waters. 'Monster,' exclaimed Glenarvon, 'I will revenge that deed even in thy blood.' There was no need: – the monk drew slowly from his bosom the black covering that enshrouded his form. Horrible to behold! – that bosom was gored with deadly wounds, and the black spouting streams / of blood, fresh from the heart, uncoloured by the air, gushed into the wave. 'Cursed be the murderer in his last hour! – Hell waits its victim.' – Such was the chaunt which the sable crew ever and anon sung in low solemn tones.

Well was it understood by Glenarvon, though sung in a foreign dialect. 'Comrades,' he exclaimed, 'do you behold that vessel? Am I waking, or do my eyes, distempered by some strange malady, deceive me? Bear on. It is the last command of Glenarvon. Set full the sails. Bear on, – bear on: to death or to victory! – It is the enemy of our souls you see before you. Bear on – to death, to vengeance; for all the fiends of hell have conspired our ruin.' They sailed from coast to coast – They sailed from sea to sea, till lost in the immensity of ocean. Gazing fixedly upon one object, all maddening with superstitious terror, Lord Glenarvon tasted not of food or refreshment. / His brain was burning. His eye, darting forward, lost not for one breathing moment sight of that terrific vision.

Madness to phrenzy came upon him. In vain his friends, and many of the brave companions in his ship, held him struggling in their arms. He seized his opportunity. 'Bear on,' he cried: 'pursue, till death and vengeance –' and throwing himself from the helm, plunged headlong into the waters. They rescued him; but it was too late. In the struggles of ebbing life, even as the spirit of flame rushed from the bands of mortality, visions of punishment and hell pursued him. Down, down, he seemed to sink with horrid precipitance from gulf to gulf, till immured in darkness; and as he closed his eyes in death, a voice, loud and terrible, from beneath, thus seemed to address him:

'Hardened and impenitent sinner! the measure of your iniquity is full: the / price of crime has been paid: here shall your spirit dwell for ever, and for ever. You have dreamed away life's joyous hour, nor made atonement for error, nor denied yourself aught that the fair earth presented you. You did not controul the fiend in your bosom, or stifle him in his first growth: he now has mastered you, and brought you here: and you[a] did not bow the knee for mercy whilst time was given you: now mercy shall not be shewn. O, cry upwards from these lower pits, to the friends and companions you have left, to the sinner who hardens himself against his Creator – who basks in the ray of prosperous guilt, nor dreams that his hour like your's is at hand. Tell him how terrible a thing is death; how fearful at such an hour is remembrance of the past. Bid him repent, but he shall not hear you. Bid him amend, but like you he shall delay till it is too late. Then, neither his arts, nor talents, nor / his possessions, shall save him, nor friends, though leagued together more than ten thousand strong; for the axe of justice must fall. God is just; and the spirit of evil infatuates before he destroys.'[48]

APPENDIX A: PREFACE TO THE SECOND EDITION OF *GLENARVON*

Glenarvon was written and committed to the press without permission, communication, advice, or assistance[1] – this may account for, though it cannot excuse all the slighter, and many, it is trusted, of the more serious errors of the composition. But if indeed the charge of immoral tendency, which some have preferred against these volumes, be well-founded, what palliation can in any degree extenuate so great an offence, or what praise can compensate for so odious an imputation? The Author must bow with submission to the adverse judgment of the public, if that judgment be once pronounced decidedly, and upon due consideration; but the flattering hope had been indulged, that the general tendency of the work was favourable to the interests of virtue. It is too late, it is presumed, to enquire whether those interests are, or are not, injured by the description of desperate characters, depraved conduct, and daring crimes? Such have been from the earliest to the most recent times, the subjects of fiction; and such ever have been the themes of tragedians of all countries; of the writers of novels, romances, and romantic poems; and the present period presents us with almost daily examples, which at least equal, if they do not surpass their prototypes of old, in the horrors, and atrocities, which they describe.

The scene of the following pages is laid, for the most part, in Ireland, in the time of the Irish Rebellion. The events have no foundation in fact, and with respect to the characters, the painter well knows, that, when he is sketching the personages of history, or the creatures of his imagination, the lineaments, with which he is most familiar, will sometimes almost involuntarily rise beneath the touch of his pencil. The same cause has perhaps produced in this work, those resemblances, if resemblances they be, which have been recognized, admitted, claimed with so much eagerness, and then condemned with so much asperity. Yet a distinction is always to be drawn between the attempt at painting human nature as it is, and the base desire of deforming, and degrading it. The crimes related in these volumes are evidently imaginary; the situations fictitious; much of the ridicule which has received a personal application, is harmless in itself, and directed against trifling peculiarities; some imputations there are, no doubt of a heavier nature, and these were conceived to have been justified by injury and provocation. The language of resentment is generally more violent, than the occasion demands, and he who uses it, is of all mankind the least qualified to judge impartially of its propriety; but those who suffer deeply, will express themselves strongly; those who have been cruelly attacked, will use the means of resistance, which are within their reach; and observations, which appear to a general observer, bitter and acrimonious, may perhaps wear another character to him who is acquainted with the circumstances, which occasioned them. This work is not the offspring of calm tranquillity, and cool deliberation, it does not bear the marks of such a temper, or of such a situation. It was written under the pressure of affliction, with the feelings of resentment which are excited by misrepresentation, and in the bitterness of a wounded spirit, which is naturally accompanied by a corresponding bitterness both of thought and expression.

> 'The blood will follow, where the knife is driven;
> 'The flesh will quiver, where the pincer tears,
> 'And sighs and tears by nature grow on pain.'[2]

These avowals being fairly, and distinctly made, an appeal is still confidently urged to those, who have read impartially, whether, whatever may be the character of the more general reflections, the features of the few supposed portraits are overcharged and distorted, as if by the hand of malevolence, or whether their beauties, are not studiously heightened and brought forth, and their defects in some measure thrown into shade and concealed.

When we cast a glance around us upon the frailty of human nature, and the errors and follies of the world, we must, it is to be feared, confess that malignity, had malignity guided the pen, might, without departing from truth, or in the slightest degree infringing the sacred confidence of friendship, have found it easy to expose foibles far more ridiculous, and to cast aspersions far more ill natured and injurious. – One observation further there is an anxiety to press upon the consideration of the public. The Author cannot be accused of having sought the favour of those who are generally admired, and courted, of those who are powerful in influence and popularity, who are surrounded by friends and supporters, and who give, in a great measure, the tone and turn to the conversation of society, and the opinions of the world; nor on the other hand, is the shaft of satire in any one instance directed against the weak, the fallen, or the defenceless.

In the vain, frivolous and unrestrained character of Calantha, and in the kind, the generous, the noble one of Avondale, it was intended to enforce the danger of too entire liberty either of conduct, or of opinion; and to shew that no endowments, no advantages, can ensure happiness and security upon earth, unless we adhere to the forms, as well as to the principles of religion and morality. Nor will it be held by the truly wise, or the truly pious, to be too heavy an imputation upon the character of Lord Avondale, that he is represented as having in early youth suffered his mind to be overpowered, and his judgment in some measure misled by the vain wisdom, and false philosophy, which have distinguished and disturbed the times, in which it has been our fortune to live. The error attributed, is one which unhappily has been in our day neither unusual, nor unnatural; it is one, into which have fallen men of the most powerful talents, and the warmest hearts, betrayed often by a confidence in their own strength; and with the candid and tolerant the question will ever be, not whether the delusion has prevailed for a time, but whether it has been afterwards shaken off by the returning rectitude of the feelings, and the growing vigour of the understanding, if this character had been represented, (as would have been easy) without blame or blemish, it would also have been without probability, without interest, without admonition. This transient error, which darkens for a moment the splendor of Avondale's virtues, is adduced not as forming an apology for the misconduct of Calantha, but as accounting for the tenderness and mercy, her husband afterwards evinced, when remembering that perhaps he had too little sought to strengthen and confirm in her, those principles, which none more deeply venerated, or more strictly observed than himself. He commiserated her fate and wept upon her grave.

The character of Calantha, of the Miss Seymours, of Lady Dartford, may be in part applied to many—they are not out of nature, nor overstrained; those of Miss St.-Clare and Lady Margaret Buchanan are more entirely fictitious.[3] Their situation, their disposition, their vices, their projects have not the remotest allusion to any person who ever existed, or to any event that ever took place. Designing ill-will and erring curiosity, may exert themselves to discover realities in murders, intrigues, marriages and separations, which have been only introduced for the sake of giving some interest to the narrative; but good sense, and discernment, will easily distinguish between such ill-founded applications, and those observations in which, it is trusted, the fair freedom of remark, and censure, which belongs to the British press, has neither been exceeded, nor abused.

It is needless further to explain the plan, and object of each particular passage, or character, which is introduced into the composition. Unless that object be delineated with such clearness, as to exhibit itself to the mind of the reader in the moment of perusal, it is vain to suggest and point it out in the preface. The whole has been written with the general design of inculcating the necessity of seeing both actions and opinions, in their true light, and as they really are; of founding religion, not like Calantha, upon enthusiasm, but upon reason and faith; of founding morality, upon principle and experience, not upon ignorance of evil. If in any part of the work, any deviation from this prescribed course can be discovered : if any sentiment throughout these volumes, appears even to approach to the toleration of vice and immorality, it is vain now to say, how from the heart it is wished unwritten; but in censures, which spring from very different motives, in misconstructions, misrepresentations, and, above all, in the charge of malevolence, the author never will silently and tamely acquiesce.

APPENDIX B: INTRODUCTION TO THE FOURTH EDITION OF *GLENARVON*[1]

From far beyond the Pleiades,[2] from far beyond the constellation of Orion – borne on the wings of Hope, I came to visit you. – 'Children of the Earth, hearken unto my words, and turn not aside from the warning voice of one, who still even, though in exile, loves you.'[3] – In the bright Planet where I was born, I lived happy, for I was innocent; and who that is innocent is not happy? Yet the unvaried monotony of so even a course fatigued me, and the desire of something new, led me into that which was evil: it is the progress of my terrestrial pilgrimage that I would fain bequeath to you: I presume not to hope, that my example will amend you; neither do I wish to intrude upon you any admonition. I lived on earth, as mortals live – I erred, as mortals err – and now, though far removed by death, my thoughts still turn with interest to your sphere.

The inhabitants of every particular planet, differ in quality and power from each other. / To us the charms of perpetual youth and innocence had been granted: our airy and pliable forms sometimes ascended over the surface of the Earth, fresh and beautiful as the early blossoms of the year. Yet we never attain to that full maturity, and those powers of intellect, which are allowed to the inhabitants of the more perfect planets; we are to them but as spring to summer.

And though our ethereal nature and the ordinances of our existence qualify us to range at large throughout the universe, yet it is only once during the period of our lives, that we are permitted to exert the power which we possess – and this is to us the period of temptation – if then we fall, we fall for ever – but if we resist, we return to enjoy the delights of eternal sunshine, reward and pleasure. – –

What millions of histories could I recount! What wonders, passing human credibility, could I describe! – But wherefore should I thus wander from my subject? – It is enough, that the days of innocence passed tranquilly along, and the wished for moment of liberty at length arrived. The Virgin Queen[4] of our bright star / appeared before us: she summoned us by name around her. – To each she distributed certain talismans, or charmed gifts which, as long as we retained them on our breasts, entitled us to her protection – and as she placed the precious spells upon hearts then spotless and secure, she warned us repeatedly to attend to their admonition. – This badge, which we were enjoined to wear, at all times, consisted of a precious jewel, in brightness and colour similar to fire – in form it represented the Bird of the sun – and such was its power that when any danger impended, over the being in whose breast it was placed, the incessant fluttering of its wings gave warning to avoid it.– Beloved and pure children of my heart, said our Queen, addressing us, fail not to attend to its admonitions, for, if you neglect them, the day will come when they will cease to be repeated. – To each of you some prohibition is enjoined. – Yours is this, she continued, looking upon me – Shun the earth, a sphere which, however small in extent, contains more of vanity and folly, than any other in the vast expanse of the Creation. – As she spoke, she waved her hand, the signal of liberty – when, in a moment, the air resounded with the quivering of / wings, and the light inhabitants of our Planet arose, as if, with one accord, fanning the breeze with their extended plumes – and ascending like a flight of birds towards the heavens. – Then, for the first time, we beheld, in one comprehensive view, the universal plan of nature –innumerable systems performing their various, but distinct courses, unclouded by mists, and unbounded by horizon – endless variety in infinite space. Then first we heard the full harmonious cadences of the angelic choirs' celestial music! uttered by happy spirits, in praise of the great Author of existence – and directing our flight onwards from sphere to sphere – from world to world – we felt joyful in ourselves – and rejoiced in the wonders and varieties of Creation. – It was extatic happiness, but it was of short duration; – for who can endure liberty? And who that yields to insatiate passion, can resist his fate? A power stronger than reason, to which the faculties of my soul resigned themselves, impelled me forward to my ruin. I viewed with indifference the millions of peopled spheres through which I passed, till after darting around earth – half oppressed by its atmosphere, and half regretting the sin of disobedience, / which thus cast a stain upon pure nature, I alighted upon it – 'It was in the beautiful season of the early summer, and amid the stillness of night that I first beheld the land that I love,' and gazed, delighted, upon the dark mountains and the green valleys of Erin.[5] – The song of the Banshees mourning for the sorrows of their country, and the heroes who had fallen in battle broke upon the silence of night: while my wings poised me upon the breeze to listen to the strain, I beheld the spirits of the departed arise in solemn grandeur – freed from the shackles of mortality, a flame of glory distinguished the souls of heroes – and pointing upwards, formed a path of light before them. Thus passed away the hours of the night, a night so still and clear, that in the blue vault of Heaven, every distinct star shone forth with sparkling lustre: but when the rising sun illumined, with its golden rays, the wide expanse of the mighty atlantic, I still heard the voice of lamentation, and approaching near the rocky shore – plainly discovered one of the beautiful Genii of the Earth.[6] – His sable wings cast a deep shade upon his form; he struck, at intervals, the chords of his lyre and accompanied the melody with his voice – singing / in sweet and mournful notes. It seemed as if alone one soul of sadness dwelt in a paradise of unenjoyed sweets. Then first the tears of mortality fell from my eyes, and in weeping for the sorrows of man – I thought not of the misery I was preparing for myself. Fair Spirit of some more favoured planet, said he, as he gazed upon me, why do you thus sully the purity of your nature, by visiting the abode of misery – and conversing with the race of man? – We are but as the flowers that wither, or as the clouds that pass along and shadow, for a moment, the brightness of the heavens. All here is desolation and woe; 'fly ere it be too late.' He spoke, and turning from me, looked upon the deserted ruins of an ancient priory, and the remains of a wrecked vessel scattered upon the shore.

It was pleasant to hear his voice, though it was mournful – and when he upraised his eyes and gazed upon me, a gleam of brightness spread itself over every feature, and a smile, all-lovely and radiant, gave to them a momentary expression of joy, – day by day, I returned to listen to his instructions – he unfolded to me the secrets of ages, and opened my mind to / the words of wisdom – he traversed with me the countries of the earth, and pointed out to me every where the vanity of man; – one hour I beheld a monarch, in all the pride of conquest, the next I saw him a prisoner and a slave – at morn I heard the festive song of parents, who rejoiced in the birth of an infant, at night I saw the funeral torch that lighted the hope, the pride of his family to the grave; each individual appeared following, regardless of danger, some object that led him onward with ardour, and left him disappointed when it was attained – every where I marked the steps of folly and presumptions, every where of punishment and pain. The earth seemed to bring forth fruits, gems and riches in abundance, but man, alone, appeared to turn from the proffered blessings and repine. I fled with horror from crime and oppression, but a new and restless desire agitated my mind, as I followed my guide with the blind devotion of love – oh that it were permitted me, I exclaimed, to dwell in these strange and ever varying scenes – unlike the monotony of what I have hitherto gazed upon, every moment as it passes, carries with it a powerful interest – I would not, / as other mortals do, forget the end, for which I was created – lose sight of yon bright heaven, to which I now eagerly aspire – my heart should not be misled by splendid baubles, and idle vanities, but from the hour in which it were permitted me to dwell on earth, I would live but to enjoy its gifts, and render all around me happy – I would succour the unfortunate, humble the pride of the oppressor, my course should be one bright, and continued stream of honour; I would yield to every virtuous impulse, but curb even in its birth every evil passion, and spurn from me in abhorrence, every object that so unworthily tempts, misleads and infatuates mankind.

To renounce your etherial nature, and to become an inhabitant of the earth for a few short years, is possible, said my artful guide, but can you indeed desire it? all that is great and high must be for that interval relinquished, – your soul, too mighty and subtle for a mortal frame, must be shackled and pinioned in a perishable body – the glory of the heavens will fade, with every other remembrance, from your weakened mind, and years must pass, ere you regain even sufficient sense to guide you – / see those fair cherubs, who play around the hamlet of their parents, he continued, pointing to children who sported along the vallies over which we passed, they are innocent, as the angels above, but cannot protect themselves, even from the commonest evil – it is as such that you must become – as ignorant as helpless, before you can even begin to act in the manner you profess. – A dark, and threatening cloud, at that moment, shadowed over the countenance of the Genii. The bird of the sun fluttered his wings tremulously on my bosom, as if warning me to depart – he perceived it; – suddenly, a lake – ....a palace arose before my view, my imagination was troubled – –

It is the lordly mansion of Altamont, he cried: – all flourishes around – but see, he continued, its owner, its possessor, mourns, – he has no child to inherit his estate, to bear his name; he prays even now, he prays, for that, which, if granted, will cause his misery and disgrace.

Spirit of the air, child of the sun, – if indeed, it is thy rash desire, I can place thee in this fair domain, – thou shalt be heiress of the whole surrounding scene – the riches of the earth / shall be poured forth at thy feet – pleasure shall dance around thee, thou shalt be beloved, even as I perhaps, had loved thee, and then, added he, with an incredulous and contemptuous smile, shew to the sons of earth a great and unrivalled example of human excellence; – as he spoke, he approached, and seized the gem that yet withheld me from his power, then, with a shriek of triumph, arose from my side. – The thunders rolled in the heavens, the lightnings darted around me, the earth trembled, and all the elements in hostile contest with each other, at once, confused, terrified and overwhelmed my senses – the crush was as if the mountains had been crumbled into dust, and the mighty waters of the sea had rushed from their channels – the power of thought was lost amidst the tumult – I sunk, till by degrees I was involved in profound darkness with no memory of the past, and no hope of the future.

It was in the land of death that I awoke.[7] Oh! cold and dreary that sepulcher, where myriads of disembodied spirits slowly and sullenly over a dark sea of burning fire sail in the same unvaried, uninterrupted course, for ever and for ever, without even the fear of worse / to make the present supportable, without hope, from one eternal dream, or reality of endless unceasing apathy – and there, all that seemed lovely and beautiful in life, appeared before me in varying shadows, for nothing was real, and all crumbled into dust, when the wild winds, pent up beneath the body of the waters, shook the caverns as they struggled and roared from below – and there were spirits of flame, who had burst the fetters that confined them upon earth, and potentates, kings, demagogues and slaves, for the shade of every thing that had existed from the foundation of the earth, was there, and all was mournful and cold. –

Then came among us one more sorrowful in look, than every other, for he more than every other, had misused the gifts, with which the creator of all things had permitted him to be endowed; I recognized my guide, and turned to him, to reproach him; and many more were there, all votaries of pleasure, who had broken the fetters, which reason and virtue had imposed – a voice terrible to me, for while it spoke, the chill of death struck on my heart, then, as if my senses slept, addressed me.

'Fallen spirit, thou hast listened to the illusions / of fancy, and hast sought for happiness in forbidden joys – thou hast quitted the paths of innocence and peace, and hast cast the sin of disobedience on thy soul – heaven has heard and granted thy request, thou art now in the land of death – arise and fulfil thy destiny – Calantha be thy name – ever follow the blind dictates of passion, be the slave of every strong emotion, pleasure and delight shall spring up around thee, but thou shalt cast all away, even as now, awake, and live, for God is just, but the spirit of evil infatuates before it destroys.'[8]

NOTES

Volume I

1. *Disperato dolor ... ne favelle*: 'I renew a hopeless despair, that makes my heart still ache, at the thought, before the words follow.' From Dante Alighieri's *Inferno*, canto 33, in which is recounted the terrible fate of Ugolino, a traitor whose children were starved and killed with him in revenge. Dante finds Ugolino gnawing on the skull of Archbishop Ruggieri, who was instrumental in his demise, and challenges him to tell his tale. In the second edition, a different epigraph appears: 'Les passions sont les vents qui enflent les voiles du vaisseau: elles le submergent quelquefois, mais sans elles il ne pourrait voguer. Tout est dangereux ici-bas, et tout est nécessaire.' (The passions are the winds which fill the sails of the vessel: they submerge her sometimes, but without them she could not sail. Everything is dangerous, here below, and everything is necessary.) This text is a slight modification of a passage from Voltaire's *Zadig*, chapter 22: '"Ce sont les vents qui enflent les voiles du vaisseau," repartit l'ermite: "elles le submergent quelquefois; mais sans elles il ne pourrait voguer. La bile rend colère et malade; mais sans la bile l'homme ne saurait vivre. Tout est dangereux ici-bas, et tout est nécessaire."' ('The passions are the winds which fill the sails of the vessel,' resumed the hermit. 'They submerge her sometimes, but without them, she could not sail. Phlegm, indeed, makes men peevish and sick; but then there is no living without it. Everything is dangerous, here below, and everything is necessary.') I am indebted to Néhal Abuelata for her assistance in translating the passage in French from Voltaire's *Zadig*. Overt references to this epigraph appear in the pages of volumes 1 and 3 of *Glenarvon* : She alludes to the 'tempest of our passions,' 'the fierce passions that disturb mankind,' and claims 'there are passions implanted in the heart's core, which reason cannot subdue; and God himself compassionates, when a fellow-creature refuses to extend to us his mercy or forgiveness'. See above, pp. 25, 47, 245. Lamb chose another epigraph for the fourth edition of *Glenarvon*: 'Contemptu famae contemni virtutem.' This epigraph (*to despise fame is to despise merit*) is from the *Annals* of Tacitus, Book 4, para. 38.
2. *Everard St. Clare*: the reader will notice in *Glenarvon* many variations on the name 'Clare', including St Clara, Clarence, and Clare of Costolly. Lamb seems to have an uncanny ability to choose names that echo in Byron's life, here with a probable reference to Byron's close friend, with whom Lamb also communicated, the Earl of Clare.
3. *In the town of Belfont. ... name he had assumed.*: Lamb revised the first paragraph of *Glenarvon*, as indicated in the copy of the novel held in the National Bibliotheek van Nederland, containing Lamb's notes for the printer. Had her changes been observed, the opening sentences of the novel would have read: 'In the town of Belfont, in Ireland, lived a learned physician of the name of Everard St. Clare. His brother, whose fine but wild imagination raising him too far above the interests of common life, had squandered away

his small inheritance; and had long roved through the world, foretelling in poetic visions, to those who would hear him, that which futurity would more fully develop. – Camioli was the name he had assumed.'

4. *Glenaa*: like Glenarvon, is derived from 'glen' – a mountain-valley, usually narrow and forming the course of a stream.
5. *Banshees*: supernatural beings supposed by Irish and Scottish peasants to wail under the windows of a house where one of the residents is about to die.
6. *Bright shone the stars ... toward the heavens.*: In her notes for the printer for the second edition, Lamb made a new paragraph beginning with 'Bright shone the stars.' Had her changes been incorporated, the text would have read: 'Bright shone the stars that night, and to the exalted imagination of the aged seer, in sleep it lay, that the spirits of departed heroes, freed from the bonds of mortality, were ascending in solemn grandeur before his eyes; – the song of the Banshees, mourning for the sorrows of their country, broke upon the silence of night; – and he heard or thought he heard the air resound with the quivering of wings, as with one accord innumerable spirits arose, fanning the breeze with their extended plumes, and ascending toward the heavens.' *Glenarvon*, Lamb's edited copy of first edition, National Bibliotheek van Nederland. Most of this passage, starting with '– the song of the Banshees,' was cut from the second edition.
7. *Then, for the first time, Camioli beheld, in one comprehensive view, the*: Lamb revised this passage to read 'Then, for the first time, Camioli, in one comprehensive view, the – ', then cut it later. Revision from Lamb's edited copy of first edition, National Bibliotheek van Nederland. See also textual variants.
8. *soft sweet*: changed to 'sweet soft' in Lamb's edited copy of first edition, National Bibliotheek van Nederland, but not incorporated in second edition.
9. *but for*: changed to 'but' in Lamb's edited copy of first edition, National Bibliotheek van Nederland, (but not incorporated in second edition).
10. *ruined priory ... deserted halls of Belfont*: probable allusion to the ruins of Byron's ancestral home, Newstead Abbey, in Nottinghamshire, which had been a monastery until Henry VIII dissolved it in 1539 and in the subsequent year granted it to the poet's ancestor, Sir John Byron, who converted the priory into a house.
11. *Cold are thy waters, Killarney*: the Irish city in County Kerry sits nigh a lake: Lough Leane.
12. *the arches and colonades of the Castle of Belfont*: again, probably based on Byron's ancestral home, Newstead Abbey.
13. *Previous, however,*: changed to 'Previous,' in Lamb's edited copy of first edition, National Bibliotheek van Nederland, but not incorporated in second edition.
14. *Castle Delaval*: Lamb chooses the name of her mother-in-law's (Lady Melbourne's) grandmother.
15. *river Elle*: from the river in Brittany, France.
16. *Inis Tara*: The Hill of Tara was considered the ancient seat of the high kings of Ireland; 'Inis' – Gaelic for 'island.'
17. *Lord de Ruthven*: Lamb almost certainly alludes to Grey de Ruthyn, whose story she heard from Byron and Byron's friends. Byron and his mother rented his family seat, Newstead Abbey, to the nineteenth Baron Grey de Ruthyn (1780–1810), then twenty-three years old, starting in January 1803, for £50 a year for five years, when Byron would come of age. Byron's mother appears to have fallen in love with Ruthyn, and Byron fell out with him inexplicably in January 1804, perhaps because Ruthyn made an unwanted sexual

advance to Byron, or perhaps his advance was welcomed but the relationship became a source of distress for Byron.
18. *Culloden*: The Battle of Culloden (16 April 1746) pitted the French-supported Jacobites (mostly Scots Highlanders) against the British Government. It was the last battle of an uprising that had begun in 1745. The Jacobites were utterly defeated in their attempt to restore the House of Stuart to the throne, and after the battle many of them were slaughtered by forces of the British army general, the Duke of Cumberland, son of King George II.
19. *Duke of Altamonte*: some of the Duke's characteristics may have been drawn from Lamb's uncle, the Duke of Devonshire.
20. *because all cannot be obtained, to which he once aspired*: changed to 'because all to which he once aspired cannot be obtained', in the edited copy of the first edition, National Bibliotheek van Nederland, but not incorporated in second edition.
21. *Mrs. Seymour*: a character amalgamated of traits drawn from Lamb's mother and her aunt Georgiana. Lamb also probably drew upon her childhood governess, Selina Trimmer.
22. *William Buchanan*: this character's social position is modelled on that of Lamb's first cousin, William, Marquis of Hartington (also known as 'Hart'), who became the sixth Duke of Devonshire in 1811. Hart had been hopelessly in love with his cousin, Lady Caroline, and collapsed when he heard of her betrothal to William Lamb. William Buchanan is, however, indifferent to Calantha as a prospective wife, and his steely resolve and amorality owe more to Sir Godfrey Vassal Webster, Lady Holland's son by her first marriage, with whom Lamb had an affair in 1810–11.
23. *Lady Margaret Buchanan*: some contemporary readers thought this character was based upon the Duchess of Devonshire, but most recognized it as a portrait of Lamb's mother-in-law, Lady Melbourne, an astute member of the 'gynocracy' (as Byron dubbed it), who may even have had an affair with Byron, with whom she was very intimate during and after Lamb's own liaison with the poet.
24. *Lord Dartford*: possibly based upon Lord Dartford of *The Fugitive*, by Joseph Richardson (1755–1803), a comedy produced in London's King's Theater and printed in a third edition in 1792. Dartford is described as 'a man void of feeling, sentiment, or sincerity – uniting in him every contradiction of depravity; cold, gay, ostentatious, and interested – But he is a man of birth – Despicable distinction.' *The Fugitive* Act II, sc. 3. Joseph Richardson was a Member of Parliament and close friends with playwright and politician Richard Brinsley Sheridan, who was an intimate of Lamb's social circle.
25. *visiting Rome and Florence.*: Byron had travelled in Europe and the Middle East, and returned just prior to his mother's death in 1811.
26. *chevalier*: knight.
27. *harrow up thy soul*: a phrase from *Hamlet* V.i: '... I could a tale unfold whose lightest word / Would harrow up thy soul, freeze thy young blood ... etc.'
28. '*Stesso sangue, Stessa sorte*': the same blood, the same fate.
29. *Mrs. Seymour and her daughters*: Sophia and Frances Seymour are drawn from Lamb's cousins, both daughters of the Duchess of Devonshire, Harriet (nicknamed Hary-O) and Georgiana (nicknamed Little G).
30. *affections*: Here Lamb planned to insert the following passage: 'Calantha was a Roman Catholic; and she rigidly adhered to that faith. All who differed from this persuasion were in Mrs Seymour's opinion lost; & her daughters had not only the happiness of believing that they were themselves saved but as they looked apound them they had also the additional delight of thinking that those who differed from them were lost – –.' See

Lamb's edited copy of first edition, National Bibliotheek van Nederland for changes not incorporated in second edition.

31. *In the company of one or other of these, Calantha*: Lamb's planned revisions include this passage, 'In the company of St. Clare and Alice, Calantha'. *Glenarvon*, Lamb's edited copy of first edition, National Bibliotheek van Nederland.
32. *CHAPTER IX.*: This chapter was misnumbered 'X,' omitting IX. All subsequent chapters were therefore misnumbered. The errors, which persisted into subsequent editions, have all been silently corrected here.
33. *Henry Mowbray, Earl of Avondale*: character clearly modelled upon William Lamb, with whom Lady Caroline fell hard in love, and who returned her affection steadfastly through many years of domestic grief after their marriage in 1805.
34. *said he*: In Lamb's handwritten remarks and corrections to her printer, the following note appears on page 103 of the first volume of the copy held in the Netherlands: 'Never put said he & said she always the reverse – '. *Glenarvon*, Lamb's edited copy of first edition, National Bibliotheek van Nederland.
35. *Leitrim*: County Leitrim lies in the northrn part of Ireland.
36. *bride his early fancy had chosen*: When William met Lady Caroline as a young girl, he is reputed to have said, 'Of all the Devonshire House girls, that is the one for me'. David Cecil, *Melbourne* (New York: Bobbs-Merrill, 1954), p. 57.
37. *with shrieks of despair she was torn from her father's bosom*: this account of the wedding reproduces several events from Lady Caroline's own marriage, including her collapse after the ceremony. See Paul Douglass, *Lady Caroline Lamb: A Biography* (New York: Palgrave, 2004), p. 51.
38. *Lord Avondale's religious opinions*: William Lamb's religion was not like Lamb's passionate belief. After sitting through a long evangelical sermon, he once commented dryly: 'Things have come to a pretty pass when religion is allowed to invade the sphere of private life.' He is also reputed to have said that he could not be considered a pillar of the church, but rather a 'buttress', for he "supported it from the outside." See Lord G. W. E. Russell, *Collections and Recollections* (London, 1903), p. 64.
39. *He foresaw not the peril to which he exposed her*: Lamb complained that William had undermined her naïve religious faith, thinking she possessed a stronger character than she actually did. During her 1810 affair with Godfrey Webster, she told her mother-in-law that William had weakened her principles, 'that horror of vice of deceit of any thing that was the least improper that Religion which I believed in then without a doubt & with what William pleasd to call superstitious enthusiasm ... they were safeguards to a character like mine & nobody can tell the almost childish innocence & innexperience I had preserved till then – all at once this was thrown off & William himself though still unconscious of what he has done'. *The Whole Disgraceful Truth: Selected Letters of Lady Caroline Lamb*, ed. P. Douglass (New York: Palgrave, 2006), p. 53.
40. *It was also for Calantha's misfortune ... its wildness and its uncertainty*: Changes made in this paragraph (see textual variants) indicate that Lamb was softening any implied criticism of William Lamb.
41. *At Allenwater*: spelt 'Allanwater' consistently in the second edition, but inconsistently one or the other in the first.
42. *Monteith*: based upon Lamb's favorite spot in England, the Melbournes' country estate, Brocket Hall, in Hertfordshire, near Welwyn, although the behaviour of the "society" there was identical with that of the Melbourne's London residence, Melbourne House.

Editorial Notes   367

43. *Lady Monteith*: i.e., Lady Mowbrey, Lord Avondale's aunt, a character possibly based on Lady Melbourne, whose characteristics, like those of Lamb herself, can be detected in multiple characters, including Lady Margaret.
44. *The threatening storm of rebellion*: the novel's historical setting is the period leading up to the rebellion of the United Irishmen in 1798, which was thoroughly put down with much bloodshed.
45. '*A young musician*': Viviani's and Gondimar's musicianship suggests the possibility that Isaac Nathan, who had collaborated with Byron to write the *Hebrew Melodies* (1815–16), and who supplied the music printed in *Glenarvon* might have provided part of the inspiration for their characters.
46. *natural to the human form and constitution*: here and in the following paragraph, Lamb lays out arguments she had read in Mary Wollstonecraft's 1792 manifesto, *Vindication of the Rights of Woman*.
47. *moment she enjoys*: Lamb's passion for dancing was in full swing with the London craze for waltzing when she met Byron in 1812, but he 'made me swear I was never to Waltz'. *The Whole Disgraceful Truth*, p. 203.
48. *Lady Mandeville and Lady Augusta Selwyn*: the former is based upon Lamb's close friend, the intellectual Lady Oxford, who betrayed her with Byron in fall 1812; the latter is based possibly on Lady Jersey, renowned for her beauty and wit, who took a liking to Byron and stuck by him when he left his wife in 1816, or possibly Lady Cahir, who introduced the playwright Richard Brinsley Sheridan to Lamb's family.
49. *which attracted*: Byron is reported by Lady Blessington as describing Lady Oxford, the model for Lady Mandeville: 'She resembled a landscape by Claude Lorraine, with a setting sun, her beauties enhanced by the knowledge that they were shedding their last dying beams ... '. *Lady Blessington's Conversations of Lord Byron*, ed. E. J. Lovell Jr. (Princeton, NJ: Princeton University Press, 1969), p. 149.
50. *but you do not understand Greek, do you?*: Lamb undertook the study of Greek from Lady Oxford and from William, her own husband.
51. *but vicious*: a Freudian slip, perhaps – corrected to 'but not vicious' in the second edition. See textual variants.
52. *Mr. Tremore was ... bear the name*: Tremore (whose name is later spelt 'Fremore,' to which it is corrected throughout the second edition) is a parody of the acerbically witty poet, Samuel Rogers. Lamb has turned him from his cadaverously thin actual size into a man of 'huge circumference,' as she says in the next sentence. The other characteristics she gives him seem to have been his own, if exaggerated. He sometimes played a conciliatory role when Byron and Lamb had fights during their affair.
53. *certain jests and bon mots ... adapted for certain conversations*: the practice of preparing clever remarks and rejoinders in advance for certain probable conversations was well-established in Lamb's era. Few talkers were so fluent as Lamb, and most had to prepare, employing a method Byron later satirised in *Don Juan*, xiii.98: 'What unexpected woes / Await those who have studied their *bon mots*!' 'Woes' await for those who have cribbed their witticisms from smart sources ahead of time, and must then somehow 'allure the conversation / By many windings to their clever clinch.'
54. *petit souper très- bien assorti*: a small dinner, well appointed.
55. *le beau capitaine, le chef des brigands*: the handsome captain, the chief of the thieves.
56. *frappé*: struck, impressed.
57. *petit maître*: little master.
58. *mon enfant*: my child.

59. *déjeûné paré*: breakfast (or lunch) party.
60. *her husband neglected her*: Lamb did complain that William paid no attention to her, and told her friend Lady Morgan that, 'I might flirt and go about with what men I pleased'. *Lady Morgan's Memoirs: Autobiography, Diaries and Correspondence*, 2nd edn (London: William H. Allen, 1863), vol. 2, p. 199.
61. *Lord Trelawny*: Trelawny (spelt sometimes 'Trelawney') may be based upon Granville Leveson-Gower, who had a years-long affair with Lamb's mother, Lady Bessborough, with whom he had two illegitimate children; but he ended in marrying Lamb's cousin, Harriet, daughter of the Duke and Duchess of Devonshire, just as, here, Trelawney marries Calantha's cousin, Frances. If so, Leveson-Gower took no offence at being included as a character, and he supported Lamb when she was attacked after the publication of *Glenarvon*.
62. *first gipsey*: in the second edition, Lamb clarified it was the Friar speaking. See textual variants.
63. *thus disguised*: i.e., dressed as a friar. This is made clear in the revision to the second edition. See textual variants.
64. *His hands were decorated with rings ... which much delighted Calantha*: The description fits the personality of Lamb's lover in 1810–11, Sir Godfrey Vassal Webster (1789–1836), son of Lady Holland by her first husband, and a notorious bad boy.
65. *Mowbrey*: The name is spelt 'Mowbray' everywhere else in the first edition, but was corrected universally to 'Mowbrey' in the second.
66. *Calantha thought of nothing but Zerbellini*: Lamb delighted in dressing up her page boys, for whom she had special uniforms designed to her specifications, and also in dressing up herself as a page boy, in which guise she appeared in Byron's rooms on several occasions. She had herself painted by Thomas Phillips in page's livery holding a platter of grapes and being gazed upon by a spaniel, an allusion to the appearance of the devil as a feminine page in a novel she and Byron had shared reading: Jacques Cazotte's *Le diable amoureux* (1772). After Byron jilted her, Lamb burned him in effigy, and her pages and footmen supposedly sported buttons on their livery with the motto 'Ne Crede Biron' [*Believe not in Byron*]. Byron's family motto was 'Crede Biron'.
67. *Duke of Myrtlegrove*: apparently based upon the fifth Duke of Devonshire, Lamb's uncle (nicknamed 'Canis,' perhaps for his love of dogs), whom she liked. The name, like 'Glenarvon' and 'Avondale', is yet another allusion to leafy forests.
68. *the account of Rome which Lucian has placed in the mouth of Nigrinus*: Lucian of Samosata was an Assyrian satirist and rhetorician who wrote in Greek. In his dialogue *Nigrinus* he makes that Platonic philosopher a critic of Rome, contrasting its low culture and greed with the high culture of Athens. Viviani is making a similar assault on the avarice and ignorance of London.
69. *Chaste – pure! ... never – never.*': Cuts from this paragraph in the second edition (see textual variants) are meant to lessen the overt sexuality of the relationship between 'Viviani' and Calantha, no doubt in deference to the offended tastes of several of Lamb's friends and family members.
70. *Fremore*: Tremore is referred to as 'Fremore' from this point on, and the spelling is kept for the second edition.
71. *Princess of Madagascar*: a send-up of Lamb's friend and confidante, Lady Holland, so convincingly drawn that twenty years after *Glenarvon* appeared, friends still called Lady Holland the 'Princess Madagascar' behind her back, J. Clubbe, '*Glenarvon* Revised – and Revisited,' *The Wordsworth Circle*, 10 (1979), pp. 209, 213. Lady Holland, being

divorced, was not a proper person to consort with, but Lamb did. Lamb also had an affair in 1810 with Lady Holland's son by her first marriage, Sir Godfrey Vassal Webster.
72. *Nabob*: a corrupted form of the Indian title Nawab (a person of high status). In contemporary usage: a merchant of great wealth and status, like those East India Company men who had made fortunes and returned to England; in broader usage: an influential person with an extravagant lifestyle.
73. *Barbary House*: i.e., Holland House, in Kensington.
74. *petits mots obligeants*: small words of kindness.
75. '*darkness visible*': Milton's phrase for the atmosphere of hell in *Paradise Lost*: ' ... from those flames / No light but rather darkness visible', I:62–3.
76. *This yellow hyena*: like Tremore/Fremore, another parody of Samuel Rogers, but this time in a form more like his actual cadaverous appearance. All this satirical description was cut in the second edition. See textual variants.
77. *Hoiaouskim*: this character is based on John Allen, whom Lady Holland employed as her physician, according to Lloyd Sanders, *The Holland House Circle* (London: Methuen, 1908), p. 73.
78. *The sun may shine fairly ... the Princess of Madagascar*.: This last paragraph of the twenty-ninth chapter of volume one of *Glenarvon* exhibits Lamb's animus toward Lady Holland for her hypocrisy and amorality. Lamb had exchanged many hot letters with Lady Holland during the time of Lamb's affair with, Sir Godfrey Vassal Webster, Lady Holland's son by her first marriage – for example, this passage from a letter of July 1811:
[A]s to the gnats & mites that dare to peck at me let them look to themselves – I will turn upon before long with the vengeance which one bated & pursued at length is taught to feel & level them to the dust from which they sprung – what are these things that dare to speak of me – at best only my equals & by what I can find many of them inferior to me in the satiric powers they would stab me with – grant me but health & life & if I chuse it you shall see them flatter & follow me & lick the dust I tread on – Lady Holland if this is the case I shall be courted by you [–] that which is loved becomes lovely in your eyes.
The Whole Disgraceful Truth: Selected Letters of Lady Caroline Lamb, p. 72.
79. *accursed hazard*: a precursor of modern dice games. There were at least two kinds: French hazard, in which the players bet against the bank, and English, or 'chicken hazard,' in which they played against each other.
80. '*Honey,' quoth she ... 'Humph,' quoth he*: adapted from 'The Lady that Loved a Swine,' a nursery-rhyme in which 'Humph' is to be pronounced in as swine-like a manner as possible:
There was a lady loved a swine.
'Honey,' said she,
'Pig hog, wilt thou be mine?'
'Humph!' said he.
81. *The curricle was beautiful*: a curricle was a light two-wheeled carriage, usually drawn by two horses abreast, fast and smart.
82. *innoxious*: Not noxious or hurtful; harmless, innocuous.
83. *'Nous nous aimions dés l'enfance .... en auriez fait autant.'*: Jean-François Marmontel (1723–99), from his comic opera, *Annette et Lubin* (1762), in which a shepherdess becomes pregnant by a shepherd who is her cousin:
'We've loved each other since childhood,
Always together at every moment.'
'in our place
You would have done the same.'

84. *chevelure*: head of hair.
85. *Anabel was the name given to the little infant*: Another example of Lamb's chosing names that cut uncomfortably close to her circle of acquaintances. Lord Byron's wife was called 'Annabella,' short for 'Anne Isabella'.
86. *Mi Lady; ne prendra-t-elle pas ce petit bonnet?*: My Lady, won't you take the bonnet?
87. *Titania ... Oberon ... boldly refused*: *A Midsummer Night's Dream* (I:2), in which Titania and Oberon, queen and king of the fairies, argue, and Oberon asks that she give him her personal attendant, an Indian boy, but she refuses.
88. *Lady Trelawney*: Sophia Seymour's sister, Frances, by virtue of having married Lord Trelawney, is now Lady Trelawney.
89. *no claim to that title*: like Glenarvon's father, Byron's grandfather was a naval officer. Byron's father was a womanizer who married in order to spend his wives' fortunes. The emphasis here seems to be on the lack of a *moral* claim to the Glenarvon title.

Volume II

1. *Disperato dolor ... ne favelle*: 'I renew a hopeless despair, that makes my heart still ache, at the thought, before the words follow.' From Dante Alighieri's *Inferno*, canto 33. See note 1 to volume 1, above, for details of the modifications to this epigraph in the second and fourth editions of the novel.
2. *discontented Catholics ... waiting to see her father*: Catholic emancipation was a key goal of the 1798 Irish Rebellion.
3. *'smile whilst I murder'*: *Henry VI, Part III* (III.2) – Richard, the Duke of Gloucester, confesses he will do anything to attain the throne: 'Why I can smile, and murder whiles I smile ... '
4. *like Agave in the orgies of Bacchus*: Agave is blinded by Dionysius and, during a Bacchanal orgy of incredible violence, either kills or causes to be slain her own son, Pentheus.
5. *will speak a word for him thoft*: reference unclear. The *OED* defines 'thoft' as a rower's bench.
6. *intituled*: i.e., 'entitled'.
7. *barouche*: A four-wheeled carriage with a seat in front for the driver, and seats inside for two couples to sit facing each other.
8. *ribbands*: early spelling of the modern word 'ribbons'.
9. *Calantha endeavoured to rouse herself ... could not easily be overcome*: Lamb's response to Byron's physical appearance was strongest in regard to his face. After seeing him the first time, she told her friend Lady Morgan that she wrote in her diary, 'That beautiful pale face will be my fate'. *Lady Morgan's Memoirs*, vol. 2, p. 200.
10. *His name I cannot ... this I will say*: Here is a rare instance of direct first person address from the narrator, a passage that would have tended to confirm *Glenarvon* as autobiography. Lamb changed it in the second edition. See textual variants.
11. *'Oimè si muoja! ... si muoja'*: Oh my, she is dying! Your Excellency, she is dying'.
12. *the penal statutes ... tythes*: The penal statutes were to be repealed since they disenfranchised Catholics. Similarly, tithing (collection of a percentage of wealth produced annually) benefited the Anglican church alone.
13. *Glenarvon seemed, however, to differ in practice from his principles ... in no other manner*: Lamb exposes here the hypocrisy of Whig principles of liberation in contrast to their practice of maintaining their social status, hypocrisy in which Byron was implicated.

14. *Heloisa*: Lamb wavers between 'Eloise', 'Heloise' and 'Heloisa' in the first and second editions.
15. *all that is new or rare ... in your estimation*: an echo of a phrase Byron apparently used when, early in their relationship, he gave Lamb a rose, saying, according to Prothero and Coleridge, 'Your Ladyship, I am told, likes all that is new and rare, for a moment'. *The Works of Lord Byron: A New, Revised, and Enlarged Edition, With Illustrations*, 13 vols, ed. Rowland E. Prothero and Ernest Hartley Coleridge (London: John Murray; New York: C. Scribner's Sons, 1898–1905), vol. 2, p. 451.
16. *all that others said ... she could feel*: an echo of one of Byron's letters to Lamb: 'All that you so often *say*, *I feel*, can more be said or felt?' (*Byron's Letters and Journals*, vol. 2, p. 171).
17. *The heart of a libertine ... chaste even in thought*: revisions to this passage show Lamb was trying to play down the carnal nature of the relationship between her protagonists. See textual variants.
18. *éclat,*: brilliant success.
19. *had effect*: at this point, Lamb inserts an entirely new song not included in the first edition, beginning 'If to lose all that love thee ... ' See textual variants.
20. *The Broken Heart*: In John Ford's play of that title (1633) the main character is named 'Calantha'. See the introduction to *Glenarvon* above for further explanation of this literary allusion.
21. *as Hyperion to a satyr*: *Hamlet* (I:ii), in which Hamlet compares his father to his usurping uncle: 'So excellent a king, that was to this / Hyperion to a satyr...' Hyperion was a titan, son of Gaia and Uranus.
22. *invade Ireland*: the French really did send a force of approximately 1,000 troops to Ireland in support of the rebellion in August 1798, without material success.
23. *a ring*: Lord Byron almost certainly did give Lamb a ring (though not with the Irish inscription described here), the location of which is now unknown.
24. *Even were you a Clarissa ... I am no Lovelace*: In Samuel Richardson's novel, *Clarissa* (1748), Lovelace rapes Clarissa and she dies.
25. *none ever but Lord Avondale read as well*: William Lamb read aloud to Lamb frequently, especially in the months after they were first married.
26. *heart is seered*: the spelling of 'seered' remains unchanged in the second edition.
27. *Glenarvon*: silently corrected from 'Glenarnon'. This error was corrected in the second edition, only to reappear in the third.
28. *'for God's sake, approach me not'*: Here and elsewhere in the second edition Lamb seems to have sought to deflect charges of a blasphemous tendency in *Glenarvon* by eliminating 'God' and substituting 'heaven' or 'mercy'. See textual variant for this passage.
29. *It seemed as if the wind ... had struck upon the chords*: an allusion to the Aeolian harp which fascinated some of the romantic poets, including Coleridge and Shelley.
30. *By that smile which made me blest ... What fate attends Glenarvon's love*: in the second edition these verses are formatted slightly differently: the first, third, fifth and sixth lines are indented.
31. *I may still be proud of my child*: an example of the elements that made readers identify Mrs. Seymour as based on Lamb's mother, Lady Bessborough, or perhaps her aunt, Georgiana, Duchess of Devonshire.
32. *he again pressed her to his bosom*: in keeping with her attempt to play down the carnal nature of the relationship between Glenarvon and Lady Avondale, Lamb cut this phrase in the second edition. See textual variants.

33. *Other men think only ... a thousand times for her*: If an observation of Lord Byron's character, this is an interesting insight into his skill with the opposite sex.
34. *Scottish bard*: Robert Burns (1759–96).
35. *The sacred lore ... petrifies the feeling*: Robert Burns, 'Epistle to a Young Friend May 1786', verse 6.
36. *CHAPTER XXVII*: The misnumbering of Chapter XXVI went uncorrected in the second edition. See silent corrections.
37. *He now opened to her the dark recesses of his heart ... each new confession.*: These phrases recall Lamb's claim that Byron revealed to her his criminal activities, perhaps including homicide and homosexual acts, in an attempt to drive her away.
38. *CHAPTER XXVI*: The misnumbering of Chapter XXVII went uncorrected in the second edition. See silent corrections.
39. *And I am your's for ever ... own free act and deed*: The editors have here followed Lamb's corrections in the second edition, clearing up a punctuational puzzle, although not entirely satisfactorily. See silent corrections.
40. *even in the delirium ... the transports of love*: Lamb again changed the language in the second edition to diminish the overtness of the carnal relationship between Calantha and Glenarvon. See textual variants for volume II.
41. *He placed a ring upon her finger ... look yet once upon me*: Lamb and Byron apparently went through a mock wedding ceremony. They exchanged several rings, including 'a wedding one' that Byron insisted Lamb '*bestowed* upon *herself* & insisted on my placing it on her finger'. See *Byron's Letters and Journals*, vol. 3, p. 355.
42. *For the sake of that resemblance*: Here the second edition of *Glenarvon* inserts a footnote: 'See Chaucer's Troilus and Creseide.' See textual variants.
43. *mais triste pensée pour moi*: but a sad thought for me.
44. *He unites the malice ... as I do*: Lamb's characterization of Glenarvon as socially bisexual is couched in the phrases of Lady Margaret, but points toward Lamb's own observations of Lord Byron himself.
45. '*si vous vous faites brebis le loup vous mangera*': a proverb: He that makes himself a sheep, the wolf will eat. Emanuel Straus, *Dictionary of European Proverbs*, 3 vols (New York: Routledge, 1994), vol. 1, p. 954.
46. *CHAPTER XXXVI*: The misnumbering of this chapter went uncorrected in the second edition. See silent corrections.
47. '*Eterna fede*': eternal fidelity.
48. '*Eterno dolor*': eternal sorrow.
49. *German sentiments*: Lamb's generation associated the Germans with sentimentalism and emotionality. Their phrase for what is today called a *ménage aux trois* was 'German trio.'

Volume III

1. *Disperato dolor ... ne favelle*: 'I renew a hopeless despair, that makes my heart still ache, at the thought, before the words follow.' From Dante Alighieri's *Inferno* canto 33. See above, p. 357, n. 1, for details of the modifications to this epigraph in the second and fourth editions of the novel
2. *There are trials, which ... mercy or forgiveness*: revisions to this last sentence of the first paragraph of the third volume completely reverse its meaning. See textual variants.
3. *Erin m'avourneen – Erin go brah*: Ireland, my beloved – Ireland forever. From 'The Exile of Erin,' traditional Irish song.

4. *the rights of man*: Thomas Paine's seminal work by this title had appeared in 1789 after being approved by the National Assembly of France on 26 August of that year.
5. *live free or die*: This phrase was part of a toast written by General John Stark in 1809 and – since Stark was too ill to attend – delivered by letter to the anniversary reunion of soldiers who had fought at the Battle of Bennington. It also recalls words attributed to Patrick Henry in a speech delivered to the Virginia House of Burgesses in 1775: 'Give me liberty, or give me death.'
6. *Irishmen ... steady step to victory*: Lamb instructed the printer to mark Glenarvon's entire speech, beginning when he throws 'his dark mantle off' and concluding with 'steady step to victory', with 'inverted comma's – to show that it is taken from a printed speech'. These line-by-line quotation marks were inserted in the second edition, but have not been reproduced in the textual variants here as they are distracting. Apparently, Lamb wanted the reader to imagine that the speech was taken from a printed source, though it appears to be entirely her own creation. *Glenarvon*, Lamb's edited copy of first edition, National Bibliotheek van Nederland.
7. *like a rose torn from ... I have left her*: Lamb returned often to the 'Last Rose of Summer' theme epitomized in the song of that title in volume five of Thomas Moore's *Irish Melodies*. She even painted herself as the personification of the last rose of summer. The watercolor is held in the Bessborough Collection at Stanstead.
8. *Think of me when I am away ... the ecstasy of being loved*: revisions to this paragraph for the second edition seek to lessen the implied carnality of the relationship between Glenarvon and Calantha. See textual variants.
9. *Clytie*: water nymph spurned by Apollo, who pined away for him and was transformed into a sunflower so that her face constantly followed Apollo in his course across the sky. Lamb compared herself to a sunflower in her relationship to Lord Byron; see *The Whole Disgraceful Truth*, p. 79.
10. *heaved the log*: a method of estimating speed. Knots were tied at seven-fathom intervals on a line tied to a log that would float. The log was heaved, and the number of knots was counted as the line paid out. If five knots passed in half a minute, for example, the ship's speed was five nautical miles an hour.
11. *They that go down into the great deep; they see the wonders of the Lord*: adapted from the Bible, Psalms 107:23–4.
12. *Miss Monmouth*: character alludes to Byron's wife, Annabella Milbanke, who was Lamb's husband's cousin.
13. *I am no longer your lover ... leave me in peace*: Lamb reproduces a version of a letter Byron wrote to her, which reads, 'Our affections are not in our own power ... am no longer your lover ... correct your vanity, which has become ridiculous – exert your caprices on others, enjoy the excellent flow of spirits which make you so delightful in the eyes of others, and leave me in peace'. See *Byron's Letters and Journals*, vol. 2, p. 242.
14. *It was a scene of horror ... confusion and pain*: According to the account Caroline later gave Lady Morgan, Byron's letter telling her he was no longer attached to her arrived with a coronet on the seal under which she recognized the initials of Lady Oxford. 'It was that cruel letter I have published in *Glenarvon*', Caroline wrote, 'it destroyed me: I lost my brain. I was bled, leeched; kept for a week in the filthy Dolphin Inn, at Rock. On my return I was in great prostration of mind and spirit'; see S. Owenson, Lady Morgan, *Lady Morgan's Memoirs: Autobiography, Diaries, and Correspondence* 2nd edn, 2 vols (London: William H. Allen, 1863), vol. 2, p. 201.

15. *a broken heart*: another allusion to John Ford's *The Broken Heart* (1633). This exact phrase occurs eight times in volume 3 of *Glenarvon*.
16. *a braid of her own*: Lady Caroline had petitioned repeatedly for a lock of Byron's hair, and Lady Melbourne helped her by reproaching Byron for balking at supplying such a 'trifle': '[R]eally by yr reluctance to have yr Hair touched, or to part with any of it,--I am tempted to think there is some particular charm attached to it--& yt some of yr powers will be lessen'd, I will not say lost ... something like Sampson'. See letter of Lady Melbourne to Lord Byron, 25 March 1813 in Elizabeth Milbanke Lamb, Viscountess Melbourne, *Byron's 'Corbeau Blanc': The Life and Letters of Lady Melbourne*, ed. J. D. Gross (Houston, TX: Rice University Press, 1997), p. 140. Under this teasing, Byron acceded. But instead of his own hair he sent a lock of Lady Oxford's. He gloated that if she ever discovered the cheat, it would have an effect upon her comparable to a lock from the head of the Medusa. See *Byron's Letters and Journals*, vol. 3, pp. 37, 40.
17. *C'est piquant cela: j'admire!*: It is so cutting: I like it!
18. *his titles and estates ... restored to him*: Glenarvon's repossession of his estates and titles marks the point at which he abandons all pretense of leading the Irish rebellion. Lady Margaret plays a crucial role in this change of circumstances.
19. *Oh listen not to the voice of the charmer, charm she ever so sweetly*: In the second edition this phrase is placed in quotation marks, indicating it is drawn from a printed source; origin unknown to the editors.
20. *leaving them under your care*: Under British law of the period, Lord Avondale would have had the right to take sole possession of his offspring, leaving Calantha with no recourse.
21. *'Is he gone?' were*: In every other first edition of *Glenarvon* the editors have seen, this phrase contains the word 'were', but the copy of *Glenarvon* held in the Koninkliijke Bibliotheek of the National Bibliotheek van Nederland, containing Lamb's notes for the printer, prints 'was,' which has been corrected in ink by her to 'were.'
22. *'Had my mother lived ... breaks my heart*: the passage reminds us that Mrs Seymour is based partly upon Lamb's mother, Countess Bessborough.
23. *post-chaise and four*: a carriage usually having a closed body on four wheels and seating two to four persons, drawn by four horses.
24. *'It is not an open enemy ... we took sweet counsel together*: taken from Psalms 55:12–14.
25. *arbutus*: a large genus of flowering plants of temperate regions of the Mediterranean and North America. The species in the Mediterranean and Western Europe are called strawberry trees from the resemblance of the fruit to a strawberry.
26. *St. Clare*: in Lamb's corrections to the first edition preserved in the copy of *Glenarvon* in the Netherlands, this name was changed to 'Elinor', but the correction was not made in the second edition. Glenarvon, Lamb's edited copy of first edition, National Bibliotheek van Nederland.
27. *with a master-hand that he struck the chords*: an echo of Lamb's first extant letter to Lord Byron: 'Oh that like thee Childe Harold I had power / With Master hand to strike the thrilling Lyre...' See *The Whole Disgraceful Truth*, p. 78.
28. *a ship is given to him ... Sir Richard Mowbrey*: Glenarvon has completely betrayed his fellow Irishmen, as well as Calantha, in joining the British Fleet and becoming engaged to be married.
29. *I cannot be humble*: Lamb was prone to describe herself as proud and keenly aware that her sense of justice 'prevents my being humble or penitent'. *The Whole Disgraceful Truth*, p. 121.

30. *Texel*: pronounced 'Tessel,' a municipality and an island in the Netherlands, part of the Frisian Islands, and thus no more part of Irish geography than the river Elle. The point here is that Glenarvon has betrayed the cause of Irish freedom and is now fighting on the side of the British.
31. *An idol,' replied Glenarvon ... a hypocrite*: In describing Viviani, his pseudonym, Glenarvon consciously describes himself.
32. *Kendal*: spelt 'Kendall' at the end of Chapter 31 of the third volume of *Glenarvon*. See above, p. 338.
33. *wherry*: light rowboat used chiefly on rivers to carry passengers and goods.
34. *He entrusted the Lord of Delaval to my care*: i.e., Macpherson is entrusted with a kidnapped child who is heir to the current Duke of Delaval, in whose place the unfortunate Billy Kendal has been sacrificed.
35. *'In the dead of night ... he denied it.'*: Macpherson thinks Gondimar has stolen the boy from him in Florence, but leaves the issue in doubt, then seems to become firm on the point in the next paragraph. Lamb corrected this possible misdirection of the narrative by cutting the first and last sentences of this passage. See textual variants.
36. *resolved not to let him escape*: Aware of possible confusion in Macpherson's narrative, Lamb added a phrase in the second edition here to indicate that the duke knew 'what part of Macpherson's narrative to believe.' See textual variants.
37. *seeing the dagger*: Silently corrected from 'seizing the dagger,' based on Lamb's notes for corrections to the printer in the copy held in the Netherlands indicates 'see-ing'. *Glenarvon*, Lamb's edited copy of first edition, National Bibliotheek van Nederland.
38. *shall it be obeyed?*: Lamb's notes to the printer in the copy of *Glenarvon* held in the Netherlands indicate she wished a paragraph break to be introduced here, but that change was not made. *Glenarvon*, Lamb's edited copy of first edition, National Bibliotheek van Nederland.
39. *– Upon the night*: Lamb's corrections to the first edition preserved in the copy of *Glenarvon* in the Netherlands call for a new paragraph here, but the change was not made in the second edition. *Glenarvon*, Lamb's edited copy of first edition, National Bibliotheek van Nederland.
40. *'England, thou hast destroyed thy sister country,' she cried*: Lamb amended the beginning of this speech in the second edition to deflect some criticism away from Glenarvon for his treachery, saying 'rage against Glenarvon' ought not to motivate the crowd, and asking, 'how has he offended you?' See textual variants.
41. *Erin go brah*: 'Ireland Forever', from 'The Exile of Erin', traditional Irish song.
42. *Nay, start not, Clarence*: Elinor has called her horse by Glenarvon's Christian name, just as Lamb later named her own horse 'Glenarvon'.
43. *poisoned in an emince*: i.e., poisoned by an 'emincé', a dish of meat cut into thin slices, covered with sauce and baked. The typographical error 'eminee' persisted into the second edition, despite Lamb's note to her printer to fix it, as indicated in the copy of *Glenarvon* held in the Netherlands. It is silently corrected here to avoid confusion. *Glenarvon*, Lamb's edited copy of first edition, National Bibliotheek van Nederland.
44. *carried to the grave by mistake*: Samuel Rogers, upon whom Fremore is apparently partly based, appeared so emaciated that once when he was emerging from the Roman catacombs, a friend turned to him and shook hands, saying to his skeletal friend, 'Good-bye, Rogers'. See M. Joyce, *My Friend H: John Cam Hobhouse, Baron Broughton of Broughton de Gyfford* (London: John Murray, 1948), p. 50.

45. *Ah, no! it was the form of Alice*: By placing this sentence in quotation marks, Lamb seems to conflate the narrator's voice and Glenarvon's.
46. *Visions of death and horror persecute me*: alludes to Shakespeare's *Richard III*, in which Richard is visited by the ghosts of those he has murdered or wronged: 'Richard, thy wife, / That wretched Anne thy wife, / That never slept a quiet hour with thee, / Now fills thy sleep with perturbations'. See *Richard III* (V.iii.161–3).
47. *that famed Dutch merchantman ... before the wind*: according to folklore, the 'Flying Dutchman' is a haunted ship doomed to sail the seas forever with its ghostly crew.
48. *the spirit of evil infatuates before he destroys*: an ancient Latin proverb, 'Quos Deus vult perdere, eos dementat': God infatuates those whom he means to destroy. Often erroneously attributed to Euripides.

Appendix A

1. *without permission, communication, advice, or assistance*: This is the public position of Lamb and her husband, but the evidence suggests that William Lamb knew quite a lot about *Glenarvon* before its publication.
2. *The blood will follow ... by nature grow on pain*: From the play *The Revenge* (1788) by Edward Young (1683–1765), V.ii.
3. *Miss St.-Clare and Lady Margaret Buchanan ... entirely fictitious*: Lamb apparently seeks here to distance herself from any perception that these characters are founded upon persons of her acquaintance. Elinor St Clare is a rebel and a defiant sinner whose suicide punctuates the main plot, and Lady Margaret Buchanan is a schemer who condones homicide. Resemblances between Lady Margaret and Lamb's mother-in-law, Lady Melbourne, would have been particularly painful to acknowledge.

Appendix B

1. *Introduction to the Fourth Edition of Glenarvon*: The full title page describes this text as 'the original Introduction', which apparently refers to an introduction the author composed for the first edition, but which was not printed. This introduction first appears in the fourth edition.
2. *Pleiades*: A cluster of stars in the constellation Taurus, known in Greek mythology as the Seven Sisters.
3. *Children of the Earth ... in exile, loves you*: Lamb employs biblical phraseology found ubiquitously in the King James version, e.g., Deuteronomy 18:19: 'And it shall come to pass, that whosoever will not hearken unto my words which he shall speak in my name, I will require it of him'. She apparently wants to set a cosmic scene like that of Genesis.
4. *The Virgin Queen*: often an epithet for Elizabeth I (1533–1603).
5. *Erin*: Ireland.
6. *one of the beautiful Genii of the Earth*: an apparent reference to the Byron/Glenarvon character of the novel's narrative.
7. *It was in the land of death that I awoke*: Lamb's 'Introduction' functions as a prologue, then, in which the spirit of Calantha is transported across space and time to be incarnated at Altamont and Castle Delaval.
8. *God is just, but the spirit of evil infatuates before it destroys*: An exact repetition of the final lines of *Glenarvon*, but applied here to Calantha herself, rather than to Lord Glenarvon. See above, p. 352.

SILENT CORRECTIONS

Silent corrections made to the 1816 first edition copy text.

Volume I

6	blossom] blosom
16	lover.] lover.'
16	Altamonte.'] Altamonte.
17	Farewell.'] Farewell.
18	Elle.] Elle
18	lost.] lost,
28	youth,'] youth,
28	say, 'is [say,' is
28	instruction;' [instruction;
28	great.'] great.
29	tract,] track,
31	CHAPTER IX.] CHAPTER X.
33	mountains?] mountains?'
34	CHAPTER X.] CHAPTER XI.
36	CHAPTER XI.] CHAPTER XII.
36	'Stesso] 'Stessa
37	miserable.'] miserable.
39	CHAPTER XII.] CHAPTER XIII.
40	castles.'] castles.
41	CHAPTER XIII.] CHAPTER XIV.
42	"Obey your father,"] 'Obey your father,'
42	contemplative?....'] contemplative?....
43	becoming inconsistency;] becominginconsistency;
44	CHAPTER XIV.] CHAPTER XV.
44	Glenaa;] Glanaa;
44	Clara,'] Clara,
44	'your] your
46	'and be] and be

46	controuled.'] controuled.
47	CHAPTER XV.] CHATPER XVI.
47	my temper] 'my temper
48	thus.'] thus.
48	'I will] I will
49	CHAPTER XVI.] CHAPTER XVII.
50	breath] breathe
51	you.'] you.
52	CHAPTER XVII.] CHAPTER XVIII.
54	Talent opposed] Talentopposed
55	before left] before he left
56	CHAPTER XVIII.] CHAPTER XIX.
57	'Oh no!'] Oh no!'
58	Glenaa] Glanaa
59	CHAPTER XIX.] CHAPTER XX.
60	never.'] never.
60	Buchanan'] Buchanan
61	CHAPTER XX.] CHAPTER XXI.
62	'the thing] the thing
62	and how?'] and how?
64	CHAPTER XXI.] CHAPTER XXII.
64	apartment;] appartment;
64	girl.] girl.'
64	surround.'] surround
64	'Gondimar,] Gondimar,
65	I ask.'] I ask.
66	CHAPTER XXII.] CHAPTER XXIII.
68	unhappy.'] unhappy.
68	turning] turing
73	CHAPTER XXIV.] CHAPTER XXV.
74	'Are you] Are you
74	to you for] for you to
74	to it.'] to it.
74	'Do you not] Do you
74	'I do;] I do;
75	CHAPTER XXV.] CHAPTER XXVI.
75	'Why do] Why do
76	– Lady] – 'Lady
76	'you] you
76	destiny.'] destiny.
76	the friar.] the friar
77	'this] this

77	'it may be] 'it may
80	CHAPTER XXVI.] CHAPTER XXVII.
81	Count] 'Count
81	negative.] negative.'
81	'You lived] You lived
82	mad,] mad.
83	CHAPTER XXVII.] CHAPTER XXVIII.
83	gravity; 'but] gravity;' but
83	'Lord] Lord
84	'all passion is founded on ...'] all 'passion is founded on ...
84	idol.'] idol'
86	CHAPTER XXVIII.] CHAPTER XXIX.
86	entered it.'] entered it.
87	Mr.] Mr,
87	trifling] trifiing
87	necessary,] necessarry,
88	whisper,] whisher,
88	'Well,] Well,
88	'will she] will she
88	follies,] folies,
89	CHAPTER XXIX.] CHAPTER XXX.
89	'But who] But who
89	swine –] swine).
90	stopping?'] stopping?
90	shall I?'] shall I?
90	'You do] You do
91	Macvicker] Mavicker
91	girls.'] girls.
91	'have you] have you
91	innoxious] innoxtious
91	for making] or making
92	world.'] world'.
92	same?'] same?
92	Lady Mandeville] 'Lady Mandeville
92	persuasion?] persuasion?'
92	brightening] 'brightening
92	'at Madame] at Madame
94	CHAPTER XXX.] CHAPTER XXXI.
94	'who is he?'] who is he?
95	'but you] but you
95	– every one] – 'every one
95	'but perhaps] but perhaps

95	love.'] love.	
97	CHAPTER XXXI.] CHAPTER XXXII.	
100	CHAPTER XXXII.] CHAPTER XXXIII.	
100	solicitude,] solitude,	
101	else.] else.'	
101	Ireland.'] Ireland.	
101	'is Lord] is Lord	
102	Glenarvon.'] Glenarvon.	

Volume II

108	'Are not] Are not
110	kingdom.'] kingdom.
112	'What!] What!
112	'Clare] Clare
112	boy; 'and] boy;' and
113	them.] them.'
113	as she] asshe
114	ever seen] everseen
118	senses.'] senses.
118	glance.] glance.'
119	Gondimar.] Gondimar,
119	called in.] called in.'
120	Costoly,] Costolly,
120	Costoly?'] Costolly?'
121	adventure.] advenventure.
122	Lady Margaret] Lady, Margaret
123	inconsistencies] inconsistences
124	exclaimed] exclaimed,
124	Shall I] 'Shall I
124	wife – or – But] wife – or –' 'But
125	Lady] 'Lady
125	smiled.] smiled.'
128	Kennedy,'] Kenedy,'
137	Glenaa] Glanaa
147	confused,] confused.
152	more alarming] morealarming
156	herself] hereself
157	'I was,'] 'I was,
158	Avondale] Avondole
158	smiling.] smilng.
158	yet: – But] yet:' – 'But
158	she] ske

159	whispered]	wispered
159	conscientious]	concientious
159	discomfiture]	disconfiture
160	occasionally]	occasionly
160	Glenarvon:]	Glenarvon:'
160	scarce]	scarse
160	change]	change:
162	this evening,]	this, evening,
166	opportunity.']	opportunity.'..
167	surprised]	suprised
172	GLENARVON]	GLENARNON[1]
172	much.']	much.
173	Thou'lt]	Thoult
173	Lord]	lord
177	know it.']	know it.
179	'Be calm,]	'Be cam,
179	'Oh!]	Oh!
179	Your most obedient servant. GLENARVON.']	'Your most obedient servant. 'GLENARVON.'
180	stubbornly]	stub bornly
182	contrary,']	contrary,
182	infatuation.]	infatuation.'
185	'I judge]	I judge
186	'and you distract me.]	and you distract me.'
186	risk']	risk
186	'of our]	of our
186	recurred]	recured
188	to her.]	to her
189	Elinor']	Elinor
189	truth']	truth
189	'you may]	you may
189	weeping; but perhaps,']	weeping;' but perhaps,
190	lowe]	lore
190	so? Alas!]	so?' 'Alas!
190	alone]	one
192	CHAPTER XXVI.]	CHAPTER XXIV.
194	believe?' – His]	believe? – 'His
196	CHAPTER XXVII.]	CHAPTER XXVI.
196	on it!']	on it!
197	dream.']	dream'
199	all?']	all?
201	appealing]	'appealing

201	'For] For	
203	'my heart] my heart	
203	many.'] many.	
203	'They will] They will	
203	from me.'] from me.	
204	the agonies] theagonies	
204	you:] you:'	
204	curse me.'] curse me.	
204	wilt thou] wiltthou	
205	ever:' 'but] ever: but	
205	deed.] deed.'	
205	Lady Margaret] Lady Magaret	
205	said Calantha. 'Oh] 'said Calantha. Oh	
208	I cannot:' 'Meet] I cannot: meet	
208	satisfied.'] satisfied.	
209	Calantha.] Calantha	
209	now] know	
216	she wrote] shewrote	
216	loved not.] loved not	
218	appeared] appeard	
219	Lord] lord	
219	Lord] lord	
220	her. Hurrying] her hurrying	
220	Lord] lord	
220	his] fiis	
220	Lady] lady	
220	Lord] lord	
220	too long.'] too long.	
221	it would] il would	
221	sorrows,' she said: 'you] sorrows.' She said: you	
221	will live,'] will live,	
222	immediately] mediately	
222	ask it?'] ask it?	
224	'But] But	
224	with them'] with them	
225	'Oh] Oh	
226	'It was] It was	
226	"It] 'It	
226	Glenarvon."] Glenarvon.'	
226	"Now] 'Now	
226	mother,"] mother,'	
226	"if] 'if	

226	heart;"] heart;'
226	"Save,] 'Save,
226	me,"] me,'
226	'Linden] Linden
226	'I will] I will
227	'From] From
227	'Sunday] Sunday
227	'Tuesday] Tuesday
227	"Alice:] 'Alice:
227	you,"] you,'
227	him again'] him again
228	destroy it.'] destroy it.
228	Mac Allain] MacAllain
228	senseless] senselesss
229	'at least in my presence.'] at least in my presence.
229	contemptuously.] contemptuously?
230	'By my soul I do; and look,'] 'By my soul I do;' and look,
230	'with what] with 'what
230	you,] you.
230	'Your rage,] Your rage,
231	*brebis*] *brebi*
232	CHAPTER XXXVI.] CHAPTER XXXIV.
234	not I;'] not I;
236	left] felt
236	consciousness] conciousness
238	sensibility,] senisbility,
238	whatever] 'whatever
238	from] form

Volume III

245	CHAPTER I.] CHAPTER LXXII.
248	CHAPTER II.] CHAPTER LXXIII.
252	CHAPTER III.] CHAPTER LXXIV.
254	sufficient?'] sufficient?
258	CHAPTER IV.] CHAPTER LXXV.
260	CHAPTER V.] CHAPTER LXXVI.
260	CHAPTER VI.] CHAPTER LXXVII.
261	ecstasy] ecstas
263	CHAPTER VII.] CHAPTER LXXVIII.
266	averted] everted
269	CHAPTER VIII.] CHAPTER LXXIX.
269	'Glenarvon,'] Glenarvon,'

269	Expose] expose
271	CHAPTER IX.] CHAPTER LXXX.
274	CHAPTER X.] CHAPTER LXXXI.
276	CHAPTER XI.] CHAPTER LXXXII.
279	CHAPTER XII.] CHAPTER LXXXIII.
282	CHAPTER XIII.] CHAPTER LXXXIV.
284	CHAPTER XIV.] CHAPTER LXXXV.
286	every menace,] everymen ace,
289	CHAPTER XV.] CHAPTER LXXXVI.
290	desires] desises
291	CHAPTER XVI.] CHAPTER LXXXVII.
294	CHAPTER XVII.] CHAPTER LXXXVIII.
294	reward you.'] reward you,'
295	jolts, ruts,] jolts, ruts'
295	thunder.] thunder.'
297	CHAPTER XVIII.] CHAPTER LXXXIX.
297	'Well,] 'We'll,
300	CHAPTER XIX.] CHAPTER XC.
303	CHAPTER XX.] CHAPTER XCI.
304	arbutus] arbutes
304	my country's.'] my country's.
306	CHAPTER XXI.] CHAPTER XCII.
308	CHAPTER XXII.] CHAPTER XCIII.
308	'Do] Do
310	CHAPTER XXIII.] CHAPTER XCIV.
310	Glenaa] Glanaa
310	St. Clare: that] St. Clae. hat
311	of you.' 'I too] of you. I too
313	CHAPTER XXIV.] CHAPTER XCV.
314	recovered,] recovered.
314	Gondimar,] Gondimer,
317	CHAPTER XXV.] CHAPTER XCVI.
320	CHAPTER XXVI.] CHAPTER XCVII.
322	CHAPTER XXVII.] CHAPTER XCVIII.
325	CHAPTER XXVIII.] CHAPTER XCIX.
327	CHAPTER XXIX.] CHAPTER C.
328	obey."'] obey.'
331	remained;] remaind;
332	CHAPTER XXX.] CHAPTER CI.
333	seeing] seizing
334	'sound there] 'soundthere
335	CHAPTER XXXI.] CHAPTER CII.

339	CHAPTER XXXII.] CHAPTER CIII.
339	away.'] away.
339	'Lead on:] Lead on:
341	Ruthven.] Ruthen.
343	CHAPTER XXXIII.] CHAPTER CIV.
344	Glenaa] Glanàa
345	CHAPTER XXXIV.] CHAPTER CV.
346	emince] eminée
347	CHAPTER XXXV.] CHAPTER CVI.
348	Harry.' – 'Do] Harry. – Do
348	i'faith.] I'faith.
351	'O Fiorabella,'] 'O fiora bella,'[2]

A LISTING OF PRINCIPAL EDITIONS OF *GLENARVON*

Glenarvon. 3 vols. London: Henry Colburn, 1816. Anon.

Glenarvon. 3 vols. London: Henry Colburn, 1816. 2nd edn. with Preface. Anon.

Glenarvon. 3 vols. London: Henry Colburn, 1816. 3rd edn. with Preface and three engravings placed in the front matter of each of the three volumes. "By Lady Caroline Lamb" is printed in some copies of this edition. Text is almost identical to that of the second edition, with only a few variants in volume 2.

Glenarvon. 3 vols. London: Henry Colburn, 1817. 4th edn with a new epigraph, a new Introduction (described as the 'Original Introduction'), and the Preface to the 2nd edn. Text otherwise identical to that of the 3rd edn.

Glenarvon. 2 vols. Philadelphia: Mose Thomas, 1816. Pirate of Colburn's second edition.

The Fatal Passion, London: C.H. Clarke, 13, Paternoster Row. n.d. [1865].

TEXTUAL VARIANTS

Following is a list of textual variants between the 1816 first edition copy text of *Glenarvon*, the second and third editions of 1816 and the fourth edition of 1817. The third edition printed by Henry Colburn follows the second almost exactly, except for the inclusion of engravings on the title page, and the listing in some copies of Lady Caroline Lamb's name as author, as described below, and a very small number of changes in volume two. All variants below occur in the second edition, unless specifically noted. A fourth edition of *Glenarvon* was printed by Henry Colburn in 1817, identical in every respect to the third, except for the inclusion of an 'Introduction' and an epigraph from Tacitus on a freshly printed title page with the date '1817'. The title pages printing Lamb's drawings for each of the three volumes are still dated "1816", however. Copies of this somewhat rare fourth edition are held in the Carl Pforzheimer Collection of the New York Public Library, the Lehigh University Library, the Herzogin Anna Amalia Bibliothek in Weimar, Germany, the Byron Society of America Collection, and the United States Library of Congress. An advertisement appeared in the *London Literary Gazette and Journal of Belle Lettres, Arts, Sciences, etc.*, on Saturday, 9 September, 1820, (p. 592), claiming to reprint the fourth edition, but the editors have not been able to establish that it ever appeared.

American and French editions of *Glenarvon* are in all cases pirated from the printings of Colburn, the only variants being typographical errors. An exception is the edition of the novel published by C. H. Clarke in London as *The Fatal Passion* (circa 1865). This rare version of *Glenarvon* follows Colburn's second edition, and was published in a cheap format as a single volume. However, it has been severely cut, stripped entirely of its numerous song lyrics, the musical settings by Isaac Nathan, and with numerous other passages excised. At least 20,000 words have been cut from the text of Colburn's second edition. The chapters have been re-shaped, as well, with chapter 1 consisting in Lamb's original chapters 1–3, chapter 2 consisting in Lamb's original chapters 4–6, and so on. Having been pirated – and cut so drastically – long after the author's death in 1828, *The Fatal Passion* is noted as a curiosity, but the editors have not attempted to collate it as an independent edition in parallel with those which were revised by Lamb herself.

Volume I

Colburn's second edition changes the title page in this way:

2nd TP-b: Disperato dolor ... che ne favelle] Les passions sont les vents qui enflent les voiles du vaisseau: elles le submergent quelquefois, mais sans elles il ne pourrait voguer. Tout est dangereux ici-bas, et tout est nécessaire. [*Passions are the swells which fill the sails of the vessel. They submerge it sometimes, yet without them, it could not navigate. Here below, everything is dangerous, and everything is necessary.*]

Editor's note: The new epigraph is a slight modification of a passage from Voltaire's *Zadig* (1759), chapter 22: 'Ce sont les vents qui enflent les voiles du vaisseau,' repartit l'ermite: 'elles le submergent quelquefois; mais sans elles il ne pourrait voguer. La bile rend colère et malade; mais sans la bile l'homme ne saurait vivre. Tout est dangereux ici-bas, et tout est nécessaire.' ['*They* [the passions] *are the swells which fill the sails of the vessel*,' resumed the hermit: *'they submerge it sometimes, yet without them, it could not navigate. Phlegm, indeed, makes men peevish and sick; but then there is no living without it. Here below, everything is dangerous and everything is necessary.*']

Colburn's third edition changes the title pages in this way:

Title P-a: VOL. I] [*a steel plate engraving has been put on the title page showing a Cupid figure raising its arms toward a heart-shaped object that has wings and is apparently flying away. Underneath is this motto:* 'L'on t'a trop cherie?' '*[You have been much too cherished?]* See above, p. 2.

2nd TP-a: IN THREE VOLUMES.] IN THREE VOLUMES. BY LADY CAROLINE LAMB.[3]

5a	absence] absence,
5b	Wizzard's] Wizard's
5c	exalted imagination] imagination
5d	– the song of the Banshees, mourning for the sorrows of their country ... variety of creation.] – Glenarvon's form appeared before him – his patron! his benefactor! – he spoke of times long past, of scenes by all forgot, pointed with a look of despondency to his infant son! – 'Who shall protect the orphan that is destitute?' he cried – ' who shall restore him to the house of his fathers!'
6a	yet delightful,] and terrible,
6b	him.] Camioli
6c	Camioli] the Bard
6d	his child] her
6e	mantle),] mantle,) [*sic*]
6f	'why do I ... desolation and woe. But I] 'I
6g	you, my lovely one,] you
6h	Clara] Clara,
6i	Elinor according to promise,] Elinor
6j	eyes] eyes,
6k	mighty. Mourn] mighty. – Mourn

Textual Variants 391

6l	trouble. Bright] trouble. . . . Bright
6m	colonades] colonnades
6n	strangers] stranger
6o	it for] it as if for
7a	fir and elm.] beach and fir.
7b	Wizzard's] Wizard's
7c	– he] he
7d	– his] his
7e	– and] and
7f	has] had
7g	has] had
7h	The] Yet the
8a	has been, by the caprices of fortune] has, by the caprices of fortune, been
8b	intended.] designed.
8c	Mediocrity,] Mediocrity
8d	obtained, to which he once] obtained to which he had
8e	enjoy.] enjoy. He had married into a Roman Catholic family.
8f	duchess, he] Duchess, he had
8g	spirit. In] spirit: in
8h	he] he also
8i	and] while
8j	for some time occupied his hours] (the titles descending in the female line,) occupied his thoughts
8k	instructing them in the same studies, by the same masters,] causing them to be instructed in the same studies,
8l	together] together,
9a	them to give way . . . each other;] them in their intercourse with each other, to give way to their violent tempers, without restraint;
9b	moment, when the Duke . . . undeceived.] moment when the Duke hoped to exult in the success, he had to contemplate the failure, of his project.
9c	Happily, a new event . . . to undertake it.] Happily, a most important event occurred at this time in his family, which turned his thoughts into another channel.
9d	hours] hours'
9e	for] for,
9f	lady Calantha] Lady Calantha,
9g	helpless] helpless,
9h	to kneel and do] to do
9i	encreasing] increasing
9j	disappointment] disclosure
10a	sincerely] sincerely,
10b	overweaning] overweening
10c	controuled] controled

10d	time, in the prosecution of her sudden and accursed designs, having] time, having
10e	innocence,] innocence;
10f	air] air,
10g	sailing, accompanied] sailing, in the prosecution of her accursed designs, accompanied
10h	equipages, horses and attendants,] equipages and attendants
10i	own native] native
10j	object,] object
10k	Duke] Duke,
10l	pleasure;] pleasure:
10m	now belonging] belonging
11a	had, in mind and person, won] won
11b	grace,] grace
11c	smiles] smiles,
13a	said she] she said
13b	Whatever] – Whatever
13c	to sully] or sully
13d	expences] expenses
13e	conniving] of conniving
13f	detaining] detaing [*sic*]
13g	unnecessary;] in this instance unnecesary;
13h	boast, was] boast was,
13i	nature,] nature
13j	He, after this,] He then
13k	intentions. – Love] intentions – love
13l	chevalier] Chevalier
13m	chevalier] Chevalier
14a	and Lady Margaret expected] Lady Margaret then expected
14b	fixed.] supposed to be fixed.
14c	her;] her:
14d	'Go,] – 'Go,
14e	friend] friend,
14f	cheeks] cheek
14g	even a thought] one serious thought
15a	and only when . . . .opprest her.] nor till alone in her own apartment did she suffer herself to give vent to the fury which opprest her.
15b	doubted;] doubted:
15c	bitter,] bitter
15d	Margaret] Margaret,
15e	calmness,] calmness
15f	thoughts: he saw at once] thoughts, he at once saw
15g	Angel,] angel,

15h	Daemon;] daemon;
15i	out of its] from its
15j	and, by] and by
15k	the dying embers of every] every
15l	said he,] he said,
15m	before hand with you] before-hand with you,
16a	much,] much
16b	his perverted heart] his heart
16c	well,] well
16d	she was mistress] her sex is sometimes mistress
16e	said,] said:
16f	'Seal the compact . . .' 'My son] 'My son
16g	shudder,] shudder
16h	counsel:] counsel;
16i	the rest.' He spoke,] the rest.' He spoke [i.e., paragraph break introduced here]
16k	me] me,
17a	Gondimar, who had . . . his designs,] Gondimar proposed returning to Italy. Previous to his departure, he sought his friend Viviani, who was at this time concealed in the town of Belfont, and who, in order to promote his designs,
17b	return] Return
17c	yourself] itself
17d	is little worth you. I love her not,] is not worthy of you. You love her not,
17e	imagination,] imagination
17f	in my heart] in me
17g	passion,] passion –
17h	this,] this
17i	Before] The evening before
17j	'months have glided by in vain . . . She evades] 'Months have glided by, and still she evades
17k	thing;] thing:
17l	foundation,] foundations,
18a	money] money,
18b	and] and,
18c	his hand trembled. He found her . . . whispered vows] his hand trembled: he approached her, and whispered vows
18d	any remaining scruple.] her remaining scruples.
18e	he looked,] he had looked
18f	favorable] favourable
18g	already] already,
19a	bashful or] bashful and
19b	honors. See there, there . . . 'Lady,] honors. 'Lady
19c	said she,] she said,

19d	words half suffocated] words. Half suffocated
19e	imagination. She] imagination, she
19f	brightness above the dark elm trees;] brightness;
19g	whispering leaves of the trees,] whispering branches of the pines,
19h	appeared,] appeared
19i	porticos] porches
19j	terror and despair. –] terror, and despair ....
19k	impressive] impressive,
19l	unheeded although impressive,] unheeded, although impressive
20a	fixed,] fixed
20b	motionless,] motionless
20c	her; – but] her. But
20d	avail,] avail
20e	flower,] flower
20f	that the] that a
20g	eyes] eyes,
20h	fancied that they] fancied they
20i	an ancient] ancient
20j	wilt] will
20k	fair] fair,
21a	life,] life
21b	flowret] flow'ret
21c	mountains] mountain's
21d	singing] singing,
21e	thus] thus,
22a	share,] share
22b	suffering] suffering,
22c	faults] faults,
22d	merits] merits,
22e	by,] by
22f	enjoyed] enjoyed,
22g	friendship] friendship,
22h	to share the disappointment, and lighten] to lighten
22i	But while the soul of the Duchess] But while her soul
23a	prosperity: – such] prosperity. – Such
23b	– You] You
23c	it; but] it. But
23d	better,] better
23e	vivacity,] vivacity
23f	smiles,] smiles
23g	leave,] leave
23h	care: – her] care, her

23i	– are] – these are
23j	Protect] To protect
23k	is the] is also the
23l	presence:......] presence.'
23m	bosom,] bosom
23n	tried,] tried
23o	her from error,] her,
23p	human heart] heart
23q	others:] other:
23r	Calantha, the] Calantha; a
23s	alarming: but] alarming. But
24a	offence] offences
24b	those] these
24c	succeeded in his breast, to] combated in his breast
24d	– 'Woman,] 'Woman,
24e	– not] Not
24f	doom: – I] doom. I
24g	tigress] tygress
24h	at last: – spurn me,] at last. Spurn me
24i	now? A] now? – a
24j	When] And when
24k	Viviana, as certain,] Viviani as certain
24l	manhood, – 'is it in the compass of probability] manhood – 'is it within the compass of possibility
24m	her and left her. – Very] her, and left her. Very
25a	Creator,] Creator
25b	piety, even] piety – even
25c	spirits] spirit
25d	care worn] care-worn
26a	thraldom: – she] thraldom. She
26b	intention] intention:
26c	request: – provided he was] request; – provided he were
26d	acceded; his] acceded. His
26e	From thence] Thence
26f	distance,] distance
26g	direct] divert
26h	parting,] parting
26i	continued she,] she continued
26j	hair: place] hair – place
26k	of both] of
26l	that you are to wear it ever, for my sake.'] that, for my sake, you are to wear it ever.'

26m	attached] attached,	
26n	regret,] regret	
26o	that] which	
27a	for Viviani.] Viviani.	
27b	– The] The	
27c	from] and from	
27d	them; and] them:	
27e	secure,] secure	
27f	preferred enduring] preferred	
27g	remorse,] remorse	
27h	heart,] heart	
27i	Duchaess;] Duchess:	
27j	authority;] authority:	
27k	praiseworthy and desirable.] desirable.	
28a	overcome.] overcome. She was a Roman Catholic, and all who differed from that persuasion were, in her opinion, utterly lost.	
28b	contradictions] contradiction	
28c	Seymour –] Seymour:	
28d	answer] answers	
28e	impelled.] impelled!	
28f	rightly, –] rightly,	
28g	it,] it	
28h	words] words,	
29a	invent,] invent	
29b	attention] attention,	
29c	Father] father	
29d	the very defects] those very defects	
29e	much too often is renounced] much is too often renounced	
29f	truth] truth,	
29g	despised;] despised:	
29h	herd;] herd:	
29i	God;] God:	
29j	trivial] trivial,	
29k	expence,] expense,	
29l	education; masters, tutors] education: masters, professors,	
29m	learn;] learn:	
29n	accomplishment; yet] accomplishment. Yet	
30a	acquirements,] acquirements	
30b	dance,] dance	
30c	draw; with] draw; at the same time, with	
30d	harsher] severer	
30e	that] which	

30f	herself;] herself:	
30g	was] and he was	
30h	possible] possible,	
30i	Emmet] Emmet,	
30j	had: –] had:	
30k	fond,] fond: – these	
30l	would she] she would	
30m	then] and	
30n	below, or climbing] below: or she would climb	
30o	gazing] gaze	
30p	thought; but at] thought. At	
30q	sun beam] sun-beam	
30r	amusement] amusement,	
31a	wildness,] wildness	
31b	she had attained her] attaining their	
31c	had already] had	
31d	– the same feeling for the same object,] the same feeling for the same object	
31e	She] she	
31f	Mowbray,] Mowbrey,	
31g	bitterly with her partiality;] with her partiality:	
31h	Mowbray] Mowbrey	
31i	his nephew;] him;	
31j	He had entered the army young;] Lord Avondale had entered the army young:	
31k	like] and like	
31l	happiness] happpiness,	
32a	temptation] temptations	
32b	principles and perverted his inclinations.] principles, and inflamed his imagination.	
32c	where upon his first return from abroad] where, upon his first return from abroad,	
32d	duty] duties	
32e	required.] might require	
32f	him;] him:	
32g	life, been exposed;] life been exposed:	
32h	art, with] art – with	
32i	nature] nature.	
32j	height, and smiled] height; and he smiled	
32k	conceit] conceit,	
32l	heartlessness] heartlessness,	
32m	walks; of] walks; and of	
32n	to where] whither	
32o	she heard] and heard	

33a	Allain,] Allain	
33b	Elle,] Elle;	
33c	madning] maddening	
33d	controul] control	
33e	Calantha,] Calantha:	
33f	offer;] offer:	
33g	master; will] master; – will	
33h	hopes,] hopes	
33i	command.'] command. [sic]	
33j	'you] you [sic]	
33k	thence.'] them.'	
33l	'They] They [sic]	
33m	Avondale,] Avondale	
33n	there, my lord,'] thither, my lord?'	
33o	she felt] but she felt	
34a	not,] not, however	
34b	was, nevertheless,] was,	
34c	independant] independent	
34d	– a frank and winning manner, –] a frank and winning manner,	
34e	Avondale, however,] Avondale	
34f	produced,] produced!	
34g	arrive] arrive,	
34h	entirely] utterly	
35a	fears to enter] fear of entering	
35b	Avondale] Avondale,	
35c	love like other arts] love, like other arts,	
35d	sensation] sentiment	
35e	lovers] lover's	
35f	Margaret when first she] Margaret, when she first	
35g	indignation:] indignation;	
35h	where] in which	
35i	encrease] increase	
35j	force;] force:	
35k	cruelty.] absolute cruelty.	
36a	immediately,] immediately	
36b	quitted;] quitted:	
36c	slowly] slowly,	
36d	loved,] loved	
36e	arms.] arm.	
36f	– Calantha] Calantha	
36g	said she,] she said,	
37a	her,] her	

37b	'Oh] 'Oh,
37c	callous to] careless of
37d	has taken place: – I observed] engrosses your thoughts: – even now I observed
37e	child.'] child.' –
37f	Calantha,] Calantha
37g	fortune] fortune,
37h	if] if,
37i	manners] manners,
37j	favour,] favour
38a	other,] other
38b	entreaties] entreaties,
38c	him.] him. –
38d	said he:] he said:
38e	and,] and
38f	too] soo [sic]
38g	not.'] not'
39a	you] you,
39b	shared,] shared
39c	account,] account
39d	himself,] himself
39e	Mowbray,] Mowbrey,
39f	– she] she
39g	hearts'] heart's
39h	castle] castle,
39i	nephew] nephew,
39j	conduct to his nephew] conduct
40a	man in every point of view] man, in every point of view,
40b	description in all ages] description, in all ages,
40c	Margaret,] Margaret
41a	controul] control
41b	Calantha's] her
41c	to be] was to be
41d	humour] humour,
41e	mother] mother,
41f	girl,] girl;
41g	hand,] hand;
41h	wide] wide,
41i	continent;] continent:
42a	achieve] achieve,
42b	said she,] she said,
42c	Why,] Why
42d	animated] quick

42e	may inadvertently] may, inadvertently,
42f	words must,] words, must
43a	that,] that
43b	information. To] information, to
43c	and awaken] awaken
44a	upon] on
44b	store to Calantha,] store,
44c	replied] replied,
44d	Child,] Child
44e	them;] them:
44f	Margaret,] Margaret
44g	Calantha] Calantha'
44h	encreasing] increasing
44i	spirits,] spirits
45a	– Mrs.] Mrs.
45b	passed] passed,
45c	sister,] sister
45d	declaring that] declaring, that,
45e	this,] this
45f	from infancy] from her infancy
45g	were however] were, however,
45h	– and] and
45i	Duke however] Duke, however,
46a	– A] A
46b	rarely or never] never or rarely
46c	through] by means of
46d	and] and,
46e	staff;] staff:
46f	regiment which] regiment, which
46g	ever known] known
46h	moment,] moment
46i	and] and,
46j	– remember] remember
46k	Calantha: 'by day, by night,] her: 'by day – by night,
46l	– she] she
47a	true.] true,
47b	encreasing] increasing
47c	honour] honor
47d	not so;] not so!
47e	you.' ....] you?'
47f	frank] frank,
47g	Avondale;] Avondale,

47h	– fear me not: – your principles, I venerate; your religion I will study – will learn – will believe in. – What more?'] fear me not: your principles I venerate: your religion I will study, will learn, will believe in. What more?'
47i	sought,] sought
48a	– But] But
48b	remonstrances, he replied: – 'I] remonstrances he replied: 'I
48c	– can] can
48d	you;] you,
48e	all;] all,
48f	– My Calantha you torture me,] My Calantha, you torture me
48g	you –] you
48h	– 'It] 'It
48i	– 'I must command: – my will.' – 'Your will, shall be my law,'] 'I must command: my will – ' 'Your will shall be my law,'
48j	'you shall be my mistress – my guide – my monitress – and I, a willing slave.' –] 'you shall be my mistress, my guide, my monitress, and I a willing slave.'
48k	freedom,] freedom
48l	and who] and, who,
48m	awaited,] awaited
48n	exclamation –] exclamation:
48o	sufficient] sufficient,
48p	nay] nay,
48q	tame,] tame
48r	fervently: –] fervently:
48s	happy –] happy;
48t	possesses –] possesses;
48u	heaven.] Heaven.
48v	errors] errors,
48w	heart,] heart
49a	Mowbray,] Mowbrey,
49b	eyes,] eyes
49c	Calantha perhaps] Calantha, perhaps,
49d	ardent] ardent,
49e	Of] In
49f	it] he
50a	tenderness:] tenderness;
50b	educated.] educated. She, as has been heretofore related, was a Roman Catholic, and had adopted with that excess and exaggeration, which belonged to her character, the most enthusiastic devotion to that captivating and delusive worship.
50c	both of faith and morality,] and observances,
50d	whole,] noble,
50e	too clearly,] clearly, and fatally,
50f	prudish reserve,] rigour,

50g	chaste,] rigid,
50h	rigid,] severe,
51a	profaneness and impurity;] unrestrained enquiry, and daring speculation;
51b	were now, without ... open before her;] the works of Historians, Philosophers, and Metaphysicians, were now eagerly devoured by her;
51c	Lord Avondale smiled; and soon the alarm] and soon the surprise
51d	at the wit,] of the wit
51e	but no caution ... which overstrained] but of what avail was caution to Calantha – ever in extremes, she threw off at once the shackles, the superstition, the restrictions, which, perhaps, overstrained
51f	doctrines,] doctrines
51g	you.'] you. [*NEW PARAGRAPH*] Such is the transient nature of enthusiasm; such the instability of over zeal; and so short the adherence to the firmest, and most austere determinations, which are not founded in right principle, and accompanied by a tranquil and humble spirit. To a mind so ardent, and so irregular as Calantha's, knowledge and information are full of danger and hazard. It is impossible to foresee the impressions which may be made, or in any degree to regulate the course which may be taken by such an imagination. Some mistaken conclusion is eagerly seized upon, some false interpretation is easily seized upon,[4] and tenaciously maintained, and reason labours in vain to counteract and remedy the mischief. The productions of such a soil are all strange, new, uncertain; and the cultivator sees with astonishment a plant arise, entirely different from the usual result of the seed which has been sown, mocking his toil, and frustrating his expectations.
52a	I know not.] who can say?
52b	it,] it
52c	suspicions] suspicions,
52d	home] home,
52e	being,] being
52f	which,] which
52g	them,] them
52h	immediately] immediatey [*sic*]
52i	agitation.] agitation [*sic*]
53a	open,] open
53b	was;] was:
53c	Allenwater,] Allanwater,
53d	uttered therefore] uttered, therefore,
53e	– they] they
53f	enjoyment ... obtaining.] enjoyment of which the heart is capable.
53g	if in union] in union
53h	do] does
53i	tortures,] tortures
53j	to it,] to it
53k	Allenwater,] Allanwater

53l	Aunt Lady Mowbray] aunt, Lady Mowbrey,
53m	sister Lady Elizabeth Mowbray] sister, Lady Elizabeth Mowbrey
53n	dearer] dearer,
53o	prised] prized
53p	society, – brilliant, beautiful] society – brilliant, beautiful,
53q	mind] mind,
53r	world] world,
53s	temptation,] temptation
53t	others.] others; but her heart, too warm, too kind, repented even any momentary severity she might have shewn.
54a	– The] The
54b	She] Lady Avondale
54c	her –] her,
54d	– I] I
54e	them:] them.
54f	family;] family,
54g	had,] had
54h	all the] all her
54i	opinions] opinions,
54j	enthusiasm] enthusiasm,
54k	the profane,] some
54l	– she] she
54m	censured] censured,
54n	tolerated] tolerated,
54o	in] n [*sic*]
54p	vilified: –] ridiculed:
54q	constant – was daily: it never ceased – it] constant, was daily; it never ceased, it
55a	Mowbray,] Mowbrey,
55b	a defect.] defect.
55c	Mowbray] Mowbrey
55d	caressed and laughed] caressed, and laughed,
55e	is Henry,'] is, Henry,'
55f	Ireland, –] Ireland,
55g	boy; –] boy;
55h	abroad,] abroad
56a	– Acts] Acts
56b	forces were increased;] posts were reinforced;
56c	individual minds that] minds which
56d	so easily] as easily
56e	so readily] as readily
56f	abroad – much] abroad; much
56g	to spend] to pass

56h	Buchanan who had till then]	Buchanan, who had, till then,
56i	that event,]	her marriage,
56j	shake it.]	shake it off.
57a	examplary,]	exemplary
57b	when, in fact,]	when in fact
57c	her,]	her
57d	venting his desire of vengeance, which, from its magnitude, might]	vengeance, which might, by its magnitude,
57e	unless when . . . make him sing,]	an evil which Calantha endeavoured to avert as often as she could, by inducing the latter to sing,
57f	unheeding either the noise or the gaiety,]	heeding neither the noise nor the gaiety,
57g	strangers]	stranger's
57h	exalted?']	extolled?'
57i	replied,]	replied
58a	Sophia: –]	Sophia:
58b	the list, that I would die to save; that I]	list whom I would die to save; whom I
58c	kindness,]	kindness
58d	'imputed]	'and imputed
58e	love breathing]	love-breathing
58f	empassioned]	impassioned
58g	Sybel?']	Sybil?'
58h	now,]	now
59a	Calantha,]	Calantha
59b	acquaintance]	acquaintance,
59c	opinions]	opinions,
59d	as fair]	fair
59e	heard,]	heard
60a	offer,]	offer
60b	friend,]	friends,
60c	you, – remember, that]	you – remember, that,
60d	would]	will
60e	you, and]	you; and
60f	never.']	never!'
60g	– I am yet innocent. – Pardon a first offence.']	I am yet innocent. Pardon a first offence.' –
60h	– Your]	Your
60i	manner,]	manner
60j	'Oh]	'Oh,
60k	him.']	him.' –
60l	daughter,]	daughter's,
60m	were]	were,
60n	adventure;]	adventure; –

60o	felt;] felt:	
61a	TIME] TIME,	
61b	reverse: –] reverse:	
61c	past;] past:	
61d	regrets,] regret]	
61e	affections only, it seemed,] affections, only it seemed	
61f	advice] advice,	
61g	You would perhaps, and then] You would, perhaps; and then,	
61h	mire.'] mire.' –	
61i	on.'] on.' –	
61j	'Yet, perhaps, sir, they are] – 'Yet, perhaps, Sir, they are,	
61k	rather] rather,	
61l	Please then] Please, then,	
61m	recollect] recollect,	
61n	head: –] head:	
61o	women:] women,	
62a	people,] people;	
62b	school;] school:	
62c	you] your	
62d	passed, by Alice,] passed by Alice	
62e	seems] seems,	
62f	'Gone,' cried Lady St. Clare! . . . 'and where? and how?'] 'Gone!' cried Lady St. Clare – 'the thing is impossible.' – 'Gone!' cried Sir Everard – 'and where? and how? –	
62g	coachman] coachman,	
62h	doctor] doctor,	
62i	surmises,] surmises	
62j	ever] ever,	
62k	and in consequence] and, in consequence,	
62l	tie,] tie	
62m	her,] her	
62n	misfortune. –] misfortune.	
62o	letter] letter,	
63a	him] him,	
63b	concern,] concern	
63c	herself,] herself	
63d	Dartford who had returned to London] Dartford, who had returned to London,	
63e	was however too innocent,] was, however, too innocent	
64a	party, at Castle Delaval,] party at Castle Delaval	
64b	presence except secretly] presence, except secretly,	
64c	wife – so gentle,] wife? So gentle,	
64d	you Viviani] you, Viviani,	

64e	seems indeed] seems, indeed,
64f	purity,] purity
64g	danger,] danger
64h	passions,] passions
64i	thrown aside, and … therein. Oh I] thrown aside. Oh, I
65a	melody.] melody!
65b	dancing too,] dancing, too,
65c	not amidst] not, amidst
65d	dances: –] dances:
65e	boasts too] boasts, too,]
65f	they] but they
65g	Oh] Oh,
65h	fall. Let her but] fall! Let her
65i	a few] only a few
65j	safety.' –] safety.'
66a	subservient spiritless] subservient, spiritless,
66b	husband; one smile, from] husband: one smile from
66c	energy – one frown, repress every feeling of gaiety,] energy; one frown repress every feeling of gaiety;
66d	pleased;] pleased:
66e	school-boy:] school-boy;
66f	votaries, –] votaries,
66g	acquaintance – every new amusement; and her mind] acquaintance, every new amusement, and her mind,
66h	affection,] affeection
66i	flattery,] flattery
66j	sweeter,] sweeter
66k	as much,] as much
66l	evil;] evil,
66m	virtue,] virtue
67a	study, –] study,
67b	regret] regret,
67c	deed,] deed
67d	wildly] wildly,
67e	trembles] trembles,
67f	rein] rein,
67g	objects it censures] objects of its censure
67h	recommendation] recommendation,
67i	honourable] honourable,
67j	itself] itself,
67k	town] town,
67l	once] once,

67m	come] come,
67n	had perhaps,] had, perhaps,
67o	hers] her's
68a	mankind. –] mankind.
68b	she, who bestowed,] she who bestowed
68c	comfort,] comfort
68d	but happily] but, happily
68e	faults,] faults
68f	Mandeville,] Mandeville
68g	Calantha. 'A woman] Calantha, 'a woman
68h	age,] age
68i	victims their] victims which their
68j	Avondale'] Avondale,'
68k	at least,] at least
68l	'Alas] Alas, [sic]
69a	a toy] a toy,
69b	visits:] visits;
69c	'I see'] "I see,'
69d	confidence, –] confidence,
69e	carriage] carriage,
69f	and without] and, without
69g	not yet] not
70a	loved] beloved
70b	Pindar: –] Pindar:
70c	her contempt] contempt
70d	but] but not
70e	when a woman affirmed] when indeed a women affirmed [sic]
70f	malevolent,] malevolent
70g	think otherwise.] think her otherwise.
71a	attendant,] attendant
71b	to you Mr. Clarendon,] Mr. Clarendon to you,
71c	Tremore,] Fremore,
71d	Tremore,] Fremore,
71e	Tremore] Fremore
71f	– he] he
71g	greek] Greek
71h	tolerated,] tolerated
72a	heart] heart,
72b	spare – to reclaim] spare or to reclaim
72c	offender.] offender. When the World is spoken of in these volumes, it means alone that frivolous part of the community who dwell with delight upon the busy scene before them, and take interest in the momentary diversions which every little novelty and every little event occasions.

73a	face,] face
73b	Augusta: –] Augusta:
73c	*très-bien assorti.*] *très bien assorti.*
73d	animals,] animals
73e	it: –] it:
74a	'Are you] 'Now are you
74b	now much] much
74c	of it. They] of it; for they
74d	thorough bred, though full] through bred though, and yet full
74e	visitation. I] visitation; yet I
74f	– there] there
74g	'I do;] 'O yes I do;
74h	it is called singing. They tell me] it is called singing… As to you, they tell me
74i	heaven] heaven,
74j	to-night,] to-night
74k	'Neither,] 'Neither
74l	society. He is the best] society; and I leave him entirely to himself in return: for he is the best
74m	marriage,] marriage
74n	somewhere] some where
74o	pleased. He] pleased. and he [*sic*]
74p	Lady Augusta left Calantha.] Lady Augusta descended the stairs, her voice murmuring on to herself as she re-entered her carriage, and drove from the door.
75a	imagined,] now imagined
75b	anxious for her safety,] interested for her welfare,
75c	turning] turning,
75d	mask,] mask
75e	mask. –] mask.
75f	jest,] jest
75g	me; or will they wait to hear,] me, or will they wait to hear
75h	them.'] them?'
75i	ball;] ball,
75j	house,] House,
75k	turn] turn,
76a	now recognised] recognised
76b	now under] under
76c	'Caprice'] Caprice,'
76d	first gipsey,] Friar
76e	fate,] fate
76f	ills,] ills

76g	care] Care	
76h	rays,] rays.	
76i	flattery] flattery,	
76j	The transient favorite . . . as health decline,]	
	Insatiate vanity shall pine,	
	As honour, and as health decline,	
	The transient favorite of a day,	
	Of folly and of fools the prey;	
76k	friar. 'No, no' he cried] friar. – 'No, no' he cried,	
77a	fate,] fate	
77b	Or weep alone for others woe.]	
	Or weep alone for others' woe;	
	Nor malice shall, with venom'd dart,	
	Have power to reach thy spotless heart.	
77c	tribe, cease Aaron' said a female gipsey advancing:] tribe cease, Aaron,' said a female gipsey advancing;	
77d	Whatever] Yet, whatever	
77e	figure, and countenance] figure and countenance,	
77f	power'] power,'	
77g	for it] for it,	
77h	the lady you have attacked,] the lady the friar has attacked,	
77i	ill natured thing.'] ill-natured thing.' –	
77j	goodnature] good-nature	
77k	archly:] archly;	
77l	The gipsey] The gipsey and friar	
77m	her party;] their party;	
77n	said she.] she said.	
77o	name'] name.'	
77p	favour.'] favour.' –	
77q	'I] – 'I	
77r	– but] but	
77s	'Had] – 'Had	
77t	sorte' – said he] *sorte*,' he said	
77u	said she:] she said;	
77v	said he;] he said;	
77w	childhood;] childhood:	
77x	face,] face	
78a	conversed during the greater part of the evening] conversed, during the greater part of the evening,	
78b	the Friar,] her companion,	
78c	him,] him	
78d	thus disguised,] in the dress of a friar,	

78e	answered: –] answered:
78f	him;] him:
78g	say this,] say this
78h	appeared that the eye was given her] appeared, that the eye was given to her
78i	her's;] hers;
78j	was therefore] was, therefore,
78k	– Lord] Lord
78l	'Accepted] – 'Accepted
78m	'Oh, pray,] – 'Oh, pray
78n	him, –] him,
79a	spying-glass: –] spying-glass:
79b	till morning,] that night,
79c	not long been in bed,] been long in bed,
79d	five o'clock] three o'clock
80a	Calantha.] Calantha. –
80b	came. –] came.
80c	encreased] increased
80d	her.' –] her – '
80e	now.'] now.' –
80f	little] a little
80g	do so,] do so
80h	Lady –] Lady;
80i	neck: –] neck:
81a	Gondimar] Gondimar,
81b	gave; and] gave: and,
81c	whisper –] whisper:
81d	arisen] arisen?
81e	near the piano-forte, striking] at the piano-forte, and struck
81f	Glenarvon,] Glenarvon
81g	Gondimar] Gondimar,
81h	wait for the child, or] stay with the child for
82a	it] yet it
82b	play mate;'] play-mate,'
82c	said] said,
82d	heart;'] heart,'
82e	found] found,
82f	day] day,
82g	Duke,] Duke
82h	and carelessness. 'Are you mad,' said the Italian] or vanity. – 'Are you mad,' said the Italian,
82i	therefore] therefore,
82j	Indeed] Indeed,

82k	actions,] actions;
82l	observed that if she ever had] observed, that if she ever had had
82m	reflect] reflect,
82n	willing] willing,
83a	conversed together] conversed
83b	repeated in a solemn tone the description of Rome] repeated, in a solemn tone, the desription of Rome,
83c	Nigrinus] Nigrinus,
83d	temptations] temptations,
83e	Calantha] Calantha,
83f	flatterers] flatterers,
83g	shape,] shape
83h	woe is it;] woos it, alas! the willing
83i	luxury and self indulgence.'] luxury, and self-indulgence.'
84a	corruption] corruption,
84b	soil,] soil
84c	'And think you,] And think you [*sic*]
84d	Avondale,] Avondale
84e	Gondimar – falling back] Gondimar, falling back,
84f	you:] you –
84g	do,] do;
84h	scorn.] scorn,
84i	party coloured] party-coloured
84j	consumed, my soul. . . dares to ask.] consumed.
84k	infancy –] infancy,
84l	souls] souls,
84m	vows. Chaste – pure . . . never – never.'] vows.
84n	Margaret you say] Margaret, you say,
84o	cold,] cold
84p	heart] heart,
84q	ears,] ears
85a	vengeance.'] vengeance?'
85b	abhorrence,'] abhorrence?'
86a	Trelawny] Trelawney
86b	reward: –] reward:
86c	entered] quitted
86d	view, for she . . . an ordinary manner.] view.
86e	called,] called
87a	*obligeants*] *obligeantes*
87b	refuted;] refuted –
87c	tapers,] tapers
87d	seated. A poet of an emaciated . . . reason to complain.] seated.

87e	the Princess] her	
87f	Avondale; the *dead*, I mean the sick poet, did the same;] Avondale,	
88a	the sallow complexioned Poet,] Mr. Fremore,	
88b	favour,] favor,	
88c	replied the poet.] said Mr. Fremore.	
88d	Fremore, joining in the discourse,] Fremore,	
88e	but,] but	
88f	tyrannies:] tyrannies;	
88g	part,] part	
88h	The Poet's] Mr. Fremore's	
88i	her.] her. –	
88j	– you,] you,	
88k	in] within	
89a	cheek?] cheek!	
89b	'But] – 'But	
89c	'You] – 'You	
89d	'I do; but indeed – '] – 'I do; but indeed – I know enough. I have friends, have I not? and who, that has friends, is ignorant of what is said? it is the office of a friend, I believe,' said Lady Avondale, smiling, 'to say to us what a foe would not.'	
89e	two.'] two.' –	
89f	'You] – 'You	
89g	– I] I	
89h	he)] he,	
89i	'Truly] – 'Truly	
89j	for in life: every thing annoys me: I am sick of all society, Love,] for: every thing annoys me: I am sick of all society – love,	
89k	abhorrence.'] abhorrence.' –	
89l	Buchanan, – riding, – your mother – your – your cousin.'] Buchanan – riding – your mother – your – your cousin.' –	
89m	jargon?'] jargon?' –	
90a	ah] ah!	
90b	faster,] faster	
90c	said,] said	
90d	anything] any thing	
90e	pulls.'] pulls.' –	
90f	don't] do'nt [*sic*]	
90g	stopping?'] stopping?' –	
90h	termed it;] termed it:	
90i	Oh] Oh,	
90j	Will,] Will!	
90k	me,] me	
90l	Let] – Let	

90m	however,] however
90n	lord, in the library] lord in the library,
90o	ever could] could ever
90p	said,] said. –
90q	alarm,] alarm
90r	Avondale; 'you are of no use whatever;'] Avondale.
90s	found] found,
90t	thoughts. Calantha was of no use… the reflection with pain.] thoughts.
91a	said she.] she said.
91b	just as he was said to have] just as it is said that he has
91c	Poor thing,] Poor thing!
91d	her. –] her.
91e	this.' 'Bless us,] this.' – 'Bless us!
91f	sudden,'] sudden!'
91g	Augusta!] Augusta; –
91h	Heavens,] Heavens!
91i	Seymour,] Seymour
91j	spirit.'] spirit.' –
91k	heavens,] heavens!
91l	husband!'] husband!' –
91m	Augusta:] Lady Augusta:
91n	object.'] object.' –
91o	child.'] child?' –
91p	glass] glass,
91q	heart,] heart
91r	myself,] myself
92a	objects.] objects
92b	love,] love
92c	dont] don't
92d	to day] to-day
92e	– we cry:] we cry;
92f	christian] Christian
92g	hats] hats,
92h	greek] Greek
92i	ever have] have ever
92j	very clever at making bargains.'] *very clever* at making – bargains.'
92k	moment,] moment. –
92l	Augusta] Augugusta [*sic*]
92m	grecian] Grecian
92n	no] No
92o	to it. –] to it.
93a	Buchanan] Buchanan,

93b   – every] every
94a   Mowbray] Mowbrey
94b   Calantha] Calantha,
94c   by,] by
94d   care. –] care.
94e   gone: – winter again approached. –] gone; – winter again approached.
94f   deserted,] deserted
94g   Aunt] aunt
94h   caps – chains – rings –] caps, chains, rings,
94i   Viviani?'] Viviani,'
94j   send] to send
94k   Titania,] Titania
95a   smiled,] smiled
95b   contempt;] contempt,
95c   replied rather fretfully;] replied, rather fretfully,
95d   Calantha] Calantha,
95e   'Ah] 'Ah,
95f   too,] too
95g   – Obey –] Obey,
95h   engagement] engagment [*sic*]
95i   world?] world
95j   hope,] hope
96a   a child – a fool,' –] a child, a fool,'
96b   – you] you
96c   superior – aye –] superior, aye,
96d   love –] love,
96e   affection.] affection. –
96f   Calantha –] Calantha
96g   estranged] estranged!
96h   Calantha;] her
96i   souls,] souls
96j   then,] then
96k   spendthrifts,] spendthrifts
96l   contemn,] contemn
96m   best,] best
97a   whilst with all the ostentation of generosity] whilst, with all the ostentation of generosity,
97b   base, –] base,
97c   ruin – the misery –] ruin, the misery,
97d   character] character,
97e   chearful,] chearful,
97f   remarks] remarks,

97g	make,] make	
97h	vanity,] vanity	
97i	truth] truth,	
97j	heart,]heart	
98a	pain] pain,	
98b	– study, nay, labour] study, nay, labour,	
98c	happiness: regret] happiness; and regret	
98d	Mowbray] Mowbrey	
98e	laughingly] laughingly,	
98f	true;] true:	
98g	Calantha:] Calantha;	
98h	desired; but now that she saw him estranged, absent, involved] desired: but now he was often absent, and appeared to be involved	
98i	hundreds,] hundreds	
98j	friends: –] friends:	
98k	ridicule.] ridicule; and even at home, with Lady Elizabeth and Lady Mowbrey, she felt that she had conducted herself in a manner they could not approve; she received a thousand proofs of their kindness and affection, but she pined also for their esteem.	
98l	thought;] thought:	
98m	nothing;] nothing:	
98n	but] but,	
99a	but,] but	
99b	feeling;] feeling!	
99c	sorrow;] sorrow!	
99d	whom in return] whom, in return,	
99e	her;] her:	
99f	Calantha's] Her	
99g	folly;] folly:	
99h	imprudence;] imprudence: –	
99i	me – the world befriends me – she continually thought;] me,	
99j	My relations. . . Convinced] Convinced.	
100a	passion –] passion.	
100b	moment,] moment –	
100c	gone] gone,	
100d	attached,] attached	
100e	clouded and cheerless. –] clouded, and cheerless.	
100f	or] or,	
100g	her;] her:	
100h	perishableness] perishable character	
100i	morning in the month of May, Calantha] morning, they	
100j	Allenwater,] Allanwater,	
100k	her] them	

100l	moment,] moment
100m	her,] her
101a	parted. It was also... to the Castle.] parted.
101b	occasion:] occasion;
101c	as Calantha concluded,] it may be supposed,
101d	Calantha,] Calantha
101e	romance,] romance
101f	view.'] view [*sic*]
101g	'I was reading... think of nothing else.] 'Possibly – but I was reading the address to the United Irishmen, and could see, therefore, and think of nothing else.
101h	I wish] I wish,
101i	Glenarvon,] Glenarvon
101j	Navy] navy
101k	Island.] island.
101l	sex;] sex,
102a	words,] words
102b	evening, took Calantha apart,] evening took Calantha apart

Volume II

Colburn's second edition changes the title page in this way:

2nd TP-b: Disperato dolor... che ne favelle] Les passions sont les vents qui enflent les voiles du vaisseau: elles le submergent quelquefois, mais sans elles il ne pourrait voguer. Tout est dangereux ici-bas, et tout est nécessaire. [*Passions are the swells which fill the sails of the vessel. They submerge it sometimes, yet without them, it could not navigate. Here below, everything is dangerous, and everything is necessary.*]

Editor's note: The new epigraph is a slight modification of a passage from Voltaire's *Zadig* (1759), chapter 22: 'Ce sont les vents qui enflent les voiles du vaisseau,' repartit l'ermite: 'elles le submergent quelquefois; mais sans elles il ne pourrait voguer. La bile rend colère et malade; mais sans la bile l'homme ne saurait vivre. Tout est dangereux ici-bas, et tout est nécessaire.' ['*They* [the passions] *are the swells which fill the sails of the vessel,*' resumed the hermit: '*they submerge it sometimes, yet without them, it could not navigate. Phlegm, indeed, makes men peevish and sick; but then there is no living without it. Here below, everything is dangerous and everything is necessary.*']

Colburn's third edition changes the title pages in this way:

Title P-a: VOL. II] [*a steel plate engraving has been put on the title page showing a Cupid figure pointing to a butterfly that is flying into the flames rising from an urn. Underneath is this motto: 'Mon plaisir me coûte de la vie.'* [*My pleasure costs me life.*] See above, p. 104.

2nd TP-a: IN THREE VOLUMES.] IN THREE VOLUMES. BY LADY CAROLINE LAMB.[5]

Textual Variants 417

Colburn's fourth edition changes the title page in this way:

2nd TP-b: Disperato dolor . . . che ne favelle] Contemptu famae contemni virtutem. Tacitus [To depise fame is to despise merit. Tacitus] See above, p. 363, n. 1, for details of this change to the epigraph in the fourth edition.

107a	was] were
107b	the one] that which
107c	for fear] least
107d	Doctor,] Doctor
108a	all,] all
108b	pardon,] pardon
108c	'its] 'Tis
108d	'Its] 'Tis
108e	it's] it is
108f	he's] he is
108g	'Don't bring] 'Do not I beseech you, bring
108h	gives a blacker shade to his character, in my opinion.'] gives in my opinion,' a blacker shade to his character, [sic]
108i	a] the
108j	foolish: not but what you did so before.] foolish:
109a	Duke,] Duke
109b	I'll] I will
109c	'can you ask] can you ask [sic]
109d	As to my girls, I really feel for them: my] My
109e	Captain] General
109f	can't] cannot
110a	infection; the poison in] infection: the poison is in
110b	lives] persons
111a	downs,] downs
111b	there,] there
111c	Wizzard's] Wizard's
111d	had remained] remained
111e	Trelawney,] Trewlawney [sic]
112a	hypocrite] hypocritic
112b	straight] strait
112c	much edified] edified
112d	said he,] he said,
112e	that,] that
112f	live?' –] live?'
112g	Lady Trelawney] lady Trelawney [sic]
112h	Henry Mowbray,'] Harry Mowbrey,'
112i	him.] him.' [sic]

112j	Costally,']	Costolly,'
112k	bow,]	bow
112l	lord,]	Lord,
112m	party,]	party
112n	cliff,]	cliff
112o	Augusta;]	Augusta,
113a	covered]	both covered
113b	pass;]	pass,
113c	contrasting]	contrasted strongly
113d	pale,]	pale and
113e	dared ask]	dared to ask
113f	he:]	he,
113g	hanged, however;]	hang'd, howéver; [sic]
113h	to obtain]	for
113i	to take them up.']	before they secure them.'
113j	doctor]	Doctor
114a	turrets;]	turret;
114b	summons:]	summons; and
114c	he waited]	waited
114d	'but]	but [sic]
114e	meddle]	meddles
114f	'Are]	Are [sic]
114g	low in a mysterious manner]	low, in a mysterious manner,
114h	perhaps]	perhaps,
114i	frightened,']	frightened.'
115a	fair.]	fair.. [sic]
115b	can]	Can
115c	Oh]	Oh!
115d	me.]	me:
115e	virtue]	virtue,
115f	course – all]	course, all
115g	troubled –]	troubled;
115h	perhaps inhabited by beings thoughtless and gay.]	perhaps, inhabited by beings as thoughtless and gay:
115i	memory]	any memory
115j	were]	are
115k	scarce]	scarcely
115l	is here]	is there here
116a	glossy]	glassy
116b	wintry]	winter
116c	one moment]	a moment
116d	she]	and she

116e	shaded] shaded over	
116f	Such a] Such	
116g	features –] features,	
116h	dreams,] dream,	
116i	sung:] sung: –	
117a	one moment beheld] beheld	
117b	this new,] this sudden,	
117c	rencontre] recontre [*sic*]	
117d	thoughts.] thoughts,	
117e	her,] her	
117f	your heart] you	
117g	Lady;] Lady?	
117h	it's] it is	
118a	chamber.] room.	
118b	room,] apartment	
118c	the old] that old	
119a	'It's] 'It is	
119b	'Well, doctor?'] 'Well doctor,'	
119c	air.'] air:'	
119d	smile,] smile	
119e	– Sir] Sir	
119f	honour,] honour	
119g	'Its] 'It's	
119h	point;] point:	
120a	said she.] she said.	
120b	here.] here:	
120c	ould] auld	
120d	female;] famale; [*sic*]	
120e	Kelly] Nelly	
121a	countenance,] coutnenance. [*sic*]	
122a	and, to] and to	
122b	pursuing] pursung [*sic*]	
122c	behind:] behind	
122d	His name I cannot at present declare; yet this I will say:] His name cannot at present be declared; yet this may be said:	
123a	when,] when	
123b	her out,] her	
123c	morning adventures] adventures	
123d	Ireland] Ireland,	
123e	new, an] new and	
123f	observed:] observed;	
123g	heard,] listened,	

123h   every] to every
123i   repeated.] which she heard repeated.
123j   rest, nor write, nor read; and the fear of again seeing it,] rest nor employ her mind in her customary occupations; yet the fear of again seeing that countenance,
123k   Margaret –] Margaret *2nd and 3rd edns*; Margaret – *4th edn*
124a   It was] But it was
124b   she said.] Lady Margaret said.
124c   insect] insect,
124d   cheek,] cheeks,
124e   'Calantha' she said] 'Calantha,' she said,
124f   child,] boy,
124g   you my child] you, my child,
124h   father yesterday] father, yesterday,
124i   Margaret,] Margaret
125a   was sitting] was
125b   in it – oh it made me sick – and] in it, and
125c   – These] These
125d   weakness – do not love.] weakness, do not, love.
125e   sorrows –] sorrows,
125f   me –] me;
125g   aye,] aye
125h   that] this
125i   castle] Castle
125j   up;] up:
125k   of] for
126a   thence,] from thence,
126b   pointing] pointed
126c   very little] short
126d   him;] him:
126e   desperate-like;] "*desperate-like*;"
126f   the county of Leitrim] county Leitrim
127a   my Alice.] Alice.
127b   Cyrel's father,] Cyril's father
127c   time,] time
127d   all one,] without effect,
127e   O'Flarney,] Flarney [sic?]
127f   say,] say
127g   present time.] present.
127h   own –] own
127i   birth-day:] birth-day;
127j   me;] me:
128a   there.'] into danger.'

128b	that;] that:
128c	he;] he,
128d	for sure, there's] and ain't there
128e	he went] why he went
128f	Linden,] Linden
128g	suppose,] suppose
128h	sure] sartain
128i	Wizzard's] Wizard's
128j	time,] time
128k	I know well] don't I know well,
128l	coming, and there is not one] coming, aye, and indeed is there one
128m	them,] them
128n	coming'] coming.'
128o	least.' As] least:' as
128p	Castle.] castle.
128q	found,'] found, Sir,'
128r	his was] he were
129a	scene.'] scene. [*sic*]
130a	and soften] to soften
130b	thing.] thing; but as
130c	and Lord] Lord
130d	They heard with] They soon heard however, though with
130e	incurred] rendered them liable to
130f	Linden and two others… all intercessions] All intercessions
130g	made, even by his fellow soldiers and comrades, to rescue] made, to rescue
131a	above] at the foot of
131b	taken with] taken, were with
131c	were executed] executed
131d	exposed] had exposed
131e	penetrated, under] perceived through
131f	letter] letters
131g	respectability took] respectability, erased
131h	club, opposite] club which had been established opposite to
132a	of this.] of this, their unusual deportment.
132b	heights,] height
132c	carried. The whole kingdom, indeed,] carried that the whole kingdom
132d	Even the few of their own countrymen… Numerous absentees] Numerous absentees, it was popularly said
132e	bankers and stewards of estates,] agents and stewards
132f	tenants; and all this caused the greatest discontent.] tenants.
132g	assurances of relief made;] assurance of relief given;
132h	even a] even the establishment of a

132i	violent,] violent	
132j	was in] might be considered in	
133a	claim for the titles] claim to the titles which	
133b	assurance that his claim would be considered,] assurance, even that his right would be recognised,	
133c	upon] on	
133d	personage,] personage	
133e	whom many] whom some	
133f	ancient] antient	
133g	guide, he had centered upon] guide he had centered in	
133h	that] which	
133i	a changing prince,] the lawful prince,	
133j	destruction. Flushed with the glow… him from enjoying.] destruction.	
133k	Glenarvon] He	
134a	He plunged, therefore, into… Florence invited him. He gave] He quitted it, and returned to Italy – there amidst the luxurious dissipation of Rome or Florence, he gave	
134b	Intervals of gloom succeeded… heart at rest.] He had been wronged and knew not how to pardon. Many had deceived him and he existed henceforward but to mislead others.	
134c	unfortunate] first	
134d	Giardini, with] Giardini, had, with	
134e	justice, was affixed] justice been attributed	
134f	tortures of remembrance… excite, he] tortures of recollection, he	
134g	easily won] won	
134h	exile,] exile	
134i	father's] father	
134j	departed,] departed;	
134k	affirmed;] affirmed,	
135a	concerning this Glenarvon.] of him.	
135b	presence at that particular time, in Ireland, occasioned many conjectures.] motives for visiting Ireland in such a conjuncure could not be misinterpreted or mistaken.	
136a	obtained his interest, none knew, or] excited his interest, none knew, nor	
136b	than] then [sic]	
136c	habitation,] habitation	
136d	welcomed] welcomed in	
137a	merry] tumultuous	
137b	most extravagant absurdity.] wildest extravagance.	
137c	steps;] teps; [sic]	
137d	her,] St. Clara	
137e	power;] power:	
137f	rest;] rest:	

Textual Variants   423

137g	if wounded, which never rested] which, if irritated, never rested,
138a	breast.] breasts. [*sic*]
138b	with] with,
138c	often-times] oft-times
138d	immediately] immediatly [*sic*]
139a	Mowbray] Mowbrey
139b	the Lower House for their distinguished condujct and assistance] Parliament for their distinguished conduct
139c	4th] 1st
139d	The ships had been. . . station at Cork.] They were now appointed to command upon the Cork station, with a considerable force, as serious apprehensions were entertained lest the enemy should attempt a descent in the south of Ireland.
139e	acquaintance] acquaintance of theirs
139f	could make up their minds] determined
139g	4th] 1st
139h	Margaret,] Margaret
139i	June 1st,] May 28th,
139j	29th, ult.] 26th, ult.,
140a	3rd,] 31st,
140b	some time, it appeared, in much anxiety.] them some time.
140c	each] them all
140d	Eloise,] Heloise,
140e	ship-builders,] ship-builders
140f	cove] Cove
140g	reserve:] reserve,
140h	ship,] ship;
141a	and,] and
141b	but,] but
141c	Mowbray,] Mowbrey,
141d	4th,] 1st,
141e	and he had received the recommendation of Admiral Howe.] and that he had received the warmest recommendations of their great Commander and famed Admiral Howe! . . [*sic*]
141f	spoken] spoken of
141g	rendered] renders
141h	nature;] nature,
141i	true;] true,
142a	not] nor
142b	Face to face she] Sir George Buchanan had long since known, observed, and distinguished him in his profession, and the firm friendship of the seaman, would not be deterred by any rumours, however current or unfavourable, from paying him that respect, which he knew to be due not more to his rank, than to his merit

	and prowess. Glenarvon had availed himself of the invitation, and face to face Calantha now
142c	quieted,] quieted
142d	Glenarvon's] his
142e	like a shot] prone
142f	voice;] voice
142g	was nature,] were nature,
142h	around her. The affectation… scarce accountable.] around her, and with a sudden affectation, to which she had hitherto been a stranger, assumed a new manner, in order to conceal the interest which she felt, and feared she was betraying.
142i	ever] ever,
143a	heard,] heard
143b	scene] hour
144a	Calantha!] Calantha! when the mind once cherishes a discontented spirit, every event that occurs tends to strengthen it in the delusion it loves to indulge. Calantha only thought herself neglected. To her perverted eyes every thing appeared in a false light. Thus she accused Lord Avondale when in fact she herself was alone to blame.
144b	Heloisa] Eloise
144c	languid] languid,
144d	it;] it:
144e	called] roused
144f	her to do so.] her.
144g	monopolized] seized upon
145a	morning] morning,
145b	Donallan's gardens;] Donallan garden
145c	Yet is it unflattering to fly,] Yet to fly,
145d	Is this so very marked a sign] Are these such very marked signs
146a	sufficiently] sufficiently,
146b	manner:] demeanour
147a	go there;] go;
147b	the party, on the government side… their tenets] those who upheld the government, was lest the rebels should prove superior, and murder them for their opinions.
147c	I will not say] It is unnecessary to relate
147d	castle; it was not of a nature to repeat;] castle;
147e	a mark of preference; at least it seemed so;] so marked a preference; at least it seemed to do so;
147f	her life,] life,
147g	saw;] saw
147h	and,] and
147i	'Not me,'] 'Not I,'
147j	say!'] say.'

148a	husband:] husband;	
148b	lust;] passion,	
148c	The whirlwinds of passions] As whirlwinds they	
148d	chaste] pure	
148e	That day… following, he took his leave.] On the following day Lord Glenaravon took his leave.	
148f	more than ordinarily] more even than usually	
148g	admiration.] approbation.	
148h	Calantha] From that time Calantha	
148i	her;] her:	
148j	desire.] hope and view.	
148k	insense] incense	
148l	lowly –] lowly,	
149a	after,] after	
149b	words,] words	
149c	other;] other:	
149d	shuddering on the very edge… fathomless chasm] already in the dark labyrinth of sin, and shuddering on the very edge of the bottomless chasm,	
150a	now considered as] now	
150b	came –] came,	
150c	appeared,] came,	
150d	excited,] excited	
150e	Buchanan,] Buchanan	
150f	assembly rooms] assembly-rooms	
150g	this eventful] the eventful	
150h	condescension.] popular condescension.	
150i	solely to his Uncle,] upon his uncle,	
150j	'which] 'Which	
150k	him: – he] him. He	
151a	from] form [sic]	
151b	'Was me! Do] 'Oh!	
151c	All were silent: – suddenly] Suddenly	
151d	modest diffidience,] diffidence,	
151e	effect.] effect.	

If to lose all that love thee, should e'er be thy lot,
By the world, that now courts thee, contemn'd or forgot;
When thy own fickle heart has all others estranged,
Then remember St. Clara, who never had changed.

Who had followed thy steps, though in sickness and sadness,
More firm to the last than the foes who upbraid her;
Who had followed thy steps, though to death and to madness,
Then mourn o'er the grave where thy falsehood has laid her.

Ah, say not! Ah, think not! she e'er can recover,
The blow never fails from the hand of a lover;
Full home it was struck, and it fell on a breast
By remorse and unkindness already deprest.

A smile, oft in death, may illumine each feature,
When hope, fondly cherished, forever is past;
And the heart that is noble and high in its nature,
Though deserted and scorn'd, will be firm to the last.

151f	extorted a stronger feeling... lawless and guilty love.] excited a strong feeling of sympathy and indignation
151g	lost by comparison] lost, by comparison,
151h	evening;] evening,
152a	imagine the cause;] define the motive;
152b	delectable amusement;] amusement;
152c	pique;] pique:
152d	'You] You [sic]
152e	you: –] you:
152f	motive –'] motive.'
152g	said he,] he replied,
153a	any thing] anything
153b	Then] Then,
153c	said he,] he said,
153d	alone,] only
154a	imagined,] imagined
154b	impossible;] imposible; [sic]
154c	no doubt sufficiently] sufficiently
154d	excuse,] excuse
154e	affect to disguise?] for a moment disguise?
154f	period; for otherwise... improbable and false.] period.
155a	A calm, a deliberate tyrant,] Calmness and deliberation
155b	a violent one] violence
155c	force and violence] force
155d	disturbed] distorted
155e	if misturned, desparate and hardened.] if it turn from the right course, desperate and hardened. Hypocricy and falsehood, however disgusting, are perhaps less dangerous symptoms than that fearless openness. The former at least proves a sense of shame, and whilst this exists all virtue is not extinct.
155f	what had once so fully] those quarrels and reconciliations which had once so entirely
155g	happiness] happines [sic]
155h	contrasted even] contrasted
155i	husband, to] husband with

156a	light radiance] light
156b	victims: –] victims:
156c	rouze] rouse
156d	scorching flames] flames
156e	then] and then
156f	accustomed;] accustomed:
156g	eminent] iminent [*sic*]
156h	cold,] cold
156i	Glenarvon] Glenarvon,
156j	neglect] neglect,
157a	which for one moment] which, for one moment,
157b	spoke with decision] spoke, with decision,
157c	club;] directory –
157d	change:] change;
157e	that sort:] this sort:
157f	now;] now:
157g	lent] leant
157h	own:] own;
158a	put] pressed
158b	moments] moment's
158c	heart:] heart;
158d	danger,] danger
158e	which the strictest propriety had rendered necessary.] of the strictest propriety prescribed.
158f	advances – too fatal... with the same idol;] advances; she imagined that all others, like herself, were enamoured of the same idol;
158g	could not] could *3rd edn*
159a	French in open boats] French, in open boats,
159b	noise] noise,
159c	do so] do so too,
159d	As he spoke... upon her finger.] He gave her a ring.
159e	an harp] a harp
159f	greek church,] Greek Church,
159g	an agreeable variety] much to the rational pleasure of the society
159h	princess] Princess,
159i	Glenarvon] Glenarvon,
159j	Oh! he is really sincere,] 'Oh! he is really sincere,'
159k	amuse –] amuse,
160a	pretty] handsome
160b	Glenarvon] Glenarvon,
160c	faults,] faults;
160d	around] round

160e	any.] any inmate.	
160f	husband] husband,	
160g	said: – he] said: he	
160h	exuberant] exuberent [*sic*]	
160i	Mowbray] Mowbrey	
160j	of it:] of the partiality:	
160k	now,] now	
160l	talents,] talents	
161a	d – d] damn'd	
161b	events,] events	
161c	question,] question	
161d	mountains,]mountains	
161e	describe,] describe	
161f	vinyards] vineyards	
162a	time] time,	
162b	luxuriently] luxuriantly	
162c	said] said,	
162d	her? She knew not what. . .she had then felt.] her?; her? She knew not what she answered; and she afterwards wished she could forget what she had then felt. *3rd edn.*[6]	
162e	who] who,	
162f	youth;] youth,	
162g	as he] as she	
162h	not willingly retreating.] unwilling to pause or to retreat.	
163a	Mandeville,] Mandeville	
163b	redder far than the rose.] far redder than the flower.	
163c	'Ah] 'Oh	
164a	She retired to her room:] She arose from her bed:; She retired to her room: *3rd edn.*	
164b	her] har [*sic*]	
164c	had] hed [*sic*]	
164d	one prayer.] or one indulgence.	
164e	not] not,	
164f	curb] allay	
164g	aught] ought	
164h	wife, and more] wife	
164i	cause,] cause	
164j	ice, and] ice, and,	
166a	disquiet.] disquiet, deeply grieved at her altered manner – too proud to seek the confidence he perdeived that he had lost – disappointed in the character and conduct of the woman he had chosen as a companion and solace, he watched not her actions, he penetrated not her feelings, but finding that his presence was distasteful to her, he avoided her: he even thought that he no longer loved one	

who in every popint had acted in the manner he least approved. Some there are whose affections change with their esteem and good opinion. Unhappily for Lord Avondale this was not his nature. Long habit had rendered Calantha dear. He thought that he had become indifferent, but he knew not that the empire with which she seized over his heart [*sic*].

166b	The rose he had given her was faded;] The flower Glenarvon had given her was faded:
166c	myself] myself,
166d	me –] me,
166e	oh God!] oh Heavens!
166f	off] away
166g	apparently] and
167a	Avondale – he had a fierce] Avondale: he had a proud
167b	not,] not
167c	'what could you be saying] 'what were you saying
167d	heart.] heart
167e	reasoned;] reasoned,
167f	faltering] faultering
167g	exultingly,] exultingly.
167h	struggle, –] struggle:
167i	loved:] loved;
168a	When he] When she [*sic*?]
169a	vice] vice,
169b	prayer;] prayer:
169c	were] was
169d	eyes,] eyes
170a	linger;] linger:
170b	mine you are mine] Mine you are – mine
170c	Starting however] Starting, however,
172a	evening] evening,
172b	stedfastly] steadfastly
172c	said] said,
172d	last alone] last *3rd edn.*
172e	'for God's sake,] 'in mercy,
172f	'I will] I will [*sic*]
173a	'Farewell.'] To the air of one of the '*Old Irish Melodies*.') 'Farewell.'; 'Farewell.' 3*rd edn.*[7]
173b	gone] gone,
173c	my hand.'] my hand.' He smiled in scorn as he said this.
173d	moment,] moment
173e	lighted.] descended from it.
173f	'well then] 'Well then
173g	repeated,] repeated

175a	shores] shores,
175b	then,] then
175c	dear] dear;
175d	its] her
175e	approach] appraoch [sic]
175f	'Beautiful] 'Beautiful,
175g	you.'] you. [sic]
175h	ease;] ease:
175i	laughing,] laughing
176a	reappeared] re-appeared
176b	else] more
176c	thoughts,] thougths, [sic]
176d	had beheld] beheld
177a	chains] chains,
177b	yes;] yes,
178a	Avondale] AVONDALE
178b	Calantha;] Calantha:
178c	did:] did;
178d	warmth.] warmth:
178e	well,] well
178f	false'] false,'
178g	favourite'] favourite.'
178h	passed. The morning after] passed; the next morning
178i	Ruthven] Ruthven,
178j	others,] others
178k	Calantha,] Calantha
179a	the] he [sic]
179b	too. Oh!] too. – Oh!
179c	look with less confidence in future.'] to be less hasty in reposing confidence hereafter.'
179d	Calantha, with supprest indignation.] Calantha with indignation.
179e	would] had
179f	smiled,] smiled
180a	moment,] moment
180b	character: –] character:
180c	the day Lord Glenarvon was from home,] the day of Lord Glenarvon's departure,
180d	looked not upon herself with one sentiment of condemnation.] regarded her own conduct without compunction or condemnation.
180e	his;] his:
180f	secresy] secrecy
180g	Avondale?] Avondale!
181a	Calantha,] Calantha

181b	her heart] heart [*sic*]
181c	from him.] from him, or alas from any one.
181d	cross-examined and distrusted.] distrusted.
181e	thought,] thought
181f	him] him,
181g	advice.] advice:
181h	to stake] at stake
182a	calml;] calm:
182b	Father,] father,
182c	Aunt] aunt
182d	about him.] on the subject.
182e	affected all things,] strove anxiously
182f	did it] succeeded
182g	Margret, laughing at her,] Margaret
182h	feeling,] feeling
182i	'With who?'] 'With whom?'
183a	Lady Avondale] She now *2nd edn*; Lady Avondale *3rd edn*.
183b	Lady Avondale] She *2nd edn*; Lady Avondale *3rd edn*.
183c	customary languor] languor
183d	Lady Avondale] She *2nd edn*; Lady Avondale *3rd edn*.
183e	excited the indignation it deserved.] excited at least as much indignation as it deserved.
183f	God] Heaven,
184a	obedience] submission *2nd edn*; obedience *3rd edn*.
185a	reproach,] reproach
185b	forgive,' 'raise] forgive.' 'Raise
185c	her,] her.
185d	reclaim,] reclaim;
186a	this, this is mine.' Saying this. . . 'I love you to madness,'] if the heart be mine of what avail? I love you to madness,
186b	'Nonsense] 'Nonsense,
186c	know,] know;
186d	'Oh God! what guilt.] 'Oh Glenarvon, what guilt!
186e	sake?] sake.
186f	her,] her;
186g	friend] friend,
186h	recurred,] recurred;
186i	ah] ah!
186j	As he spoke, he. . . his tears fell over her.] As he spoke his tears fell upon her hand.
186k	me. – Remember,] me – remember,
187a	Calantha!'] Calantha?' [*sic*]
187b	moments,'] moment's,' [*sic*]

187c   wickedly,] wickedly;
187d   madness.'] madness.'
            It may appear strange, but all this time the world and friends appeared more fond of Calantha than at any other: they courted, they flattered her they no longer feigned that Glenarvon was insincere – and they seemed to gaze with new intent, new admiration upon the object of his attention. – Never was she apparently so beloved, so sought after – in particular by the Princess of Madagascar, her party and her followers. Is it then virtue, or its semblance, that the world of fashion admire? – Alas no – they seek every thing that can give them momentary amusement – wealth, rank, novelty and power, whereever [*sic*] it may be found – but from misfortune, poverty and distress, they turn away! – Had Calantha been discarded and wretched they had believed her guilty – now they cherished, they sought after, they flattered her, and she believed in their professions, but Glenarvon mocked her for her credulity. *2nd edn*;
            madness.'
            It may appear strange, but all this time the world and friends appeared more fond of Calantha than at any other: they courted, they flattered her they no longer feigned that Glenarvon was insincere – and they seemed to gaze with new intent, new admiration upon the object of his attention. – Never was she apparently so beloved, so sought after – in particular by the Princess of Madagascar, her party and her followers. *3rd edn*.
188a   which] which,
188b   niece and a dimness coming over his eyes,] niece, a dimness came over his eyes, and
188c   The fall was said to have] The fall, it was feared, had
188d   my] My
188e   'take it,'] 'Take it,'
189a   subdued,] subdued
189b   'he] 'He
189c   lady; and tell him] Lady; and tell him,
189d   for a moment her eye;] her eye for a moment; but
189e   'he] 'He
189f   said he] he said
189g   Elinor'] Elinor,'
189h   truth' said Glenarvon] truth,' said Glenarvon,
189i   frown,' said he, 'or] frown, or
189j   do:] do?
189k   kindness!'] kindness?'
189l   once,'] once?
189m   then] then,
190a   truth:'] truth:
190b   so?] so!
190c   like.] understand.
190d   Calantha:] Calantha;

192a	love,] love
192b	plea] mask
192c	ofttimes] besides ofttimes
192d	betrayed him.] betrayed him. How different was he in mind, in person, and heart from other men! His very nobleness of soul prevented him from conceiving what some perhaps had soon observed, and wounded pride estranged him from a woman who now appeared avowedly to shun his society.
192e	Mowbray] Mowbrey
193a	time felt remorse.] time, saw her conduct in its true light.
193b	gloom: – it] gloom: every little act of kindness he had once shewed her recurred; all his manly virtues: his open unsuspicious nature: – it
193c	vice.] crime.
193d	so as to render such a step] in a way to render such step
193e	no remorse] only momentary fits of remorse
193f	no fear] no lasting fear
193g	thoughtful of] thoughtful for
194a	me] me,
194b	wicked'] wicked,'
194c	goad] urge
195a	ardent,] ardent
195b	he thus spoke: then clasping her. . . every future hope.] he thus spoke: [*sic*]
195c	Calantha. It was not love, it was distraction.] Calantha.
195d	though but] though
195e	At night she seldom slept. . . He felt,] He felt,
195f	her life itself were gone] was gone
196a	their's,] theirs,
196b	'but my dream, sweet one. . . Shall I repeat it?'] 'Shall I repeat my dream?'
196c	it;] it:
196d	now; but] now;
197a	serious. –] serious.
197b	continued he,] he continued,
197c	thing] thing,
197d	she again] she
197e	oftentimes, that day,] oftentimes that day
197f	Linden;] Linden:
197g	form] form,
197h	recall,] recall
198a	were it] it were
198b	little part in the disease; passion absorbed] little part now: passion soon absorbed
198c	now at times] now, at times,
198d	dissimulation,] dissimulation;
198e	moved] moved –

199a	dinner that day] dinner, that day,	
199b	Calantha,] Calantha	
199c	heart,] heart	
199d	them:] them;	
199e	Calantha] her	
199f	that has been retained.'] retained.'	
200a	said:] said;	
200b	'Great God, how] 'how	
200c	night,] night	
201a	fixed.] therefore fixed.	
201b	go. Will] go.' 'Will [*sic*]	
201c	hear us?] hear us?' [*sic*]	
201d	Castle?] Castle? [*sic*]	
201e	sleak] sleek	
201f	said he] he said	
203a	comforts] comfort	
203b	her to weep.] her.	
203c	from me,' he said.] from me.'	
203d	depravity,] depravity	
203e	see how] could'st thou see how	
203f	calm,] calm	
204a	'Calantha' at length Glenarvon… once more to my heart –] 'Calantha,' at length he said,	
204b	go] Go	
204c	remember that,] remember, that	
204d	part,'] part.'	
205a	thus suffer.'] suffer thus.'	
205b	fiercely,] fiercely;	
205c	'do] 'Do	
205d	God's] Heaven's	
205e	interfering] interfering,	
205f	watched;] watched:	
206a	and that this might convince her that] and that	
206b	word] word further	
206c	behaviour of late.] behaviour.	
206d	heart,] heart	
207a	you,] you	
207b	make use of.] employ.	
207c	vengeance] veangeance [*sic*]	
207d	trembling] trembled	
207e	miserable;] indeed wretched;	
208a	and, holding] and holding	

208b	'Where?] 'Where?' [sic]
208c	ill;] ill:
208d	blood receding to his heart] blood, receding to his heart,
208e	admire you] admire
208f	his lips] while his lips
208g	God] Heaven
208h	death or disgrace] disgrace or death
209a	me] me,
209b	me?' 'Upon] me? Upon [sic]
209c	must] mnst [sic]
209d	for you] for you.
209e	expect] I expect
209f	prefered] preferred
209g	God.] God,
210a	superstition;] superstition:
210b	time:] time!
210c	ruin;] ruin:
210d	in] into
210e	to the glory, the ecstacy. . . the joys of Heaven:] to the glory, of being thine! Return Glenarvon, adored, beloved.
210f	'take] 'Take
210g	'take] 'Take
210h	I know there are some] There are many
211a	its excess: –] their excess,
211b	to-night] to-night,
211c	promise.'] promise!'
212a	Calantha] Then she
212b	noise] noise,
212c	had] hd [sic]
212d	Nor ray of hope,] Nor hope,
213a	agony.] alarm.
213b	us:] us;
213c	lovers'] lover's
213d	relinquish?] relinquish!
213e	you?] you!
213f	flight . . . .'] flight.
213g	the delirium of passion, even in the transports of love,] the mad infatuation of passion,
213h	God. She] father, she had disobeyed his sacred command, she had broken her solemn promise; she
213i	God] Heaven
213j	your's] yours
214a	phrenzy] frenzy

214b	change my sentiments] change
215a	eyes.] eye.
215b	ring,] ring
215c	Glenarvon?' she said with a faint smile!] Glenarvon?'
215d	Calantha's] Her
215e	lady,] Lady
215f	Clara,] Clare
215g	said;] said:
216a	him,] him
216b	warmest,] warmest
216c	God's] Heaven's
216d	Good God!] Glenarvon!
216e	said Glenarvon,] he replied,
216f	God] Being
216g	purity and generous] purity, and generous,
216h	my] My
217a	to God] that
217b	assurance;] assurance:
217c	hopes,] hopes
217d	her:] her;
217e	Is it the] Is it in the
217f	Till now] Till this period
217g	hopes; and the crime... feared to commit.] hopes.
217h	inflamatory] inflammatory
217i	most] had most
217j	herself,] herself
217k	that during] that, during
217l	disgust.] dislike.
217m	lover,] lover
218a	that... a female figure,] that?... a female figure
218b	cheeks;] cheeks:
218c	'Oh] 'Oh!
218d	God] Heaven
218e	you,' cried] you.' cried [*sic*]
218f	started:] started,
218g	resemblance,] resemblance, [footnote inserted: 'See Chaucer's Troilus and Creseide.]
218h	her lover,] the lover
218i	feeling] feeling,
218j	curse for] curse on
219a	exertion;] exertion:
219b	lost] neglected

219c	has been] is
219d	woman whom Mr. O'Kelly,] woman, whom Mr. O'Kelly
219e	sure] sure,
219f	wept, and] wept, at [*sic*]
219g	door,] door
220a	stairs,] stairs
220b	house] house,
220c	agony,] agony:
220d	said he,] he said,
220e	all;] all:
220f	despair,] despair
221a	that] that,
221b	said he:] he replied:
221c	comfort: –] comfort:
221d	to God] that
221e	ever,] ever
221f	death.] death; –
221g	hand,] hand
221h	her 'for] her, 'For
221i	only hope now. Oh! Calantha!] only hope, now you will not believe!
222a	slumbers] slumbers,
222b	immediately admitted him.] admitted him immediately.
222c	It] The letter
222d	lady,] Lady,
222e	lady,] Lady,
223a	power] powe [*sic*]
223b	her] Alice
223c	this,] this
223d	avails, even] avail, nor would they even
223e	avert] divert
223f	unavailable] unavailing
223g	quell.] allay or restore.
223h	have,] have
223i	and] end [*sic*]
224a	St. Alvin's] St. Alvin
224b	My father, that evening,] That evening,
224c	forever] for ever
225a	Oh God] Heaven
225b	permit] permit of
225c	said,] said
225d	journey] journey,
225e	heard,] heard

226a	follow:]	follow;
226b	he spoke to me of love. . . I said, as I madly] he spoke to me with kindness. I thought he had been my friend but it proved other wise. I madly	
226c	In mercy oh my God] In mercy, oh	
226d	the boy] him	
227a	over – My father forgive me. – We sailed;] over. – We sailed:	
227b	– there was one voice clear,] there was one voice clear	
227c	– it] it	
227d	a bride awaits him, I was told.] A bride awaits him, I am told.	
227e	ask.] ask. . .	
227f	Father,] father,	
227g	down,] down	
227h	bitter bitter] bitter, bitter	
227i	– They] They	
228a	malignity,] malignity	
228b	awakes,] awakes	
229a	'yes,'] 'Yes,'	
229b	and kissed her.] her.	
229c	God:] Heaven;	
229d	married:] married;	
229e	believe it,'] believe it, in defiance of them,'	
229f	weak,] weak	
229g	chaste;] pure;	
229h	rendering more] renderinge [sic]	
230a	one] any	
230b	him,'] him.'	
230c	you] yon [sic]	
232a	conduct] conduet [sic]	
232b	days;] days,	
232c	castle;] castle:	
233a	you then] you	
233b	Calantha's] A	
233c	Therefore, for God's sake,] Therefore,	
233d	the] 'the	
233e	disappointment.] disappointment.'	
233f	God!] Heavens!	
234a	having] having,	
234b	him] him on	
234c	Mowbray] Mowbrey	
234d	better.'] better' [sic]	
234e	Trelawny] Trelawney	
235a	abhorrence,] abhorrence	

235b	thing,] thing
235c	meantime] mean time
235d	indifferent;] indfferent [sic]
235e	her,] her
235f	think] imagine that
236a	honor, purity and virtue:] honor and purity
236b	stop?] check your course?
236c	villify] vilify
236d	her,] her
237a	child:] child;
237b	clasped] claspsed [sic]
237c	myself,'] myself, [sic]
238a	apartment – regardless indeed] apartment: regardless, indeed,
238b	he;] he:
238c	Mowbray] Mowbrey
238d	Lady] lady
238e	you;] you,
238f	him] him,
238g	pleasure] pleasure,
239a	alone,] alone
239b	taken] taken,
239c	prohibition] prohibition,
239d	set] sat
239e	'None Nurse] 'None, nurse
239f	'Lord] 'Lord,
239g	ribbands' .... 'Who] ribbands. Who
239h	room] room,
239i	'she's] 'she is
240a	will?' 'Sophia] will!' 'Sophia,
240b	left.] left?
240c	form] form,
240d	'let] 'Let
240e	sternly –] sternly:

Volume III

Colburn's second edition changes the title page in this way:

2nd TP-b: Disperato dolor ... che ne favelle] Les passions sont les vents qui enflent les voiles du vaisseau: elles le submergent quelquefois, mais sans elles il ne pourrait voguer. Tout est dangereux ici-bas, et tout est nécessaire. [*Passions are the swells which fill the sails of the vessel. They submerge it sometimes, yet without them, it could not navigate. Here below, everything is dangerous, and everything is necessary.*]

Editor's note: The new epigraph is a slight modification of a passage from Voltaire's *Zadig* (1759), Chapter 22: 'Ce sont les vents qui enflent les voiles du vaisseau,' repartit l'ermite: 'elles le submergent quelquefois; mais sans elles il ne pourrait voguer. La bile rend colère et malade; mais sans la bile l'homme ne saurait vivre. Tout est dangereux ici-bas, et tout est nécessaire.' ['*They* [the passions] *are the swells which fill the sails of the vessel*,' *resumed the hermit*: '*they submerge it sometimes, yet without them, it could not navigate. Phlegm, indeed, makes men peevish and sick; but then there is no living without it. Here below, everything is dangerous and everything is necessary.*']

Colburn's third edition changes the title pages in this way:

Title P-a: VOL. III] [*a steel plate engraving has been put on the title page showing aweeping Cupids around an urn labeled 'Calantha.' Underneath is this motto*: '*Il n'est plus temps.*' [*It is no longer time* [*to...*]]' See above, p. 242.

2nd TP-a: IN THREE VOLUMES.] IN THREE VOLUMES. BY LADY CAROLINE LAMB.[8]

Colburn's fourth edition changes the title page in this way:

2nd TP-b: Disperato dolor . . . che ne favelle] Contemptu famae contemni virtutem. Tacitus [To depise fame is to despise merit. Tacitus] See above, p. 363, n. 1, for details of this change to the epigraph in the fourth edition.

245a	change. But, when the flame is unsupported] change; but, when unsupported
245b	hell;] hell,
245c	power,] power
245d	sinner –] sinner,
245e	There are trials, which. . . mercy or forgiveness.] There is no trial which human frailty cannot resist[9] – there is no passion implanted in the heart's core, which reason cannot subdue, if we call upon our God to assist us; but, when unsupported by his strength, every temptation that assails us may overcome us, and the remembrance of our own weakness should teach us to be humble in ourselves.
245f	Even] Yet even
246a	where] whither
246b	fate – she found herself] fate, she found herself,
246c	walk] walk,
246d	shore] shore,
246e	Wizzard's] Wizard's
246f	where to fly, or what to do.] whither to fly, or how to act.
246g	terror. He] terror; he
246h	ill,'] ill, [*sic*]
246i	moments] moment's
246j	in him,] to him,
246k	have been] been
246l	shall] shall,

246m	victim – what] victim! what
246n	given;] given,
246o	mine,] mine;
246p	thee,] thee
246q	thee,] thee
246r	duty,] duty;
246s	– but now when thou art mine;] but now, when thou art mine,
246t	me –] me,
246u	grief and increase my own.] grief, and increase my own?
246v	him:] him.
246w	O! Glenarvon. I believe in you,] Glenarvon! I believe in you
247a	keenly, not] keenly
247b	of weight.] of little weight.
247c	power:] power;
247d	Heaven,] Heaven
247e	now – I] now; I
247f	rippled over the sea] rippled
247g	tear] hurry
247h	now touched] touched
247i	breeze,] breeze
247j	those that] those who
247k	approached:] approached;
247l	passed:] passed;
247m	retainers] retainers,
247n	gone;] gone,
247o	brave.' They now] brave!' Calantha and Glenarvon now
248a	hour. She] hour; she
248b	forget] forget,
249a	enveloped] envelloped
249b	chill'd – are] chilled? Are
249c	this scene.] the scene.
249d	Conner,] Connor,
250a	arms. Beg,] arms; beg,
250b	in to] into
250c	nothing,] nothing;
250d	you:] you;
250e	grievances. Only] grievances; only
250f	by twos, by threes.] by two's, by three's.
250g	blood:] blood;
250h	wronged:] wronged;
250i	God] *Being*
251a	countrymen:] countrymen;

251b	power:] power,
252a	joy] enthusiasm
252b	'Elinor] 'Elinor,
254a	clift,] cliff,
254b	'God reward] 'Heaven bless
255a	the agony of her soul] her agony
255b	her,] her
255c	''Tis] 'It is
255d	alone;] alone:
255e	to his bosom,] hand,
255f	now that we are united by every tie; that] now that
255g	your prayer; but the kiss… has made me mad.] your prayer.
255h	but now that fierce passions… the fruits of guilt.] but not now; oh not now!
256a	flock,] flock
256b	If he clasp thee thus, 'tis] 'Tis
256c	myself:] myself;
256d	now; fear neither man nor God.] now;
256e	fastened it:] fastened it –
256f	ring:] ring;
256g	between us;' and, kneeling… abandon, or forget thee:] between us, friend of my best affections; never, will I abandon or forget thee;
256h	one] one,
256i	see:] see;
256j	interrupted he,] he interrupted,
256k	given:] given;
256l	away:] away;
256m	pillow; and when… in Glenarvon's arms.] pillow.
256n	friendship,' he said; 'but] friendship, but
256o	and vice with thousands of common lovers,] and vice
256p	Whilst] While
256q	rose in summer,] rose of summer,
257a	shews] shew
257b	Upon thy burning lips… take it thence.] Never let, or father or husband teach thee to forget me.
257c	dare not forget me.] dare not.
257d	others:] others,
258a	the rapture of receiving… erroneous or unprofitable.] the happiness of receiving them.
258b	virtue:] virtue;
258c	like this] like
258d	'thank God,] 'thanks be to Heaven,
258e	ruin:] ruin;
258f	remorse.] repentance.

258g	Calantha,] my gentle mistress,
258h	heart] hear [*sic*]
258i	last:] last;
259a	done what they had gladly done] followed him whom all had gladly sought,
259b	paused;] paused:
259c	long cherished] long-cherished
259d	him;] him:
259e	parted:] parted;
260a	end;] end,
260b	yet:] yet;
260c	well,] well
260d	anxiety] anxiety,
260e	others:] others;
260f	Calantha] She
260g	down,] down
260h	there. This] there; this
260i	said:] said;
261a	period;] period:
261b	isles,] Isles,
261c	engenders!] engengers! [*sic*]
261d	God] Heaven
262a	'Remember to] 'Remember and
262b	dignity,] dignity
262c	seems,] seems
263a	Calantha] Calantha,
263b	darkness:] darkness;
263c	it] it,
263d	whatever;] whatever:
263e	not necessary] unnecessary
264a	things that] things
264b	all] all,
264c	God] Heaven
264d	crime; and God, they say, is just. The] crime; The [*sic*]
265a	dinner.] dinner!
265b	it;] it:
266a	Lady Avondale] And Lady Avondale
266b	was;] was:
266c	Lady Avondale walked to Belfont. She called upon] She walked to Belfont. She met with
266d	her coldly.] her coldly. Lady St. Clare drew up her head, and dropt her an austere courtesy. Several ladies of equally unblemished reputation, were the first to shrink from 'a fallen sinner.'
266e	feel] see

266f	fell justly;] fell with justice;
267a	please;] please her;
267b	return to;] return to:
267c	his God. 'Oh, God of mercy!'] his Creator. 'Oh Father of mercy,'
267d	he gave. He] he gave, He [*sic*]
270a	call you] call upon you
270b	perhaps?] perhaps:
270c	this?] this.
270d	you] you,
270e	despair] despair,
270f	falsehood;] falsehood:
271a	God] Heaven
271b	that Being] her Creator
272a	has been] have been
272b	remorse] remorse,
272c	death? Oh, God; it is no coward's act!] death? – it is no coward's act.
274a	is annihilated] is as it were annihilated
274b	evil. Calantha] calamity. Calantha,
274c	reigns] reign
274d	religion;] religion:
274e	a] 'a
274f	enshrined.] enshrined.'
274g	after,] after
275a	love gifts] love-gifts
275b	betrayed;] betrayed:
275c	'T was] They were
275d	It was] They were
275e	that] which
275f	To] to
275g	remorse] remorse,
275h	desperation. Instead] desperation; instead
275i	breaking-heart,] breaking heart,
275j	see:] see;
275k	Sophia,] Sophia
276a	Monmouth's seat] Monmouth'ss eat [*sic*]
276b	confidence: tears] confidence. Tears
276c	misery] misery,
276d	insufficient,] insufficient
276e	chains] chain
276f	'T were] It were
276g	made use of.] employed.
276h	at her for her folly, and despised her for her] at her folly, and despised her

276i	never will]	will never
277a	Glenarvon]	Glenarvon,
277b	sneer;]	sneer:
277c	are]	is
277d	herd;]	herd:
277e	hair,]	hair, one of these glorious creatures,
277f	cowardly]	cowardly,
278a	yet:]	yet;
278b	already, apparently,]	already apparently
278c	grace;]	grace:
278d	lady]	lady herself
278e	instance,]	instance
279a	there]	thither
279b	for]	in favour of
279c	rage;]	rage:
280a	the sorrows of the owners of the castle.]	the secret sorrows of those who pledged them, or of their superiors.
280b	breaking,]	breaking;
280c	gossamer;]	gossamer:
280d	underneath]	beneath
280e	playful]	playful,
281a	repent]	repent,
281b	journey on;]	journey on:
281c	Oh]	'Oh
281d	sweetly.]	sweetly.' [*sic*]
282a	father,']	fathers,'
282b	was]	wert
283a	were hard]	were ever hard
283b	approaches.']	is come.'
283c	rests]	rest
283d	curse:']	curse!'
283e	horrid]	hurried
283f	Glenarvon.]	Glenarvon!
284a	relatives]	relations
284b	words]	words,
284c	vain]	vain,
284d	ill judged]	illjudged
285a	folly, concluding in crime,]	folly and error
285b	shewn,]	shewn
285c	imploring]	imploring,
285d	which though]	which, if
285e	Such a pang]	Such pang

285f	comforted] had comforted
286a	but,] but
286b	her;] her:
286c	solace;] solace:
286d	you .... but] you – but
287a	received;] received:
287b	earth;] earth:
287c	severity,] severity
287d	trembling.... 'Calm] trembling – 'Calm
287e	heart] hear [sic]
287f	attachment] attachment that perhaps never yet was equalled,
288a	again'..... 'Oh!] again' – 'Oh!
288b	heart?.... Have] heart? – Have
288c	mercy.... I am] mercy – I am
289a	you;] you:
289b	said,] said
290a	Calantha] Calantha,
290b	slave, of a noble,] slave of a noble
290c	Heaven:] Heaven.
290d	who] who,
291a	neglect to] neglect of
291b	commands. Tears] commands, and tears
292a	No;] No:
294a	Lard] Lord
294b	Henry.] the children.
295a	lard!] lord!
295b	I'm] I'am [sic]
295c	hope, my lady,] hope
295d	Oh!'....] Oh!' –
295e	God] Heaven
295f	'Oh!.... 'Stop] 'Oh! – Stop
295g	hill. Drive for your life: a guinea for every mile you go.'] hill.' [sic] Drive for your life:
295h	shrieked:] shrieked;
296a	fetched,] fetched
296b	enterprise:] enterprize:
296c	Be] be [sic]
296d	letters;] letters:
297a	uniform;] uniform:
297b	rail] ra'al
297c	the] that
297d	God!] Heavens!

298a	There's] There is
298b	God!'] Heavens!'
298c	stern....] stern. –
298d	lady] Lady
298e	I will never leave you.] My uncle and the world may scorn me; but I will do for thee, what many have done for those less worthy. Whatever the sacrifice, be it life, or even fame, I swear by Him who created me, to forgive, to stand by thee to the last. Every one has – every one may forsake thee, but I – never, never!
298f	friend. But were it to seal my ruin, I must, I do pardon thee.] friend: thou hast renounced thy religion to follow after the vanities and false light of a cold and vain philosophy. – I, too, have erred, for I left thee without a guide; and now I will dedicate every hour of my life to restore and reclaim thee.
298g	Heaven] May heaven
299a	mercy.] Heaven.
299b	Calantha.] Calantha.

And did she thus die, some may perhaps exclaim, unpunished for her crime! Did she not live to feel its consequences in all their magnitude and bitterness – to hid under smiles of levity the anguish of her soul – to mask under the appearance of pride and insensibility, the remorse, the terror, the despair, she felt – to receive from strangers unmerited kindness – to hear from malice all that she too well deserved?[10] Did she not linger on to see the husband she adored reproached by the cold and stern, for his mercy to herself – to trace in his countenance the bitterness of a proud but injured spirit[11] struggling to conceal its sufferings and its wrongs, perishing, by slow degrees, of the cruelest of all maladies – disappointment, regret, injured honour, and blasted happiness?[12] Oh did the God who made her, in commiseration for what she had already felt, spare her this trial? – He did in mercy; and on a bed of death, she lay insensible to the present, as to the past.[13]

300a	faltering] faultering
300b	however they had injured her;] although they might have injured her;
300c	Christians] christians
301a	'Aye] 'Aye,
301b	did she ever] never did she
301c	distress?'] distress.'
301d	that....'] that –'
301e	prest] pressed
301f	together....farewell!] together – farewell!
301g	led thee to] caused
301h	act.] act. My vengeance till this hour, for thy sake, was sheathed.
301i	heart, and thou] heart; and, oh, Calantha, how thou
302a	enquiry.] enquiry. How many daily sacrifice themselves for the wives of others. – How many for a mistress renounce both fame and country!
302b	and I led her myself into temptation and ruin.] and I left her myself, when temptation and ruin surrounded her.

303a intentions?' 'I presume... nor fame, nor parentage.] intentions? Long, long have I desired this interview. For one cause alone, I sacrificed myself, my feelings – my just resentment.
303b charge to carry,] charge,
304a 'If it is thy mad wish, then be it so, and now stand off. . . . as he watched him in the distance.] – St. Clare, at that moment, rushed forward with a troop of followers; and placing herself between the furious combatants: 'Avondale,' she cried, 'thou shalt not raise thy hand against Glenarvon. By this bleeding heart, I adjure you – by Calantha's last prayer, and the solemn vow you made her, sully not thy upright honour with this mockery and exhibition. Who doubts thy prowess, and thy power? Splendid is the ray that surrounds the youthful head of Avondale: – yon miserable victim has yet to live and to repent 'Oh, hear me,' she continued, throwing herself forward before him: 'reserve that arm to defend an injured country. Calantha's spirit cries to thee from the grave: oh, hear that prayer, and remember thy solemn vow. Let the worthless live to repent and suffer.'

'I sought thee not,' said Glenarvon, fiercely breaking from St. Clare; 'but since it is thy rash desire to strike at one who defies thee – take this.' – He rushed forward as he spoke, and struck his dagger into Lord Avondale's bosom, then departed. 'Let *me* pursue. Let *me* revenge,' said St. Clare, as she consigned Lord Avondale to the care of her followers. – 'Monster, bereft of every principle, this is too horrible. I did not think thee capable of this.' –– Glenarvon fled not from her pursuit: he continued his course unmoved. 'I could have loved that man,' he said and sighed. –

304b him: – but O!] him: but – Oh!
304c he turned with bitterness from the steep, and descended] he descended
304d Glenarvon] He
304e valley:] valley;
304f bay,] Bay,
304g heard: I know not; but approaching her,] heard. Approaching her,
304h replied;] replied:
304i Calantha's] Avondale's
305a pardon?'] pardon!'
306a FROM] It was at Kelly Cross that Lord Avondale remained until he was sufficiently recovered from his wound to proceed. From
306b bay,] Bay,
306c lords;] lords:
307a people;] people:
307b enquiries] inquiries
307c cheerless,] cheerless
307d heart,] heart
308a bay] bow
308b Verny,] Terny,
308c another:] another;
308d this;] this:
308e it;] it:

308f	weary;] weary:
309a	Carter, and Tyrone, now come] Carter, Grey, and Terney, now came
310a	tears;] tears:
310b	doors;] doors:
311a	age;] age:
311b	heart,] heart
311c	such things] such
311d	unhappy,'] unhappy?'
313a	her allies,] the allies,
313b	proceeded] proceeding
315a	Viviani?] Viviani!
316a	secret] secret,
317a	M. De Ruthven,] Colonel De Ruthven,
317b	night:] night;
319a	me] me.
321a	produce?] produce
321b	possible?] possible
322a	year,] year ****,
323a	got the boy sent] procured the boy to be sent
324a	gravely,] gravely, and as if conquering some sudden emotion,
325a	answer,] answer
327a	paid for his passage] engaged a packet
328a	search,] search
328b	stopt] stopped
328c	village] villiage [*sic*]
329a	surely,] sorely,
329b	trees;] trees:
329c	dark: the] dark. the [*sic*]
330a	my lord who spoke, – my master] my lord –' 'Who?' cried the Duke. 'My master
330b	my letters.] myl etters. [*sic*]
330c	In the dead of night. . . . seized the boy. I had] I had
330d	name:] name;
330e	and affluence. I think it was. . . But he denied it.] and affluence.
331a	phrenzy] frenzy
331b	escape.] escape: he knew also what part of Macpherson's narrative to believe.
333a	ties.] duties.
335a	some] at some
338a	St. Alvin's] St. Alvin
339a	militia, but will serve us at the moment.'] militia: he is a rat.'
340a	songs] song
340b	hurried] horrid

342a	now]	now, perhaps,
342b	'England,]	'Let not rage against Glenarvon actuate your resolves: whatever he may have done, "we shall not live to see his like again." Shew not such pleasure in trampling upon the high: my vengeance is just resentment – but how has he offended you? England,
345a	forborne to teach,]	prevented him from believing,
345b	joyfully]	tranquilly
346a	The dead, or yellow poet was twice carried by mistake to the grave. It is further said,]	It is said,
347a	the last engagement, in which he lost his life,]	he departed to join the fleet,
351a	signal songs of the sailors,]	signals of the boatswain,
351b	merchantman,]	pirate,
351c	gave]	soon gave
352a	and you]	you

Notes:

1. GLENARNON: this error was corrected in the second edition, only to reappear in the third.
2. 'O fiora bella,': Lamb's corrections to the first edition preserved in the annnotated copy of a first edition of *Glenarvon* held in the Koninkliijke Bibliotheek of the National Bibliotheek van Nederland, state clearly 'Fiorabella' – and not 'fiora bella'. The name 'Fiorabella' also appears in the third chapter of volume one of *Glenarvon*, and so the correction is made silently here to avoid confusion.
3. *IN THREE VOLUMES. BY LADY CAROLINE LAMB*: The editors have seen two versions of this title page for the third edition, one with and one without Lamb's name as author. The slight changes necessary to insert the name suggests that Colburn may have printed the third edition without her name, then printed more copies with the name added.
4. *Some mistaken conclusion is eagerly seized upon, some false interpretation is easily seized upon*: the repetition was not apparently intended by Lamb, whose corrections to the first edition preserved in the copy in the Netherlands read: 'Some mistaken conclusion is eagerly seized upon, some false interpretation is hastily approved & tenaciously maintained...' *Glenarvon*, Lamb's edited copy of first edition, National Bibliotheek van Nederland.
5. *IN THREE VOLUMES. BY LADY CAROLINE LAMB*: See note 3 directly above.
6. *3rd edn*: i.e., this passage was dropped in the second edition and restored in the third.
7. *'Farewell.'*: i.e., the phrase 'To the air of one of the "*Old Irish Melodies.*"') [sic.] was added in the second edition (lacking an opening parenthesis mark) and was omitted in the third.
8. *IN THREE VOLUMES. BY LADY CAROLINE LAMB*: See note 3 directly above.
9. *which human frailty cannot resist*: in the copy in the Netherlands which Lamb annotated, this phrase is followed by one not included in the second or third editions: 'if supported by religion'.
10. *to hear from malice all that she too well deserved?*: in Lamb's corrections to the first edition preserved in the copy of *Glenarvon* in the Netherlands, there are cancelled words: 'could even her enemy have wished her such a fate'.

11. *spirit*: the word 'heart' is written above this word in Lamb's corrections to the first edition preserved in the copy of *Glenarvon* in the Netherlands.
12. *perishing, by slow degree... and blasted happiness?*: this clause is omitted from the emendations included in Lamb's corrections to the first edition preserved in the copy in the Netherlands.
13. *insensible to the present, as to the past*: in Lamb's corrections to the first edition preserved in the copy of *Glenarvon* in the Netherlands, there are alternative words, cancelled: 'insensible to her husband'.